FUNDAMENTALS OF
HUMAN
SEXUALITY

HOLT, RINEHART AND WINSTON, INC. NEW YORK CHICAGO SAN FRANCISCO ATLANTA
DALLAS MONTREAL TORONTO LONDON SYDNEY

Herant A. Katchadourian, M.D. | Donald T. Lunde, M.D.

DEPARTMENT OF PSYCHIATRY, STANFORD UNIVERSITY

FUNDAMENTALS OF
HUMAN
SEXUALITY

Cover illustration, *The Kiss* by Edvard Munch (woodcut, 1897), is used by permission of the Graphische Sammlung Albertina, Vienna.

Cover design by Colin Chow
Book design by Cecilia Gonzalez and Colin Chow

It is a curious and poignant fact that some of the subjects that affect human lives most powerfully receive little attention in scientific research or in higher education. Sex is such a subject. This situation is beginning to change for the better, and this book is a remarkable contribution to the improvement. I know of no other book on human sexuality that matches it in clarity, cogency, and dependability of information.

Five years ago it was my privilege to invite Herant Katchadourian to join the faculty of the Stanford University School of Medicine. Shortly thereafter, I asked him to replace me on a committee on university health. The members of this committee were quickly impressed with his extraordinary qualities and asked him to undertake an innovative course on human sexuality for Stanford undergraduates. The third time the course was offered, with Donald Lunde as collaborator, over a thousand students enrolled, making it the largest single course at Stanford. This textbook grew out of that course, which continues to attract an enthusiastic response from the student body.

The scientific literature on sex is in its infancy. Although popular books abound, full of flashy claims and disputable speculations, there is a striking lack of adequate textbooks on human sexuality for college-level instruction. This is in pronounced contrast to the large number of excellent textbooks in such subjects as biology and psychology. No doubt this reflects the fact that sex has always been a delicate subject, a not quite respectable field for scientific inquiry or scholarly analysis. Similarly, there has been concern that sex education will lead to sexual promiscuity or aberration. By now it should be apparent to any reasonable person that there is no scarcity of interest in sex nor in exploring the avenues of sexual experience. What is lacking is accurate information and thoughtful consideration of alternative courses of action.

So far as I know, this book is the first successful attempt to produce a textbook on human sexuality that, in scope, reliability, and level of sophistication, compares favorably with the better textbooks in the biological and social sciences. The availability of this book should greatly facilitate the teaching of human sexuality in colleges and may prove to be a potent incentive to start such courses where none exist now.

The primary emphasis in this book is on information, not advice. The information has been selected with care and the reader is clearly told when he is being presented

Foreword

with empirical data, what are the limitations of the evidence, and when one must rely upon hypothetical constructs. Whenever pertinent, alternative explanations are offered for the same behavior or phenomenon. The material is presented in a fashion that should make it readily comprehensible for beginning college students, yet the information is sufficiently sophisticated to make the book valuable for advanced students as well. Since people of all ages have generally lacked scientifically based education about sex, this book can be useful to a broad range of readers.

There are few topics where the need for an integrated view is as great as in the area of sex. Although much remains to be learned about the biological, psychological, and cultural aspects of sex, we know enough to realize that these elements cannot be separated from each other, nor can one be ignored in favor of the other. One of the major strengths of this book is that it approaches human sexuality as a comprehensive and integrated topic by thoughtfully distributing emphasis across different areas, and by viewing sexual behavior in an evolutionary, historical, and cross-cultural perspective.

The authors have ranged widely across biological sciences, social sciences, and clinical medicine in arriving at their assessment of the current state of knowledge about sex. They are not inhibited by the narrow confines of a single discipline, nor are they preoccupied with any doctrinaire ideological position. They are open-minded, broadly informed, and freely inquisitive. They often find present evidence inadequate to answer questions definitively, yet they do not avoid difficult issues. Their assessment of evidence is consistently judicious and useful. Moreover, their appraisals are expressed with wit and grace and the book is enjoyable to read.

Finally, it is significant to note that this textbook on human sexuality for college instruction is written by two psychiatrists, both members of the faculty of Stanford University, who have broad backgrounds in the behavioral and biological sciences. During the past decade, this university has made a deep commitment to pooling the strengths of various disciplines to achieve a deeper understanding of man. In the Department of Psychiatry of the School of Medicine, where the authors teach and do their research, specialists come from a variety of disciplines: psychiatry, clinical psychology, developmental psychology, physiological psychology, endocrinology, biochemistry, genetics, anthropology, and statistics. In the undergraduate Human Biology program, where the Human Sexuality course is now given, the Departments of Biology, Genetics, Pediatrics, Sociology, and Psychiatry play leading roles. The problems of man do not come in neat packages that fit the traditional academic disciplines. They are far-reaching, complex, and fascinating. Drs. Katchadourian and Lunde have approached human sexual behavior in this spirit and the book they have produced is thus hard to classify, easy to read, and a genuine contribution to our understanding of man.

David A. Hamburg, M.D.

Department of Psychiatry, Stanford University

As this text is an outgrowth of our course on human sexuality at Stanford, it is appropriate that we first give due recognition to those who helped initiate and sustain the course. Robert M. Moulton, Jr., chaired the committee on university health where the need for such a course was first discussed. His interest and support, along with that of Robert R. Sears (who was at the time Dean of Humanities and Sciences at Stanford and a member of the committee) were crucial. Since then help and encouragement have come from many quarters. David A. Hamburg's broad conception of psychiatry legitimized our involvement in this field. The university unfailingly provided the necessary financial and administrative support. We have been the grateful recipients of much encouragement from the faculty as well as from other members of the Stanford community. Ultimately, of course, our most important supporters have been our students, for without their enthusiastic response neither the course nor this book would exist today.

We started this venture with the conviction that serious attention would have to be paid to artistic and literary contributions to this field in order to achieve an adequate portrayal of the sexual life of man. We are particularly grateful therefore for the collaboration of Lorenz Eitner, Osgood Hooker Professor of Fine Arts and chairman of the Art Department, Stanford University, and Strother B. Purdy of the Department of English, Marquette University. Their contributions have greatly enriched this book.

During the early phases of the preparation of this book, we profited greatly from visits to the Institute for Sex Research at the University of Indiana. Director Paul Gebhard and others on his staff have been helpful in numerous ways. The Institute is well known for its publications, but deserves wider recognition for the informal, yet important, educational job it fulfills.

A number of colleagues and friends read parts of the manuscript and made specific, as well as general, comments. We are particularly grateful in this regard to Frank A. Beach, Fred Elmadjian, Julian M. Davidson, Paul H. Gebhard, H. Duane Heath, Raeburne Heimbeck, Erich Lindemann, George L. Mizner, Stephen A. Robins, John Romano, Judge George W. Phillips, Jr., Sherwood L. Washburn, Archdeacon John Weaver, and Lee H. Yearley.

Acknowledgments

In the preparation of this book we were assisted by David P. Boynton, Jane Mayo Roos, Jan Hughes, Estelle Whelan, Susan F. Riggs, and Carol Lee Smith. The manuscript was typed by Ann Dunn Morey and Ann Edmonds.

The division of labor between co-authors was as follows: Katchadourian wrote the introductory chapter, the chapters on anatomy, physiology, sexual behavior, autoeroticism, sexual intercourse, the introductory section on contraception, and the section on sexual malfunctions; Lunde wrote the chapters on hormones, conception and pregnancy, morality, law, the concluding chapter, and the sections on contraceptive methods and diseases of the sex organs. The chapter on sexual deviation was written by Lunde and revised by Katchadourian.

This book was written over a period of two years, mostly in the evenings and on weekends. Our families have thus labored with us throughout this process. Furthermore, from the book's conception to its birth, we have benefitted from the good judgment and critical sense of our wives.

Herant A. Katchadourian
Donald T. Lunde

Stanford University

Contents

FUNDAMENTALS OF
HUMAN
SEXUALITY

Given the universality of sex, we would expect a great deal to be known about it. But this is not the case, partly because sexual behavior is variable and partly because all societies regulate sexual activity. This control restricts both the observation of sexual behavior and the access to information about it. We can therefore neither generalize from personal experience nor investigate freely.

Of the innumerable questions that can be asked about the sexual life of man, three are of primary importance: Why do we behave sexually? How do we behave sexually? And how should we behave sexually? Our task in this book is to provide information to help answer these questions.

Why We Behave Sexually

There are certain physiological functions like eating, whose primary purpose is immediately obvious. Even though food preferences vary widely among individuals and groups, everyone must eat something: fish or fowl, raw or cooked, with or without fork and knife, and so on. Similarly, unused food matter must be eliminated from the bowels regardless of the social customs attached to the process. No society can interfere with the physiological functions of eating and elimination without jeopardizing life.

What about sex? Can it be compared to either of these two functions? Both comparisons have been tried, but neither is quite adequate. We can, of course, refer metaphorically to "sexual hunger." In fact, at certain times men and animals may prefer copulating to eating. Nevertheless, sex is not an activity necessary to sustain life, except in the broad sense of species preservation. In fact, there is no generally agreed upon evidence that abstinence from sexual activity is even necessarily detrimental to health.

The comparison to elimination also has some superficial validity, as most men do ejaculate periodically. But women experience orgasm and do not ejaculate so the comparison is not appropriate. At best therefore we can speak only of periodic neurophysiological "discharge" through orgasm, with the understanding that sexual activity is not literally the "discharging" of anything that would otherwise be "dammed up."

Although comparisons to other body functions may thus be inadequate, we can hardly deny that the origins of human sexual behavior are rooted in biological makeup. But we must also consider other factors because, although important, biology is not all there is to sex. How we behave is a result of three types of forces—biological, psychological, and social. In dis-

FUNDAMENTAL QUESTIONS ABOUT HUMAN SEXUALITY

cussing these determinants of sexual behavior, we do not intend to imply that a choice among these factors is necessary; it is understood that they are complementary rather than mutually exclusive.

Biological Origins of Sexuality

Biological explanations of sexual behavior have generally been based on the concept of instinct. This notion of an innate force has proved quite useful, but scientists have so far failed to define specifically enough what terms like "instinct" and "drive" mean.

As sex and reproduction are so intimately linked in most living beings, we tend to forget that there are also asexual modes of reproduction and organisms that duplicate themselves merely by dividing into two identical "daughter cells." Sexual reproduction, in which two dissimilar cells (sperm and egg) combine to form a new being, is nevertheless the reproductive mode of most animals, including man.

It is thus understandable that one explanation of sexual behavior is simply the need to reproduce. Sex, in this sense, is part of a larger reproductive "instinct," a deep-rooted biological incentive for animals to mate and perpetuate their species. But lower animals cannot possibly know that mating results in reproduction. For that matter, we do not know who made the momentous discovery, at some point in prehistory, that coitus leads to pregnancy. As lower animals are ignorant of this association, what mysterious force propels them to mate?

Although the reproductive consequences of copulation are obvious to us, sexual behavior cannot be scientifically explained in teleological terms, as behavior in which animals engage in order to reproduce. Besides, a great deal of animal and human sexual activity serves no reproductive function.

A simpler and more likely explanation is that man and other animals engage in sex because it is pleasurable. The incentive is in the act itself, rather than in its possible consequences. Sexual behavior in this sense arises from a psychological "drive," associated with sensory pleasure, and its reproductive consequences are a by-product (though a vital one). We are only beginning to understand the neurophysiological basis of pleasure. It has been demonstrated, for example, that there are "pleasure centers" in the brain (in the thalamus, hypothalamus, and mesencephalon) that, when electrically stimulated, cause animals to experience intense pleasure. (Stimulation of certain adjacent areas causes extreme discomfort or pain.) When an animal has the opportunity to stimulate these pleasure centers, it will persist in doing so to the exclusion of all other activity: It will not take time to eat even when starving.

What about sex hormones? They are a fascinating but currently problematic subject of study. We know, for instance, that they begin to exert their influence before birth and are vital in sexual development. Yet, in the mature animal they seem relatively dispensable to the maintenance of sexual functioning. Although these hormones are intimately linked to sexual functioning, the link is clearly not a simple one, and we have yet to discover a substance that might represent a true "sex fuel."

Thus, the biological basis of our sexual behavior involves certain physical "givens," including sex organs, hormones, intricate networks of nerves, and brain centers. How these components are constructed and how they work will occupy us in Part 1 of this book.

Psychological Determinants of Sexual Behavior

If biological explanations of sexuality were totally satisfactory, it would not be necessary for us to go farther. But, as they do not at this time suffice, we must look for additional factors to explain sexual behavior.

In discussing psychological determinants of behavior, we often must deal with different levels of analysis of the human organism. In one sense, psychological or social forces are merely reflections and manifestations of underlying biological processes. For example, Freud argued that the libido, or sex drive, is the psychological representation of a biological sex instinct.

In another sense, psychological factors are more independent, even though they must be mediated through the neurophysiological mechanisms of the brain, for neither thought nor emotion can occur in an empty skull. But these mechanisms are considered only as the intermediaries through which thought and emotion operate, rather than as their primary determinants. Let us again use hunger as an example. When the brain motivates a person to eat, in response to a feeling of hunger (due to certain sensations in the gastrointestinal system or to a decrease in blood sugar), the response of the individual is relatively independent of psychological and social considerations. Although such factors have some influence on the individual's behavior, they are not the main determinants. On the other hand, when a person dislikes pork or is expected to abstain from eating it, he acts from personal preference or religious conviction. His motivation is still mediated through the brain, but it originates in learned patterns of behavior, rather than in biological factors. We have used the example of hunger, rather than of sex itself, because in the latter the biological imperative is less clear.

Theories of the psychological motivation for sexual behavior are thus fundamentally of two types. In the first, which includes psychoanalytic theory, psychological factors are considered to be representations or extensions of biological forces. In contrast, many learning theories assume that patterns of sexual behavior are largely acquired through a variety of psychological and social mechanisms. In Chapter 8 we shall discuss this issue in greater detail.

While the causes or determinants of a given type of behavior must not be confused with the purposes that it serves, and though such distinctions are not always easy to recognize, it is, nevertheless, also useful to examine the various aims of sexual behavior. For instance, when a person engages in sex expressly to satisfy physical desire or to relieve "sexual tension," we may say that sex occurs "for its own sake." But for most people sex has an emotional component as well; it takes on added significance as an expression of affection or love for the partner. We can argue, of course, whether this affective component ought to be a basic part of sex or a desirable addition to it, but this question comes under the third main section of this chapter.

Certain secondary (though not necessarily unimportant) goals of sex are clearly "nonsexual" in origin. The contribution of sex to self-esteem is, for instance, most important. Each of us needs a deep and firmly rooted conviction of personal worth. Although no one can hope to be universally loved and admired, we must receive some appreciation from "significant others" and from ourselves. An important component of a person's self-esteem is his sexual standing in his own eyes, as well as in those of others. The role of sex in self-esteem varies among individuals and groups, and some sexual attributes have more widespread significance than do others. For example, confidence of virility is vital to most males, and impotence before old age is humiliating. A man who is often impotent is likely to lose confidence in himself and to feel uncertain and incompetent even in areas in which sexual virility has no direct bearing. Others may be driven to compensate for their sexual weaknesses by acquiring political power, wealth, or knowledge or through antisocial behavior.

In contrast, women have traditionally been much less concerned about their ability to experience orgasm, though this attitude is changing, at least in the West. In some conservative groups in the Middle East, for instance, a women who fails to reach coital orgasm may be aware of a lack, but her self-esteem is not affected by it. The disaster for her is not frigidity but sterility.

The more striking changes in female awareness of orgasm have been occurring in the West, particularly in countries long influenced by the "Victorian ethic." Respectable Victorian women, for instance, risked actual loss of self-esteem if they experienced sexual pleasure (at least, so the predominantly male chroniclers of the age tell us). In contrast, the sophisticated modern Western woman is rapidly becoming as preoccupied with orgasm as males are and as vulnerable to loss of self-esteem at failure. For most women, however, the association between sex and self-esteem has always seemed less direct than for men. Women are more concerned with being attractive, desirable, and lovable, and deficiencies in these attributes are more apt to damage their self-esteem than sexual responsiveness as such. Also, these attributes and sexual responsiveness are often mutually enhancing: A woman who feels admired and desired is more likely to respond sexually and a responsive woman in turn is more ardently desired.

Sexuality is clearly an important component of an individual's self-concept, or sense of identity. Awareness of sexual differentiation precedes that of all other social attributes in the child: He knows himself as a boy or girl long before he learns to associate himself with national, ethnic, religious, and other cultural groupings.

Although developing an awareness of one's biological sex is a relatively simple matter, the acquisition of a sense of sexual identity is a more complex culturally relative process. Traditionally we have assumed that biological sex (maleness and femaleness) and its psychological attributes (masculinity and femininity) are two sides of the same coin. In traditional and stable societies this assumption may have been (and may still be) valid. But in the technologically advanced and structurally more fluid societies such direct correspondence between biological sex and psychological attributes is being challenged more and more vigorously as occupational and social roles for men and women become progressively blurred. There is an extensive literature on the topic of sex differences to which we shall make further references, and we shall discuss the entire topic more fully in Chapter 8.

Finally, sex figures prominently in an individual's moral or spiritual identity. At least in Western cultures, it is used as a moral yardstick more consistently than any other form of behavior, at both the personal and public levels: Many of us feel greater guilt and are often punished more severely for sexual transgressions than for other offenses. Common as sexual themes are in our mass media, the level of tolerance is nowhere near that for aggression and violence.

Although both personal and public attitudes are changing in this regard, a common first reaction as to whether or not a person (particularly a woman) is moral or "honorable" is to think in sexual terms. We are not implying that this should or should not be so, but are merely pointing out the enormous influence that sex has on our standing as individuals and members of society.

Social Factors in Sexual Behavior

Just as psychological functions are intimately linked with biological forces, they are equally tied to social factors. In fact, distinctions between what is primarily psychological and what is social often tend to be arbitrary. As a rule, in referring to social or cultural factors the emphasis is on the interpersonal over the intrapsychic and on group processes over internal ones.

Sexuality is often considered a cohesive force that binds the family unit together. In this sense it is subservient to a social goal, and social organizations reciprocally facilitate sexual aims by providing sexual partners and contacts. Sexuality can, of course, also have a divisive influence, and this potential may be one reason for the ambivalence with which sex is viewed in many societies.

Sex also functions as a form of communication. Through it we express affection and love—as well as anger and hatred. When, after coming home from a party, a wife who is herself sexually aroused refuses to sleep with her husband because he has been flirting with other women, she is using sex to communicate a message ("I am angry") and a lesson ("Next time behave yourself"). On the other hand, a woman who is sexually unstimulated may engage in coitus to reward her husband for good behavior. Similarly, promiscuous sexual activity may communicate messages like "I am lonely," "I am not impotent," "I dare to misbehave," and so on.

Sex also symbolizes status. The dominant male animals in a troop and the men with power in society usually have first choice of the more desirable females, as well as the juicier cuts of meat. Beauty is naturally pleasing to the eye, but beyond this attraction the company of a beautiful woman is a testimony and a tribute to a man's social standing, even though she may be tedious in bed. A woman's status is more often enhanced by the importance than by the looks of her man. The value of sex as an indicator of status prompts men in some cultures to keep mistresses; similarly, in prison a dominant inmate may have a "girl" (a sexually submissive male). In both instances, the actual sexual interest may be quite desultory.

The association of sex and aggression is very broad and encompasses biological, psychological, and social considerations. We shall make additional references to this point in Chapters 7 to 12. We need only point out here that aggressive impulses may be expressed through sexual behavior and vice versa and that there is a fluid and intimate relation between these two powerful "drives" in all kinds of sexual liaisons.

For some people sexual activity is a form of self-expression in a creative, or aesthetic, sense. What matters most is not simple physical pleasure as such but the broadening of sensual horizons with each experience and the opportunity to express and share these experiences in a very special and intimate way with another person. Such feelings, though very real, are difficult to describe.

In various places and at various times, sex has been used for the loftiest, as well as for the basest, ends. Although sexuality is foreign to the major modern Western traditions of religious worship, other religions have had distinctly sexual components, as the erotic statuary adorning Indian temples (Figure 13.4) and phallic monuments from Classical times (Figure 13.2) attest. Some Muslim men still offer brief prayers before coitus.

On balance, sex has been more crassly and mercilessly exploited than has any other human need. The female body in particular has been a commodity since remotest antiquity. Although women have benefited financially from prostitution, men have had more than their share of profits from this commerce. Prostitution is the most flagrant example of the use of sex for practical gain, but it is by no means the only one. Sexual favors are exchanged for other services between spouses and friends. Sex is used to maintain social standing, to gain popularity, to ensnare and hold spouses, and so on. The overt and covert use of sex in advertising hardly needs to be pointed out.

Other uses of sex are legion. The ancient Romans wore amulets in the form of male sex organs (Figure 2.6). Some people use sex to cure headaches, to calm their nerves, or to end insomnia. Sex can thus be used for "nonsexual" as well as "sexual" ends. Conversely, sexual gratification can be achieved through orgasm as well as by the displacement and sublimation of the sexual drive with countless ordinary and extraordinary "nonsexual" activities.

How We Behave Sexually

As causation is complex, it is understandable that we do not have satisfactory answers to our first question. We might hope, however, that answers to our second question would be relatively easy, for all that is theoretically required is observation of behavior rather than attempts to fathom human motivation. But, in fact, we are frequently in the dark on questions of how as well, and this ignorance may be an important cause of our ignorance in the first instance. After all, if we do not know enough about how people behave, how can we investigate why they behave as they do?

A comprehensive view of human sexual behavior would require knowledge of current sexual behavior in our own society, the history of sexual behavior and how it has changed over the centuries, sexual behavior in other cultures and its historical roots, and, finally, sexual behavior of animals.

Although it is customary (for good reason) to decry our ignorance in these matters, we actually do have a great deal of information (and a great deal more misinformation) on human sexual behavior, even though it is uneven and scattered. Most of this information can be found in three sources: art and literature, clinical reports, and ethnographic and statistical surveys.

Since the Paleolithic cave painters of c. 15,000 years B.C., artists have portrayed sexual activities. As a result we have a wealth of information, despite repeated and often successful attempts to conceal, distort, and destroy

it. In Chapter 13 Lorenz Eitner surveys this record.

Writers of all periods have also recorded descriptions, observations, and speculations on the sex life of man (see Chapter 14 by Strother Purdy). More recently films have become an important vehicle for the portrayal of sexual behavior (see Chapter 15 by Strother Purdy).

Clinical interest in sexual functioning also goes back to antiquity, but more intensive (some people think excessive) concern with sexual behavior is a twentieth-century phenomenon. The primary interests of the clinician have been aberrations and malfunctions. We can, of course, also learn a great deal about the normal through studies of the abnormal, as long as inferences are made with full awareness of the potential pitfalls.

Surveys of sexual behavior are generally of two types. In the first, observations are primarily descriptive. Anthropologists and travelers have, for instance, provided fascinating accounts of sexual activities in distant lands. The second type of survey is more systematic in attempting to describe sexual behavior in quantifiable terms, relating the activities of specially selected samples to other significant characteristics. The Kinsey studies are the best known examples of this type of survey. In Chapters 7 to 12 we shall make extensive use of data from both types of surveys, as well as from clinical sources. The more important sources of information that we have used are discussed later in this chapter.

Interest in animal behavior has until recently been restricted to zoologists. Now, however, we are becoming more aware of the relevance of data on animal behavior (particularly that of primates) to the understanding of human behavior. Just as cross-cultural data provide us with comparisons of how various societies organize certain behaviors, cross-species comparisons may eventually permit us to trace the biological roots of our behavior. We can, of course, also learn about biology from cross-cultural studies and about social systems from cross-species comparisons, for there are biological constants in all cultures and social organization is not an exclusively human characteristic.

How We Should Behave Sexually

Our third question is primarily, though not exclusively, a moral one. In addition to more strictly moral judgments, we must take into account, for instance, health considerations, factors that will enhance sexual satisfaction, and social customs and conventions that carry no moral weight but define courtesy, decency, and so on. At worst these codes are hollow rituals that needlessly complicate life, offer arrogant badges of status, and serve as tools of intimidation. At best they make social intercourse more comfortable and gracious. Although we must bear in mind these wider implications of this question, we shall be concerned here mainly with the more specifically moral aspects of sexual behavior.

Sexual morality requires judgments on a wide range of specific activities. Some activities are exceedingly rare. Others are so destructive or disruptive that no society, no matter how tolerant, can possibly condone them. We certainly cannot have "free rape" and it is highly doubtful that any society can manage widespread "free love" (in which anyone can sleep with anyone else whenever they choose). Even if morality could be set aside, it would be unrealistic to believe that we could always benefit from such arrangements without paying any price for them. For practical purposes, moral issues become matters of general concern when violations are attractive to many people (adultery or homosexuality, for example) and not barred by overwhelming practical considerations.

According to an old saying, a stiff penis has no conscience. The world, however, is not populated by penises and vaginas but by men and women, and they do have consciences. In fact, the moral questions related to sex, as well as to any other area of life, may well be the most critical ones. They certainly are the most difficult.

There are several well-known approaches to the discussion of sexual ethics. First is the straitlaced attitude, which at its worst stands for dullness, hypocritical double standards, tedious lists of "don'ts" with a few "dos" (that are hardly worth doing), and an outlook that generally inhibits all that is spontaneous, imaginative, and exciting in sex.

The opposite alternative is the callously libertine approach advocated by assorted sexual "liberators." Their central message is a cavalier insistence on discarding sexual shackles, casting off "Victorian" (and often long dead and buried) inhibitions, and "letting oneself go." The proponents and practitioners of this ethic are not always concerned with the consequences of their acts and even less bothered by offending the sensibilities of others.

Then there is the intermediary stance that is becoming increasingly prevalent, whereby permissiveness is tempered with consideration. There is little concern here with abstract principles; the attitude is rather one of "as long as it gives pleasure to all concerned and hurts no one, it is moral."

In the search for a sexual ethic, it is tempting to bypass basic moral issues by dismissing them as "philosophical" abstractions of no practical immediacy and instead to try to go directly to specifics of sexual behavior. This shortcut usually fails, for before we can sensibly discuss whether premarital sex, for example, is right or wrong, we must agree on what "right" and "wrong" mean. Nor can we be satisfied with the mere enunciation of moral generalities, for the specifics of sexual acts must also be recognized: Agreeing that sexual exploitation is wrong is insufficient to determine whether or not certain episodes of premarital sex are wrong. Premarital sex may or may not be exploitative, and, besides, exploitation is not the only kind of immorality.

The answer to a given moral question is dependent upon the content and application of specific principles. For example, the following considerations could enter into judgments about heterosexual intercourse: Children are best raised by their parents; sex is most satisfying in the context of stable relationships; and secrecy is inimical to honest relationships. In a particular sexual act these components (*content*) of moral judgment are then *applied* to the specific act. In the case of extramarital intercourse, it is likely that children resulting from the union will not be raised by both parents or that children in an existing marriage will lose a parent; that the relationship will be unstable; and that the relationship will have to be kept secret. Therefore adultery could be judged morally wrong on any or all counts.

In contemporary Western society, however, neither the content of moral judgments nor their applications are agreed upon. In the above example, some people would argue that it is preferable to raise children in communes, that casual sexual encounters can be satisfying and need not result in pregnancy, that it is possible to have stable relationships without the benefit of marriage, and that what you do not know will not hurt you. There are marked differences of opinion in these matters between groups divided along generational, educational, and socioeconomic lines. Even within clergy of the same denomination opinions are likely to be conflicting.

Faced with these uncertainties we are forced to reconsider basic ethical issues. But we cannot do that in a book of this kind. We could take a "neutral" position and raise many questions and answer none, which would offer no practical help. To take a polemical stance in defense of

one or another moral code would be inconsistent with the basic purpose of this book. The least objectionable solution to this dilemma appears to us to present various ethical alternatives and argue for "common sense" positions which, although lacking the force of moral truth, may serve as workable points of reference. We shall, therefore, next examine certain features of moral judgments that are especially pertinent to sexual behavior. These include the distinctions between private and public morality, absolute and relative moral stands, and changes in moral values.

Private and Public Morality

Moral principles seem to derive their authority from various sources: divine revelation, social customs, legal statutes, and so on. When religious institutions are strong, they tend to enforce their moral codes through the civil authorities. As the industrial West has become progressively more secularized, church and state have, at least in principle, separated their spheres of influence. In other cultures the law of the land is still based on religious documents (for example, the Koran in Saudi Arabia). Even in the West there are, of course, wide differences on this point, depending upon particular religious institutions and political systems: The Catholic Church in Italy and the Lutheran Church in Sweden exercise different kinds of influence.

In the realm of sexual behavior there is increasing awareness of the need to distinguish between private and public behavior, especially when the former involves acts between consenting adults conducted in private. The trend now is toward viewing such behavior as beyond the right of society to regulate it. In England homosexual acts that conform to this definition are no longer illegal, which does not mean that the English necessarily view homosexuality as healthy or moral. In this country homosexuality is still a criminal offense, and in many states the law is even concerned about which orifice of the wife is penetrated by the husband.

Sexual behavior becomes public when it is carried out before others or when others' individual rights are violated. Although standards obviously vary, all societies attempt to regulate public sexual behavior in one way or another. There is no record of a totally "free" community in this respect. Judgments, moral as well as legal, are important in both private and public life, but they should not be confused.

Our intent here is not to equate morality with legality but rather to draw attention to how and why we discriminate between certain forms of behavior. In some cases, such as marital coitus, we view the act as immoral and illegal only if it is performed in public. Yet, oral-genital contact is, at least in theory, deemed morally and legally objectionable even if engaged in in private.

Absolute versus Relative Standards

Should moral judgments be absolute and independent of all other considerations, or should they be relative, depending upon circumstances? This question has been debated for centuries, yet each thoughtful person must face it for himself.

Absolute moral stances are usually based on religious conviction but may also be supported by universal philosophical principles. For example, "You shall not commit adultery" (Exodus 20:14) is an absolute command that makes no allowances for "special situations."

Absolutist standards are clear and unambiguous, assuming one understands the basic premises. They obviate soul-searching on every occasion and help people to live according to their beliefs by minimizing personal choice and the likelihood of self-deception. While thus doing justice to the spirit, however, they tend to neglect the flesh. They may be useful as reminders of the basic weakness of man, but they do not function effectively as regulators

of his behavior or do so only at the cost of severe sexual deprivation.

Another difficulty with absolute codes is their rigidity. There are special circumstances in which most people are inclined to forgive if not to condone certain behavior. For instance, to use an extreme example, what does one say to a mother in the ghetto who prostitutes herself to feed her children? Hypothetically there may be other solutions to her poverty, but what if practically there are none? In condemning such a woman are we obeying the letter of the moral law but violating its spirit? Because of such considerations, even absolutist doctrines do frequently make tacit concessions to circumstance and thus become to some degree relative.

The more frankly relativistic approach provides the individual with a sense of autonomy, without so many stifling rules and regulations. He is captain of his fate. The moral absolutist who believes that premarital intercourse is wrong must face each opportunity with gloom. He is damned with guilt if he yields and damned with frustration if he does not. The moral relativist faces frustration too should he decide to abstain, but otherwise he is free to yield with joy. He thus approaches each opportunity with spontaneity and hope, for he can decide on the merits of the situation. A devout religious believer would shake his head at this logic, for it makes of morality a purely human enterprise. A cynic would shake his head because it seems unrealistically optimistic.

At worst a relativistic morality can be purely self-serving. One does what one wants to do and then rationalizes it. Justifications may be serious ("He loves me") or trivial ("I let him do it because it was New Year's Eve"). At its most responsible, relative morality is conditional on some profound principle like *agape* or selfless love. But even then it is not clear how we can be certain that the necessary conditions are fulfilled or what happens to sexual desire in their absence. What if the consequences of an act performed for the loftiest of motives prove harmful to one or the other participant or to a third party?

Morality and Change

That individuals and institutions change their moral views over time can hardly be disputed. Furthermore, change is usually initiated by the young, and often appears bewilderingly rapid to those experiencing its effects. The following statement is more than forty years old but could as well have been written today:

> The younger generation is behaving like a crazy man who for one lucid moment has suddenly realized that the physicians in charge are all demented, too. The elders who have for so long been the sacred guardians of civilization have bungled their task so abominably as to have lost irrevocably their influence for sobriety and sanity with the youth of the world. The failure of the church to treat sex and natural impulse with dignity and candor is the largest single fact in that disintegration of personal codes which confronts us in these hectic times: the inevitable swing of the pendulum from concealment to exhibitionism, from repression to expression, from reticence to publicity, from modesty to vulgarity. This revolutionary transition is inevitable and essentially wholesome, for all its crudity and grotesquerie.[1]

Members of the "younger generation" to which this paragraph refers are now the grandparents of the contemporary college population.

It is also possible to argue, however, that today we are going through a particularly rapid and far-reaching process of change in our attitudes toward sex. For instance, a 1969 poll of 1,600 Americans in various walks of life revealed that 81 percent considered a policeman who takes money from a prostitute to be worse than the prostitute; 71 percent thought that a doctor who refuses a house call to a seriously ill patient is worse than a homosexual; 54 percent regarded a politician who accepts bribes as more reprehensible than an adulterer.[2]

There is no doubt that the availability of reliable and reasonably safe contraceptives has already had a major influence, for moral and legal codes of sexual behavior have probably originated in large measure in concern about illegitimate offspring. The integrity of the family unit has had to be fiercely protected, for no culture can trifle with the upbringing of its progeny and hope to survive very long. It is possible, however, that such worries have now become less realistic and that certain traditional values like reproductive fertility are beginning to be viewed negatively.

As changes in deep-rooted sexual mores tend to be slow, no matter how dizzying they may appear, we have yet to experience the full impact of the new separation of sex from reproduction. Montagu ranks the significance of "the Pill" with that of the discovery of fire, learning how to make tools, the development of urbanism, the growth of scientific medicine, and the harnessing of nuclear energy.[3] In Chapter 18, we shall hazard some guesses about the future impact on sexual behavior and morality of available contraceptive devices and those likely to become available.

Fundamental Standards for Sexual Behavior

Given the uncertainties about why and how people behave sexually and the confusion between judgments of private and public behavior, the dilemma of absolute versus relative moral standards, and changing moral values, how do we decide how we should behave sexually here and now?

New Year's resolutions notwithstanding,

---

[1] Calverton and Schmalhausen (1929), p. 11.

[2] Changing morality . . . (1969).

[3] Montagu (1969), p. 11.

most of us do not regulate our sex lives formally. At best we have general feelings about how we should behave sexually. Most of us conform out of inertia or fear and break rules mainly on impulse. We reject some activities totally because of the enormity of their social consequences or the threats that they pose to our self-esteem. We find others unappealing or difficult of access. When we change our moral views, we usually do so with guilt and primarily to justify acts already committed. Hopefully, some of us also just grow wiser with time.

Our behavior and attitudes are determined by complex and often unconscious processes that explain the apparent irrationality with which we conduct our lives. That is "human nature," and little can be done to change it. We are not, however, totally helpless in this respect, even though it may be convenient to assume that we are. At some point every thoughtful and responsible person must exercise his "free will" and make choices. The first, and basic, choice is whether he wants to be a "moral" person, by whatever standard, or to take what he can for himself and the rest of the world be damned. The ambiguities and difficulties in making ethical judgments can be used as an excuse for avoiding them altogether: As no one really "knows" what constitutes right and wrong, why pay attention to them at all? Why not do as we please and let other people fend for themselves?

Unless we begin with a readiness at least to make reasonable efforts to act "morally," it is pointless to engage in discussions of sexual ethics. Yet, even such honest willingness to be moral may be insufficient by itself without additional guidelines. The Golden Rule,[4] or some version of it, is probably as universal an ethical yardstick as any available. Its central purpose is to make us concerned about how our acts influence the welfare of others as well as our own. In Kant's terms, it forces us to consider the consequences of our behavior if everyone else were also to behave likewise.

The Golden Rule is nevertheless no moral panacea. Its literal application would obviously be relativistic; in the extreme it would lead to absurd situations: A masochist, for example, would be entitled to hurt someone else because he presumably welcomes such treatment himself. Since we often do not know what is in our own best interest, how can we treat others in the light of how we would want them to treat us? Thus even if we all agreed to act upon such a rule, we would still need to know how to behave in actual practice under ambiguous and changing social conditions. Such "Golden Rules" therefore are not blueprints for action but "a point of view from which to consider acts."[5]

A corollary test of moral intent, aside from observation of the Golden Rule, is to test how far a person is willing to extend his area of concern. Even some avowed criminals have loyalties to limited circles of friends, perhaps simply as extensions of their own self-interest. To qualify as a moral code, concern must extend beyond such self-seeking attachment to circumscribed groups. In general, the wider the circle of concern, the more genuine is the moral awareness. Ultimately some recognition must be extended to everyone, on the basis of his humanity alone and regardless of social or psychological characteristics and affiliations. It takes very little effort to be considerate of those whom we love, need, or fear. The value of morality is in influencing behavior when such factors are not operative. Willingness to be a "moral" person is a necessary first step but does not automatically resolve the problem of mo-

---

[4] Matthew 7:12.

[5] Dewey (1960), p. 142. See also page 2 of Dewey for a list of works that have strongly influenced the development of the theory of morals.

rality. We also have to know how to act morally. Given the strength of sexual needs, the multiplicity of sexual aims, and the pressures of specific situations, it seems reasonable to seek a fundamental standard to guide us in satisfying our sexual needs in pleasurable yet "moral" ways. Our choice of such a standard is likely to reflect (through agreement or rebellion) the values of our families and culture. But, in order to be meaningful and workable, the standard must be a basically personal set of principles, self-enforced. Such standards cannot therefore be either proposed or adopted wholesale. They must be evolved over time and through experience. The most that other people can do for us is to suggest certain considerations that may be useful in this process, and that is what we intend to do here.

In order to do justice to sexual needs, as well as to realistic limitations on sexual expression, a fundamental standard must be located at a sensible point between absolute and purely relative on the moral continuum. Furthermore, this position must be fairly stable without being rigid. Bohannan differentiates between ethical principle, which is absolute, and morality, which is relative.[6] In this sense the standard of behavior should be a workable combination of ethical and moral principles.

These recommendations are easier offered than followed. When yesterday's sin becomes today's virtue, what do we say to those (or ourselves) who after years of self-denial discover that the rules of the game have changed? How do we learn discipline and teach it to our children, knowing that standards may change once again?

There are no ready answers to these questions. Above all we must be at peace with our own consciences. But we also must learn to live in society, and it is not always easy to reconcile these two imperatives.

---

[6]Bohannan (1969), Chapter 13.

To live in society in reasonable peace we have to know its rules and to be able to differentiate between those that can be broken with relative impunity and those that cannot. But what if the rules are irrational or unfair? Is adjustment to society the ultimate goal? The answers again involve personal choices. Most people follow the main trends of sexual behavior, and this majority provides stability. Many people, however, refuse to conform themselves, and some attempt to change others' behavior as well. Those who do should remember that deviation from the norm and forging ahead of one's time are the prerogatives of prophets and fools: One must be sure of his calling. Despite these imponderables, can we isolate some components of a fundamental standard of sexual behavior? There are at least five that seem worth major consideration.

Acceptance of Sexual Realities. Knowledge and acceptance of sexual realities are indispensable to sexual fulfillment and honesty. First comes the willingness to recognize biological facts, including practical knowledge (not necessarily from formal study) of the sexual organs and their functions. More important is acceptance of sexual feelings as legitimate biological and psychological manifestations, rather than as afflictions that must be exorcised or only grudgingly tolerated.

Next is a willingness to accept behavioral facts, to recognize how people behave, regardless of how we think that they ought to behave. People have remarkable capacities for self-deception. When an investigator reports statistics on the prevalence of some socially unacceptable behavior, there is always a public outcry. People object not because they have more reliable data but because the findings "don't make sense." "There cannot be so many homosexuals," they may say, but what they mean is that there should not be so many homosexuals. The tendency to think in stereotypes is often as strong as the tendency to deny:

According to some people, for example, any artist or intellectual, any man who is refined or gentle, is a homosexual. The behavioral realities are there, whether we recognize them or not. By ignoring, distorting, or denying them we merely fool ourselves. On the other hand, recognizing reality does not necessarily require condoning it.

Of all the various phases of our sex lives perhaps the most crucial is how well we face up to our own sexual thoughts and feelings. It is not possible to come to terms with ourselves as long as we refuse to confront our own sexuality. Some extraordinary individuals willingly recognize their sexual needs, yet delay or inhibit satisfying those needs for what they consider to be higher causes. That is one thing; simply to look away is another. We must be honest with ourselves and others in all things but especially in sex, for in this area pretense wears thin, bravado sounds hollow, and in bluffing others we bluff ourselves.

Enhancing Sexuality. Sexuality is not a wild horse that must be tamed and then exercised periodically. It is a potential with which we are born and which must be developed and nourished. It is every bit as important to be concerned about fulfilling our sexual capabilities as about fulfilling our intellectual or artistic capabilities.

The biological origins of sexual functioning do not ensure its automatic operation. Monkeys reared in isolation, for instance, do not know how to interact sexually. They are physically healthy and the sex drive is present, but the behavior that would lead to gratification is disorganized. Sexuality thus requires a certain milieu in which to develop. It needs warm contacts with other people, and it needs nurture.

To start with, there must be acceptance of the fundamental value of sex, in addition to acceptance of its reality. Such acceptance must come early and be incorporated into the personality structure of the child. His intimate relationships must enhance this feeling and permit the growth of his sexuality while instilling the restraints required for successful social living.

A fundamental standard must therefore include incentives as well as prohibitions. There is at times the assumption that one can do no wrong sexually as long as one does nothing at all. This approach is too negative and makes sexuality appear a necessary evil at best.

When a person enters a relationship that has a legitimate sexual component, is he not obligated to act effectively in a sexual way? When a parent does not provide for his family to the best of his ability or fails to care for his children we rightfully condemn him. But what about the spouse who makes no effort to maintain and improve his or her sexual attractiveness, who is lazy and inept in bed, and who tries to pass off sexual incompetence as innocence or decency?

Integrating Sex into Life as a Whole. Ultimately sex must make sense in the context of one's overall life. At certain periods sexual pressure is overwhelming, and sometimes we go to great lengths for its sake. But these instances are unusual and transitory and generally give way to more prosaic but steady sexual needs.

The place that sex occupies in our overall lives varies from one person to another. It is possible that we are born with different genetic predispositions in drive strength. Physical characteristics certainly have great influence on personality development and sexual behavior. For example, a pretty girl discovers very early the impact of her appearance upon others. The families that raise us and the community values that we learn to share or reject combine to shape our sexual behavior.

For some people sex becomes the pivot of their lives. Others hardly seem to care. The important point is not how many orgasms we achieve during a week or in a lifetime but whether or not our sexual needs are satisfied in a manner consistent with the strength of our desires, the requirements of our consciences, and the basic goals and purposes of our lives.

As we shall discuss in Chapter 12, some sexual dissatisfactions are caused by false or excessive expectations. Gratifying as sex may be, we can derive only so much from it. It cannot be substituted for all other needs, just as substitution of other satisfactions for those of sex can also be stretched only so far.

A fundamental standard that does not facilitate the integration of sexuality into life as a whole has limited usefulness. There are those who feel or act morally in all respects but sexually; sex is thus their secret vice. To a degree such schisms are unavoidable, but beyond certain limits they constitute points of weakness that are vulnerable to stress.

The Relation of Sex to Marriage. The aspect of heterosexual intercourse that raises the most frequent moral concern is whether it occurs within or outside of marriage. Marriage in its various forms is a universal institution. Sex almost always plays a part in it, but, of course, marriage involves much more than sex. At least in principle, however, there are important cultural differences in whether or not sex is restricted to marital partners.

In the West the traditional expectation has been that sex will be restricted in this way. In practice there have been many departures from this expectation, particularly among men. Currently the trend is toward less rigidity on this point for both sexes, particularly in relation to premarital sex. Statistical estimates of the incidence of virginity have been one of the more popular forms of sex research on university campuses. Current assessments vary, but half the student population in some colleges may well be engaging in coitus with some frequency. Extramarital coitus poses different kinds of problems, for it involves consideration of the spouse's feelings as well as of one's own conscience. The incidence of extramarital sex is apparently also on the rise, but again there are wide variations among social groups.

Because of the long-term mutual commitments of married couples, marital sex has particular significance. The marital relationship entails much more than sex. Nevertheless, sexual imcompatibility is a frequent cause of marital discord. Of course, marital discord arising from other sources also leads to sexual problems. The issue is not how much sex is necessary or "good" for the couple but whether or not sex plays a mutually satisfactory role in the relationship.

These areas are those to which a fundamental standard must apply. The matter has been discussed time and again and continues to be a major topic.[7] We shall have occasion to return to it in Chapters 10, 17, and 18.

Sex and Love. Each era and culture has had its views on love, and many of man's most eloquent expressions have been those of love. It is a tribute to the enduring strength of the sentiment to which it refers that the word "love"—hackneyed, abused, and exploited as it has been—still retains so much meaning.

A common, and justified, criticism of "sex manuals" is that they neglect appropriate consideration of love: Either they omit mention of it altogether, or they include only insipid platitudes. By the same token, however, essays on love tend to neglect or etherealize sex to a point at which it seems more suited to angels than to human beings.

The relation of sex to love, like that of sex to marriage, is a frequent source of controversy. The well-known Western ideal attempts to combine all three: sex, love, and marriage. But

---

[7] For views in contemporary academia, see Farnsworth and Blaine, eds. (1970), pp. 133–151; Student Committee on Human Sexuality (1970).

relatively few people seem able to attain this ideal or to sustain it over periods of years. Currently some people are willing to settle for love and sex alone, and love too may be on its way out as a necessary condition for sex. This change is viewed as moral degeneration by some people and as sexual regeneration by others.

There is, of course, a vast literature on love, as well as many historical and analytical studies of the concept of love.[8] Love is generally viewed as a complex emotion. There are different kinds of love and each act of love has a number of components. Thus, we differentiate sex (or lust), *eros* (or the urge toward higher states of being and relationships), *philia* (friendship, or brotherly love), and *agape* (or *caritas*, selfless love as exemplified in the love of God for man), and so on.[9]

Should sex, which is equally complex, not be viewed as an entity in its own right? If we can have love with or without sex, why can we not legitimately have sex with or without love? Everyone must ultimately face this question, and a well-thought-out fundamental standard may be preferable to the usual compromises reached under the pressures of the moment.

The Study of Sex

The vast store of presently available information and misinformation on sex has been gathered largely through informal observation and inference. Only a small part of it is the result of careful, systematic study. As even the latter often has serious shortcomings and because the notion of sex research itself raises certain pertinent questions, we shall briefly review those studies upon which we have relied most heavily in this book.

Studies in the Biology of Sex

There is a striking disparity between our scientific knowledge about reproduction and that about sex. Reproduction has been the object of intensive study: The anatomy of the reproductive system, its physiology and endocrinology, pregnancy and childbirth, contraception, and diseases of the sex organs are all subjects of highly developed medical specialties, each with its own extensive literature. The study of the nonreproductive aspects of human sexuality is, by contrast, still rudimentary, and it is the aspect with which we shall be concerned here.

In some areas there is considerable information carried over from research on reproduction; for instance, the study of anatomy is equally valuable in teaching about sexuality. Research on reproductive hormones is less directly relevant. This field is relatively new, however, and it has enormous potential. The study of all phases of animal sexuality is another area of major interest.

The physiology of coitus and orgasm is the area most sadly neglected in medical research. Even the most sophisticated physiology textbooks give this topic only cursory treatment. Aristotle observed that the testes are lifted within the scrotal sac during sexual excitement; more than twenty centuries passed before this fact was confirmed under laboratory conditions.

So far there has actually been only one extensive investigation of the physiology of orgasm, the one conducted by Masters and Johnson.[10] Their work is widely known, and numerous summaries of it are available.[11] We shall therefore outline it only briefly here.

---

[8]For a study of love in the Western world, see de Rougemont (1956). Some books on love have attracted wide attention; see, for example, Russell (1968); Fromm (1956).

[9]May (1969).

---

[10]Masters and Johnson (1966).

[11]See, for example, Brecher and Brecher (1966), Part I; Belliveau and Richter (1970), Chapter 4.

Masters and Johnson were primarily interested in investigating the physiology of orgasm in a laboratory setting. Their subjects were 694 normally functioning volunteers of both sexes between the ages of eighteen and eighty-nine years. The group included 276 married couples and 106 women and 36 men who were not married at the beginning of their participation in the project (though 98 in this group had been married before): a total of 382 women and 312 men. Many were from a university community in St. Louis, Missouri, and the group was predominantly white.

Applicants were screened by detailed interviews and physical examinations, and all those considered to have physical abnormalities, to be emotionally unstable, or to be motivated primarily by exhibitionism were eliminated. The subjects thus did not constitute a random sample of the general population, and in this sense they were not "average people." But they were not specifically selected for their sexual attributes; the only such requirement was that they be sexually responsive under laboratory conditions. In socioeconomic terms the group was as a whole better educated and more affluent than is the general population, though there was some representation across social classes. The subjects have, of course, remained anonymous and their biographical details are not available.

The research procedure was to observe, monitor, and sometimes film the responses of the body as a whole and the sex organs in particular to sexual stimulation and orgasm. Both masturbation and sexual intercourse were included in the experiment. In order to observe vaginal responses, a special penis-like object was used; it was made of clear plastic, which permitted direct observation and filming of the inside of the vagina. All research subjects were told in advance about the exact nature of the procedures in which they would participate, and the unmarried subjects were assigned mainly to studies that did not involve coitus.

The laboratory in which the research took place was a plain, windowless room containing a bed and monitoring and recording equipment. The subjects were first left alone to engage in sex, and only when they felt comfortable in this setting were they asked to perform in the presence of the investigators and technicians manning the equipment (recording heart rates, blood pressures, brain waves, and so on). It was the type of setting in which hundreds of experiments of all kinds are conducted in medical centers all over the world. The only unique element was the specific physiological function under study.

During almost a decade (beginning in 1954) at least 10,000 orgasms were investigated. Because more of the subjects were women and because females were sexually more responsive than were males under the circumstances, about three-quarters of these orgasms were experienced by women.

Although no one has yet attempted to replicate Masters and Johnson's research, the scientific validity of their physiological findings has been widely accepted. We shall discuss these findings in detail in Chapter 3. The study of human sexual response was merely the first phase of this research. Masters and Johnson have since embarked on a program of treatment for sexual malfunctioning[12] and are currently in the process of expanding their investigative work into other areas of sexual behavior. Their work on sexual malfunctions is discussed in Chapter 12.

Studies in Sexual Behavior

Research on sexual behavior has had a short though checkered history,[13] but is now less controversial than it has been. Although the origins of behavioral sex research go back to the nineteenth century, it is largely a twentieth-century phenomenon.

Henry Havelock Ellis (1859–1939) is probably the most widely recognized pioneer in sex research. He was a physician in Victorian England, but his contributions went beyond clinical study, and his major work evolved over several decades into a vast compendium of sexual knowledge: from anthropological and med-

---

[12] Masters and Johnson (1970); abstracted in Belliveau and Richter (1970).

[13] See Ellis, A., and Abarbanel, eds. (1967), pp. 25–33; Diamond, ed. (1968), Chapter 23; Brecher (1969).

ical literature to clinical case histories, life histories, and so on.[14] Ellis was subjected to considerable public vilification, but eventually his contributions were duly recognized. There are several biographies of him,[15] in addition to his autobiography.[16] Other pioneers around the turn of the century were August Forel, Iwan Bloc, A. Moll, Magnus Hirshfeld, and Richard von Krafft-Ebing. We shall make further reference to Krafft-Ebing's work in Chapter 11.

Sigmund Freud was born three years earlier than Ellis, and they died in the same year. Freud was not a sex researcher, in the sense that he did not deliberately initiate the investigation of sexual behavior; rather he developed his theories of human sexuality from his clinical work in psychoanalysis.[17] Nevertheless, his influence, both directly and through his followers, in making sexuality a focus of attention probably has outweighed that of any other person or group. Freud's multivolume collected works[18] include countless discussions of sexuality in human development and its "normal," as well as pathological, manifestations. The same is true of the writings of other psychoanalysts, though some have dealt with sexual issues more extensively than have others.[19] We shall make further references to psychoanalytic theory in Chapters 7–12.

Some sex research has also been conducted by anthropologists. With some notable exceptions (like Bronislaw Malinowski[20]), most early anthropologists paid less attention to (or at least reported less material on) the sexual practices of the cultures that they studied than to other features. A considerable body of anthropological data on sexual behavior has nevertheless accumulated over the years. Much of this information (pertaining to 190 societies) has been abstracted and made more accessible by Ford and Beach in a volume that also includes extensive material on sexual behavior among animals.[21] This work is the main source for the cross-cultural and animal data offered here.

Of all contemporary anthropologists Margaret Mead has probably done most to attract the attention of the general public to differences in norms of sexual behavior (particularly relating to premarital sex) in other cultures.[22] Through her work, as well as that of other anthropologists, many more people have become willing to view cross-cultural alternatives as potentially valuable models rather than as merely exotic oddities.

All the sex research mentioned so far has been clinical or descriptive in nature. Indispensable as such work is, it fails to provide a comprehensive view of the sexual behavior of large populations (as opposed to that of special groups and individuals). Also, as such findings are usually not presented in quantitative terms, they do not lend themselves to systematic statistical analysis, which in turn seriously hampers investigation of correlations and possible causal relations between component variables.

The investigations of Alfred C. Kinsey (1894–1956) and his collaborators have so far been the one major attempt at taxonomic study of human sexual behavior. The primary goal of this approach is to make understanding of individuals possible through examination of

---

[14] Ellis, H. (1942).

[15] For example, Peterson (1928); Goldberg (1926); Collis (1959); Calder-Marshall (1959).

[16] Ellis, H. (1939).

[17] Jones, E. (1953).

[18] Freud (1957–1964).

[19] See, for instance, Stekel (1930); Reik (1970); Reich (1961); Deutsch (1944–1945); Ferenczi (1950); Benedek (1952); Bonaparte (1953); Bieber *et al.* (1962); Marmor, ed. (1965); Marmor, ed. (1968), Chapter 6.

[20] Malinowski (1929).

[21] Ford and Beach (1951).

[22] Mead (1929, 1935, 1949).

their behavior in relation to that of the group as a whole. In order to determine whether a man is "tall" or "short," it is not enough to know his height accurately; we also need to know the range of heights in the group to which he belongs. The frequency and length of orgasm and so on are also meaningless unless we have standards of comparison from the general population. Basically, that is the purpose of the statistical approach in any field. It is one tool—though by no means the only or always the best tool—for the study of a given problem, yet it is indispensable to any systematic study of behavior.

Some taxonomic studies were conducted before the Kinsey survey,[23] and others have been conducted since, but none has come close to matching the scope of Kinsey's work. Because we have therefore relied primarily on the Kinsey data in this volume, we shall review only the Kinsey studies here.

Kinsey left no autobiography. There are, however, many brief accounts of his career,[24] one of them by a close associate, and detailed biographies are now being written.[25]

Kinsey was an entomologist (specializing in the gall wasp) at the University of Indiana, but his interest in sex research was aroused when he discovered in mid-career the inadequacy of our knowledge of human sexual behavior. His method of study was taxonomic, and his main research tool was the detailed personal interview. He and his associates collected more than 16,000 histories from people in all walks of life across the United States. Kinsey alone collected 7,000 such histories: an average of two a day for ten years.[26] He died, however, long before he could fulfill his goal of interviewing 100,000 individuals.

The procedures that his researchers followed in gathering and analyzing the data are described in detail in the introductory chapters of the first two volumes of the Kinsey studies.[27] There is also a considerable body of writing about his work. Probably no other book published during the past several decades has elicited as widespread a response as has the first Kinsey report, on the sexual behavior of the human male. Reaction to this work included a systematic and serious analysis by the American Statistical Association,[28] as well as thoughtful and less thoughtful opinions from pundits across the country.[29]

The more relevant criticisms of the Kinsey study are aimed at the sampling and interviewing techniques. The men and women whose sexual histories provided Kinsey with his data were not statistically representative of the population of this country. Kinsey was quite aware of this fact and made no claims to the contrary: "This is a study of sexual behavior in (within) certain groups of the human species . . . not a study of the sexual behavior of all cultures and of all races of man."[30] Although the Kinsey sample involved forty times as many subjects as had been included in any previous study, it was hampered by reliance on volunteers. "Self-selected" subjects do not constitute a random sample. Kinsey was also aware of this shortcoming and tried to minimize its effects. Given the nature of his research and the numbers of subjects required, however, he had to take all applicants. Because of these and related considerations, therefore, the Kinsey data are, strictly speaking, applicable only to his sample and cannot be generalized for the country as a whole or even for part of it. Yet, if interpreted cautiously, they still yield the best clues that we have to the patterns of sexual behavior of the population in this country several decades ago.

The second objection is more obvious. Does the average person talk freely to a relative stranger about the intimate details of his sex life? This question cannot be answered with any certainty, and Kinsey was, of course, well aware of the possibility of

[23] They are summarized in Kinsey *et al.* (1948), pp. 23–31.
[24] For example, see Brecher (1969), Chapter 5.
[25] Brecher and Brecher (1966), pp. 111–123.
[26] Brecher (1969), p. 116.

[27] Kinsey *et al.* (1948, 1953).
[28] Cochran *et al.* (1954).
[29] See Chall (1955).
[30] Kinsey *et al.* (1953), p. 4.

distortion. But, although it is true that in an interview of several hours much may be omitted or fabricated, this risk would exist even if the subjects could be interviewed over periods of years. The critical issue is then to know whether the magnitude of distortion totally invalidates the data or can be approximately corrected. Even without these defects the Kinsey data would probably be dated by now. Yet there is no better information.

In the furor raised by some of Kinsey's findings (especially those on premarital sex and homosexuality) his important contributions on sexual physiology and other aspects of sexuality have been overlooked by the general public. Even had Kinsey and his associates collected not one single item of new information they would still have rendered an invaluable service through their meticulous research into existing sources of sexual information. The Institute for Sex Research (usually called the Kinsey Institute) at the University of Indiana, presently headed by one of Kinsey's collaborators, Paul H. Gebhard, has probably the most extensive library and film collection in this field. Over the years the Institute has thus served a major educational function, while continuing to conduct research on sexuality.

Another important study to come from the Institute, one to which we shall refer in Chapter 11, is a survey of the personalities and life histories of more than 1,500 convicted sex offenders divided into fourteen categories.[31] Although this study is also limited by the nature of its sample (including only convicted male sex offenders, rather than a random sample of people exhibiting deviant forms of sexual behavior), it remains the major contribution in this field.

Problems in Sex Research

Beside the multitude of problems inherent in investigation of any complex human function, there are additional difficulties in sex research, notably questions about the propriety of such research itself. As usual, the polar positions in the controversy are most easily

stated. One is that sex is a natural biological function and that its physiology must be elucidated by the most effective methods available. The scientific study of other body functions has been most effectively conducted in the laboratory, and sexuality is no exception. This approach involves observing, recording, and quantifying data in ways that can be readily understood and replicated. Even though sex has well-known emotional components, its physiology is still best studied under the glare of laboratory lights rather than in the glow of moonlight. As far as behavioral research is concerned, we must likewise ascertain the facts in the most expeditious manner possible.

The objections to this approach originate from a variety of sources. One argument is that sex is more than just another physiological function and that certain moral considerations ought to regulate its study. For example, though a woman may experience the same physiological changes during orgasm with her husband or with a stranger, the fact is secondary to the issue of her committing an "immoral" act in the latter instance. Some people argue too that it is indecent to watch others making love, regardless of the purpose of the observation or the relationship of the pair.

Another type of objection is that the statistical and laboratory approaches miss the essence of sex by focusing on its physiological or quantifiable aspects: that it is appropriate to think in terms like "total outlet" and "sexual-response cycle" in connection with animals and machines but not with human beings.

Proponents of sex research correctly reply that man has fought progress in this area every inch of the way. There was a time when physicians even had to deliver babies under cover because exposing the mother's genitals would have seemed indecent. If this particular standard of decorum had been sustained we would not have the science of obstetrics today. Many people who were shocked by Kinsey's work

---

[31] Gebhard *et al.* (1965).

were not offended by Havelock Ellis, who had shocked his own contemporaries, however. Many of those who now object to physiological research accept Kinsey's work because he only inquired about what people did and did not ask them to perform for him. Such is progress. The pioneers blaze the trail, and the rest of us must be dragged behind, some kicking and screaming all the way.

This logic would have seemed unassailable some years ago, but it no longer does. Even though "pornography" has always sold, works on sex (serious as well as exploitative) have now become extremely lucrative, as books of very modest literary value on best-seller lists attest. The law is becoming more lenient and the public more tolerant, trends that we shall discuss further in Chapter 18.

The questions about sex research that are being raised today rarely result from public outcries any longer but come from concerned individuals. Their concern is not directed exclusively at sex research itself but at the larger issue of contemporary sexual attitudes. Are we losing our capacity for shame? Is the price of free public sexual expression a diminution of our sensitivities to the point of an irrevocable loss? Are we taking the mystery out of sex and even its meaning? [32]

Some critics claim that a new sexual tyranny is arising, as men, and more especially women, now feel shame and guilt at failing to experience orgasm (or orgasm at certain levels of intensity)—a reversal of the traditional pattern. Is there an inverse relation between the emphasis on sexual technique and the experiencing of sexual passion? As the Victorians sought love while avoiding sex, do we seek sex while avoiding love? Are we turning our sex organs

into machinery in our already highly mechanized world? [33]

These questions are disturbing to sophisticated and sensitive men and women; they are not like the objections of Anthony Comstocks and assorted turn-of-the-century prudes. There are no ready answers, and these questions will continue to be asked. But the real question actually is not whether or not sex research should continue (or whether or not free sexual expression ought to be permitted in the arts and in literature). Most reasonable people will agree that sex research should continue if we are to remain true to a quest for the truth. The relevant questions are how we should best study sex and what to do about the use and abuse of the resultant data.

The remarks of Alan Gregg in his introduction to the first Kinsey volume in 1948[34] are equally applicable now, more than two decades later.

Certainly no aspect of human biology in our current civilization stands in more need of scientific knowledge and courageous humility than that of sex. The history of medicine proves that in so far as man seeks to know himself and face his whole nature, he has become free from bewildered fear, despondent shame, or arrant hypocrisy. As long as sex is dealt with in the current confusion of ignorance and sophistication, denial and indulgence, suppression and stimulation, punishment and exploitation, secrecy and display, it will be associated with a duplicity and indecency that lead neither to intellectual honesty nor human dignity.[35]

---

[32] Tyrmand (1970).

[33] May (1969).

[34] Gregg was then Director for the Medical Sciences of the Rockefeller Foundation, the major financial supporter of the Kinsey study.

[35] Kinsey *et al.* (1948), p. vii.

BIOLOGY

"Praise be given to God, who has placed man's greatest pleasure in the natural parts of woman, and has destined the natural parts of man to afford the greatest enjoyment to woman."

The Perfumed Garden

The human body has no other parts as fascinating as the sexual organs. Venerated and vilified, concealed and exhibited, the human genitals have elicited a multitude of varied responses. They have been portrayed in every art form, praised and damned in poetry and prose, mutilated with religious fervor, and amputated in insane frenzy.

Many of us combine a lively interest in the sex organs with an equally compelling tendency either to deny such interest or to be ashamed of it. There are men and women who have been married for years, who have engaged in sexual intercourse countless times, but who have never looked frankly and searchingly at each other's genitals. Nor is this aversion merely a matter of prudishness. To many people, the sex organs appear neither beautiful nor sexy when viewed directly. Unfortunately, although concealment may promote desire, it also perpetuates ignorance.

The performance of basic procreative functions obviously does not require any formal knowledge of anatomy. Even accomplished lovers do not need to know much about the structural details of the sex organs. For most of us, however, some knowledge of sexual anatomy, particularly of the genitals, is helpful in understanding sexual functions. Anatomy, the study of structures, is related to physiology, which deals with functions, as geography is related to history: It is the description of the theater where the action takes place.

The various organs of the body are organized into systems. Each system serves a primary function such as digestion or respiration, and some parts of the body serve two or more systems. Both food and air, for instance, pass through the throat. The reference in all anatomical descriptions is to the upright body.

As sexual activity has been traditionally associated with procreation, the sex organs are considered part of the reproductive system. In lower animals this equation of sex with procreation is generally valid. As we climb the evolutionary scale, however, sexual activity becomes increasingly independent of reproduction and is indulged in for its own sake. We cannot procreate without sex, but we do not always engage in sex in order to procreate. This separability of sex and reproduction is an issue of far-reaching psychological and social consequence, one still unresolved in most human societies.

CHAPTER

ANATOMY
OF THE SEX ORGANS

Male Sex Organs

The reproductive system in either sex is located partly inside the body cavity and partly outside it. Although all the sex organs belong to a single system, the internal ones are regarded as primarily organs of procreation, whereas the external ones, the genitals, are associated more closely with sexual activity itself. The external organs are thus more likely objects of erotic and social interest.

The internal sex organs are housed in the *pelvis* (see Figure 2.1). The bones of the pelvis consist of the triangular end of the vertebral column (*sacrum*) and a pair of "hip bones," which are attached to the sacrum behind and to each other in front (at the *symphysis pubis*), thus forming a circle at their rim. Each "hip bone" actually consists of three separate bones (*ilium, ischium, pubis*) that are fused together. The components of the bony pelvis are in turn fixed and permit no movement.

The pelvic cavity is a bottomless basin crowded with organs belonging to the reproductive, urinary, and digestive systems (see Figure 2.2). Separating these organs from one another and supporting and attaching them to the bony framework of the body are various tough fibrous structures analogous to canvas sheets (*fasciae*) and cords (*ligaments*). These structures, along with the various muscles in the area, form a multilayered "hammock" in which the genital organs are embedded or from which they are suspended.

External Genitals

The external sex organs of the male consist of the *penis* and the *scrotum*. The *testes,* or *testicles,* and their attachments within the scrotal sac, though outside the body cavity, are generally not considered part of the external genitals.

The penis ("tail") is the male organ for copulation.[1] It contains three parallel cylinders of spongy tissue (see Figure 2.3), through one of which runs a tube (*urethra*) that conveys both

---

[1] *Phallus* is the Greek name for "penis." Many colloquial terms refer to the erect penis as a pricking, probing, piercing instrument. Nefzawi's *The Perfumed Garden* has more exotic descriptions like "housebreaker," "ransacker," "rummager," and "swimmer" (1964 ed., pp. 156–157).

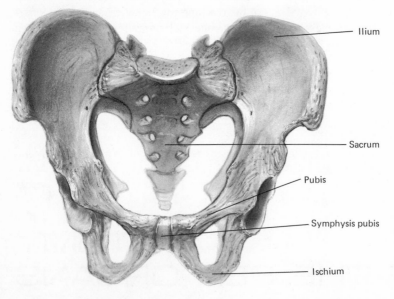

Ilium

Sacrum

Pubis

Symphysis pubis

Ischium

Figure 2.1. Male bony pelvis. From Dienhart, *Basic Human Anatomy and Physiology* (Philadelphia: Saunders, 1967), p. 35. Reprinted by permission.

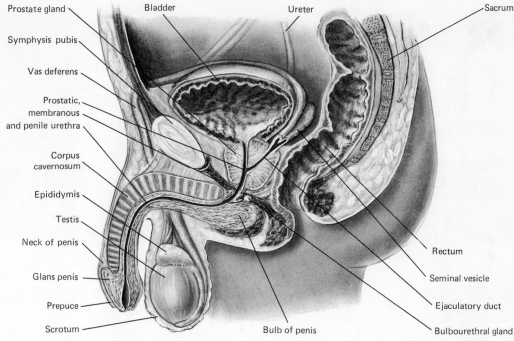

Figure 2.2. The male reproductive system. From Dienhart, *Basic Human Anatomy and Physiology* (Philadelphia; Saunders, 1967), p. 207. Reprinted by permission.

urine and semen. The portion of the penis that is attached to the pelvis is its *root*; the free, pendulous portion of the penis is known as its *body*.

The three cylinders of the penis are structurally similar. Two of them are called the cavernous bodies (*corpora cavernosa*), and the third is called the spongy body (*corpus spongiosum*) (see Figure 2.3). Each cylinder is wrapped in a fibrous coat, but the cavernous bodies have an additional common "wrapping" which makes them appear to be a single structure for most of their length. When the penis is flaccid, these bodies cannot be seen or felt as separate structures, but in erection the spongy body stands out as a distinct ridge on the underside of the penis.

As the terms "cavernous" and "spongy" suggest, the penis consists of an agglomeration of irregular cavities and spaces, very much like a dense sponge. These tissues are served by a rich network of blood vessels and nerves. When the penis is flaccid, the cavities contain little blood. During sexual arousal they become engorged, and their constriction within their tough fibrous coats causes the characteristic stiffness of the penis. We shall discuss the mechanism of erection further in subsequent chapters.

At the root of the penis, the inner tips (*crura*) of the cavernous bodies are attached to the pubic bones. The spongy body is not attached to any bone. Its root expands to form the *bulb* of the penis, which is fixed to the fibrous "hammock" that stretches in the triangular area beneath the pubic symphysis. The crura and the bulb constitute the root of the penis.

The smooth, rounded head of the penis is

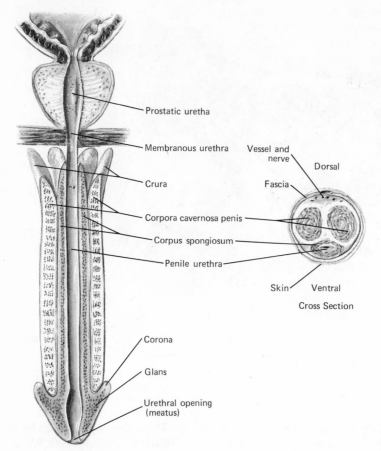

Prostatic uretha

Membranous urethra

Crura

Corpora cavernosa penis

Corpus spongiosum

Penile urethra

Vessel and nerve

Dorsal

Fascia

Skin

Ventral

Cross Section

Corona

Glans

Urethral opening (meatus)

Longitudinal Section

Figure 2.3. The penis. From Dienhart, *Basic Human Anatomy and Physiology* (Philadelphia: Saunders, 1967), p. 211. Reprinted by permission.

known as the *glans* ("acorn") *penis*. This structure is actually formed entirely by the free end of the spongy body, which expands to shelter the tips of the cavernous bodies. The glans penis has particular sexual importance. It is richly endowed with nerves and extremely sensitive. Most tactile stimulation of the penis is transmitted through the glans. The rest of the penis is far less sensitive. Although the glans as a whole is highly excitable, its underside, where a thin strip of skin (*frenulum*) connects it to the adjoining body of the penis is particularly sensitive, as is its rim, or crown (*corona*),

which slightly overhangs the superficial constriction called the *neck* of the penis. This neck is the boundary between the body of the penis and the glans. At the tip of the glans is the longitudinal slit for the urethral opening.

The skin of the penis is hairless and unusually loose, which permits expansion during erection. Although the skin is fixed to the penis at its neck, some of it folds over and covers part of the glans (like the sleeve of an academic gown), forming the *prepuce*, or *foreskin*. Ordinarily the prepuce is retractable and the glans readily exposed. Circumcision (which we shall discuss later) is the excision of the prepuce. In the circumcised penis, therefore, the glans is always totally exposed.

Under the prepuce and in the corona and the neck are small glands that produce a cheesy substance (*smegma*) with a distinctive smell. This is a purely local secretion of no known function that must not be confused with the semen that is discharged through the urethra.

The human penis (unlike that of all other carnivora) has no bone. Nor does it have muscles within it. The *bulbocavernosus* and *ischiocavernosus* muscles surround the bulb and the crura respectively, but their function is primarily in helping eject urine and semen through the urethra. Although these muscles may have an indirect role in contributing to venous congestion, the process of erection does not directly involve muscles, nor can the penis be moved voluntarily except for slight jerking motions.

The scrotum is a multilayered pouch. Its thin outermost skin is darker in color than is the rest of the body. It has many sweat glands, and at puberty it becomes sparsely covered with hair. The second layer consists of loosely organized muscle fibers (*dartos muscle*) and fibrous tissue. These muscle fibers are not under voluntary control but do contract in response to cold, sexual excitement, and a few other stimuli. Under such conditions the scrotum appears compact and heavily wrinkled. Otherwise it hangs loose, and its surface is smooth. When the inner side of the thigh is stimulated, the dartos muscle contracts slightly (the *cremasteric reflex*).

The scrotal sac contains two separate compartments, each of which houses a testicle and its *spermatic cord* (see Figure 2.4). The spermatic cord is a composite structure from which the testicle is suspended in the scrotal sac. It includes the tube (*vas deferens*) that carries the sperm from the testicle, as well as blood vessels, nerves, and muscle fibers. When these muscles

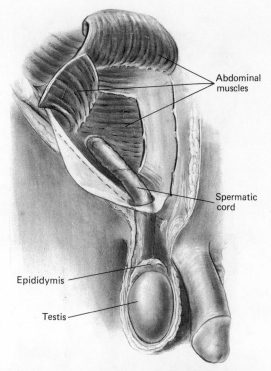

Figure 2.4. Spermatic cord in the inguinal canal. From Dienhart, *Basic Human Anatomy and Physiology* (Philadelphia: Saunders, 1967), p. 209. Reprinted by permission.

contract, the spermatic cord also contracts and pulls the testicle upward within the scrotal sac.

The spermatic cord enters the abdominal cavity from the scrotal sac by traversing a region of the abdominal wall called the *inguinal canal.*

Size of the Penis. Variation in size and shape from individual to individual is the rule for all parts of the human body. Nevertheless, the size and shape of the penis are often the cause of curiosity and amusement as well as apprehension and concern. Representations of enormous penises can be found in numerous cultures, including some from remote antiquity (see Figure 2.5). These anatomical exaggerations are generally not mere caricatures or monuments to male vanity but symbols of fertility and life.

Figure 2.5. Mochica pottery. Courtesy of William Dellenback, Institute for Sex Research, Inc.

The average penis is three to four inches long when flaccid and somewhat more than six inches in erection. Its diameter in the relaxed state is about $1\frac{1}{4}$ inches and increases another $\frac{1}{4}$ inch in erection. Penises can, however, be considerably smaller or larger (erect penises larger than 13 inches have been measured).[2]

The size and shape of the penis, contrary to popular belief, are not related to a man's body build, race, virility, or ability to give and receive sexual satisfaction. Furthermore, variations in size tend to decrease in erection: The smaller the flaccid penis, the proportionately larger it tends to become when

erect. The penis does not grow larger through frequent use.

The folklore surrounding penis size, though generally unsubstantiated, is nevertheless quite interesting. Arab and Indian sources are quite specific in this regard. According to *The Perfumed Garden,* for example, "the virile member, to please women," must be at most as long as the breadth of twelve fingers (about nine inches) and at least as long as the breadth of six fingers (about four and one-half inches).[3]

Two of the best-known Indian "love manuals" (*Kama Sutra* and *Ananga Ranga*) classify men in three categories on the basis of penis size: the hare-man (with an erect penis six finger breadths long); the bull-man (nine finger breadths); and the horse-man (twelve finger breadths). These works also attempt to correlate penis size with personality traits.[4]

Circumcision ("cutting around") is the excision of the foreskin and is practiced around the world both as a ritual and as a sanitary measure. The operation is simple: The prepuce is pulled out in front of the penis, and part of it is cut off. The remaining skin leaves the glans and the neck of the penis completely exposed (see Figure 2.4). If the operation is performed under hygienic conditions, the wound heals promptly, and there are usually no complications.

Circumcision is medically obligatory if the foreskin is so tight that it cannot be easily retracted over the glans (*phimosis*). Otherwise, it is optional, although in most North American hospitals it is now usually performed on male infants (with parental consent) on the second day after birth. Its advocates point out that after circumcision smegma does not accumulate under the prepuce and that it is therefore generally easier to keep the penis clean. Also, cancer of the penis seems to be less frequent among the circumcised and cancer of the cervix less common among their spouses, though the causal relation has not yet been satisfactorily established.

It is generally assumed that the circumcised male

[2]Dickinson (1949), Fig. 112.

[3]Nefzawi (1964 ed.), p. 72.

[4]Vatsyayana, *The Kama Sutra* (1963 ed.), p. 87; Malla, *The Ananga Ranga* (1964 ed.), pp. 55–58.

is more rapidly aroused during coitus because of his fully exposed glans penis. Circumcision is also believed to cause difficulty in delaying ejaculation. Current research has failed to support these beliefs: There seems to be no difference between the excitability of the circumcised and uncircumcised penises.[5]

Phallic Worship. The worship of the male genitals is one of the oldest religious practices known. It is usually interpreted as related to fertility cults: the expression of man's desire for the perpetuation of the race and his identification with the reproductive powers of nature. In ancient Greece phallic worship centered around Priapus and the Dionysiac cults. Priapus was the son of Aphrodite (goddess of love) and Dionysus (god of fertility and wine). Usually represented as a grinning little man with an enormous penis, Priapus was very much in evidence during the many festivals honoring Dionysus, which were occasions for orgiastic abandon.

Under the Roman Empire, phallic worship took on a less festive, rather grim form. During the yearly festival, the notorious Day of Blood, some frenzied participants actually mutilated their own genitals. In fact, self-castration during this festival became a prerequisite for admission into the priesthood. The Romans apparently also wore amulets representing the male genitals in various forms (see Figure 2.6).

In India, Shiva (or Siva), one of the three supreme gods of Hinduism, was symbolically represented and worshipped as an erect penis (the lingam). It was believed that marriages would be more fertile if virgin brides were first deflowered by the lingam, usually a stone phallus. Phallus worship has also been prominent in Japanese and some American Indian fertility rites.

Internal Sex Organs

The reproductive system (see Figure 2.2) can be viewed as consisting of three functional units: organs for the production of sperm (the testes), a system of ducts for the storage and transport of sperm (epididymis, vas deferens,

---

[5]Masters and Johnson (1966), p. 190.

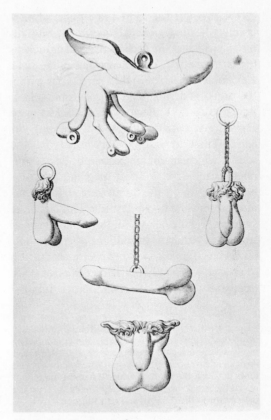

Figure 2.6. Roman amulets.

ejaculatory duct, urethra), and the apparatus for delivery of the sperm (the penis). The components of the first two units are the internal sex organs.

The testes ("witnesses": from the ancient custom of placing the hand on the genitals when taking an oath) are the *gonads,* or reproductive glands, of the male. They produce sperm, as well as the male hormone testosterone.

The two testicles are about the same size (2 x 1 x 1¼ inches), although the left one usually hangs somewhat lower than the right one. The weight of the testicles varies from one person to another but averages about one ounce and tends to lessen in old age.

Each testicle is enclosed in a tight, whitish, fibrous sheath (*tunica albuginea,* "white tunic"),[6] which at the back of the organ thickens (*mediastinum testis*) and penetrates the testicle. Its ramifications (*septa*) then spread out within the organ and subdivide it into conical *lobes* (see Figure 2.7). Each lobe is packed with convoluted *seminiferous* (sperm-bearing) *tubules.* These thread-like structures are the sites at which sperm are produced. Each seminiferous tubule is 1–3 feet long and the combined length of the tubules of both testes measures several hundred yards. This elaborate system of tubules allows for the production and storage of hundreds of millions of sperm. The process of *spermatogenesis* or sperm production (discussed more fully in Chapter 5) takes place exclusively within the seminiferous tubules:

---

[6] This anatomical feature is responsible for the sterility that may follow mumps in adulthood. When this virus infection involves the testicles, the swelling organs push against their unyielding covers, and the pressure destroys the delicate tubes in which the sperm develop. When the same virus infects the female ovaries, the organs simply swell up and then return to their normal size and function.

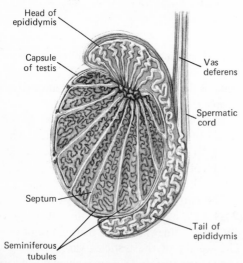

Figure 2.7. Testis and epididymis. From Dienhart, *Basic Human Anatomy and Physiology* (Philadelphia: Saunders, 1967), p. 207. Reprinted by permission.

Microscopic cross sections thus show sperm at various levels of maturation (Figure 2.8). The first or earliest cell in this maturational chain is the *spermatogonium* which in subsequent stages of development is successively called a *spermatocyte* (primary and secondary); *spermatid;* and finally, when mature, *spermatozoa* or sperm. The seminiferous tubules of the newborn are solid cords (Figure 2.8A) where only undifferentiated cells are evident. Following puberty the tubules develop a hollow center (Figure 2.8B) into which the sperm are released.

The second major function of the testes is the production of the male sex hormone. As hormones are secreted directly into the bloodstream, glands that produce them need no ducts and are known as *ductless,* or *endocrine,* glands. The testicular cells that produce the male hormone are found between the seminiferous tubules and are therefore known as *interstitial cells* (or *Leydig's cells*): They are scattered in the connective tissue in close association with blood vessels. The cells responsible for the two primary functions of the testes (reproductive and endocrine) are thus quite separate and never in contact.

The seminiferous tubules converge in an intricate maze of ducts which ultimately leave the testis and fuse into a single tube that forms the beginning of the system of paired genital ducts already mentioned. Figure 2.9 shows the route that sperm follow through these larger ducts in order to be ejaculated.

The epididymis ("over the testis") constitutes the first portion of this paired duct system. Each is a remarkably long tube (about 20 feet) that is, however, so tortuous and convoluted that it appears as a C-shaped structure not much longer than the testis to whose surface it adheres (see Figure 2.7).

The vas deferens, or *ductus deferens* ("the vessel that brings down"), is the less tortuous and much shorter continuation of the epididymis. It travels upward in the scrotal sac for

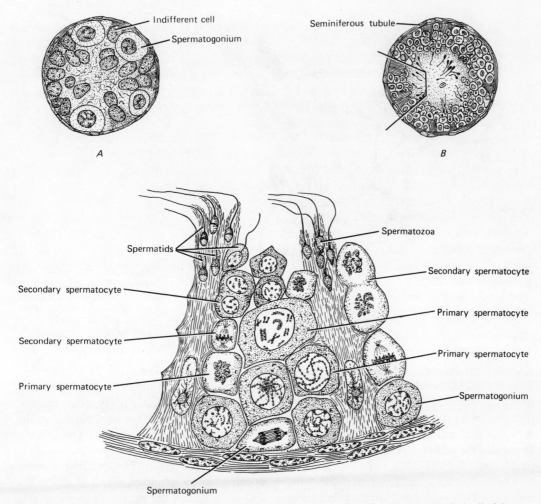

Figure 2.8. Human testis tubules, in transverse section. (*A*) Newborn (× 400); (*B*) adult (× 115); (*C*) detail of the area outlined in (*B*) (× 900). From Arey, *Developmental Anatomy,* 7th ed. (Philadelphia: Saunders, 1965), p. 41. Reprinted by permission.

a short distance before entering the abdominal cavity; its portion in the scrotal sac can be felt as a firm cord.[7]

The terminal portion of the vas deferens is enlarged and once again tortuous; it is called the *ampulla* ("flask"). It passes to the back of the urinary bladder (Figure 2.10), narrows to a

---

[7] That the vas is so easily located and surgically accessible makes it the most convenient target for sterilizing men. The operation (vasectomy, "cutting the vas") is very simple: Under local anesthesia, a small incision is made in the scrotum, and the vas is simply either tied or cut. To stop all passage of sperm, the operation must, of course, be performed on both sides. The man is then sterile, but his sex drive, potency, and ability to have orgasms are not affected. He will continue to ejaculate, but his semen will contain no sperm. It is sometimes possible to reestablish fertility by untying or suturing the severed vas. This procedure is, however, very delicate and not always successful.

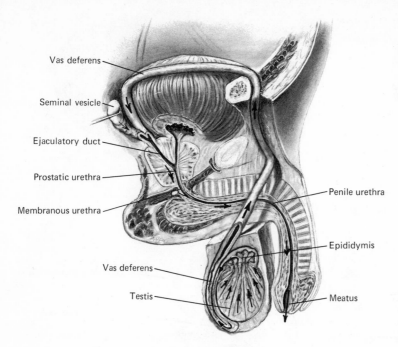

Vas deferens

Seminal vesicle

Ejaculatory duct

Prostatic urethra

Membranous urethra

Penile urethra

Epididymis

Vas deferens

Testis

Meatus

Figure 2.9. Passage of spermatozoa. From Dienhart, *Basic Human Anatomy and Physiology* (Philadelphia: Saunders, 1967), p. 212. Reprinted by permission.

tip, and joins the duct of the seminal vesicle to form the *ejaculatory duct*. This portion of the paired genital duct system is very short (less than one inch) and quite straight. It runs its entire course within the *prostate gland* and opens into the prostatic portion of the *urethra* (see Figures 2.2 and 2.10).

The *urethra* has a dual function in the male, conveying both semen and urine. It begins at the bottom of the urinary bladder and periodically empties accumulated urine. (It must not be confused with the two *ureters*, each of which begins in one kidney and carries urine into the bladder.) The urethra is about eight inches long and is subdivided into prostatic, membranous, and penile parts (see Figures 2.2 and 2.3).

The prostatic portion of the urethra is more easily dilated than are the others. In its posterior wall are the tiny openings of the two ejaculatory ducts. The multiple ducts of the prostate gland also empty into the prostatic urethra like a sieve (see Figure 2.3).

Voluntary control of urination is made possible by the muscle fibers (*urethral sphincter*) surrounding the short membranous urethra: When sufficient urine has accumulated in the bladder the resulting discomfort prompts the person to relax the urethral sphincter to allow the passage of urine. The external urethral opening has no sphincter, which is why at the end of urination the urine left in the penile portion must be squirted out through the contraction of the bulbocavernosus and ischiocavernosus muscles.

The penile part of the urethra has already been discussed. It pierces the bulb of the corpus spongiosum, traverses its whole length, and terminates at the tip of the glans in the external urethral opening (see Figure 2.3). The *bulbourethral glands* (to be discussed) empty into this portion. The urethra is the most common site of gonorrheal infection in men. (Gonorrheal urethritis is discussed in Chapter 12.)

Accessory Organs

Three accessory organs perform auxiliary functions in the male. They are the prostate gland, two seminal vesicles, and two bulbourethral glands.

The prostate is an encapsulated structure about the size and shape of a large chestnut and consisting of three lobes. It is located with its base against the bottom of the bladder. It consists of smooth muscle fibers and glandular tissue whose secretions account for much of the seminal fluid and its characteristic odor. As we have described, it is traversed by the urethra and the two ejaculatory ducts, and prostatic fluid is conveyed into this system through a "sieve" of multiple ducts.

The prostate is small at birth, enlarges rapidly at puberty, but usually shrinks in old age. Sometimes, however, it becomes enlarged and interferes with urination, necessitating surgical intervention. (It may be removed piece by piece through the urethra or in open surgery.) The size of the prostate is determined by means of rectal examination.

The seminal vesicles are two sacs, each about two inches long. Each ends in a straight, narrow duct, which joins the tip of the vas deferens to form the ejaculatory duct. The function of the seminal vesicles was once assumed to be the storage of sperm (each holds about two to three cubic centimeters of fluid), but it is currently believed to be primarily involved in contributing fluids which initiate the motility of sperm.

The bulbourethral glands (*Cowper's glands*) are two pea-sized structures flanking the penile urethra, into which each empties through a tiny duct. During sexual arousal these glands secrete a clear, sticky fluid that appears as a droplet at the tip of the penis (the "distillate of love"). There usually is not enough of this secretion to serve as a coital lubricant. As it is alkaline, however, it may help to neutralize the acidic

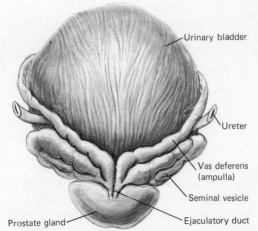

Figure 2.10. The bladder, seminal vesicles, and prostate gland—posterior view. From Dienhart, *Basic Human Anatomy and Physiology* (Philadelphia: Saunders, 1967), p. 210. Reprinted by permission.

urethra, which is harmful to sperm, in preparation for the passage of semen. Although this fluid must not be confused with semen, it does often contain stray sperm, which explains pregnancies resulting from intercourse without ejaculation.

Female Sex Organs

Despite dramatic differences in appearance, the female sex organs are built according to the same basic plan as are those of the male. Organs of the two sexes can thus be compared according to developmental origin, as well as to function although similar developmental origin may or may not be reflected in similar functions. For example, the *ovaries* develop from the same type of tissue as do the testes, and their functions are similar as well: the production of germ cells (eggs, corresponding to sperm). On the other hand, whereas the anatomical counterpart of the penis is the *clitoris*, its functional counterpart is the *vagina* with which it operates in a complementary fashion, like a lock and key.

Later in this chapter we shall trace the parallel development of the sex organs in the two sexes. Meanwhile, it is useful to consider the female reproductive organs as being external or internal as well as having a tripartite functional division corresponding to that of the male: production of germ cells (in the ovaries), transport of these cells (through the *uterine tubes* to the *uterus*), and reception of the ejaculate from the penis (in the vagina). As fertilization occurs inside the female body, the female duct system carries sperm as well as eggs and the fertilized product of these two cells. The uterus, of course, is also the location where the embryo develops to maturity. The female sex organs have therefore, in addition to their functions corresponding to those of the male, a fourth and uniquely maternal function.

Many of the female sex organs, like those of the male, are housed in the pelvic cavity. The female pelvis is, however, broader, in order to permit passage of the infant's head during birth (see Figure 2.11). Women with narrow or male type pelvic outlets frequently cannot give birth

naturally, and their children must be delivered through *abdominal (Cesarian) section* of the uterus (discussed in Chapter 5).

In order to accommodate anatomical differences, the supporting structures—fascia, ligaments, and muscles—are quite different in the female, but the basic plan and purpose of the multilayered "hammock" suspended across the lower opening of the pelvis remain the same.

External Genitals

The external genitals of the female are collectively called the *vulva* ("covering") or the *pudendum* ("a thing of shame"). They include the *mons pubis* (or *mons veneris,* "mount of Venus"), the *major* and *minor lips,* the clitoris, and the vaginal opening.

The mons pubis is the soft, rounded elevation of fatty tissue over the pubic symphysis. After it becomes covered with hair during puberty, the mons is the most visible part of the female genitals.

The major lips (*labia majora*) are two elongated folds of skin that run down and back from

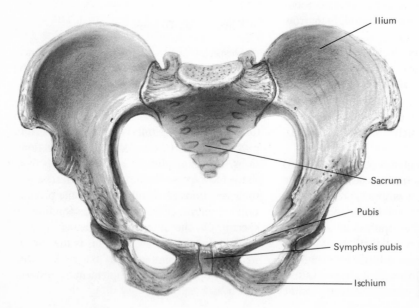

Ilium

Sacrum

Pubis

Symphysis pubis

Ischium

Figure 2.11. Female bony pelvis. From Dienhart, *Basic Human Anatomy and Physiology* (Philadelphia: Saunders, 1967), p. 35. Reprinted by permission.

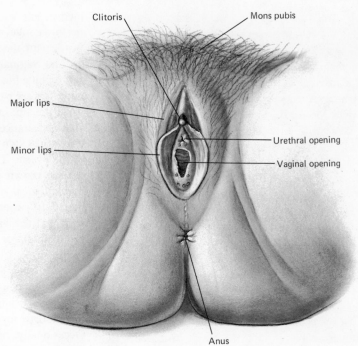

Clitoris   Mons pubis

Major lips

Minor lips

Urethral opening

Vaginal opening

Anus

Figure 2.12. External female genitalia. From Dienhart, *Basic Human Anatomy and Physiology* (Philadelphia: Saunders, 1967), p. 217. Reprinted by permission.

the mons pubis. Their appearance varies a great deal: Some are flat and hardly visible behind thick pubic hair; others bulge prominently. Ordinarily they are close together, and the female genitals appear "closed."

The major lips are more distinct in front, where they meet at the *anterior commissure.* Toward the anus, they flatten out and merge with the surrounding tissues. The outer surfaces of the major lips are covered with skin of a darker color, which grows hair at puberty. Their inner surfaces are smooth and hairless. Within these folds of skin are bundles of smooth muscle fibers, nerves, and vessels for blood and lymph. The space between the major lips is the *pudendal cleft*; it becomes visible only when the lips are parted (see Figure 2.12).

The minor lips (*labia minora*) are two pinkish, hairless folds of skin located between the major lips. The space that they enclose is the vaginal *vestibule* into which the vaginal and

urethral orifices, as well as the ducts of the Bartholin's or greater vestibular glands, open. The minor lips merge with the major lips behind. In front each divides in two: The upper portions form a single fold of skin over the clitoris and are called the *prepuce of the clitoris*; The lower portions meet beneath the clitoris as a separate fold of skin (*frenulum of the clitoris*).

From front to back the structures enclosed by the minor lips are thus: the clitoris, the external urethral orifice, the vaginal orifice, and the openings of the two greater vestibular glands. The anus, which is completely separate from the external genitals, lies farther back.

The clitoris ("that which is closed in") resembles a miniature penis. It consists of two corpora cavernosa (but no corpus spongiosum), the tips (crura) of which are attached to the pubic bone. Most of its body is covered by the upper folds of the minor lips, but its free,

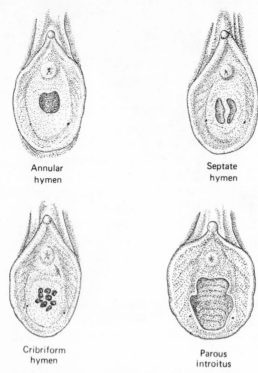

Annular
hymen

Septate
hymen

Cribriform
hymen

Parous
introitus

Figure 2.13. Types of hymens. From Netter, *Reproductive System* (Summitt, N.J.: Ciba, 1965), p. 90. Reprinted by permission.

rounded tip (the glans) projects beyond it. The urethra does not pass through it.

As does the penis, the clitoris becomes engorged with blood during sexual excitement. Because of the way it is attached, however, it does not become erect as does the penis. Functionally it corresponds more closely to the glans of the penis: It is richly endowed with nerves, highly sensitive, and a major focus of sexual stimulation. The clitoris has also been subjected to ritual mutilation.[8]

The external urethral orifice is a small,

median slit with raised margins. The female urethra conveys only urine and is totally independent of the reproductive system.

The vaginal orifice or *introitus* is not a gaping hole but rather is visible only when the inner lips are parted. It is easily distinguishable from the urethral opening by its larger size. The appearance of the vaginal orifice depends to a large extent upon the shape and condition of the *hymen*. This delicate pinkish membrane has no known physiological function, but its psychological and cultural significance is enormous. It varies in shape and size and may surround the vaginal orifice (annular), bridge it (septate), or serve as a sieve-like cover (cribriform) (Figure 2.13). There is, however, almost always some opening to the outside.[9]

Most hymens will permit passage of a finger (or sanitary tampon) but usually cannot accommodate an erect penis without tearing. Occasionally, however, a very flexible hymen will withstand intercourse. This fact, coupled with the fact that the hymen may be torn accidentally, makes the condition of the hymen unreliable as evidence for or against virginity. In childbirth the hymen is torn further and only fragments remain attached to the vaginal opening (parous introitus).

Defloration. The tearing of the hymen during the first coitus has received a great deal of attention in "marriage manuals." Under ordinary circumstances it is an untraumatic event. In the heat of sexual excitement the woman feels minimal pain. Bleeding is generally also slight. What makes first intercourse a painful experience for some is not the "heroic" effort of breaching this "formidable" barrier. Rather, it is the muscular tension that an

---

[8]Clitoridectomy, or female circumcision, is rare but has been practiced in the Middle East and in certain tribes of Africa and Latin America. The term "circumcision" is misleading in this connection, for it is the clitoris itself, rather than its "prepuce," that is amputated.

[9]In rare instances, the hymen consists of a tough fibrous tissue that has no opening (*imperforate hymen*). This condition is usually detected after a girl begins to menstruate and the products of successive menstrual periods accumulate in the vagina and uterus as an enlarging mass. It is corrected by surgical incision, usually without aftereffects.

anxious, unprepared, or unresponsive woman experiences that may cause pain. Clumsy attempts at penetration of an unlubricated vagina guarded by a tense and spastic introitus do not, of course, facilitate matters. In anticipation of such difficulties, some women with no premarital sexual experience have their hymens cut surgically before their wedding nights. Usually they do so with the knowledge and consent of their grooms to avoid doubts of virginity or disappointment at being "cheated" of the experience of defloration. The frequency of this practice is unknown.

The hymen is an exclusively human body part. Other primates and lower animals do not have it. Why and how the hymen evolved is not clear, but most human societies seem to have "made the most" of it. There is hardly a culture that has not been preoccupied with its proper disposal. In medieval times some lords claimed the prerogative of "plucking the maidenheads" of their female subjects (*droit du seigneur*) on their wedding nights. Where defloration has been thought to pose a magical threat, special men have been assigned to carry it out. Among the seminomadic Yungar of Australia, girls were deflowered by two old women a week before marriage. If a girl's hymen was discovered at this time to be not intact, she could be starved, tortured, mutilated, or even killed. The old Kurdish custom of parading the blood-stained bed sheets on the wedding night as proof of the bride's chastity is well known. In other cultures horns, stone phalluses, or other assorted implements have been used in ritual deflorations. In view of the widespread practices, one wonders to what extent surgical defloration in our culture serves the same basic psychological needs.

We shall have occasion to return to some of these considerations later. We digress at this point simply to emphasize the tremendous discrepancy that may develop between the physiological and social significances of a given body part.

Internal Sex Organs

The internal sex organs of the female consist of the paired ovaries and uterine (*fallopian*) tubes, the uterus, and the vagina, along with a few accessory structures. The ovaries, like the testes, have a dual function: the production of germ cells or *ova* ("eggs") and of female sex hormones (*estrogen* and *progesterone*). The ovary is almond-shaped, smaller ($1\frac{1}{2} \times \frac{3}{4} \times 1$ inches) and lighter ($\frac{1}{4}$ ounce) than the testis; it shrinks further in old age. In their usual positions the ovaries lie vertically (see Figure 2.14) flanking the uterus (see Figure 2.15). They are held in place by a number of folds and ligaments, including the *ovarian ligaments,* which attach them to the sides of the uterus. These ligaments are solid cords and are not to be confused with the uterine tubes which open into the uterine cavity.

In contrast to the testis, the ovary has no tubes leading directly out of it. The ova leave the organ by rupturing its wall and becoming caught in the fringed end of the uterine tube. To permit the exit of ova, the ovarian capsule is thus quite thin. Before puberty it has a smooth, glistening surface. After the start of the ovarian cycle and the monthly exodus of ova, its surface becomes increasingly scarred and pitted.

The ovary contains numerous capsules, or *follicles,* in various stages of development, embedded in supporting tissues: These are located toward the periphery of the organ (the *cortex,* or "bark") (see Figure 2.16). The central portion of the ovary, the *medulla* ("marrow"), is rich in convoluted blood vessels.

Each follicle contains one ovum. Every female is born with about 400,000 immature ova: It seems unlikely that additional new ova are generated during the rest of a woman's life. At puberty some of these follicles start maturing, and each month one follicle ruptures, discharging the ovum. The empty follicle becomes a yellowish structure (*corpus luteum*). This ovarian cycle has great reproductive and hormonal significance and will be discussed in detail under those respective headings in Chapters 4 and 5.

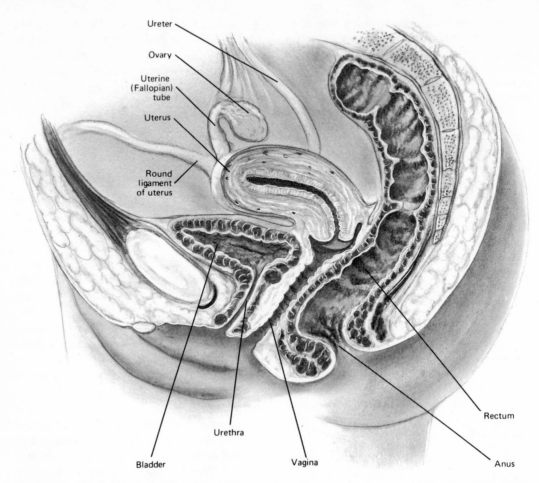

Figure 2.14. The female reproductive system. From Dienhart, *Basic Human Anatomy and Physiology* (Philadelphia: Saunders, 1967), p. 213. Reprinted by permission.

The two uterine, or fallopian,[10] tubes are about four inches long and extend between the ovaries and the uterus. The ovarian end of the tube, the *infundibulum* ("funnel"), is cone-shaped and fringed by irregular projections, or *fimbriae,* which may cling to or embrace the ovary but are not attached to it. After leaving

the ovarian surface, the ovum must find its way into the opening of the uterine tube. Although not every ovum succeeds in doing so, the process seems to be aided by a mysterious attraction between the uterine tube and the ovary. There have been instances in which women missing an ovary on one side and a uterine tube on the other have nevertheless become pregnant—all the more remarkable considering that the ovum is about the size of a needle tip and the opening of the uterine tube

[10]Named after a sixteenth-century Italian anatomist, Gabriello Fallopio, who mistakenly thought that the tubes were "ventilators" for the uterus.

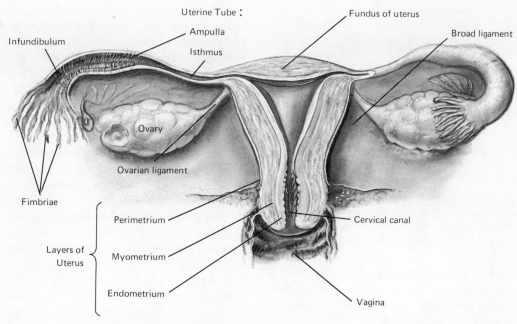

Uterine Tube :
Ampulla
Isthmus
Infundibulum
Fundus of uterus
Broad ligament
Ovary
Ovarian ligament
Fimbriae
Perimetrium
Layers of Uterus
Myometrium
Endometrium
Cervical canal
Vagina

Figure 2.15. Internal female reproductive organs. From Dienhart, *Basic Human Anatomy and Physiology* (Philadelphia: Saunders, 1967), p. 215. Reprinted by permission.

is only a slit about the size of a printed hyphen.

The second portion of the tube (the *ampulla*) accounts for over half its length. It has thinner walls and is joined to the less tortuous *isthmus*, which resembles a cord and ends at the uterine border. The last segment of the tube (the uterine part) runs within the wall of the uterus itself and opens into its cavity (uterine opening).

The cavity of the uterine tube becomes progressively smaller between the ovarian (two millimeters) and uterine (one millimeter) ends; the numerous folds projecting into the cavity also gradually disappear (see Figure 2.17). The lining of the uterine tube has a deep velvety texture because of the numerous hairlike structures (*cilia*) lining it. If the ovum were the size of an orange, these cilia would be comparable in size to eyelashes.

The function of the uterine tubes, unlike that of the male genital ducts, is more than mere

storage and conveyance of germ cells. The fertilization of the ovum usually occurs in the infundibular third of the uterine tube, where sperm that have traversed the vagina and the uterus meet the ovum. Passage of the ovum

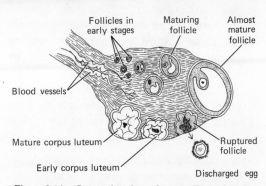

Follicles in early stages
Maturing follicle
Almost mature follicle
Blood vessels
Mature corpus luteum
Early corpus luteum
Ruptured follicle
Discharged egg

Figure 2.16. Composite view of ovum. From Crawley, Malfetti, Stewart, and Vas Dias, *Reproduction, Sex, and Preparation for Marriage* (Englewood Cliffs, N.J.: Prentice-Hall, 1964), p. 16. Reprinted by permission.

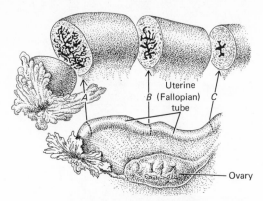

Uterine
B (Fallopian)
tube

Ovary

Figure 2.17. Uterine tube. (*A*) Infundibular; (*B*) ampullar; (*C*) isthmic. From Eastman and Hellman, *Williams Obstetrics,* 13th ed. (New York: Appleton-Century-Crofts, 1966), p. 31. Reprinted by permission.

through the tube takes several days, and, if fertilization has occurred, the structure that reaches the uterine cavity is already a complex, multicellular organism.[11]

The ovum, unlike the sperm, is not independently motile: Its movement depends upon the sweeping action of the cilia lining the tube and the contractions of its wall during the passage of the ovum.

Although the uterine tubes are nowhere as surgically accessible as is the vas deferens of the male, they are still the most convenient targets for sterilizing females. The usual procedure is to tie or sever the tubes (*tubal ligation*) on both sides. The result, as with vasectomy in the male, is sterility without concomitant impairment of sexual characteristics, desire, or ability to reach orgasm.

The uterus, or womb, is a hollow, muscular organ in which the embryo (known as the fetus after the eighth week) is housed and nourished

until birth.[12] It is shaped like an inverted pear and is usually tilted forward (anteverted) (see Figure 2.14).[13] The uterus is held, but not fixed, in place by various ligaments. Normally three inches long, two inches wide at the top, and an inch thick, it expands greatly, of course, during pregnancy. There is no other body organ that is ordinarily forced to a comparable adaptation.

The uterus consists of four parts (see Figure 2.15): the *fundus* ("bottom"), the rounded portion that lies above the openings of the uterine tubes; the body, which is the main part; the narrow *isthmus* (not to be confused with the isthmus of the uterine tube); and the *cervix* ("neck"), the lower portion of which projects into the vagina.

The cavity of the uterus is wider at the point at which the uterine tubes enter but narrows toward the isthmus: The *cervical canal* then expands somewhat and narrows again at the opening (the *external os*) into the vagina (see Figures 2.15 and 2.18). Because the anterior and posterior uterine walls are ordinarily close together, the interior, when viewed from the side (in sagittal section), appears to be a narrow slit (see Figure 2.14).

The uterus has three layers (see Figure 2.15). The inner *mucosa*, or *endometrium*, consists of numerous glands and a rich network of blood vessels. Its structure varies with the period of life (prepubertal, reproductive, and postmenopausal) and the point in the menstrual cycle. We shall discuss these variations later in con-

---

[11] On rare occasions the fertilized ovum becomes implanted in the wall of the uterine tube itself, causing one form of ectopic ("out of normal place") pregnancy, which ultimately results in the death of the fetus and may cause the tube to rupture, with potentially serious consequences for the mother.

[12] The Greek word for uterus is *hystera,* a term that supplies the root for words like "hysterectomy" (surgical removal of the uterus) and "hysteria" (a condition believed by the ancient Greeks to result from a uterus' wandering through the body in search of a child).

[13] Attempts at self-abortion or abortion by untrained individuals often end in disaster because of this anatomical feature. When a probe or long needle is introduced, the tendency is simply to push it on into the uterus; instead the instrument pierces the roof of the vagina and penetrates the abdominal cavity.

nection with sex hormones and pregnancy. The second, or muscular, layer (*myometrium*) is very well developed. Intertwined layers of smooth muscle fibers endow the uterine wall with tremendous strength and elasticity. These muscles are vital for propelling the fetus at the time of birth by means of a series of contractions. The muscular layer of the uterus is continuous with the muscular sheaths of the uterine tubes and the vagina. The isthmus of the uterus and the cervix contain fewer muscle fibers and more fibrous tissue than do the body and the fundus. The third layer, the *perimetrium* or *serosa*, is the external cover.

The vagina ("sheath") is the female organ of copulation and the recipient of the semen. Through it also pass the discharge during menstruation and the baby during birth. It does not serve for the passage of urine.

The vagina is ordinarily a collapsed muscular tube, a potential, rather than permanent, space. Its main surfaces are formed by the anterior and posterior walls, which are about three and four inches long respectively. Its side walls are quite narrow. It also appears as a narrow slit in sagittal section (see Figure 2.14).

The vaginal canal is slanted downward and forward. At its upper end it communicates with the cervical canal (usually open only the width of the lead in a pencil), and the lower end opens into the vestibule between the minor lips.

The external vaginal opening, or introitus, is flanked by elongated masses of erectile tissue (*bulb of the vestibule*). These masses are the counterparts of the bulb of the penis and are encircled by the bulbocavernosus muscles. We shall return to the functional significance of this muscle.

The inner lining, or vaginal *mucosa*, is like the skin covering the inside of the mouth. In contrast to the uterine endometrium it contains no glands, although its appearance is affected by hormone levels. In the adult premenopausal woman, the vaginal walls are corrugated but

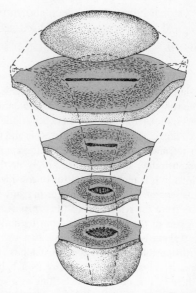

Figure 2.18. Reconstruction of uterus showing shape of its cavity and cervical canal. From Eastman and Hellman, *Williams Obstetrics*, 13th ed. (New York: Appleton-Century-Crofts, 1966), p. 44. Reprinted by permission.

fleshy and soft. Following menopause they become thinner and smoother. The middle vaginal layer is muscular but far less developed than is that of the uterine wall. Most of these fibers run longitudinally. The outer layer is also rather thin. The vaginal walls are poorly supplied with nerves. Like the body of the penis, the vagina is a rather insensitive organ. But the area surrounding the vaginal opening is highly excitable.

Behind the vestibular bulbs are two small glands (*Bartholin's* or *greater vestibular glands*), the ducts of which open on each side of the lower half of the vestibule, in the ridges between the edge of the hymen and the minor lips. These glands are the female counterparts of the male bulbourethral (Cowper's) glands. Their function is also somewhat obscure. Formerly assumed to be central in vaginal lubrication, they are now considered to play only a minor role in this process. The primary source of the vaginal lubricant has been shown to be the vaginal walls themselves (discussed in Chapter 3).

Size of the Vagina. Because of its function in sexual intercourse, the vagina, like the penis, has been the subject of great interest and speculation.[14] Popular notions differentiate between tight and relaxed vaginas, those that grasp the penis and those that do not, and so on. Some aspects of these notions are demonstrable, and others are purely mythical. Functionally it is more meaningful to consider the introitus separately from the rest, for in many ways it differs from the remainder of the organ as much as the glans of the penis differs from its body.

The vagina beyond the introitus is a soft and highly distensible organ. Although it looks like a flat tube, it actually functions more as a balloon. Thus there is, first of all, no such thing as a vagina that is permanently "too tight" or "too small." Properly stimulated, any adult vagina can, in principle, accommodate the largest penis. After all, no penis is as large as a normal infant's head, and even that passes through.

The claim that some vaginas are "too large" is more tenable. Some vaginas do not return to normal size after childbirth, and tears produced during the process weaken the vaginal walls. Even in these instances, however, the vagina expands only to the extent that the penis requires. When we add to its anatomical features the relative insensitivity of the vaginal walls, we can reasonably conclude that the main body of the vaginal cavity does not either add to or detract from the sexual pleasure of coitus in any major way. Most of the time there is no problem of "fit" between penis and vagina.

The introitus is another matter. First, it is highly sensitive. Both pain and pleasure are intensely felt there. Second, the arrangement of the erectile tissue of the bulb of the vestibule and, more important, the presence of the muscular ring of the bulbo-cavernosus around it make a great deal of difference in how relaxed or tight it will be. It must be emphasized that these muscles permit a significant degree of voluntary control over the size of the opening. Not that a woman can open her vagina as freely as she can open her mouth. But she can relax or tighten the vaginal opening as she can relax or tighten the anal sphincter (though usually to a lesser extent). Furthermore, in common with all other muscles of the body, those around the introitus can be developed by exercise.

The introitus is thus literally the gateway to the vagina. If a woman is tense, her introitus will also be tense. She may feel tense because of physical pain or anxiety. If attempts are made to force the penis in, she will, of course, feel further pain. In rare instances the resulting muscular spasm (*vaginismus*) is so intense that the vagina simply cannot be penetrated.

A relaxed introitus, however, is not all that sexually sophisticated individuals look for in their partners. It is desirable that the penis feel firmly (though not spastically) grasped. Some women can convey the sensation of "milking the penis." These intricacies and refinements of coitus are often difficult to evaluate. People are not at their most objective at such times, and some tend to fabricate and fantasize sensations. At any rate, whatever mechanism is involved, it is reasonable to assume that the introitus, rather than the vagina as a whole, is responsible for sensations. Control of the introitus and appropriate development of its musculature are also key factors in a woman's ability to reach orgasm, as we shall have occasion to discuss.

Contrary to popular belief, the penis cannot be "trapped" inside the vagina. This misconception arises from observation of dogs, to which this phenomenon can occur. The penis of the dog expands into a "knot" inside the vagina and cannot be withdrawn until ejaculation or loss of erection occurs. Other horrors haunt some men: fantasies that the vagina has teeth (*vagina dentata*) or is full of razor blades or ground glass are known and understandably influence sexual functioning.

[14] The many colloquial names for the vagina attest to the interest elicited by this simple organ. In *The Perfumed Garden* it has been called the "crusher," "the silent one," "yearning one," "glutton," "bottomless," "restless," "biter," "sucker," "the wasp," "the hedgehog," "the starling," "hot one," "delicious one," and so on. The *Ananga Ranga* classifies women according to vaginal size (deer-woman, six finger breadths deep; mare-woman, nine finger breadths deep; elephant-woman, twelve finger breadths deep) and links these sizes to personality traits.

Breasts

The *breasts* are not part of the sex organs but, because of their erotic significance, we shall discuss them briefly. Although males also have breasts, they are not as fully developed as are those of females. Breasts are characteristic of the highest class of vertebrates (mammals), which suckle their young.

The adult female breasts are located in front of the chest muscles and extend between the second and sixth ribs and from the midline of the chest to below the armpit. Each breast consists of lobes or clusters (about fifteen to twenty) of glandular tissue, each with a separate duct opening on the nipple. The lobes are separated by loosely packed fibrous and fatty tissue, which gives the breast its soft consistency (see Figure 2.19).

The *nipple* is the prominent tip of the breast into which the milk ducts open. It consists of smooth muscle fibers which, when contracted, make the nipple erect. The area around the nipple (*areola*) is pinkish: It becomes darker during pregnancy and remains so thereafter. The nipple, richly endowed with nerve fibers, is highly sensitive and plays an important part in sexual arousal. The sensitivity of the nipples or breasts is unrelated to their size and shape.

Developmental Anatomy of the Sex Organs

The study of the developmental anatomy of the various systems and organs of the body is a separate science (embryology), and a comprehensive survey of the development of the reproductive system is far too complex an undertaking for us to attempt here. We shall therefore select only a few aspects of this process to illustrate how sex organs develop and to emphasize the basic *structural* similarities between the male and female reproductive systems. Intrauterine growth and development in general will be discussed in conjunction with conception and pregnancy.

The genital system makes its appearance during the fifth to sixth week of intrauterine life, when the embryo has attained a length of five to twelve millimeters. At this undifferentiated stage, the embryo has a pair of gonads and two sets of ducts (see Figure 2.20), as well as the rudiments of external genitals (see Figure 2.21).

At this time, one cannot reliably determine the sex of the embryo by either gross or microscopic examination. The gonads have not yet become either testes or ovaries, and the other structures are also undifferentiated. This lack of visible differentiation does not mean that the sex of the individual is still undecided; sex is determined at the very moment of fertilization and depends upon the chromosome composition of the fertilizing sperm. The hormonal mechanisms involved in the process of sex differentiation will be discussed in Chapters 4 and 5.

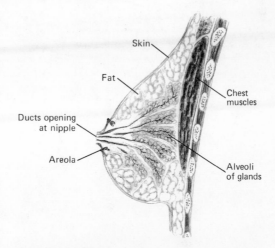

Skin

Fat

Chest muscles

Ducts opening at nipple

Areola

Alveoli of glands

Figure 2.19. Vertical section of the breast. From Dienhart, *Basic Human Anatomy and Physiology* (Philadelphia: Saunders, 1967), p. 217. Reprinted by permission.

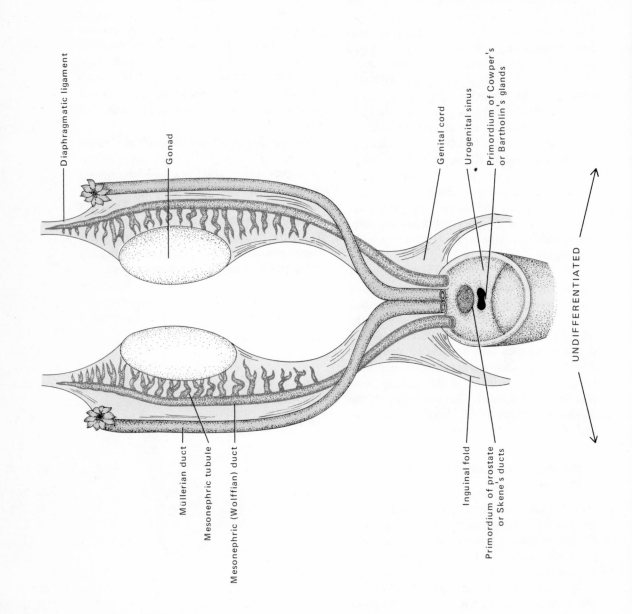

Diaphragmatic ligament

Gonad

Genital cord

Urogenital sinus

Primordium of Cowper's
or Bartholin's glands

Müllerian duct

Mesonephric tubule

Mesonephric (Wolffian) duct

Inguinal fold

Primordium of prostate
or Skene's ducts

UNDIFFERENTIATED

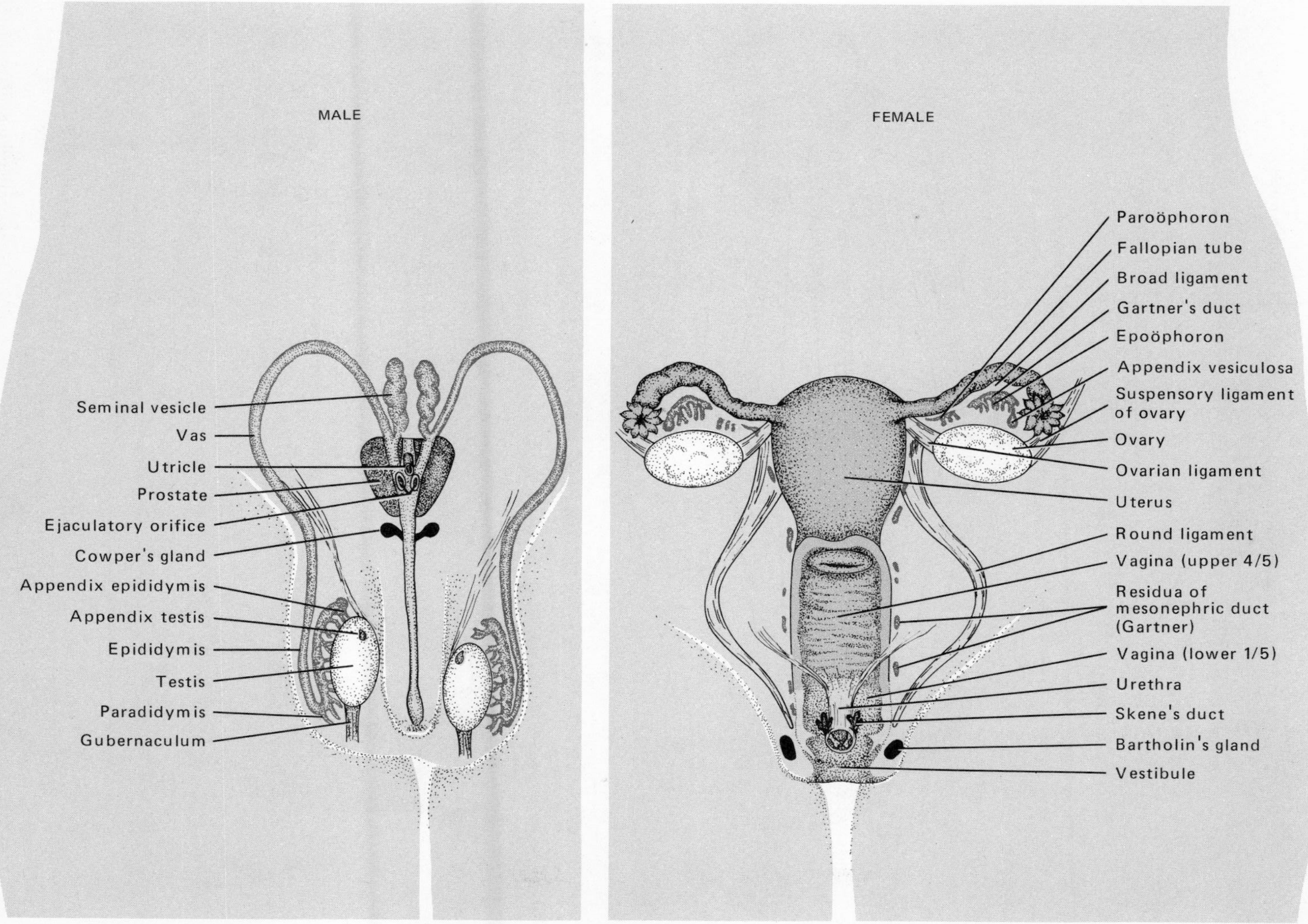

MALE

FEMALE

Seminal vesicle
Vas
Utricle
Prostate
Ejaculatory orifice
Cowper's gland
Appendix epididymis
Appendix testis
Epididymis
Testis
Paradidymis
Gubernaculum

Paroöphoron
Fallopian tube
Broad ligament
Gartner's duct
Epoöphoron
Appendix vesiculosa
Suspensory ligament of ovary
Ovary
Ovarian ligament
Uterus
Round ligament
Vagina (upper 4/5)
Residua of mesonephric duct (Gartner)
Vagina (lower 1/5)
Urethra
Skene's duct
Bartholin's gland
Vestibule

Figure 2.20. Homologues of internal male and female genitalia; development from undifferentiated into differentiated stage. © Copyright 1965 by CIBA Pharmaceutical Company, Division of CIBA-GEIGY Corporation. Reproduced, with permission, from The Ciba Collection of Medical Illustrations, by Frank H. Netter, M. D. All rights reserved.

UNDIFFERENTIATED

Glans area
Epithelial tag
Urethral fold
Urethral groove
Lateral buttress
Anal pit
Anal tubercle

Genital tubercle

Tail (cut away)

45-50 M M.

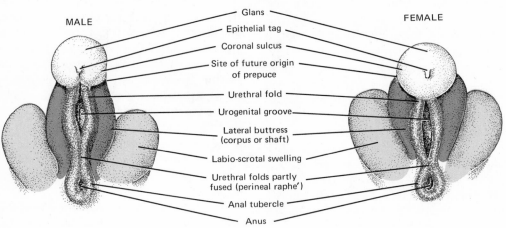

MALE

FEMALE

Glans
Epithelial tag
Coronal sulcus
Site of future origin
of prepuce
Urethral fold
Urogenital groove
Lateral buttress
(corpus or shaft)
Labio-scrotal swelling
Urethral folds partly
fused (perineal raphe')
Anal tubercle
Anus

FULLY DEVELOPED

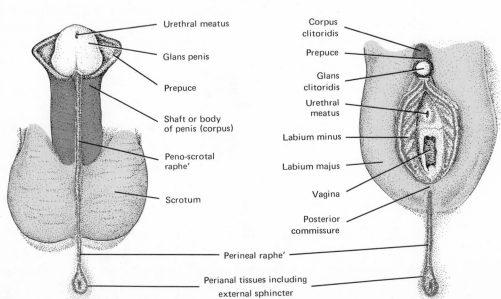

Urethral meatus
Glans penis
Prepuce
Shaft or body
of penis (corpus)
Peno-scrotal
raphe'
Scrotum

Corpus
clitoridis
Prepuce
Glans
clitoridis
Urethral
meatus
Labium minus
Labium majus
Vagina
Posterior
commissure

Perineal raphe'
Perianal tissues including
external sphincter

Figure 2.21. Homologues of external male and female genitalia; development from undifferentiated into differentiated stage. © Copyright 1965 by CIBA Pharmaceutical Company, Division of CIBA-GEIGY Corporation. Reproduced, with permission, from The Ciba Collection of Medical Illustrations, by Frank H. Netter, M. D. All rights reserved.

Differentiation of the Gonads

The gonad that is destined to develop into a testis gradually consolidates as a more compact organ. Some of its cells are organized into distinct strands (*testis cords*), the forerunners of the seminiferous tubules. Other cells form the basis of the future internal duct system. By the seventh week (when the embryo is fourteen millimeters long) enough differentiation may have occurred so that the organ is recognizable as a developing testis. On the other hand, if by this time the basic architecture of the future testis is not discernible, it can be provisionally assumed that the undifferentiated gonad will develop into an ovary. More definitive evidence that the baby will be a girl comes somewhat later (about the tenth week), when the forerunners of the follicles begin to become visibly organized. After these basic patterns are set, the testis and ovary continue to grow accordingly. These organs do not attain full maturity until after puberty. The differences between the gonads of the newborn and the adult of each sex, briefly outlined above, will be further elaborated in Chapters 4 and 5.

Descent of the Testis and Ovary

Concomitant with the development described, both the testis and the ovary undergo gross changes in shape and position that are of special significance. At first, the testis and the ovary are slender structures high up in the abdominal cavity. By the tenth week they have grown and shifted down to the level of the upper edge of the pelvis. There the ovaries remain until birth; they subsequently rotate and move farther down until they reach their adult positions in the pelvis.

In the male this early internal migration is followed by the actual descent of the testes into the scrotal sac. As early as the third month preparations are underway. Sacs (*processus vaginalis*, growths that have nothing to do with the female vagina) invade the scrotum in the seventh month and are normally followed by the testes within the next month or so (see Figure 2.22). After the descent of the testes, the passage above is obliterated. The lower part of the processus vaginalis persists as a testicular covering (*tunica vaginalis*, not to be confused with the *tunica albuginea*, or the fibrous coat of the testes).

Two clinical problems may arise during this process. First, one or both of the testes may fail to descend into the scrotum before birth, as happens in about 2 percent of males born. In most of these boys they do descend by puberty. However, if they do not do so spontaneously, hormonal or surgical intervention becomes necessary. Otherwise the higher temperature of the abdominal cavity would interfere with spermatogenesis, resulting in

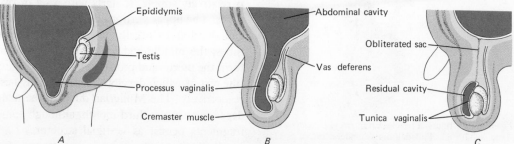

Figure 2.22. Descent of the human testis and its subsequent relations, shown in diagrammatic hemisections. From Arey, *Developmental Anatomy,* 7th ed. (Philadelphia: Saunders, 1965), p. 333. Reprinted by permission.

sterility if both testes have failed to descend into the scrotum. Undescended testes are also more likely to develop cancer.

The second problem arises when the passage traversed by the testes is not eliminated or reopens when the tissues become slack in old age. An abnormal passage is created, and intestinal loops may find their way into the scrotal sac, creating a condition known as *inguinal hernia*, or *rupture* (see Figure 2.23). It too can readily be corrected by surgery.

Differentiation of the Genital Ducts

In the undifferentiated stage the gonad has two sets of ducts: the *Müllerian* (the potential female) and the *mesonephric*, or *Wolffian* (the potential male ducts, see Figure 2.20). The former develop separately; the latter are taken over from the urinary system. The human embryo develops three forms of the kidneys

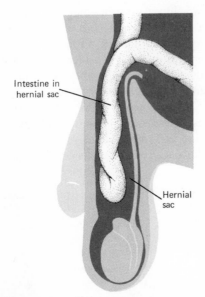

Intestine in
hernial sac

Hernial
sac

Figure 2.23. Inguinal hernia. From Arey, *Developmental Anatomy*, 7th ed. (Philadelphia: Saunders, 1965), p. 334. Reprinted by permission.

successively: First comes the *pronephros*, a functional form in lower animals but not in man. Next appears the *mesonephros*, which functions briefly (although it is the definitive form of kidney in other anamniote animals). These early forms are essentially sets of tubules leading into common ducts. Before the mesonephric tubules and ducts are discarded by the urinary system, they are taken over by the genital system. The *metanephros* is the final type of embryonic excretory organ, and it develops into the human kidney.

In the embryonic male the developing testis outgrows the mesonephros, the tubules of which start to degenerate. Those that survive are reorganized and incorporated into the cords of the testis, as collecting ducts, starting in about the third month. The mesonephric (Wolffian) duct, into which they formerly emptied, itself becomes the main genital duct; its upper part becomes the convoluted epididymis, and the lower part evolves into the vas deferens and ejaculatory duct. Mesonephric tubules that neither degenerate nor become functional persist as "blind tubules" (*paradidymis, appendix of epididymis, aberrant ductules*) and are of no significance. The mesonephric duct system in the female degenerates. Vestigial structures persist here and there as "blind canals" or segments of ducts (*epoöphoron, paroöphoron,* and so on) and are also of no practical significance.

The genital passages of the female develop from the Müllerian duct system. The process is relatively simple. It starts with a set of two tubes. The upper portions remain independent and develop eventually into the two uterine tubes; the middle and lower portions fuse to form the uterus and probably the upper vagina (the rest of which develops from other tissues) respectively. The Müllerian ducts in the male degenerate in the third month, although some fragments persist as vestigial structures (*appendix testis, prostatic utricle,* and so on).

Differentiation of the External Genitals

The external, like the internal genitals, are at first sexually undifferentiated (see Figure 2.21). As we have indicated, by the seventh week the sex of the embryo can be ascertained provisionally by means of microscopic study of the gonads. Several more weeks are necessary for the more distinctive development of the external genitals. The sex of the four-month-old fetus is unmistakable. The differentiation of male and female external genitals is illustrated in Figure 2.21. This process usually proceeds in a predictable and orderly manner. However, anomalies of development occasionally result in paradoxical conditions of bisexuality or hermaphroditism (discussed in Chapter 4).

Homologies of the Reproductive Systems

Organs or parts of animal bodies that are similar in origin and structure (but not necessarily in function) are said to be homologous. They contrast with body parts that are analogous, that is, similar in function but not in origin and structure (like the gills of a fish and the lungs of a land animal).

Both the internal and external sex organs of males and females are homologous. Theoretically it ought to be possible to make a complete list of such pairs, but practically such pairing is not possible. Furthermore, many remnants of the discarded duct system are of no consequence. Figures 2.20 and 2.21 indicate some of the more important homologous pairs in the reproductive systems of the two sexes.

Sexuality starts and ends with life itself. Its manifestations range from overt acts to behavior whose sexual origins are matters of conjecture. Sexual activity is cyclical: Like the wheels of a clock, sexual cycles of different dimensions are concurrently in operation. In the broadest sense each human life constitutes one full cycle, which is then repeated in the lives of succeeding generations. Each pregnancy, each orgasm, is likewise a cyclical event with a predetermined course and predictable manifestations.

The physiological goal of sexual activity is the attainment of orgasm. A great deal of such activity, of course, falls short of this goal, and the frequency and means by which orgasm is achieved through a lifetime vary tremendously. In studies of sexual behavior, orgasm is used as a practical measure, for it can be easily recognized and its occurrence counted. Its physiological manifestations are independent of the means by which it is brought about.

In this chapter we are primarily concerned with physiological processes. There is an inherent danger in this approach, and it can be legitimately asked whether or not it is ever possible to separate the physiological functions of the body from their psychological concomitants. We do not intend to claim a dichotomy between mind and body, but practical considerations dictate that we examine the various facets of human sexuality a few at a time. Furthermore, as Kinsey has stated, "Whatever the poetry and romance of sex and whatever the moral and social significance of human sexual behavior, sexual responses involve real and material changes in the physiologic functioning of an animal."[1] It is these physiological processes that we shall deal with in this chapter.

It is common knowledge that an episode of sexual "discharge" begins with mounting excitement, which culminates in orgasm and is followed by a period of relaxation and sexual satiety. In more formal descriptions various stages have been ascribed to this process. Ellis envisaged two phases: tumescence and detumescence. More recently Masters and Johnson have proposed four phases: excitement, plateau, orgasm, resolution. The purpose of such subdivisions is to facilitate observation and description. It is not intended to obscure the basic unity of sexual activity, which proceeds in a continuous manner with the manifestations of various phases overlapping and merging into one another imperceptibly.

---

[1] Kinsey *et al.* (1953), p. 594.

CHAPTER

3

PHYSIOLOGY OF SEXUAL FUNCTIONS

Sexual Stimulation

The ability to respond to sexual stimulation is a universal characteristic of all healthy beings. Although the nature of the stimulus varies widely, the basic physiological response of the body is the same. The varieties and intensity of sexual arousal that each person experiences during a lifetime are, however, legion. Sometimes this excitement achieves full expression in orgasm; most of the time it progresses no farther than lingering thoughts or vague, evanescent yearnings.

What triggers such responses? Potentially anything and everything. The stimuli may be "sexual" in the ordinary sense of the term, or they may involve factors that have no erotic interest for most people. In a study of the circumstances in which younger boys have erections, it was found that a wide variety of athletic activities (swimming, boxing, riding, skiing), emotionally charged events (coming home late, receiving report cards, being chased by the police), and even sitting in church or hearing the national anthem were included.[2] Nonsexual sources of erotic stimulation are not really random, however. They generally involve activities and situations that have intense emotional components. Unfortunately, no comparable data are available for girls where sexual arousal is more difficult to determine.

Over time such indiscriminate erotic responses gradually give way to more selective patterns. By the late teens sexual response is by and large limited to direct stimulation of the genitals or to obviously erotic situations. In later years conditions leading to erection become even more limited and increasingly dependent on actual physical stimulation.

Age is one determinant of responsive capacity. It has been assumed that gender is

another and that males are more easily aroused, but the evidence is inconclusive. The number and variety of sexual stimulants are, of course, bewildering. To impose some order, it is usual to classify erotic stimuli on different parameters: physical versus psychological, those to which responses are innate versus those to which they are learned, and so on. Such classification attempts are, however, doomed to failure, for most stimuli have both physical and psychic components, and all behavior has internal and external determinants.

All modalities of sensation can be and usually are involved in erotic arousal, but for most human beings touch predominates, followed by vision. Among other animals other sensory modalities like smell and taste (as in insects) may be more potent.

Stimulation through Touch

Tactile stimulation probably accounts for most instances of sexual arousal among mammals. In man, though other modalities are also important, touch remains the predominant mode of erotic stimulation. It is, in fact, the only type of stimulation to which the body can respond reflexively and independently of higher psychic centers. Even a man who is unconscious or whose spinal cord is injured at a point that prevents impulses from reaching the brain (but leaves sexual coordinating centers in the lower spinal cord intact) can still have an erection when his genitals or inner thighs are caressed.

The perception of touch is mediated through nerve endings in the skin and deeper tissues. These end organs are distributed unevenly, which explains why some parts (fingertips) are more sensitive than others (the skin of the back): The more richly innervated the region, the greater is its potential for stimulation.

Some of the more sensitive areas are believed to be especially susceptible to sexual arousal and are therefore called *erogenous zones*. They include the glans penis (particularly the corona

---

[2]Kinsey *et al.* (1948), pp. 164–165.

and the underside of the glans), but not the shaft of the penis; the clitoris; the labia minora and the space they enclose (vestibule), but not the vaginal canal; the area between the anus and the genitals; the anus itself; the breasts (particularly the nipples); the mouth (lips, tongue, and the whole interior); the ears (especially the lobes); the buttocks; and the inner surfaces of the thighs.

Although it is true that these areas are most often involved in sexual stimulation, they are not the only ones by any means. The neck (throat and nape), the palms and fingertips, the soles and toes, the abdomen, the groin, the center of the lower back, or any other part of the body may well be erotically sensitive to touch. Some women have reached orgasm when their eyebrows were stroked or when pressure was applied to their teeth alone.[3]

The concept of erogenous zones is not new: Explicit or implicit references to them are plentiful in "love" manuals, and the practical value of such knowledge is self-evident.[4] A knowledge of erogenous zones may greatly enhance one's effectiveness as a lover. It must be noted, however, that these zones are often indistinct and do not correspond to any given pattern of nerve distribution. Also, the ultimate interpretation of all stimuli by the brain is profoundly affected by previous experience and conditioning. A specific "erogenous" zone may thus be quite insensitive in a given person, or

it may be sensitive to the point of pain. One cannot therefore approach another person in a mechanical, push-button manner and expect to elicit automatic sexual arousal.

Although it is true that one is more likely than not to respond to stimulation of common erogenous zones, the subtle lover will seek to learn the unique erogenous map of his partner, which is the result of both biological endowment and life experiences.

Stimulation through Other Senses

Vision, hearing, smell, and taste are to lesser extents also important avenues of erotic stimulation. These modalities, in contrast to touch, do not operate reflexively, however. We learn to experience certain sights, sounds, and smells as erotic and others as neutral or even offensive. We are not born with the notion that roses have an attractive odor or that feces (particularly those of others) smell bad. A young child would touch his feces and lick his finger if his mother let him. Regardless of the claims of cosmetics manufacturers, there are no scents and colors that are "naturally erotic," but scents and colors can be exciting if we have been conditioned to associate them with sexual arousal.

The reflexive basis of tactile stimulation does not mean that such stimulation is not subject to experiential modification. As discussed earlier, any part of the body surface may be rendered erotically sensitive or insensitive through experience and mental associations. Yet usually the reflexive aspect of tactile stimulation continues to operate. With vision, hearing, and smell all responses are learned.

There is consequently boundless diversity in the sexual preferences and dislikes of individuals, as well as of cultures. This diversity makes it impossible to generalize about the effectiveness of any one source of stimulation. Why a certain female profile or a male sexual characteristic should be found exciting in one culture but not in another or only during a certain

---

[3] Kinsey *et al.* (1953), p. 590.

[4] The *Kama Sutra* refers to the armpit, throat, breasts, lips, "middle parts of the body," and thighs as suitable locations for stimulation (Vatsyayana, 1963 ed., p. 99). The approach in the *Ananga Ranga* is more complex: The sensitivities of parts are claimed to shift with the periods of the lunar month so that, as one must "kiss, bite and chew softly" the lower lip on the thirteenth day of the first half of the month (light fortnight), the upper lip should receive such attentions on the third day of the second half (dark fortnight). Other body parts mentioned include the genitals and breasts, the eyes, and even the big toe (Malla, 1964 ed., p. 46).

period of a given culture is cause for endless speculation.

The sight of the female genitals is probably as nearly universal a source of excitement for men as any that exists. Paradoxically, viewing the male genitals does not seem to excite women as much, even though men fantasize that it does. In cultures in which nudity is acceptable, open preferences for certain features of external sex organs develop. Among some peoples of South Africa, for instance, large, pendulous minor lips ("Hottentot aprons") were considered very attractive in women. By pulling and stretching these parts during childhood and adolescence women caused them to hypertrophy. Alteration and mutilation of the genitals do not, however, always have erotic purposes.

Even though erotic standards differ and change, the impact of visual stimuli are unmistakable, as our preoccupation with physical attributes, cosmetics, and dress indicates. We could argue, of course, whether or not aesthetic concerns are erotically motivated in all instances. Furthermore, the ability to experience and elicit sexual feelings does not always depend upon shape and form, as experience with beautiful but frigid women or handsome but inept men readily demonstrates.

The effect of sound is perhaps less telling but nevertheless quite significant as a sexual stimulant. The tone and softness of voice as well as certain types of music (with pulsating rhythms or repeated languorous sequences) can serve as erotic stimuli. But these responses are learned, so that what stimulates one person may simply distract or annoy another.

The importance of the sense of smell has declined in man, both generally and in sexual terms. Nevertheless the use of scents in many cultures, as well as preoccupation with body odors, attests its considerable influence.

We would expect the smell of vaginal secretions and semen to have erotic properties. Yet most people do not openly admit to recognizing

such properties—possibly because of inhibitions about discussing sexual matters. As far as most other body odors are concerned, if "marriage manuals" ever mention them it is to suggest emphatically that they be eliminated or masked. Observation of sexual behavior among animals indicates not only that our sense of smell has declined but also that we have lost our enjoyment of whatever body smells we do perceive. Sexual stimulants will be discussed further in connection with aphrodisiacs.

Emotional Stimulation

Sexual stimulation through purely mental activity is infinitely more complex. All sensory input must ultimately be interpreted in the brain before a particular sensation is experienced. But, apart from this process, the brain can use memory and imagination to initiate sexual excitement without sensory stimuli.

A full understanding of the known neurophysiological processes underlying sexual functions would require a comprehensive knowledge of the functions of the nervous system in all their awesome complexity. A great many of these processes are, of course, not specific to sexual functions. For instance, touch receptors (Meissner's corpuscles) embedded in the skin merely inform the brain that a certain area of the skin is being stimulated; it is up to the brain to interpret this touch as a lover's caress.

There are special nerve endings and end organs that respond specifically to cold, warmth, pain, touch, and the like, but none that is specialized to respond selectively to sexual stimulation. The nerve endings in the glans penis are thus no different from those in the fingertips. Also sensory messages are transmitted from the body to the brain and spinal cord, and responses are transmitted to the body parts through the same networks of nerves, regardless of whether or not the activity is sexual. In this sense nerves, like telephone cables, are ignorant of the content of the messages they carry.

The specifically sexual aspects of nervous activity involve certain reflex processes like orgasm and the still little understood functions of the brain that deal with sexual motivation and pleasure.

The neurophysiology of sexual emotion is still being investigated. It has recently been shown, for instance, that in certain parts of the brain (thalamus, hypothalamus, mesencephalon) there are areas that respond to stimulation with intense pleasure. These areas are paired with adjacent ones yielding the opposite responses; the pairs are therefore called *pleasure* and *pain,* or *reward* and *punishment, centers.* If an electrode is implanted in one of these pleasure centers in an animal and the animal is permitted to stimulate the center by pressing a lever, it persists in this activity to the exclusion of all other behavior, including eating when it is hungry.[5] Nevertheless, in our current state of knowledge, sexual arousal cannot yet be adequately explained on purely neurophysiological grounds.

Sexual Response: General Characteristics

In response to sexual stimulation, the body reacts as a whole. The components of this total response are, however, many and varied. To facilitate description we shall first outline the general behavioral characteristics of sexual response patterns and then deal with the physiological changes in the sex organs and various body systems.

We shall be dealing throughout with the ordinary patterns of human sexual response. Our descriptions are not, however, intended as standards of "normality" or "healthiness."

There are innumerable variations on these patterns, and they are also perfectly "normal" and "healthy." The biological basis of sexuality does not imply that its manifestations are relentlessly uniform.

As sexual excitement and orgasm are widely experienced phenomena, we may wonder about the need to describe them. But most of us cannot generalize from only our own experiences. There is far too much variation among individuals to permit it, and, furthermore, most of us are in no mood for dispassionate observation at those times. There is in fact a blurring of our perceptual ability during sexual arousal, as a result of which we are not quite fully conscious of our own sensations and physiological responses.

Approach to Orgasm

In response to effective sexual stimulation, a sensation of heightened arousal develops. Thoughts and attention turn to the sexual activity at hand, and the person becomes progressively oblivious to other stimuli and events in the environment. Most people attempt to exert some control over the intensity and tempo of their mounting sexual tensions. They may try to suppress it or to ward it off by diverting their attention to other matters. Or they may deliberately enhance and prolong the feeling by dwelling on its pleasurable aspects. If circumstances are favorable to fuller expression, these erotic stirrings are difficult to ignore. On the other hand, anxiety or strong distractions may easily dissipate sexual arousal during the early stages.

Although excitement sometimes intensifies rapidly and relentlessly, it usually mounts more unevenly. In younger people the progression is steeper, whereas in older ones it tends to be more gradual. As the level of tension rises, external distractions become less effective, and orgasm is more likely to occur.

The prelude to orgasm is pleasurable in itself

---

[5] Olds (1956).

and can be quite satisfying. In fact, following a period of sustained excitement one may voluntarily forego the climax. But lingering tensions usually do create irritability and restlessness if unrelieved by orgasm.

It is generally believed that men respond more rapidly to sexual stimulation and are capable of reaching orgasm more rapidly than women are. A great deal of advice in marriage manuals revolves around this very point: Because women supposedly respond more slowly, they must be stimulated for longer periods if they are to reach orgasm and so on. This belief has a certain validity, for in clinical practice the "slower" wife usually does complain that she is "left behind." Yet there is no known physiological basis for this claimed difference, and females can respond more or less as quickly as men do to effective sexual stimulation.

The average female, for example, takes somewhat less than four minutes to reach orgasm during masturbation, whereas the average male needs between two and four minutes. Some women may achieve climax, however, in as little as fifteen to thirty seconds. The disparity between the sexes in achieving coital orgasm is therefore related not to fundamental physiological differences but to the mechanical and psychological components of sexual intercourse.

The behavioral and subjective manifestations of sexual excitement vary so widely that no one description can possibly encompass them all. With mild sexual excitement, relatively little may be visible to the casual observer; on the other hand, in intense excitement behavior may be quite dramatic.

The person in the grip of sexual excitement appears tense from head to toe. The musculature of the entire body is taut. As tension mounts, the individual clasps with his hands and legs whatever may be within reach, and even a frail woman seems suddenly to be endowed with tremendous strength. Involuntary and irregular muscular twitches and jerks gradually take on a more rhythmic pattern best exemplified by pelvic thrusts—the hallmark of mammalian coitus.

The activities of the muscles, though the most dramatic, are by no means the only sexual responses of the body. The skin becomes flushed; salivation increases; the nostrils may flare; the heart pounds; breathing grows heavy; the face is contorted and flushed; the person feels, looks, and acts quite unlike his ordinary self.

These phenomena may be quite mild. The results of muscular tension and vasocongestion are inevitably present but are not always reflected in a highly visible manner. The person may remain still or show only occasional and minimal overt responses. His movements may be deliberate and gentle. Thrusting may involve only the buttocks and be barely noticeable. Changes in facial expression may be minor. But, no matter how attenuated his behavioral manifestations, he must experience distinct increases in his heart rate and heavier breathing; otherwise he is simply not aroused.

We have so far omitted all reference to changes in the sex organs, for we shall deal with them in detail later. We have also left out idiosyncratic manifestations: Some stutterers, for instance, speak more freely when sexually aroused. The gagging reflex may disappear, which explains the ability of some people to take the penis deep into their mouths. Spastics may coordinate better; those suffering from hay fever may obtain temporary relief; bleeding from cuts decreases. The perception of pain is markedly blunted during sexual arousal, which partly explains masochistic endurance of sadistic practices.

Orgasm

Voluntary control of the excitement level becomes progressively more difficult to maintain during sustained stimulation, and at the moment of orgasm it is completely lost. In the more elaborate language of the past:

> . . . while tumescence is largely under control of the will when the moment of detumescence [that is, orgasm] arrives, the reins slip from the control of the will; the more fundamental and uncontrollable impulses of the organism gallop on unchecked; the chariot of Phaëthon dashes blindly into a sea of emotion.[6]

Orgasm (from the Greek *orgasmos*, "to swell," "to be lustful") is one of the most intense and profoundly satisfying sensations that a person can experience. In physiological terms it consists of the explosive discharge of accumulated neuromuscular tensions. More subjectively defined, it is a high pitch of tension, in which time seems to stand still for a moment. There is drive toward release and utter helplessness to stop it. In a matter of seconds it is all over, but while it lasts it seems eternity.

The patterns of response during orgasm vary among individuals and according to age, fatigue, length of abstinence, and so on. There is some evidence, however, that, within limits, each person has a fairly characteristic set of responses during his sexually active life. On strictly physiological grounds, there is no reason why men and women should react differently during orgasm. However, psychological factors and different standards of propriety may markedly alter the behavior of the two sexes. Differences in orgasmic response may also arise from physical considerations, such as whether the person is experiencing orgasm when lying down or standing up, and so on.

At one extreme, the overt manifestations of orgasm may be so subdued that an observer may hardly be able to detect them; on the other hand, the experience may be an explosive convulsion. Most commonly, there is a visible combination of genital and total body responses: sustained tension or mild twitching of the extremities while the rest of the body becomes rigid, a grimace or muffled cry, and rhythmic throbbing of the sex organs and pelvic musculature before relaxation sets in. Less commonly, reactions are restricted to the genitals alone. The pelvic thrusts are followed by subdued throbbings, and general body response seems minimal.

In intense orgasm the whole body becomes rigid, the legs and feet are extended, the toes curl in or flare out,[7] the abdomen becomes hard and spastic, the stiffened neck is thrust forward, the shoulders and arms are rigid and grasping, the mouth gasps for breath, the eyes bulge and stare vacantly or shut tightly. The whole body convulses in synchrony with the genital throbs or twitches incontrollably.

At the climax the person may moan, groan, scream, or utter fragmented and meaningless phrases. In more extreme reactions there may be uncontrollable laughing, talking, crying, or frenzied movement. Such climaxes may last several minutes.

Orgasm is experienced by both men and women as intense pleasure, though its subjective components do vary somewhat between the two sexes. In adult males the sensations of orgasm are linked to ejaculation,[8] which occurs in two

---

[6]Ellis, H. (1942), Vol. II, Part One, pp. 115–116. Phaëthon was the son of Helius, the sun god in Greek mythology, who was allowed by his father to drive the chariot of the sun through the heavens for a day. Unable to check the celestial horses, Phaëthon drove them first so high that everyone on earth shivered and then so close to the earth that the fields were scorched. Zeus, enraged, struck him with a thunderbolt (Graves, 1959, Vol. 1, p. 156).

[7]In Japanese erotic art curled toes indicate sexual excitement. The characteristic posture of the stiffened and extended feet and hands is called *carpopedal spasm*.

[8]Ejaculation and orgasm are two separate processes. Orgasm can be experienced by both sexes and probably at all ages. It consists of the neuromuscular discharge of accumulated sexual tensions. Ejaculation on the other hand is experienced only by males following puberty, when the prostate and accessory glands become functional. Females do not ejaculate. The fluid that lubricates the vagina is produced during arousal and does not correspond to the male semen.

stages. First, there is a sense that ejaculation is imminent, or "coming," and that one can do nothing to stop it. Second, there is a distinct awareness of the contracting urethra, followed by fluid moving out under pressure.

In the female, orgasm starts with a feeling of momentary suspension followed by a peak of intense sensation in the clitoris, which then spreads through the pelvis. This stage varies in intensity and may also involve sensations of "falling," "opening up," or even of emitting fluid. Some women compare this stage of orgasm to mild labor pains. It is followed by a suffusion of warmth spreading from the pelvis through the rest of the body. The experience culminates in characteristic throbbing sensations in the pelvis. The female orgasm, unlike that of the male, can be interrupted.

Because of the intensity of feeling, the reduction in sensory perception described earlier is most marked during sexual climax. The person may become quite insensitive to blows or even to more painful stimuli, and at the peak of sexual excitement one may bite and scratch with only a vague realization that he is doing so. Vision, hearing, taste, and smell—all sensations—become partly numbed. Particularly in a more intense climax the person may lose consciousness for a few seconds.

It is paradoxical that, at the peak of sexual gratification, the person does not display an expression of joy or contentment. On the contrary, his contorted face and straining movements seem to suggest torment. Incidentally, should a woman smile placidly while presumably experiencing orgasm, it is probable that she is merely pretending.

Aftereffects of Orgasm

Whereas the onset of orgasm is fairly distinct, its termination is more ambiguous. The rhythmic throbs of the genitals and the convulsions of the body become progressively less intense and less frequent. Overwhelming neuromuscular tension gives way to profound relaxation.

The manifestations of the postorgasmic phase are the opposite of those of the pre-orgasmic period. The entire musculature is relaxed. The person feels an overwhelming need to rest. His head feels too heavy for his neck to support. The grasping hands and curled toes relax, and the arms and legs can be moved only with effort. The pounding heart and accelerated breathing revert to normal. Congested and swollen tissues and organs resume their usual colors and sizes. As the body rests, the mind reawakens, and the various senses regain their full acuity gradually.

The quiescent state of body and mind following sexual climax has given rise to the belief that all animals are sad following coitus.[9] Actually, for most people the predominant sensation is one of profound gratification, or peace and satiation. The contorted expression yields to one of calm. The eyes become luminous and languid, and a subtle flush lights the face. Women are said to be at their loveliest at this time.

The descent from the peak of orgasm may occur in one vertiginous sweep or more gradually. Particularly at night the profound postcoital relaxation contributes to natural weariness, and the person may simply fall asleep. Others feel relaxed but perfectly alert or even exhilarated.

It is not unusual to feel thirsty or hungry following orgasm. A smoker may crave a cigarette. Often there is a need to urinate, sometimes to move the bowels. Idiosyncratic reactions are myriad: Some people feel numb or

---

[9] The original remark, ascribed to Galen (A.D. 130–200) was "Triste est omne animal post coitum, praeter mulierem gallumque" ("Every animal is sad after coitus except the human female and the rooster").

itch, some want more physical contact, and others want to be left alone. It is difficult to separate physiologically determined responses from psychological, or learned, patterns of behavior in this area.

Regardless of the immediate postorgasmic response, a healthy person recovers fully from the aftereffects of orgasm in a relatively short time. Protracted fatigue is often the result of activities that may have preceded or accompanied sex (drinking, lack of sleep), rather than of orgasm itself. When a person is in ill health, however, the experience may be more taxing in itself.

Orgasm in Lower Animals. The expressions of orgasm are clearly discernible among mammals. In the male animal there is no question that orgasm occurs regularly, and ejaculation marks it clearly. Female animal orgasm is more difficult to detect. In female mammals other than humans neuromuscular tensions do not seem to subside abruptly following coitus but rather dissipate slowly. Furthermore, female animals in heat remain responsive to sexual stimulation after coitus rather than losing interest as males do.

Even though most infrahuman females seem to be orgasmically nonresponsive, there are records of specific instances in which female chimpanzees have seemed to exhibit all the signs of orgasm. Physiological measures of blood pressure in these animals during sexual activity also demonstrate similar elevations and depressions for both sexes, which constitutes indirect evidence for the occurrence of sexual climax. The evidence from animals indicates that orgasm evolved late for females. Whereas orgasm in males is clearly the continuation of mechanisms present in infrahuman species, the human female is unique in her ability to reach orgasm so readily and unmistakably.[10]

The Sexual Response Cycle

Although the general response of the body to sexual stimulation has been fairly well documented, accurate physiological observations during orgasm have been lacking. Current research is, however, beginning to fill this void. The sexual response patterns shown in Figures 3.1 and 3.2 summarize observations by Masters

---

[10]Ford and Beach (1951), p. 30.

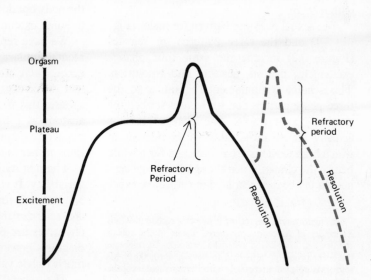

Figure 3.1. The male sexual response cycle. From Masters and Johnson, *Human Sexual Response* (Boston: Little, Brown and Company, 1966), p. 5. Reprinted by permission.

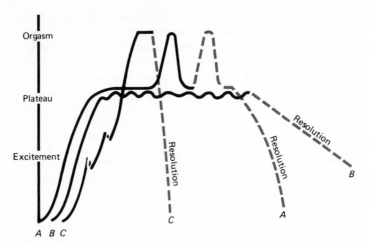

Figure 3.2. The female sexual response cycle. From Masters and Johnson, *Human Sexual Response* (Boston: Little, Brown and Company, 1966), p. 5. Reprinted by permission.

and Johnson of about 10,000 orgasms (see Chapter 1).[11] They represent generalized patterns, rather than consistent reactions of individuals. These graphic summaries do not, of course, show the common deviations from basic responses. Such deviations, however, occur mostly in the durations of phases, rather than in the sequence of response in each. We can therefore view these curves as typical while keeping in mind the wide range of variation within them.

The sexual response pattern for males (Figure 3.1) and the three patterns for females (Figure 3.2) include the same four phases: excitement, plateau, orgasm, and resolution. This scheme is fundamentally similar to the three-phase pattern that we have described for the body as a whole. The plateau phase is actually an advanced stage of excitement in which high tensions are maintained for a while before the climax. Even though this stage cannot readily be differentiated in subjective expe-

rience, we shall refer to it because the original data have been described in this manner.

These response patterns are generally independent of the type of stimulation or sexual activity that produces them. The basic physiology of orgasm is the same, regardless of whether it is brought about through masturbation, coitus, or some other activity. Differences resulting from the type of stimulation do not affect the fundamental changes manifested by the body but do affect the intensity of responses to some extent.

We have repeatedly emphasized the fundamental similarity of sexual responses in the two sexes. There are, however, a number of important differences between male and female responses that must be noted. Some result from anatomical differences; others cannot be explained structurally and possibly reflect variations in nervous system organization.

The first major difference is in the range of variability. It is already apparent from Figures 3.1 and 3.2 that, whereas a single sequence characterizes the basic male pattern, three alternatives are possible for females. Even this diagram, however, does not fully convey the much richer variety of female responses.

The second difference between the sexes

[11] This figure has an interesting historical precedent. When Alexander of Macedon conquered Persia in the fourth century B.C. he married a Persian princess. To celebrate the event properly, he is said to have had 10,000 of his soldiers couple simultaneously with Persian maidens at the stroke of midnight on his wedding night.

involves the presence of a refractory period in the male cycle. (A cell, tissue, or organ may not respond to a second stimulation until a certain period of time has elapsed after the preceding stimulation. This period is known as "refractory.") As indicated in Figure 3.1, the refractory period immediately follows orgasm and extends into the resolution phase. During this period, regardless of the nature and intensity of sexual stimulation, the male will not respond. He cannot achieve full erection and another orgasm. Only after the refractory period, the duration of which has not yet been specified with precision, can he do so. In principle, a man can then go on to have another orgasm. In practice, his ability to do so is quite limited.

Females do not have such refractory periods (Figure 3.2). Even in the pattern closest to that of the male (line A), as soon as the first orgasm is over the level of excitement can mount immediately to another climax. Women can thus have multiple orgasms in rapid succession. If they do not, the cause lies in specific circumstances of the occasion, including the males' inability or unwillingness to provide the necessary sustained stimulation.

Apart from these differences, these basic response patterns in the two sexes are the same. We shall review briefly: In males (Figure 3.1) and females (Figure 3.2, line A) excitement mounts in response to effective and sustained stimulation, which may be psychogenic (erotic thoughts and feelings) or somatogenic (physical stimulation) but usually involves both. Excitement may mount rapidly or more slowly, depending upon various factors. If erotic stimulation is sustained the level of excitement becomes stabilized at a high point: the plateau phase. Sometime during this stage the point of no return is reached, and orgasm follows. This abrupt release is succeeded by a gradual dispersion of pent-up excitement during the resolution phase.

The lengths of these phases vary greatly, but in general the excitement and resolution phases are the longest. The plateau phase is usually relatively short, and orgasm usually takes only a minute or less. Although the diagrams do not indicate them, there may be several peaks in the plateau phase, each followed by a return to a lower level of excitement. It is also possible, of course, that excitement may not reach the point of orgasm. The overall time for one complete coital cycle may range from a few minutes to many hours.

The other two patterns for females (Figure 3.2, lines B and C) represent minor departures from the more common response, in that the plateau phase is omitted. In line B excitement mounts and immediately breaks into a series of rapid orgasms, which the woman experiences as one sustained climax followed by a protracted resolution phase. Line C is characterized by more abrupt increments in excitement, culminating in a single sustained climax, followed by a precipitate resolution of tensions. Both these alternative responses are more intense than is the more common one and are reflected in particularly marked physiological changes.[12]

During the various phases of the sexual response cycle numerous specific physiological changes occur, some in the genitals, some in other parts of the body. As we describe these reactions, we must keep in mind that not all these responses continue through the entire cycle. Some physiological responses (like erection of the penis) set in right away and persist throughout the entire cycle, whereas others occur only during part of a given phase (for instance, additional coronal engorgement late in the plateau phase).

---

[12] Such sustained orgasms have been labeled *status orgasmus*, or "orgasmic states," in contrast to single orgasms. This is analogous to the distinction between single convulsions and convulsive states in epilepsy.

Physiological Mechanisms
of Sexual Response

Two underlying mechanisms explain how various organs respond to sexual stimulation: *vasocongestion* and *myotonia*.

Vasocongestion is the engorgement of blood vessels and increased influx of blood into tissues. Ordinarily the flow of blood through the arteries into various organs is matched by the outflow through the veins, so that a fluctuating balance is maintained. Under various conditions blood flow into a region will exceed the capacity of the veins to drain the area, and vasocongestion will result. Blood flow is primarily controlled by the smaller arteries (arterioles), whose muscular walls constrict and dilate in response to nervous impulses. The ultimate causes may be physical (for example, heat) or psychological (for example, embarrassment). Congested tissue, because of its excess blood content, becomes swollen, red, and warm. Sexual excitement is accompanied by widespread vasocongestion involving superficial and deep tissues. Its most dramatic manifestation is the erection of the penis. Erection has been called the "blushing of the penis." The response varies in different organs and at different times but is necessarily present in sexual excitement.

Myotonia is increased muscle tension. Even when a person is completely relaxed or asleep, his muscles maintain a certain firmness, or "muscle tone." From this baseline muscular tension increases during voluntary flexing or involuntary orgasmic contractions. During sexual activity, myotonia is inevitable and widespread. It affects both smooth and skeletal muscles and occurs both voluntarily and involuntarily. Although evidence of myotonia is present from the start of sexual excitement, it tends to lag behind vasocongestion.

Vasocongestion and myotonia are the underlying sources of practically all physio-

logical manifestations during sexual activity, and the reader should keep them in mind during our discussion of general and specific physiological responses.

Reactions of Male Sexual Organs

Penis. Of all the sex organs, the penis undergoes the most dramatic changes during sexual excitement and orgasm. Erection is correctly regarded as evidence of sexual excitement. Nevertheless, there are instances in which erections occur in the absence of sexual stimulation or erotic feelings.

Erection is experienced on innumerable occasions by practically all males and may occur in earliest infancy (some baby boys have erections right after birth), as well as in old age. During their sexually active years, men experience erections daily both while they are awake and while they are asleep.[13] Erection is, of course, not an all-or-none phenomenon; there are many gradations between the totally flaccid penis and the maximally congested organ immediately before orgasm. For practical purposes, a penis that can be inserted into a normally responsive vagina may be considered fully erect.

Mechanism of Erection. Erection is a vascular phenomenon that is triggered by a nervous reflex. Nervous reflexes have three components. First are the "receptors," or sense organs, which detect the stimuli and transmit them to centers in the spinal cord or the brain. These centers ("transmitters") interpret the sensory input and convey the appropriate response to the third component, the end organs ("effectors"), thus completing the reflex arc. The end organ may be a muscle that contracts or a gland that secretes in response to such stimulation. An example of a simple reflex is withdrawal of the

---

[13] Fisher *et al.* (1965).

hand after touching a hot object. Another well-known example is the knee-jerk response to tapping of the patellar tendon. Reflexes are involuntary in the sense that their response is automatic and does not require a "decision" by the brain. The brain is, of course, conscious of these responses and may be able to inhibit the reflexive response to a variable extent.

A similar reflex network links the genital organs and adjoining areas (like the insides of the thighs) to an "erection center" in the lowest (sacral) portion of the spinal cord. The outgoing impulses are carried to the blood vessels that supply the spongy tissues of the penis. Ordinarily the cavernous and spongy bodies receive modest amounts of blood from the arteries and are drained by the veins. After effective tactile stimulation, like stroking of the insides of the thighs or of the glans penis, nerve impulses converge in the spinal erection center. This center in turn activates nerve fibers connected to the muscular coating of the arterial walls. There are two sets of such fibers. One set (the parasympathetic system) causes the arterial walls to relax and expand their lumina; the other (the sympathetic system) causes them to contract, thus narrowing their lumina. The response to sexual stimulation is activation of the parasympathetic system and inhibition of sympathetic fibers, which immediately result in expansion of the arterial lumina and rush of blood into the cavernous and spongy tissues of the penis.

The veins, hampered by their valves and the compression of their thin walls by the swelling organ, cannot handle the outflow of blood. The penis is thus rapidly engorged, so that it stiffens and stands erect. Loss of erection results from a reversal of this process: Sympathetic nerve fibers constrict the arteries, cutting down the inflow of blood, and drainage through the veins increases until the organ returns to a flaccid condition.

The processes described so far are the re- flexive aspects of penile erection. They are independent of the brain, in the sense that they can occur without assistance from higher centers. For instance, a man whose spinal cord has been severed above the level of the spinal reflex center may still be capable of erection. He will not "feel" the stimulation of his penis; for that matter, he may even be totally unconscious. But his penis will respond, blindly as it were.

The independence of reflex centers does not mean that they cannot be influenced by the brain, however. Intricate networks link the brain to the reflex center in the spinal cord. Purely mental activity may thus trigger the mechanism of erection without physical stimulation, or it may inhibit erection despite persistent physical stimulation. Usually the two components operate simultaneously and complement each other. Spurred by erotic thoughts the man initiates physical stimulation of the genitals; conversely, physical excitement inspires erotic thoughts.

The instances in which erection seems to be nonsexual in origin involve tension of the pelvic muscles (as when lifting a heavy weight or straining during defecation). Irritation of the glans or a full bladder may have the same effect. Erections that occur in infancy are explained on a reflex basis also.

Erection occurs with remarkable rapidity. In men younger than forty years of age, less than ten seconds may be all the time required. There are, of course, tremendous differences among individuals, as well as among occasions for the same individual. Younger men generally respond more rapidly, but slowing down with age is not inexorable.

The excitement phase may be short, and activity may rapidly proceed to the more stable plateau phase. More often the earlier phase is quite protracted, and the varying firmness of erection reflects the waxing and waning of sexual excitement and desire. During this period a man is quite vulnerable to loss of erection.

Even if sexual stimulation continues uninterrupted, alarming distraction can cause partial or total detumescence.

During the plateau phase the penis undergoes two further though relatively minor changes. Although full erection is achieved at the end of the excitement phase, further engorgement occurs, primarily in the corona of the glans. Erection is then more "permanent," and the man may temporarily turn his attention away from sexual activity yet remain tumescent. In addition, the glans occasionally shows a deepening of the reddish-purple color resulting from venous congestion. Unlike the preorgasmic color change of the minor labia in the female, this change does not predict whether orgasm is to follow or not.

Erection is the most delicate of the male sexual functions. Chronic failure, known as *impotence,* can take many forms. The man may simply be unable to achieve erection under any circumstance or may be impotent only during some sexual activities or with some partners. Failure may be complete or partial; in the latter instance the penis, though erect, is not firm enough to permit sexual intercourse. Finally, a man may be unable to maintain an erection long enough to participate in coitus satisfactorily ("premature ejaculation").

At one time or another every man experiences some loss of potency. Fluctuations and occasional failures in sexual capacity do not constitute impotence. It is only when the problem is persistent that it is considered a malfunction. Impotence is further discussed in connection with sexual disorders (see Chapter 12).

The converse of impotence is a rare condition known as priapism[14] which is a pathological condition, rather than a sign of exceptional virility. The cause may be unknown or may be

a demonstrable disease (infection, tumor, and so on) that triggers and maintains the mechanism of erection. Such persistent erections are usually unaccompanied by sexual desire and may be quite painful. Not infrequently they cause permanent damage to the penis and end in impotence. Priapism is not to be confused with satyriasis, which refers to "excessive" sexual desire in the male (see Chapter 7).

During orgasm the characteristic rhythmic contractions begin in the accessory sexual organs (prostate, seminal vesicles, and vas) but very soon extend to the penis itself (see Figure 3.3). Orgasmic contractions involve the entire length of the penile urethra, as well as the muscles sheathing the root of the penis. At first they occur regularly at intervals of approximately 0.8 seconds, but after the first several strong contractions they become weaker, irregular, and less frequent.

Ejaculation ("throwing out"), as already indicated, is not precisely synonymous with orgasm but is its cardinal manifestation in the adult male. This forcible ejection of spermatic fluid through the urethra is unequivocal evidence that orgasm has taken place. The fluid, which flows in variable amounts (usually about 3 cubic centimeters, or a teaspoonful), is known as "semen," "seminal fluid," or "spermatic fluid." It consists of sperm (which account for very little of its volume) and the secretions of the prostate (which impart to it a characteristic milkiness and odor), of the seminal vesicles, and to a much lesser extent of Cowper's glands.

Ejaculation consists of two distinct phases. During the first (emission, or first stage orgasm) the prostate, seminal vesicles, and vas deferens pour their contents into the dilated urethral bulb. At this point the man feels the inevitability of ejaculation. In the second phase (ejaculation proper, or second stage orgasm) the semen is expelled by the vigorous contractions of the muscles surrounding the root of the penis and the peristaltic contractions of the genital

---

[14]Named after Priapus (see Chapter 2).

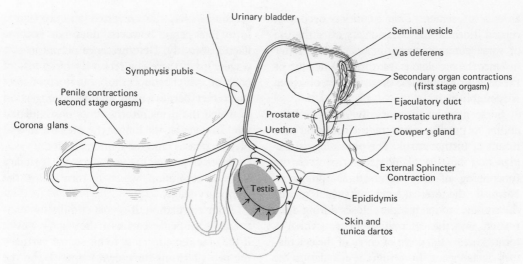

Figure 3.3. The male pelvis: orgasmic phase. From Masters and Johnson, *Human Sexual Response* (Boston: Little, Brown and Company, 1966), p. 184. Reprinted by permission.

ducts. The subjective experience at this point is one of intense pleasure associated with orgasmic throbs and the sensation of spermatic flow.

The initial vigorous thrust during orgasm pushes the semen out with some force, but usually the fluid is propelled barely beyond the tip of the penis. At times, however, it may be projected to a distance of several feet. At any rate, after the initial ejaculation, the remaining semen flows out in gentle spurts. In successive orgasms the flow of fluid is progressively less.

The amount of fluid and the force with which it is ejaculated are popularly associated with strength of desire, potency, fertility, and so on. These beliefs are difficult to substantiate, however.

There is also a popular notion that semen is generated entirely by the testes, for during prolonged abstinence the testes may feel tense and full. This feeling, which may be uncomfortable, is relieved by ejaculation. Nevertheless, the contribution of the testes to semen is restricted to sperm and the minimal fluid that carries them. The pelvic sensation of fullness

before orgasm results from vasocongestion and sustained muscular tensions. Women have similar experiences.

Mechanism of Ejaculation. Ejaculation, like erection, is reflexive. Its center is also in the spinal cord but is located somewhat higher (in the lumbar portion) than is the erection center. The nervous impulses that trigger ejaculation travel to the genital area through the sympathetic nerves. The ejaculation process is a purely nervous phenomenon, with no vascular component. Furthermore, it is much more autonomous, in that once ejaculation has been triggered it cannot be stopped until it has been completed.

Apart from premature ejaculation, disturbances of this process are very rare. Occasionally a man with a normal erection fails to ejaculate, no matter how hard he tries. More often the ejaculation reflex is triggered, but the fluid, instead of flowing out normally, empties into the urinary bladder (*retrograde ejaculation*). The sensation of orgasm in this condition is unchanged, but the man is usually alarmed by the absence of semen. This condition occurs in certain illnesses and occasionally after the use of some common tranquilizers. In the latter instance the problem is transitory: When use of the drug is discontinued the usual flow of semen is reestablished.

Some men have reportedly developed the ability to produce retrograde ejaculation as a means of birth control. The physiological explanation of this phenomenon involves the functioning of the two urethral sphincters. Normally the internal sphincter (which guards the entrance to the bladder) closes during ejaculation, and the external sphincter (which is located below the point of entry of the ejaculatory ducts) opens. In retrograde ejaculation the external urethral sphincter closes, and the internal sphincter opens, thus permitting the semen to back up into the bladder.

The ability to delay ejaculation voluntarily is one of the most admired attributes of male virility. It enables a man to provide protracted sexual gratification for his partner, as well as prolonging his own enjoyment. Specific techniques for delaying ejaculation will be discussed later. The fundamental principle is to modulate excitement while maintaining erection, rather than permitting it to build up relentlessly. Such control includes mental distraction (thinking about a neutral or even unpleasant topic) and muscular relaxation (slow pelvic thrusts or cessation of movement).

Coitus reservatus (the *karezza* of India) represents the ultimate in control of ejaculation. Men trained in this practice are able repeatedly to approach ejaculation without completing it. They claim that they thus achieve the equivalent of many orgasms. This practice was at one time standard in the nineteenth-century communistic Oneida colony in upstate New York.[15]

In the resolution phase the changes of the

preceding phases are reversed, and erection is lost. The penis, however, does not become flaccid abruptly. Detumescence occurs in two stages: First, there is a relatively rapid loss of erection, which reduces the organ to a semierect state; then there is a more gradual decongestion in which the penis returns to its unstimulated size. In general, the longer the excitement and plateau phases (and the more marked the vasocongestion process), the longer the primary stage of resolution, which in turn delays the secondary stage.

After ejaculation, if sexual stimulation continues (if the penis remains in the vagina or even if the man remains close to his sexual partner), the penis remains tumescent longer. If, on the other hand, he withdraws, is distracted, or attempts to urinate, detumescence is more rapid. A man actually cannot urinate with a fully erect penis because the internal urinary sphincter closes reflexively during full erection to prevent intermingling of urine and semen.

Scrotum. The changes in the scrotal sac, though distinct, are not as dramatic as are those in the penis. During the excitement phase the scrotal skin contracts and thickens with a resulting loss of the normal baggy appearance. The initial response of the scrotum to sexual excitement is thus similar to its reaction to cold (and also to fear and anger). If the excitement phase is quite prolonged, the scrotum relaxes, even though the sexual cycle is not yet completed. During the plateau and orgasmic phases there are no further changes. In the resolution phase there is usually a rapid loss of the thickening of the scrotal skin. The scrotum shows no color changes.

Testes. The changes undergone by the testes, though not visible, are quite marked. During the excitement phase both testes are lifted up within the scrotum (see Figure 3.3), mainly as a result of the shortening of the spermatic cords

---

[15] Bishop (1969).

and the contraction of the scrotal sac. During the plateau phase, this elevation progresses farther until the organs are actually pressed against the body wall. Full testicular elevation is necessary for orgasm and anticipates it.[16]

The second major change is a marked increase in size (about 50 percent in most instances) because of vasocongestion. During orgasm there are no further changes. In the resolution phase the size and position return to normal. Again the process may be rapid or slow (the pace is usually consistent for a given person), and, the longer the plateau phase, the more protracted is the process of detumescence.

Cowper's Glands. The bulbourethral (Cowper's) glands show no evidence of activity during the excitement phase. If tension is sustained, a drop or so of clear fluid, probably produced by these glands, appears at the tip of the penis. These tiny structures are rudimentary in men. Their female homologues, the Bartholin glands, tend to be slightly more active. In contrast, in some animals (for example, stallions, rams, bears, and goats) these glands secrete profusely during sexual arousal.

Men do, however, vary a great deal in the production of this mucoid material. Although most secrete only a drop or none at all, a few produce enough to wet the glans or even to dribble freely. The presence of this fluid is reliable evidence of a high level of sexual tension, but its absence does not ensure the opposite.

It has been assumed that this secretion acts as a lubricant during coitus. Because of its scanty and inconsistent presence, however, this function is unlikely. A more plausible explanation is that it neutralizes the urine-contaminated acidic urethra, protecting the sperm during their passage.

Whatever its source and function, its association with voluptuous thoughts has been well known. Medieval scholars called it the "distillate of love" and correctly distinguished it from semen. It has also been mentioned in ancient literature.[17]

Although quite unrelated to semen, this secretion sometimes contains stray sperm that have seeped out before ejaculation. Intercourse may thus result in pregnancy even though the male withdraws his penis before orgasm, which often explains unexpected pregnancies when the participants vehemently maintain that coitus stopped before intravaginal ejaculation.

Prostate and Seminal Vesicles. The responses of the prostate gland and the seminal vesicles are similar and will therefore be described together. Overt changes are restricted to the orgasmic phase (see Figure 3.3), during which they do play a major role. As indicated earlier, ejaculation actually begins with the contractions of these accessory structures as they pour their secretions into the expanded urethra. The admixture of sperm from the throbbing vas deferens with the secretions of the seminal vesicles (whose walls also pulsate spasmodically) occurs in the ejaculatory duct. Sperm that may have been stored within seminal vesicles, along with those coming through the vas, are thus propelled through the duct into the urethra. These accessory organs actually participate in the rhythmic convulsions of orgasm. Their

---

[16]The elevation of the testes during sexual excitement was noted by Aristotle in the fourth century B.C.

[17]The *Priapeia,* epigrams on Priapus by various Latin poets, includes the following poem (quoted in Ellis, H. [1942], Vol. II, Part One, p. 153):

You see this organ, after which I'm called
And which is my certificate, is humid;
This moisture is not dew nor drops or rain,
It is the outcome of sweet memory,
Recalling thoughts of a complacent maid.

contractions, along with the filling of the urethra, are responsible for the sensation that orgasm is imminent.

Reactions of Female Sex Organs

Vagina. The vagina, the main female organ of copulation, corresponds functionally to the male penis (but the clitoris is the penile homologue). The physiological responses of the vagina and penis to sexual stimulation are complementary: As the penis prepares for insertion, the vagina prepares to receive it. These reactions are of course not limited to sexual intercourse. Effective stimulation, of whatever origin, brings about the standard vaginal and penile responses.

The vagina exhibits three specific reactions during the excitement phase: lubrication, expansion of its inner end, and color change. The warm, moist vagina betrays sexual desire. The term "lubricity" is an appropriate synonym for "lust." Moistening of the vaginal walls is actually the very first sign of sexual response in a woman and usually occurs within ten to thirty seconds after erotic stimulation.

The lubricatory function of the clear, slippery, and mildly scented vaginal fluid is self-evident. As the fluid is alkaline, it has also been assumed to help neutralize the vaginal canal (which normally tends to be acidic) in preparation for the transit of semen. The source of this fluid was, however, unknown until recently. Earlier it was assumed that the fluid was a female ejaculate, analogous to male semen and therefore essential to conception. This misconception, which was prevalent until the seventeenth century, had some unusual repercussions. It formed the basis for theological tolerance of female masturbation if orgasm did not occur naturally during coitus; the argument was that, unless the woman complemented male semen with her own ejaculation, conception could not occur. Such a failure would negate what was considered the primary function of coitus.

As the vaginal wall has no secretory glands, it was assumed that the lubricant emanated from either the cervix, the Bartholin glands, or both. It has recently been convincingly demonstrated, however, that this fluid does ooze directly from the vaginal walls. The secreting mechanism is as yet unclear, but in all likelihood it is related to vasocongestion in the vaginal walls.[18]

The Bartholin glands do produce a discharge, but, in analogy to the secretion of the male Cowper's glands, it tends to be scanty, erratic, and of lubricating value only in the area of the introitus if at all. Incidentally, the clear vaginal fluid that results from sexual excitement must not be confused with the chronic vaginal discharges produced by various infections (see Chapter 12). Some secretions from the cervix may also be present, but they too do not contribute substantially to vaginal lubrication.

The second major change during the excitement phase is the lengthening and expansion of the inner two-thirds of the vagina. The ordinarily collapsed interior vaginal walls expand to create a space where the ejaculate will be deposited. The stretched walls of the vagina thus lose some of their normal wrinkled appearance.

Finally, the ordinarily purple-red vaginal walls take on a darker hue in response to sexual stimulation. This discoloration, initially patchy, eventually spreads over the entire vaginal surface. These color changes reflect the progressive vasocongestion of the vaginal walls.

During the plateau phase, the focus of change shifts from the inner two-thirds to the outer one-third of the vagina. During the excitement phase the outer end of the vagina may have dilated somewhat, but in the plateau phase it becomes congested with blood, and the vaginal lumen becomes at least a third narrower. These congested walls of the outer third of the

---

[18]Masters and Johnson (1966), p. 70.

vagina constitute the *orgasmic platform*. It is there that rhythmic contractions during orgasm are most apparent. During the plateau phase the "tenting effect" at the inner end of the vagina progresses still farther, and full vaginal expansion is achieved. Vaginal lubrication, on the other hand, tends to slow down, and if the excitement phase is unduly protracted further production of vaginal fluid may cease altogether in the plateau phase.

During orgasm (see Figure 3.4), the most visible effects occur in the orgasmic platform. This area contracts rhythmically (initially at approximately 0.8 second intervals) from three to fifteen times. After the first three to six contractions (corresponding to the first ejaculatory contractions of the penis), the movements become weaker and more widely spaced. This orgasmic pattern varies from person to person and in the same person from one orgasm to another. The more frequent and intense the contractions of the orgasmic platform, the more intense is the subjective experience of climax. At particularly high levels of excitement these rhythmic contractions are preceded by spastic (nonrhythmic) contractions of the orgasmic platform that last two to four seconds. The inner portion of the vagina does not contract but continues its "tenting."

These observations confirm that the vagina is not a passive receptacle for the penis but an active participant in coitus. This fact has been well known to those who have observed the quivering of the vaginal opening in the throes of orgasm. Sexual sophisticates have sung the praises of the vagina that eagerly admits, envelops, and "milks" the penis to a voluptuous climax.

During the resolution phase the orgasmic platform subsides rapidly. The inner walls return much more slowly to their usual form. With decongestion the color of the vaginal walls lightens over a period of ten to fifteen minutes. The process of lubrication may rarely continue into this phase, and such continuation indicates lingering or rekindled sexual tension: With sufficient stimulation, a second orgasm may follow rapidly.

It has been a tenet of orthodox psychoanalytic theory that females experience two types

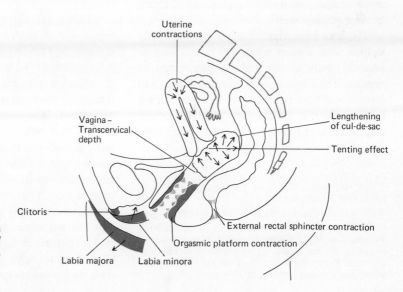

Figure 3.4. The female pelvis: orgasmic phase. From Masters and Johnson, *Human Sexual Response* (Boston: Little, Brown and Company, 1966), p. 77. Reprinted by permission.

of orgasm: vaginal and clitoral. This notion was originally proposed by Freud[19] and subsequently reiterated by other psychoanalysts.[20] This dual orgasm theory assumes that in young girls the clitoris, like the male penis, is the primary site of sexual excitement and expression. With psychosexual maturity the sexual focus is said to shift from the clitoris to the vagina, so that after puberty the vagina emerges as the dominant orgasmic zone. Should this transfer not occur, the woman remains incapable of experiencing vaginal orgasm and is restricted to the "immature" clitoral type. In a sense, such a woman is "frigid": incapable of achieving the fully satisfying vaginal orgasm that is the hallmark of the sexually healthy and mature woman.

Kinsey and his associates raised doubts about the whole concept of dual orgasm (and thus incurred the wrath of some psychoanalytic theorists). They pointed out that the vagina is a rather insensitive organ; during pelvic examinations many women simply cannot tell when the vaginal wall is being gently touched, and in surgical practice the vagina has been found to be rather insensitive to pain. Also microscopic studies fail to reveal end organs of touch in most vaginal walls.

The data from Masters and Johnson's study support the Kinsey point of view. Physiologically there is one and only one type of orgasm. The clitoris and the vagina respond in identical fashion, regardless of which is stimulated or, for that matter, even if neither one is directly involved (as when orgasm occurs after

breast manipulation only). This finding does not mean that the subjective experience of orgasm, elicited by whatever means, is always the same. The similarity is in the physiologic manifestations only. The subjective experience of orgasm resulting from masturbation or coitus, or from coitus in a given position or with a specific person, can certainly vary tremendously. But the basis of these differences is psychological.

The Kinsey researchers, also, encountered many women who claimed that deep vaginal penetration yielded a special type of satisfaction. They explained this finding on several grounds: the psychological satisfaction of total and intimate involvement with another person; tactile stimulation resulting from total body contact and the effect of the partner's weight; stimulation of the labia, clitoris, and vestibule through pressure from the male genitals and body (in other words stimulation of other areas perceived as stimulation of the vagina); stimulation of perineal muscles; and direct stimulation of the vaginal wall (in those few women whose organs are equipped with sensory nerve endings).

Clitoris. The clitoris is an exclusively sexual organ, and in contrast to its male homologue it plays no part in reproduction and is totally independent of the urinary system. In response to sexual excitement, the clitoris becomes tumescent through vasocongestion, just as the penis does. The overhanging prepuce of the clitoris does not, however, permit it to stand erect as does the penis. That the clitoris does not function exactly as a miniature penis is also apparent from its relatively slow response to stimulation. The immediate counterpart to penile tumescence is vaginal lubrication, rather than clitoral vasocongestion.

The clitoris is highly sensitive. Practically all women perceive tactile stimulation in this area, and most women respond erotically to

[19] *New introductory lectures on psychoanalysis* (1933), in Freud (1957–1964), vol. XXII.

[20] For example, Ferenczi (1936); Abraham (1948); Knight (1943); Fenichel (1945); Deutsch (1945); Benedek (1952). In more current psychoanalytic literature, there is a shift away from the dual orgasm hypothesis, under the influence of recent physiological data. See, for example, Sherfey (1966) and Salzman (1968).

such manipulation.[21] Its shape and ability to trigger voluptuous sensations have led to comparisons with an electric bell button.[22]

During the excitement phase both the glans and the shaft of the clitoris become congested. This response is more consistent for the glans and may result in doubling of its diameter. The vasocongestive response is more rapid and more marked if the clitoris and adjoining areas of the mons are stimulated directly. The fundamental sequence of changes, however, is independent of the method of stimulation.

The shape, size, and position of the clitoris in the unstimulated state and its visible tumescence during the excitement phase have no relation to the likelihood of orgasm. Important as it is for sexual stimulation, the clitoris gives no reliable clues to the subsequent course of the sexual cycle. Visible tumescence of its glans, when it does occur, coincides with the vasocongestive response of the minor labia and comes quite late in the excitement phase (when the penis has been erect for some time and the vagina is fully lubricated). The clitoral glans, once tumescent, remains so throughout the sexual cycle.

During the plateau phase the entire clitoris (glans and shaft) shows a peculiar response. It is retracted under the clitoral hood and almost disappears from view. This reaction is particularly rapid and striking in response to direct stimulation and may result in the clitoris' receding to half its unstimulated length. As the initial enlargement of the organ indicates sexual excitement, its subsequent retraction may understandably be misinterpreted as indicating

loss of sexual tension. When excitement abates the clitoris reemerges from under the hood. During a protracted plateau phase there may be several repetitions of this retraction-emergence sequence, which may confuse the uninformed male who is attempting to stimulate his partner's clitoris.

During orgasm the clitoris remains hidden from view. Following orgasm it promptly (in five to ten seconds) reemerges from its retracted position. The rapidity and timing of this response are comparable to the first postorgasmic loss of penile erection. Final detumescence of the clitoris, on the other hand (like the second stage loss of penile erection), is much slower (usually taking five to ten minutes but sometimes as long as half an hour). When orgasm has not occurred, the engorgement of the glans and shaft of the clitoris may persist for hours and cause discomfort.

Major Lips. The labia of women who have not given birth (nulliparous labia) are anatomically somewhat different from those of women who have (parous labia). These structural alterations influence the types of physiological response during the sexual cycle, especially in the major lips.

Nulliparous major lips become flattened, thinner, and more widely separated, "opening" and exposing the external genitals. This slight opening reveals the congested moist tissues between. During the plateau and orgasmic phases nulliparous major lips show no further changes. During the resolution phase they return to their decongested size and shape and resume their midline contact. Resolution proceeds rapidly if orgasm does occur. Otherwise the changes brought about during excitement take longer to dissipate. Following a protracted period of arousal, congestion may be so intense that the labia remain swollen for several hours after all sexual stimulation has ceased.

Parous major lips are larger and more

---

[21] In gynecological examinations conducted for the Kinsey study, 98 percent of the subjects were able to perceive tactile stimulation of this organ; in contrast, less than 14 percent could detect being touched in the interior of the vagina (Kinsey *et al.,* 1953, pp. 574 and 580).

[22] ". . . a veritable electric bell button which, being pressed or irritated, rings up the whole nervous system" (quoted by Ellis, H., 1942, Vol. II, Part One, p. 130).

pendulous and may contain permanently distended (varicose) veins. Instead of flattening, they become markedly engorged and may double or triple in size during arousal, but they do nevertheless expose the entrance to the vaginal orifice. There are no changes during the next two phases. Resolution is more rapid if orgasm occurs. Otherwise this phase takes longer, depending upon how distended the labial veins have become and how effectively they can be drained.

The changes in the major lips are comparable in scope and consistency with those in their male homologue, the scrotal sac. In both, the responses are common but not particularly dramatic. The underlying mechanisms are, however, different: In the scrotum the response is muscular contraction, whereas in the major lips it is vasocongestion.

Minor Lips. The alterations in the minor lips during the sexual cycle are quite impressive and remarkably consistent. As the excitement phase progresses to the plateau level, they become severely engorged and double or even triple in size in both parous and nulliparous women. These tumescent lips project between the overlying major lips and become quite apparent, which may explain the parting of the major lips during excitement.

Color changes reflect the extent of venous congestion and are therefore affected by any existing venous distension in parous women. During the plateau phase the minor lips become progressively pink or even bright red. In parous women the resulting color is a more intense red or a deeper wine color.

This vivid discoloration of the minor lips has been observed so consistently that they have been called the "sex skin" of the sexually excited woman.[23] If erotic stimulation continues

beyond this point, orgasm is inevitable, but if stimulation is interrupted, orgasm will not occur. On the other hand, orgasm does not occur unless labial congestion first reaches this peak. In this sense, the "sex skin" is comparable to the full testicular elevation of the male: Both herald impending orgasm.

In the resolution phase the swollen and discolored minor lips return to normal. The loss of color occurs in two steps: Within the first ten to fifteen seconds following orgasm the deeper red color gives way to a pinkish tone; subsequently there is a slower and less regular return to the unstimulated pale appearance.

Bartholin's Glands. Bartholin's glands respond to sexual stimulation by secreting a few drops of mucoid material rather late in the excitement phase or even in the plateau phase. They appear to be most effectively stimulated by the action of the copulating penis over a long period of time, and parous women have 'a more generous production. The contribution of these glands to vaginal lubrication or to neutralizing the acidic vaginal canal is relatively minor.

Uterus. Despite its being hidden from view the uterus has long been known to participate actively in the changes of the sexual response cycle. It has often been assumed that the contractions of the uterus during coitus cause the semen to be sucked into its cavity. There is no evidence to support this assumption. One also encounters references in literature to the enjoyment resulting from ramming the penis against the uterine cervix. This too is totally unsubstantiated. In fact, the cervix is remarkably insensitive: It can even be cut without pain.

The uterus responds to sexual stimulation initially by elevation from its usual position. (This reaction does not occur if the uterus is not resting in its normal anteverted position.)

---

[23] Masters and Johnson (1966), p. 41.

This reaction pulls the cervix up and contributes to the tenting effect in the vagina. Full uterine elevation is achieved during the plateau phase and maintained until resolution, when it returns to its usual position over a period of five to ten minutes.

In addition, the uterus clearly shows the effects of the two main physiological phenomena: vasocongestion and myotonia. The former is manifested in a distinct increase in size during the earlier phases, which returns to normal following orgasm; the latter is apparent in the activity of the uterine musculature, culminating in distinct contractions.

Orgasmic contractions start in the fundus and spread downward. Although they occur simultaneously with those of the orgasmic platform, they are less distinct and more irregular. The cervix shows no specific change until the resolution phase, when the external cervical opening may dilate to some extent immediately after orgasm: The more intense the orgasm, the greater is the likelihood of this cervical reaction. Because of inevitable changes in the cervix during childbirth, this reaction is best seen in the nulliparous woman.

Extragenital Reactions

As indicated earlier, the responses of the body to sexual stimulation are not restricted to the sex organs. As extragenital manifestations are quite similar in the two sexes, we shall describe them together.

Breasts. Even though male breasts also respond to sexual stimulation, changes during the sexual cycle are far more striking in the female. Our description, therefore, refers primarily to the latter. Erection of the nipple is the first response of the breast to sexual stimulation. It occurs in the excitement phase and is the result of the contraction of "involuntary" muscle fibers rather than vascular congestion. Engorgement of blood vessels is, however, responsible for the enlargement of the breasts as a whole, including the areolae.

In the plateau phase the engorgement of the areolae is more marked. As a result, the nipples appear relatively smaller. The breast as a whole expands farther during this phase, particularly if it has never been suckled (it may increase as much as a fourth of its unstimulated size); a breast that has been suckled may change little in size or not at all. During orgasm the breasts show no further changes. In the resolution phase, along with the rapidly disappearing sexual flush, the areolae become detumescent, and the nipples regain their fully erect appearance ("false erection"). Gradually breasts and nipples return to normal size.

Changes in the male breast are inconsistent and restricted to nipple erection during the late excitement and plateau phases. Male nipples are rarely stimulated directly during heterosexual activity (sometimes they are during homosexual contact), but the nipple reactions nevertheless appear in more than half the instances observed.

Skin. The significance of skin changes accompanying emotional states is well known. We blush in embarrassment, flush in anger, turn pale in fear. These surface reflections of inner feelings are manifest in the infusion or draining of blood from the vessels in the skin and are controlled by the autonomic nervous system. It is thus hardly surprising that sexual activity results in definite skin reactions, consisting of flushing, temperature change, and perspiration.

The flushing response is more common in women. It appears as a discoloration, like a rash, in the center of the lower chest (epigastrium) during the transition from the excitement to the plateau phase. It then spreads to the breasts, the rest of the chest well, and the neck. In some women large surface areas of the body become mottled as in a measles rash. This sexual flush reaches its peak in the late plateau phase and is an important component of the excited, straining, and uniquely expressive physiognomy of the woman about to experience the release of orgasm. During the resolution phase the sexual flush disappears very quickly; the order reverses its spread so that discoloration leaves the chest last.

Temperature changes during the sexual response cycle have not been measured. Although there is no evidence that the temperature of the body as a whole changes, people do frequently report feelings of pervasive warmth following orgasm, and there are popular references to sexual excitement as a "glow," "fever," or "fire." Superficial vasocongestion is the likely explanation of this sensation.

Perspiration (apart from that caused by physical exertion) occurs fairly frequently during the resolution phase. Among men this response is less consistent and may involve only the soles of the feet and the palms of the hands. There may be a great deal of physical activity during a sexual encounter and, when the atmosphere is warm, sweating is greatly increased and may occur throughout the sexual cycle. Perspiration is one of the means by which the overheated body cools itself.

Cardiovascular System. Just as the heart races and pounds during fear, anger, and excitement, it also responds to sexual stimulation by beating faster. This reaction is usually not immediate, and mild, transient erotic thoughts may not alter the heart rate. But significant levels of sexual tension and certainly orgasm do not occur without some elevation of the pulse rate. Erotic thoughts, no matter how powerful, if unaccompanied by concomitant physiological changes are devoid of emotion and offer only a shadow of genuine sexual experience. In the plateau phase the heart rate rises to 100 to 160 beats a minute (the normal resting heart rate is 60 to 80 beats a minute). The blood pressure also registers definite increases parallel to that in the heart rate. These changes are quite significant

and comparable to levels reached by athletes exerting maximum effort or by men engaged in heavy labor. They entail considerable strain on the cardiovascular system, which is easily handled most of the time; people with heart disease, however, require medical guidance in this regard.

Respiratory System. Respiration and heart rate are interrelated through complex physiological mechanisms, so that they respond concurrently to demands on the body: The most common example is physical exercise. Changes in respiratory rate lag behind those in heart rate. Faster and deeper breathing becomes apparent in the plateau phase, and during orgasm the respiratory rate may go up to forty a minute (the normal rate is about fifteen a minute, inhalation and exhalation counting as one). Breathing, however, becomes irregular during orgasm, when the individual may momentarily hold his breath and then breath rapidly. Following orgasm he may take a long deep breath or sigh as he sinks into the resolution phase. Along with the pulse and blood pressure, respiration returns to normal rate and depth.

The flaring nostrils, heaving chest, and gasping mouth that accompany sexual experience are popularly known and caricatured in the stylized panting of comedians to suggest erotic excitement. Some of the panting and grunts uttered during orgasm result from involuntary contractions of the respiratory muscles, which force air through the spastic respiratory passages. Following orgasm the soft palate relaxes, and the person may make snoring noises.

The changes manifested by the cardiovascular and respiratory systems are partly caused by muscular exertion and are nonspecific to sex. Apart from these changes, however, are some that occur in response specifically to sexual stimulation. Changes in facial expression and gasping for breath during orgasm raise the possibility that the individual suffers a lack of oxygen (anoxia), but this surmise has not been conclusively documented.

Digestive System. The response of the digestive tract to sexual stimulation can be best observed at its beginning and end: the mouth and the anus. During sexual arousal the secretion of saliva increases and the person may literally water at the mouth. In some instances he may drool or even spray saliva. During intense erotic kissing (or mouth-genital contact) increased salivation is very apparent.

The anus is a sensitive area, which, apart from its proximity to the genitals, appears to be intimately involved in both eliciting and responding to sexual stimuli. Some people react to anal stimulation erotically, whereas others are indifferent or disgusted. Anal stimulation is not an exclusively male homosexual practice; it occurs in heterosexual relations also. Penetration of the anus is likely to be painful to the uninitiated, however.

Stimulation of the anus has well-known repercussions in the body: Stretching the anal sphincter induces inhalation, but contraction makes exhalation difficult. The rhythmic contraction of the anus, along with the flexing of the buttocks, induces sexual tension. Some women are able to reach orgasm through this maneuver alone.

Sexual activity elicits anal responses (noted long ago by Aristotle). During the excitement and plateau phases, the rectal sphincter contracts irregularly in response to direct stimulation. The more striking reactions, however, occur during orgasm, when involuntary contractions can be seen to occur at approximately the same 0.8 second intervals as do the throbs of the orgasmic platform and the penile urethra. Anal contractions do not always occur and usually involve only two to four spasms. The rectal sphincter relaxes while the manifestations of orgasm are still in progress elsewhere.

Urinary System. The male urethra is an integral part of the penis, and its changes during the sexual response cycle have already been described in that connection. In some women the urethra undergoes a few irregular contractions during orgasm. Unlike the anal spasms these contractions are asynchronous and quite feeble. The urge to urinate after orgasm has already been mentioned. In some women urination may be frequent and uncomfortable after prolonged coital activity ("honeymoon cystitis") because of the mechanical irritation of the urinary bladder.

The urinary meatus in both sexes is quite sensitive. Its stimulation is also sexually arousing for some people. Particularly in females masturbation may involve manipulation and insertion of various objects like pins into the urethra. Occasionally these slip into the urinary bladder and must be removed surgically.

Reactions in Older People

Sexuality has generally been viewed as the prerogative of those in youth and middle age; older people have been assumed to lose sexual ability and interest progressively. Although in fact they generally do, expectations have often been exaggerated to the point at which older men and women are considered asexual; when they do evince erotic interest, it is frequently regarded as unnatural and undignified at best.[24]

Aging is a mysterious process that is poorly understood and even less successfully retarded. The arrest, or at least the slowing down, of temporal decay remains one of the universal and unfulfilled dreams of mankind. Although obviously affected by complex factors, aging is

---

[24] Some men have always had fears of intercourse with older women: "As to coiton with old women, it acts like a fatal poison. . . . Do not rummage old women. . . . Beware of mounting old women [even] if they cover you with favours. . . . The coitus of old women is a venomous meal." (Vatsyayana, 1964 ed., p. 149)

specific to species and genetically determined. What concerns us here, however, is only the vicissitudes of the sex drive and the reactions of the body with age.

Aging affects the sexual functioning of men and women in various ways, some of which are common to both and some specific to each. Information on this problem is scarce and still incomplete, for obtaining it has so far proved difficult even for investigators who have otherwise been successful pioneers in sex research. Our remarks must therefore be taken as tentative clinical observations.

The impact of aging on sexual physiology seems to be fairly consistent and predictable in general terms, but these observations are not applicable to every individual. Some men and women function in old age as if they were many decades younger. What accounts for the persistence of sexual vigor in such people is not clear. In addition to many important biological and psychological factors, there seems to be some correlation with the intensity and regularity of sexual activity: Individuals who lead active sex lives in their youth and throughout adulthood appear to carry this pattern into their old age.

Changes in the sexual physiology of older people are the result partly of visible anatomical alterations involved in aging and partly of less obvious causes. In general there is slowing and attenuation of body responses in both sexes. The older person does not react in a novel or abnormal manner; some of the reactions already described continue uninterrupted, whereas others are modified and a few cease altogether. Basically the older man and woman respond as before and continue to be capable of orgasm. In considering departures from earlier functioning, this central fact must not be forgotten.

For the older male the key concern is potency: the ability to initiate and sustain penile erection, which slows with age. Instead of the several seconds required in the prime of youth, the older man needs more time to achieve erection, no matter how exciting the stimulation is.

Once erection has been achieved, however, it can be maintained longer, perhaps because of better control based on experience or because of changes in physiological functioning. Should the older person lose his erection before orgasm, he will encounter great difficulty in reviving it. The excitement phase in older people, in contrast to younger people, is not characterized by successive degrees of penile tumescence. Although erection can be maintained throughout the excitement and plateau phases, it is not sustained at its maximum, which is achieved just before orgasm only. During orgasm contractions start at the same intervals of 0.8 seconds but die out after very few throbs. Ejaculation is no longer so vigorous, and in very old age the semen simply seeps out.

The response of other male organs is similarly attenuated: Scrotal changes may not occur at all, testicular elevation is limited, and after fifty-five years of age the testicles may not increase in size during the sexual response cycle.

During the resolution phase whatever physical changes have occurred disappear with dramatic speed; in fact, some bodily responses disappear before they can be detected. Penile detumescence occurs in a matter of seconds after orgasm, rather than in a lingering two-stage process. It is as if the body, having mustered all its energies for the climax, collapses in exhaustion. Few older men seek multiple orgasms, and even fewer can achieve them, but, given a chance to recharge during a longer refractory period, some men can and do go on to have additional orgasms.

The impact of age on the female sex organs is more severe. The postmenopausal woman exhibits progressive and marked anatomical changes: Their hormonal basis is discussed in the next chapter.

The vaginal walls lose their thick, corrugated texture, their purplish complexion, and their elasticity, and appear thin and pale. The vagina continues to function but is less responsive: Lubrication takes longer (several minutes) and is less profuse; the tenting effect is limited and delayed; the orgasmic platform develops but not fully. The size of the lumen of the older woman's vagina is nevertheless comparable to that of a younger woman, for, as the introitus has become narrower, even the less developed orgasmic platform sufficiently obstructs it. This point is of some interest in view of the importance attached to the grip of the excited vagina on the penis.

In the orgasmic and resolution phases the older vagina is comparable to the older penis: Orgasmic contractions are fewer and less intense, and resolution is prompt and precipitate.

Thinner vaginal walls, delayed or inadequate lubrication, and the loss of tissue flexibility may lead to painful coitus. But these problems can often be remedied medically and by the use of lubricants.

The uterus is another organ that undergoes marked changes. Within a decade after its procreative functions have ceased, it is reduced to a misshapen mass, its body shriveled to the size of the cervix. Uterine elevation during the sexual response cycle is less marked and occurs later, and no vasocongestive enlargement can be detected in the postmenopausal uterus. Uterine contractions have not been measured during orgasm, but older women report spasms that can at times be quite painful, comparable to labor pains. Sometimes they are sufficiently distressing to prevent an older woman from seeking sexual gratification.

The responses of the labia alter considerably with advancing age. Again actual anatomical changes occur during menopause: The major lips lose their subcutaneous fatty deposits and appear thin. They show no visible response to sexual stimulation (particularly if they are nulliparous). The minor lips do produce vasocongestive response, but swelling is less, and the striking preorgasmic color change is attenuated or absent. Clitoral response seems to remain largely unchanged even in very old age; resolution is, however, unusually rapid.

Extragenital responses in both sexes decline in variable degrees. The heart and respiratory reactions persist and are more taxing. The breasts continue to respond with nipple erection, but vasocongestion in the female breast is greatly reduced. The responses of the anal sphincter and urethra are also attenuated.

Older women develop a tendency toward burning during urination following intercourse. The underlying mechanism is similar to that of "honeymoon cystitis" and results from irritation of the bladder and urethra by the penis. Whereas in newlyweds frequency or novelty of intercourse may be responsible, the cause in older women is the thinner, partly atrophied, vaginal wall, which gives inadequate protection to the bladder. Discomfort may persist for several days following coitus. It does not follow orgasm through masturbation.

In summary, we find that men and women of advanced age are handicapped to some extent by inevitable physical changes. Men are less virile and must husband their strength. Women are more sensitive to pain and discomfort. None of these obstacles is so great that it cannot be remedied, however. Insufficient lubrication can be overcome with patience or the application of an artificial lubricant. Some anatomical changes can be delayed or avoided through hormone treatment (although this approach requires caution). Physiologically the older man and woman remain sexually capable. As they adjust to other physical limitations, they can

Table 3.1. Reactions of Sex Organs During the Sexual Response Cycle

Male	Female
EXCITEMENT PHASE	
Penile erection (within 3–8 seconds)	Vaginal lubrication (within 10–30 seconds)
As phase is prolonged:	*As phase is prolonged:*
Thickening, flattening, and elevation of scrotal sac	Thickening of vaginal walls and labia
As phase is prolonged:	*As phase is prolonged:*
Partial testicular elevation and size increase	Expansion of inner $\frac{2}{3}$ of vagina and elevation of cervix and corpus
	As phase is prolonged:
	Tumescence of clitoris
PLATEAU PHASE	
Increase in penile coronal circumference and testicular tumescence (50–100% enlarged)	Orgasmic platform in outer $\frac{1}{3}$ of vagina
Full testicular elevation and rotation (orgasm inevitable)	Full expansion of $\frac{2}{3}$ of vagina, uterine and cervical elevation
Purple hue on corona of penis (inconsistent, even if orgasm is to ensue)	"Sex-skin:" discoloration of minor labia (constant, if orgasm is to ensue)
Mucoid secretion from Cowper's gland	Mucoid secretion from Bartholin's gland
	Withdrawal of clitoris
ORGASMIC PHASE	
Ejaculation	*Pelvic response (no ejaculation)*
Contractions of accessory organs of reproduction: vas deferens, seminal vesicles, ejaculatory duct, prostate	Contractions of uterus from fundus toward lower uterine segment
Relaxation of external bladder sphincter	Minimal relaxation of external cervical opening
Contractions of penile urethra at 0.8 second intervals for 3–4 contractions (slowing thereafter for 2–4 more contractions)	Contractions of orgasmic platform at 0.8 second intervals for 5–12 contractions (slowing thereafter for 3–6 more contractions)
Anal sphincter contractions (2–4 contractions at 0.8 second intervals)	External rectal sphincter contractions (2–4 contractions at 0.8 second intervals)
ORGASMIC PHASE, CONT.	
	External urethral sphincter contractions (2–3 contractions at irregular intervals, 10–15% of subjects)
RESOLUTION PHASE	
Refractory period with rapid loss of pelvic vasocongestion	Ready return to orgasm with retarded loss of pelvic vasocongestion
Loss of penile erection in primary (rapid) and secondary (slow) stages	Loss of "sex-skin" color and orgasmic platform in primary (rapid) stage
	Remainder of pelvic vasocongestion as secondary (slow) stage
	Loss of clitoral tumescence and return to position

Table 3.2. General Body Reactions During the Sexual Response Cycle

Male	Female
EXCITEMENT PHASE	
Nipple erection (30%)	Nipple erection (consistent)
	Sex-tension flush (25%)
PLATEAU PHASE	
Sex-tension flush (25%)	Sex-tension flush (75%)
Carpopedal spasm	Carpopedal spasm
Generalized skeletal muscle tension	Generalized skeletal muscle tension
Hyperventilation	Hyperventilation
Tachycardia (100–160 beats per minute)	Tachycardia (100–160 beats per minute)
ORGASMIC PHASE	
Specific skeletal muscle contractions	Specific skeletal muscle contractions
Hyperventilation	Hyperventilation
Tachycardia (100–180 beats per minute)	Tachycardia (110–180 beats per minute)
RESOLUTION PHASE	
Sweating reaction (30–40%)	Sweating reaction (30–40%)
Hyperventilation	Hyperventilation
Tachycardia (150–80 beats per minute)	Tachycardia (150–80 beats per minute)

adjust to sexual ones. Time takes its toll, but it need not quench sexual desire or cripple its fulfillment.

Summary of Physiological Responses

The multiplicity of changes involving various organs of males and females makes it difficult to maintain an overall view of the progression of events during each phase of the sexual re-

sponse cycle. Tables 3.1 and 3.2 are intended to highlight the temporal interrelations of the reactions of different body parts and should convey an impression of the orderly yet variable progression of events.[25]

---

[25] The tables are adapted from Beach, ed. (1965), pp. 517 and 522. A more detailed set of tables can be found in Masters and Johnson (1966), pp. 286–293.

Reproduction could not occur were it not for sex hormones. The development of the anatomical equipment and the physiological processes essential to reproduction are dependent upon the production of certain chemical substances (hormones) by the sex glands. In this chapter we shall describe the hormonal processes that occur during the reproductive years, the period beginning with puberty and ending in the female with menopause.

Basic Endocrinology

Some familiarity with what hormones are and how they work will facilitate the reader's understanding of such phenomena as puberty and menstruation, which we shall cover later in this chapter. *Endocrinology* is the study of the secretions of the endocrine, or *ductless*, glands. In contrast to other glands (like the salivary glands) the endocrine glands secrete their products directly into the bloodstream. These products are hormones, and they exert profound physiological effects upon specific tissues or organs, to which they travel through the bloodstream. Endocrine glands include such structures as the thyroid, parathyroid, adrenal, and pancreas glands. For our purposes, however, we shall concentrate on the sex glands (the ovaries and testes) and the *pituitary* gland, which controls the secretions of the other endocrine glands.

The pituitary gland is the most complex of all the endocrine glands. It is a pea-sized structure located at the base of the brain and connected to it by a system of microscopic blood vessels and nerve fibers. In recent years it has been demonstrated that the brain can exert a modifying influence on the activity of the pituitary gland through this connecting system, and a whole new field of study, *neuroendocrinology,* has developed. The biochemical and physiological details of this mechanism are beyond the scope of this book. Suffice it to say that previous "mysteries" about the effects of psychological states and other brain-related phenomena on hormonal activity are now being elucidated.

The pituitary gland has been called the "master gland" because it secretes hormones into the bloodstream that in turn stimulate the other endocrine glands to produce their specific hormones. The hormones of the pituitary gland are molecules called *polypeptides,* and chemically they resemble fragments of larger protein molecules.

Two pituitary hormones are of particular interest here because they stimulate the sex glands: the *follicle-stimulating* hormone (FSH) and the *luteinizing* hormone (LH). In the female

SEX HORMONES AND THE REPRODUCTIVE PERIOD

FSH and LH stimulate the ovaries to manufacture and secrete the female sex hormones, *estrogen* and *progesterone*. In the male LH is usually called *interstitial-cell-stimulating hormone* (ICSH) because it stimulates the interstitial cells of the testes to manufacture and secrete the male sex hormone, *testosterone*. All the sex hormones belong to a group of chemical substances called *steroids*. All steroids resemble in structure (but not in activity) that well-publicized chemical culprit, cholesterol. Steroid hormones are widely used compounds in medicine. Birth-control pills consist of mixtures of synthetic female sex steroids. The drug cortisone, identical to a steroid hormone manufactured by the adrenal glands, is used for treatment of a wide variety of ailments from arthritis to poison oak.

The early history of endocrinology is essentially the history of the discovery of the effects and the chemistry of steroid hormones. The classical methods of studying hormone activity involve depriving the organism of the hormone and observing the changes that occur, then administering doses of the hormone to demonstrate reversal of the effects noted during deprivation.

The effects of testosterone deprivation were first recorded among castrated males in ancient Egypt, China, and elsewhere. Aristotle noted in the fourth century B.C. the effects of castration on men and birds. Castration of a rooster prevents growth of the cock's comb, and in 1849 Berthold showed that this effect could be reversed by transplanting testes from another rooster to a castrated one. In 1889 the French physiologist Charles Brown-Sequard claimed to have experienced increased potency after treating himself with a testicular extract.[1] This and other highly publicized dramatic effects (longevity, youthful appearance, energy, and virility) attributed to extracts of the sex glands

tended to give endocrinology a somewhat disreputable flavor among the more conservative members of the medical profession.

Although we now understand many of the effects of sex hormones and that the pituitary gland "instructs" the sex glands what hormones to secrete and when, it still is not clear which brain mechanism regulates the pituitary gland. For instance, the changes in physical appearance at puberty clearly result from dramatic increases in the production of stimulating hormones by the pituitary, but what triggers the pituitary to pour out these hormones? The best answer for the moment is that some sort of "biological clock" in the brain triggers the pituitary gland at a certain stage of maturity. We shall return to this notion later in the chapter.

Sex Hormones and the Sex Drive

The conclusion that humans are endowed with a "sex drive" is not as obvious as we might think. As we shall discuss in later chapters, a certain amount of sexual activity leading to reproduction is obviously essential to the survival of the species. As man has reproduced extensively in his short tenure on this planet, we might be tempted to assume that this fact alone is sufficient evidence of the existence of an innate sex drive, or instinct, in human beings. If by "instinct" we mean an innate, unlearned pattern of sexual behavior specific to Homo sapiens, the evidence seems to be against it. The multiple forms of human sexual behavior are vastly different from the rather consistent courtship and mating behavior of birds, fish, and other lower animals. On the other hand, the notion of a sex drive as an internal state of tension influenced by various external stimuli and relieved by a particular sort of experience may have some validity in describing (but not necessarily explaining) human sexual behavior. Several drives have been attributed to human beings, and their existence is generally recognized in those instances in which physiological

---

[1] Tepperman (1962), p. 49.

correlates of drive-motivated behavior can be demonstrated. Hunger is an example: Contractions of the stomach and a fall in the blood-sugar level create an urge to eat, which is accentuated by the presence of food. The hunger drive is satisfied by the ingestion of food, and eating normally ceases until the individual once again experiences hunger. Breathing, sleeping, and various other body functions can be explained in similar fashion. But the question of whether or not there are physiological correlates of the sex drive in human beings remains unanswered. There is evidence suggesting that sex hormones do play some role in motivating the individual toward sexual activity. Other mammals show distinct decreases in sexual behavior when deprived of sex hormones by removal of the ovaries or testes. Conversely, sexual behavior can be induced by administration of sex hormones to lower animals.

Human sexual behavior, however, is so profoundly influenced by learning experiences that it is extremely difficult to sort out the effects of sex hormones on the sex drive. Some intriguing observations have been made in recent years, however, which merit further study. They can be summarized as follows: Deprivation of sex hormones through removal of the ovaries or testes has little or no effect upon the sex drive in adults. Administration of female sex hormones to males seems to diminish the sex drive in some instances; administration of male sex hormones seems to enhance the sex drive in some women.

Female Reproductive Endocrinology

Puberty

A girl's first menstrual period (menarche) occurs several years after the beginning of the physical changes that define puberty. Puberty begins somewhere between the ages of nine and twelve for most girls. Menarche usually occurs between the ages of eleven and fourteen.

External Changes. The most obvious change in the outward appearance of a girl during puberty is the development of the rounded contours that distinguish the adult female profile from that of the male. This process begins with an increase in secretion of FSH by the pituitary gland.

FSH stimulates the ovaries to produce *estrogen* (a collective noun referring to a group of chemically related female sex hormones produced by the ovaries). The estrogen, in turn, travels through the bloodstream to the breasts, where it stimulates growth of breast tissue. (This and other hormonal pathways at puberty are summarized in Figure 4.1.) The pigmented area around the nipples (the areola) becomes elevated, and the breasts begin to swell as the result of development of ducts in the nipple area and an increase in fatty tissue, connective tissue, and blood vessels. The milk-producing part of the breast (*mammary gland*) does not develop fully during puberty and indeed does not become fully mature and functional until pregnancy.

At the same time that estrogen is inducing the development of fatty and supporting tissue in the breasts of the young girl, a similar process is occurring in the hips and buttocks. These changes may be more pronounced in one region than in another in a particular woman. In some cultures the size and shape of the buttocks are important indices of femininity. In others greater emphasis is placed upon the breasts.

Another visible change at puberty is the appearance of *pubic* and *axillary* (underarm) *hair*. This hair is coarser and has more pigment than does that of the scalp, and its growth is stimulated partly by estrogen and partly by hormones secreted by the adrenal glands, also in response to a stimulating hormone (adrenocorticotrophic hormone, or ACTH) from the pituitary gland.

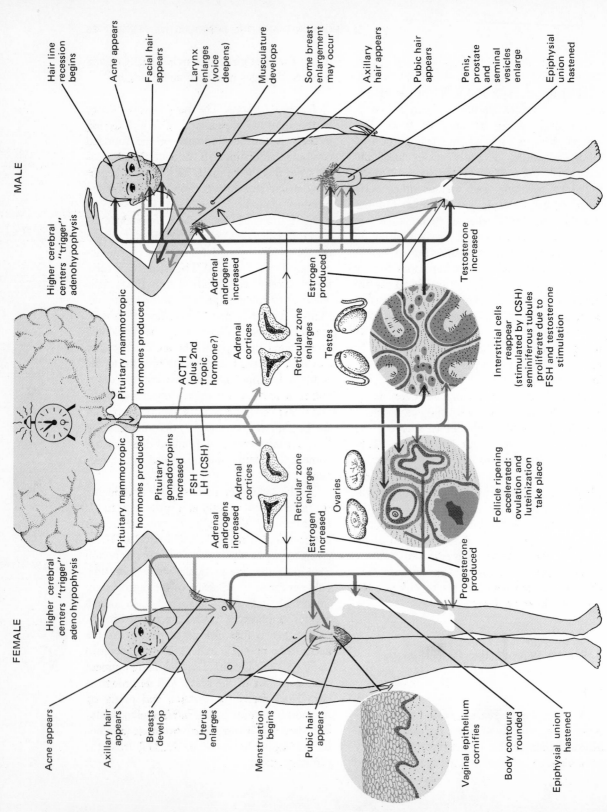

MALE

Hair line recession begins
Acne appears
Facial hair appears
Larynx enlarges (voice deepens)
Musculature develops
Some breast enlargement may occur
Axillary hair appears
Pubic hair appears
Penis, prostate and seminal vesicles enlarge
Epiphysial union hastened

Higher cerebral centers "trigger" adenohypophysis

Pituitary mammotropic hormones produced

ACTH (plus 2nd tropic hormone?)

Adrenal cortices
Reticular zone enlarges
Testes

Adrenal androgens increased
Estrogen produced
Testosterone increased

Interstitial cells reappear (stimulated by ICSH) seminiferous tubules proliferate due to FSH and testosterone stimulation

Higher cerebral centers "trigger" adeno hypophysis

Pituitary mammotropic hormones produced

Pituitary gonadotropins increased
FSH
LH (ICSH)

Adrenal cortices

Adrenal androgens increased
Reticular zone enlarges
Estrogen increased
Ovaries

Follicle ripening accelerated: ovulation and luteinization take place
Progesterone produced

FEMALE

Acne appears
Axillary hair appears
Breasts develop
Uterus enlarges
Menstruation begins
Pubic hair appears
Vaginal epithelium cornifies
Body contours rounded
Epiphysial union hastened

Figure 4.1. Effects of sex hormones on development at puberty. © Copyright 1965 by CIBA Pharmaceutical Company, Division of CIBA-GEIGY Corporation. Reproduced, with permission, from The Ciba Collection of Medical Illustrations, by Frank H. Netter, M. D. All rights reserved.

The adrenal glands are paired glands situated just above each kidney. In the female they produce small amounts of androgens (a group of related compounds produced in much larger amounts in the male), which stimulate growth of pubic and axillary hair and are perhaps related to the female sex drive. In addition, the adrenal glands produce cortisone, adrenalin, and other substances. Excessive secretion by the adrenal glands, a pathological condition known as "Cushing's disease," may result in excessive growth of facial hair.[2]

A frequent source of embarrassment at puberty is the appearance of facial *acne,* a condition that is generally transient and seems to be related to the changes in hormones occurring at this time in life. Although it generally presents no more than a cosmetic problem, acne may sometimes be severe and require medical treatment. It tends to be more severe in girls whose menstrual cycles are grossly irregular.[3]

Estrogen also causes accelerated growth of the external genitals at puberty, including enlargement of the labia and associated structures. The clitoris enlarges under the stimulation of androgens from the adrenal glands. At the same time, there is a noticeable increase in skeletal size, which is related to increased secretion of the growth hormone by the pituitary gland.

Internal Changes. Estrogen specifically stimulates growth of the uterus and vagina during puberty. The muscular wall of the uterus enlarges, and its glandular lining also develops. The lining of the vagina is extremely sensitive to estrogen, and its thickness is proportional to the amount of this hormone present at any given time. Examination of a mucus smear containing cells from the vaginal walls is a simple and clinically useful test for determining how much estrogen is present. As the vaginal wall matures, the pH of the secretions that moisten its surface changes from alkaline to acid.[4]

Under the influence of estrogen the female pelvis enlarges during puberty and assumes different contours from those of the male pelvis. Ultimately estrogens also prevent further growth of the long bones of the skeleton (counteracting the effects of the growth hormone), and usually no further increase in height occurs after about age seventeen in girls. An estrogen deficiency in late puberty may cause great height in a girl, for estrogen normally applies brakes to skeletal growth. Many other factors are, of course, involved in determining the height of a given individual.

Estrogen secretion not only increases in quantity during puberty, mediating the various external and internal physical changes that we have just described; it also takes on a cyclical pattern of secretion, which results in certain cyclical phenomena in the female, the most obvious of which is the menstrual cycle. The first menstruation occurs usually between the ages of eleven and fourteen years and may come as a shock to the girl who has not been prepared for it. For the first few years after the menarche the girl's menstrual periods tend to be irregular, and ovulation does not occur in each cycle. For some time after her first period, then, the girl is relatively infertile, but she can nevertheless become pregnant.

Related Considerations. In many societies menarche has been regarded as the time when a girl becomes a woman, and girls often marry shortly after the first menstruation. Puberty

---

[2]Lloyd (1964), p. 333.

[3]Lloyd (1964), p. 184.

[4]The pH scale is a commonly used index of acidity and alkalinity, based on hydrogen ion concentration. The scale runs from 0 to 14; the neutral point is 7. Values from 7 to 14 indicate an alkaline state, from 7 to 0 an acid state.

rites often occur at the time of the first menstruation. These rites are sometimes only family affairs, but in other societies the ritual is quite elaborate. Among some California Indian tribes, for instance, a girl was segregated from the rest of the tribe during her first menstrual period. She lived in a special hut built for this purpose and had to eat and bathe in a prescribed manner, using special implements. The Chiricahua Apaches also had elaborate ceremonies at menarche and believed that at this time girls possessed certain supernatural powers, including the powers to heal and to bring prosperity.

In our culture puberty does not mark the entrance into adulthood. Nevertheless girls are quite sensitive in responding to the physical maturity of others in the peer group. Studies have shown, unexpectedly, that girls who mature late score highest on peer-group ratings of popularity and prestige.[5]

An interesting but unexplained observation is that the average age of menarche in Western countries has been gradually declining. In 1860, for example, a girl usually had her first period between sixteen and seventeen years of age, whereas in 1960 it usually occurred between twelve and thirteen. This phenomenon is usually attributed to better nutrition, but other factors may also be involved. Animal studies do not entirely support the notion that better nutrition alone hastens the beginning of puberty.

A number of rare diseases can result in precocious sexual development. They include tumors of the hypothalamic region of the brain (causing the pituitary gland to stimulate the ovaries prematurely) and tumors of the ovaries (resulting in premature outpouring of estrogen). Girls with such disorders are often capable of becoming pregnant, and pregnancies in girls as

young as five and six years have been known to occur.[6] In addition to generalized sexual precocity (in which all of the changes of puberty occur several years earlier than usual), isolated aspects of puberty may occur unexpectedly. In premature *thelarche* the breasts mature in childhood. In premature *pubarche* pubic hair grows in childhood. These conditions are usually benign in origin.

Synthetic estrogens are readily available nowadays, particularly in the form of contraceptive pills and, if taken by children, will produce premature development of feminine characteristics.

The Menstrual Cycle

Menstruation, periodic uterine bleeding, is a phenomenon that occurs only in female humans, apes, and some monkeys. An ovarian, or estrus, cycle occurs in other mammals but is not accompanied by bleeding. The length of the ovarian cycle is specific for each species: In the human, it is approximately twenty-eight days, in the chimpanzee thirty-six days, in the cow twenty days, in the sheep sixteen days, and in the mouse five days. Cats and dogs usually ovulate only twice a year.

For the first few years after menarche a young woman's menstrual cycles may be very irregular in length, but by age eighteen or twenty her periods usually assume a certain rhythm. Although there is considerable variation among mature women in the frequency of menstrual periods, most cycles fall into the range of twenty-six to thirty-four days, with a mean of about twenty-eight days. The dura-

---

[5] Hamburg and Lunde (1966), p. 3.

[6] The youngest documented pregnancy occurred in Peru in the widely publicized case of Lina Medina. This little girl became pregnant and was delivered by cesarean section of a six-and-one-half-pound male infant at the age of five years and seven months. The birth occurred on May 15, 1939, and was attended by several American physicians. The girl had menstruated regularly since the age of three and had become pregnant at four years and ten months.

tion of menstrual bleeding varies between three and seven days in most women.

The occurrence of irregular menstrual cycles in women after the age of twenty may be related to various factors, some of which are not well understood. Certainly psychological states are important, particularly prolonged or severe emotional stress. It was not uncommon for women to cease menstruating while imprisoned in concentration camps during World War II (often before malnutrition or physical illness had developed). Gynecologists also report that some girls cease menstruating or menstruate irregularly while at college but have regular cycles when they are home for the summer.

Sometimes an unmarried girl who has intercourse and fears pregnancy will have a "late" menstrual period. This delay seems related to her emotional state, but we cannot usually rule out the possibility that she has indeed conceived but spontaneously aborted very early.

The phases of the menstrual cycle, like the events of puberty, are essentially under the control of hormones. The first phase is called the *proliferative* (in which the lining of the uterus—the *endometrium*—shed during the preceding menstruation, is reconstructed) or *preovulatory* (before the release of a mature egg from the ovary) phase. This phase lasts about fourteen days in a twenty-eight-day cycle (see Figure 4.2). During this time the pituitary gland secretes FSH, which increases ovarian estrogen production. The estrogen, in turn, is responsible for the regrowth of the endometrium and also stimulates one of the ovarian follicles to mature (see Figure 4.3). This follicle will ultimately rupture during ovulation.

Estrogen stimulates the growth of the glandular surface of the endometrium, and a thickness of about 3.5 millimeters is attained during this phase. In addition, estrogen stimulates the size and productivity of the mucous glands of the cervix. Cervical mucus produced under estrogen stimulation is plentiful, thin, and highly viscous; it has an alkaline pH and contains nutrients that can be used by the sperm.[7] As mentioned previously, rising estrogen levels also stimulate growth of the vaginal lining so that maximum thickness is achieved at ovulation.

---

[7] One of the effects of birth-control pills is to alter the constituents of the cervical mucus, creating a more hostile environment for the sperm.

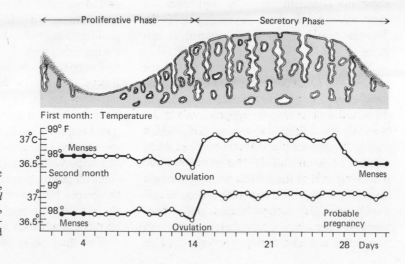

Figure 4.2. The phases of the menstrual cycle. From Benson, *Handbook of Obstetrics and Gynecology,* 3rd ed. (Los Altos, Calif.: Lange Medical Publications, 1968), p. 26. Reprinted by permission.

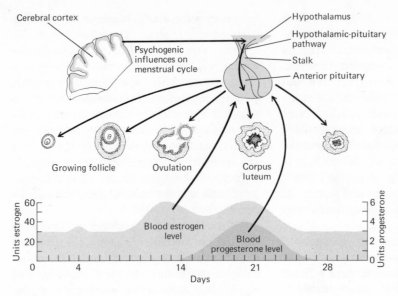

Figure 4.3. Ovulation during the menstrual cycle. From Benson, *Handbook of Obstetrics and Gynecology,* 3rd ed. (Los Altos, Calif.: Lange Medical Publications, 1968), p. 26. Reprinted by permission.

The amount of fluid within the maturing follicle increases steadily during the proliferative phase, and at a critical point the follicle ruptures, and the mature egg (ovum) is released into the fallopian tube. This process is *ovulation,* which occurs about fourteen days before menstruation. In a twenty-eight-day cycle, ovulation thus occurs on about the fourteenth day, but in a thirty-four-day cycle, it occurs on about the twentieth day. The significance of these schedules to those depending upon the "rhythm method" for birth control is obvious.

The period after ovulation is called the *secretory,* or *postovulatory,* phase of the menstrual cycle. The pituitary gland, responding to the stimulus of increased estrogen levels in the bloodstream, begins to secrete LH, which travels through the bloodstream to the recently ruptured ovarian follicle and stimulates the remaining cells of the follicle to develop into a microscopic glandular structure called the *corpus luteum.* The corpus luteum, under continued LH stimulation, produces two female sex hormones, estrogen and progesterone. (This

new source of estrogen accounts for the second peak in the estrogen level seen in Figure 4.3.) Under the combined influence of estrogen and progesterone, the glands of the endometrium that have developed during the proliferative phase become functional and produce nutrient fluid by the eighteenth day of a twenty-eight-day cycle, corresponding to the time when the ovum is free within the uterine cavity and dependent upon uterine secretions for nourishment. In addition, there is increased proliferation of blood vessels within the uterus during this phase.

Progesterone inhibits the flow of cervical mucus that occurs during ovulation and diminishes the thickness of the vaginal lining.

If fertilization does not occur, the pituitary gland responds to the increased blood levels of estrogen and progesterone much as a thermostat responds to an increase in temperature and shuts off production of FSH and LH, depriving the corpus luteum of the chemical stimulation to produce estrogen or progesterone. The corpus luteum then withers away.

The final phase of the menstrual cycle is

actual menstruation, the shedding of the endometrium through the cervix and vagina. The trigger for menstruation appears to be the fall in the estrogen level at the end of the cycle. (The change in progesterone level that occurs simultaneously is not necessary for menstruation.)

The menstrual discharge consists primarily of blood, mucus, and fragments of endometrial tissue. About sixty milliliters (two ounces) of blood are lost in an average menstrual period.[8] For a woman on an adequate diet, such blood loss can be easily tolerated. Heavy menstrual bleeding in a woman on a deficient diet can, however, lead to anemia. The duration of menstrual bleeding is usually from three to seven days, and periods longer than one week usually indicate some abnormal condition.

As the estrogen level continues to fall, the pituitary gland again responds as would a thermostat and turns on its secretion of FSH, thus initiating the proliferative phase of the next menstrual cycle.

Symptoms and Syndromes. Painful menstruation (*dysmenorrhea*) is the most common symptom related to the menstrual cycle. Almost every woman at some time experiences pelvic discomfort during a menstrual period, but its frequency and severity vary considerably. Some women occasionally have painful periods but are able to continue their activities with the aid of mild analgesics like aspirin. Others are disabled to the point of being bedridden for a day or two during each menstrual period. The primary complaint of women with this condition is cramps in the pelvic region, but there may also

be headaches, backaches, nausea, and general discomfort.

The cause of menstrual pain is unknown, but seems to be related in part to uterine spasms ("cramps"). In women for whom it is a monthly problem it generally begins at an early age. In fact, for a woman to have her first painful menstrual period after the age of twenty is relatively uncommon. Women who suffer from menstrual cramps usually notice a dramatic improvement after childbirth. The mechanism by which childbirth "cures" menstrual pains is not known.

In addition to pelvic pains, a few women experience so-called "menstrual migraines" with their periods. These headaches are essentially the same as are other migraine headaches, except that they occur particularly during menstration or just before the beginning of menstrual flow.

During the four to seven days preceding menstruation, most women experience symptoms that make them aware of the imminence of their periods. When these symptoms are severe they constitute a syndrome known as *premenstrual tension.* They include fatigue, irritability, headache, pain in the lower back, and sensations of heaviness in the pelvic region. There may be actual weight gain of several pounds because of retention of fluids. Women with premenstrual tension are often emotionally labile and more easily upset at this time of the month. Psychic distress, particularly depression, is most apt to occur during the premenstrual period. In addition, school and work performance tends to decline during this time. A few women undergo rather dramatic personality changes before menstruation. Women who commit violent crimes usually do so in the week just before their periods. Indeed, in France a woman who commits a crime during her premenstrual period may use this fact in her defense, claiming "temporary impairment of sanity." The symptoms of premenstrual

---

[8] Traditionally, women have used externally worn sanitary napkins to absorb the menstrual discharge. The trend now is toward tampons worn internally. Tampons are cylinders of absorbent cotton inserted into the vagina and removed by an attached string. They can be used whether or not a woman has had coitus, since most hymens will easily permit their passage.

tension are probably related to the shift in hormone levels occurring at this time, but other factors are also involved.

A separate condition also related to cyclical changes in hormones and retention of fluid is premenstrual pain and swelling of the breasts, known as *mastalgia*. This condition is less common than, but may occur in conjunction with, premenstrual tension.

An unexplained phenomenon is *Mittelschmerz*, pain occurring in midcycle during ovulation. This symptom is most common in young women. It consists of intermittent cramping pains on one or both sides of the lower abdomen lasting for about a day. Occasionally the symptoms of ovulation have been mistaken for appendicitis, much to the embarrassment of the surgeon who decides to operate and finds a healthy appendix.

Related Considerations. There is no medical reason why a woman should refrain from intercourse while she is menstruating. Nevertheless, many societies strictly prohibit this practice and consider women "unclean" during menstruation. The Old Testament, the Koran, and Hindu law books all specifically prohibit such intercourse, on the grounds that women are polluted and dangerous at this time and will defile anyone who has contact with the menstrual discharge. In addition, certain societies impose additional restrictions on women during their periods. They may have to follow diets and may be forbidden to participate in certain activities. There may be special rules about bathing at this time, as in orthodox Judaism.

Several South American and African tribes believed that a man would become physically ill if he had sexual relations with a menstruating partner. Some nomads of northeast Asia believed that a woman would become sick and eventually sterile if she copulated while bleeding. Other tribes believed that a menstruating woman who had any physical contact with a man could cause him to lose his virility and his hunting ability. In such societies women were physically isolated from their communities during menstruation.

Lower Animals. In monkeys and apes, copulation during the menstrual period is relatively rare. The degree to which sexual behavior in these species is under hormonal control is not entirely clear, but the relation of sexual behavior to sex hormones in lower mammals is well known. Females come into "heat," that is, become receptive to the sexual advances of males, at specific points in their estrus cycles, which coincide with ovulation and maximum levels of female sex hormones. Mating at this time obviously enhances the probability of reproduction, and there is essentially no sexual activity in lower mammals except when the females are fertile and likely to conceive. Removal of the ovaries of a guinea pig or hamster has been shown to eliminate sexual activity, but the female can be made sexually receptive again with injections of estrogen and progesterone.

The human female is unique in that she is always or never "in heat," depending upon how we look at it. In any event, human sexual activity is not linked to specific periods of the estrus cycle, as it is in most other mammals. Studies have shown, however, that there are predictable variations in the frequency of intercourse during the menstrual cycle in large groups of women, with peaks occurring at midcycle and just before menstruation.[9] Which sex hormone these variations are related to, if any, is not clear. Some studies show that the period of maximum progesterone secretion is usually one of least sexual activity. On the other hand, there is some evidence that the androgens secreted by the adrenal glands play a role in the sex drives of women, and surgical removal of the adrenal glands has a more predictable

---

[9]Udry and Morris (1968).

effect on libido than does removal of the ovaries. Women who receive androgenic hormones for medical reasons sometimes also report dramatic increases in sexual desire while under treatment.

Menopause

The term *menopause* refers to the permanent cessation of menstruation due to the physiological changes associated with aging. A broader term, encompassing the various changes that occur in connection with the altered functioning of the ovaries is *climacteric* ("critical period"). The latter generally includes the years from age forty-five to sixty—the years of the "change of life."

Menstruation most commonly ceases between the ages of forty-six and fifty. There is no correlation between age of menarche and age of menopause. Menstrual periods usually become very irregular several years before menopause, and this interval is one of relative infertility, as is that just after menarche. Pregnancy beyond age forty-seven is rare. Pregnancy has been medically documented as late as sixty-one, however.

The mechanism of menopause, unlike that of puberty, is not related to the pituitary gland. The latter continues to pour out FSH, but for some reason the ovaries gradually fail to respond, and very little estrogen is produced.

The symptoms of the climacteric are rather well known and affect almost all women to some degree, but only about 10 percent of them are obviously inconvenienced by these problems. The best known of the symptoms is the *hot flash,* or *flush,* the experience of waves of heat spreading over the face and the upper half of the body. It may be followed by perspiration or chills and may last for a few seconds or much longer. Other physical symptoms include headaches, dizziness, heart palpitations, and pains in the joints. These symptoms are sometimes relieved by treatment with estrogens.

Severe depression (*involutional melancholia*) may occur at this time in women with no previous history of mental illness. The cause is unknown. Less severe depression during menopause may be partly related to the hormonal imbalance of this period but is probably also related to the woman's realization that she is losing her reproductive capacity, combined with the fact that her children are often leaving home at about this time and other psychological factors.

Certain changes in the genitals occur during the years after menopause, including a gradual shrinking and atrophy of the uterus and shrinking of the vaginal lining. Some women experience a new awakening of sexual desire after menopause, perhaps because they no longer need worry about pregnancy.

Male Reproductive Endocrinology

Puberty

Puberty begins somewhat later and lasts longer in boys than it does in girls. It is initiated at age ten or eleven in boys by the same pituitary hormones that mediate it in girls, FSH and LH. But in males, as noted earlier, LH is called "interstitial-cell-stimulating hormone" (ICSH) because of the difference in the site of its action.

ICSH reaches the interstitial cells of the testes through the bloodstream and stimulates them, initiating the process of puberty. Little is seen in the way of striking external changes, but the interstitial cells begin producing the primary androgen (male sex hormone), a compound known as *testosterone.* This one substance is essentially responsible for the development of all the physical changes (including development of *secondary sex characteristics*) that occur during puberty (see Figure 4.1).

External Changes. The first noticeable changes resulting from testosterone stimulation include enlargement of the testes and penis and the appearance of fine straight hair at the base of the penis. At first the penis increases in circumference more than in length. By age twelve it is still, on the average, about 1.5 inches long in the relaxed state and less than three inches long in erection.

As the testes enlarge, however, their capacity to produce testosterone increases, and at age thirteen or fourteen rapid growth of the penis, testes, and pubic hair begins. By this age most girls will have had their first menstrual period, although they will not necessarily be ovulating yet.

Axillary hair does not appear until about age fifteen in most boys, and at the same time some fuzz appears on their upper lips. Adult beards do not appear for two or three more years, however, and indeed by age seventeen 50 percent of boys in the U.S. have not yet shaved, and many others shave only infrequently. Continued development of facial and chest hair, under androgen stimulation, continues beyond age twenty in many young men, along with recession of the hairline (see Figure 4.4).

A very noticeable change that occurs during puberty, though strictly speaking an internal change, is the deepening of the voice, related to growth of the *larynx* ("voice box") in response to hormonal stimulation. The deepening of the voice may be gradual or fairly abrupt, but on the average it occurs by age fourteen or fifteen.[10]

Acne becomes a source of embarrassment to many boys at age fifteen or sixteen, as does another transient phenomenon, enlargement of the breasts, or *gynecomastia*. The latter occurs in about 80 percent of pubertal boys and is

---

[10]Castration before puberty, of course, eliminates the source of testosterone that causes the voice to change. The famed *castrati* of Italy were men whose testes had been removed before puberty and who consequently kept their high-pitched voices all their lives. The voice of the castrated male and of the prepubertal boy has always had its admirers, presumably because of a purer tonal quality.

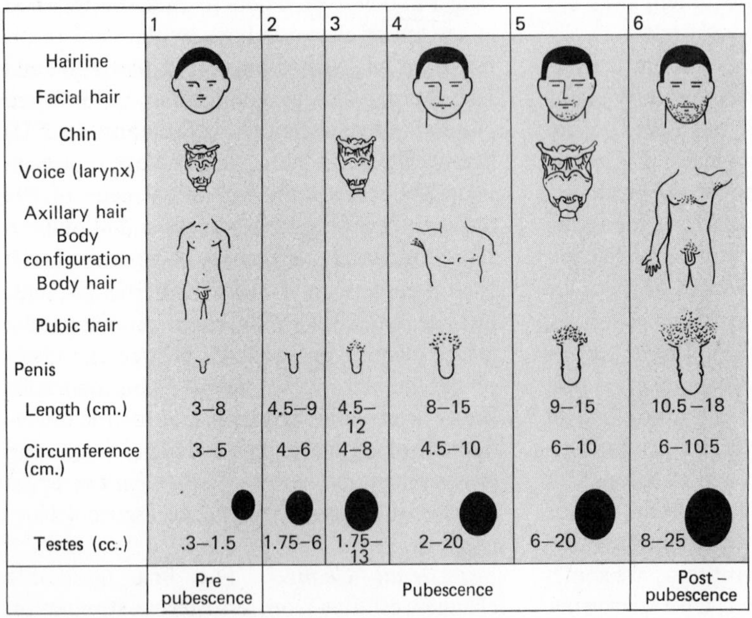

	1	2	3	4	5	6
Hairline / Facial hair / Chin						
Voice (larynx)						
Axillary hair / Body configuration / Body hair						
Pubic hair						
Penis						
Length (cm.)	3–8	4.5–9	4.5–12	8–15	9–15	10.5–18
Circumference (cm.)	3–5	4–6	4–8	4.5–10	6–10	6–10.5
Testes (cc.)	.3–1.5	1.75–6	1.75–13	2–20	6–20	8–25
	Pre-pubescence	Pubescence				Post-pubescence

Figure 4.4. Development of some secondary sex characteristics in men. From Wilkins, L., Blizzard, R., and Migeon, C., *The Diagnosis and Treatment of Endocrine Disorders in Childhood and Adolescence,* 3rd ed. (Springfield, Ill.: Charles C Thomas, 1965), p. 200. Reprinted by permission.

probably related to small amounts of female sex hormones produced by the testes.

Overall growth in both height and weight occurs during puberty. But, whereas the girl develops fat deposits in breasts and hips at this time, the boy's new weight is in the form of increased muscle mass, and he consequently develops a quite different physique. And, whereas the female pelvis undergoes enlargement at puberty, more striking expansion occurs in the boy's shoulders and rib cage at this time. Of course, there is also a definite spurt in the linear growth rates of boys at puberty, and this process continues until age twenty or twenty-one, when the male hormones finally put the brakes on growth of the long bones of the skeleton. As previously noted, female sex hormones induce this "braking" process more rapidly, which accounts for the generally smaller height of women.[11]

Internal Changes. Whereas the changes in external appearance just described give the appearance of biological maturity to the growing boy, significant internal changes must also occur before the capacity for reproductive activity is actually achieved.

The pituitary hormone FSH, which stimulates maturation of the ovum in the female, is also essential in the production of mature sperm in the male. With the increase in FSH secretion during puberty, germ cells in the lining of the seminiferous tubules of the testes (see Chapter 2) begin to divide and differentiate into mature sperm. Mature sperm are first present in the ejaculatory fluid at age fifteen, on the average, but, as with the other changes at puberty, there is wide variation among individuals, encompassing the range from ages eleven to seventeen.

FSH is a necessary but not sufficient stimulus for the production of mature sperm. Other hormones, particularly thyroid hormone, must also be present in sufficient concentrations. In addition, a temperature lower than normal body temperature is essential to mature sperm production. In undescended testicles, which are still in the abdominal cavity, mature sperm cannot be produced.

The organs that supply the fluids for the semen enlarge significantly during puberty. The prostate gland is particularly sensitive to the stimulation of testosterone. By age thirteen or fourteen the prostate gland is producing fluid that can be ejaculated during orgasm, but this fluid will probably not contain mature sperm. Just as the menarche does not necessarily indicate that a girl has ovulated, so the ability to ejaculate does not indicate that a boy is already fertile.

At about this same age a boy begins to have "wet dreams," or *nocturnal emissions* of seminal fluid (see Chapter 9). In a few societies the occurrence of the first "wet dream" is considered a sign that the boy has reached adulthood.

Related Considerations. Many societies have specific puberty rites for boys, generally to signify that they have reached adulthood. As there is no event for boys comparable to menarche, an arbitrary age like thirteen may be taken as the time for initiation. In some societies, however, particular manifestations like the appearance of facial hair or the first "wet dream" are required. Women are often excluded from such male puberty rites, and sexual information is often transmitted to boys during these ceremonies. In addition, circumcision may be performed at this time (see Chapter 2). Many tribal peoples require the performance of certain acts of physical strength, skill, and endurance, and, in addition, a boy may be required to participate in certain sexual activities.

With the exception of the bar mitzvah

---

[11] This statement does not imply that a tall girl has a deficiency of female sex hormones or that a tall boy has a deficiency of male hormones. Other factors, including heredity, influence stature.

among Jews, our society does not have formal puberty rites for boys. Nevertheless, like girls, boys are very sensitive to the physical transformations that occur in their peers during puberty and respond accordingly. Early-maturing boys have thus been found to have greater peer-group prestige and are most often ranked as "leaders" among boys of pubertal age. It should be noted, however, that in adulthood the late maturers are often found to be more adventurous, flexible, and assertive than are early maturers.[12]

Premature puberty (*sexual precocity*) may occur in boys and may be related to disorders similar to those that cause it in girls. In about 50 percent of the examples of precocious sexual maturity in boys, there is no apparent cause. Enlargement of the breasts before puberty is not a symptom of sexual precocity in boys and almost always results from exposure to estrogen in some form. Estrogen may be present in certain cosmetic creams and absorbed through the skin, or it may be ingested accidentally in pill form.

Hormones and Fertility in the Male

There is no fertility cycle in men as there is in women. Sperm are normally produced throughout the reproductive years, and the healthy man is consistently fertile at all times of the month and year. This phenomenon corresponds to the fairly consistent secretion of testosterone by the testes, in contrast to the cyclical secretion of sex hormones in the female.

Lower Animals. In the animal world there are some exceptions to this continuous male fertility. Some species, like deer and sheep, have specific "rutting seasons" during which the males are fertile and sexually active. During the rest of the year these animals are infertile and generally uninterested in

sexual activity. In certain wild rodents, the testes are actually drawn into the body cavity except during the mating season, when they descend into the scrotum. During the period that the testes are inside the abdominal cavity they produce neither sperm nor male sex hormones.

Although testosterone secretion and spermatogenesis are generally constant in man, variations may occur in certain situations. Severe emotional shock has been known to cause temporary cessation of sperm production in some men. Studies of soldiers in combat show that testosterone levels rise and fall in response to the degrees of stress to which the men are exposed.[13] These findings should not seem surprising in light of the interrelations of sex hormones, pituitary hormones, and the brain, to which we alluded earlier in this chapter.

Other factors may also affect fertility in men either temporarily or permanently. Certain drugs, including some used in the treatment of cancer and at least one antibiotic (*Furadantin*), may cause temporary sterility. A prolonged exposure to high temperature, as in an illness involving a high fever or in frequent and prolonged hot baths, may inhibit sperm production. Mumps may cause permanent sterility in men through the mechanism described in Chapter 2. Severe or prolonged radiation can cause sterility or the production of abnormal sperm. In the days when fluoroscopes were commonly used in fitting shoes some shoe salesmen were rendered sterile by prolonged exposure to radiation.

Eunuchism

Castration, the removal of the male sex glands, was practiced in many cultures until recently. It was most common in the Near East and probably first performed in ancient Egypt, where hundreds of young boys would be cas-

[12]Hamburg and Lunde (1966), p. 4.

[13]Rose (1969), p. 136.

trated in a single religious ceremony and their genitals offered as sacrifices to the gods. A eunuch (from Greek *eunoukhos,* "guardian of the bed") is a castrated male, and eunuchs have perhaps been most famous as harem guards. Although most eunuchs were slaves to Muslim rulers, they occasionally worked themselves into positions of great influence and power. The sex drive varied greatly among eunuchs, but some were apparently very active sexually. If the operation had been performed after puberty, the penis was of adult size and capable of erection. Although deprived of androgen from the testes, the castrated male still produced some androgen in his adrenal glands.

The psychological implications of the fear of castration have been given great importance by Freud, and his theory is discussed in Chapter 8.

Although castration is generally regarded as an ancient practice only, it should be noted that in special instances it is legally performed in state and prison hospitals today—on mentally retarded patients and on certain sex offenders (see Chapter 16).

Aging in the Male

There is no male equivalent of the menopause in the female. Whereas the ovaries essentially cease to function at a fairly specific time in a woman's life, the testes continue to function in men indefinitely, though there may be gradual declines in the rates of testosterone secretion and sperm production. There are well-documented reports of men of ninety years of age having fathered children, and viable sperm have been found in the ejaculations of men even older.

There are certain syndromes that occur in men in their forties, fifties, and later that are believed to be related to changes in hormone levels. The most common problem is enlargement of the prostate gland, which occurs in 10 percent of men by age forty and in 50 percent of men who reach age eighty. The reader will recall that the prostate gland is a chestnut-shaped structure encircling the urethra. Consequently, when it becomes enlarged it interferes with the flow of urine and causes difficulty in voluntarily initiating urination, as well as frequent nocturnal urination. Enlargement of the prostate is not related to masturbation, excessive sexual activity, or venereal disease, common myths to the contrary.

The symptoms of "prostate trouble" can usually be readily remedied by surgical removal of the part of the gland that is impinging upon the urethra. Nonsurgical treatment is not effective. For reasons that are not understood, administration of female sex hormones causes shrinkage of prostatic cancer but does not affect benign enlargement of the prostate.

Depression, irritability, and other symptoms similar to those of the menopause may occur with increasing frequency in aging men, but they are not particularly correlated with any known hormone changes. It should be noted again that in both men and women there is no reason related to hormones why advancing age need cause cessation of sexual activity, and indeed for many older people it does not (see Chapter 3).

Genetic Defects and Sex Hormones

Individuals who exhibit external genital characteristics of both sexes have traditionally been called *hermaphrodites.* Ancient Greek and Roman art and literature are replete with images and reference to the deity Hermaphroditus (see Figure 4.5). Herodotus and Plato both referred to an ancient tribe living north of the Black Sea and said to be ambisexual. Plato theorized that such people represented a third sex, which had died out over time. To other writers, however, hermaphrodites seemed to have supernatural qualities. From the time of Theophrastus (382–287 B.C.) through the

Figure 4.5. The Palermo Hemaphroditus found in Centuripe. From Jones and Scott, *Hermaphroditism, Genital Anomalies and Related Endocrine Disorders* (Baltimore: Williams & Wilkins, 1958), p. 7. © 1958 by The Williams & Wilkins Co., and reprinted by permission.

Roman Empire, Hermaphroditus was considered a god, the offspring of Hermes (god of occult science) and Aphrodite (goddess of love).

In medical terminology, a true hermaphrodite (*hermaphroditus verus*) is an individual who has both ovarian and testicular tissue. The condition is extremely rare—only sixty cases have been reported in the entire world medical literature of the twentieth century. Such an individual may have one ovary and one testicle or sex glands that contain mixtures of ovarian and testicular tissues. A hermaphrodite usually has masculine genitals but feminine breasts. There often is some sort of vaginal opening beneath the penis, and many hermaphrodites menstruate. Development of the uterus is often

incomplete, with only one fallopian tube present, for instance.

The development of both male and female sex organs is caused by the simultaneous presence, in significant amounts, of both male and female sex hormones during embryological development (see Chapter 2) and at puberty. As male sex hormones can also be produced by the adrenal glands, a female may present a virile appearance because of a genetic defect in the adrenal glands that results in pouring forth of large amounts of androgens. Such individuals are called *pseudohermaphrodites,* and the disorder associated with this condition is *congenital adrenal hyperplasia.* Although such a woman may have normal internal female genitalia, including ovaries, her clitoris is often enlarged and resembles a penis (see Figure 4.6). In addition, the folds of the labia may be fused in such a manner as to resemble a scrotum, with the result that such a female may be reared as a male. When reared as girls, pseudohermaphrodites do not usually have homosexual or bisexual orientations. The sexual activity of both true and pseudohermaphrodites usually reflects their assigned gender roles—those raised as boys usually choose female sexual partners and vice versa. (There is one unusual case on record, however, of a hermaphrodite who had intercourse alternately with men and women, using the vaginal opening or the enlarged clitoris to suit the occasion.)

Pseudohermaphroditism can be corrected by a combination of medical (hormone) and surgical treatment (see Figure 4.7), but it is important that the proper diagnosis be made early. Psychological difficulties are quite common in individuals who have lived for several years or more with mistaken or ambiguous sexual identities, as might be expected.

In recent years a series of disorders associated with abnormal sex-chromosome patterns has been identified. A normal female has two X chromosomes (one from the mother and one from the father), and a normal male has one X chromosome (from the mother) and one Y chromosome (from the father) (see Chapter 5). But occasionally an individual ends up with an unusual combination of sex chromosomes, with or without associated physical or mental defects. The most common such anomalies are the XXX (*triple-X syndrome*), XXY (*Klinefelter's syndrome*), XO (*Turner's syndrome*), and XYY (newly discovered and not yet completely described) patterns.

Triple-X females have been called "superfemales" but are not unusually feminine (or masculine) and may be mentally retarded.

Klinefelter's syndrome (XXY) is characterized by a particular physical appearance. A man who has it is usually tall and thin, has a small penis and small testes, and may develop breasts at puberty. He is sterile and may have some mental impairment. He is usually relatively inactive sexually.

A patient with Turner's syndrome has only one sex chromosome (X). She appears to be a physically immature (prepubertal) female. Ovaries are absent or present only in rudimentary form. Various other physical defects may be associated with this disorder, the most consistent one being short stature. Intelligence may be, but is not necessarily, impaired.

The XYY syndrome has received a great deal of publicity because a high percentage of these men have been found among men imprisoned for crimes involving violence or sex. XYY individuals are thoroughly masculine in appearance, tend to be more than six feet tall, and show a normal range of intelligence. Any causal connection between their abnormal sex-chromosome pattern and their behavior patterns remains to be established, however. Courts in France and Australia have accepted the presence of the XYY syndrome as grounds for acquittal or mitigation of punishment in criminal cases, but existing evidence does not validate the implied connections.

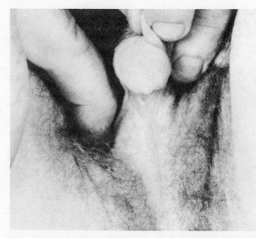

Figure 4.6. Characteristic external genitalia of a female hermaphrodite. From Jones and Scott, *Hermaphroditism, Genital Anomalies and Related Endocrine Disorders* (Baltimore: Williams & Wilkins, 1958), p. 212. © 1958 by The Williams & Wilkins Co., and reprinted by permission.

Aphrodisiacs

The search for substances that may increase sexual drive or potency is as old and, so far, as unsuccessful as is man's search for the fountain of youth. "Erotic potions" are described in medical writings from ancient Egypt (*circa* 2000 B.C.). Among various societies since that time all the following and many more preparations have been recommended: pine nuts, the blood of bats mixed with donkey's milk, root of the valerian plant, dried salamander, cyclamen, menstrual fluid, tulip bulbs, fat of camel's hump, parsnips, salted crocodile, pollen of date palm, the powdered tooth of a corpse, wings of bees, jasmine, turtles' eggs, henna (externally applied), ground crickets, spiders or ants, the genitals of hedgehogs, rhinoceros horn, the blood of executed criminals, artichokes, honey compounded with camel's milk, swallows' hearts, vineyard snails, certain bones of the toad, sulfurous waters, powdered stag's horn, and so on. We have already mentioned the equivocal (at best) evidence that sex-hormone preparations have

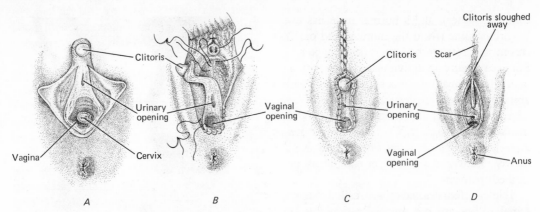

Figure 4.7. The surgical treatment of pseudohermaphroditism. (*A*) The genitalia before surgery. Note the hypertrophied clitoris. (*B*) The body of the clitoris is excised, but the glans is spared. (*C*) Closure. (*D*) The genitalia following surgery. In more recent versions of this operation, the glans of the clitoris is not spared, since it tends to slough off anyway. From Jones and Scott, *Hermaphroditism, Genital Anomalies and Related Endocrine Disorders* (Baltimore: Williams & Wilkins, 1958), p. 227. © 1958 by The Williams & Wilkins Co., and reprinted by permission.

aphrodisiac properties. Two other substances are still widely enough used (or at least discussed) to merit fuller comment here: *cantharides* (Spanish fly) and *yohimbine.*

Cantharides is a powder made from certain dried beetles (*Cantharis vesicatoria*) found in southern Europe. When taken internally, it causes acute inflammation and irritation of the urinary tract and dilation of the blood vessels of the penis, producing, in some instances, prolonged erections. Spanish fly is a dangerous drug and can produce severe systemic illness. Legend has it that in sixteenth-century Provence cantharides was used to cure fever. One woman reported that, after she gave the drug to her husband, he had intercourse with her forty times in forty-eight hours and then died.

Yohimbine is an alkaloid chemical derived from the bark of the African yohimbe tree (*Pausinystalia yohimbe*). Its use was first ob-

served by Europeans among natives in the nineteenth century; samples were brought back to Germany for analysis. The drug stimulates the nervous system and is also dangerous in large doses. It is available (by prescription) in the United States in capsule form, in combination with *nux vomica* (also a nervous system stimulant) and testosterone.

Drugs like alchohol and marijuana are not true aphrodisiacs but may affect sexual behavior by producing relaxation and releasing inhibitions.

A drug commonly thought to have anti-aphrodisiac properties is *saltpeter* (potassium nitrate). Rumors occasionally circulate among boys in boarding school or men in prison that saltpeter is added to the food to eliminate the sex drive and sexual activity. Saltpeter tends to increase urine flow but has no particular effect on sexual interest or potency.

When we consider the consequences of a sperm's uniting with an egg, it is perhaps surprising how little is generally known about this process. Similarly, when we consider the complexity of the newborn infant, it is difficult to visualize its development within the uterus during the nine months of pregnancy. Furthermore, the experiences of the expectant mother are in many ways unique and perhaps not fully appreciated by those who have not known, for instance, the sensation of a tiny foot kicking outward against the confines of one's abdomen. The events and experiences that culminate in the birth of a child are the subject of this chapter.

CONCEPTION

The Sperm

Description and Mechanism of Production

Human sperm were first scientifically described by the Dutch microscopist Anton van Leeuwenhoek (1632-1723) in a letter to the Royal Society of London in November 1677 and in a second, more detailed report the following year. (The discovery was actually made by a student, Ludwig Ham, however.)

Leeuwenhoek noted that the sperm resembled other microscopic organisms that he had observed swimming about in specimens of pond water, and he therefore named them *spermatozoa* ("seed animals"). Although he believed these cells to be essential constituents of the reproductive system of man, other observers thought that they were only miscellaneous organisms contaminating the seminal fluid. Not until 100 years later did Lazaro Spallanzani (1729-1799) demonstrate that seminal fluid that had been filtered (thus removing the sperm) was incapable of causing pregnancy when injected into the vagina of a female dog. Even then, some scientists continued to believe that the sperm did not become part of the offspring but simply stimulated the development of the eggs. Not until the twentieth century was it discovered that the sperm cell actually fuses with the egg to initiate life.

Sperm are produced in the seminiferous tubules of the testes, beginning with cells called *spermatogonia,* which lie along the internal linings of the tubules. The spermatogonia divide into *spermatocytes,* which in turn undergo a special division in which each pair of chromosomes splits, so that the resulting *spermatids* have twenty-three chromosomes, rather than the forty-six that all other cells of the body have.

CHAPTER

CONCEPTION, PREGNANCY, AND CHILDBIRTH

Of the forty-six chromosomes present in each body cell there are twenty-two pairs and two additional chromosomes (see Figure 5.1). These two are the "sex chromosomes." In the male, one is an X chromosome and one a smaller Y chromosome. When sperm are formed and the chromosomes divided, one sperm will contain an X chromosome and one will contain a Y chromosome. On the other hand, females have two X chromosomes in each cell; when cell division occurs in the ovaries, each egg ends up with one X chromosome.

The spermatid undergoes a process of transformation into a mature sperm (see Figure 5.2), involving constriction of the nucleus of the cell into the *head* of the sperm. The head is pear-shaped in side view and oval in a view from above. A small amount of cellular material

Idiogram of Human Male

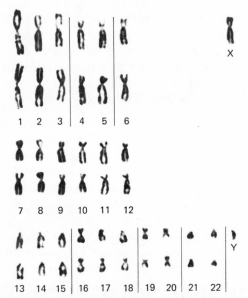

Figure 5.1. The human chromosomes (autosomes 1-22, sex chromosomes X and Y), from a male cell in culture. The forty-six chromosomes are from a photomicrographic print (cut single) arranged in pairs, and grouped according to sizes and relative lengths of the arms. From Tjio and Puck, *P.N.A.S.* 44 (1958): 1232.

forms a conical shaped *middlepiece* directly behind the head, and a bundle of fibers grows out beyond the middlepiece to form a *tail*, which enables the sperm to swim (see Figure 5.3).

Compared to the egg, the sperm is a small structure. The head is only about five microns long, the middlepiece another five microns, and the tail thirty to fifty microns long (1 micron equals .000039 inch or .001 millimeter). A quantity of sperm sufficient to repopulate the world could be fitted into a space the size of an aspirin tablet.

The sperm move up the seminiferous tubules to the epididymis (see Figure 2.7) and are stored there awaiting ejaculation. If ejaculation does not occur in thirty to sixty days the sperm degenerate and are replaced by new ones that are constantly being formed.

The Journey of the Sperm

The probability that a given sperm cell will ever fertilize an egg is extremely low. During the lifetimes of most men, literally billions of sperm are ejaculated and die: Their particular combinations of genes thus never achieve expression. The most common reason is, of course, that coitus occurs at times when the women have not been ovulating, for humans, in contrast to most animals, do not restrict their sexual activity to those periods when the females are fertile, or "in heat." But, even if coitus has occurred during ovulation, there are still many obstacles to successful fertilization of the egg.

The spermatic fluid in a normal ejaculation has a volume of 2.5 to 5 cubic centimeters, approximately enough liquid to fill a teaspoon. This small amount of fluid contains 150–600 million sperm which comprise only a very small proportion of the total volume of semen. The ejaculated fluid is whitish and semigelatinous; it is deposited somewhere in the vagina during male orgasm. If intercourse has occurred while the woman has been supine and if she has remained in this position for some time afterward, there is a greater possibility that some of the sperm will proceed through the cervix to the uterus. If she has been in an upright position during intercourse or has arisen immediately afterward, the force of gravity will cause the semen to flow away from the uterus.

Even when the woman lies on her back, seminal fluid may be lost, partly because of variations in the anatomy of the female genitals. The most common such variation is caused by obstetrical trauma during childbirth, resulting in damage to the tissues supporting the vagina. On the other hand, it should be noted that sexual excitement leads to engorgement of the blood vessels around the vaginal opening, creating a temporary "orgasmic platform" that facilitates retention of seminal fluid in the vagina.

Another mechanism that may result in loss of seminal fluid is continued penile thrusting after ejaculation. Each withdrawal movement by the male tends to disperse the sperm. Sometimes the ejaculate may fail to reach the distal portion of the vagina because of incomplete penetration by the male. This failure may be unavoidable because of his extreme obesity or a condition known as *hyrospadias,* in which the urethral opening is located near the base of the penis, rather than at its tip.[1]

Assuming, however, that the spermatic fluid has reached the general vicinity of the cervix and is allowed to remain there, we may consider what further factors will influence its fate. We mentioned in Chapter 4 that the pH of the cervical secretions varies. The sperm are very

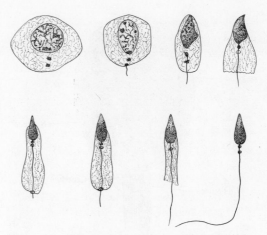

Figure 5.2. Eight successive stages in the transformation of a spermatid cell into a mature sperm. After Stieve, *Habch. d. Mikroskop. Anat. d. Menschen,* 7, 1930. From Stern, *Principles of Human Genetics,* 2nd ed. (San Francisco: W. H. Freeman and Company, 1960), p. 11. Copyright © by W. H. Freeman and Company, and reprinted by permission.

sensitive to the pH of their environment. If the secretions in the vagina are strongly acidic, the sperm are quickly destroyed. (This fact is behind the use of vinegar, or acetic acid, as a douche for contraceptive purposes.) Even in a mildly acidic environment (for example, when the pH is 6.0) the movement of the sperm ceases. The optimum pH for sperm survival and motility is between 8.5 and 9.0. In such an environment the sperm begin to swim toward the cervix against the fluid currents of the cervical secretions, which is their natural tendency. Sperm are capable of swimming at a rate of one to three centimeters an hour (about one inch), but once inside the uterus they may be assisted by muscular contractions in the uterine wall. Sexual stimulation and orgasm are known to produce contractions of the uterus, a phenomenon of which pregnant women in particular are often acutely aware. Whether or not these contractions aid the sperm in their journey through the uterus is not known for sure, but it is known that sperm may arrive in the

[1] In such instances artificial insemination can be used to impregnate women. The male ejaculates into a container to which a glycerine compound is added. The spermatic fluid is then injected into the vagina or directly into the uterus. Sperm may also be quick-frozen and stored for months or even years and still remain viable for future use.

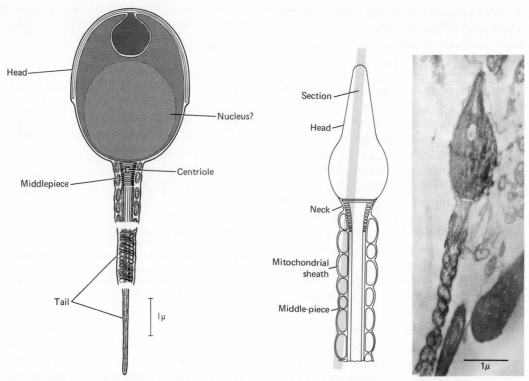

Figure 5.3.   A human sperm. *Left:* A "frontal" section (based on electronmicroscopic studies). From Schultz-Larsen. *Right:* Electronmicrograph of a somewhat tangential "longitudinal" section through head and middlepiece. Diagram shows approximate plane of section. From Lord Rothschild, *British Medical Journal,* 1 (1958), p. 301.

fallopian tubes much sooner than would be expected from their own unassisted rate of propulsion: within an hour to an hour and a half after intercourse, in fact.

Once in the fallopian tube, the sperm complete the final two inches or so of their journey toward the ovum by swimming against the current generated by the minute, waving, hair-like structures known as "cilia" that line the tube. Of course, about half the sperm that succeed in gaining access to the uterus end up in a tube containing no egg, even if the woman has ovulated (except on the rare occasions when a woman ovulates simultaneously from both ovaries). It is estimated that, of the original several hundred million sperm in the ejacula-

tion, only about 2,000 reach the tube containing the egg. And only one actually unites with the egg.

The Egg

Description and Mechanism of Maturation

Although the egg is one of the largest cells in the human body, it is small compared to the eggs of other species, scarcely visible to the naked eye. It is a spherical cell about 130 or 140 microns in diameter (about $\frac{1}{175}$ inch) and weighs about .0015 milligram, or approximately one-twenty-millionth of an ounce.

The discovery of the human egg has been attributed to Karl Ernst von Bar (1792–1876), generally recognized as the father of modern embryology. Von Bar studied a group of female dogs in various stages of pregnancy and succeeded in finding minute specks of matter in dogs in which the embryos had not had time to develop. He noted that these small objects in the fallopian tubes were smaller than the follicles of the ovaries, which had previously been thought to be eggs themselves. He then verified that the follicles contained minute bodies identical with those he observed in the fallopian tubes, which had been assumed to represent the actual germ material essential for reproduction. Later studies of humans confirmed these findings.

We noted in Chapter 2 that at birth the ovaries contain about 400,000 primitive egg cells (*primary oocytes*), and it is generally believed that no new germ cells are produced by the human female after birth, in significant contrast to the continuous production of sperm in the male throughout his life. Although only about 400 eggs are essential to provide one a month during a woman's reproductive life, exposure to radiation or drugs may alter all the germ cells at once and do permanent damage.[2]

An egg matures while still in the ovary, encased in a larger spherical structure known as a *graafian follicle* (see Figure 5.4). The egg divides while still within the follicle, producing a large *secondary oocyte* and a minute *first polar body*, each containing forty-six chromosomes. The final step in maturation of the egg occurs

---

[2] Possibly related to such "aging" of eggs is the increased incidence of certain defects, particularly mongolism, in children born to older women. A woman in her forties is 100 times more likely to have a mongoloid child than is a woman of twenty. This finding has been clearly correlated with the mother's age, although it is not known what causes chromosome defects as women grow older.

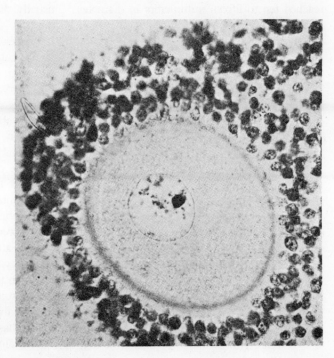

Figure 5.4 Human oocyte from a large graafian follicle (×480). From Eastman and Hellman, *Williams Obstetrics*, 13th ed. (New York: Appleton-Century-Crofts, 1966), p. 60. Reprinted by permission.

after ovulation, within the fallopian tube, when division of the genetic material in the cell occurs, resulting in an egg containing twenty-three chromosomes and a second polar body containing twenty-three chromosomes. The latter is extruded and disintegrates.

The mature egg, then, is a spherical cell, containing, in addition to the genetic material (chromosomes), fat droplets, protein substances, and nutrient fluid (see Figure 5.5). It is surrounded by a gelatinous capsule (*zona pellucida*), the final obstacle to the sperm cell seeking to fertilize the egg. (A layer of small cells, the *corona radiata*, which surrounds the egg within the follicle has usually disappeared by this time.)

Ovulation and Migration of the Egg

The hormonal mechanism that stimulates ovulation has been described in Chapter 4. At the time of ovulation the graafian follicle has reached ten to fifteen millimeters in diameter

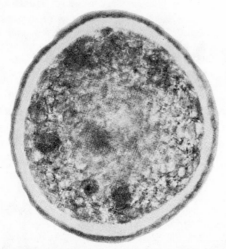

Figure 5.5. A fresh ovum washed from the tube; the protoplasm is enclosed by semitransparent zona pellucida and consists largely of lipoid masses ($\times 405$). From Eastman and Hellman, *Williams Obstetrics,* 13th ed. (New York: Appleton-Century-Crofts, 1966), p. 60. Reprinted by permission.

and protrudes from the surface of the ovary. It is filled with fluid, and its wall has become very thin. The egg has become detached within the follicle and is floating loose in the fluid. At ovulation the thinnest part of the follicle wall finally bursts, and the egg is carried out with the fluid. Although the fluid does build up a certain amount of pressure within the follicle, the process of ovulation is less like the explosion of an air-filled balloon and more like the leakage from a punctured sack of water.

Occasionally a follicle fails to mature and to rupture; the result is a *follicle (retention) cyst,* one of the most common forms of *ovarian cysts* (a fluid-filled sac in the ovary). Such cysts may vary from microscopic size to one or two inches in diameter. It is possible for several cysts to be present simultaneously in one or both ovaries. If large they may produce pain in the pelvis and cause painful intercourse, and the ovary may be tender to external pressure. Cysts of this kind rarely present serious problems and usually disappear spontaneously within sixty days.

The exact mechanism by which the egg finds its way into the fallopian tube is still a mystery. Although the fringed end of the tube is near the ovary, there is no direct connection that would ensure that the egg did not simply fall into the abdominal cavity. Indeed, it sometimes does, but, even more fascinating, it has clearly been established that an egg from an ovary on one side of the body can somehow reach the tube on the other side. There is the well-documented instance of a woman who had her right tube and left ovary removed surgically yet succeeded in having two normal pregnancies afterwards.

In any event, once the egg has entered the fallopian tube, it begins a leisurely journey to the uterus, taking about three days to move three to five inches. The egg, in contrast to the sperm, has no means of self-propulsion but is carried along by the current of the small cilia lining the tube. There are also periodic contractions of the muscles in the walls of the fallopian tubes, which are believed by some investigators to aid in transporting the eggs, although this belief has not been definitely confirmed.

If the egg is not fertilized during its journey through the fallopian tube, it disintegrates.

Fertilization

The moment when sperm and egg unite is the moment of conception, and, though it is commonly believed that conception occurs within the uterus, it actually takes place about half-way down the fallopian tube. If intercourse has taken place within about thirty-six hours before ovulation, viable sperm may already be present in the tube, swimming about in apparently random fashion, when the egg arrives on the scene. Conception must occur within about forty-eight hours of ovulation, or the egg will be incapable of being fertilized. Assuming the time of ovulation is known and the woman has intercourse one or two days before or after this time, she may become pregnant. Otherwise, it is impossible.

Although many sperm surround the egg at the time of fertilization, only one sperm actually penetrates it; this sperm adds its twenty-three chromosomes to the twenty-three in the egg, providing the necessary complement of forty-six for the new human being. It is believed that the additional sperm assist by secreting a particular enzyme (*hyaluronidase*) that aids in eliminating excess cellular material that may still cling to the outside of the egg.

The mechanism by which a sperm actually penetrates the capsule of the egg is unknown, but it apparently bores through it somehow. In some animals, sperm have been observed to enter the eggs and to continue to move well into the interior with the aid of their tails. In other animals only the heads and middlepieces enter the eggs.[3]

By means of another unknown mechanism the wall of the egg becomes impervious to other sperm once the first one has successfully penetrated. Whether or not this sperm represents the "best" of the available specimens is a matter of conjecture, but, in any event, the particular genes that it carries will determine the sex and many other characteristics of the child. If it carries an X chromosome, the child will be a girl. If it carries a Y chromosome, the child will be a boy.

Parthenogenesis. The development of an egg into a mature adult in the absence of fertilization is known as *parthenogenesis.* Aristotle observed that the drone males of a honeybee colony develop from unfertilized eggs. This phenomenon occurs in several species of insects but has not been observed to occur normally in any species of vertebrate animal. If one pierces an unfertilized frog's egg with a fine needle, however, it may develop into a mature frog, for reasons that are not clear. Artificial stimulation of the unfertilized eggs of higher animals has not induced full development, though stimulation of rabbit eggs causes them to go through some of the early stages of development.

The fertilized egg begins to divide into multiple cells as it moves down the fallopian tube. The original egg becomes two cells, these two become four, the four become eight, and so on. There is no significant change in volume during these first few days, but the initial egg

---

[3] A group of English scientists recently succeeded in fertilizing a human egg with a sperm in a test-tube preparation (*Medical World News,* April 4, 1969, p. 27). This experiment has once again raised the specter of eugenic breeding, which shocked readers of Aldous Huxley's *Brave New World* four decades ago. The possibility of "test-tube babies" raises many important moral questions. It is quite likely that an egg fertilized in this way could be inserted into a woman's uterus and would develop normally.

has become a round mass subdivided into many small cells. This round mass of cells is called a *morula* (from the Latin *morum,* "mulberry"), and the cells of the morula arrange themselves around the outside of the sphere during the third to fifth days after ovulation, leaving a fluid-filled cavity in the center. This structure, called a *blastocyst,* floats about in the uterine cavity, and sometime between the fifth and seventh days after ovulation attaches itself to the uterine lining and begins to burrow in, aided by enzymes that digest the outer surface of the lining, permitting the developing egg to reach the blood vessels and nutrients below (see Figure 5.6). By the tenth to twelfth day after ovulation the blastocyst is firmly implanted in the uterine wall, yet the woman still cannot know that she is pregnant, for her menstrual period is not due for several more days.

Notions about Pregnancy in Primitive Societies

As most sexual intercourse does not result in conception, it is perhaps not surprising that primitive peoples have developed a variety of beliefs about the origin of life. Two South Pacific tribes, the Arunta and the Trobrianders, believed that intercourse was purely a source of pleasure unrelated to pregnancy. Natives of these tribes believed that conception occurred when a spirit embryo entered the body of a woman. The spirit was believed to enter the uterus either through the vagina or through the head. In the latter instance, it was thought to travel through the bloodstream to the uterus.

Other people, though recognizing that intercourse is essential to conception, believed that supernatural powers determined whether or not specific acts of intercourse would cause pregnancy. The Jivaro tribesmen in the Amazon region believed that women were particularly fertile during the phase of the new moon. Perhaps this belief reflects association of the lunar cycle with the menstrual cycle, both of which are about the same length. In addition, the Jivaro, along with the Hopi Indians and several other tribes, believed that each new child was a reincarnation of a deceased member of the tribe. The Hopi believed that pregnancy represented reincarnation of a child who had died in infancy, whereas the Jivaro believed that babies were the reincarnations of ancestors, not necessarily those who died in infancy. It was common practice among tribes that believe in reincarnation to examine the newborn children for birthmarks or other peculiarities that deceased relatives were known to have had. Such signs were considered proof of reincarnation.

Many tribes, including the Hopi, the Masai tribe of Africa, and the Maori of New Zealand,

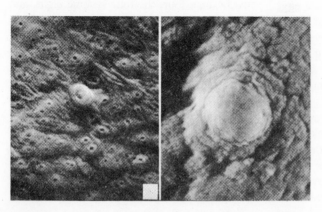

Figure 5.6. Low- and high-power photographs of the surface of an early human implantation obtained on the twenty-second day of cycle, less than eight days after conception; the site was slightly elevated and measured 0.36×0.31 millimeters. *Left:* the actual size of the ovum indicated by the white square at the lower right; the mouths of uterine glands appear as dark spots surrounded by halos. From Eastman and Hellman, *Williams Obstetrics,* 13th ed. (New York: Appleton-Century-Crofts, 1966), p. 123. Reprinted by permission.

have associated the likelihood of pregnancy with given phases of the menstrual cycle. All these tribes believed that the period of maximum fertility was just after a woman's menstrual period had ended. But as the Hopi also believed that intercourse must take place repeatedly, rather than just once, for conception to occur, a Hopi couple would probably end up having intercourse at the time of ovulation: doing the right thing for the wrong reason.

In practically all societies that recognize the relation between intercourse and pregnancy, there have been at least occasional circumstances in which alternative explanations for conception have been assumed. Believers in witchcraft, currently a subject of renewed interest in the Western world, have always held that a woman can conceive after a union with Satan or some related demon. The Jivaro considered grossly deformed children to be the results of such unions.

A few tribes, like the Kiwai of New Guinea and the Baiga of India, believed that a girl could become pregnant from something that she had eaten, implying that a substance taken in through the mouth may have been contaminated with semen, which then found its way to the uterus.

In some tribes the mother's wearing of certain charms was thought to influence the sex of the child. Other, more elaborate methods of influencing the sex of the infant have been described by Landtman[4] in his study of the Kiwai tribe.

Infertility

Even in overpopulated societies, failure to conceive is often a problem of great concern to the individual involved. Between 10 and 15 percent of all marriages in the United States are involuntarily childless. Although it is com-

mon in many societies to attribute sterility to females, about 40 percent of infertile marriages result from sterility in the male partners. Therefore it is important that, whenever a couple wishes to have children and is unsuccessful for about a year, both the husband and the wife should see a physician, for either or both may have disorders that can be treated.

Conditions that interfere with a man's ability to ejaculate into the depths of the vagina are one cause of infertility and have been described earlier in this chapter. More commonly, the problem is a low sperm count, which can result from many factors. An ejaculation that contains fewer than 35 million sperm per cubic centimeter (a total count of fewer than 100–150 million sperm in the seminal fluid) will almost never result in fertilization of the egg. Frequent ejaculation (one or more times a day for several consecutive days) will lower the sperm count; this deficiency, obviously, is easily remedied. Usually, however, the problem is more serious. Infectious diseases that involve the testes may cause sterility. The most common such disease is mumps. Infections of the prostate gland may also affect fertility. Direct damage to the testes through trauma or radiation may result in decreased sperm production or mechanical obstruction to the movement of the sperm.

Cryptorchism (failure of the testes to descend into the scrotum from the abdomen during development) affects about 2 percent of postpubertal boys bilaterally and results in sterility because sperm do not mature at the higher temperature to which they are exposed within the abdomen. This condition can sometimes be remedied either medically or surgically before puberty. If one testicle is present in the scrotum, fertility is usually not impaired.

Certain hormone disorders, particularly hypothyroidism and diabetes, may be associated with low sperm counts. Men with such disorders can often be successfully treated. Hormone disorders may also result in infertility in

---

[4]Landtman (1927), pp. 228–229.

women. Deficiencies of thyroid, adrenal, or pituitary hormones, in particular, can cause failure to ovulate; these deficiencies can be treated by replacement of the appropriate hormone in pill form or by injection.[5] Failure to ovulate may also be associated with malnutrition, vitamin deficiency, anemia, or severe psychic stress (see Chapter 4).

Infections of the vagina, cervix, uterus, tubes, or ovaries may cause infertility by inhibiting or preventing passage of sperm or eggs to the site of fertilization. Treatment involves identification of the particular microorganism causing the infection and administration of the appropriate antibiotic.

There are also various congenital malformations of the female reproductive tract, as well as tumors (particularly cervical or uterine), that may prevent fertilization. Many of these conditions can be corrected surgically (some of these conditions are described in more detail in Chapter 12). A woman may inadvertently be preventing conception by using certain commercial douches or vaginal deodorants containing chemicals that destroy, or inhibit the motility of, sperm.

If a couple consults a physician for infertility, he will take complete medical histories, and each partner will undergo a physical examination, with particular emphasis on the reproductive organs. Laboratory tests to rule out infections, anemia, and hormone deficiencies will be performed. The husband will be instructed to bring in a complete ejaculation for sperm analysis. The wife will be instructed to keep a morning temperature chart during her next several menstrual cycles. The purpose

of this chart is to determine if and when she is ovulating, as indicated by a rise in basal body temperature (BBT) approximately in midcycle (the use of such charts to avoid conception in the practice of the "rhythm method" is described in Chapter 6).

If these tests indicate that the male is producing adequate numbers of apparently normal and motile sperm and that the female is ovulating, then further tests to determine why conception is not occurring will be indicated. The most common site of obstruction of the egg in its journey from the ovary is obviously the fallopian tube, and the so-called "Rubin's test" is performed to determine if the tubes are obstructed. The test involves forcing carbon dioxide under pressure into the uterus through the cervix. If the tubes are open, there will be a drop in pressure as the gas passes through them. If there is an obstruction, the pressure will increase. The most common site of obstruction of the sperm in their journey is the cervix; an analysis of the cervical mucus may also be in order to rule out an abnormality at this point. Once a correctable problem has been identified, treatment may begin. If no abnormalities can be found, couples are sometimes advised to adopt children. For reasons that are not known, a previously infertile couple may sometimes succeed in having children of their own after having adopted a child.

In many societies barrenness is a source of great shame and even social ostracism for a woman. Failure to conceive after a certain period of time is considered sufficient grounds for divorce among orthodox Jews, as well as in many primitive tribes. It was not unusual for a woman of the Lango tribe of East Africa to commit suicide if she failed to have children. The high premium placed on having children is especially understandable in societies with high mortality rates and in nonindustrial economies, in which many hands are needed to produce the necessities of life.

---

[5] The pituitary hormone FSH has recently been made available to physicians, but the exact dosage necessary to induce ovulation cannot be accurately determined. As a given dose may cause six or eight ova to ripen and pass into the fallopian tubes simultaneously, there has been an increased incidence of multiple births among women receiving this hormone.

Among the Bena and Mbdunu tribes of Africa new sexual partners might be taken by a man and among the Ifugao people of Oceania by a man or woman to determine whether or not a different partner would result in a fertile union. This practice did not necessarily involve divorce from the original spouse. It is rare, however, for a male to be publicly identified as sterile. One exception was found among the Ashanti tribe of Africa, in which a sterile man was scorned for having a "wax penis."

Various medicines or rituals were used in some societies to enhance fertility. Kiwai women were encouraged to eat spiders or spider eggs to cure sterility. The Andamanese women ate a certain kind of frog that itself produced numerous offspring. Some Polynesian men drank large quantities of coconut milk to promote fertility, for they believed that semen was specifically derived from this food (which it vaguely resembles).

PREGNANCY

The average length of human pregnancy is 266 days, or approximately nine calendar months.[6] It is traditional obstetrical practice to divide pregnancy into three-month periods, called *trimesters*. We shall discuss each trimester from the perspectives of the expectant mother's

---

[6] There is, of course, great variation from this mean in both directions. Premature births are well known. Extended pregnancies also occur; the length of pregnancy assumes legal importance in establishing the legitimacy of a child when the husband has been away for more than ten months. In the United States the longest pregnancy upheld by the courts as legitimate was 355 days. In England in *Preston-Jones* v. *Preston-Jones,* conducted in the House of Lords in 1949, the husband claimed adultery on the grounds that the interval of sexual abstinence between himself and his wife before birth of the child in question would have meant a pregnancy of 360 days. Although he was initially overruled, he finally won his case in the Court of Appeals.

experiences and developments within the uterus. The details of each stage in fetal development are available in textbooks on embryology. Our aim here is to enable the reader to visualize more clearly the fascinating steps that intervene between conception and birth, without becoming bogged down in details and complex terminology.

The First Trimester

First Symptoms of Pregnancy

Many readers of this book will recall vividly a time when they themselves or acquaintances failed to menstruate as expected. The experience may have been particularly joyful if it signaled the news that mutual desire for a child was to be fulfilled. On the other hand, it may have been an experience of fear and guilt, the unintended consequence of sexual intercourse. Or the news may have been met with mixed feelings, as when a young couple wanted to have children "but not yet." But the knowledge that a woman has missed her period is rarely met with indifference by those concerned.

A woman may miss her period for many reasons other than pregnancy, however, as we have pointed out in Chapter 4. Various illnesses and emotional upsets may result in failure to menstruate. In addition, women under twenty and over forty may skip periods occasionally for no apparent reason. A woman who has recently delivered a child, particularly one who is still nursing, may not menstruate for five or six months or more. She cannot rely on the absence of menstruation as an indication of pregnancy and may indeed become pregnant without having had a menstrual period since her previous pregnancy. She need only have ovulated.

Conversely, a woman may continue to have cyclic bleeding, though in smaller quantities and for shorter durations than usual, during pregnancy. Such bleeding, often called "spotting," occurs in about 20 percent of pregnant women and is not necessarily ominous. It is particularly common among women who have had children before. On the other hand, "spotting" may be an early sign of miscarriage.

Another early symptom of pregnancy is enlargement and tenderness of the breasts. The physiological mechanisms that lead to enlargement of the breasts have been described in Chapter 4. When hormonal stimulation of the mammary glands begins after conception, a woman will initially become aware of sensations of fullness and sometimes of tingling in her breasts. The nipples, in particular, become quite sensitive to tactile stimulation early in pregnancy.

Many women experience so-called "morning sickness" during the first six to eight weeks of pregnancy. Usually it consists of queasy sensations upon arising, accompanied by an aversion to food or even to the odors of certain foods. This nausea may be accompanied by vomiting and great reluctance to be near food. Some women experience "morning sickness" in the evening, but about 25 percent of pregnant women never experience any vomiting at all. On the other hand, about 1 in 200 pregnant women in the United States experiences vomiting so severe that she must be hospitalized. This condition is known as *hyperemesis gravidarum* and may have serious consequences (including malnutrition) if not properly treated. Occasionally therapeutic abortion may be required in order to save the life of the mother, but this necessity is quite rare.

A phenomenon known as "sympathetic pregnancy" is sometimes observed in the husband of a pregnant woman. He too becomes nauseated and vomits along with his wife. The etiology of this condition is implied in its name.

More frequent urination is another symptom of early pregnancy and is related to increased pressure on the bladder from the swelling uterus. This symptom tends to disappear as the uterus enlarges and rises up into the abdomen, but frequent urination again becomes a common complaint toward the end of pregnancy, when the fetal head descends into the pelvis and exerts pressure on the bladder.

Fatigue and a need for more sleep are often most striking early in pregnancy and may be quite puzzling to a girl who is usually very energetic. The sensation of drowsiness early in pregnancy may be so overwhelming as to make sleep irresistible, even in the midst of conversation.

Early Diagnosis of Pregnancy

A sexually active woman who has missed her menstrual period, is having "morning sickness," and has noticed breast enlargement and tenderness, increased frequency of urination, and extreme fatigue has reason to suspect that she is pregnant. If she is particularly anxious to verify this suspicion, she may see a physician for a "pregnancy test." Actually there are many ways in which a physician can determine whether or not a woman is pregnant, none of which is 100 percent accurate early in pregnancy, however.

The sixth week of pregnancy (i.e., about four weeks after missing a period) is the earliest point at which a physician can determine with any reliability that a woman is pregnant.[7] By this time certain changes in the cervix and uterus are apparent upon pelvic examination. Of particular usefulness to the physician is *Hegar's sign,* which refers to the soft consistency of a compressible area between the cervix and body of the uterus and becomes apparent in the sixth week of pregnancy. To an experienced clinician it is a fairly reliable indication.

---

[7] It is tragic that some women have in panic assumed that they were pregnant because of late menstrual periods and have had illegal abortions, resulting in severe complications and even death, when in fact they have not been pregnant.

The examination is performed by placing one hand on the abdomen and two fingers of the other hand in the vagina (see Figure 5.7).

Various laboratory tests may also be performed in the sixth week, and if properly administered they are 95–98 percent accurate. (Some laboratory tests for pregnancy may be positive as early as the fourth week, two weeks after the "missed period.") If the test is negative at this time, however, it does not necessarily mean that the woman is not pregnant. The percentage of such "false negative" test results diminishes after six to eight weeks. The so-called "frog test" takes advantage of the fact that there are elevated amounts of gonado-tropins (sex-gland-stimulating hormones) in a woman's urine after about six weeks of pregnancy. If a specimen of this urine is injected into the dorsal lymph sac of a male frog, he will ejaculate microscopically visible sperm within about two hours. This test was developed in 1947 and is still rather widely used because it is cheap and simple to perform. A newer pregnancy test involves administering progesterone alone or in combination with estrogen, either orally or by injection. If the woman is not pregnant uterine bleeding will usually occur within seven to ten days.

Regardless of the tests performed, we must emphasize that it is impossible to make an *absolute* diagnosis of pregnancy during the first three to four months after conception.

False Pregnancy (*Pseudocyesis*). Occasionally a woman may become convinced that she is pregnant despite evidence to the contrary. About 0.1 percent of all women who consult obstetricians fall into this category. Usually they are young women who intensely desire children, but some are women near menopause. A certain percentage of these women are unmarried; in fact, the phenomenon was not unknown among nuns in medieval convents, who took their marriage vows with Christ literally and believed that they had been impregnated by Christ.

Women suffering false pregnancy often experi-

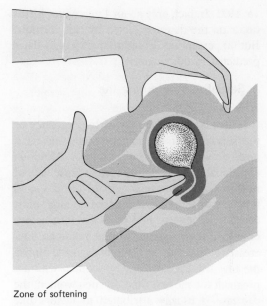

Zone of softening

Figure 5.7. Hegar's sign. From Benson, *Handbook of Obstetrics and Gynecology,* 3rd ed. (Los Altos, Calif.: Lange Medical Publications, 1968), p. 42. Reprinted by permission.

ence the symptoms of pregnancy, including morning sickness, breast tenderness, a sense of fullness in the pelvis, and the sensation of fetal movements in the abdomen. They often cease to menstruate, and physicians may observe contractions of the abdominal muscles that resemble fetal movements. Even though pregnancy tests are negative, a woman suffering from a severe mental illness like schizophrenia may persist in her delusion for years.

Once pregnancy has been reasonably established, the first question that the woman asks is usually "When is the baby due?" The expected delivery date (EDC, or expected date of confinement) can be calculated by the following formula: Add one week to the first day of the last menstrual period, subtract three months, then add one year. For instance, if the last menstrual period began on January 8, 1971, adding one week (to January 15), subtracting three months (to October 15), and adding one year gives an expected delivery date of October

15, 1971. In fact, only about 4 percent of births occur on the dates predicted by this formula. But 60 percent occur within five days of dates predicted in this manner.

Sexual Activity during the First Trimester

There is no reason why early pregnancy or the suspicion of pregnancy should inhibit a healthy woman's sexual activities. Although occasional morning sickness may cause lack of interest during the early part of the day, and fatigue may be a deterrent in the evening, most couples are able to find mutually satisfactory occasions for continued sexual relations. Decreased sexual interest is rarely reported during the first trimester, except by women who are pregnant for the first time. In such women, the decrease is usually attributed to factors like nausea and fatigue, but probably equally important is general increased anxiety. Then, too, physiological changes during this period can make sexual stimulation somewhat painful. In particular, the vasocongestion of the breasts that occurs during sexual excitement may be painful to a woman who is already experiencing tenderness there.

There is no evidence to support the notion that intercourse during the early months of pregnancy can cause abortion of the fetus. Nevertheless, concern about injuring the fetus during intercourse is often reported by women during the first trimester, particularly if they are pregnant for the first time or have had previous miscarriages. It is interesting that some primitive peoples believe continued intercourse after conception essential to the continuation of pregnancy; they believe that the sperm serve to nourish the developing fetus.

Intrauterine Events of the First Trimester

Development of the Placenta. Earlier in this chapter we left the small, spherical blastocyst freshly embedded in the inner lining of the uterus. A disk-shaped layer of cells develops across the center of the blastocyst, and from this *embryonic disk* the fetus develops. The remaining cells develop into the *placenta,* the *membranes* that will contain the fetus and the *amniotic fluid,* and the *yolk sac* (which in humans is insignificant in function).

The placenta is the organ that exchanges nutrients and waste products with the mother. It is constructed from both fetal and maternal tissue and during the first trimester develops into a bluish-red, round, flat organ about seven inches in diameter and one inch thick. It weighs about one pound and constitutes, along with the fetal membranes, the "afterbirth." The blood vessels of the placenta are connected to the circulatory system of the mother through the blood vessels in the wall of the uterus. The circulation system of the fetus is connected to that of the placenta by the blood vessels of the *umbilical cord,* which is attached to the placenta. Oxygen and essential nutrients reach the fetus through the umbilical vein, and waste products from the fetus reach the maternal system through the two umbilical arteries.

The placenta also functions as an endocrine gland, producing hormones essential to the maintenance of pregnancy. The hormone *human chorionic gonadotropin* (HCG) stimulates continued production of progesterone by the corpus luteum during the first trimester. Gradually, however, the placenta begins to produce large amounts of progesterone and estrogens. It also produces other hormones like cortisol and androgens in small amounts. There is evidence that placental production of progesterone and estrogens falls off just before delivery and that this drop plays a role in initiating labor.

Fetal Complications Transmitted through the Placenta. It is very important to realize that substances other than nutrients may also reach the developing fetus through the placental circulation system. Various drugs taken by the mother may have harmful effects on the developing fetus, particularly during the first trimester. In recent years the effects of the sedative thalidomide have been widely publicized. This drug causes abnormal development of the arms and legs (*phocomelia*). In infants suffering from this condition the hands and feet are attached to the bodies by short stumps rather than by normal arms and legs.

Synthetic hormone preparations resembling progesterone have been administered during the first trimester to women showing signs of possible miscarriage. When the fetus has been female, these hormones have sometimes resulted in "masculinization" of the external genitals, including enlargement of the clitoris, so that it has resembled an infant's penis.[8]

Regular use of addictive drugs like heroin and morphine by the mother produces addiction in the fetus. When the infant is born, it must be given further doses of the drug to prevent withdrawal effects that may be fatal.

Certain viruses are also known to have damaging effects on the fetus during the first trimester. The most common is the virus of rubella, or German measles. If a woman has rubella during the first month of pregnancy, there is a 50 percent chance that the infant will be born with cataracts, congenital heart disease, deafness, or mental deficiency. In the third month of pregnancy the risk of such abnormalities decreases to 10 percent. The high probability of serious damage to the fetus is the basis for the argument that women who contract German measles during the first trimester of pregnancy should be allowed to have abortions.

Development of the Fetus. The first trimester is a period during which the rather simple structure of the embryo is transformed into the very complex organism called the "fetus," though with relatively little change in size. (In medical terms the word "fetus" refers to the developing infant after the eighth week of pregnancy. The "ovum" becomes an "embryo" one week after fertilization.)

The embryonic disk described earlier becomes somewhat elongated and ovoid by the end of the second week after fertilization. The embryo is about 1.5 millimeters long at this point. The actual sizes of the embryo at various stages in the first seven weeks are depicted in Figure 5.8.

During the third week, growth is particularly noticeable at the two ends of the embryo. Differentiation of the *cephalic* (head) end is particularly notable in comparison to that of the rest of the body. By the end of the third week or the early part of the fourth week the beginnings of eyes and ears are visible. In addition, the brain and other portions of the central nervous system are beginning to form. By the end of the fourth week two bulges are apparent on the concave (front) side of the trunk. The upper one represents the developing heart and is called the *cardiac prominence*; the lower one is the *hepatic prominence* and is caused by the protrusion of the developing liver (see Figure 5.9). At this point the embryo is only about four millimeters long and weighs about 0.4 gram (about $\frac{1}{7}$ of an ounce). A prominent "tail" is present in the young embryo, but it is almost gone by the eighth week.[9]

Between the fourth and eighth weeks the facial features—eyes, ears, nose, and mouth—become clearly recognizable (Figure 5.10).

---

[8] A follow-up study of ten such girls has been conducted at Johns Hopkins University, and it was found that nine were "tomboyish" in their behavior; they preferred outdoor and athletic activities to playing with dolls and the like. These findings suggest that the effects of these hormones during early development may extend beyond the development of the genitals (Ehrhardt and Money, 1967.)

---

[9] In rare instances the tail fails to regress, and there are documented cases of human infants born with tails. The tails are usually removed surgically at an early age, but in one case reported in the medical literature a twelve-year-old boy had a tail nine inches long.

Fingers and toes begin to appear between the sixth and eighth weeks (Figure 5.11). Bones are beginning to ossify, and the intestines are

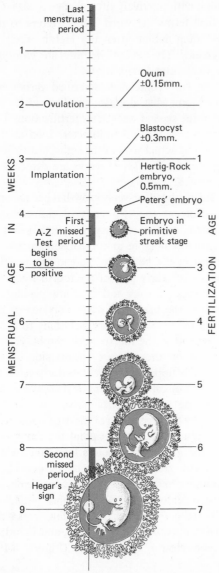

Figure 5.8. Actual sizes of embryos and their membranes in relation to a time scale based on the mother's menstrual history. From B. M. Patten, *Human Embryology,* 3rd ed., p. 145. Copyright © 1968 by McGraw-Hill, Inc. Used with permission of McGraw-Hill Book Company.

forming. By the seventh week the gonads are present but cannot yet be clearly distinguished as male or female. Similarly, the external genitals cannot be identified as male or female until about the third month (see Chapter 2).

Between the eighth and twelfth weeks the embryo increases in length from about 1.5 to about 4 inches and in weight from about 2 grams to about 19 grams (approximately $\frac{2}{3}$ ounce). The skin takes on the pinkish color of normal human skin, and the internal genitals become recognizable as male or female. Although still very small, the fetus resembles clearly a human being, and from this point on development consists primarily of enlargement and further differentiation of structures that are already present.

Complications of the First Trimester

The defects caused by certain drugs and infectious diseases during the first trimester have already been mentioned. These problems do not ordinarily become apparent until after birth, however.

Miscarriage, or *spontaneous abortion,* occurs most often during the first trimester of pregnancy. Between 10 and 15 percent of all pregnancies end in spontaneous abortion; that is, the pregnancies terminate in miscarriages before the fetuses have any chance of survival on their own. About 75 percent of spontaneous abortions occur before the sixteenth week of pregnancy, and the great majority occur before the eighth week. The first sign that a woman may miscarry is vaginal bleeding, or "spotting." If the symptoms of pregnancy disappear and the woman develops cramps in the pelvic region, the fetus is usually expelled. About 50 percent of such miscarried fetuses are clearly defective in some way. About 15 percent of miscarriages are caused by illness, malnutrition, trauma, or other factors affecting the mother. In the remaining 85 percent the reasons are

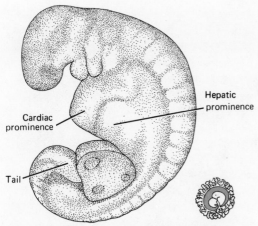

Figure 5.9. A human embryo about four weeks after fertilization (crown-rump length 3.9 millimeters). Retouched photograph (×20) of embryo 5923 in the Carnegie Collection. Sketch, lower right, shows actual size of embryo. As modified by B. M. Patten for *Human Embryology,* 3rd ed., p. 70. McGraw-Hill Book Company. With permission.

not apparent. A woman who has had one spontaneous abortion usually can conceive again and have a normal pregnancy.

In addition to pregnancies that end in spontaneous abortion, it is estimated that another 10 percent of all pregnancies are terminated by *induced abortion.* Probably about 750,000 illegal, or "criminal," abortions are performed in the United States each year.[10] An estimated 50 percent of them are performed by people other than physicians, and complications like hemorrhaging and infection are not uncommon.

The term *therapeutic abortion* refers to the surgical termination of pregnancy in accordance with legal and medical criteria. These criteria vary from state to state and from physician to physician. Until recently therapeutic abortions were performed in the United States mainly when it was believed that continued pregnancy

would endanger the life of the mother. (For example, when serious heart disease might prove fatal under the added strain of pregnancy). In the past few years, however, some states have revised their laws on therapeutic abortion, so that it is now legal to perform this operation when there is reason to believe that continuation of the pregnancy will seriously impair the physical *or mental* health of the mother or when the pregnancy results from rape or incest. Laws in most states still do not provide for therapeutic abortion when there is reason to believe that the fetus has been damaged, as when the mother has had German measles (see Chapter 16).

Contrary to popular belief, most abortions are performed on married women.

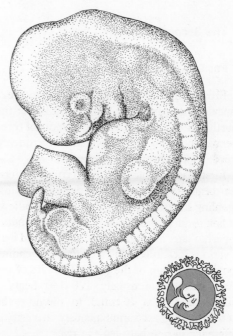

Figure 5.10. A human embryo a little more than six weeks after fertilization (crown-rump length 14 millimeters). Retouched photograph (×8) of embryo 1267A in the Carnegie Collection. From B. M. Patten, *Human Embryology,* 3rd ed., p. 74. Copyright © 1968 by McGraw-Hill, Inc. Used with permission of McGraw-Hill Book Company.

---

[10] This figure is a rough estimate based on several surveys conducted prior to the legalizing of abortions in several states in recent years. The impact of the new abortion laws on criminal abortions is not apparent yet.

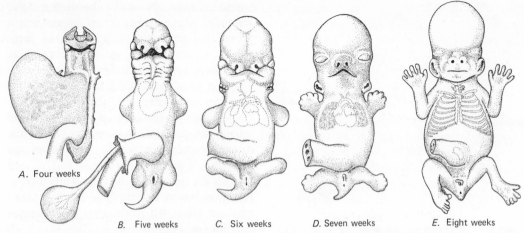

A. Four weeks

B. Five weeks   *C.* Six weeks   *D.* Seven weeks   *E.* Eight weeks

Figure 5.11. Frontal views of a series of human embryos, drawn as they would appear if the body curvatures had been straightened. From B. M. Patten, *Human Embryology,* 3rd ed., p. 146. Copyright © 1968 by McGraw-Hill, Inc. Used with permission of McGraw-Hill Book Company.

The Second Trimester

Positive Diagnosis of Pregnancy

From a medico-legal point of view, pregnancy cannot usually be proved until after the fourth month. By that time one or more of three specific signs, anyone of which is considered proof of pregnancy, are present.

First, it is possible to hear and count the fetal heartbeat. Its sound is often described as resembling the ticking of a watch under a pillow. At first it can be heard best just above the pubic bone, but later in pregnancy it can be heard best at various locations in the abdomen, depending upon the position of the fetus. The rate of the fetal heartbeat is usually 120–140 beats a minute, and it is essential to monitor the mother's heartbeat simultaneously to verify a difference in rate between the two.

Second, fetal movements can be confirmed, usually by the end of the fifth month, by means of feel and observation. By placing his hand on the mother's abdomen the experienced physician can distinguish spontaneous fetal movements from muscular or intestinal contractions

that may resemble them. Later on the kicking of the fetus becomes visually apparent.

Third, X-ray films of the abdomen can demonstrate unequivocally the outlines of the fetal skeleton. The fetal skeleton is not visible on X-ray, however, until the fifth or sixth month of pregnancy in most instances. (Visibility on X-ray is dependent upon calcification of the skeleton.) Because of the potential hazards of radiation to the fetus, X-rays are only used when there is a clear necessity for information which cannot be obtained by other means.

Experiences of the Mother

During the second trimester the pregnant woman becomes clearly aware that she is expecting. She usually experiences the sensations caused by the fetus' kicking and moving about in her abdomen ("quickening"). In addition, her waistline begins to expand (particularly in women who have borne children previously), and her abdomen begins to protrude, necessitating a change from regular to maternity clothes. Her condition now becomes publicly recognizable.

The second trimester is generally the most

peaceful and pleasant period of pregnancy. Nausea and drowsiness present during the first trimester tend to disappear during the second. Concerns about miscarriage are generally past, and it is too early to start worrying about labor and delivery. Barring complications or illness, the pregnant woman can be quite active during the second trimester. She can continue to work if she wishes, do housework, travel, and participate in recreation and sports. Rather than eliminating specific activities, most physicians nowadays urge "moderation in all things."

Sexual Activity during the Second Trimester

In contrast to their feelings in the first trimester, most women report greater interest in sexual activity and greater sexual satisfaction during the second. Indeed, many women claim that sexual intercourse is more satisfying during this period than at any other time, including when they are not pregnant.

The reasons for this improvement are partially known. As noted, nausea and extreme drowsiness generally disappear in the second trimester. Breast tenderness or pain resulting from sexual stimulation also disappears. There is significantly increased vaginal lubrication during sexual stimulation from the second trimester on, particularly in women who have had children before.

The full range of coital positions can generally be used until late in the second trimester, but then certain positions become either too tiring or too awkward for the woman.

Development of the Fetus

Beyond the twelfth week the fetus is clearly recognizable as a human infant (see Figures 5.12 and 5.13), although it is much smaller than

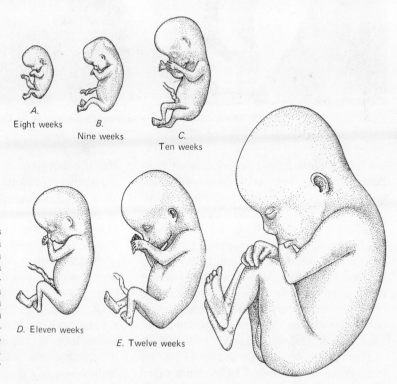

Figure 5.12. Human embryos between eight and sixteen weeks, actual size. *A–D* from photographs of embryos in University of Michigan Collection. *E* and *F* redrawn, with slight modification, from DeLee, "Obstetrics." From B. M. Patten, *Human Embryology,* 3rd ed., p. 150. Copyright © by McGraw-Hill, Inc. Used with permission of McGraw-Hill Book Company.

A.
Eight weeks

B.
Nine weeks

C.
Ten weeks

D. Eleven weeks

E. Twelve weeks

F. Sixteen weeks

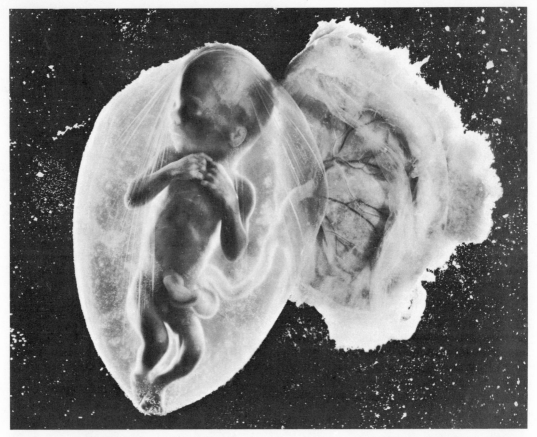

Figure 5.13.   Fetus, about four months, eight inches long. From Nilsson et al., *A Child Is Born* (Boston: Seymour Lawrence, Inc., 1965), pp. 116–117. Reprinted by permission.

it will be at birth. It has a proportionately large head, with eyes, ears, nose, and mouth. The arms and legs, which began as "limb buds" projecting from the trunk, now have hands and feet, fingers and toes. The digits of the hands and feet begin with the formation of four radial grooves at the ends of the limb buds, lending the initial appearance of webbed hands or feet (see Figure 5.14). In some children remnants of this webbing remain after birth, causing embarrassment to the parents, perhaps, but usually of no real significance.

Hair appears on the scalp and above the eyes in the fifth or sixth month. The first hairs, called *lanugo,* are fine, soft, and downy. The skin at

the fifth and sixth month is quite red because the many small blood vessels below its surface show through. Beginning in the seventh month, however, layers of fat build up beneath the skin, so that the baby develops the characteristic chubby pinkness.

Beside further maturation of the internal organ systems during the second trimester, there is a substantial increase in the size of the fetus. At the end of the third month the fetus weighs about one ounce and is only about three inches long. By the end of the sixth month it weighs about two pounds and is about fourteen inches long. By this time the eyes can open, and the fetus moves its arms and legs sponta-

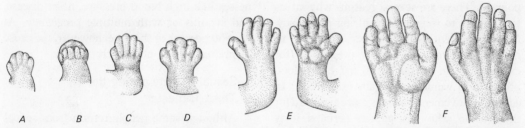

Figure 5.14. Stages in early development of the hand. (*A*) Anterior limb bud of an embryo 12 millimeters long; (*B*) anterior limb bud of an embryo 15 millimeters long; (*C*) anterior limb bud of an embryo 17 millimeters long; (*D*) hand and forearm of an embryo 20 millimeters long; (*E*) two views of the hand and forearm of an embryo 25 millimeters long; (*F*) two views of the hand of a fetus 52 millimeters long. After Retzius, from Scammon, in Morris, *Human Anatomy.* From B. M. Patten, *Human Embryology,* 3rd ed., p. 148. Copyright © 1968 by McGraw-Hill, Inc. Used with the permission of McGraw-Hill Book Company.

neously and vigorously. If delivered at the end of six months, the fetus usually survives for a few hours to a few days. With heroic efforts, 5 to 10 percent of babies weighing about two pounds (800 to 1,000 grams) survive. The smallest infant known to have survived weighed less than one pound at birth (it weighed 400 grams; 1 pound = 455 grams). The fetus was estimated to be twenty weeks old at the time of delivery.

The Third Trimester

Experiences of the Mother

During the last three months of pregnancy the expectant mother becomes more acutely aware of the child that she carries within her swelling abdomen (see Figure 5.15). The fetus becomes quite active, and its seemingly perpetual kicking, tossing, and turning may keep the mother awake at night. Weight, if not controlled up to this point, may become a problem, as the woman realizes that she has already gained her "quota" and still has three months to go. Often working against her is an increased appetite that is partly caused by the hormonal changes of pregnancy. Most physicians set an ideal of about twenty pounds weight gain for a full-term pregnancy. The average infant at nine months weighs only about 7.5

pounds. The rest of the weight gain is accounted for by the placenta (about one pound), the amniotic fluid in the uterine cavity (two pounds), the enlargement of the uterus (two pounds), enlargement of the breasts (about 1.5 pounds), and retained fluid and fat accumulated by the mother (the remaining six or more

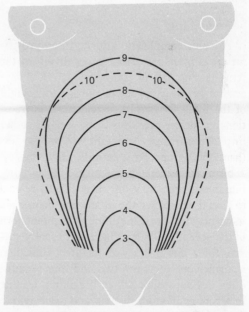

Figure 5.15. Relative height of the top of the uterus at the various months of pregnancy. From Eastman and Hellman, *Williams Obstetrics,* 13th ed. (New York: Appleton-Century-Crofts, 1966), p. 263. Reprinted by permission.

pounds). There are several reasons why attention is paid to weight gain during pregnancy. Most important is the higher incidence of medical complications during pregnancy (for example, strain on the heart and high blood pressure) in women who gain excessively. In addition, movement becomes more awkward for the woman who has gained perhaps forty pounds, and she tires more easily. Finally, probably more good figures have been permanently ruined by excess fat acquired during pregnancy and never lost than from any other single cause!

By the ninth month of pregnancy a woman is usually anxious to "have it over with" and to "see what it is." There is speculation about the sex of the child, prospective names are considered, and the nursery is made ready. As the delivery date approaches, a woman may also become anxious about whether or not the baby is going to be "all right"—healthy and without congenital defects.

Prematurity

A major complication during the third trimester is premature labor and delivery of the fetus. As the date of conception is not always accurately estimated and as the age and weight of the fetus are highly correlated, it is traditional to define prematurity by weight, rather than estimated age. An infant who weighs less than 2,500 grams (five pounds, eight ounces) at birth is considered premature. The mortality rate among premature infants is directly related to size: The smaller the infant, the poorer are its chances for survival. Although an infant born in the seventh month or later can usually survive for a few hours without great difficulty, a smaller one (between two and four pounds) often develops difficulty in breathing, leading to severe respiratory distress and death within forty-eight hours.

It is estimated that about 7 percent of births in the United States are premature. Prematurity may be associated with various maternal illnesses like high blood pressure, heart disease, and syphilis or with multiple pregnancy. At least 50 percent of the time, however, the cause of prematurity is not clearly known.

Sexual Activity during the Third Trimester

Although some people refrain from sexual activity during the third trimester because they are afraid of causing premature labor, there is no medical evidence to support this fear, provided that the woman is in good health. It is true that orgasm is accompanied by rather strong contractions of the uterus during the third trimester, but they do not ordinarily induce labor. Late in the third trimester the uterus may go into spasm for as long as a minute following orgasm, but this experience is not painful (though it may be reported as an "odd sensation").

There is no question that sexual activity tends to decrease during the third trimester, and there are several obvious reasons why. Some physicians advise their patients not to have intercourse at all during the third trimester, and almost all advise total abstinence during the last four to six weeks of pregnancy, primarily in order to avoid infecting the fetus.

Regardless of physicians' advice, many women are uncomfortable during late pregnancy, and symptoms like backache and fatigue tend to diminish their sexual interest. They frequently report, however, that they are surprised at their sexual responsiveness when they are approached by their husbands during this period.

Some couples practice intracrural (between the thighs) intercourse or mutual masturbation during the last month of pregnancy.

Final Development of the Fetus

The third trimester is a period of growth and maturation for the fetus, which by now has developed all the essential organ systems. By the end of the seventh month the fetus is about sixteen inches long and weighs about three pounds, twelve ounces. If delivered at this time, the baby has about a 50 percent chance for survival.

At the same time the fetus has usually assumed a head-down position in the mother's uterus. This position, called *cephalic presentation* (since the head appears at the cervix first during delivery), is the most common position for delivery and presents the fewest complications. During the seventh month, however, about twelve percent of fetuses are still upright in the mothers' uteruses (the so-called *breech presentation*), and a few are oriented with the long axis in a transverse position (called *shoulder presentation*). In addition to the baby's small size and immaturity, there is thus the added risk of a more complicated breech delivery early in the third trimester. At full term (nine months) only about 3 percent of babies are still in the breech position.

By the end of the eighth month the fetus is about eighteen inches long and weighs about five pounds, four ounces. If delivered at this time, it has a 90–95 percent chance of survival.

During the ninth month the fetus gains more than two pounds, and essential organs like the lungs reach a state of maturity compatible with life in the outside world. In addition, less crucial details like hair and fingernails assume a normal appearance and may even grow to such lengths as to require trimming shortly after delivery. At full term the average baby weighs 7.5 pounds and is 20 inches long.[11] Ninety-nine percent of full-term babies born alive in the United States survive, a figure that could be improved even further if all expectant mothers and newborn babies received proper medical care.

---

[11] There is great variation in birth weights, however, ranging usually from five to nine pounds. Weights of ten or eleven pounds are not uncommon, and the largest baby known to have survived weighed 15.5 pounds at birth. Stillborn babies as heavy as twenty-five pounds have been delivered.

CHILDBIRTH

As the end of pregnancy approaches, the expectant mother experiences contractions of her uterus at irregular intervals; the woman who has not delivered previously may rush to the hospital in the middle of the night, only to be sent home because she is experiencing *false labor*. The mechanism that finally initiates labor is unknown.

Three or four weeks before delivery the fetus "drops" (see Figure 5.16) to a lower position in the abdomen. The next major step in preparation for delivery is the softening and dilation of the cervix. The mother may be unaware of this process, but usually just before labor begins there is a small, slightly bloody discharge (*bloody show*) which represents the plug of mucus that has been occluding the cervix. In about 10 percent of pregnant women, however, the membranes encapsulating the fetus burst (*premature rupture of the membranes*), and there is a gush of amniotic fluid down the woman's legs. Usually labor begins within twenty-four

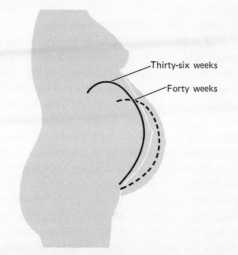

Thirty-six weeks

Forty weeks

Figure 5.16. Height of the uterus at various weeks during late pregnancy. From Benson, *Handbook of Obstetrics and Gynecology,* 3rd ed. (Los Altos, Calif.: Lange Medical Publications, 1968), p. 48. Reprinted by permission.

hours after such a rupture, but if it does not there is risk of infection, and the mother must be hospitalized for observation. (While intact, the fetal membranes serve as a barrier to infection.)

Labor

True labor begins with regular uterine contractions ("pains"), which dilate the cervix. Labor is divided into three stages, the first of which is the longest, extending from the first regular contractions until the cervix is completely dilated (about ten centimeters in diameter). This stage lasts about fifteen hours in the first pregnancy and about eight hours in later ones. (Deliveries after the first are generally easier in all respects.) Uterine contractions begin at intervals as far apart as fifteen or twenty minutes, but they occur more frequently and with greater intensity and regularity as time passes. When the contractions are coming regularly four or five minutes apart the woman usually goes to the hospital, where she is admitted to a labor room (essentially a regular hospital room) for the remainder of the first stage. Her husband is usually allowed to remain with her during this time.

The second stage begins when the cervix is completely dilated and ends with delivery of the baby (see Figures 5.17 and 5.18). The woman is taken to a delivery room (similar to a surgical operating room), and the husband may or may not be allowed to be present, depending upon the laws of the state, hospital regulations, the discretion of the physician, and the wishes of the couple. The second stage may last from a few minutes to a few hours. If any anesthetic is used, it is usually given before this stage begins. General anesthesia for childbirth is becoming less popular. Its disadvantages include all the risks to the mother that general anesthesia entails under any circumstances plus a slowing effect upon labor and depression of the infant's activity (particularly respiration).

Caudal or spinal anesthetic is currently very popular. The anesthetic is inserted by needle into the spinal canal, producing temporary loss of sensation (and paralysis) below the waist only. Advantages include the mother's awareness through delivery and the infant's freedom from anesthetic effects.

In the third stage the placenta separates from the uterine wall and is discharged as the *afterbirth* (placenta and fetal membranes). The uterus contracts to a significantly smaller size during this stage, and there is variable bleeding. The third stage of labor lasts about an hour, during which time the physician examines the mother and baby carefully, and sews up any tears of the *perineum*[12] that may have occurred (or the episiotomy incision if there has been one; an episiotomy is a simple incision in the perineum to facilitate passage of the baby's head). These "stitches" may cause itching and discomfort for several days after delivery, but they usually heal readily without complications.

Cesarean Section. Occasionally, as when the baby is too large (or the woman's pelvis is too small) to accommodate vaginal delivery, a cesarean section is performed. In this operation the baby is removed from the uterus through an incision in the abdominal and uterine walls. About 5 percent of deliveries in the United States are by cesarean section. With modern surgical techniques, the incidence of complications in this kind of delivery is no greater than that in vaginal delivery. It is not necessarily true that a woman who has had one cesarean section must have all her later children by this method: A cesarean delivery may be followed by normal vaginal deliveries. On the other hand, it is possible also to have several children by cesarean section, despite the common notion that a woman can endure only one such operation. The recovery period is somewhat longer after a cesarean section, and hospitalization usually lasts seven to ten days.

---

[12] The *perineum* is the skin and deeper tissues between the vaginal and anal orifices.

(It is unlikely that Julius Caesar, for whom this operation was named, was actually delivered by cesarean section. Although it is known that the operation was performed in ancient times among both civilized and primitive peoples, it was almost always performed after the mother had died, in hopes of saving the baby. Caesar's mother lived for many years after his birth. Cesarean section was definitely being performed on living women in the seventeenth century, but the operation at that time involved *removing* the uterus with the baby still inside and then sewing up the abdomen. The current practice of removing only the baby and leaving the uterus in place dates from 1882.)

Natural Childbirth

The term "natural childbirth" was coined by the English physician Grantly Dick-Read in 1932. During the Victorian era the use of anesthetics like chloroform had come into vogue as a means of relieving the pains of labor and delivery.[13] Dick-Read postulated that the pain of childbirth is primarily related to fear and subsequent muscular tension during labor. Very briefly his method of "natural childbirth" involves eliminating fear through education about the birth process before delivery, in order to break the cycle of fear, tension, and pain. The method is best described in his book *Childbirth without Fear.*

A second type of "natural childbirth" originated in Russia but was popularized by the French physician Bernard Lamaze. The "Lamaze method" is based on Pavlov's description of conditioned-reflex responses and is sometimes called the "psychoprophylactic method" of childbirth.[14] It involves conditioning the pregnant woman mentally to dissociate uterine contractions from the experience of pain, through repeated reinforcement of the notion that such contractions are not painful.

[13] Queen Victoria, in fact, was delivered of her eighth child while under chloroform anesthesia, thus adding to its popularity in England.

[14] Chertok (1967), pp. 698–699.

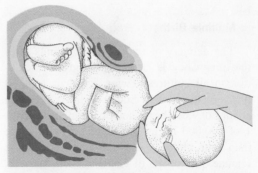

Figure 5.17. Gentle traction to bring about descent of anterior shoulder. From Eastman and Hellman, *Williams Obstetrics,* 13th ed. (New York: Appleton-Century-Crofts, 1966), p. 423. Reprinted by permission.

Prescribed exercises requiring voluntary relaxation of the abdominal muscles are also part of the program. After having been successfully conditioned to experience uterine contractions without reflex muscular contractions and pain, a woman may have a relaxed and painless delivery.

The term "natural childbirth" is unfortunate, for it implies that any other method of childbirth is "unnatural" and therefore "wrong." Many women and children are alive today, however, only thanks to the use of such "unnatural" techniques as forceps delivery and cesarean section.

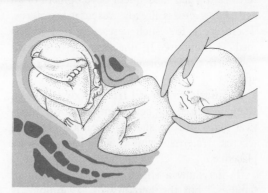

Figure 5.18. Delivery of anterior shoulder completed; gentle traction to deliver posterior shoulder. From Eastman and Hellman, *Williams Obstetrics,* 13th ed. (New York: Appleton-Century-Crofts, 1966), p. 423. Reprinted by permission.

Multiple Births

The delivery of two or more infants after one pregnancy is an event of great fascination in all cultures. Twins occur in 1 of 90 births in the United States. Triplets occur in about 1 of 9,000 births and quadruplets in about 1 of 500,000 births. Multiple births of more than four children are extremely rare. The Dionne quintuplets of Canada, born May 28, 1934, were the first quintuplets known to survive. All five were girls, and they weighed a total of thirteen pounds, six ounces at birth. Because of their small sizes and usually premature delivery, the mortality rate among infants in a multiple birth is significantly higher than otherwise. Twins are born an average of twenty-two days before the EDC. Their mortality rate is two to three times that of single births.

There are two types of twins, identical and fraternal. Two of three sets of twins are fraternal, developed from two separate eggs fertilized simultaneously. It is apparently biologically possible for twins to have different fathers. This phenomenon is called *superfecundation* and has been clearly documented in animal studies. Another bizarre occurrence is *superfetation,* the fertilization and subsequent development of an egg when a fetus is already present in the uterus. There are a few such cases reported in the medical literature. In one instance, a woman gave birth to two normal children three months apart.

Identical twins result from subdivision of a single fertilized egg before implantation. Identical twins usually share a common placenta, whereas fraternal twins usually have separate placentas.

Twins show a slight tendency to "run in families," but the heredity of "twinning" is rather vague. Fraternal twins are more likely to reoccur than are identical twins.

The Postpartum Period

A woman nowadays usually leaves the hospital three or four days after an uncomplicated delivery, though the length of the stay varies somewhat from place to place. With a first baby the first week home may be a bit of a turmoil for the young mother, who is trying to cope simultaneously with the needs of the baby (feeding, bathing, changing diapers) and the calls of many well-meaning friends and relatives anxious to see "the new addition." Fatigue may be a major complaint at this point, along with a general "letdown" feeling.

About two-thirds of all women experience transient episodes of sadness and crying some time during the first ten days after delivery, a phenomenon known as the "postpartum blues" syndrome. Women (and their families) are often puzzled by this reaction, for it comes when they are expected to be especially happy and celebrating the arrival of the new child. Doubts about their competence as mothers, fatigue, feelings of rejection or neglect by their husbands, and the drastic hormone changes that occur at this time are some factors involved.[15]

Resumption of Ovulation and Menstruation

There is wide variation in timing of the resumption of normal menstrual cycles after delivery. For about four weeks the woman has a bloody vaginal discharge called *lochia* (from Greek *lokhios,* "pertaining to childbirth"). One or two months later a mother who is not nursing may have a menstrual period. If she is nursing, however, her periods may not resume for as long as eighteen months, although five months is more common. The first few periods after pregnancy may be somewhat irregular in length

---

[15]Yalom *et al.* (1968).

and flow, but women who have had painful periods before pregnancy often find that they suffer no such discomfort after childbirth.

It should be emphasized that ovulation occurs *before* the first postpartum menstrual cycle and that consequently a woman can become pregnant without having a menstrual period after the birth of her baby. It should also be noted that women can conceive while nursing. The notion that nursing is "nature's method of contraception" is false.

Sexual Activity

There is considerable variation in patterns of sexual activity after delivery. Fatigue, physical discomfort, and the obstetrician's injunctions play an important part in determining when a woman resumes sexual relations after childbirth. Although doctors commonly advise women to refrain from intercourse for six weeks after delivery, there is no medical reason why a healthy woman cannot have vaginal intercourse as soon as the episiotomy or any lacerations of the perineum have healed and the flow of lochia has ended. The only medical concern is the possibility of infection through the vagina. Couples who practice intracrural intercourse, manual manipulation of the genitals to orgasm, or sexual activity other than vaginal intercourse early in the postpartum period are not hampered by this concern.

Studies have shown that a certain percentage of men feel driven to extramarital sexual affairs during the period of abstinence "six weeks before and six weeks after" that is rigidly adhered to by some women. That this explanation is a rationalization is certainly possible, because the imaginative couple that considers regular sexual activity desirable can certainly find satisfying forms of gratification during periods when vaginal intercourse is inadvisable.

It is interesting to note that women who nurse their babies tend to report greater postpartum sexual interest than do women who do not. Some women relate this interest directly to sexual stimulation produced by the suckling of the child, and a few actually experience orgasm while nursing their babies. Feelings of guilt at this experience are also expressed by some mothers, who consequently resume sexual activity with their husbands as soon as possible in order to allay their fears that they are indulging in some form of sexual perversion.

PREGNANCY AND CHILDBIRTH IN OTHER SOCIETIES

Primitive people have developed various beliefs and practices in connection with pregnancy and childbirth. Many tribes believed that the fetus developed from a combination of male semen and menstrual blood. The Venda tribe of East Africa believed that "red elements" like muscle and blood were derived from the mother's menses (which ceased during pregnancy because the menstrual blood was being absorbed by the developing fetus). The "white elements" like skin, bone, and nerves were believed to develop from the father's semen.

Some societies imposed dietary restrictions upon pregnant women, often from fear that the fetus might otherwise take on undesirable characteristics of food plants or animals. For example, if the mother ate rabbit, the child might have weak legs, if she ate trout, he might exhibit characteristic quivering movements. In addition, Ashanti women were forbidden to look upon any deformed object or creature during pregnancy lest their children be born with similar deformities.

The majority of primitive tribes that have been studied prohibited sexual intercourse during the last month of pregnancy on the grounds that it might kill the child or cause premature delivery, an interesting observation, considering the similar concern in modern societies and the absence so far of substantial medical evidence for or against this belief.

Abortions were performed in some primitive societies, particularly if the women were unmarried or pregnant as the result of adultery. Usually the fetuses were killed *in utero* by violent beating upon the abdomen, and this was followed by mechanical extraction of the fetus or spontaneous stillbirth.

Contrary to popular opinion, childbirth was not considered a routine and painless event by most primitive peoples. Among many tribes elaborate dietary and exercise regimens were practiced to prevent painful and difficult deliveries. Various rituals might be performed to ensure easy delivery, and particular attention was paid to confession of sexual indiscretions at this time, for difficult deliveries were often attributed to violations of the tribal sexual codes.

Childbirth usually took place with the woman in a sitting or squatting position. Assistants were almost always present, usually older women designated as tribal midwives. Men were usually excluded from such scenes, though they might be assigned some rituals or tasks to perform away from the places where the births were taking place.

The placenta was almost always viewed as a potentially dangerous object and was carefully disposed of, usually by burying in a special place. There was also usually a taboo on sexual intercourse for several weeks or more after delivery, another striking similarity to taboos in modern societies.

Deformed babies and multiple births were viewed with alarm in most primitive societies. Twins, triplets, and babies with congenital deformities were usually killed at birth. Twins were often believed to result from adultery or impregnation by an evil spirit. A more benign explanation was offered by the Kiwai tribesmen of New Guinea, who believed that a woman would give birth to twins if she ate bananas from a tree with two bunches!

For the first time in the history of man, it is now possible to regulate conception reliably, and on the success of such regulation the future of mankind may hinge. Contraceptive practice goes back to remote antiquity. The oldest surviving documents on the subject come from Egypt in 1900–1100 B.C. A sample prescription calls for pulverized crocodile dung in fermented mucilage, combined with honey and sodium carbonate, to be applied to the vulva.[1] The practice of coitus interruptus is mentioned in *Genesis* 38:8-9, as well as in the Talmud. Absorbent materials, root and herb potions, pessaries, and more permanent means of sterilization were used by the Greeks and Romans and have been used subsequently by many peoples around the world.

Although it is interesting to explore and speculate about the predominant motivations for such measures in ancient and foreign cultures, there is no evidence that before modern times there was a concerted effort on the part of any society to limit population as a matter of general policy. The historical incentives for birth control were usually personal or idiosyncratic: Slaves, harlots, and illicit lovers tried to avoid pregnancy, and other people sought to regulate the sizes of their families for various reasons. Such personal incentives continue to be important, but there is now mounting concern that entire nations and even humanity as a whole must urgently check galloping population expansion.

The alarm was first sounded by the English economist and sociologist Thomas Robert Malthus (1766–1834). His thesis was simply that, given the geometrical increase of populations and the arithmetical increase of the means of subsistence, poverty and hunger are unavoidable unless war, famine, and disease take their toll time and again. Although Malthus' original predictions have not yet been borne out, the specter of disaster continues to loom before us.

Malthus' warning spurred the beginnings of the birth-control movement in England. During the past century this movement has picked up great momentum. Two of its outstanding leaders have been women: Marie Stopes in England and Margaret Sanger in the United States. In 1958 the Lambeth Conference of Bishops of the Church of England vigorously endorsed the use of contraceptives to control family size. In the United States similar action was taken in 1961 by the National Council of Churches, representing many Protestant denominations. The Roman Catholic Church has, on moral and

---

[1] Noonan (1967), p. 23.

CONTRACEPTION

doctrinal grounds, remained rather firm in its opposition to birth control by any means other than abstinence during periods of fertility.

ARGUMENTS FOR AND AGAINST BIRTH CONTROL

Contraception remains a controversial issue. Opposition to birth-control programs, though weakening gradually, is still formidable in many parts of the world. Although somewhat outside our immediate areas of concern, the urgent nature of these problems requires that we deal with some of the more cogent arguments for and against the use of contraceptives (see also Chapter 17). The various incentives or imperatives for separating sexual from reproductive functions can be subsumed under three headings.

Prevention of Illness and Deformity

Certain hereditary illnesses (like hemophilia) and certain deformities in one or both parents or in close relatives may make it likely that children will also be ill or deformed. A healthy mother may be in danger of giving birth to a deformed child if she has been ill during pregnancy (for example, with German measles) or has taken certain drugs (like thalidomide). In such instances should pregnancy be avoided or terminated?

Some people will argue for and others against this solution, yet all will argue from moral principles. According to one argument, man has no right to tamper with nature. He should neither interfere with conception nor artificially terminate pregnancy under any circumstance. On the other hand, some people argue that to permit the birth of a child into certain misery and to allow him to burden his family and society are immoral.

When serious genetic defects are present medical opinion tends to favor contraception, abortion, or even sterilization. Yet in less certain and therefore more controversial instances, like mental retardation, medical opinion is more divided. "Genetic counseling" is an important medical obligation, but it can also be perverted into a vicious political and racist weapon.[2]

Preventing Unwanted Pregnancies

The overwhelming majority of people who currently use contraceptives do so for personal and private reasons: avoiding pregnancy out of wedlock, postponing pregnancy for economic and psychological reasons (as when the future of a marriage is uncertain), limiting family size because of economic, health, and other considerations.

Moral judgments in these matters vary widely. Although some people do not use contraceptives under any circumstances, most people approve their use for certain purposes: "Their use is legitimate if a woman's life will be otherwise endangered by pregnancy"; "Married people may use them"; "People about to be married may use them"; "All adults may use them."

The use of contraceptives is becoming progressively more legitimate, despite opposition. If moral considerations were not involved, the realistic approach would be to prescribe contraceptives to the entire postpubertal population upon demand. The common fear is, of course, that dispensing information and contraceptive devices tacitly encourages youngsters to engage in intercourse. Increasing numbers of adolescent pregnancies seem to indicate, however, that lack of contraceptive knowledge

---

[2] For instance, sickle-cell anemia is an incurable, and often fatal, hereditary disease of the blood which occurs almost exclusively in black people. The racial implications of counseling people with this disease not to have children is obvious, as is the medical dilemma of knowingly perpetuating the illness.

or of the willingness to use it are not discouraging many teen-agers from engaging in sex.

There are, on the other hand, countless educated and financially secure adults who become pregnant only unintentionally or for questionable reasons: to perpetuate family names, to please the grandparents, to bolster failing relationships, to "tie a man down," to force partners into marriage, to conform socially, and so on.

The true motivations for having children are often rationalized or unconscious. Parents often view children as extensions of themselves. Through his children a parent may seek to gratify his own unfulfilled childhood needs, to replay early dramas and this time to come out the "winner." A parent may regard his offspring as means to fill his own inner void, to give meaning to his life, and to consolidate his faltering sense of self-worth. Pregnancy may result from conscious or unconscious hostility, as an aggressive or punitive act against the sexual partner who does not want parenthood.

A surprising number of sophisticated unmarried young men and women risk unwanted pregnancies because taking contraceptive measures implies forethought. They feel that such precautions rob sex of its spontaneity and turn it into a calculated and dehumanizing activity. Such "refined" considerations frequently, however, conceal confusion and guilt about premarital sex. Consider, for instance, a couple in college. They are fond of each other and would like to have intercourse, but one or the other feels that they should not. They engage in progressively heavy petting, which ultimately does culminate in intercourse without contraceptives. Although stricken with remorse, they try to alleviate their guilt by claiming that they did not plan intercourse, that they could not help it. (Occasionally alcohol is used as the scapegoat in these encounters.) Premarital sex has definite moral implications that must be faced. A person may decide for

or against it for a variety of reasons, but the difficult decision-making process cannot be evaded without risks to both parties involved.

Alleviating Population Pressure

There is a great deal of discussion and considerable confusion these days about the consequences of unchecked population growth in the world; there are also disagreements about how to resolve the problem. On one hand, some experts, usually demographers and agronomists, are relatively confident that food resources will expand sufficiently to keep up with demand, at least for the rest of this century. Their confidence rests on the success of the "green revolution": the recent increase in production of certain foodstuffs (mostly wheat and rice) through the use of new strains that have, in some instances, trebled ordinary yields per acre.

Other experts, mainly biologists, are more alarmed. They view the problem in almost apocalyptic terms. They point out that we need not wait for famines in the distant future. They are with us now, for an estimated 10 to 20 million people die each year from nutritional deficiencies. While acknowledging the spectacular gains in agricultural science, they seriously question that food production can keep pace with population, given the facts that most arable land is already in use and that there are serious difficulties in storing foodstuffs and transporting them to distant, less fertile countries or to areas within the same country.

Even though these disagreements occasionally become acrimonious and bewildering to laymen, the areas of agreement among these experts far outweigh their differences. No one who knows anything about the problem would, for example, deny that mankind will face a serious threat should population growth continue unchecked.

The facts and figures speak for themselves. From the dim beginnings of mankind, it took until 1830 for the population of the world to reach 1 billion. This figure was doubled within the next 100 years. By 1975 it is expected to have doubled again, reaching 4 billion. It will then take only another twenty-five years for the world's population to reach a staggering 6–8 billion people.[3]

Additional statistics pile up with numbing effects. About 40 percent of the population in "developing" countries, for instance, is less than fifteen years old. The repercussions of this fact can be ominous. Wealthy industrialized countries are generally expanding less rapidly and will be able to meet their own nutritional needs for the foreseeable future. Yet we can take little comfort in this fact, for even a wealthy nation like the United States has poverty and hunger in its midst. Also these richer nations tend to use disproportionate amounts of the world's resources. These considerations are relevant, for the problem of population cannot be considered in isolation from general ecological concerns. It is clear that consumption and pollution are related to affluence, as well as to simple population density.

What should be done? There are now hundreds of international, national, state, private philanthropic, and voluntary organizations grappling with various aspects of these problems. The consensus is that the battle is not being won. Predictions for the future range from muted concern to paralyzing gloom. Failure to meet this challenge so far can be attributed to a complex of causes.

First, experts claim that not enough is being done in areas in which some success has already been shown: voluntary family-planning programs, for instance. Second, a definition of ideal family size as four, rather than five or more, and the willingness to accept restrictions are still not common. Children might have to be limited to an average of two per family if population growth is to be stabilized. Increasing numbers of parents—though still far too few—are willing to limit themselves to two. Some are even willing to forego the privilege of biological parenthood in favor of adoption. As our psychological and social needs for children are deeply rooted, changing both individual and social attitudes is an overwhelming task.[4]

Third, from various quarters come conscious and determined objections to birth-control programs and practices, for a variety of reasons. The Roman Catholic Church opposes them on doctrinal and moral grounds. Minority groups and developing nations perceive such programs as excuses for perpetuation of racist and imperialistic dominance by the current world powers. Some political radicals view population control as counter-revolutionary. Although many people may agree in principle that there is need for population control, the majority clearly think that *other* people should practice it.

That we are failing to slow the population tide is conceded by most informed people. Proposals that go beyond the voluntary use of contraceptives are being offered, but many are unacceptable to most people or unrealistic. Proposals for widespread abstinence from sex are one example, for feeding nations with nutritious but unpalatable food substances are another, for colonizing other planets are a third.

There are other impractical solutions. It is estimated, for instance, that to sterilize the 40

---

[3] Although the issue of overpopulation is usually expressed in global terms, the problem is, of course, more localized both at present and in future potentials. For example, whereas the "doubling time" for the population of Brazil is 22 years and for that of El Salvador 19 years, it will take Denmark 88 years and Australia 175 years to double their populations at their current growth rates. The problem in Australia, in fact, is seen as underpopulation, rather than overpopulation.

---

[4] See Pohlman (1968).

million males in India who already have three or more children would require 100,000 surgically trained personnel each performing twenty vasectomies a day five days a week for about eight years. Meanwhile, of course, there would be a steady supply of new candidates.

Many alternatives besides enforced family planning have been proposed. They include extensions of voluntary fertility controls (liberalizing abortion laws), intensified educational campaigns, incentive programs, tax and welfare benefits and penalties, shifts in social and economic institutions (like providing women with acceptable alternatives to motherhood), and augmented political action and research efforts to find still other solutions.[5] Finally, there are schemes for public control, which range from the merely fantastic (addition by the state of mass fertility-control agents to the water supply) to the frightening (compulsory sterilization).

Population growth is rather like cell growth. While an organism is young, life depends upon rapid and relentless cell multiplication. As it reaches maturity, this process slows. What is needed from then on is basically replacement of old and dying cells with new cells. When there is an injury, cell multiplication accelerates to compensate for the damage. The organism thus maintains life without perpetually growing. Only in pathological conditions does cell multiplication exceed replacement needs. When the process gets out of hand, we have cancer. An individual cell of this dreaded illness may be nothing more than an exuberantly dividing, otherwise normal cell. But, as division occurs at the wrong time and at the wrong rate, the cells invade and interfere with the other functions of the body and the person dies.

Similarly, when the human race was young, survival depended upon successful propagation.

When mankind suffered massive losses, it was essential to "replace" the dead. But, now that we are crowding the usable portions of the earth, unchecked growth spells doom. For those of us who cherish children, the imperative of contraception is a bitter pill indeed. For those with moral and religious reservations, it is a source of endless agonizing.

As an example of how the times have changed, consider the following. Wolfgang Amadeus Mozart was one of seven children, five of whom died within six months of birth. He himself fathered six children, only two of whom lived past six months. He died at the age of thirty-five years and ten months, from a cause unknown to the medical profession of his time. These facts of his life are typical of most of human history, but not of the present.[6] There is now a great need for safer, more reliable means of contraception, a particularly poignant need, considering that as many as 75 percent of the babies born in this country may be either unwanted or unplanned. This figure is based on interviews of all pregnant women who came to a university medical center obstetrics clinic during a one-month period.

Only one-fourth of the women interviewed reported that their pregnancies had been planned and that both parents of each couple looked forward to the baby's arrival. The remaining three-fourths fell into three groups of about equal size, according to whether their "rejection" was rated severe, moderate, or mild.

A woman considered to show "severe rejection of pregnancy" would be extremely agitated and upset about being pregnant and would state unequivocally her objections to having a child. She would generally either have practiced a "reliable" contraceptive method that had failed or would volunteer the information that she had attempted to have an illegal abortion or would have had an

[5]Berelson (1969).

[6]Thomlinson (1967).

abortion had it been legal. (This study was conducted in California one year before the abortion law was liberalized.)

Women in the category of "moderate rejection of pregnancy" expressed ambivalence about their pregnancies but gave very firm reasons for not wishing children. They also had generally been using contraceptive methods that had failed them. Women in the category of "mild rejection of pregnancy" were unhappy about being pregnant at that particular time, though they declared previous plans to have children at some later date. The women were often using methods of contraception that they knew to be somewhat unreliable, for example, the rhythm method. In summary, although varying degrees of regret over pregnancy were revealed in this study, only 25 percent of the sample definitely wanted the children that they were about to deliver.[7]

CONTRACEPTIVE METHODS

The Pill

History

Observations in the early twentieth century led to recognition that ovulation does not occur during the luteal phase of the menstrual cycle (see Chapter 4) or during pregnancy. At those times the levels of the hormone progesterone are elevated, because of increased secretion by the corpus luteum in the latter part of the menstrual cycle and in the first trimester of pregnancy and by the placenta during the remainder of pregnancy (see Chapter 5). Progesterone was isolated and purified in the laboratory in 1934, and administration to rabbits was shown to inhibit ovulation and to prevent pregnancy. Estrogen was isolated chemically at about the same time as was progesterone and by 1940 was being used clinically

in the treatment of certain menstrual disorders. It was observed that both progesterone and estrogen separately or in combination could inhibit ovulation by suppressing the release of gonadotrophic hormones (FSH, LH) from the pituitary gland (see Chapter 4). But various unacceptable side effects (particularly "breakthrough bleeding" during the menstrual cycle) were associated with the use of the natural hormones on a regular basis. Rather large doses of progesterone were required to inhibit ovulation, and the effects were not entirely predictable.

In 1954, however, Carl Djerassi succeeded in synthesizing in the laboratory a group of steroid chemicals called *progestagens*. The term is derived from the word "gestation" and refers to the ability of these compounds to induce "pseudopregnancy" in females: certain changes in the lining of the uterus (endometrium) and elsewhere in the reproductive organs that are similar to those in pregnancy. These synthetic compounds were found to be far more potent than are natural hormones, and consequently much smaller doses could be used. Gregory Pincus (recognized by many as the "father of the Pill") and coworkers J. Rock and C. R. Garcia began testing about 200 of these new compounds on animals. Several were found to be particularly effective as antifertility agents, and the first large-scale field trials on human beings of a contraceptive pill were initiated by Pincus and his colleagues in San Juan, Puerto Rico, in 1956. The chemical compound that they used in this first pill was norethynodrel (to be known later under the trade name Enovid). The drug was highly successful in these initial trials, and within a few years the era of "the Pill" had clearly begun.

Effects

Although it is assumed that the primary mechanism preventing pregnancy through pills is the inhibition of ovulation, it is not entirely

---

[7] Yalom *et al.* (1968), p. 18.

clear whether or not such inhibition is the only factor. The only certain way to determine whether or not a woman has ovulated is direct visual examination of the ovaries and fallopian tubes through a microscope.[8] This procedure requires major surgery, but relevant observations can be made during a hysterectomy (surgical removal of the uterus). If an egg were found in the fallopian tube of a woman taking the Pill, it would argue against assuming inhibition of ovulation. But, if an egg were not found—and none has been thus far—its absence would not prove that the woman had not ovulated earlier in her cycle (or would not have ovulated later).

Pituitary Gland. Most contraceptive pills contain combinations of synthetic compounds resembling progesterone and small amounts of synthetic estrogen. Studies of animals and humans have shown that the progestagens tend to inhibit pituitary secretion of LH and that the estrogenic compounds tend to inhibit pituitary secretion of FSH. It will be recalled that these two pituitary hormones are essential to ovulation (see Chapter 4).

Ovaries. There is some evidence that the Pill has a direct effect upon the ovarian follicles by preventing maturation of the ova. On the other hand, studies of animals receiving the Pill have shown that ovulation can be induced by administering exogenous FSH and LH, supporting the notion that the ovaries are still responsive to pituitary hormones.

Fallopian Tubes. Fertilization normally occurs in the fallopian tube, as described in Chapter 5. There is evidence that in animals progesterone and estrogenic compounds influence motility of eggs within the tube by interfering with both muscular contractions and mucous secretion. It is also possible that the Pill increases the rate at which the egg travels to the uterus, causing it to arrive before it is sufficiently mature or before the lining of the uterus is ready.

Uterus and Cervix. A delicate balance of progesterone and estrogen is necessary for the endometrium to develop in such a manner as to be receptive to implantation. Changes in the endometrium have been observed in women taking contraceptive pills and may contribute to infertility. In addition, the character of the cervical mucus is definitely altered by the pill (for example, it is thicker and has a different pH) and may act as a barrier to penetration of the uterus by the sperm.

Types of Pills and Their Usage

There are two basic types of birth-control pills now available commercially (with a physician's prescription). The most widely used are mixtures of one of the synthetic progestagens and estrogen compounds. Each pill contains 0.5-10.0 milligrams of the progestagen (depending upon the specific compound used and also upon the manufacturer). A much smaller amount of estrogen is used, varying from 0.075 to 0.15 milligram per pill. These "combination" pills are usually taken for twenty days of the cycle, beginning on the fifth day after the start of menstruation. If the pills are not begun until the sixth day of the cycle, they are still effective, but to wait until the seventh or eighth day is to risk failure.

After twenty days the pills are stopped. "Withdrawal bleeding" (considered by some doctors not to be "true" menstruation because ovulation has presumably not occurred) usually begins three to four days after taking the pills has stopped. The first day of withdrawal bleeding is considered the first day of the next

---

[8] There are, of course, indirect indications like elevation of the basal body temperature (BBT) and of excretion of a progesterone metabolite called "pregnanediol."

cycle, and the pills are resumed on the fifth day. Combination pills have such brand names as *Enovid, Ortho-Novum, Ovulen, Provest,* and *Norinyl.*

The second type of birth-control pill is the "sequential type," with such brand names as *C-Quens, Oracon,* and *Norquen.* Again twenty pills are taken during each cycle on the same schedule described, but the first fifteen pills contain *only* estrogen. The other five pills contain a combination of estrogen and progesterone. The rationale behind this regimen is that it follows more closely the natural sequence of hormonal events during the menstrual cycle: primary estrogen secretion during the first half of the cycle, both estrogen and progesterone secretion during the latter half. While not quite as effective, this type of pill is said to have fewer side effects.

Many new contraceptive pills are coming onto the market, but they differ from older types mainly in the specific proportions of the progestagen and estrogen compounds. The trend has been toward smaller doses of progestagen, in order to reduce side effects. Whereas most early birth-control pills contained 10.0 milligrams of progestagen, later this amount was reduced to 5.0 milligrams and then to 2.5 milligrams by several manufacturers. Some pills now contain as little as 1.0 milligram of progestagen. There appears to be no loss of effectiveness with the lower doses.

Some manufacturers now produce and recommend a 21:7 pill program. The pills are the same as before, but the woman takes twenty-one pills, then stops for seven days, then repeats the series again, regardless of when menstruation begins. The main advantage of this regimen is that the woman always starts taking her pills on the same day of the week. Another way to help a woman to remember is to have her take a pill every day—twenty-one hormone pills followed by seven placebo (inert) pills packaged in such a way as to prevent her from taking the wrong pill on any given day.[9]

The "morning after" pill has been widely publicized but is not yet commercially available. This pill, taken only after a woman has had intercourse, contains a potent synthetic estrogen and is believed to prevent implanation of the egg in the uterus. It is still being tested and has not yet been approved for general use.

Long-acting hormone preparations that would have to be taken only once a month orally or by injection are also being studied and tested. Two problems have so far been encountered: irregular uterine bleeding and an unpredictable interval (as much as several months or more) between cessation of treatment and resumption of normal ovarian functioning and ovulation.

Another subject of research is a pill for men. Studies have already shown that administration of standard (female) birth-control pills to men results in inhibition of spermatogenesis (sperm formation). The mechanism is similar to that presumed in women: suppression of the secretion of pituitary gonadotrophins (essential to sperm formation and maturation). But the administration of female sex hormones to males usually results in distinct decreases in libido after two or three weeks, and this method is therefore rated as unacceptable by most subjects.

Administration of the male sex hormone testosterone also suppresses sperm production by suppressing pituitary functioning. But animal studies have shown that the dose of testos-

---

[9]As there is relatively little difference in composition among most birth-control pills, competitors have tried to improve packaging as a selling point. Some pills come in fancy plastic cases, rather than in paper containers. Some packages have built-in calendars or other "reminders," and some have dispensers indicating the pill to be taken each day by date, which eliminates the worrisome question "Did I take my pill today?"

terone is very critical, for too much of this hormone appears to stimulate sperm production directly, despite suppression of the pituitary. Research in the area of contraceptives for men has lagged far behind comparable work on pills and other devices for women. This lag may partly reflect an attitude (at least among men) that contraception should be women's responsibility (see Chapter 18).

Effectiveness and Side Effects

There is no question that birth-control pills, properly used, are the most effective contraceptive measure available today (short of surgical sterilization). The combination pills, taken as directed, are 100 percent effective in preventing pregnancy by the second month of usage. Effectiveness is slightly less than 100 percent during the first month of usage. The sequential pills are also highly effective, but pregnancies have occurred in women on this regimen, for two reasons. The first is that the sequential pills are not quite as effective in suppressing ovulation as are the combination pills. Estimates based on indirect signs of ovulation show that it still occurs in 2–8 percent of the cycles of women taking sequential pills. This problem could perhaps be resolved by increasing the doses of estrogen in the first fifteen pills. The second reason why sequential pills are less effective is that the endometrium and cervical mucus may be closer to normal, for this regimen follows the normal physiological pattern of the menstrual cycle more closely.

The usual cause of pregnancy in women taking the pill, however, is not the type of pill but failure to take it regularly. Forgetting one pill is usually not significant, provided that the woman takes two the following day. But there is a fair risk of failure if pills are skipped for two days or more.

In countries with low literacy rates there have been problems in educating women in the use of the pill. Following in the "amulet tradition," some women string the pills and wear them as necklaces, hoping to ward off pregnancy in this way. Others cannot see the need for using them except in conjunction with intercourse itself. If their husbands are away for a few days, they may simply put the pills away until the men return. In such countries the pill is obviously not the ideal method of contraception.

In the United States the Pill has had wide acceptance. Whereas only about 400,000 American women were using it in 1961, by 1965 at least 4 million were using it, and by 1970 an estimated 9 million had used it.[10] Reliable data on short-term side effects are available and indicate that such effects are fairly common during the first few months that women take the Pill. The most common complaints are nausea and weight gain. Nausea occurs in about 10 percent of women during the first month of treatment, in about 3 percent during the second month, and very rarely from the third month on. Weight gains occur in 5–25 percent of women, depending upon the particular preparations used. Partly these gains result from greater fluid retention caused by progestagens. They can be countered by drugs (diuretics) or sometimes by switching to different birth-control preparations. Most weight gains, however, are caused by actual accumulation of fat, especially in the thighs and breasts. They occur mainly in the first month of using the Pill and are partly related to increased appetite, not unlike the increased appetite that occurs in pregnancy. The additional pounds gained in the first few months often remain as long as the woman is on the Pill, however. Weight

---

[10] Advisory Committee on Obstetrics and Gynecology (1966), p. 5; Calderone, ed. (1970), p. 288.

gains are most common with high-dosage combination pills and least common with sequential pills.

Breakthrough bleeding, or minor "spotting," while taking birth-control pills is annoying but can often be remedied by switching to a different preparation.

Less common short-term side effects include tenderness of the breasts, headaches, nervousness, depression, alterations in libido patterns, menstrual irregularities, and general malaise. Women with histories of liver disease (e.g., hepatitis) may find the ailments reactivated by the Pill, and they must take it only under strict medical supervision.

Lactation may be somewhat suppressed in a nursing mother who is taking the Pill, and the hormones in the Pill may be transferred to the infant in small amounts through the mother's milk. There is no evidence that contraceptive pills either enhance or decrease subsequent fertility in a woman who has taken them for several years and then stops. Nor is there evidence that chronic use of the pills either hastens or postpones menopause.

Certain beneficial side effects of the pills have led to their prescription when contraception is not the major goal, for example to relieve premenstrual tension and to eliminate irregularity and pain associated with menstrual periods. Some women report a general sense of well-being, as well as increased pleasure in sexual intercourse, while taking the Pill. The latter effect probably results partly from elimination of the fear of unwanted pregnancy.

Blood Clots and the Pill

Large-scale studies seem to indicate that there is a small, though statistically significant, increase in the incidence of blood clotting with subsequent complications, in women who take the Pill. A blood clot (*thrombus*) may, for instance, form in one of the deep veins of the leg in association with a local inflammation (*thrombophlebitis*). The clot may then break loose (as an *embolus*) and travel toward the lungs, where it may occlude a major blood vessel (as a *pulmonary embolus*). The result can be fatal. Women with histories of difficulties with blood clots (*thromboembolic* disease) may be advised not to use contraceptive pills. On the other hand, it should be noted that the incidence of deaths associated with pregnancy and labor is about eighteen times greater than that associated with thromboembolic disease in users of the Pill.

Cancer and the Pill

At present there is no clear evidence that chronic use of birth-control pills either increases or decreases the likelihood that a woman will develop cancer of the cervix, uterus, or breast. Animal studies have shown that long-term administration of large doses of estrogen can induce cancer of the endometrium, but this finding has not been documented in humans. In fact, large doses of estrogens in humans have sometimes had therapeutic effects on cancer of the breast.

A definitive analysis of any possible relation between cancer and the Pill will probably not be available until about 1980, for it is known that a latency period of twenty years or more can occur between exposure to a cancer-stimulating (*carcinogenic*) substance and the onset of the disease.

Intrauterine Devices

History

The use of intrauterine devices was known in ancient Greece and is mentioned in the writings of Hippocrates. Arab camel drivers have been familiar with a variety of this method of contraception for centuries. As it was undesirable for a female camel to be pregnant on a long trip, a round stone was inserted in the uterus of each before a journey across the desert was undertaken. This practice is still employed in the Sudan and Tunisia.

A variety of intrauterine devices for humans was popular during the nineteenth century both for contraception and in the treatment of such gynecological disorders as displacement of the uterus. These devices fell into disrepute in the early twentieth century, but in 1930 the German physician E. Gräfenberg developed a ring of coiled silver wire, of which he inserted duplicates in 600 women for the purpose of contraception. He reported a failure rate of only 1.6 percent. In the next few years, however, several gynecologists published articles condemning the use of intrauterine devices on the grounds that they might lead to serious infection of the pelvic organs. That some of the most vocal critics had had no experience with this method did not lessen their influence, and intrauterine devices again fell into disrepute until 1959. In that year two promising reports were published, one by the Israeli W. Oppenheimer, who had worked with Gräfenberg, and one by the Japanese physician A. Ishihama. Oppenheimer reported having used the Gräfenberg device in 1,500 women over a period of thirty years with no serious complications and a failure rate of only 2.4 percent. Ishihama reported on the use of a ring developed by another Japanese physician, T. Ota, which had been used in 20,000 women, with a failure rate of 2.3 percent and no serious complications. Ota was the first to use plastic instead of metal in an intrauterine device. These reports triggered a new enthusiasm for intrauterine devices made of inert synthetic materials.

Countries where poverty and overpopulation were critical problems rapidly adopted the use of intrauterine contraceptive devices (IUCDs). In India, for instance, only 2,000 IUCDs had been inserted by 1964, but by 1968 2 million had been inserted in that country alone, and a total of 6–8 million were in use throughout the world. Recently the IUCD has become popular in the United States as well, for reasons that will become obvious in the ensuing discussion.

Effects

How the IUCD prevents pregnancies in humans is unknown. Although considerable research has been devoted to it, the mechanism is unclear. Studies have shown that IUCDs are effective in every species of animal tested, but the mechanism varies from species to species. In sheep, for example, the IUCD has been shown to inhibit the movement of sperm, thus preventing fertilization. In cows, on the other hand, it is the functioning of the corpus luteum that is impaired, and, though fertilization may occur, implantation in the uterus is inhibited. In the rhesus monkey, a fertilized ovum can be found in a tube but not in the uterus of an animal fitted with an IUCD, suggesting that the site of action is the uterus, rather than the fallopian tubes.

In humans, studies have shown *no systemic effects* (for example, no alteration of pituitary or sex-hormone secretion) from the IUCD. This finding is in marked contrast with those related to the Pill, of course, which affects the pituitary glands, ovaries, breasts, uterus, liver, and other organs. Examination of the ovaries and fallopian tubes of women fitted with IUCDs shows normal morphology and functioning. Tissues and secretions of the cervix and vagina are also normal. A transient inflammation of the lining of the uterus occurs for a few days after insertion of the IUCD, but it goes away and cannot therefore explain the contraceptive effect.

Eggs and sperm can be found in the fallopian tubes of women with IUCDs, indicating that ovulation and movement of sperm are not affected. By the process of elimination, then, we conclude that the contraceptive action of the

IUCD is probably localized in the uterus, most likely interfering with implantation in some way that is still unknown.

Types of IUCDs

Intrauterine devices are made in various shapes and from various materials. A metal ring was the first widely used device, but it has the disadvantage that dilation of the cervix is required to insert or remove it. The same is true of the Ota ring, which is made of plastic and has been widely used in Japan and Taiwan. The zipper ring is, however, made from coils of nylon thread and can be inserted through the cervix without prior mechanical dilation.

Most IUCDs currently in use are made of plastic that is flexible and can be stretched into linear form to facilitate insertion. The first such device was the Margulies spiral, introduced in 1959, which has the shape of a coil with a beaded tail. The tail remains in the cervical canal with the last two beads protruding into the vagina. The woman can reach up into the vagina and palpate the beads, thus ensuring that the device is properly in place. The disadvantage, however, is that intercourse is sometimes painful for the male, who encounters the beaded tail with his sensitive glans penis.

Shortly after the introduction of the Margulies spiral, several other flexible devices, including the bow, the double spiral, and a stainless-steel spring were also introduced. These devices all have nylon threads that hang down through the cervical opening into the vagina, enabling the wearer to check that the device is in place. The threads are small enough not to interfere with intercourse, however. These newer plastic devices also contain small amounts of barium in the polyethylene, which allows for visualization of the device on an X-ray picture.

Most popular of all the new plastic devices is the Lippes loop. It comes in four sizes, ranging from 22.5 millimeters in diameter (for women who have not had children) to 30 millimeters. It is easily inserted by a physician, who stretches the loop into linear form and pushes it into the uterus through a plastic tube that is inserted in the cervical opening (see Figure 6.1).

Effectiveness

There is substantial agreement among various studies of the effectiveness of IUCDs. Figures show a failure rate varying from 1.5 to 3 percent during the first year of use; that is, of 100 women using IUCDs, approximately two become pregnant during the first year of use. The failure rate tends to decline after the first year of use.

Although in theory some of the more traditional contraceptives described later in this chapter approach the IUCD in effectiveness, in practice they all have higher failure rates because of the various possibilities of human or mechanical error. When the IUCD is used, there is nothing that either partner must remember to do to make it effective (except that the woman must periodically check to ensure that the device has not been expelled).

Side Effects and Complications

The two most common side effects associated with IUCDs are irregular bleeding and pelvic pain, which occur in 10–20 percent of women using them. As do most of the minor side effects associated with the Pill, these problems tend to disappear after the first two or three months of use. Bleeding, or "spotting," may occur during the menstrual cycle, and menstrual periods may be heavier than usual after insertion of the IUCD. Uterine cramps or general pelvic pain may also occur, and complaints of bleeding or pain constitute the major reasons for removal of IUCDs. One study of 16,734 women reported that 833 IUCDs were removed for these reasons.[11]

There are two rare but more serious com-

[11]Borell (1966), p. 53.

plications, both related to the actual insertion of the IUCD: infection and perforation of the uterus. In the study mentioned above, infection of the pelvic organs (uterus and tubes) was observed in 171 women, though hospital records showed that half of them had previous histories of such infections. As insertion of an IUCD seems to exacerbate such conditions, women who have recently suffered pelvic infections are generally advised against using IUCDs. Careful attention to antiseptic technique when inserting the IUCD and careful screening for a history of prior infection can virtually eliminate the problem of infection.

Perforation of the uterus is very rare (it occurs perhaps once in 10,000 attempts), but it can be fatal. As with infection, the incidence of this complication varies with the skill and care of the physician inserting the device. A 1967 survey of all gynecologists in the United States disclosed a total of four instances in which death appeared to have been caused by insertion of IUCDs. Six other deaths were reported in which the relationship was not clear.[12] This mortality rate is significantly lower than that associated with pregnancy and delivery.

Spontaneous expulsion of the IUCD is most likely to occur during menstruation, during the first year of use, in younger women, and in women who have had no children. Smaller IUCDs are more apt to be expelled into the vagina than are larger ones. The various "tails" on the newer IUCDs enable women to check and verify that the devices are still in place, for they are sometimes expelled and discarded with tampons and sanitary napkins without the women realizing that they have been lost.

Cancer and the IUCD

There is no evidence so far that an IUCD increases the risk of cancer of the cervix or

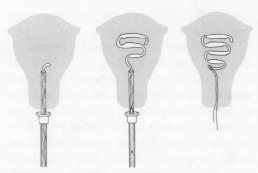

Figure 6.1. Insertion of the Lippes loop. Courtesy of Ortho Pharmaceutical Corporation.

uterus. Plastics of the type commonly used in IUCDs have also been used extensively by surgeons for prosthetic devices in various parts of the body and have never been known to cause cancer.

Subsequent Fertility and the IUCD

An IUCD can be easily removed when a woman wishes to become pregnant and appears to have no effect whatever upon subsequent fertility. Studies have shown that, after removal of IUCDs, 60 percent of women become pregnant within three months and 90 percent within one year. These figures are comparable to those for women who have never used any form of contraception.

The Diaphragm and Related Devices

Until the advent of the Pill and the IUCD, the diaphragm (invented in 1882) and other mechanical devices designed to cover the cervix were widely used for contraception. Many women objected to the aesthetic or nuisance aspects involved in the repeated insertion and removal of these devices, however. Nevertheless, the simplicity of and absence of side effects related to these devices still outweigh the disadvantages as far as many women are concerned.

---

[12]Advisory Committee on Obstetrics and Gynecology (1968), pp. 44–45.

Effects

The principle of the diaphragm is straightforward. A thin rubber dome is attached to a flexible, rubber-covered metal ring; it is inserted in the vagina so as to cover the cervix and thus to prevent passage of sperm into the cervical canal (see Figure 6.2). For added protection, the inner surface of the diaphragm (that is, the surface in contact with the cervix) is coated with a layer of contraceptive jelly before insertion.

Diaphragms come in various sizes and must be individually fitted by a physician. They are usually about three inches in diameter. In addition, following the birth of a child or any other circumstance that may have altered the size and shape of her vaginal canal, a woman must be refitted.

The diaphragm when used with jelly must be inserted within six hours before intercourse for the jelly to be effective. Unless a woman knows in advance that she is going to have intercourse on a particular occasion, she must stop and insert her diaphragm in the midst of lovemaking, or she can decide to "take a chance this one time" and ignore it.[13] The latter choice is one of the reasons for failure of the diaphragm method. When the diaphragm has been properly inserted, neither partner is aware of its presence during intercourse. After intercourse, the diaphragm must be left in place for a minimum of six hours and may be left as long as sixteen hours. It should then be removed and washed; additional jelly should be applied before reinsertion.

Effectiveness

The failure rate for the diaphragm varies between 5 and 20 percent in different studies. There are several reasons for this variation in failure rate. First, the diaphragm is not always used when it should be or inserted correctly.

---

[13] The only exception is during menstruation, when it is virtually impossible to become pregnant. Some women use the diaphragm during menstruation for aesthetic reasons, for it keeps the lower portion of the vagina free of blood and causes no harm. It is removed eight or ten hours later as usual.

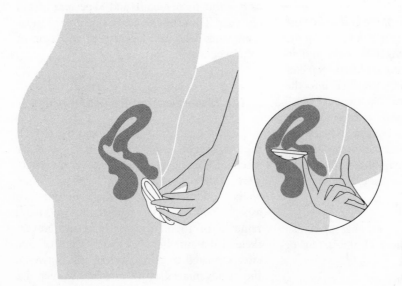

Figure 6.2. Insertion and placement of diaphragm. Courtesy of Ortho Pharmaceutical Corporation.

Second, even if it is coated with jelly and correctly in place before intercourse, it may have slipped by the time of ejaculation. Studies by Masters and his colleagues have shown that the diaphragm may become dislodged during intercourse, exposing the cervix, especially if it fits loosely, if the woman has not had a refitting since the birth of her last child, or if she participates in vigorous intercourse with multiple withdrawals of the penis in a position other than flat on her back (especially when she is on top of the man).[14]

Related Devices

Several other mechanical devices are similar to the diaphragm in principle and are called *cervical caps*. Although invented by New York physician E. B. Foote in the nineteenth century, and popular in Europe for a long time, these devices have, for some reason, never achieved wide use in the United States. The most popular version in Europe is shaped like a large thimble with a raised rim and may be made of rubber, plastic, or metal. It fits over the cervix much as a thimble fits over the finger (see Figure 6.3). The failure rate for cervical caps is about 8 percent. Not all women can use them, because of the sizes and shapes of their cervixes. It requires more dexterity to insert a cap than to insert a diaphragm, but once the cap is in place it can be left for days or even weeks. A cap may also be dislodged during intercourse, but this is less common than with the diaphragm.

Spermicidal Substances

Various foams, creams, jellies, and vaginal suppositories that kill sperm on contact are available. These substances are readily obtainable in drugstores without prescription and are simple to use. Usually there is a plastic appli-

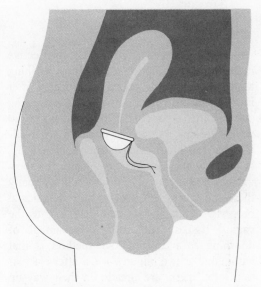

Figure 6.3. A cervical cap in position. From *International Planned Parenthood Federation Medical Handbook*, p. 53. Reprinted by permission of the International Planned Parenthood Federation, 18–20 Lower Regent Street, London SW1, England.

cator that enables a woman to introduce the cream or other substance into her vagina before intercourse. Vaginal foam is actually a cream packaged in an aerosol can. The foam has been shown to provide the best distribution within the vagina and is the most effective of these methods.[15] The least effective are the foaming vaginal tablets and suppositories, which are distributed more unevenly and depend partly upon mixing with natural lubricants and dispersion during the movements of intercourse. If ejaculation occurs before sufficient lubrication, mixing, and dispersion have occurred, these agents are of little benefit. Furthermore, the foam tablets in particular often cause temporary vaginal irritation upon insertion.

The failure rates for foams, creams, and jellies are in the vicinity of 20 percent, for tablets and suppositories closer to 30 percent.

[14]Calderone, ed. (1970), p. 234.

[15]Calderone, ed. (1970), p. 241.

Douching

A time-honored but rather ineffective method of contraception is douching, washing the sperm out of the vagina immediately after intercourse. This method is simple, requiring only a bidet or a douche bag and plain tap water. Various commercial products are available for douching; vinegar, lemon juice, soap, or salt may also be added to enhance the spermicidal properties of the solution. Actually these substances add little to the spermicidal properties of tap water and may irritate the vaginal tissues. The major disadvantage of douching as a contraceptive method is that within one or two minutes *or less* after ejaculation some sperm are already on their way up the cervical canal and beyond reach of the douche. The woman must literally run from bed to bathroom if the douche is to be even mildly effective. The overall failure rate for the douche as a contraceptive method is 30–35 percent.

Condoms

The condom is perhaps the most widely used mechanical contraceptive and is the only mechanical device used by the male. A condom is a thin, flexible sheath worn over the erect penis to prevent entry of the semen into the vagina (Figure 6.4). Condoms are also known as "rubbers," "prophylactics," "French letters," and "skins." The first ones were produced in England in the early eighteenth century from the intestines of sheep and other animals. Although more expensive than rubber condoms, "skin condoms" are still used because they are said to conduct heat better and thus to interfere less with sensation during intercourse.

Rubber condoms are by far the most widely used type. It is estimated that about 750 million are sold annually in the United States alone. The rubber condom is cylindrical with a ring of thick rubber at the open end. The thickness of the sheath is about 0.0025 inches. Each is packaged rolled and ready for use, sometimes also with a small amount of lubricant to facilitate use.

The advantages of condoms include their ready availability at drugstores and the protection that they offer against transmission of venereal diseases. One disadvantage of condoms is that they tend to reduce sensation and thus to interfere with sexual pleasure for both partners. They also require interruption of sexual activity after erection but before inser-

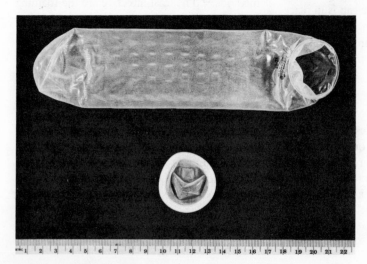

Figure 6.4. Condom, rolled and unrolled. Scale is in centimeters.

tion of the penis in the vagina. Furthermore, failure rates for the condoms may approach 15 percent. They can burst under the pressure of ejaculation, tear or leak, or slip off during intercourse. Using condoms with spermicidal foam or cream increases their effectiveness.

Withdrawal

Withdrawal of the penis from the vagina just before ejaculation (*coitus interruptus*) is probably the oldest known method of birth control[16] and is still common throughout the world. The decline of the birth rate in western Europe from the late eighteenth century onward is believed to have been primarily caused by the currency of this method.

Obviously, coitus interruptus requires high motivation and great will power just at the moment when a man is inclined to throw caution to the winds. Nevertheless, the method costs nothing, requires no contraceptive materials, and has no physical side effects, though many people find it psychologically unacceptable.

Various studies report failure rates when withdrawal is the only contraceptive measure ranging from 15 to 30 percent, partly because men may not withdraw completely or quickly enough and partly because small amounts of semen may be extruded before orgasm and ejaculation.

The Rhythm Method

The rhythm method involves periodic abstinence during the presumed fertile period of the menstrual cycle (see Chapter 4). This

---

[16] As we mentioned at the beginning of this chapter, there is reference to this method in *Genesis* 38:8–9: "Then Judah said to Onan, 'Go in to your brother's wife, and perform the duty of a brother-in-law to her, and raise up offspring for your brother.' But Onan knew that the offspring would not be his; so when he went in to his brother's wife he spilled the semen on the ground, lest he should give offspring to his brother."

method is unreliable, particularly for women whose menstrual cycles are irregular. If a woman has kept track of her periods for ten or twelve months, she can calculate her fertile period from Table 6.1. The "safe period" for intercourse includes only those days not included in the "fertile period."

For the woman with a regular twenty-eight-day cycle, the fertile period extends from day ten through day eighteen. For women with cycles ranging from twenty-four to thirty-two days, the periods of abstinence must extend from the sixth through the twenty-second day, an unacceptable span for many couples. Nev-

Table 6.1.   The Fertile Period

Shortest Cycle (Days)	Day Fertile Period Begins
22	4
23	5
24	6
25	7
26	8
27	9
28	10
29	11
30	12
31	13
32	14
33	15
34	16

Longest Cycle (Days)	Day Fertile Period Ends
22	12
23	13
24	14
25	15
26	16
27	17
28	18
29	19
30	20
31	21
32	22
33	23
34	24

ertheless, to have intercourse during this period is akin to playing Russian roulette, for there is no way to know in advance whether or not "the chamber is loaded."

The BBT (basal body temperature) chart does indicate when ovulation has occurred in a given cycle, but it is not helpful before ovulation. Ideally, the BBT rises at ovulation (see Figure 6.5). A woman must take her temperature immediately upon awakening every morning, before arising, moving about, eating, drinking, or smoking. Minor illnesses like colds and sore throats may also throw off the temperature curve.

If the BBT chart is to be used to determine the "safe period," then the woman is advised to abstain from intercourse from the end of her menstrual period until three days after the time of ovulation indicated by the rise in her temperature curve. A significant rise (indicating ovulation) is considered to be any increase of 0.4° F. or more (above the average temperature of the five days preceding the initial shift in BBT) that is sustained for three days.

The success of the rhythm method varies with each couple's ability and motivation to

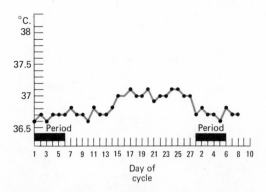

Figure 6.5. BBT chart showing ovulation about the thirteenth day (36°C = 98°F). From *International Planned Parenthood Federation Medical Handbook*, p. 62. Reprinted by permission of the International Planned Parenthood Federation, 18-20 Lower Regent Street, London SW1, England. .

follow the directions exactly. Failure is high among women with irregular menstrual cycles. Large-scale studies of couples using this method have shown failure rates varying from 15 to 35 percent, depending upon these variables. The primary reason for use of the rhythm method is that it is the only birth-control method approved for Roman Catholics (see Chapter 17).

Sterilization

Voluntary surgical sterilization has become increasingly common in recent years among both men and women in the United States and in countries like India, where it is encouraged by the government, especially for males.

Male Sterilization

The operation that sterilizes the male is the *vasectomy*, a relatively simple procedure that can be performed in a doctor's office or a village hut in about fifteen minutes. A small amount of local anesthetic is injected into each side of the scrotum, and a small incision is made on each side in order to reach the vas deferens (see Chapter 2). Each vas is tied in two places with ligatures, and the intervening segment is then cut and usually removed to prevent the two cut ends from growing together. No change in sexual functioning occurs as the result of this operation. The sex glands continue to function normally, secreting male sex hormones into the bloodstream. The man continues to ejaculate, for the seminal fluid contributed by the testes through the vas deferens constitutes only about 10 percent of the total volume. The only difference is that the fluid is now free of sperm. (Sperm may still be present up to eight weeks after a vasectomy, however, for they may be stored—but not produced—beyond the site of the vasectomy.)

Vasectomy is 100 percent effective as a birth-control measure, and there is no physical

Table 6.2 Summary of Contraceptive Methods

Method	User	Effec-tiveness Rating	Advantages	Disadvantages
Birth-control pills	Female	Excellent	Easy and aesthetic to use	Continual cost; side effects; requires daily attention
IUCD	Female	Excellent	Requires little attention; no expense after initial insertion	Side effects, particularly increased bleed-ing; possible expulsion
Diaphragm with cream or jelly	Female	Very good	No side effects; minor continual cost of jelly and small initial cost of diaphragm	Repeated inser-tion and removal; possible aesthetic objections
Cervical cap	Female	Very good	Can be worn 2-3 weeks without removal; no cost except for initial fitting and purchase	Does not fit all women; potential difficulties with insertion
Condom	Male	Very good	Easy to use; helps to prevent venereal disease	Continual ex-pense; interrup-tion of sexual activity and possible impair-ment of gratification
Vaginal foam	Female	Good	Easy to use; no prescription required	Continual expense
Vaginal creams, jellies, tab-lets, and suppositories	Female	Fair to good	Easy to use; no prescription required	Continual expense; unattractive or irritating for some people
Withdrawal	Male	Fair	No cost or preparation	Frustration
Rhythm	Male and female	Poor to fair	No cost; acceptable to Roman Catholic Church	Requires signifi-cant motivation, cooperation, and intelligence; useless with irre-gular cycles and during postpartum period
Douche	Female	Poor	Inexpensive	Inconvenient; possibly irritating

reason why it should lead to impotence or loss of libido. Psychological ramifications are highly individual, however. Some men may experience a new sense of "freedom," whereas others may feel that they have lost their virility.

Although occasionally a vasectomy may be "reversed" by recoupling the severed ends of the vas deferens, this operation is not always successful. The male who has a vasectomy must be prepared to give up the potential for fathering children permanently. Approximately 2 percent of married American males had had vasectomies by middle age, according to a 1964 study.[17] The percentage has probably increased in recent years.

Female Sterilization

The most common surgical procedure expressly for sterilizing women is popularly called "tying the tubes."[18] The operation is similar in principle to the vasectomy, although there are more than 100 various techniques available for performing it. Severing the fallopian tubes prevents the eggs from reaching the uterus just as severing the vas prevents the sperm from reaching the penis. Sterilization of a woman is a major surgical procedure that must be performed in a hospital operating room, for it involves entering the abdominal cavity, usually through an incision in the abdominal wall. Sometimes the operation is performed in con-

junction with a cesarean section or other surgery in the abdominal cavity.

As with the vasectomy, tying the fallopian tubes has no physiological effects on sexual functioning. Reversal of the procedure is usually not possible, but it has been done. About 4 percent of American women have had their fallopian tubes tied, but many more have been effectively sterilized by another surgical procedure, the hysterectomy.

A hysterectomy is a surgical removal of the uterus. It can be performed in one of two ways: through an incision in the abdominal wall (abdominal hysterectomy) or through the vagina (vaginal hysterectomy). The ovaries are left in place (unless some disease necessitates their removal). The secretion of female sex hormones thus remains normal. A hysterectomy is usually not performed solely for purposes of sterilization but most often occurs because of some pathology of the uterus: for example, uterine tumors ("fibroids" and the like) or cancer of the cervix.

A summary of the comparative effectiveness of the contraceptive methods discussed in this chapter is provided in Table 6.2.

Abortion

Although not a means of contraception as such, abortion has become increasingly popular as a method of population control, most notably in Japan and more recently in the United States. The medical, legal, and moral aspects of abortion are discussed in Chapters 5, 16, and 17.

---

[17] Calderone, ed. (1970), p. 390.

[18] The medical term for the procedure is *bilateral subtotal salpingectomy,* removal of part of each tube (*salpinx*).

PART

2

BEHAVIOR

In dealing with the structure and functions of the sex organs, we have been, as it were, investigating the house but disregarding its inhabitants. Now we must turn to people themselves to see how they behave sexually and why.

Our ignorance of the biology of sexual functions is mild compared to our ignorance of the psychology of sexual behavior. Although reams have been written about the psychology of sex, forcible conviction is generally more apparent than demonstrable fact. Science has not yet substantially added to what astute people know from experience.

The problem of assessing sexual behavior is bewildering. What is normal? healthy? moral? How do we decide? What is legal is relatively clearer, but even law is based on assumptions about normality and morality that are often alarmingly arbitrary.

In the remainder of this book we shall attempt to deal with these issues. In this chapter we shall examine the statistics on human sexual behavior as reported by Kinsey and his associates. In Chapter 8 we shall outline sexual development through childhood and adolescence. Chapters 9, 10, and 11 provide more detailed discussions of the varieties of sexual behavior.

In this chapter we shall be concerned primarily with what people do, rather than with what they ought to do, in their sex lives. We do not underestimate the importance of moral considerations, but we believe that understanding of the facts must come first and that the facts can best be understood if approached with the minimum possible prejudgment.

Just as the physiology of sex can be understood only within the context of total body functioning, sexual activity must be viewed within the framework of human behavior in general.

What Sexual Behavior Is

In the ordinary sense, "behavior" is how we act—what can be witnessed by others, in contrast to inner feelings and thoughts. This dichotomy between "inner" and "outer" is, of course, arbitrary, for we seldom act without thinking or feeling, and we rarely fail to reflect thought and emotion in our actions. Behavior is, therefore, better viewed as the integrated whole of these inner and outer aspects.

All behavior, including sexual behavior, has several main characteristics.[1] First, it is integrated and indivisible. When we describe it as

---

[1] See Engel (1962), p. 4.

SEXUAL BEHAVIOR

conscious, unconscious, or innately or socially determined, we refer simply to different components of behavior, not to different behaviors. Second, all behavior expresses the total organism, the personality as a whole. Third, all behavior is part of a lifelong developmental sequence and can be understood only as links in a chain of events. Finally, all behavior is determined by multiple forces. Each act has biological, psychological, and social determinants, which are themselves quite complex. We do not think, feel, or do anything for one single reason.

Range of Sexual Behavior

The question "What is sexual behavior?" is deceptively simple; it is actually impossible to answer. Most people would agree that it involves more than just coitus, but how much more is another matter. A physiological definition based on tumescence of sex organs or orgasm, though not without merit, leaves out vast areas of activity that are commonly recognized as sexual. Furthermore, it would include certain behavior, like erections in very young boys, of which the sexual nature can be questioned.

Closer scrutiny of human behavior reveals that any and all objects and activities may have sexual significance. The concept then becomes so nearly global that it cannot possibly be quantified for comparison and analysis. Confronted with these alternatives we must resort to working definitions that, though deficient in some respects, are at least operationally useful. For example, although we are aware of the many varieties of sexual expression, we shall deal primarily with those that culminate in orgasm. Just as with the physiology of sex, orgasm will serve as our unit of behavioral measurement.

In a sense this approach is most regrettable, for it obscures the myriad nuances and the subtlety of sexuality in favor of a "mechanical"

definition. Unfortunately, we have no other alternative to chaos. If we are to discuss what people do, we must have a unit of measurement. We shall not stop there, however, but shall attempt also to capture some of the less quantifiable, more ephemeral, but no less important manifestations of human sexuality.

Even after such drastic concessions, we can still say very little in quantitative terms about how people actually live their sex lives. There are five or six general ways in which they can achieve orgasm, but how often do they use each, who prefers which, and how does it all add up? We do not really know. But almost everyone seems to have known all along that we actually behave quite differently from the ways in which we are "assumed" to behave.

It was established in the Kinsey surveys that the vast majority of people of both sexes usually attain orgasm through one or more of six main methods: masturbation, nocturnal sex dreams, heterosexual petting, coitus, homosexual relations, and contacts with animals. Other activities like voyeurism, sadism, masochism, and fetishism are rare as exclusive means for achieving orgasm. They may, however, accompany any of the main six.

An important problem for sex research is the documentation of actual sexual behavior in large populations. Before we have such a global picture, to attempt to explain in depth any aspect of sexual activity is likely to be misleading. The study of a given individual must begin with determination of his position in a relevant group; we therefore need to know how all kinds of people behave, not only those deemed well or ill, normal or abnormal.

There is still no definitive information on the sexual behavior of large communities anywhere in the world. We shall refer often later to the distribution and frequencies of various types of sexual behavior. The presentation of such data in percentages and other mathematical forms tends to lend a certain scientific dignity and to imply accuracy. There is nothing in these pages, however, that can be taken to reflect accurately the behavior of whole nations or all mankind. What we do have are fragments of information on some facets of sexual activity in some groups. The resulting picture is like the image in a broken mirror with many missing pieces. It is to be hoped that enough is reflected to suggest the broader outlines.

Everything we know indicates that sexual behavior is extremely varied. Like the stars, individual patterns of activity are countless, but they cluster in definite constellations, some of which are apparent to the naked eye and others only to trained observers.

This extreme variability is another reason for caution in drawing conclusions from information obtained from groups. Even when careful study has uncovered the patterns of behavior in a given community, this information cannot be automatically applied to any member of that community. Averages tell us about groups but not individuals. Understanding each person requires a special study of each: There are no shortcuts. But such studies can yield more meaning if we know the averages and variations for the group.

Most of us behave most of the time in ways that allow a certain classification of sexual activities. Many similarities in sexual behavior depend upon the fundamental biological unity (though not uniformity) of man and all living beings. Many of the differences arise from different modes of social adaptation and the complexity inherent in human societies. The more advanced a species is on the evolutionary scale, the more complex are the determinants of its sexual behavior.

Judgments of Sexual Behavior

Of all the varieties of human behavior sex is the most controversial, conflict-ridden, and subject to contradictory judgment. In dealing with the biology of sex, we managed to skirt this issue, but now that we must deal with behavior we no longer can.

Assessments of behavior, sexual or otherwise, are generally made according to four criteria. First is the statistical norm: How common is the behavior? Second is the medical norm: Is the behavior healthy? Third is the ethical norm: Is the behavior moral? Fourth is the legal norm: Is the behavior legitimate?

It would be helpful if these four criteria were mutually reinforcing, or at least not contradictory. For instance, unprovoked murder during peacetime is infrequent, obviously unhealthy for the victim, morally inadmissible by almost everyone, and illegal in practically all societies. It would be difficult, however, to find other such clear-cut examples. In actual practice we must judge behavior primarily according to one or another of these criteria, but there is a strong tendency to seek corroboration from the rest. In fact, one set of judgments is often predicated on another. For example, an act is considered immoral or illegal because it is unhealthy or offends the majority (or the reverse). In addition, we seek to strengthen arguments against behavior that we wish to suppress: An activity that we consider immoral seems worse if it is indulged in by only a few, is unhealthy, and is also illegal.

The application of such judgments to sexual behavior in heterogeneous and pluralistic societies has resulted in much confusion. The meaning of the statistical norm has been distorted, partly through ignorance and partly deliberately. Medical judgments have often lacked scientific support. Morality has been confused with tradition and the idiosyncrasies of those in power. Statutes and ordinances have frozen into law many dubious factual claims and moral conclusions. Not infrequently the original determination that an act is unhealthy or uncommon turns out to be incorrect or no longer applicable, but the moral and legal judgments based on it persist.

Statistics on Sexual Behavior

People often attempt informally to quantify observations, but the widespread use (and misuse) of formal statistics is a relatively recent and predominantly Western practice. Although statistics are primarily a research tool, certain terms like "average," "percentage," and so on have become common in everyday usage. For some of us all such figures have become synonymous with facts. In an overreaction to such credulity others of us harbor deep mistrust of all statistics.

The proper application of statistical methods is indispensable to understanding of any scientific phenomenon, including sexual behavior. Even apart from deliberate deception, however, the publication of statistical results entails considerable risks of confusion, for even elementary concepts like "average" can be easily misunderstood. In the brief discussion that follows we shall attempt to clarify the statistical terms that are used in the remainder of this chapter.

In confronting behavioral data from large populations, two questions must be answered: What are the various averages of activity in the group, and what is the range of variation in the frequency of each such activity?

An average conveys a quick impression of some measure of activity in a group. If we are told that the average height of athletes on a team is six feet, then we think immediately of a group of tall men. There are three types of averages: the mean, the median, and the mode. Each tells us something different about the group, but each can be quite misleading if taken alone.

The mean is what we generally think of as the "average." It is obtained by adding the value of the variable for each member of the group and then dividing the sum by the total number of members in the group. The mean is most useful in answering the question "How often does such an activity occur in the group?" It is not so useful as an indicator of how often the average person engages in the activity. For instance, in a group of ten people half of whom have one orgasm each and the rest three orgasms each per week, the mean number of weekly orgasms is two per person. In another group, in which nine people have no orgasms but the tenth person has twenty orgasms during the week, the mean is the same, although the sexual patterns of the two groups are obviously quite different. The smaller the population, the more a few unusual cases can influence the mean.

Most of the averages in this chapter are means. Although they summarize the practices of large groups and are therefore less subject to the type of distortion just illustrated, they must nevertheless be interpreted with caution. When variations are extreme, a relatively small group of people with exceptionally high or low frequencies of a given behavior can have a telling effect on the mean.

The median is another type of average. Although less often used than the mean, it actually provides better answers to the question "How often does the average person engage in an activity?" The median is the midpoint in a linear series; half the individuals in the series have higher frequencies, and the other half have lower frequencies. In a series of eleven people, the first of whom has one orgasm a week, the second two, and so on, the median is six orgasms per week. If the series includes an even number like ten, then the median is the mean of the two central values (5.5). If the tenth or eleventh person were to have twenty or more orgasms, the median would not change, but the mean would. Medians are thus unaffected by extremes of performance by a few people. On the other hand, they fail to reflect differences in frequencies for the group as a whole. Another shortcoming is that in groups in which more than half the members score zero, the median is meaningless.

The third type of average is the mode, the most frequently occurring measurement in the group. The usefulness of this measure depends upon whether the frequencies are clustered. When each rate of activity occurs only once or twice in a group, then the mode cannot tell us very much.

Although averages are useful summaries, they convey at best limited pictures and at worst misleading ones. For more complete understanding we must also know the range of variation within the group: the distance between the smallest and highest measures or frequencies. In our example of the athletic team, if we were told that the shortest man is six feet tall, then we could be more certain that we were dealing with a group of tall men than we ever could be on the basis of any average. Even ranges are not enough, however, and ultimately we need to know the entire frequency distribution: some orderly and systematic summary of the whole range of activity. Such frequency distributions are more readily intelligible in the form of graphs.

In statistical descriptions of behavior we compare an individual's behavior with that of a group or locate his performance on a distribution curve. But what is a distribution curve?

Most measurable characteristics that occur in nature vary widely but within limits: There are, for instance, no men twenty feet tall. Furthermore, most measurements cluster around the means, and fewer and fewer occur as one approaches either extreme. Plotting the heights of 1,000 men yields a close approximation to a perfect, symmetrical curve, as shown in Figure 7.1.

Such an ideal curve is known as a "normal," or "bell-shaped," distribution curve, and it has a number of special characteristics. First, the mean, median, and mode are all at its midpoint (and are therefore the same). Second, there is a definite clustering around this midpoint: Almost 70 percent of all men deviate from it by no more than two inches (one "standard deviation"); 95 percent deviate by no more than four inches (two "standard deviations"). Anyone who is shorter than sixty-four inches and taller than seventy-two inches is quite unusual. It therefore makes sense to speak of sixty-eight inches as an "average height."

No frequency distribution in nature yields such perfectly symmetrical curves. Besides, there is nothing "abnormal" in even a markedly asymmetrical curve (like that in Figure 7.2), but it is difficult then to speak of a distinct majority or of averages and a few deviations; statistical norms become less meaningful.

The Kinsey Data

The statistics on sexual behavior reported by Kinsey and his associates are the most comprehensive data available in this field. As discussed earlier, however, this information has

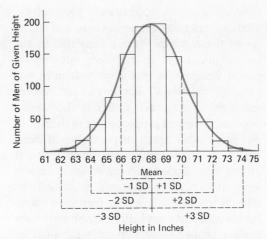

Figure 7.1. Distribution of statures of 1,000 men (hypothetical figures), with normal curve superimposed. From Hill, *Principles of Medical Statistics* (London: Oxford University Press, 1966), p. 97. Reprinted by permission.

a number of important shortcomings (see Chapter 1). Furthermore, as the data were gathered more than two decades ago, their applicability to current behavior becomes increasingly problematic with the passage of time. Information becomes obsolete at different rates, however, and it is not necessary to reject categorically all data simply because they were gathered some time ago.

In view of the various limitations, it may be asked whether or not we ought to rely on the Kinsey findings to the extent we do. Unfortunately, we have nothing better, and, if both the strengths and the weaknesses of the Kinsey material are understood properly, it can continue to provide a useful frame of reference in which to examine the broader aspects of human sexual behavior.

In discussing the Kinsey data we shall refer often to the "Kinsey sample." This sample comprised 5,940 female and 5,300 male residents of the United States whose sexual histories were gathered by the Kinsey staff. This population of 11,240 people included individuals of a wide variety of ages, marital statuses, educational levels, occupations, geographical locations, religious denominations, and so on. As all these groups were represented in the sample population in sufficient numbers to permit comparison, the Kinsey sample was properly "stratified." But it was not "representative" in that each group in the sample population was not proportionate to the size of that group in the American population at large. For example, lower educational levels and rural groups were underrepresented. Some sectors were, in fact, not represented at all: All the subjects whose histories were used were white. Kinsey collected many histories from nonwhites but not enough to permit statistical analysis. This one fact alone should make clear why these data have never been claimed to reflect exactly how Americans behaved sexually two decades ago; they certainly do not do so now.

Statistical generalizations about large groups provide us with useful summary statements, but always at some cost. Consider, for example, the finding that single men between the ages of thirty-six and forty years achieved 22 percent of their orgasms through homosexual activity. Married men in this same age group achieved 0.5 percent of their orgasms through homosexual activity. Given these extremes, what can we say about the "average" role of homosexuality in the sex lives of men between the ages of thirty-six and forty? Statements about men in general and about men and women together are potentially even more misleading.

The units of behavioral statistics are the specific bits of information from given individuals. For example, if a couple has had intercourse once during a week, that is a fact. Whatever we say about the average frequency of coitus for them or about the average frequencies of coitus for people "like" them consists only of approximations and probability estimates, even though presented in precise mathematical terms.

Given the wide variability in sexual behav-

ior, the more specific the data are for a particular group, the more meaningful they will be. In the example already cited, it is better to examine the data for single and married men separately and even in smaller subcategories defined by variables like educational level and occupation. As statistical manipulations are meaningless when performed with insufficient numbers, compromises must be made in subdividing such categories.

Finally, although the Kinsey sample consisted of only one large group of people, in dealing with these data it is easy to become confused by references to different kinds of samples. There are three distinctions that are especially important to remember. First, the data for the "total sample population" comprise the "raw" information from all subjects in the study. This total population included certain individuals who had never experienced orgasm or had not done so through one or another of the means under investigation. These people were excluded from certain computations, and the remaining group constituted the "active sample." Such "active samples," in contrast to the "total sample," did not comprise fixed numbers of the same individuals. For example, when the variable studied was total sexual outlet, the active sample excluded those who had never experienced orgasm (had zero total outlets); when it was masturbation, the active sample excluded those who had never reached orgasm through masturbation (even though they may have done so through other means); and so on. Active samples thus permit comparisons between individuals who differ only quantitatively in respect to a given behavior in a specific period of time by excluding those who are "qualitatively" different, having not shared in the behavior at all.

The third type of sample is the "American population," or the "U.S. sample," reflecting an attempt to adjust figures for the total sample population so that they more accurately describe the national population in terms of age, sex, marital status, and so on. This attempt does not make the original data more "representative" but may correct some of the additional errors arising from disproportionate representation of certain groups. Kinsey and his associates computed such corrections for much of the male data but not for the female data because of certain technical problems. All the Kinsey figures used in this book are based on the total or active samples and not on the U.S. sample unless otherwise specified.

Frequency of Sexual Activity

How much sex should a person have? Although each culture apparently assumes a range of permissible sexual activity for those with access to legitimate sources, that range is rarely, if ever, spelled out.

The frequency of sexual behavior has health implications in the minds of most people. For example, young men from better-educated, less strictly religious families are often told that masturbation is all right, provided that it is not "excessive." Occasionally there are differences between husband and wife over how often they will make love. These conflicts are inevitably assessed against hypothetical standards of what is "reasonable" and "healthy."

To estimate how much sex a person was having Kinsey combined all sexual activities over a period of time and viewed them as the person's "total sexual outlet." Theoretically any and all forms of erotic expression should have been included. As this ideal was impossible, Kinsey counted only orgasms achieved through the six main types of sexual activity listed earlier.

To speak of "sexual outlets" conveys a certain view of the nature of sexuality. It implies a pressure from within that needs release, a blind urge that demands gratification in one way or another. Sexuality in a way becomes like hunger and elimination. The former comparison implies the intense yearning characteristic of sexual desire, the latter the mounting tension, periodic release, and ensuing comfort and sensual gratification also associated with orgasm. Unfortunately, the riddle of sex is not to be solved through analogy, for neither comparison fits very well.

The term "outlet" is used here for convenience and should not be taken as a reflection of our theoretical stance. People in large groups do seem to be trying to satisfy fundamental needs in various ways, but the avenues to satisfaction and the intensity of activities vary, depending upon many factors.

Frequency must be measured over specific periods of time. As our lives are generally organized around weekly schedules, Kinsey found the week a useful unit of measure. Furthermore, sexual activities change over the years, and Kinsey therefore examined them over five-year periods. In the following pages "total outlet" refers to the total number of orgasms achieved during an average week through masturbation, sex dreams, petting, coitus, homosexual activities, and animal contacts; the "average week" is based on given five-year periods of a person's lifetime.

Frequency of Total Outlet among Males

The mean frequency of total sexual outlet for white males between adolescence and eighty-five years of age was calculated by Kinsey to be nearly three orgasms in an average week.[2] To reiterate earlier cautions, this figure should not be taken to mean that the "average man" necessarily had this many weekly orgasms, and it certainly does not mean that such

---

[2] In these and subsequent examples the figures cited are approximations based on the more specific data in the Kinsey surveys. Some minor discrepancies between text and figures have also been carried over.

frequencies are standards of normality, health, virility, and so on.

Before we go on to the more common levels and averages, we must emphasize the extreme variation among apparently healthy people living under reasonably similar conditions. Some men in this group had experienced very few orgasms over long periods: One man in apparently good physical health had had only one orgasm in thirty years. Others reported many orgasms each week, week after week. One man, also apparently in good physical health, claimed to have averaged thirty orgasms a week for thirty years.

Much more significant than such single figures is the frequency pattern of the number of orgasms per week for the same population (see Figure 7.2). It is important to note that a higher percentage of men attained about one orgasm a week than any other single frequency. The weekly mean of three orgasms was thus inflated by the more active rates.

The asymmetrical nature of the curve indicates that men cannot be readily grouped as typical, or average, on the basis of frequency of orgasm and that high-frequency and low-frequency individuals cannot be clearly distinguished as deviating from the norm. In this group, whereas three-quarters of men had one

to six orgasms a week, almost a quarter fell outside this range. It is apparent that weekly rates of male orgasm fall on a continuum: Some men are a little more active than are others, who are in turn more active than are the rest, and so on. Although the range between the two extremes may be tremendous, there are intermediate frequencies all along.

The frequency of total outlet was related to a variety of factors, of which age was the most important. In Figure 7.3 we see how the average number of orgasms experienced each week was related to the age group of the individual. The first group consisted of boys fifteen years old and younger (but past puberty), the next group of those between sixteen and twenty years of age, and so on in five-year spans.

The most active groups appear to have been those below the age of thirty. After thirty the frequency of orgasms steadily declined with advancing age. It is startling to realize that the level of activity did not gradually rise to a peak but was already close to its maximum in the youngest age group. This trend runs contrary to the popular notion that sexuality is awakened during adolescence, gradually reaches its peak during the "prime of life," and then wanes.

The curve for the mean is higher than that for the median at every point. The peak mean

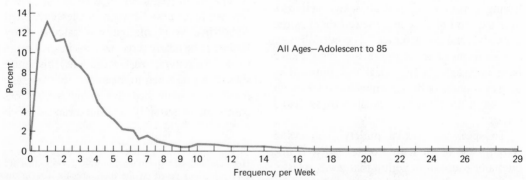

Figure 7.2. Individual variation in frequency of total sexual outlet among males. From A. C. Kinsey *et al.*, *Sexual Behavior in the Human Male* (Philadelphia: Saunders, 1948), p. 198. Courtesy of the Institute for Sex Research.

(for the group between twenty-six and thirty years old) was three orgasms a week, whereas the median was only a little more than two (2.24). This disparity means that an average week for this age group included three orgasms per person but that the average person had only about two orgasms each week.

Frequency of Total Outlet among Females

Comparisons of sexual behavior in the two sexes must be undertaken with care, so that differences are neither exaggerated nor minimized. Also the significance of female sexuality must be recognized in its own right rather than only in relation to that of the male.

Because of certain important differences in male and female sexual behavior, comparisons can be carried out only up to a point. For example, orgasm is a less satisfactory measure of female than of male sexuality. Less of what is obviously sexual behavior culminates in orgasm for women; even when orgasm does occur it is more difficult to recognize and count it because of the absence of ejaculation. Also, as the sexual behavior of women is in general more stringently controlled than is that of men, behavioral criteria alone yield a less accurate picture of true female sexual potential. To counteract these distortions it is therefore necessary to consider all female sexual behavior, even that which does not culminate in orgasm, and to look at the data on certain subgroups, like married women, with particular care, for social constraints on these women are fewer, and their behavior thus probably more closely reflects natural tendencies.

The range of individual variation in frequency of total sexual outlet among females is so much greater than among males that questions about "average number of orgasms per week" cannot be answered meaningfully. The Kinsey volume on the female does not have a counterpart to Figure 7.2, nor does it report

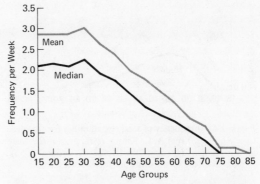

Figure 7.3. Frequency of total sexual outlet for males, by age groups. From A. C. Kinsey *et al., Sexual Behavior in the Human Male* (Philadelphia: Saunders, 1948), p. 220. Courtesy of the Institute for Sex Research.

data that would permit the construction of such a graph for females. We shall therefore illustrate rates for a few specific groups in order to obtain a general notion of the approximate range of rates of total outlet among females.

In the Kinsey sample about a third of the single females between the ages of sixteen and twenty, twenty-six and thirty, and forty-six and fifty experienced an average of one orgasm every other week. In the age group between sixteen and twenty about 5 percent reached one orgasm a week and a smaller percentage had two or more orgasms per week. Between twenty-six and thirty and between forty-six and fifty about 10 percent had one orgasm a week, and in the younger group a somewhat larger number had more.[3]

Among married females between twenty-one and twenty-five about one-third had mean total sexual outlets of one to two orgasms a week. Somewhat more than 5 percent averaged three orgasms a week, and another 5 percent reached five to seven orgasms a week. In this age group fewer than 20 percent of women had only one

---

[3]Kinsey *et al.* (1953), p. 540.

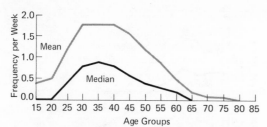

Figure 7.4. Frequency of total sexual outlet for females, by age groups. From A. C. Kinsey *et al., Sexual Behavior in the Human Female* (Philadelphia: Saunders, 1953), p. 548. Courtesy of the Institute for Sex Research.

or fewer orgasms every other week. Between thirty-six and forty one of four women had no more than one orgasm every other week, but an equal number averaged one a week. Between fifty-one and fifty-five almost two out of three women experienced fewer than one orgasm a week. About 20 percent still reached one or two weekly orgasms, but women with higher frequencies were quite rare.[4]

Figure 7.4 shows the mean and median frequencies of total sexual outlet among various age groups. This figure is the counterpart for females of Figure 7.3. Comparison of the two figures reveals several differences. First, the frequencies of total sexual outlet for females were lower than were those for males in all comparable age groups. This finding confirms the common notion that women as a group are orgasmically less active than men, but it also seems to contradict earlier references (Chapter 3) that showed women to be more capable of multiple orgasm than are men. The apparent confusion arises from the fact that Masters and Johnson were actually counting the number of orgasms during an episode of sexual activity, whereas Kinsey obviously could not have expected his subjects to recall accurately how many orgasms they had reached during past

sexual acts and had to be content with their memories of the number of sexual acts that culminated in orgasm at all. This contradiction illustrates the ambiguities in sweeping generalizations about whether men or women are more "highly sexed" and so on. Females revealed themselves as having higher total outlets than most people would have expected, however. The differences between the two sexes are, after all, not that striking: Whereas the most active male group achieved an average (mean) of three orgasms a week, its female counterpart experienced almost two orgasms (1.8) during the same period of time.

The disparity in medians is somewhat more marked: The average male in the peak group experienced somewhat more than two (2.2) weekly climaxes, whereas the average female had almost one (0.9).

Among females the wider disparity between the means and medians indicates wider individual variability. There must have been some women whose levels of activity were so much higher than the rest that their performances unduly inflated the mean values for the group as a whole. More detailed study of the female sample shows that this assumption is valid.

The second, and more intriguing, sex difference is revealed by the shapes of these curves, which indicate quite different patterns of relation between age and frequency of sexual outlet among males and females. Whereas men achieved high levels of sexual activity right after puberty and by the age of fifteen, the youngest female group was quite inactive sexually. Its weekly mean was 0.3 orgasms a week (one orgasm in about every three weeks). The median was zero, which does not, of course, mean that the average girl had no orgasms at all, but that more than half the girls in this age group did not experience weekly orgasms (see our earlier definition of "median").

Between the ages of sixteen and twenty males

---

[4]Kinsey *et al.* (1953), p. 541.

attained their highest rates of sexual outlet and maintained them for a full decade. For females the period between sixteen and thirty years was one of gradually increasing activities culminating in orgasm. But they maintained this peak frequency for a full decade, whereas in males it steadily declined. The fall in female frequencies was thus preceded by reductions in male frequencies by about ten years. Because of the overall higher male weekly rates, at no time was a given group of females having more orgasms a week than were the males in the corresponding age group. The mean curve for females is closest to the mean curve for males in the age group of forty-one to forty-five years.

Many female groups were more active than were certain male groups. For instance, female groups in their peak decade (thirty-one to forty years old) had more frequent outlets than did all male age groups beyond forty-five years put together (note the portions of the male mean curve that fall below the high point of 1.8 sustained on the female curve).

Once the decline had begun, increasing age brought the two sexes progressively together. Although men maintained a slightly higher frequency than women, in advanced old age the rates for both sexes were very low.

The progress of the median was quite similar. The average female between puberty and age fifteen was, unlike the male, sexually quite inactive in terms of achieving orgasm. Her rates increased steadily, but she did not attain her peak until she was almost thirty years old. Even then she averaged only about one orgasm a week, whereas males between adolescence and the same age had more than twice that many. She sustained this weekly rate until she was almost forty and then had progressively fewer orgasms. By the age of sixty-five, whereas the average man attained an orgasm about every other week, the average woman achieved very few.

Differences in Frequencies for Males and Females

Such differences between the total outlets of the two sexes have both theoretical and practical interest. Are they biologically or socially determined? What are the underlying causes of both? Definitive answers are not yet available, but studies of animals and of different cultures have shed some light. We shall have occasion to examine some of these findings.

From a practical point of view, the discrepancy in timing between levels of sexual output and eligibility for social institutions designed to meet sexual needs is quite obvious. Marriage, for instance, is not possible for many men until they are in their late twenties. Furthermore, men generally marry younger women. Total sexual outlets may not be the cardinal consideration in these matters, but the fact that disparities exist must not be overlooked, particularly in cases of sexual incompatibility. More than a third (36 percent) of the women in the Kinsey sample had not yet experienced orgasm at the time of their first marriages. Most men, on the other hand, had had hundreds of orgasms over long periods. In fact, many men were already declining in the frequency of their total sexual outlets.

More specifically, in the generation born after 1910 men marrying for the first time had had an average of almost three orgasms a week in the previous ten years: a mean of 1,500 orgasms per person. Among their brides, no more than one or two in ten had had even one orgasm a week in the preceding *five* years: There had been only about 223 orgasms per person in that time. (If we were to consider the ten-year period preceding marriage, this number would not double, for female frequencies are lower in younger groups.)

Males had also had more variety in the types

of sexual outlet, as we shall see later. The obvious conclusion is that most men and women, at least of those in the Kinsey sample, entered married life with widely disparate sexual backgrounds. Currently this disparity is probably less marked, though we have no actual data to support this supposition.

The notable variability among individuals (especially women) makes the application of group rates to given individuals hazardous if not meaningless. In the Kinsey sample, within each age group of either sex there were individuals whose weekly rates of sexual outlet were totally out of keeping with the group mean or median. People in the least active groups, perhaps an adolescent girl or an old woman, may have regularly experienced more orgasms during an average week than did some men in the most active years (ages fifteen to thirty). Such deviation from group averages is in itself no indication of pathology. This point must be kept in mind when we discuss individuals with particularly low or particularly high frequencies of total sexual outlet.

The differences in the sexual behavior of the two sexes are, of course, not exhausted by these

Figure 7.5. William Hogarth, *Before* (left) *and After* (opposite). Courtesy of the Metropolitan Museum of Art, Harris Brisbane Dick Fund, 1932.

statistics. Throughout subsequent chapters we shall have occasion to examine the ways in which men and women act differently. Figure 7.5 illustrates Hogarth's view that, although women may be "hard to start," they may be even "harder to stop."

High Levels of Sexual Activity

Men and women considered to have exceptionally active sex lives are a source of wonder and preoccupation in many cultures. Are they specially endowed beings, or are they sick? Is one born with a higher sexual capacity, or does one develop it? If the latter, what is the secret?

Although we may ponder such questions from time to time, most of us manage with our ordinary levels of sex drive. Many people, however, try either to suppress it or to intensify it, and some seem to devote their entire lives to such attempts. Both efforts are losing battles, as adolescents struggling with their impulses to masturbate and aging men attempting to shore up sagging virility demonstrate.

The satyrs of Greek mythology were part-human, part-animal beings who lived in forests

and mountains and formed part of the entourage of Dionysus, the god of wine and fertility. They were jovial, lusty creatures and have become symbolic of the sexually active male. Such "extreme" activity, with pathological overtones, has come to be known as "satyriasis."

Nymphs were a more varied lot and less single-mindedly dedicated to sexual pursuits. They were young and beautiful maidens, mostly amorous and gentle. Some, however, were quite wild and behaved more as satyrs did. The sexually hyperactive woman is therefore known as a "nymphomaniac" ("inflicted with nymph madness").

Clinicians who argue that sexual hyperactivity is pathological, even when the "patients" seem not to be in any distress, come into conflict with social scientists' interpretations. Clinicians deal with sick people who come to them because they are suffering. These patients' sexual functioning has often been impaired along with other aspects of their lives; sometimes it takes the form of frantic activity that appears pointless and is devoid of joy. The pathological basis of such behavior is so obvious that many clinicians become firmly convinced that similar processes must be at work in every other instance of apparent sexual hyperactivity.

Social scientists disagree. They note that clinicians have no idea how many people in the general population exhibit sexual behavior that does not differ materially from that of patients. A clinician never sees most of these people because they do not seek his services. How can he infer that these people are also sick when they voice no complaints and their behavior in other areas appears to be quite adequate?

The latter argument cannot be easily attacked, but it does have limitations. Findings from population studies must provide a base line for assessing individual behavior, but insights can be gained only from careful examination of individuals, which is clearly impossible in studies of large populations. If we can avoid adopting a doctrinaire position, the information from these two sources can be quite complementary.

In view of the data presented here, the range of variation in sexual outlets in a large population makes it clear that individuals cannot be arbitrarily defined as abnormal or unhealthy simply by the frequency of their sexual activities. They may be happy or unhappy about these activities, but their feelings are often determined by social considerations.

On the other hand, sexual activity, like any other human behavior, is affected by neurotic conflicts. Some people are sexually hyperactive *because* they are neurotic; other sexually hyperactive persons simply happen also to be neurotic. An apparent coexistence of neurosis and very frequent sexual outlet does not mean that the two are necessarily causally related in either direction. Attempts to differentiate these people may be an unrewarding task, but to lump them together (when we still know little about differences in drive levels and their determinants) is nevertheless unwarranted.

Although each historical period seems to have had its sexual prodigies, some have been more celebrated than have others. Usually the exploits of the socially prominent or the flamboyant become more widely known; no one hears of the staggering "records" that otherwise ordinary husbands and wives may set.

In the folklore of sexual prowess fact and legend are intermingled and elaborated. The Roman Empress Valeria Messalina (A.D. first century) and her husband's son-in-law, the Emperor Nero, both have reputations for prolific sexual activity.[5] Catherine II of Russia

---

[5] Claudius I was first married to Messalina, and they had two children, Britannicus and Octavia. After Messalina's adulterous activities were discovered she was put to death and Claudius married Agrippina, the mother of Nero by a previous marriage. The Emperor was persuaded to adopt Nero, who later became the guardian of Britannicus and husband to Octavia. Nero eventually poisoned both his wife and his mother.

(1729–1796) seems to have been as enterprising in her sexual life as she was politically. The names of Casanova and Don Juan have, of course, come to represent the hyperactive male perpetually in search of sexual conquest.

Giovanni Giacomo Casanova de Seingalt (1725–1798), a Venetian, was expelled from school as a boy for immorality. He became an adventurer and traveled widely around Europe. After a lifetime of intrigue he retired to the castle of a prominent friend to write and study. His multivolume memoirs (originally written in French) are regarded as an important historical document.

Don Juan is not a historical character but the literary prototype of the profligate. Although his counterparts can be found in the legends of many peoples, the Spanish version is most widely known. In this story Don Juan seduces the daughter of the commander of Seville and kills him in a duel. He eventually meets his own end when a statue of the commander comes to life and drags him to hell. The theme of Don Juan has been the inspiration for many artistic works. The earliest known dramatization is attributed to Gabriel Téllez (*El burlador de Sevilla*); it was written in 1630. Perhaps most famous are Molière's *Le Festin de Pierre* (1665) and Wolfgang Amadeus Mozart's opera *Don Giovanni* (1787). Other works include George Gordon Lord Byron's *Don Juan* (1819–1824), Juan Ignacio de Esproneeda's *Estudiante de Salamanca* (1840–1842?), Richard Strauss' *Don Juan* (1888), and George Bernard Shaw's *Man and Superman* (1903).

Study of large segments of the population reveals that frequent sexual outlet is neither rare nor legendary. More than 7 percent of males in the Kinsey sample (more than one in fifteen) averaged seven orgasms a week. One in four of these men was less than thirty years old.

Such high frequencies were partly the result of the ability (in about a third of these males) to reach multiple climaxes during a single sexual episode. These individuals were ordinary people in most other ways. They came from varied ethnic, social, educational, and occupational groups. The circle of acquaintance of each of us probably includes at least several such men.

Sexual performance under special circumstances gives further indication of man's biological capacities. Some male prostitutes (mostly homosexual) are, for instance, able to ejaculate five, six, or even more times a day for many years.

Women with high frequencies of sexual outlet were fewer in the Kinsey sample, but certainly many were as active as the most active males. Conventions and social expectations are more inhibiting of expressions of female sexuality. On the other hand, women are physiologically better equipped to achieve multiple orgasms during a single sexual episode (see Chapter 3). Some women attain multiple climaxes every time that they have intercourse throughout long and active sexual lives; occasionally such a woman may reach a dozen or more climaxes in an hour, which probably no man is capable of doing.

Low Levels of Sexual Activity

Sexually "underactive" people are a far less celebrated lot. They do not inspire artists, and moralists lose no sleep over them. Like "high-frequency individuals" they are distributed among the general population and by no means constitute a distinct group.

Sexual abstinence for days or weeks is, of course, quite common. About one in ten males between puberty and thirty-one years of age in the Kinsey sample routinely averaged only one orgasm every two weeks. About 3 percent of this same age group had about one orgasm each in ten weeks. The number of males with low outlets increases steadily after the age of thirty-five.

That there are more sexually inactive females than males is almost certain. A considerable proportion of unmarried females engages in no sexual activity that leads to orgasm, including, in the Kinsey sample, almost eight out of ten girls between menarche and age fifteen. As age increased, this proportion changed, but even between the ages of thirty or so and forty, the peak years of female sexual activity, about a third had no orgasms. More than a quarter of all unmarried women never had had this sexual experience.

Among married women the proportion that had never experienced orgasm was smaller but still considerable. It was largest in the younger age groups (ages sixteen to twenty), in which about one in five had not attained orgasm. Between the ages of twenty-one and twenty-five this proportion dropped to about one in ten.

The "previously married" (separated, divorced, and widowed) group scored between the married and never married on this continuum. Of the youngest members of this group, a third had had no orgasms; at age thirty only one in five had had no orgasms, and at age fifty the ratio had dropped farther.

The measurement of sexual outlet by orgasm presents a problem, as noted earlier. In addition to the numbers of women who do not attain orgasm, there are many more who only rarely engage in activities leading to sexual climax. It is a mistake to conclude that the sex lives of these women are necessarily unfulfilling, however. For one thing, orgasm is more difficult to detect in women: They are more likely to deny it or to fail to recognize it. As a result, indices of frequency for females are more subject to error. Furthermore, as many women insist, their sexual needs seem less dependent upon achievement of orgasm; sexual embraces may be satisfying without it.

As has high frequency, "underactivity" has been ascribed a number of unwarranted meanings. But, whereas "moralists" have tended to cloud the former issue, it is the "sexual liberators" who are responsible for much confusion about the latter.

No one has yet died or suffered demonstrable damage from lack of sexual activity as such. There is no reliable evidence that "high" or "low" levels of total sexual output are in general either caused by or the causes of physical or psychological pathology. There are special instances in which such deviations from ordinary levels of outlet result from physical, psychological, or both such factors. Conceivably, when extraordinary restrictions are placed upon sexual expression or when an individual is precociously or excessively stimulated, some damage may result. But it is one thing to properly recognize specific instances and another to draw wholesale generalizations from them.

As women have become freer to feel and to express their sexuality, a certain preoccupation with orgasm has evolved. It is difficult to say whether men or women are primarily responsible for endowing this physiological process with such cultish attributes. The available data show that a very wide range of types of total outlet involving people from all walks of life exists in the community. The sensible approach seems to be to accept the frequency of sexual outlet for each person as such and to pass judgment on whether the person is sexually ill or well only on the basis of more comprehensive criteria, including the individual's own assessment of his sexual functioning.

Varieties of Sexual Experience

If variety is, in fact, the spice of life, then sexual behavior is spicy indeed. Throughout history some men and women have resorted to every imaginable type of activity in pursuit of sexual gratification. They have copulated with each other, with members of their own sexes, and with animals. They have used their bodies in solitude, in pairs, in triads, and in greater numbers. Every orifice that can possibly be penetrated has been penetrated, and every inch of skin has been caressed, scratched, tickled, pinched, licked, and bitten for love. Orgasms have come amid murmurs of tender affection and screams of pain, in total awareness and while fast asleep. An important aspect of this diversity is also the fact that some members of the population lead very restricted sex lives and that there are some apparently healthy people who go through life without ever experiencing orgasm.

How do we explain these vast differences? Do we not all share the same biological heritage? Are our cultures so diverse as to permit such a bewildering range of behavior? Several considerations are pertinent in trying to answer these questions.

Some of the observed differences are undoubtedly real. Variation is a cardinal rule of all biological phenomena, and cultures are by definition diverse. The ranges of variation are quite narrow in some physiological matters (like the degree of heat that sperm can tolerate) and much broader in others (like the numbers of sperm in normal ejaculates). Certain behaviors (for example, incest) are also strictly prohibited in all cultures, whereas other behaviors (premarital sex, homosexuality) are viewed with widely varying tolerance among cultures. Such real differences exist among individuals within a group as well as among groups of various dimensions.

Other apparent differences in sexual behavior are based on ignorance and willful concealment. Some of us still labor under the impression that the overwhelming majority of mankind engages in coitus exclusively; some of us think of homosexuals as a small minority who have contact only with their own sex. We have laws that prohibit certain acts (for example, genital kissing) between spouses, thus implying that the practices in question are rare and contrary to community standards, whereas they appear to be quite common among married couples. As we discussed in Chapter 1, answers to the question "How do we behave sexually?" come as unpleasant surprises to some people. If we could be quite open about what we do in our sex lives, a great many apparent differences in sexual behavior might be revealed as considerably less sharp.

Finally, to an important extent, the magnitude of these apparent differences is a function of the particular methods of observation and interpretation used. Among psychoanalysts, for example, the definition of sexual behavior is incomparably broader than among most psychologists or anthropologists. When investigators use different yardsticks for different settings, obviously considerable disparities will emerge independent of whatever actual variation may exist in the groups under study.

Aside from differences that are only apparent, what accounts for the real differences in sexual behavior among individuals and groups? On several occasions so far we have addressed ourselves to this issue of "causes," or determinants, of sexual behavior only to offer uncertain or partial answers. Given current limitations on available information we shall instead merely examine briefly here the more common components of total sexual outlet and their correlates.

Components of Total Sexual Outlet

The six components of total sexual outlet that were found by Kinsey to account for practically all orgasms experienced by men and women were listed earlier and will be defined here.

Masturbation is self-stimulation for sexual arousal and discharge. It usually involves manipulation of the genitals but may also be achieved through breast stimulation, rhythmic muscular contractions, and other means.

"Sex dreams," also called "nocturnal emissions," include those that occur during daytime sleep. The older and more common term "nocturnal emissions" is appropriate only for males, as women do not ejaculate, even though many reach orgasm during such dreams.

Heterosexual petting includes any physical contact between members of opposite sexes undertaken for the purpose of sexual arousal but not involving actual penetration of the vagina by the penis. Accidental contacts, even though sexually stimulating, do not count. In the Kinsey study only petting that led to orgasm was counted. The figures presented here therefore reflect that limitation.

Coitus is heterosexual intercourse involving vaginal penetration by the penis. In practice, it is seldom isolated but rather comes as the culmination of petting, or foreplay. When foreplay proceeds coitus, it is considered part of the latter act, rather than as petting, although the specific activities involved—kissing, caressing, and the like—are identical.

Homosexual relations involve physical activity between members of the same sex for the purpose of erotic arousal and discharge. Much of homosexual activity consists of petting, though the term is not usually used in this context. Homosexual relations may also involve anal intercourse and oral-genital contacts. Men and women also perform these acts together, of course, so that the acts cannot be considered homosexual by definition. What makes an act homosexual is not its nature but the fact that the partners belong to the same sex.

The definition of animal contacts, like that of homosexual activity, is based on the nature of the participants, rather than of the act itself: physical contact by a person of either sex with an animal of either sex deliberately undertaken for sexual gratification. The activities are similar to human petting and intercourse but modified to allow for anatomic limitations. Further distinctions are generally not drawn.

That men and women engage in all these activities has been well known and documented throughout history. What has been unclear, however, is to what extent people rely on one means of gratification over another. In most Western societies marital coitus has traditionally been accepted as the only legitimate sexual outlet. All other forms of sexual expression have been formally condemned. Sanctions have ranged from mild disapproval to the death penalty, depending upon the nature of the act and also on the identities of the participants.

Correlates of Sexual Behavior

If two events or characteristics occur together more frequently than chance would indicate, we have a positive correlation. If they occur together less often than chance would indicate, then we have a negative correlation. Correlations do not necessarily reflect causal relations, but they may provide leads to common causes. They are thus useful as predictors. A child, for instance, will soon learn that snow and cold go together, even though he may not know which comes first. Usually it is only this type of elementary insight to which we can currently aspire in studying the correlates of sexual behavior.

The conditions and characteristics that coexist with various types and frequencies of sexual activity are so many that we need some means of sorting them out. Many daily events distract or stimulate erotic interest, and external circumstances facilitate or hamper sexual expression. Honeymooners, for example, are more apt to pursue sexual satisfaction single-mindedly than are partners in long-standing or stale relationships. Confinement with members of the same sex in prisons and the like inevitably results in increased homosexual activity, and so on.

Possible influences on sexual behavior are thus legion. What we are primarily concerned with here are not the obvious, transient, or externally imposed conditions but rather the biological and social characteristics that may be consistently related to rates and patterns of sexual outlet: gender, age, marital status, age at puberty, social class, religion, and urban or rural background.

Figures 7.6 to 7.12 illustrate the components of total sexual outlet for certain subgroups of men and women. The information on the two sexes do not necessarily correspond, for the Kinsey data are not always comparable for the two sexes. Nor is it necessary for our purposes here to undertake a complete presentation of their findings. The figures presented are primarily intended as illustrations of the influence of certain factors on the components of total sexual outlet.

Components of Total Sexual Outlet among Females

Figures 7.6, 7.7, and 7.8 show how marital status was correlated with sources of orgasm in the female sample.[6] These patterns of sexual behavior show striking though in some ways expected differences, as well as certain similarities.

For single women (Figure 7.6) in the youngest age group masturbation was the primary orgasmic outlet (84 percent of total outlet). In successive age groups this proportion declined, so that between ages thirty-six and forty coitus and masturbation provided equal proportions of orgasms (37 percent of total outlet each). In the next two age brackets masturbation moved ahead, but only enough to account for slightly more than half of all orgasms in the group between forty-six and fifty.

Nocturnal orgasms, or sex dreams, were clearly a very minor source for single women. Interestingly, they were most common (4 percent of total outlet) in the oldest age group, even though we think of nocturnal orgasms as more typical of adolescence.

Petting accounted for almost 20 percent of orgasms between the ages of sixteen and twenty-five years and continued to be frequent even in the older age groups. It is perhaps

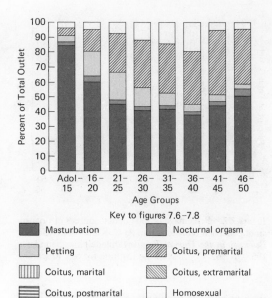

Figure 7.6. Percentages of total outlet: sources of orgasm among single females. From A. C. Kinsey *et al., Sexual Behavior in the Human Female* (Philadelphia: Saunders, 1953), p. 562. Courtesy of the Institute for Sex Research.

surprising that petting provided the same ratio (4 percent) of orgasms for adolescents who were sixteen years old and younger and for single women forty-one to forty-five years old. But it is quite likely that if all petting, not just petting to orgasm, were considered, teenagers would show a relatively higher level of activity than would older women.

Coitus was the second most important source of orgasm for single women. Beginning with the youngest age group, in which premarital coitus accounted for 6 percent of orgasms, this outlet reached its peak between the ages of forty-one to forty-five years, when it provided 43 percent of total outlets.

Homosexual contacts provided a steadily increasing proportion of the orgasms of single women up to the age span of thirty-six to forty years, when almost one out of five orgasms was reached by this means.

In comparison to single women, married

---

[6]These three figures are based on an "active sample," defined earlier: All subjects in this group had experienced orgasm through one or another means.

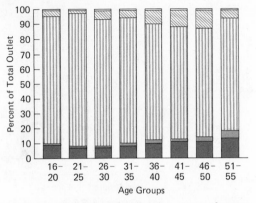

Figure 7.7. Percentage of total outlet: sources of orgasm among married females. From A. C. Kinsey *et al., Sexual Behavior in the Human Female* (Philadelphia: Saunders, 1953), p. 562. Courtesy of the Institute for Sex Research.

women showed much more "uniform" sex lives (Figure 7.7). Through all the age levels examined they registered an overwhelming reliance on coitus as a source of no fewer than four out of five orgasms. It will be noted, however, that some of these orgasms occurred during extramarital intercourse at all age levels. Between the age of forty-one and fifty, when the rates of extramarital orgasm are highest, they

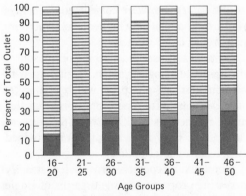

Figure 7.8. Percentages of total outlet: sources of orgasm among previously married females. From A. C. Kinsey *et al., Sexual Behavior in the Human Female* (Philadelphia: Saunders, 1953), p. 562. Courtesy of the Institute for Sex Research.

accounted for somewhat more than 10 percent of total outlet.

Although coitus was the primary source of orgasm for married women in the Kinsey sample, it was not the only source. Masturbation provided a fairly steady proportion (about 10 percent) of total sexual outlet, and there was a slight increase with age. The same was true of nocturnal orgasms but to a much lesser extent. Homosexual contacts were either absent or a negligible source of orgasm for married women.

Previously married women (that is, women who were separated, divorced, or widowed) would be expected to show a pattern intermediate between that of single and married women, for previously married women share some of the characteristics of all married women, as well as many of the actual life circumstances of single women. Actually previously married women appeared to be closer in their sexual behavior to married than to single women: Coitus was the predominant source of orgasms, even though these women did rely more heavily on masturbation, nocturnal orgasms, and homosexual contacts than married women did (Figure 7.8).

These data do not permit full elucidation of the relation of marriage to sexual outlet. To what extent is there preselection of women primarily attracted to coitus (and attractive to men similarly inclined)? To what extent is the preeminence of coitus in marriage a function of readily available partners, social and moral approval of marital sex, and so on? The pattern for previously married females indicates that both sets of factors were at work. If the differences in sexual behavior between the single and married reflected only the external consideration of marital status itself, then the pattern of the previously married would be similar to that for singles. If, on the other hand, the differences reflected only preselection, then the pattern would be the same as that of married women. In this regard comparison with widows alone would be preferable; the separated and divorced can be thought of as having rejected marriage (assuming that such choices are freely available, which often they are not).

No mention has been made so far of orgasm through animal contacts, for in none of the female groups do they constitute a frequent enough outlet to allow representation on the graphs.

Components of Total Sexual Outlet among Males

We shall next examine the data from the male Kinsey sample, according to the same subdivisions by age and marital status; in addition, however, we shall introduce the factor of education. For our purposes it suffices to examine two groups only: men with elementary-school educations and men with some college education. To simplify matters further, we shall deal only with single and married men.[7]

The Kinsey study demonstrated important associations between educational level and the components of total sexual outlet. Among single males with elementary-school educations (Figure 7.9) masturbation accounted for little more than half the total sexual outlets even at the youngest age levels. It became less significant with increasing age; between twenty-one and thirty-five it accounted for only about a quarter of orgasms. Starting at age sixteen, coitus was the primary outlet for this group. Note that these single men showed increasing reliance with age on prostitutes as sexual partners. Homosexual contacts also increased so that between thirty-one and thirty-five they

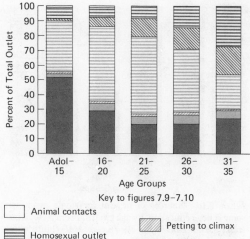

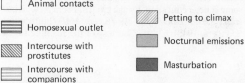

Figure 7.9. Sources of orgasm for single males with elementary-school educations, by age groups. From A. C. Kinsey *et al., Sexual Behavior in the Human Male* (Philadelphia: Saunders, 1948), p. 490. Courtesy of the Institute for Sex Research.

accounted for one-fourth of all orgasms. Nocturnal orgasms provided a modest but steady outlet for these men, but petting contributed only very slightly to total outlets.

In contrast, single males with some college education relied heavily on masturbation (Figure 7.10). In the youngest age group it accounted for four out of five orgasms. In successively higher age groups the ratio declined but not much below 50 percent. The better-educated single male's reliance on masturbation was at the expense of coitus, particularly with prostitutes. Petting and nocturnal emissions were more substantial outlets in this group, but homosexual contacts were less important than for less-educated males. There was, however, a similar increase in reliance on such contacts with age.

In contrast to the patterns of single males, those of married males (like those of married

---

[7]The data presented in Figures 7.9–7.12 are drawn from the "total sample" of the Kinsey study that has been "corrected" for the U.S. population. They are therefore not directly comparable to those in Figures 7.6–7.8. The basic trends are nevertheless the same within these male "populations," which is all that we are concerned with here.

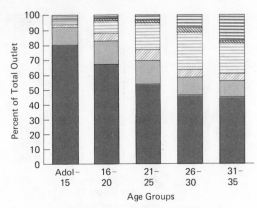

Figure 7.10. Sources of orgasm for single males with some college education, by age groups. From A. C. Kinsey *et al., Sexual Behavior in the Human Male* (Philadelphia: Saunders, 1948), p. 491. Courtesy of the Institute for Sex Research.

females) were much more uniform. As Figures 7.11 and 7.12 indicate, marriage greatly narrowed the differences between the two educational groups; coitus was the primary sexual outlet. Yet a few differences remained. Masturbation and nocturnal emissions were relatively more important sources for the better-educated group. Also the less-educated married male was shown to be more involved with extramarital coitus and homosexual contacts in his earlier years, whereas the better-educated married male became more involved with these activities in his later years.

These data on males further illustrate the important associations of sexual behavior with various biosocial variables. For example, as there are no demonstrable biological differences between less and more educated males in general, the important differences between these two groups must be explained on psychological and social grounds. In this regard, it must be emphasized, however, that education itself was not the key factor. These men were not behaving differently because of what they were taught in school. The pertinence of education was primarily as an index of "social class." It was

social class that determined the styles of life, values, and so on of these men. Similar associations could be shown, for instance, between occupational choice and patterns of sexual behavior.

So far we have singled out a few important variables to illustrate their connection with sexual behavior. As indicated earlier, other factors were also shown by the Kinsey study to be significantly related both to the frequency and to the components of sexual outlet. For example, the age at which a boy reached puberty was shown to have a correlation with future sexual activity: Those maturing earlier had higher total outlets. As this relationship held for those who married, as well as for those who remained single, it suggests the possibility of biological differences. Yet the age of menarche did not seem to matter in this respect. Religious beliefs were also shown to be related to total outlets: Among males Orthodox Jews were the least active and nonpracticing Roman Catholics the most active sexually. Among both sexes those who took religion more seriously were less likely to engage in noncoital or extramarital activities.

These observations are but a few of many that have emerged from the Kinsey data. Some of them were obvious and expected, others paradoxical and questionable. Some of these same observations are probably equally applicable today and others not. What is more important for our purposes is the realization that sexual behavior is highly varied and profoundly influenced by a host of biological and social variables, even though we remain ignorant of the precise nature and magnitude of these influences. The cross-cultural comparisons that follow are intended to highlight these points further.

In subsequent chapters additional information on prevalence, frequencies, and correlates of the major sexual outlets will be provided in connection with more detailed presentations.

Cross-Cultural Comparisons

There is a vast amount of information on sexual behavior in various parts of the world, but almost all of it is in descriptive rather than quantified form. Studies of large populations on the order of the Kinsey investigation are nonexistent. In this chapter, we shall restrict ourselves to cross-cultural comparisons of frequency of sexual outlet: Specific types of sexual behavior in other cultures will be discussed in later chapters.

Anthropologists have gathered large volumes of data from primitive cultures, some of which pertain to sexual behavior. The term "primitive" is misleading but hallowed through usage. It refers to preliterate cultures that have evolved along lines different from those on which ours has evolved. They do not necessarily represent early stages already passed through by literate societies, nor are they always simple in social organization. The sexual behavior of such groups is widely assumed to be free and unlimited. It would be useful to see whether or not the available data support this notion.

In their review of anthropological studies of almost 200 primitive societies, Ford and Beach found the quantitative data on sexual outlets to be quite limited.[8] Observation, rather than measurement, has been the traditional anthropological approach. Fragments of information have nevertheless revealed three aspects of

these cultures that are quite relevant to our immediate concerns.

First, there seemed to be tremendous variations among various primitive peoples in the

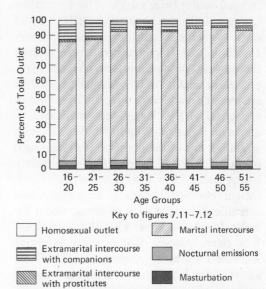

Key to figures 7.11–7.12

☐ Homosexual outlet   ▨ Marital intercourse

☰ Extramarital intercourse with companions   ▦ Nocturnal emissions

▨ Extramarital intercourse with prostitutes   ■ Masturbation

Figure 7.11. Sources of orgasm for married males with elementary-school educations, by age groups. From A. C. Kinsey *et al., Sexual Behavior in the Human Male* (Philadelphia: Saunders, 1948), p. 492. Courtesy of the Institute for Sex Research.

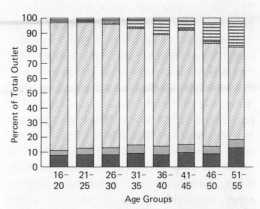

Figure 7.12. Sources of orgasm for married males with some college education, by age groups. From A. C. Kinsey *et al., Sexual Behavior in the Human Male* (Philadelphia: Saunders, 1948), p. 493. Courtesy of the Institute for Sex Research.

---

[8]Ford and Beach (1951). It must be emphasized that this survey dealt with different cultures and not with separate geographical or political units. The cultures surveyed were selected from several thousand described by anthropologists. For example, of Western cultures only that of the United States was included. Furthermore, the book is now several decades old, and the original reports from which the data were drawn are, of course, even older. Most of these cultures have undoubtedly undergone profound changes, and some may even be extinct. Nevertheless, these changes do not detract from the value of the original data for our purposes.

frequency of sexual activity. Males of the Keraki (seminomads of New Guinea) generally had coitus once a week, of the Lesu (hunters, fishers, and primitive agriculturists of New Ireland) once or twice a week, of the Chiricahua (Arizona Indians who hunted, gathered, and carried on some agriculture) two or three times a week, of the Hopi (farmers) three or four times a week, of the Crow (seminomadic hunters) every night, of the Aranda (Australian hunters and gatherers) three to five times a night, and of the Chagga (advanced agriculturists of Tanganyika) up to ten times a night.

All but one of these groups permitted men to have multiple wives; the Hopi were strictly monogamous. The institution of polygamy, though obviously relevant, is not the sole determinant of frequency of sexual outlet for males. We do not know what else is involved. It is clear, however, that in many primitive societies on which information is available adults engage in almost daily intercourse during periods when sex is permitted.

Second, every society had some restrictions upon sexual activity. There is no human society anywhere that permits a man or a woman to engage in sex at absolutely any time and place. The human erotic potential is, therefore, never given free reign in any organized social group.

Restrictions on sexual outlets have various bases: Sometimes the surviving partner of a deceased spouse must remain chaste for a certain period, which may extend to days or years. Sometimes the prohibition extends to other relatives as well. A sick person and sometimes his relatives too cannot have sex in some societies. Among some peoples no intercourse is permitted before, during, or after hunting, fishing, farming, or war. Menstruation, pregnancy, and childbirth also impose restrictions in various cultures.

Third, at least some primitive groups seemed to share our notions about the effects of frequency of sexual activity upon health. Crow Indians, active as they were, believed that too

frequent intercourse weakened the participants. The Seviang (cultivators of New Hebrides) recommended that a man with a single wife should have coitus for three nights, then rest for two; one who had two wives should copulate for two nights and rest on the third.

The effects of age are also well known in primitive societies, as the following passage illustrates.

> In their youth and young manhood (the period Lepchas call *fleng*) Lepcha men would appear to be remarkably potent; trustworthy people said that when they were first married they would copulate with their wives five or six, and even eight or nine times in the course of the night, though they would then be tired the next day. I have got no comparable information from women but such statements were often made in mixed company without the women present making any comment or in any way expressing incredulity. This potency diminishes around the age of thirty, but copulation once nightly is still the general rule for married couples. Tafoor claimed that in his youth he was almost indefatigable, but says that now he only sleeps with his wife once every three or four nights; that is the reason why he is relatively fat, for chastity induces fatness. It is believed that people accustomed to regular copulation will feel extremely uncomfortable for the first few days if for any reason their partner is removed; but it is considered that people over thirty should be able to support long periods of chastity.[9]

Some patterns of sexual behavior among primitive peoples are thus quite similar to those in the West, but there are also striking differences. Extensive comparisons of sexual behavior in various societies would go a long way toward helping us to understand the social functions and implications of sexual behavior, as well as permitting us to infer the possible biological factors at work. Regrettably such comparative data do not yet exist.

---

[9] Gorer (1938), pp. 329–330.

Thorough understanding of any behavior requires some knowledge of its genesis. This chapter deals with the genesis of sexual behavior during human development. It should be stated at the outset that there is still no comprehensive, consistent theory of psychosexual development that is generally acceptable. We have many facts, but only a few can be explained; we have many explanations, but only a few can be supported by facts. To emphasize this disparity between behavioral data and theory, we shall deal first with empirical observations of sexual behavior during childhood and adolescence. Then we shall turn to the fascinating but controversial theoretical constructs and inferences.

DEVELOPMENT OF SEXUAL BEHAVIOR

Whatever its basis, there is no disputing that sexuality begins with life and develops along with other functions of the body, in both its physiological and psychological aspects. Although evidence of infantile sexuality has been abundant in everyday life, formal recognition of it has come about relatively recently and over considerable opposition. Traditional views of human sexuality before this century assumed an orderly progression from childhood sexual innocence through awakening of sexual impulses in adolescence to their culmination in adult behavior. Although this theoretical sequence is applicable to the emergence of reproductive capacity, it is not a correct model for sexual development. Certain extreme notions of infantile sexuality, according to which the child is viewed as a lecher whose incestuous impulses are denied expression simply because of his inability to implement them, are equally misleading.

Observation of infants of both sexes indicates that at least some of them appear capable of sexual arousal and orgasm. In the absence of verbal expression, we have, of course, no way of knowing what their subjective experiences are, but, as the ensuing descriptions suggest, some infantile behavior is so strikingly similar to that of sexually aroused adults that there can be little doubt about its sexual nature.

Frank manifestations of sexual arousal and response are not commonly observed in infancy, partly because we either fail to see or refuse to recognize sexual behavior at this age level. Infants and young children are also ordinarily not stimulated sexually, and we often cannot tell whether or not a child would be sexually responsive. Apart from such considerations, we also know that there are wide differences in

CHAPTER

PSYCHOSEXUAL DEVELOPMENT

the time at which sexual behavior emerges and that only some but not all infants and children are sexually responsive at any given age. Whereas practically all of us are born with the requisite biological potential, the rate of maturation and actual functioning vary from one person to another. Some are sexually responsive within several months of birth; others have their first orgasms during puberty and still others years later. In general, as with other body functions, more and more children attain their sexual capacities as they grow older.

Although many of us have experienced conscious sexual feelings and in some instances even orgasm before puberty, the latter still serves as a turning point in psychosexual development. Several terms are used, often interchangeably, to describe this period of life. But more precisely "adolescence" (from Latin *adolescere,* "to grow up") refers to the phase of psychological development that culminates in full genital and reproductive maturity. This period overlaps with but does not precisely correspond in time to the two underlying biological phases: "puberty" (from Latin *pubertas,* "adulthood"), which begins with the appearance of secondary sexual characteristics and extends to the inception of reproductive capacity, and "nubility" (from Latin *nubilis,* "able to marry"), during which full reproductive fertility is reached.[1]

Prepubescent Sexuality

Sexual arousal in childhood is easier to detect among boys than among girls, for it takes the visible form of penile erections. Such physiological proof is not always necessary, however, and activities of a patently sexual nature may be observed in both sexes before puberty. Many of the sexual activities and interactions of

children take the form of play. Although adults are apt to dismiss play as merely amusement, it is in many ways a serious activity for the child. We shall discuss the role of play in more detail later. In the sexual sphere too the behavior of children takes the form of play. When we discuss heterosexual and other forms of sexual activity among children, we really mean sexual play in these various forms.

Erections may be observed among male infants right after birth or any time thereafter. At this early age it is difficult to ascribe as complex a reaction as sexual arousal to the infant, and it is therefore commonly assumed that such erections are reflexive. That is, they are believed to be mediated solely through the simpler networks of nerves in the spinal cord and not to depend upon the higher centers of the brain that deal with thought and emotion. Ultimately, of course, erections become the primary expression of male sexual arousal, but we do not know when and how this reflexive response becomes "eroticized."

Another dilemma involves various types of interaction like kissing, hugging, caressing, and other forms of endearment. Such interactions between adults, infants, and children are universal in one form or another and, from all that we know, vital to proper development.

Are such activities sexual? On one hand, the very thought of ascribing erotic motives to such innocent behavior can seem repulsive. On the other hand, such acts are difficult to distinguish at times from sexual foreplay. Is the primary difference, then, in conscious motivation and subjective experience? If the intent is to arouse or to become aroused, then the activity is sexual, whereas otherwise it is not? But then what if the participants are stimulated inadvertently, or the erotic motives are unconscious?

The infant shows an active interest in exploring his own body, and he initially explores in a random and indiscriminate manner. Contact with his own genitals may not always be

---

[1] Engel (1962), p. 141.

deliberate. Infants of both sexes as young as four months old are known, however, to respond to genital stimulation in a manner that at least strongly suggests erotic pleasure. As the child grows, self-exploration becomes more thorough, but, unless he is stimulated or inhibited externally, he does not seem to give his genitals special or preferential treatment. In some instances, however, the self-manipulation is clearly erotic (Figure 8.1).

When the child is two or three years old, he interacts with other children with sufficient intimacy to carry his sexual explorations over into these relations. He investigates his playmates' genitals, as well as exhibiting his own. If permitted, he does the same with adults, but in general there are, of course, stringent social prohibitions of such activity. Such cultural attitudes start to make their influence felt early in life and are part of the process of socialization.

The Kinsey data on prepubescent sexual behavior were obtained mostly from the recollections of adult subjects, but some were also gathered directly from children. The findings

on the prevalence of sex play at various ages before puberty are shown in Figures 8.2 and 8.3.[2]

Although some people claim to remember specific instances of sexual arousal and orgasm from as early as the age of three, it is only around the age of five that substantial numbers of children (about one in ten) appear to have their first sexual experiences beyond autoerotic exploration and thus qualifying as "sociosexual" behavior.

Comparison of Figures 8.2 and 8.3 also shows that boys became considerably more active in sex play than did girls, as age increased. Approximately 10–14 percent of girls were engaged in some form of sex play between

---

[2] In the Kinsey reports the term "adolescence" is used for puberty. The figure legends thus refer to play at each "preadolescent age" (Kinsey *et al.* [1948], p. 169; Kinsey *et al.* [1953], p. 111). Incidentally, the Kinsey survey was not the first to document prepubescent sexuality. For studies antedating their research, see the footnotes of Kinsey *et al.* (1948), Chapter 5; Kinsey *et al.* (1953), Chapter 4.

Figure 8.1. Infantile masturbation. From *The Erotic Drawings of Mihály Zichy* (New York: Grove Press, 1969), plate #24. Copyright © 1969 by Grove Press, Inc., and reprinted by permission.

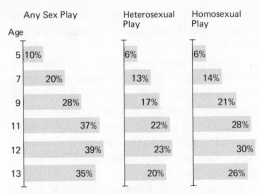

Age

Any Sex Play		Heterosexual Play	Homosexual Play
5	10%	6%	6%
7	20%	13%	14%
9	28%	17%	21%
11	37%	22%	28%
12	39%	23%	30%
13	35%	20%	26%

Figure 8.2. Percentages of prepubescent boys who had engaged in sociosexual play. From A. C. Kinsey *et al.,* *Sexual Behavior in the Human Male* (Philadelphia: Saunders, 1948), p. 162. Courtesy of the Institute for Sex Research.

the ages of five and twelve years (Figure 8.3). By contrast, there was an almost fourfold increase in the prevalence of sex play among boys between the same ages (Figure 8.2). The peak age for girls was nine, when 14 percent engaged in some form of sex play; boys attained their peak at age twelve, when 39 percent were similarly involved.

In the Kinsey study, "sex play" meant actual genital play. This definition was not as stringent

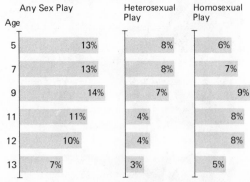

Age

Any Sex Play		Heterosexual Play	Homosexual Play
5	13%	8%	6%
7	13%	8%	7%
9	14%	7%	9%
11	11%	4%	8%
12	10%	4%	8%
13	7%	3%	5%

Figure 8.3. Percentages of prepubescent girls who had engaged in sociosexual play. From A. C. Kinsey *et al.,* *Sexual Behavior in the Human Female* (Philadelphia: Saunders, 1953), p. 129. Courtesy of the Institute for Sex Research.

as that of "sexual outlet," which required culmination in orgasm (see Chapter 7), but it certainly excluded casual physical contact between children with uncertain erotic intent. On the other hand, Kinsey thought that his reported percentages were altogether too low and that probably nearly all boys (but only about a fifth of all girls) had engaged in sex play sometime before reaching puberty.

These actual or estimated percentages should not be taken to mean that children are constantly involved in sex play. For most children it is a sporadic activity. For example, one out of four boys who had engaged in sex play had done so only during one year, and some had participated in such play only once before puberty. Only one in three boys had persisted in such play on and off over five or more years. These limitations applied even more strongly to prepubescent girls.

Finally, in both sexes prepubescent sexual activity did not increase with the approach of puberty. In fact, there was a slight but noticeable decline in sex play once the peak ages were passed. There is evidence that in some cultures the development of sexual behavior does not manifest such a "break" between childhood and the attainment of sexual maturity. Among other anthropoids also the sexual activity of the young animal merges imperceptibly with adult behavior. These observations suggest that the pattern shown in the Kinsey data may have been culturally determined.

Types of Prepubescent Sex Play

Much prepubescent sex play is motivated by curiosity and influenced by the availability and sex of companions. To the extent that a child's companions are of the same sex, his sex play will likely be "homosexual." And, when a boy lies on top of a girl, it is viewed as coital play. As children are often quite unaware of the significance of such acts, we should refrain from ascribing adult sexual motives to them. These activities are largely experimental, imitative, exploratory play, sexual only in a general sense—unless, of course, an older, more experienced person stimulates the child and initiates him into a more frankly erotic response. It is particularly important not to label the sex play of children as deviant or perverse, no matter what it entails. To do so would be like calling a child who believes in ghosts and fairies "delusional" or "mentally ill."

Self-exploration and self-manipulation are the most common forms of sex play. Occasionally an individual may actually remember masturbating, sometimes to the point of orgasm, as early as at three years of age. Particularly among girls (more than 85 percent), orgasm is first experienced through self-stimulation. Although boys indulge in considerable handling of their own genitals, fewer seem to carry it to climax: Fewer than 70 percent reach their first orgasms this way.

Fondling the penis and manual stimulation of the clitoris are the most common autoerotic techniques. Children easily discover the erotic potentials of rubbing against beds, other furniture, toys, and the like. Girls in particular are apt to stimulate themselves by rhythmic movements of the buttocks while lying down. A child may, however, learn to masturbate from seeing someone else do it or from actually being taught by someone more experienced. Such experiences are more common among boys than among girls.

Next to autoerotic activities, the most common forms of prepubescent sex play are exhibiting and handling one's genitals in the presence of companions. These types of sex play are the precursors of future sociosexual encounters. Figures 8.2 and 8.3 show the extent to which such sex play occurred at various ages and the sexes of the companions involved in the Kinsey data. Although the differences are slight and of uncertain significance, the sex play of boys appears to be more homosexually than

heterosexually inclined. The pattern among girls is quite erratic.

Preteen-aged boys are generally group- or gang-oriented. Sexual activities, as well as other behavior, thus tend to occur in these contexts; genital exhibition, demonstration of masturbation, group masturbation, and similar activities are quite common (see Figure 8.4). They satisfy social needs that are far broader than the mere release of sexual tension. Occasionally sex play with companions becomes more like adult homosexual behavior, with oral-genital contacts and attempts at anal intercourse.

What is the relation of preadolescent homosexual play to adult homosexual behavior? According to the Kinsey data, fewer than half of all males continued homosexual play before puberty into adolescent and adult activity. At lower educational levels the likelihood of such continuation was greater (one out of two) than among college-educated men (a little more than one in four). As the socioeconomically lower youngster has relatively free access to coitus, his preference for homosexual contacts nonetheless may indicate stronger homosexual inclinations. Although prepubescent homosexual play more often than not stops at puberty, most adult homosexuals do trace their sexual preference to prepuberty. That is, whereas prepubescent homosexual acts do not necessarily lead to adult homosexuality, an adult homosexual is likely to have started homosexual practices before reaching puberty.

Among prepubescent girls in one out of three instances the activity did not go beyond genital exhibition and superficial exploration. Interestingly, girls were more likely to engage in mutual genital examination among themselves than with boys, and the same was true for vaginal insertions. Also only 5 percent of girls with prepubescent homosexual experience continued it into adolescence.

The first heterosexual play experiences occur somewhat earlier for most boys than do their

Figure 8.4. Boys masturbating. From *The Erotic Drawings of Mihály Zichy* (New York: Grove Press, 1969), plate #30. Copyright ©1969 by Grove Press, Inc., and reprinted by permission.

initial homosexual encounters, which usually occur at about age nine. Boys, rather than girls, are usually the instigators of heterosexual play, which 40 percent of men and 30 percent of women recall having experienced before puberty. Again, genital exhibition and handling are the most common activities.

The child's first glimpse of the genitals of the opposite sex, particularly of an adult, is impressive, and he rarely forgets it. Obviously, the experience owes at least some of its impact to the mystery and secrecy surrounding the sex organs. Male genitals are more accessible to view; 90 percent of women report having seen male organs (most often those of their fathers) by adolescence.

Activities beyond those listed are difficult to evaluate. Finger insertions, for instance, are more apt to be part of an exploratory sequence and not to go farther in than the girl's introitus. Children have also well-known games like "playing house," "papa and mama," and "doctor." The titles vary, but the scripts are the same. During such play there is usually a good deal of lying on top of one another, but even when children occasionally undress the activity does not proceed beyond mere genital apposition. In the Kinsey sample more than 10 percent of boys but only a small proportion of girls were reported to have engaged in such "coital play."

Adult types of sexual activity during preadolescence are much more likely to occur when one partner is older and more experienced. In the hands of an adult, a child can be trained to engage in practically all forms of sexual activity, including oral-genital contact and coitus.

Prepubescent Orgasm

As so much sex play is random and exploratory, we may wonder how much of it really has sexual meaning and how much of it is mere play. One practical distinction would, of course, be the occurrence of orgasm.

Although almost everyone now concedes that children play sexual games, it may be more difficult to accept the observation that they can also actually experience orgasm, sometimes even before the age of six months. In attempting to test this observation, we run into two difficulties. First, as infants cannot talk, we have no way of knowing their subjective experiences. Even older children have difficulty describing the nature of their erotic feelings. Second, females at any age do not have ejaculation with orgasm, and prepubescent orgasm in males is

not accompanied by ejaculation (for the prostate is still not fully developed). We thus have only the evidence that we can observe. But, as we shall illustrate, the similarities between the observable indications and those of adult orgasm are so striking that there can be little doubt of their sexual nature.

In response to sexual stimulation some male infants experience erection and other physiological changes that accompany arousal in adult males. Their muscles tense, and they perform rhythmic pelvic thrusts that culminate in distinct climaxes of convulsive movements of the arms and legs, and penile throbs. A child may cry at the height of this activity, but he is soon quiet, loses his erection, and exhibits the relaxation of the postorgasmic phase in adults.

A more graphic description has been provided by the mother who watched her three-year-old girl masturbate:

Lying face down on the bed, with her knees drawn up, she started rhythmic pelvic thrusts, about one second or less apart. The thrusts were primarily pelvic, with the legs tensed in a fixed position. The forward components of the thrusts were in a smooth and perfect rhythm which was unbroken except for momentary pauses during which the genitalia were readjusted against the doll on which they were pressed; the return from each thrust was convulsive, jerky. There were 44 thrusts in unbroken rhythm, a slight momentary pause, 87 thrusts followed by a slight momentary pause, then 10 thrusts, and then a cessation of all movement. There was marked concentration and intense breathing with abrupt jerks as orgasm approached. She was completely oblivious to everything during these later stages of the activity. Her eyes were glassy and fixed in a vacant stare. There was noticeable relief and relaxation after orgasm. A second series of reactions began two minutes later with series of 48, 18, and 57 thrusts, with slight momentary pauses between each series. With the mounting tensions, there were audible gasps, but immediately following the cessation of pelvic thrusts there was complete relaxation and only desultory movements thereafter.[3]

It is impossible to say how many infants and children have such experiences or how often. Although such activity is probably not an everyday occurrence, much of it occurs unobserved. Adults tend to ignore it or at least to fail to recognize its sexual significance. As far as the capacity to attain orgasm is concerned, it has been reported in a five-month-old boy and a four-month-old girl (within the limitations mentioned earlier). There are also reports of orgasms at older ages for both sexes. Although sexual responsiveness develops at different rates, Kinsey estimated that more than half of all boys could achieve orgasm at three to four years and almost all boys could do so three to five years before reaching puberty. (No comparable data exist for girls.) These figures indicate that sexual capacity is present at these ages, but there is no reason to assume that children should therefore be deliberately stimulated sexually.

In Chapter 3 we discussed the high degree and indiscriminate nature of sexual excitability in the preadolescent male. Erection occurs more rapidly before puberty than in adulthood. Prepubescent boys are also more capable of multiple orgasms than are adolescents and adults. In the general population, however, only a few boys are stimulated to such performances.

Significance of Prepubescent Sexuality

The sexual activities of children and their often unused sexual potential raise important developmental, as well as social, questions. In the West there is no general agreement on how we should regulate the sex lives of children. The dominant traditional values have generally been restrictive: Sexual contact with adults has been strictly prohibited and sex play among children discouraged. Often even didactic sexual instruction in any form has been opposed as potentially stimulating and therefore harmful. There is, however, growing concern now that this area may be one of the most neglected in the upbringing of children and that a great deal of confusion and damage result when the children are left to "sink or swim" in their sex lives. In certain countries (for example, Sweden) there are already extensive sex-education programs in schools. Attitudes in this country are still ambivalent, and the issue often causes sharp disagreements among various segments of the population.[4]

It is often suggested that children should be educated sexually at home. Many parents find the prospect bewildering. When is one to begin such instruction, what does one say, how far does one go beyond stories of "birds and bees"? Now that many have by and large abandoned their traditionally restrictive attitudes, even sophisticated parents may feel paralyzed by uncertainty at what to encourage and what to discourage in their children. Professional advice tends to be fragmentary and more often based on the adviser's "common sense" and convictions than on tested evidence. Not, of course, that such advice cannot be quite useful nevertheless.[5] As a result, most parents currently steer a moderate course whereby they neither give coital demonstrations to their children nor punish the child every time he touches his genitals. Instead they try to respond

---

[3]Kinsey *et al.* (1953), pp. 104–105.

[4]In this country the most active organization in this area is the Sex Information and Education Council of the United States (SIECUS), formed as a voluntary health organization in 1964. Its headquarters are at 1855 Broadway, New York, New York, 10023. See Broderick and Bernard (1969), Chapters 1 to 6, for further discussions of the problems and prospects of sex education.

[5]For examples of current professional opinion in this regard, see Spock (1970), pp. 372–383; and Fraiberg (1959), pp. 210–241.

to the child's questions as they arise. But this often entails considerable uncertainty and discomfort for all involved.

Prepubescent Sexual Contacts with Adults

Children of both sexes have been sexually exploited by adults probably in all cultures. Regardless of criminal sanctions (see Chapter 16) some adults continue to approach children sexually. How prevalent this problem is we do not know exactly. In the Kinsey female sample, about one out of four women had been sexually approached by someone five or more years older than herself when she was preadolescent. Most women (80 percent) had experienced such contacts only once each, about 5 percent had had such encounters nine or more times before adulthood. About half the time the adult was a stranger, but one-third of the approaches involved friends and acquaintances, and about one in five involved relatives (uncles, fathers, brothers, and grandfathers, in order of decreasing frequency).

In about half the instances the approaches consisted of exhibition of the adult male genitals. Next came fondling the children without genital contact (31 percent) and genital manipulation (22 percent). Other forms of activity were rare. Coitus, for instance, was reported in only 3 out of 100 instances of adult sexual approach (0.7 percent of the entire female sample). A few of the girls were as young as four or five years old when these incidents occurred, but most were ten years old or older (though still prepubescent).

There are no comparable statistics for male children. Adults who approach boys sexually are more often male. It is quite possible, however, that adult females can much more easily conceal their sexual motives and "get away with" sexual approaches to children than men can, for we generally find it more "natural" that

a woman be physically affectionate toward children, even if they are relative strangers.

The impact of precocious sexual stimulation on young children is generally believed to be quite detrimental. Clinicians have traced some serious psychological disturbances in adults to such childhood experiences. The Kinsey survey, though admittedly superficial from a clinical point of view, does not seem to substantiate the notion that childhood sexual experience with adults necessarily results in serious damage. We cannot conduct experiments on this problem, of course, any more than we can inoculate children with virulent microorganisms to learn their precise effects.

The use of children as sexual objects is more frequent in poorer neighborhoods where living conditions are crowded. It is, however, severely condemned at all levels of society. This value judgment, unlike many others related to sexual behavior, is apparently not determined by class. Even in penal institutions, inmates who have molested children must be segregated because they are likely to be angrily attacked by other inmates. Most of us feel so strongly about this issue that we tend indiscriminately to equate the confused or lonely old man who may have vaguely approached a child with the psychotic sex murderer.

Adolescent Sexuality

Despite the importance of prepubescent sexuality, puberty and adolescence are the periods when adult sexuality emerges. The discovery of the importance of infantile sexuality so fascinated early psychoanalysts that adolescence for a while attracted only secondary interest, but it has more recently been restored to its position as a crucial phase for the study of sexual development.

Biologically the key features of puberty are accelerated growth, development of secondary sex characteristics, and initiation of reproductive capacity. These changes have already been discussed (see Chapter 4), and we shall not examine them again here. Certain features will, however, have to be reiterated because of their bearing on the development of sexual behavior.

First, puberty and adolescence are not points in time but periods of time. Puberty extends over three or four years in females and longer in males. Adolescence is even more protracted.[6] As puberty generally begins one or two years later in males, pubescent girls are clearly ahead of boys in reproductive development. But, as we shall see, reproductive capacity is not the same as sexual responsiveness.

Second, puberty begins at different times for different members of each sex. There is also some variation in which of the many body changes appear first. Convention and convenience dictate adoption of menarche in the female and first ejaculation in the male as the primary points of reference, but they are not entirely satisfactory because a number of changes, like growth of pubic hair, generally precede them. In fact, some young men and women may be fully developed sexually for several years before having their first ejaculations or their menarches. Nor does the appearance of these physiological processes necessarily indicate the beginnings of the psychological changes of puberty. Despite the intimate association between reproduction and sex, the two are separate functions and develop on separate schedules.

To recapitulate our earlier discussion, boys and girls seem to reach peaks of prepubescent sexual activity and then, in our culture, to manifest gradual declines. The subsequent course of events differs for the two sexes. Partly because prepubescent sex play is more prevalent among boys, despite its relative decline before puberty more of it actually continues into adolescence. In this regard, petting to orgasm was found to be more likely to persist during the transition into puberty and adolescence (among 65 percent of boys) than were other sexual outlets. Homosexual contacts were most likely to be interrupted. A year or so before the onset of puberty this relative quiescence apparently comes to an end, and boys show an upsurge of sexual activity that accelerates during the period of puberty: Sporadic prepubescent sex play is replaced by steady levels of sexual activity. In a few years most boys reach the sexual acmes of their lives. As a group they will never again attain higher levels of total sexual outlet (see Chapter 7).

Although the adolescent boy may have already experienced orgasm, his first ejaculation is an impressive and long-remembered event. Among physiologically normal males in the Kinsey sample the earliest ejaculation remembered was at about eight years of age and the latest, again among apparently healthy men, at twenty-one years of age. About 90 percent of all males had had this experience between the ages of eleven and fifteen years (the mean age was thirteen years and 10.5 months).[7] Ejaculation could, of course, occur outside these limits, in pathological conditions. Even this apparently purely biological phenomenon reflected socioeconomic influences: In the lowest educational group the mean age for first ejaculation was 14.6 years, almost a year later than in the most educated group. The differences among individuals were very great: Some boys in elementary school were sexually more mature than other boys in college.

The first ejaculation resulted most often

---

[6]Adolescence is often divided into "early adolescence," which encompasses most of the high-school years, and "late adolescence," which may extend into the twenties. These age ranges are subject to great individual and cultural variation.

[7]Kinsey et al. (1948), pp. 185–187.

from masturbation (in two out of three instances), nocturnal emissions (one out of eight instances), and homosexual contacts (one out of twenty instances). It may rarely have occurred "spontaneously" (through fantasy alone, without direct genital stimulation). Contrary to popular belief, nocturnal emissions were not the most frequent harbingers of puberty. Usually they occurred a full year after the first ejaculation had been (or could have been) experienced. First ejaculations through nocturnal emissions were more common in higher socioeconomic groups.

"Spontaneous" ejaculations, though rare, are of special interest. As the ability to have them is almost always lost after puberty, it too attests to the high and indiscriminate level of excitability in younger males. "Spontaneous" ejaculations reportedly occurred in response to various physical (but not genital) activities (chinning on bars, vibrations of a boat) and psychological provocations (watching couples petting, milking a cow, reciting in front of a class). Some ejaculations that appear to be spontaneous (as when climbing a tree) may in fact be caused by genital friction, even though the boy may be, at least initially, quite innocent of sexual intent.

The sexual development of females contrasts sharply with that of males in a number of ways. First, as prepubescent sex play was less prevalent among females, the interruption in sexual activity before puberty appeared much more marked. The pubescent girl had to begin all over, as it were. Furthermore, during female puberty there was no sudden upsurge in sexual activity comparable to that of males. Instead, women showed slow but steady increases in sexual responsiveness that reached peaks in the middle twenties and early thirties. To say that females mature more rapidly sexually is quite misleading, even though they do so in terms of reproductive capacity.

On the basis of sexual responsiveness alone

(and obviously there are many other considerations), we should match the adolescent boy with the woman almost twice his age. Our sexual customs and institutions reverse this correspondence, however. Although men usually marry younger women, marriages in which the women are older are much rarer and more likely to appear odd.

During and after adolescence adult patterns of sexual behavior become established. They will be discussed in subsequent chapters. Petting, however, because it is typically an adolescent activity and constitutes one of the major avenues of developing sociosexual relations, will be discussed here.

Petting

"Petting" refers to erotic caressing, as well as to fondling without apparent erotic intent (as in petting an animal). Erotic petting is not an exclusively Western or even human practice. Among many mammals there is a great deal of sex play that does not lead to coitus. In one form or another petting is practiced all over the world. In this country it has in the past been known by a variety of names ("bundling," "spooning," "smooching," "larking," "sparking," and so on), all of which now sound quaint and antiquated. The term "petting" itself seems to be on its way to joining this list. One current replacement, "making out," is quite ambiguous, in that it is also used for sexual intercourse.

Although terminology varies, the techniques of petting (which are basically those of foreplay) persist essentially unchanged. Petting may or may not culminate in orgasm for either participant. If it leads to coitus then it may be more accurate to call it "foreplay." Also the term "petting" is generally reserved for heterosexual encounters, even though homosexual relations may involve similar techniques.

The relative prevalence of petting at various periods provides interesting clues to changes in sexual patterns and attitudes. For example, it was shown in the Kinsey survey that successive generations of women in this country had petted in increasingly larger numbers. Of those born before 1900, 80 percent reported some premarital petting experience (15 percent to the point of orgasm). Of those born in 1900–1909, 91 percent reported such experience (32 percent to orgasm). Nearly 99 percent of those born between 1910 and 1929 reported such experience; about a third of these women had reached orgasm through petting at least once. No comparable information was obtained for males. Altogether 90 percent of women reported having engaged in premarital petting, about 30 percent to the point of orgasm.[8] It will be recalled, however, that the Kinsey sample was weighted toward the higher socioeconomic classes, which usually show heavier reliance on petting than do the poor and the less educated.

There are no current figures for petting activities in this country. Both public and scientific interest have moved beyond this issue. The fine distinctions between "necking," "petting," and "heavy petting" hardly seem to preoccupy today's youth. The question now more commonly revolves around whether or not to engage in coitus, with whom, and under what circumstances. Observations in countries that are being westernized suggest that their youth may now be going through phases similar to those experienced by Western youth in the recent past.

From the point of view of psychosexual development, the primary significance of petting is its role in initiating heterosexual psychosocial encounters. Although petting in adolescence progresses concurrently with masturbation and less often with homosexual contacts, it gradually gains in primacy; for most people it provides the bridge to adult heterosexual intercourse. Adolescents learn much about each other's bodies, sexual responses, and so on while petting. Through these encounters they also learn the social rules and customs of sexual behavior.

These tentative and often tremulous encounters frequently go beyond the specifically sexual and involve feelings of intimacy, tenderness, and love. Through these interactions adolescents learn about each other's emotions and thoughts. It is during this period that concepts of sex roles, notions of masculinity and femininity, and the other components of sexual identity begin to be consolidated.

Our remarks here are intended only to be illustrative. We do not pretend to offer a universal model of sexual development during adolescence. The same tasks may be accomplished with minimal or no physical sexual contact at all. Or adolescents may proceed directly to full-fledged sexual activity without benefit of these "trials." The outcome in the nature and quality of adult sexual life is thus not a simple function of how much sex or what sort of sex a person has during adolescence. Rather, a host of factors, sexual as well as other, interact to shape sexuality in the context of overall development.

Cross-Cultural Perspectives

Cross-cultural comparisons of child-rearing practices offer opportunities to learn from what are, in fact, "natural experiments." We may, for instance, learn about the effects of sexual contacts between children and adults, which we would be loath to experiment with among ourselves. Unfortunately, because of the limited and fragmentary nature of cross-cultural data, only some of our questions can be answered.

The development and manifestations of sexual behavior in childhood cannot be properly understood without assessment of the sexual mores of the specific group because of the powerful influence that these mores exert on

---

[8]Kinsey *et al.* (1948), p. 534; Kinsey *et al.* (1953), p. 268.

such behavior. Whether or not children engage in given forms of sexual activity has different meanings, depending upon whether the activity is encouraged, permitted, or prohibited by their groups.

Ford and Beach[9] have thus categorized cultures according to levels of adult permissiveness: restrictive, semirestrictive, and permissive. Although this classification oversimplifies matters by necessity, it is nevertheless quite useful. It is understood, of course, that in a heterogeneous and complex society there are, not one, but multiple levels of permissiveness. Nevertheless, there are still standards to which, at least in principle, the majority (or the dominant groups) adheres and that set the "moral tone" and shape the laws of that society. (Other limitations of this research were discussed in Chapter 7.)

Restrictive Societies. Restrictiveness is a matter of judgment. For example, to describe American society as restrictive of preadolescent and adolescent sexual activity may impress some people as ironic. On the other hand, it may also come as a surprise that many primitive societies are equally restrictive in their attitudes toward early sexual behavior. Restrictive societies constitute the minority in Ford and Beach's survey: Only fourteen, in addition to American society, were listed in this group. Semirestrictive societies numbered forty-eight, and thirty-two were considered permissive.[10]

Restrictive primitive societies vary in the severity of their control of preadolescent sexuality, but as a rule they attempt to keep children from learning about sexual matters and to check their spontaneous sexual activities. For instance, both the Apinaye (a primitive, peaceful, monogamous people in Brazil) and the Ashanti (a complex polygynous society in Guinea) expressly forbade children to masturbate from an early age. In New Guinea a Kwoma woman who saw a boy with an erection would strike his penis with a stick. Kwoma boys soon learned not to touch their penises even while urinating.

The secrecy that surrounded sex also often extended to reproductive functions. Humans or even animals giving birth might not be watched by children and fictitious explanations of where babies come from were offered. Special precautions were taken to keep children from surprising adults while they were engaged in coitus; children might even be placed in separate sleeping quarters at an early age.

It is interesting that even in these more restrictive societies the expression of sexuality in childhood could not be entirely checked. Children still engaged in sex play when they could even though they may have done so in fear or shame.

Restrictive attitudes toward children did not always mean that these cultures were sexually prohibitive in general. Once an individual had reached maturity (usually marked by some rite), he could immediately be permitted wide sexual freedom. Most of these cultures also shared the double standard so well known in our society. Girls were almost always more strictly guarded, and coitus before menarche (or some other sign of puberty) was believed to be injurious.

Female virginity at the time of marriage was highly valued in these cultures. The ancient Kurdish custom of parading blood-stained bed sheets on the wedding night is well known. Yungar (Australian aborigine) brides were deflowered by pairs of old women. In either culture, should the hymen have been tampered with earlier, a girl would be in serious difficulty.

Restrictive societies may go to great pains to enforce prohibitions on preadolescent sexual behavior. Warnings, chaperoning, and segregation are some preventive measures. Disgrace, punishment, and even death are invoked when

---

[9] Ford and Beach (1951).

[10] Ford and Beach (1951), pp. 178–192.

prevention fails. Among the Chagga (advanced polygynous agriculturalists of Tanganyika, now Tanzania), for instance, if a boy who had not been initiated was caught in the sex act, he and his partner were placed on top of each other and staked to the ground.

Semirestrictive Societies. The majority of cultures surveyed by Ford and Beach have been placed in the semirestrictive category. They were characterized less by differences in sexual codes for juveniles than by the lack of vigor in enforcing existing prohibitions.

For example, the Alorese (polygynous agriculturalists of Indonesia), the Andamanese (monogamous seminomadic gatherers, hunters, and fishers), and the Huichol (monogamous Mexican people who live by animal husbandry and agriculture) all formally disapproved of premarital intercourse but made little effort to check it. As long as the practice was not flaunted and did not result in pregnancy, it was generally tolerated. When pregnancy occurred the couple was pressured into marriage. Contraceptive measures were therefore frequently used by youngsters in these cultures. Methods included coitus interruptus, ejaculation between the girl's legs, placing a pad in the vagina, and washing the vagina after coitus. A pregnant girl might also have resorted to abortion.

American society, and Western society in general, has been moving toward semirestrictive standards. Masturbation now hardly carries any of its former stigma among the more educated population. Premarital coitus also appears to be increasing, or at least people are more open about it.

More than three decades ago, Terman[11] was impressed by the decline in premarital virginity in the United States between 1910 and the early 1930s. He predicted that, if this trend continued

at the same rate, very few males born after 1930 and very few females born after 1940 would be virgins when they married. Although this prediction has not yet come true, the importance of premarital virginity does seem to have declined among large segments of the population.

It is unwarranted to assume that people preserve their virginity merely in conformity with prevailing sexual mores. Because a given activity is condoned does not mean that everyone wishes to participate in it. No matter how permissive society may become, therefore, some people will probably continue to refrain from premarital sexual intercourse.

Permissive Societies. Permissiveness toward sexual behavior during the developing years does not mean complete absence of rules and regulations. All societies have prohibitions on certain sexual activities in childhood and later. Relative to the cultures already discussed, however, permissive societies showed remarkable laxity toward youngsters' sexual activity.

Among various Pacific islanders and other permissive cultures,[12] children of both sexes freely and openly engaged in autoerotic activities and sex play, including oral-genital contacts and imitative coitus. These children were either instructed in sex or allowed to observe adult sexual activity. In a few societies adults actually initiated children sexually. Siriono (polygynous nomads of Bolivia) and Hopi parents masturbated their youngsters.

In these permissive cultures sex play became progressively more sophisticated and gradually merged with adult forms of sexual activity. With the exception of incest, youngsters were generally free to gratify their growing and changing sexual needs.

---

[11] Terman (1938).

[12] The Pukapukans, Trobrianders, Lesu, Hottentot, Tikopians, Seniang, and others.

As we have already suggested, permissiveness in these groups went beyond mere acquiescence. Sexual activity was actually encouraged early in life. The Chewa (polygynous advanced agriculturists of central Africa) believed that children should be sexually active if they wished to ensure fertility in the future. The Lepcha (monogamous agriculturalists of the Himalayas) believed that sexual activity was necessary for girls to grow up: At eleven or twelve years most girls were engaging in coitus, often with adult males. Trobriand boys of ten to twelve years and girls of six to eight years were initiated into coitus under adult tutelage. Because of relative physiological sterility during adolescence, pregnancy rarely resulted from these encounters.

Cross-Species Comparisons

Comparison of human sexual development patterns with those of subhuman species is particularly instructive in clarifying the biological and cultural components of preadolescent sexuality. Subhuman primates and lower mammals show a great deal of sexual activity before puberty. Clearly sexuality precedes fertility, and the rudiments of adult sexual behavior are easily discernible in the sex play of the young of many animal species.

Infant and adolescent chimpanzees are well known for their active involvement in autoerotic (solitary masturbation is more common in males), heterosexual, and homosexual sex play. Long before reproductive maturity is reached, they attempt copulation and experiment with various positions. Males may orally stimulate females, who may, in turn, manually arouse the males.

Young monkeys imitate practically all adult sexual behavior.[13] A seven-month-old pigtail monkey (equivalent in development to a two-year-old child) was observed mounting his mother, having an erection, and making copulatory thrusts. Similar manifestations of early sexual activity have been observed among baboons and other subhuman primates of both sexes. We shall discuss the sexual development of monkeys in more detail later.

Lower mammals show comparable juvenile sexual behavior among males but not among females. Before the first period of heat the female animal is sexually unresponsive. Males, however, show mounting behavior long before reproductive maturity has been achieved.

THEORIES OF PSYCHOSEXUAL DEVELOPMENT

Theories of psychosexual development are attempts to explain the evolution of sexual functioning in the context of general development. As the term "psychosexual" indicates, sexual and psychic processes are intimately interrelated, and it is not possible to understand one apart from the other.

Currently there is no generally accepted theory of psychosexual development. Nevertheless, there are many areas of general agreement. Also certain aspects of sexual development are best explained by one theory and other aspects by some other. The theoretical points of view presented here are therefore best regarded as complementary, rather than as competitive. Our intention is not, however, to pretend a consensus that does not exist but to take from each approach what seems most valid.

Biological Basis of Sexual Development

Theories of psychosexual development are based on different hypotheses about the nature of sexuality itself. For example, psychoanalytic

---

[13] Zuckerman (1932).

theorists rely heavily on the concept of a sexual instinct, whereas behaviorists have little use for it. As we discussed in Chapter 7, even the definition of what constitutes sexual behavior is difficult to agree upon. As long as there are such basic disagreements about the nature of sexuality itself, attempts to explain its development will be difficult.

For many years the biological basis of sexual behavior was tied to the concept of a "sexual instinct." Although there is no agreement on what constitutes an "instinct," many students of behavior still find this concept useful in explaining activities that appear to be universal in members of a species, that have demonstrable physiological bases, and that are adaptive. But "instinctive" must not be equated with "innate" in efforts to reduce behavior to its "learned" and "unlearned" components. Attempts at drawing such dichotomies in behavior have generally proven fruitless. For example, it is often impossible to differentiate between behavior that is learned and genetically determined behavior that does not appear until maturation.

Despite the ambiguities, however, the biological basis of sexual behavior and the influence of biological factors in the development of such behavior can hardly be denied. In man, as in the vertebrates as a whole, adult sexual behavior is the product of the interaction of biological (genetic, hormonal, and so on) and experiential (psychological, social) factors throughout the life cycle. During intrauterine life, development is predominantly under the influence of genetically determined factors. But adult man, in contrast to very young human beings and to lower animals, appears relatively emancipated from the control of these biological forces, though to exactly what extent we do not know.[14]

The abstract arguments over the concept of instinct that preoccupied scientists in the past have now been replaced by the experimental approaches of ethologists, Konrad Lorenz and Niko Tinbergen being the two best known. Although the applicability of their findings to the study of man is often unclear, much has been learned from their work about the interaction of innate patterns of behavior and environmental factors that elicit such behavior.

It has been demonstrated that some animals respond to very specific cues from the environment. For example, a mother hen responds to the peeping of a chick. It will ignore a chick that it cannot hear (if the chick is under a glass jar, for example) but will come to the rescue of any object that peeps as if it were one. The mating behavior of the stickleback progresses quite predictably. The male fish displays its red underbelly, in response to which the female turns to him her swollen abdomen and follows him to the nest that he has built. The pair go through a number of additional moves and countermoves, and the sequence culminates when the male fertilizes the eggs laid by the female in the nest.

In these and numerous other examples the animals exhibit specific, stereotyped behavior that is innate and believed to be mediated through neurophysiological mechanisms called "Innate Releasing Mechanisms" (IRM). The external cues that stimulate these mechanisms are specific ("cue stimuli" or "social releasers"). Systematic study and demonstration of similar phenomena among humans remain to be accomplished, but the presence of such mechanisms among animals is itself of great interest, for it permits the experimental, rather than the

---

[14] There is extensive literature on this topic. For a general discussion of instincts see Curtis (1968), pp. 614–624. See

Young, ed. (1961), Vol. II, Chapter 23, for a discussion of the ontogenesis of sexual behavior in man by Hampson and Hampson and Chapter 24 for a review of the cultural determinants of sexual behavior by Mead.

speculative, study of innately determined patterns of behavior.

In earlier chapters we examined the development of the genital apparatus (Chapter 2) and the role of hormones in their development and functioning (Chapter 4). Although it is not yet possible to relate these processes in a demonstrable manner to various phases of psychosexual development, in the final analysis any adequate scheme of psychosexual development will have to integrate biological processes with the pertinent psychological and social variables.

Psychoanalytic Theory

Few intellectual movements in recent history have had an impact on Western thought comparable to that of psychoanalysis. Particularly significant for our purposes is the paramount importance accorded to sexuality in this theory. Psychoanalysis is not a unified body of thought. Although the figure of Sigmund Freud (1856–1939) dominates psychoanalysis to this day, there have been many contributors to the theory, and some have sharply disagreed with his formulation of the role of sexuality in human development.

The psychoanalytic literature is vast: Freud's writings alone fill twenty-four volumes.[15] As an introduction, we can therefore only hastily sketch Freud's model of the mind ("the mental apparatus") and introduce his concept of the unconscious before describing the psychosexual development of the individual from the psychoanalytic point of view.

It is generally agreed that the two most original concepts elaborated by Freud were those of the unconscious and of infantile sexuality. Although our primary concern is with the latter, the notion of the unconscious and the whole concept of the mental apparatus are so closely related to it that we must describe them briefly first.

Freud neither discovered nor invented the human unconscious,[16] but he did designate it as the pivotal point of his theory of mental functioning and the primary location of human motivations. What is the unconscious? We often speak as if it were part of the brain. Actually it is a characteristic of certain mental functions. Thoughts (as well as feelings) can thus be placed in three categories: conscious thoughts, of which we are aware at any given time; preconscious thoughts, which can be brought into awareness more or less at will (as when we summon up a friend's name or telephone number); and unconscious thoughts, which cannot ordinarily be brought into consciousness even with a great deal of effort. In fact we are, by definition, not even aware that our unconscious thoughts exist. Unconscious thoughts can, however, become conscious in a number of ways. They spill out in dreams, slips of the tongue, and other distorted or camouflaged forms, and they may be coaxed out through free association.

Contrary to the popular cliché that what one does not know cannot hurt him, psychoanalysts believe that what one does not know dominates his life. Unconscious thoughts and feelings are beyond voluntary control yet profoundly influence how we feel, what we think, and how we act. To explain these activities Freud proposed a hypothetical model of the mind, consisting of the id, the ego, and the superego, which are, of course, not parts of the brain but rather categories of its processes and functions.

The id embodies the drives, the psychic representations of biological instincts. Initially Freud postulated a single drive, the libido. Later he incorporated another drive (aggression) into his notion of the id. All the contents of the id are entirely unconscious. Only derivatives may come out in veiled form, passing through the dual censorship of the ego and superego. The id strives for expression through pleasure, regardless of reality considerations or social concerns.

---

[15] The definitive translation of Freud's complete works, published from 1957 to 1964 under the editorship of James Strachey, is *The Standard Edition of the Complete Psychological Works of Sigmund Freud.*

[16] Whyte (1960).

The ego is more difficult to describe. Part of it (the autonomous ego), consists of processes (perception, memory, communication systems, and so on) that mediate drives and thus promote survival. But the ego must therefore also fulfill defensive functions. Through various mechanisms, it blocks recognition of the demands of the id (repression, denial, and so on), rechannels them (through sublimation, displacement, or the like), or distorts them (as in projection). Through such mechanisms the ego manages a working compromise between drive gratification and environmental constraints and limitations. The ego is part conscious, which accounts for our faculty of self-awareness, but its defensive functions are unconscious. As the defenses are against the id, which is always unconscious, it could not be otherwise: The most effective concealment involves concealing the very fact of concealment.

The superego is popularly equated with the conscience. Part of its function is in fact to maintain a conscious awareness and to ensure the morality of one's conduct. But the superego, like the ego, is also partly unconscious, for it too must work to block the id. The superego embodies the moral and value judgments of those who have helped to shape one's life. It may be inconsistent and corruptible or excessively harsh and punitive. When its demands are not met, the ego (the self) experiences guilt.

The Libido Theory

Historically, elaboration of the concept of the unconscious preceded the theory of infantile sexuality.[17] It was the latter, however, that evoked (and still evokes) so much controversy. Freud viewed the sexual instinct as a psychophysiological process (like hunger) with both physical and mental manifestations. By "libido" (Latin for "lust") he meant the psychological manifestations, the erotic longing aspect of the sexual instinct. The libido theory was a conceptual scheme that purported to explain the nature and manifestations of the sex drive throughout development.

What did Freud mean by "sexual"? His critics have attacked him for stretching the meaning of the term unduly. Some of his followers (notably Carl Jung) have reinterpreted its sensual aspect and equated it with a more general life force. One source of difficulty has been Freud's own repeated revisions of the theory (he made more changes in the successive editions of *Three Essays* than in any other work except *Interpretation of Dreams*).

Freud did not divest "sex" of its commonly understood sense of pleasure through orgasm. Rather he extended the term to pleasurable experiences that were then ordinarily considered nonsexual. This extension was comparable to his broadening of the concept of "mental" from its ordinary sense of "conscious" to include the entire range of unconscious mental activity as well.[18]

Sexuality, in this broader sense, is the central theme of psychoanalytic theory. The necessity to keep certain thoughts out of consciousness, indeed, the very concept of the unconscious itself hinges on the issue of infantile sexuality

---

[17] Freud published his first major analysis of the unconscious in *The Interpretation of Dreams* (1900). Five years later appeared *Three Essays on the Theory of Sexuality* (also translated as *Three Contributions to the Theory of Sex*) in which the theory of infantile sexuality was first formulated. James Strachey, editor of Freud's collected works, has stated that "Freud's *Three Essays on the Theory of Sexuality* stands, there can be no doubt, beside his *Interpretation of Dreams* as his most momentous and original contribution to human knowledge" (Freud [1957-1964], Vol. VII, p. 126). Only 1,000 copies of the first edition of *Three Essays* were printed; it took more than four years to sell them. During the next ten years two more editions appeared,

earning Freud $53.08. But subsequently the book went through six editions in Freud's lifetime and has been translated into nine languages. In his introduction Freud remarked, "If mankind had been able to learn from a direct observation of children, these three essays could have remained unwritten" (Freud, [1957-1964], Vol. VII, p. 133).

[18] Jones, E. (1953), Vol. II, p. 284.

and the psychological development of the individual essentially revolves around the unfolding of the libido.

Stages of Psychosexual Development

Although Freud's writings still dominate much of psychoanalytic thought, important conceptual developments have occurred during the past several decades, particularly the growth of ego psychology. Current theories of psychosexual development, though retaining the fundamental Freudian scheme, reflect advances in psychoanalytic thinking, as well as relevant insights from related studies. A detailed discussion of these theories is not possible here. Instead we shall present in broad outline only the most salient features of the psychoanalytic developmental model.[19]

All psychoanalytic formulations start from the assumption that the newborn child is endowed with a certain libidinal "capital." Psychosexual development is then the process by which this diffuse and labile sexual energy is "invested" in certain pleasurable zones of the body (mouth, anus, genitals) at successive stages of childhood. The vicissitudes of the libido during psychosexual development determine not only the sexual functioning of the individual but also his entire personality structure and psychological (and at times physical) health.

Oral Stage. Libidinal investment in body parts is not random but follows a specific

_____

[19]All general monographs on psychoanalysis deal with psychosexual development in considerable detail. For examples (at increasing levels of complexity) see Brenner (1957), Waelder (1964), Nunberg (1969), and Fenichel (1945). This material is also covered in most textbooks on child development and psychology; see Hilgard (1956), Janis *et al.* (1969). For an exposition that draws heavily on recent biomedical research see Engel (1962). For a comprehensive view of new directions and perspectives in psychoanalytic theory, see Marmor, ed. (1968).

sequence coordinated with physiological maturation. The survival of the newborn infant depends on his competence in sucking: a universal innate response. To psychoanalysts sucking means more than simple food intake: The infant also obtains gratification through the process itself. During the first year of life his mouth thus becomes his main source of pleasure; like all pleasure it is basically erotic in nature.

The oral zone is thus the first site of libidinal investment and the mode of its gratification is through "taking in," or incorporation. This model is duplicated through other senses: The eyes, ears, and skin of the body "take in" stimuli, and as long as the latter are of appropriate intensity, these organs not only help to acquaint the infant with his environment but also provide him with pleasure.

Although the mouth remains an avenue of pleasure for everyone, its relative importance in the psychosexual configuration at any stage in the life of each individual varies greatly. For instance, thumb sucking provides only transient pleasure for some children, and they are easily distracted from it. Other children are greatly preoccupied with it into late childhood. Most children tend to revert to it (regress) under the stress of hunger, fatigue, boredom, rejection, or other unhappiness.

Thumb sucking does not generally last beyond childhood, but the use of the mouth to obtain pleasure certainly does. The pleasure of eating past the point of mere satiation is a universal experience. Kissing is, of course, both an oral and an erotic activity. Psychoanalysts include also smoking, drinking, and the use of drugs because the pattern in all is the obtaining of gratification or relief through the intake (incorporation) of external substances.

As children vary in their thumb sucking, so do adults vary in their reliance on oral gratification. The ordinary person enjoys good food but he eats primarily to relieve his hunger. He will also kiss and use his mouth in various ways as part of erotic foreplay. But he performs all these oral activities in moderation. He can dispense with some or all of them. Although an "oral streak" runs through his personality, including his sexual preferences, it does not dominate his life.

When a person is under stress, his oral needs may be intensified; he may literally eat, drink, or smoke more.[20] His need for affection may also increase, and he may seek reassurance, love, and the like. At such times he is more eager to "take in." Like intensified thumb sucking in childhood, such behavior under stress is to be expected.

Anal Stage. The erogenous zone invested with libido during the second stage of development is the anus. Concurrent with the beginning ability to control the bowels (and to experience the pleasure of evacuation), the child of about two years also becomes capable of moving about effectively and using his developing muscles to do many things.

The general modes of gratification at this stage are two: retention and elimination (counterparts of incorporation). If all goes reasonably well, the individual obtains some pleasure from defecation and may enjoy occasional messy activity. At a characterologic level, he is able to say both yes and no; to love and give yet also to withhold and to be aggressive if necessary; to accumulate and to hold on to some belongings but not to be burdened by them and also to be capable of generosity.

---

[20] In considering such behavior, we must remember that, though oral needs may be important, they are by no means the only motivation. A person may, for instance, smoke or drink because of social pressure without enjoyment. Narcotics addiction involves a physiological imperative that may even supersede whatever incorporative needs may originally have been dominant. There are also various biological and social factors in obesity that are quite independent of oral gratification.

These stages of development not only reflect changes in libidinal needs but also have an aggressive aspect. For example, in the latter part of the oral stage the infant can bite quite effectively. In the anal stage, children go through a phase of intense ambivalence in which they tend frequently to be stubborn, self-assertive, willful, and cruel, alternating rapidly between expressions of love and hate. This ambivalence is explained as a result of the primary conflict (retention against elimination) that characterizes this period.

Phallic Stage. The oral and anal stages generally extend through the first three years of a child's life. As the genitals have not yet been invested with libido, these stages together are designated "pregenital"; they are identical for males and females.

Although the term "sublimation" is used loosely to refer to channeling sexual drives to nonsexual ends, in psychoanalytic usage it refers to the transformation of pregenital drives to overtly nonsexual and socially acceptable ends. In this sense the avocation to paint would be considered partly a derivative of the anal urge to soil. As the artist's paints have been refined from crude compounds, so his offensive (to adults) childhood urge has been "purified" through the process of sublimation.

At the age of about three years, the child becomes more keenly aware of his genitals and of the pleasures of manipulating them. The zones now invested with libido are the penis in the male and the clitoris in the female. Behavior is dominated by the "intrusive mode." At this age children poke their fingers into things and make forays into the unknown to satisfy their insatiable curiosity. When they are permitted to do so, children of three or four also make deliberate sexual explorations.

The main psychoanalytic issue related to this stage is the development of the Oedipus complex.[21] The child develops an erotic attachment to the parent of the opposite sex and feelings of aggressive rivalry toward the parent of the same sex. This development places the child in a dilemma: First, he does not have the capacity to gratify his genital impulse; second, he still loves (and fears) the "rival" parent and thus suffers guilt. A boy imagines that he deserves punishment involving genital damage or "castration" (actual loss of the penis, rather than the testes). The "reasoning" behind this fear is simple. He expects punishment of the offending part. He has discovered that girls have no penises, and his fear that the penis can be lost is substantiated. A girl's reaction to the discovery that boys have penises may be to conclude that she has lost her own and to envy the male's apparent advantage ("penis envy").[22]

If development continues undisturbed, the child resolves the oedipal conflict by giving up the parent as an erotic object (while continuing to love this parent) because of his own fear of disapproval and retaliation and the obvious hopelessness of his desires. Instead, the child identifies with the parent of the same sex, hoping one day to acquire comparable prerogatives. To ensure that unacceptable wishes will not be fulfilled or continue to torment the person, the entire conflict is buried in the unconscious. The oedipal wishes nevertheless do not simply fade, and their derivatives occasionally seep into consciousness, as in fairy tales in which giants are killed and princesses rescued, inflated fantasies of strength and daring, various nightmares, phobias, and the like.

---

[21] Named after Sophocles' tragedy *Oedipus Rex*, in which the king has unwittingly murdered his father and married his mother, a theme common in disguised form in literature, myth, and folklore in many parts of the world.

[22] Psychoanalysts now concede that Freud developed his sexual theories from a male perspective; using the male as his prototype, he superimposed his model on his description of women also. See Salzman in Marmor, ed. (1968), p. 127.

Problems in Psychosexual Development

Events rarely progress smoothly in the fashion described so far, and much of the psychoanalytic literature deals with the pathological consequences of faulty psychosexual development and with the techniques for correcting them. Difficulties in this regard arise when the needs of a given stage have been either insufficiently or excessively gratified. In the first instance, as physiological maturation moves inexorably, the libido does not keep pace, as it were, and the body zone appropriate to the next phase of development does not become adequately eroticized. When gratification is excessive, then the child is reluctant to give it up. In either instance the libido becomes "fixated" at that stage. This hampers subsequent development, and the individual either fails to mature psychosexually or is at least handicapped by a tendency to "regress" to the fixation point under stress.

The adult manifestations of such libidinal fixation in infancy vary greatly but generally fall into two types. In the first instance the individual continues to seek the erotic gratification of the infantile stage in an undisguised fashion. The "anally fixated" person may, for example, seek actual stimulation of the anus through anal intercourse. He thus becomes a "passive homosexual." When the expression of the infantile erotic impulse seeks such overt gratification, the result is a "perversion." In this sense, perversions are merely the persistence of infantile forms of sexuality into adulthood. The child is considered to be "polymorphously perverse," but that is normal for his level of development.

Psychoanalysts find it permissible that some residues of pregenital impulses persist into adulthood, provided that they do not gain primacy over coitus. For example, kissing is a legitimate oral activity during foreplay. But, if a person would rather kiss than engage in coitus (when coitus is legitimately available), then kissing is a "perversion" under the circumstances.

Although perversions or sexual deviations are fairly frequent outcomes of infantile fixations, the alternative pathway is even more common. In these instances the infantile libidinal drive is repressed and permitted expression in highly disguised, symbolic form, and the result is a "neurosis."[23] The neurosis in turn may take many forms. For example, a repressed infantile sex drive may color the individual's total personality. If the fixation is at the oral stage, he will show "oral traits," perhaps an excessive and chronic preoccupation with food or some other form of oral gratification. Or he may become an "oral character" and require constant pampering as if he were an infant: always eager to receive but rarely willing or able to reciprocate. In extreme instances a person may develop psychotic delusions of "incorporating" others into his own body. If the fixation is at the anal level, the personality of an individual may be characterized by the ambivalence or stubborn, willful behavior of the two-year-old. A multitude of defense mechanisms distort and modify these impulses, of course, so that many symptom combinations are possible. Some of them have fairly obvious associations with the events of the anal stage, but others are much more obscure.

If oedipal ties are not resolved similar personality defects and sexual difficulties result. If the child does not have sustained relationships with both parents or adequate substitutes or if he is still fixated at pregenital levels, he may

never fully engage in the oedipal situation and thus may fail to resolve it.

If one parent is seductive toward the child or both parents are deeply and openly hostile toward each other, the child's oedipal hopes may be unrealistically intensified, and resolution of the conflict becomes more difficult. Should a parent become sick or die at this stage, the child may blame himself, magically ascribing the event to his own hostile wishes.

Whether parents are punitive or seductive, the presence and number of siblings, and the individual's own ranking among them are all likely to influence the outcome of the oedipal dilemma. Conceptions of sex roles, pride in one's gender, respect for the other sex, moral attitudes toward sexual activity, and other relevant issues are shaped at this stage. The extraordinary human capacity for adaptation ensures that potentially pathogenic influences are often mitigated or neutralized. Unfortunately, serious problems still do occur, particularly when an individual enters this phase with major doubts and conflicts left from the pregenital period.

Males with unresolved oedipal conflicts may become timid and sexually inhibited. They may have been so threatened by punitive fathers that they have "decided" to give up not only their mothers but all women as erotic objects. A mother who is envious and hostile toward men may relate in the same way to her son, thus causing him to shun all women. The daughters of aggressive fathers may identify with them and develop masculine character traits. Those with punitive mothers may emulate them or rebel against them and attempt to ally themselves with passive fathers. Or such girls may develop passive, even masochistic, personalities and court needless suffering.

A classical outcome of an unresolved Oedipus complex is the personality with exaggerated sexual traits. The male prototype is the

---

[23] In the early psychoanalytic literature, the term "neurosis" stood for all mental and emotional disturbances, and it is in that sense that we use it here. The current psychiatric definition of "neurosis" is more restricted and refers to certain circumscribed symptom complexes like phobias.

seductive, exhibitionistic, and narcissistic Don Juan (the "phallic-narcissistic" character) who constantly seeks sexual conquests. His relationships are shallow and unrewarding, except as demonstrations to himself and to the world of his own potency and daring (a "counterphobic" defense against castration anxiety). The predilection to court women who are married to other men may be another indication of oedipal longings.

The female counterpart of this type of male personality is the seductive and exhibitionistic but competitive and manipulative, "castrating" woman who delights in humiliating men. This type of woman is said to have a "hysterical character disorder." In their less severe forms such character traits in both sexes are viewed as charming and exciting by many people.

In the psychoanalytic scheme all mental, personality, and emotional problems are thus viewed as having sexual bases, just as perversions do: Neurosis and perversions are considered the two sides of the same coin. The infantile erotic impulse is expressed covertly in the former and overtly in the latter.

This theoretical framework is very versatile in explaining sexual phenomena, but it is also quite nonspecific. For example, male homosexuality may be explained as arising from fixations in any one of the stages. The taking of another's penis in the mouth may be considered to satisfy an oral need. Anal intercourse may satisfy anal needs. Or one may seek out another man to obtain reassurance from the sight of his penis and thus allay castration fears arising from the phallic-oedipal phase. Psychoanalysts must therefore reconstruct in each instance the specific dynamics of the infantile conflicts rather than rely on predetermined judgments for their explanations.

Genital Stage. The successful resolution of the Oedipus complex signals the end of the phallic stage and makes it possible for "genital maturity" to emerge. Not that the three- or four-year-old child is sexually adult. The next phase of development (latency) is for most youngsters a period of intellectual growth, social maturation, and fairly limited sexual activity.

At the beginning of adolescence sexuality reawakens. To the extent that past conflicts have been satisfactorily resolved, the young person is free to initiate sexual interaction along adult lines. But such conflicts may not all have been resolved. Pregenital fixations may make it difficult, if not impossible, to invest the libido in "normal" sexual objects. If the adolescent is still smarting from phallic fears and insults, he may renew the battle. He also now has the requisite sexual apparatus to make his activity potentially more effective: Unintended parenthood may occur long before he is ready for it.

It is quite common for adolescents to manifest traces of conflict from the phallic phase: for boys to be boisterous, daring, and narcissistic and for girls to be seductive, flirtatious, and exhibitionistic. Such behavior offers safe ways to test one's sexual skills, the reactions of the opposite sex, and the rules of society, as well as to work out residual pregenital wishes and impulses.

Gradually, however, "genitality" should manifest itself. The young man should cease to be preoccupied with his penis and should react sexually with his whole self. The young woman too should go beyond the intrusive mode and incorporate the "inceptive" and "inclusive" modes into her psychosexual structure.

The psychoanalytic ideal of "genitality" encompasses the integration of pregenital stages to permit the reconciliation of genital orgasm with love and to facilitate establishment of satisfactory life patterns of sex, procreation, and work. Freud's response to the question of what ought to be the central purpose of life was "work and love."

Theories of Learning

"Learning" is readily understood in an everyday sense, yet it defies a formal definition that would be generally acceptable. A simple way to approach it is to consider as learned all behavior that would not appear unless it was either specifically taught by someone else or learned by the individual through trial and error, imitation, and so on. Innate responses (like nest building by birds), new behavior that reflects maturation (like flying of birds when they are of age), and changes in performance resulting from fatigue are thus excluded. Reasoning, imagination, inventiveness, and insight are mental functions that also differ from learning in a strict sense but are, of course, dependent upon and closely related to it.

We are interested here in the learning of human sexual behavior. Unfortunately, little of the literature on learning theory treats sexual behavior specifically.[24] We shall therefore assume that learning sexual behavior proceeds along the same general lines as does all learning.

Although learning theory may seem to offer a unified approach or a single conceptual scheme, actually there is no single widely accepted learning theory. Instead there are many theories of learning, including those of Thorndike (connectionism), Guthrie (contiguous conditioning), Skinner (operant conditioning), Hull (systematic behavior), Tolman (sign learning), and Lewin (field theory), as well as those of the classical Gestalt school, the more eclectic approach known as "functionalism," and various approaches using mathematical learning models. Psychoanalytic theory is, in a sense, also a theory of learning, but, because of historical and methodological differences, it is usually neither labeled nor treated as one.

Although we cannot possibly deal with all these theories individually, we shall dwell briefly on their general nature and the ways in which adherents of some of them view the development of sexual behavior.[25] Learning theories have been generated primarily by psychologists. They have been based on carefully controlled and verified laboratory experiments with animals (most often rats) and some have also been tested on children.

As the concept of conditioning is central to most learning theories, we shall use it to illustrate how a learning theorist would explain the development and differentiation of sexual behavior. This approach is so firmly rooted in experimental work that we shall begin by reviewing briefly the animal experiments upon which classical and operant conditioning models have been based.

Classical Conditioning. The original experiments on conditioning were conducted by Pavlov.[26] His paradigm is now called "classical conditioning" to differentiate it from later-developed techniques of "operant conditioning." Pavlov's experimental model can be summarized as follows: When a hungry dog is presented with food (the unconditioned stimulus) it salivates (the unconditioned response). This response is innate in all dogs. If a bell is sounded shortly before or while the food is presented, the dog will in time learn to salivate to the sound of the bell, even though no food accompanies or follows it. As dogs ordinarily do not salivate to the sound of bells, the experimental dog is said to have become "conditioned." For him the bell is a conditioned stimulus, and salivation

---

[24] Hilgard (1956).

[25] For a comprehensive exposition of various learning theories, see Hilgard (1956). A more condensed review is presented in Janis *et al.* (1969), Chapter 3.

[26] Pavlov (1927).

to the bell alone is a conditioned response. In a sense, the bell and food have become paired in the mind of the dog.

The fate of this conditioned response depends upon subsequent experience. As long as the sound of the bell is accompanied by the appearance of food, the conditioned response (salivation to the sound of the bell alone) will be strengthened (reinforced). If food accompanies the bell less and less often, the salivating response weakens and ultimately disappears (is extinguished). But, if at this point the animal is allowed to rest and is then brought back into the laboratory, the salivation response to the bell will reappear (spontaneous recovery).

Operant Conditioning. In Pavlov's experiment the salivation of the dog always occurs in response to a specific external stimulus (food or bell). But in actual life most animal behavior is spontaneous. Dogs do not sit around waiting for food but actively look for it. To differentiate such spontaneous behavior from activity that involves mere reactions to external stimuli, the term "operant behavior" is used, and the modification of spontaneous behavior through learning is called "operant conditioning."[27] The concept of operant behavior provides a much more versatile and comprehensive framework for understanding both animal and human behavior, sexual and otherwise. In fact, some theorists believe that the applicability of classical conditioning is restricted to autonomic physiological responses like salivation in dogs.

The techniques of operant conditioning were devised primarily by B. F. Skinner during the past several decades. Again the starting point was a specific experiment. A hungry rat was placed in a dark sound-proof box, which had a small metal lever. When the rat stepped on the lever, a pellet of food was delivered. The rat ate the food and gradually learned to seek the lever, as more and more pellets were delivered (reinforcement). The rat could then obtain food at will.

In contrast to Pavlov's dog, Skinner's rat did not see the food, nor did it know that there would be food before it accidentally received the first pellet.

Lever pressing was thus not a response but a spontaneous (operant) act that became conditioned through reinforcement by the reward of food pellets. Conditioning of operant behavior is designated as "type R," to emphasize the importance of reinforcement in learning, in contrast to the emphasis in Pavlovian conditioning in which the unconditioned stimulus (food) determines subsequent learning ("type S" conditioning).

Reinforcement may be primary or secondary, positive or negative. In Skinner's experiment the food pellet that drops when the lever is pressed is an example of a primary positive reinforcer: Its presence increases the likelihood that the animal will perform in a predictable way (will press the lever). Water and sexual contact act as similar incentives. The animal will learn and perform tasks to obtain them.

A negative primary reinforcer has the opposite effect. It reduces the likelihood of an operant response, and its removal augments the probability of such a response. If the rat in the experimental box receives an electric shock in addition to receiving the food pellets on its way to the lever or when it touches the lever, it is less likely again to press the lever (the operant response) despite the food reward. Loud noise, very bright light, and extreme temperatures all act as negative reinforcers. They inhibit the operant response until the rat's hunger becomes sufficient to make the reward worth the discomfort.

In secondary reinforcement, a neutral stimulus is reinforced by repeated association with one that is not neutral. If the primary reinforcer is positive, then so is the associated secondary reinforcer; the same is true for negative reinforcers. For example, if upon pressing the lever, the rat receives a food pellet and simultaneously turns on a light and if, after it has been conditioned, the lever fails to deliver food or to turn on the light, the rat will ultimately cease to press the lever frequently (extinction). If, then, upon occasional manipulation, the lever turns on the light but fails to deliver the food pellet, the rat will nevertheless resume pressing the lever with increased frequency. The light alone has now acted as a reinforcer, even though the primary reinforcer (the food pellet) has not reappeared.

---

[27] Skinner (1938).

We have dealt so far with the basic notions of operant conditioning. From this model, ingenious and intricate experiments for manipulating the schedules of reinforcement and other variables have been devised. Although we cannot go into detail, additional principles will be mentioned when we discuss the application of learning theory to sexual behavior.

How does the concept of conditioning explain the learning of sexual behavior? Although conditioning techniques have been successfully used to train animals (for example, rats have learned to use marbles to obtain food from a vending machine, pigeons to play a modified game of table tennis, dogs to operate a pedal to obtain a bone from a refuse can) and have also been tested in classroom teaching of children, they have not been used experimentally to demonstrate the learning of so complex an activity as human sexual behavior. It is nevertheless legitimate to see whether or not the principles behind them can be extended to such behavior.

The main contribution of operant conditioning to the study of sexual behavior is perhaps in its liberating effect upon research. Centuries of speculation about the nature of the sex drive have not gone far to increase our understanding of sexual manifestations. We can now at least begin to look into the sexual learning process in terms of environmental influences while we continue to search for its biological roots.

For simplicity, we shall bypass detailed discussion of the relative influence of drives on learning. Learning theorists are themselves quite divided on this issue. In Pavlov's experiment, for instance, the primary motivator was the physiological need for food. The dog did not have to learn to respond to food. To apply this model to the learning of sexual behavior, we would have to assume the presence of a sex drive. We would then view erotic arousal in response to certain basic physical or psychological stimuli as, in a sense, the sexual

counterpart of the salivating response (unconditioned response). All other forms of sexual behavior would then be considered to be learned by association with this innate capacity.

In Skinner's experiments the influence of hunger upon learning is unequivocal, but Skinner prefers to call it the "effect of food deprivation" because "hunger" also implies certain internal changes. Food deprivation can be measured in time, whereas hunger is a subjective sensation that cannot be measured and therefore cannot be empirically studied. This same reasoning would presumably also apply to sex and we could study the effects of sex deprivation upon behavior.

Although in Pavlovian and related theories there is the general notion of a drive that activates the organism, in Skinnerian and related theories the notion is less of a push from within than of a pull from without (exerted through the mechanism of reinforcement), which shapes the learning of behavior. Without dwelling on these differences, let us now examine some specific examples of how the mechanism of conditioning may explain the learning of sexual behavior.

A little girl becomes sexually aroused while climbing a rope, riding a bicycle, or pressing herself against her mattress. She does not understand the significance of this novel feeling, but as it is pleasant, she tries to elicit it again, and this time she uses her hands. One day she carries the activity far enough to experience orgasm; she has now learned to masturbate. The pleasure thus obtained positively reinforces the activity, and it may become habitual.

A young boy may arrive at the same point through direct initiation to orgasm by a friend. He too has learned to masturbate. That this activity is learned by various people at different ages can be explained by variations in the maturation rate of the physiological apparatus and in the availability of instruction or the accidental occurrence of arousing events.

How and when the youngster masturbates

are subject to further learning. If the initial episode occurred during some athletic activity, certain features of the game may take on erotic significance. If a boy masturbates in bed, the darkness of the room, the warmth of the bed, the texture or color of the blanket, and so on may all take on sexual associations. Later on, simply going to bed or being in a warm, dark place may arouse him.

So far the activities in these examples have been carried out in private. Then one day the child is discovered by his mother. If she becomes upset or punishes her child, she provides negative reinforcement; although the youngster may continue to masturbate, he now pays a price. He cannot help but be influenced by his mother's reaction. He may stop masturbating for a while, may continue fearfully, or may even begin to feel guilty. If the punishment is severe—if a boy is beaten and even struck on the penis or if a child is convincingly threatened with loss of parental love—then the impact will be more nearly devastating. If he knows that his friends also masturbate and are not punished, there will be additional complications.

The outcome of such negative reinforcement will vary. It may only inhibit masturbating behavior or detract from its pleasure. Or it may influence sexual activity in general. If erections result in pain and loss of love to a boy, he may prefer not to have them. If he learns that sexual arousal is improper, he may avoid it, rather than feel worthless and unclean. The seeds of future sexual malfunctioning can thus be sown during such early experiences.

Boys and girls also experiment with sex play. Again the positive reinforcement is the pleasure obtained, but additional rewards include the companionship of shared experiences and so on. Even quite early a child may learn to exchange sexual favors for other rewards, a pattern that he may then carry into adult life.

From this welter of experiences emerges the sexual orientation of the individual. A particular type of orientation may result from quite different experiences. For instance, a young boy whose mother is excessively punitive or repressive in sexual matters (negative reinforcement) will come to believe that females do not like sex, that they are unapproachable or fraught with danger. A father may be so seductive in his behavior that the boy will come to prefer males as sexual objects. In both instances, boys are more likely to develop homosexual orientations. Whether or not they do become practicing homosexuals is of course another matter, which is controlled by life circumstances and social (and perhaps biological) factors.

The process of learning and behavior modification continues throughout life, although repeated early experiences may be most influential. Even an adult will be affected by the nature of his first experience with intercourse: one basis for the time-honored advice to bridegrooms to be especially gentle with their brides on their wedding nights. A man who is repeatedly made to feel sexually inadequate will probably begin to perform poorly after a while. The power of conditioning is such that it may undo years of accumulated experience: A man who has apparently had an adequate sex life but then experiences a heart attack during coitus may develop an intense fear of sex, lose interest in it, or become impotent.

The paradigm of conditioning as such has, of course, only limited usefulness, for very few sexual habits can actually be traced to specific past experiences and associations. The applicability of this concept is, however, greatly enhanced through *generalization* and *discrimination*.

The concept of generalization explains how a novel stimulus can produce a response learned in connection with a similar stimulus. A man who has learned to respond erotically to a specific item of a certain woman's underwear may also respond erotically to other items of her underwear or to female underwear in general and even, through further generalization, to all objects that evoke by their shapes, textures, colors, smells, and so on memories of the original garment (the first conditioned stimulus). Objects or features of an object that have no sexual significance as such may thus become eroticized.

To the extent that the conditioned stimulus involves common objects (such as underwear, which most women wear) it tends to have erotic significance for much of the population. When the associations are more idiosyncratic, fewer people will tend to respond to the stimulus. We can thus explain the many shared attitudes toward what is erotically stimulating, as well as the tremendous variation in preferences within and across cultures.

The principle of discrimination operates in opposition to that of generalization. Were it not for discrimination, we would all be subject to an ever-expanding field of stimuli so that practically anything would ultimately be able to arouse us. As we have already discussed (Chapter 3), immature boys are in a similar situation and are likely to have erections at the most apparently unlikely moments.

It has been demonstrated experimentally that the process of discrimination can extinguish the response to one stimulus while preserving or even reinforcing the response to a similar stimulus. During psychosexual development this mechanism does progressively narrow our responsiveness. For instance, a man gradually responds to only certain types of women, then perhaps to one woman, and finally to her only at appropriate times and places. Learned discrimination thus explains how we select sexual objects, for instance, excluding incestuous relations and a variety of erotic responses to other people and situations. We are not talking here about the moral constraints that sometimes prevent us from acting on our impulses; the facts are that a child, for example, is actually less likely to feel aroused in the presence of a naked parent and that a doctor is less likely to be stimulated while examining a patient. Learned discrimination is of course by no means foolproof. When it fails to develop fully or falters in a specific instance, the various conflicts and difficulties characteristic of so much of our sexual lives occur.

The Critical-Period Hypothesis

A significant recent advance in our understanding of the learning of behavior has to do with the concept of "critical periods." It has been established that during the early life of an animal there are limited and often highly specific critical periods during which occurs the learning that largely determines the subsequent behavior of the animal. A well-known example is Lorenz' experiment with the graylag goose: Shortly after birth the gosling begins to follow its mother. If immediately after hatching it is taken into human care it will follow the human caretaker (or wooden models of the mother). Once this pattern has been established, that is, once the gosling has been "imprinted," it will continue to follow the initial object rather than its own mother or members of its own species.

There is some evidence of an analogy between the establishment of gender role in early childhood and the phenomenon of imprinting in lower animals. It has been obtained through research, which we mentioned in Chapter 4, on certain forms of pseudohermaphroditism.[28] As far as the concept of the critical period is concerned, many apparent applications can be recognized in the various schemes of psychosexual development that we have described. It is, of course, one thing to make such plausible associations and another to demonstrate convincingly what the specific critical periods are.

---

[28] Also see Young, ed. (1961), Vol. II, pp. 1404–1405.

The Development of Affectional Systems

During the past two decades psychologists have been studying the development of affectional systems in monkeys, with fascinating results. Although this research is still in progress, enough has been learned to postulate certain general principles that appear to be quite pertinent to understanding human sexual behavior.[29] Monkeys, of course, are not the same as people, and their interactions lack the enormous complexity of human relations. On the other hand, the relative simplicity of their behavior patterns, coupled with the opportunities to manipulate them experimentally, make them excellent subjects for study.

Perhaps the most important result of this research so far is the confirmation of the notion that sex, even among nonhuman primates, involves complex behavior that can emerge effectively only when related developmental tasks have been properly met. Monkeys do not "automatically" copulate. Their ability to do so is dependent upon a long sequence of antecedent interactions with caretaker adults, as well as with peers.

In this context "love" refers to affectional feelings for others (thus excluding narcissism or self-love). It consists of five basic kinds: maternal love, paternal love, infant-mother love, peer or age-mate love, and heterosexual love. These love systems, though discrete, are not necessarily temporally distinct. Each love system prepares the individual for the next phase, with which it overlaps, and problems in one are reflected in difficulties in the others.

These integrated and interdependent affectional systems have their "sexual" components. The infant monkey clings to its mother without

an overt desire for coitus; but it is nevertheless manifesting a form of behavior that is a necessary precursor for more specifically sexual activities in the future. In this sense, the following discussions of love are not a digression from but an integral part of our discussion of sexuality.

Maternal Love

The love of the mother for the infant is as nearly universal an emotion as we could hope to find. We generally assume that maternal love is innate in females. Girls respond to babies differently than do boys, long before they reach puberty. Although such differences between the sexes could reflect cultural influences, the co-existence of innate propensities is not ruled out. For example, similar differences in attitudes toward rhesus monkey babies have been demonstrated among prepubescent male and female macaque monkeys, even though the latter had not been raised by monkey mothers and had never before seen infants younger than themselves.[30]

The maternal-love system appears in several stages. First is the stage of care and comfort. As the very survival of the infant monkey depends upon the feeding, care, and protection afforded by its mother, it spends a great deal of time being physically cradled or clinging to the mother and thus obtaining vital "contact comfort." It is in this early and intimate relationship that the infant establishes the basis for all his future associations, sexual and otherwise.

---

[29]The leader in this research is Harry F. Harlow. For a general discussion of his work see Harlow *et al.* (1971).

[30]Chamove *et al.* (1967), pp. 329–335. Such findings are particularly interesting, for they appear to provide some biological basis for the nearly universal cultural attitude that the care of the infant is the mother's privilege and obligation. From this premise follow additional conclusions about the place and role of women in society and so on: conclusions that are currently being challenged in some quarters. Incidentally, though it is true that the female animal is *usually* the primary caretaker of the young, this is not always the case.

Maternal love is initially elicited by the mere presence of the baby, but if it is to be sustained the baby in turn must respond. A monkey mother can even "adopt" a kitten as her own, but because the kitten cannot reciprocate by clinging as a monkey baby can, she will ultimately abandon it.

Among humans the life-sustaining functions of the mother can be adequately replaced with bottle feeding and so on. But close, physical, comforting contact with affectionate adult caretakers remains imperative.

The second, or transitional, stage in maternal love is characterized by ambivalence. As the infant must ultimately survive on its own, the monkey mother begins to encourage the development of independence by becoming less protective and even by rejecting and punishing at times.[31] In sexual terms this emotional "weaning" is essential if the infant is going to be able to go out as an adult and relate to mates.

The third and final stage of maternal love is that of relative separation, which among monkeys gradually leads to the severance of the affectional bond between the mother and the maturing offspring. The arrival of a younger sibling accelerates this process.

Older infants who have established peer relations are able to forgo the need for close maternal contact during the day, but at nightfall they make persistent efforts to reestablish maternal contact; as a last resort they may even seek physical comfort from adult males. Incidentally, there are interesting differences among monkey species in this regard. For example, among pigtail monkeys the infant interacts socially primarily with the mother and close

relatives. Yet bonnet monkeys appear to interact with kin and nonkin with equal frequency.[32] As pigtail and bonnet monkeys are all part of the macaque group it is clear that such "cultural" differences exist even among closely related groups in primitive animal societies.

Infant Love

The love of the infant for the mother is closely related to and reciprocal with maternal love. The two affectional systems are nevertheless distinct and can be studied separately. Unlike the mother, who develops emotional ties to the baby even while she is still pregnant, the newborn is at first quite indiscriminate in his feelings toward others. Among both humans and other primates, the infant's earliest responses are reflexively determined. They include sucking responses, the rooting reflex (stimulation of the cheek elicits exploratory head movements that help to locate the nipple), groping, grasping, clinging, and so on. Such unlearned, species-specific behavior patterns among human infants have been called "instinctual response systems."[33]

As these interactions between infant and mother are reflexive, the first stage in the development of the infant's affectional system is that of "organic affection." This stage is practically concurrent with the stage of comfort and attachment that, among monkeys, consists of actual bodily contact between infant and mother soon after birth. This stage includes both the cradling of a passive infant and active clinging by the infant to the mother. Such "contact comfort" seems to be more important than even nursing in the development of the monkey infant's attachment to the mother.

Next comes the stage of solace and security,

---

[31]Chimpanzees, unlike monkeys, are less likely to resort to physical punishment. A chimpanzee mother who is trying to wean her infant will resort to tickling and other playful techniques to distract it from the nipple. Van Lawick-Goodall (1967).

---

[32]Kaufman and Rosenblum (1969).

[33]Bowlby (1969).

in which the presence of the mother or mother surrogate enables the infant monkey (and the older human child) to wander beyond the mother's immediate vicinity to explore the environment. This initial effort is followed by greater detachment and environmental exploration, culminating in a stage of relative independence.

The parallels between the development of the maternal and infant love systems are quite clear. First, there is a phase of close and intense attachment, followed by progressive independence. When the infant's personal and social security are established, he can move out. Without this basic security the infant is socially paralyzed. On the other hand, when the attachment to the mother persists in full force, the infant remains helplessly dependent upon her. The primary function of the maternal and infant love systems is, then, to prepare the infant for the demands and satisfactions of peer relations that must be developed next.

Paternal Love

Manifestations of paternal love among monkeys and apes are infrequent and inadequately studied. It has been hypothesized that innate, biologically determined affection for the infant is much less strong in the nonhuman primate male than in the female. Male monkeys do, however, learn to love and protect infants through imitation of the mother. Conversely, the infant's affectional ties to the male are far less apparent than are his attachment to the mother, although infants will occasionally seek out adult males for comfort when no females are available.

Among humans paternal love can, of course, be just as intense as can maternal love, and, though in most cultures mothers perform the primary child-rearing functions, fathers can and occasionally do fulfill the same role. It is generally assumed that, ideally, maternal and paternal love must supplement each other in providing the infant with the full complement of love and emotional nurture during his growth and development.

Age-Mate or Peer Love

Research with monkeys indicates that the peer affectional system is probably the most important of all affectional systems in sociosexual development. The rudiments of peer love appear in early infancy and expand progressively throughout childhood, adolescence, and adulthood. The primary vehicle for the development and expression of peer love is play, through which earlier affectional systems are integrated and the love systems to follow are anticipated.[34]

Attachment to peers begins as the infant becomes capable of wandering away from the mother briefly and is permitted and encouraged to do so. In humans affectional relations with peers are usually established at about age three years (four months for monkeys) but do not reach their peak until the ages of nine to eleven years. They gradually decline during adolescence as the heterosexual affectional system emerges.

The transfer to peers of at least part of the infant's love for the mother has been explained according to different theories. In the psychoanalytic scheme the shift involves an unconscious reorganization of libidinal attachments ("cathexes") through the use of such "defense mechanisms" as displacement. Learning theorists account for it through "stimulus generali-

---

[34] Play is a complex activity that serves different functions at different ages. Presocial play (play with inanimate objects), for example, precedes social play. Presocial play may in turn be exploratory, parallel (playing beside other children rather than with them), or instigative. Social play may be free, creative, or formal. For a discussion of these various forms of play as they relate to sexual development, see Harlow et al. (1971), pp. 76–85.

zation" from mothers to peers. It has also been suggested that "contact comfort" is transferred from mother to peers. If the child is to develop normal sexual responses, he must have been provided with and must have accepted a certain degree of physical contact very early. Such contact must have been pleasurable and comforting for him to seek it in play with peers. Contact comfort does not necessarily refer to specifically genital contact but is based on general body contact. At the psychological level, the child must also be able to transfer to peers the "basic trust" that he has developed toward the adult caretaker. We shall discuss this important notion of "basic trust" later.

Heterosexual Love

The heterosexual affectional system has its roots in the earlier love systems, but it emerges as a distinct entity at the time of puberty, matures during adolescence, and operates as the primary sociosexual affectional system for most adults.[35]

The heterosexual love system in primates, including man, develops through three subsystems: mechanical, hormonal, romantic. The mechanical subsystem depends on the anatomical and physiological properties of the sexual organs, physiological reflexes, appropriate body postures and movements, and so on. As discussed in earlier chapters, some of these mechanical functions, like penile erection, are present at birth. Others, like ejaculation, develop at puberty. Some features of this mechanical subsystem (for example, sexually differentiated genitals or pelvic thrusting) are common to all primates. Others are peculiar to some. Monkeys, for example, have a basic adult sexual posture (Figure 8.5), whereas man is far more versatile in this respect (Figures 10.5 and 10.6). This basic adult monkey posture has been shown to arise out of three discrete responses during infant play: threat by the male and passivity (turning her back) and rigidity (supporting the male) by the female.

In Figure 8.6 we see the basic presexual play position adopted by a juvenile pair and in Figure 8.7 the first attempts at mounting. These monkeys are engaged in play, not in coitus, yet the female's passive position and willingness to support the male and the latter's grasping of her hindquarters and efforts at mounting have an unmistakable resemblance to the basic adult sexual posture (Figure 8.5).

The second, or hormonal, subsystem has also been discussed as it operates in man (Chapter 4). The sexual behavior of nonhuman primates and of lower animals is, of course, much more

Figure 8.5. Basic adult sexual posture. Courtesy of Wisconsin Regional Primate Research Center.

---

[35]Throughout this discussion we assume that heterosexuality is the normative affectional system in adults, which is the point of view expressed in Harlow *et al.* (1971). As we discussed in Chapter 7, neither the bases of judgments in these matters nor the issue of "normality" will be considered here.

firmly under hormonal control. Although much remains to be learned about the precise roles of sex hormones in human physiology, their importance cannot be underestimated, particularly in relation to sexual growth and maturation.

The third component of the heterosexual love system is the romantic subsystem, among monkeys the subsystem of transient heterosexual attachments. Although we cannot attempt to do justice here to human romantic love, we should point out that in a general sense comparable attachments also characterize the relations of nonhuman primates, with due allowance for their cognitive limitations. Nonhuman primates are not indiscriminately promiscuous. Rather, their associations are characterized by formation of pairs of compatible individuals. Relations between lower animals show no such selectivity, with some notable exceptions: Beavers, one species of deer, and wolves are known to form long-lasting relationships.

Although each of these three subsystems can operate independently to some extent, full heterosexual expression requires their integrated and complementary functioning. These subsystems also vary in their vulnerability to disruption. For example, social isolation early in life does not disturb hormonal functioning but seriously disrupts some mechanical functions and has a disastrous effect upon the transient affectional, or romantic, subsystem. As studies of social isolation in infant monkeys, conducted by Harlow and his associates, have provided highly pertinent insights into sexual behavior, we shall briefly describe them here.

In these experiments male and female infant monkeys were reared in isolated wire-mesh cages and thus denied the opportunity to develop infant- and peer-love affectional systems. At puberty the socially deprived males showed every evidence of normal physical development. They also achieved erection and mastur-

Figure 8.6. Basic presexual position. Courtesy of Wisconsin Regional Primate Research Center.

bated, sometimes to orgasm, at rates comparable to those of undeprived monkeys. Socially deprived females also behaved essentially in a fashion comparable to that of undeprived females, as far as hormonal functioning and autoerotic activities were concerned.

On the other hand, the effect of social isolation in infancy on adult sociosexual behavior was calamitous. Deprived males would be visibly aroused in the presence of females but would stand puzzled, not knowing what to do (Figure 8.8). They would grope aimlessly and act clumsily with receptive females or they would brutally assault them. The impact of social isolation upon females was somewhat less damaging. Although they mistrusted physical contact and would flee or attack males, they

Figure 8.7. The first attempt at mounting. Courtesy of Wisconsin Regional Primate Research Center.

could be induced in time to endure at least partial sexual contact with undeprived males. Figure 8.9 shows the inadequate sexual posturing of a socially deprived female and the sexual disinterest of a normal male in response to it.

These experiments leave no doubt that heterosexual activity cannot develop adequately in an affectional vacuum and that even the coital postures have to develop in the context of infantile and peer interactions. Although we obviously cannot and should not attempt to replicate these findings in humans, there is much in them that seems familiar from faulty

Figure 8.8. Inappropriate response by socially deprived male to receptive female. Courtesy of Wisconsin Regional Primate Research Center.

Figure 8.9. Inadequate sexual presentation by socially deprived female. Courtesy of Wisconsin Regional Primate Research Center.

human sexual development. Human interactions are infinitely more complex, of course, and the transition from peer love to the romantic subsystem involves transitional mechanisms of greater intricacy, involving trust, acceptance of physical contact, and motivation for physical proximity and behavioral sex-role differentiation. As Harlow has put it, "Sex secretions may create sex sensations, but it is social sensitivity that produces sensational sex."[36]

Psychosocial Development

Starting from basic psychoanalytic concepts, Erik Erikson has extended the formulations that we have discussed to encompass the entire life span, rather than only the early years of life. Furthermore, he has attempted to supplement the study of psychosexual development with a parallel study of psychosocial development. As intimately related to sexual behavior as psychosocial development may be, a detailed discussion here would take us too far from our

immediate, limited purposes. We shall therefore simply review briefly Erikson's theory, in order to complete our consideration of the developmental aspect of human sexual functions.[37]

In Erikson's scheme the life cycle—the entire life span from birth to death—is characterized by eight phases of psychosocial development. Each phase is defined by the primary accomplishment of a phase-specific task, even though the resolutions are generally prepared in preceding phases and worked out further in subsequent ones.[38]

---

[37] For Erikson's reformulation of psychosexual development see *Childhood and Society* (1963), Chapter 2. His scheme of psychosocial development is briefly stated in Chapter 7 of the same work, but it is more fully elaborated in *Identity and the Life Cycle* (1959), Part II, and more recently in *Identity: Youth and Crisis* (1968), Chapter 3.

[38] These eight phases, or stages, of psychosocial development and their phase-specific conflicts are: (1) infancy (basic trust versus mistrust), (2) early childhood (autonomy versus shame and doubt), (3) play age (initiative versus guilt), (4) school age (industry versus inferiority), (5) adolescence (identity versus identity confusion), (6) young adulthood (intimacy versus isolation), (7) adulthood (generativity versus stagnation), and (8) mature age (integrity versus despair).

---

[36] Harlow *et al.* (1971), p. 86.

Each phase is defined as a crisis (in the sense of a critical period, rather than of a threat of catastrophe) and labeled according to the extreme successful and unsuccessful solutions. The actual outcome for any given individual phase is, however, generally a balance between such extremes. For instance, we all emerge from phase 1 with mixtures of trust and mistrust. Theoretically there are as many gradations between such extremes as there are people.

At the risk of complicating what is intended as an outline, we must point out several additional key features of Erikson's scheme. First, he has assumed an innate ability to adapt to an average expectable environment: Given a reasonable chance, the organism as a whole will thrive in all its specific functions, sexual ones included. But the organism will have to have this reasonable environmental interaction and support, in order for its biological potentials to be fulfilled. This attempt at integration of the biological (genetic) with the environmental (societal) factors is one of Erikson's main contributions to developmental theory.

Second, Erikson views development as proceeding according to the epigenetic principle "that anything that grows has a ground plan, and that out of this ground plan the parts arise, each part having its time of special ascendency, until all parts have arisen to form a functioning whole."[39] This view is a reformulation of the fundamental principle that embryological development progresses from the simpler to the more complex through the building units or cells.[40] Viewed in this light, the child is not simply a miniature adult, just as the sperm is not a tiny fetus. Sexuality is a potential that will develop if permitted and assisted throughout the individual's life span but particularly during the formative years.

Finally, there is a "cogwheeling" of life cycles, a crucial coordination between the life cycles of the "nurturing" figures and representatives of society and that of the developing individual. As the infant proceeds through his phases with their specific tasks, his parents are passing through their own phases. This meshing provides necessary cohesion and impetus in human relations.

We have said very little so far about sex. What, then, is the relevance of this discussion to our topic? First, in its extension of psychoanalytical concepts, Erikson's formulation also assumes the presence of an all-pervasive libidinal force. Psychosocial phases 1, 2, and 3, for instance, are the counterparts of the oral, anal, and phallic stages of psychosexual development.

Second, sexuality is an important factor in the task of identity formation, the concept for which Erikson is best known. Part of the process of identity formation is the formation of its sexual aspect. Biological features are, of course, the primary "givens," but they do not necessarily determine the individual's own definitions of himself as masculine or feminine or the way that he is perceived by others. The components of such definitions and the sex-role expectations implied vary markedly from culture to culture, even though the basic biological givens remain constant. It is thus up to each individual to clarify and consolidate his own sexual character as part of the larger task of identity formation. Cultures that provide clear and consistent models and guidelines facilitate this task for their members.

Despite the upsurge in sexual activity during adolescence, only after identity formation has been fairly well consolidated does true intimacy with the opposite sex (or with anyone else) become possible. Adolescent sexuality is often experimental, part of the search for identity. People may marry in the hope of finding themselves through each other, but the need to

---

[39] Erikson (1968), p. 92.

[40] Arey (1965), p. 5.

fulfill defined roles as mates or parents often actually hampers this effort.

The task of intimacy versus isolation is specific to young adulthood (phase 6). On the strength of the accomplishments of earlier phases, the young adult develops the capacity for establishing a workable ratio between these two extremes. Intimacy requires expressing (and exposing) oneself, giving and sharing, and both sexual and more general union.

Isolation and loneliness ("distantiation"), in appropriate amounts, are also necessary. No matter how satisfying a relationship, both partners need some solitude. A certain distance in this sense helps them to keep each other in proper focus. When intimacy fails or is exploited, self-preservation is reliant on ability and readiness to repudiate it, to isolate oneself, and, if necessary, to annul such destructive ties.

The similarities in the general conclusions we can draw from Harlow's experimental work and Erikson's clinical research are quite clear. Monkeys or men cannot grow and function in isolation. Even though each individual is unique, he can be understood only in the context of his relations with his fellow beings. Sex is a complex and pervasive force that has a biological basis but can function properly (or be understood adequately) only in the context of affectional networks and life as a whole. Erikson has said:

> As an animal, man is nothing. It is meaningless to speak of a human child as if it were an animal in the process of domestication; or of his instincts as set patterns encroached upon or molded by the autocratic environment. Man's "inborn instincts" are drive fragments to be assembled, given meaning, and organized during a prolonged childhood by methods of child training and schooling which vary from culture to culture and are determined by tradition. In this lies his chance as an organism, as a member of a society, as an individual. In this also lies his limitation. For while the animal survives where his segment of nature remains predictable enough to fit his inborn patterns of instinctive response or where these responses contain the elements for necessary mutation, man survives only where traditional child training provides him with a conscience which will guide him without crushing him and which is firm and flexible enough to fit the vicissitudes of his historical era.[41]

---

[41] Erikson (1963), p. 95.

The term "autoeroticism" was coined by Havelock Ellis at the turn of the twentieth century to describe certain solitary sexual activities like masturbation, nocturnal orgasms, and sexual fantasies. To distinguish such activities from those that involve interaction between people (sociosexual) is useful if we do not forget that hard and fast distinctions are impossible. For example, when boys masturbate together in a group are they not in fact engaging in a form of sociosexual behavior? Is such group masturbation still to be considered an autoerotic activity simply because there is no physical contact between members of the group? When a man and women entertain wild sexual fantasies while looking into each other's eyes but avoiding all direct physical contact are they engaging in autoerotic activity?

Despite these problems of definition, we shall discuss in this chapter three types of sexual behavior that are commonly acknowledged to be autoerotic: erotic fantasies, sexual dreams, and masturbation.

Erotic Fantasies

There is a whole world of sexual activity that is confined to the mind, including fleeting erotic images, intricately woven fantasies, fading sexual memories, and fresh hopes, all of which are moving in and out of consciousness a good deal of the time. Erotic fantasies must be the most ubiquitous of all sexual phenomena. It is difficult to imagine any human who does not have them.[1] Fantasies are frequent preludes to other outlets, but more often they exist on their own. Theologians called sexual reveries *delectatio morosa* and differentiated such dallying with erotic images from simple sexual desire or intent to engage in coitus.

Although erotic daydreams are exceedingly common, only a few individuals are apparently able to achieve orgasm through this means alone. Some women are reportedly able to reach orgasm even in public simply by being in the presence of particularly attractive men or in exciting situations.

The propensity of adolescents to daydream is well known, especially when they are in love. In the private and safe theaters of their minds, they endlessly rehearse their favorite fantasies, sometimes in the form of continuing stories, more often as variations on the same theme.

---

[1] A medieval penitential assigned the following penances for this offense: for a deacon twenty-five days, for a monk thirty days, for a priest forty days, for a bishop fifty days. Haddon and Stubbs, *Councils and Ecclesiastical Documents,* Vol. 3; quoted in Ellis, H. (1942), Vol. II, Part One, p. 184.

AUTOEROTICISM

Sexual reveries, though more common in adolescence, actually continue through the entire life span, as does all autoerotic activity. Even happily married people with satisfactory sex lives occasionally ruminate about past experiences (particularly missed opportunities). Such memories sometimes acquire a persistent, haunting quality (see Figure 9.1). These thoughts are generally harmless and are often sustained by unconscious associations with ungratified childhood wishes that have been repressed and long forgotten.

The dramatis personae in daydreams often vary, but the individual dreamer usually remains the central character. The objects of these fantasies may be actual acquaintances or people that the dreamer knows only from afar (see Figure 9.2). Often they are fictitious figures with somewhat vague and occasionally changing features. The imaginary activities are countless and are determined by the dreamer's unconscious wishes, the extent to which the wishes are permitted into consciousness, and his imaginative gifts, which sometimes conjure up extraordinary images.

The intensity of feeling accompanying such fantasies also varies. Most often images and thoughts are relatively inert, even though they may involve patently sexual themes. At the other extreme their intensity may be overwhelming. Sexual fantasies are not, of course, always heterosexual or necessarily always pleasant. They may also revolve around homosexual or sadomasochistic themes and may cause embarassment and profound guilt to the individual.

The Functions of Sexual Fantasies

Erotic fantasies fulfill many functions. First, they are a source of pleasure to which everyone has ready access. Second, they are often substitutes for action: as temporary satisfactions while awaiting more concrete ones (tonight's date, a honeymoon in the distant future) or as compensations for unattainable goals. Despite this apparent function as wish fulfillment, an individual may not want his fantasies to come true, no matter how much he "yearns" for them. Such unrealizable daydreams are probably disguised replays of infantile (possibly oedipal) wishes.

Sexual fantasies that deal with real or imagined past events therefore fulfill a compensatory function. They allow partial, tolerable expression of forbidden wishes and to some degree relieve sexual frustrations. Fantasies cannot yield full gratification of sexual desires, but by easing the pain and pressure of past traumas and unfulfilled wishes they help to make them more bearable.

Third, some fantasies revolve around future events and can sometimes be of very definite help. As an individual anticipates problems, plans for contingencies, and mentally rehearses alternative modes of action, he lessens his own

Figure 9.1.   René Magritte, *Ready-Made Bouquet.* Courtesy of Alexander Iolas Gallery.

anxiety and prepares to cope with novel situations. There is thus a difference between fantasies that substitute for action and those that prepare for it.

Pathological Fantasies

Given the universality of sexual fantasizing, it must be assumed to be part of "normal" mental life. But does it have pathological, as well as healthy, forms? Judging quantitatively, fantasizing beyond a certain point about sex or anything else is wasteful and maladaptive. Particularly during adolescence, erotic fantasies may become excessively absorbing. If they interfere with work or if they regularly take the place of satisfying interaction with others, they may interfere with normal psychosocial development.

Can fantasies be evaluated by content? If we had a commonly accepted set of qualitative criteria to separate healthy from unhealthy forms of sexual behavior, then it would probably also apply to fantasies. But we have no such reliable yardstick of "normality." Furthermore, the individual's subjective reaction cannot be taken as the sole criterion, for some people are disturbed by thoughts of very common activities, whereas others may be unaffected by very bizarre fantasies. Even though there are no simple answers to these questions, several observations are pertinent.

Thinking about socially unacceptable behavior is very common. Sometimes it is merely silly and apparently senseless (like thinking about urinating on someone), but it may also center on highly disturbing, guilt-provoking behavior (such as homosexual, sadistic, or incestuous acts). Often it evokes a curious mixture of pleasure and distress. Fantasies of using force in sexual encounters or of being raped are quite common. Not infrequently a woman will imagine that she is a prostitute and will be simultaneously titillated and disgusted by the vision.

Figure 9.2. Young man fantasizing (artist unknown).

What do such thoughts mean, and how does one deal with them? First, it may be comforting to realize that most of these fantasies are never acted upon. We all have reservoirs of repressed wishes that occasionally surface in thinly disguised forms, residues of our earlier, undifferentiated sexuality. They do not "define" us as adults.

There is no easy way to deal with unpleasant or disturbing fantasies. Conscious attempts to dispel them often simply cause us to focus upon them more strongly. It is better to take them for what they are: isolated thoughts that do not mean very much. We can, of course, minimize opportunities for lengthy reveries. We are not as helpless in these matters as we sometimes think.

In very rare instances, a person may correctly realize that he is losing control and that he is likely to commit a seriously antisocial act. He must then seek help. It is better to find psychiatric or other professional assistance, rather than turning to family or friends. For most people, however, sexual fantasies are common and pleasurable, even though they include occasional unacceptable thoughts and cause a tinge of shame.

Sexual Dreams

Man has sought in his dreams a key to his future and a window into his past. Freud called dreams "the royal road to the unconscious." Within the last decade or so inquiries into the neurophysiology of sleep and dreaming have yielded new and intriguing findings, some of which are particularly relevant to the study of sexuality.

Psychoanalytic Concepts of Dreaming

Freud thought that the function of dreams was to protect sleep. During sleep, when the vigilance of the ego relaxes somewhat, unacceptable (often sexual) wishes threaten to break through into consciousness and thus to disrupt sleep. These wishes are permitted partial expression in disguised form and are experienced as dreams. The process of transforming unconscious wishes into dream imagery is known as "dream work." A dream therefore has two components: the manifest content (usually woven around some actual experience, "the day residue") and the latent content (which carries the real message in disguised and symbolic form).

Symbolism is a major component of dreams, though it is by no means restricted to dreaming. It is also present in art, literature, myths, legends, proverbs, jokes, and so on. In dreams symbols may be highly individual, tailored to the occasion, as it were. More frequently we use symbols that have common or universal meanings. The meaning of a dream symbol may be transparent or highly camouflaged and distorted. To complicate matters further, a given symbol may have several meanings, and the correct interpretation in any given instance must be arrived at from its context and associations.

In psychoanalytic reckoning a great many (but not all) symbols have sexual meanings. For example, long objects like sticks or tree trunks may stand for the penis. The opening of an umbrella may represent an erection. Knives, daggers, and nail files (possibly because they rub back and forth) also symbolize the penis. On the other hand, boxes, chests, cupboards, ovens, rooms, ships—in fact any enclosed space or hollow object—usually represent the female genitals. The significance of actions involving such objects or places is not hard to surmise: Going in and out of a room would signify intercourse, and whether or not the door is locked thus has great meaning. Walking up and down steps, ladders, and staircases also stands for coitus, for in both climbing and orgasm we reach the apex through rhythmic movements and with loss of breath, after which we can go down again very quickly.

These examples are but a few from Freud's extensive writings on dreams, most notably his monumental *The Interpretation of Dreams*, a psychoanalytic classic. For a fragmentary sample of his method of dream analysis, let us consider the following excerpts.

In this instance the dreamer was a young woman suffering from a phobia of open spaces (agoraphobia) based on her unconscious fears of seduction.

"I was walking in the street in the summer, wearing a straw hat of peculiar shape; its middle-piece was bent upwards and its side-pieces hung downwards" (the description became hesitant at this point) "in such a way that one side was lower than the other. I was cheerful and in a self-confident frame of mind; and, as I passed a group of young officers, I thought: 'None of you can do me any harm!'"

Freud's comments in response to the dream were as follows:

> Since nothing occurred to her in connection with the hat in the dream, I said: "No doubt the hat was a male genital organ, with its middle-piece sticking up and its two side-pieces hanging down." . . . I intentionally gave her no interpretation of the detail about the two side-pieces hanging down unevenly; though it is precisely details of this kind that must point the way in determining an interpretation. I went on to say that as she had a husband with such fine genitals there was no need for her to be afraid of the officers—no need, that is, for her to wish for anything from them, since as a rule she was prevented from going for a walk unprotected and unaccompanied owing to her phantasies of being seduced. I had already been able to give her this last explanation of her anxiety on several occasions upon the basis of other material.

> The way in which the dreamer reacted to this material was most remarkable. She withdrew her description of the hat and maintained that she had never said that the two side-pieces hung down. I was too certain of what I had heard to be led astray, and stuck to my guns. She was silent for a while and then found enough courage to ask what was meant by one of her husband's testes hanging down lower than the other and whether it was the same in all men. In this way the remarkable detail of the hat was explained and the interpretation accepted by her.[2]

The psychoanalytic literature on dream interpretation is extensive. Among numerous contributors to this field we should mention C. G. Jung, whose best known work on dreams is his "General Aspects of Dream Analysis."[3]

The Neurophysiology of Sleep and Dreaming

Sleep is not the uniform state that it appears to be, nor are dreams erratic events that punctuate it unpredictably. Rather, there is a definite sleep-dream cycle that recurs nightly. Brain waves (electroencephalogram, or EEG, tracings) show four distinct sleep patterns. One of these is characterized by a fast rhythm and bursts of rapid eye movements (REM). When a person is awakened during this phase, he will almost inevitably report that he has been experiencing vivid dreams. During the other sleep phases dreaming has been found to be more erratic and less vivid.

During an ordinary night's sleep, there are four or five active dream periods, accounting for almost a quarter of the total sleeping time: The first occurs sixty to ninety minutes after falling asleep, and the rest at approximately ninety-minute intervals. These dream periods are generally quite constant, which means that everyone dreams every night, regardless of whether or not he remembers his dreams in the morning.

These periods of active dreaming (called REM periods because of their association with rapid eye movements), furthermore, appear to be times of intense physiological activity, with rapid and irregular pulse and respiration. Also in a remarkably high number of instances (85-95 percent) partial or full erections have been observed during REM states among males, even among infants and elderly men. These erections are not necessarily accompanied by sexual dreams, and their full significance remains unclear.[4]

Sexual dreams, particularly those culminating in orgasms, are intensely pleasurable but

---

[2]Freud, *The Interpretation of Dreams* (1900), in Freud (1957-1964), Vol. IV-V, pp. 360-361.

[3]In Jung (1960), pp. 237-281.

[4]See Fisher *et al.* (1965); Gulevich and Zarcone (1969); Kleitman (1963); and Dement (1965).

can also be quite bewildering. Like all other dreams they are usually fragmentary and difficult to describe. Sometimes their sexual content is accompanied by appropriately erotic emotions. Quite often, however, imagery and affect seem contradictory: A person may dream of a flagrantly sexual activity without feeling aroused, or he may feel intense excitement while dreaming of an apparently nonsexual, even improbable, situation like climbing a pole, flying, and so on. Psychoanalysts explain such dreams in terms of their symbolic rather than their manifest content.

Fantasies and dreams are closely related. In both there is transient relaxation of conscious restraints, and repressed wishes are permitted partial expression. Daydreams generally remain relatively more subject to the dictates of logic and reality ("secondary-process thinking"), however. In dreams the vigilance of the ego is lessened to the point at which deeply buried material emerges—without much regard for ordinary logical processes and the restraints of reality. Nevertheless, although in dreams anything becomes possible ("primary-process thinking"), unconscious material rarely surfaces in stark and undisguised form.

The intelligibility of fantasies and dreams varies from obvious to enigmatic. They may represent patent or thinly veiled wish fulfillments or deeply concealed fears. Some women, for instance, have fantasies that during intercourse their vaginas will be torn apart. Some men fear that vaginas are full of razor blades, ground glass, or armed with teeth (*vagina dentata*) to mutilate the penises that venture in. Such perceived threats to the integrity of the genitals bespeak mixtures of aggressive and sexual impulses. Fleeting thoughts of this type are nevertheless quite common and should not always be taken seriously. Most dreams make no overt sense at all and can be given meaning only through detailed analysis of their symbolic content.

Nocturnal Orgasms

Visitations by "the angel of the night" (which is what the pioneer sexologist Paolo Mantegazza called nocturnal emissions) have left many a young man in an awkward situation in the morning. Although orgasms during sleep (nocturnal or daytime) do not constitute an important proportion of total sexual outlets (2–3 percent for females, 2–8 percent for males, depending upon the population subgroup), they are nevertheless of considerable interest. Substantial numbers of people experience them (by age forty-five almost 40 percent of females and more than 90 percent of males have had such experiences at least once). As involuntary acts nocturnal orgasms are less subject to moral censure, and as a "natural" outlet they supposedly act as a safety valve for accumulated sexual tensions.

The universality of the experience is well documented. Babylonians believed in a "maid of the night" who visited men in their sleep and a "little night man" that slept with women.[5] Such imaginary beings became more prominent in medieval times in the form of demons (see Figure 9.3) who would lie upon women (incubus) and under men (succubus). The West African Yoruba believed in a single versatile being who could act either as male or female and visit members of either sex in their sleep.[6]

Nocturnal orgasms occur more often in males than females. They are, therefore, generally called "nocturnal emissions" or "wet dreams," designations that are, of course, applicable only to males. For the same reason the experience is more difficult for males to conceal.

Nocturnal orgasms are almost always accompanied by dreams, but the dreamer often

---

[5] Jastrow, *Religion of Babylonia*, and Ploss, *Das Weib;* quoted in Ellis, H. (1942), Vol. I, Part One, p. 198.

[6] Ellis, H. (1942), Vol. I, Part One, p. 188.

Figure 9.3. Illustration by Frédéric Bouchot in *Diabolico Foutromanie.*

awakens in the process.[7] The manifest content of such a dream may or may not be clearly erotic, but there is always a subjective sensation of sexual excitement. Pleasure may, however, be tinged with apprehension and remorse. As in all dreams, there is usually a succession of apparently discrete images, rather than a coherent scenario. These images may be purely heterosexual, or they may have homosexual, sadomasochistic, incestuous, or other startling elements. Occasionally the dreamer will sleep right through the experience and will have only vague recollections in the morning.

It is also possible for orgasm to occur without dreams. For instance, a man with a com-

[7]His awareness of what is happening may be hazy: In some instances orgasm is completed, and he goes back to sleep without having fully awakened. At other times he may wake up startled, and if orgasm has not started it may be possible to avert it. Medieval theologians mercifully permitted believers to complete nocturnal orgasms on awakening, provided that they did not willfully enjoy them.

pletely severed spinal cord (but with intact ejaculatory spinal centers) can have nocturnal orgasms. Because of the interruption of the spinal tracks, the brain can no longer communicate with the portions of the spinal cord below the lesion, and dreaming (which occurs in the brain) cannot possibly influence the ejaculatory center in the lower spinal cord. In these instances erection and ejaculation may result from tactile stimulation caused by friction in the bed or from some other reflexive source.

Information on nocturnal orgasm among primitive groups is scarce. Male nocturnal orgasm is widely recognized, but there are few references to female experiences.

Males of several species of mammals are known to have erections and orgasms during sleep. There is also accumulating evidence of REM sleep periods in animals. These fields of investigation are still in their infancy, however.

Prevalence, Frequency, and Correlates

Orgasms during sex dreams constituted a minor outlet for both sexes in the Kinsey sample. They accounted for only 2-3 percent of the female and 2-8 percent of the male total sexual outlets, depending upon age, marital status, and other characteristics (see Chapter 7). Almost 50 percent of males, but fewer than 10 percent of women, reported experiencing orgasm during sleep more than five times a year. Approximately 5 percent of men and 1 percent of women averaged weekly orgasms through this means. This experience is one in which the range of variation among males was greater than among females.

Despite the low frequencies of orgasm, sex dreams are experienced by a wide segment of the population. In the Kinsey sample two of three women and practically all the males reported having had erotic dreams sometime in their lives. Yet by the age of forty-five only about 40 percent of women and 80 percent of

men had actually reached orgasm during such dreams.

Frequencies of nocturnal emission in males are highest among the college-educated and progressively lower in lower educational groups. There is an almost sevenfold difference between the averages of the two extremes. At all social levels frequencies are higher before marriage. Otherwise there are no differences between rural and urban groups, among various religious groups, or between those practicing and not practicing their religion. Correlations with female nocturnal orgasms are even less impressive.

Health Aspects

The attitude toward nocturnal orgasm in our society is generally benevolent, though the phenomenon has not entirely escaped concern and opprobrium. Adolescents used to be advised to empty their bladders at bedtime, not to sleep in one position or another, not to wear tight nightclothes, and so on in order to minimize the chances of night-time "pollutions." More commonly, however, this outlet is regarded as nature's way of taking care of sexual needs in the absence of other legitimate outlets. Do nocturnal orgasms actually fulfill such a compensatory function?

This possibility was tested on Kinsey's female sample. A compensatory correlation with other outlets was found in about 14 percent of respondents; as these women refrained from other forms of sexual expression, nocturnal orgasms became more frequent. This compensatory function appeared most often when other outlets had been drastically reduced or completely eliminated, as during imprisonment or after loss of a spouse. Nocturnal orgasms seemed to increase more when sociosexual outlets, rather than masturbation, were reduced.

On the other hand, when the compensatory increase in nocturnal orgasms occurred, it was nowhere commensurate with the magnitude of the reduction in other outlets: A woman who lost the chance for several coital orgasms a week might have only a few more nocturnal orgasms a year. Besides, in about 7 percent of the sample there was even a positive correlation: As other outlets became more frequent, so did nocturnal orgasms. In 10 percent of the sample this outlet was first experienced only after one or more of the other outlets had been experienced.

The evidence, at least for females, is far from supporting the idea of nocturnal orgasms as a "natural" safety valve. It is ironic that the one outlet (aside from marital coitus) that has some legitimacy among large numbers of people turns out to be one of the least effective.[8]

Masturbation

Masturbation was probably practiced long before mankind appeared in the world. The practice is prevalent among mammals and must have continued while man was evolving. As historical and anthropological records also attest its universality, certainly whether it is harmful or harmless should be known by now. Yet the voluminous literature and even more voluminous folklore on masturbation did not settle the question at all. The physiological harmlessness of masturbation has been recently established, however, and there is no need to labor the issue, even though there may be lingering doubts in some minds.

The vulgar Latin verb *masturbari* dates from the first century A.D. It is believed to have been derived from the Latin for "hand" (*manu-s*) and "to defile" (*stuprare*) or "to disturb" (*turbare*). An alternative explanation is that "mas" is derived from *mas* ("male seed,"

or semen). In view of other than manual methods of achieving the same ends, "self-stimulation" seems more accurate.[9]

What actually constitutes masturbation is as uncertain as its etymology. It is easy to agree that it involves more than simply manipulating one's own genitals. What about the woman who achieves orgasms by fondling her breasts or through erotic fantasy alone? What about infants who seem to enjoy pulling and tugging at their genitals? What about indulgence in such tactile stimulation as thumb sucking and back scratching for sensual pleasure? Are all these and countless other acts masturbatory activities in disguise? An all-inclusive conception of masturbation would have little heuristic value: We could not possibly count all episodes of thumb sucking, back scratching, and the like for study. The alternative is to restrict our definition to those deliberate acts of self-arousal that culminate in orgasm without direct physical interaction with others. Unfortunately, this definition leaves out activities that are generally accepted as forms of masturbation, to say nothing of the myriad types of behavior that psychoanalysts believe to be "masturbatory equivalents."

When we refer here to the findings of the Kinsey study we shall consider only masturbation that leads to orgasm. Otherwise we mean by "masturbation" any erotic activity that involves voluntary self-stimulation. Most often it occurs in private, but two or more people may masturbate together; mutual stimulation, however, is not masturbation but either petting

---

[8]For further consideration of the role of fantasy in sex, see Sullivan (1969), pp. 79–89.

[9]The term "onanism" is a misnomer, for the biblical event to which it refers had no connection with masturbation (Genesis 38:8–11). Pejorative terms like "self-abuse" and "self-pollution" have also been dropped in serious discussions. The vernacular expressions for masturbation are many: "jerking off," "whacking off," and so on. Most of these terms are obviously more descriptive of male masturbation than of its female counterpart.

or homosexual play. Masturbation thus involves a variety of sexual behaviors that overlap with other forms of sexual expression. The techniques of masturbation can be viewed more generally as techniques of stimulation. The same acts are also performed during petting or coital foreplay.

Techniques

Similarities in human physiological makeup impose certain general characteristics upon all forms of masturbation in both sexes. There is, nevertheless, considerable variation owing to anatomical differences, diverse life experiences, and different cultural patterns of sexual behavior.

It is impossible, and hardly necessary, to catalogue each and every method of masturbating used. Instead we shall restrict ourselves to the more common forms plus a few of the more exotic variants that illustrate how far some people go in their autoeroticism.

Predictably, the external genitals, which are most sensitive, are the primary targets of stimulation. But, as we noted earlier, individuals may be differently conditioned. The physiological mechanisms underlying all sexual responses are vasocongestion and increased muscular tension. The first is beyond voluntary control, but the second can be deliberately used to heighten sexual tension.

Genital Manipulation. Manual techniques are the most common for both sexes but particularly for males (see Figure 8.4). The most frequent form of male masturbation involves simply manipulating the penis by hand. This technique usually consists of gripping the shaft and moving the hand over it firmly to and fro or in a "milking" motion. The glans and frenulum may be lightly stroked in the earlier stages, but as tensions mount and movements become more vigorous direct contact with these areas is generally avoided because of their extreme sensitivity. It is possible, however, to continue stimulation of these parts by moving the prepuce over them.

Women also rely primarily upon genital manipulation, though to a lesser extent than males do. In one fashion or another the clitoris and the labia minora are the structures most commonly involved (see Figure 9.4). They are stroked, pressed, and rhythmically stimulated. As they are the most sensitive parts of the female genitals, the motions are usually quite gentle and deliberate. Just as males avoid direct friction of the penile glans, females avoid the glans of the clitoris. Instead, they concentrate upon the clitoral shaft, which they can stimulate on either side. If too much pressure is applied or manipulation is prolonged over an area, the site may become less sensitive. Switching hands or moving the fingers about is therefore quite common.

Although the clitoris is often cited as the primary erotic target, Masters and Johnson have discovered that women usually manipulate the mons area as a whole. In this way they can prolong the buildup of tension and avoid potentially painful contact with the clitoral glans. Sometimes rhythmic or steady pressure over the mons is all that is necessary to elicit orgasm.

The inner surfaces of the labia minora are as sensitive as is the clitoris and are frequently stimulated during masturbation. The motions involved are similar: gentle stroking, steady or rhythmic pressure, and so on. Actually these movements merge into one another, and the fingers of one or both hands move from one structure to the other, perhaps pulling on the labia and stimulating the clitoris alternately with circular strokes to excite the introitus. The outer labia are less often involved and are only incidentally stimulated.

In both male and female masturbation the buildup to orgasm follows the description given earlier (Chapter 3). Slow and deliberate initial movements become progressively more intense. As a woman approaches orgasm, she may require firm and forcible manipulation to catapult herself to pitch excitement.

Breast stimulation is confined essentially to females. About one in ten women in the Kinsey sample manipulated her own breasts (often just the nipples) as part of her autoerotic activities. On rare occasions such manipulation alone may lead to orgasm.

Friction against Objects. It is, of course, physiologically immaterial whether the genitals are excited by the hand, the heels, or the back of a chair. But behaviorally such distinctions are significant. When a person resorts to manual handling of his organs, there can be no mistake about the nature of his act. Out of shame some people resort to indirect means of achieving the same end. Adolescents may feel that they are thus actually obeying the injunction against "playing with oneself." Others, of course, use this approach simply because they find it more exciting.

The possibilities are many, for any reasonable object will do: a pillow, a towel, nightclothes tucked between the legs, a bed cover, or the mattress itself may provide a convenient surface to rub and press against, and one can often achieve orgasm without ever touching one's genitals (Figure 9.5).

Many an adolescent girl may actually discover the potential of self-stimulation through some innocent activity like climbing a pole or riding a bicycle. The health manuals of some years ago devoted considerable thought to the proper design of bicycle seats in order to minimize this hazard.

Apart from its usefulness in camouflaging masturbation, using friction against objects also may seem more akin to sexual intercourse and may facilitate coital fantasies.

Muscular Tensions. Even when the first two techniques of masturbation are used, muscular tension is also used to heighten sexual excite-

Figure 9.4. Illustration by Caylus in *Thérèse Philosophe.*

ment. Occasionally, however, a woman will attain orgasm by relying exclusively on such tension. She may, for instance, lie with her knees drawn up against her belly and move her buttocks or press them together rhythmically. The movements involved are similar to the pelvic thrusts during coitus. They must be performed with deliberate force and determination if they are to be effective.

Thigh Pressure. Thigh pressure is an exclusively female method. When a woman's legs are crossed or pressed together, steady and rhythmic pressure can be applied to the whole genital area. This method combines the advan-

Figure 9.5. Jean Honoré Fragonard, *Sleeping Girl.*

tages of direct stimulation and muscular tension. It can be indulged in practically anywhere the women may be and can be detected only by the particularly observant. Havelock Ellis described one such episode:

> . . . A few years ago, while waiting for a train at a station on the outskirts of a provincial town, I became aware of the presence of a young woman, sitting alone on a seat at a little distance, whom I could observe unnoticed. She was leaning back with legs crossed, swinging the crossed foot vigorously and continuously; this continued without interruption for some ten minutes after I first observed her; then the swinging movement reached a climax; she leant still further back, thus bringing the sexual region still more closely on contact with the edge of the bench and straightened and stiffened her body and legs in what appeared to be a momentary spasm; there could be little doubt as to what had taken place. A few moments later she slowly walked from her solitary seat into the waiting-room and sat down among the other waiting passengers, quite still now and with uncrossed legs, a pale quiet young woman, possibly a farmer's daughter, serenely unconscious that her manoeuvre had been detected, and very possibly herself ignorant of its true nature.[10]

Years ago, when people were more preoccupied with the effects of masturbation than they are today, they went to some trouble to uncover it. There are descriptions, for instance, of how in large French dress factories (equipped with

---

[10] Ellis, H. (1942), Vol. I, Part One, p. 180.

treadle-operated sewing machines) shop stewards would listen for the occasional uncontrollable acceleration of a machine as its female operator went through mounting excitement and orgasm.[11]

Fantasy. It is often claimed that for males sex is more a purely physical function, whereas for females it is psychologically more involved. If so, then it is surprising that fantasy seems to be a more integral part of male than of female masturbation.[12]

As do pure erotic fantasies, masturbatory fantasies also vary widely. Fairly frequently, especially among better-educated people, erotic photographs or literature may be used as sources of stimulation. Males also seem to be aroused by observing their own genitals.

A few people, usually women, claim to be able to reach orgasm through fantasy alone ("psychic masturbation"). One wonders, however, to what extent the activity is purely "neutral" and whether or not in fact subtle and hard-to-detect muscular tension is not accompanying the fantasies.

Vaginal Insertions. Men commonly think that females often insert their fingers or objects into their vaginas when they masturbate, but only one in five women in the Kinsey sample reported such insertions, and often they may have meant merely slight penetrations of the sensitive introitus. The vagina itself is poorly supplied with nerves, which explains why penetration is not used more often in masturbation. Some women, however, clearly derive additional pleasure from deep penetration, perhaps because it simulates coitus.

When insertions do occur, fingers are most often used. Insertion is not usually an isolated activity but is accompanied by manipulation of adjoining parts. The use of various objects is quite rare and often resorted to solely for purposes of entertaining males.

The majority of objects used in autoerotic activities are household items. Conveniently shaped vegetables and objects like bananas,[13] cucumbers, pencils, and candles have no doubt been pressed into service from time to time.

There also are special devices that are used as aids to masturbation. The most common are artificial penises. Although the frequency with which these objects are used is often exaggerated, there is ample evidence that they are available in many parts of the globe.

Artificial penises have been fashioned from gold, silver, ivory, ebony, horn, glass, wax, wood, and stuffed leather; they range from crude specimens to products of fine craftsmanship. Their most common name in English is "dildo" (from the Italian *diletto*), though the French form *godemiche* is also used. Dildos are easily identified in works of antiquity and are mentioned by Aristophanes (*Lysistrata*, v. 105). Herondas wrote an entire play (*The Private Conversation*) around an *olisbos*. These devices have sometimes been modified to permit the passage of warm liquid (usually milk) to simulate ejaculation. Contemporary versions have been further refined to befit an industrialized world and can vibrate on battery power.

Who uses dildos? No doubt some sexually adventurous women do, but mainly they seem to be used in exhibitions for male audiences.

---

[11] Pouillet (1897).

[12] Among males in the Kinsey sample who masturbated 72 percent almost always fantasized at the same time, 17 percent sometimes did, and 11 percent did not. The corresponding percentages for females were 50, 14, and 36.

[13] "O bananas, of soft and smooth skins, which dilate the eyes of young girls . . . you alone among fruits are endowed with a pitying heart, o consolers of widows and divorced women." (From a poem in *The Arabian Nights,* quoted in Ellis, H. [1942], Vol. I, Part One, p. 171.) In the mythology of Hawaii, goddesses were impregnated by bananas placed under their garments. (Ellis, H. [1942], Vol. I, Part One, p. 171.)

Dildos are also used by male homosexuals. Artificial penises are not always merely gadgets but may have ritualistic and symbolic relevance. The human penis, real and counterfeit, has much more meaning than simply as a sexual organ (see Chapter 2).

There are other ingenious devices. One is the Japanese *rin-no-tama*, two hollow metal balls, one of which is empty and is introduced first into the vagina. The other contains a smaller metal ball, lead pellets, or mercury and is inserted next. Both are held in place by a tampon. The slightest movement then makes the metals vibrate and sends shocks of voluptuous sensations through the vagina: Some geishas reportedly swing in hammocks and rocking chairs while thus equipped.

There are also vibrators of various shapes and designs. Some are cylindrical dildos; others have vibrating rubber tips or can be attached to the back of the hand, through which they transmit their vibrations. Many of these gadgets are sold as instruments for massage, or they are advertised as devices that "sooth the nerves" yet are "harmless to delicate tissues" and so on. Later we shall discuss further their use in connection with the treatment of frigidity.

Finally, there is the "masturbatory doll" to console the solitary male. It is an inflatable, lifesize rubber or vinyl doll which may even come equipped with an artificial vagina (and sometimes an anus).

Other Methods. Occasionally, masturbation revolves around organs other than the genitals or involves an unusual method of stimulation. Some women, for instance, find that running a strong stream of water over the genitals is very exciting. Wearing very tight clothing or any other practice that either creates friction or induces muscular tension may have the same effect.

In anal masturbation objects are inserted in the rectum, either in conjunction with or independently of genital manipulation. Homosexuals are obviously more likely to resort to this method. Curiosity, however, or the search for novel sensations may prompt others to try it also. When a person who has no conscious homosexual strivings tries it, psychoanalysts are likely to interpret this as evidence of "latent homosexuality," a rather vague concept we shall discuss in Chapter 11.

Urethral insertions are rare. Women and children are more likely to attempt them, and for those to whom pain is erotically arousing this approach may be tempting. Surgeons not infrequently recover hairpins and other foreign bodies from the urinary bladders of children or mentally incompetent women who often feign ignorance of how the objects came there. Some women are able to suck on their own nipples, and occasionally a man may be able to put his penis in his mouth (many try).

Masturbation is clearly a versatile procedure: The accompanying fantasies may be heterosexual or homosexual; the sadist can inflict imaginary pain, and the masochist may experience real pain; the voyeur may peep while masturbating, and so on. Under such special circumstances, however, it is customary to label the activity according to these other characteristics.

Learning to Masturbate

As infants explore their bodies, sooner or later they discover the pleasurable potential of their genitals. Some infants and preadolescent children do masturbate, in effect, but deliberate masturbation usually does not become common until the early teens. Most boys, for instance, are ten to twelve years old when they begin; at age thirteen, when most girls have experienced menarche, only about 15 percent have masturbated.

Most boys seem to learn to masturbate from one another. In the Kinsey sample nearly all males reported having heard about the practice before trying it themselves, and quite a few had watched companions doing it. (Three out of four boys were led to masturbating by hearing or reading about it. About 40 percent mentioned observing others as their primary inspiration.) Pubescent boys thus appear to be much more communicative about their sexual activities than are girls, and bolder in seeking information. Fewer than one in three boys reported discovering this outlet by himself, and fewer than one in ten was led to it through homosexual contact.

Females learn to masturbate primarily through accidental discovery of the possibility (two out of three in the Kinsey sample), and they may begin as late as the thirties. Apparently females do not discuss their own sexual behavior as openly as males do: Some women who know of male masturbation are startled to discover that the practice also occurs among females. Occasionally a woman may masturbate for years before she realizes the nature of her act, though such innocence was perhaps more common in the past.[14]

Verbal and printed sources, though less important than for males, continue to provide important leads (43 percent), and so does observation (11 percent). Furthermore, slightly more than 10 percent of girls are initiated into masturbation through petting, which is true for very few males. After a girl experiences orgasm through petting (usually as a result of manipu-

lation by the male) she may then use the same methods autoerotically. Occasionally foreplay leading to coitus fulfills the same function. Homosexual contacts account for very few initiations into masturbation for females.

Prevalence and Frequency

Even those who decry the practice concede that masturbation is very prevalent among males and much more common among females than is widely recognized. Prevalence figures from various studies differ somewhat, but all have been high.

In the Kinsey sample, 92 percent of males and 58 percent of females were found to have masturbated to orgasm at some time in their lives. An additional 4 percent of women had masturbated without reaching orgasm. If we try also to include those who have the experience while oblivious of its "true nature," about two of three women may be supposed to have masturbated. Males rarely masturbate without ejaculating, and when they ejaculate there is no mistake about it. The male percentages do not therefore really change much when those with experiences stopping short of orgasm are also included.

Figures 9.6 and 9.7 show the percentages of people in the Kinsey samples who masturbated to orgasm at some time in their lives. Such graphs (known as "accumulative incidence curves") plot answers to the question "How many people ever have such experience by a given age?" The curves do not, of course, differentiate among behavior of individuals: A person who masturbates only once in his life and one who does so many times are counted in the same way.

In Figure 9.6 we note that only a negligible percentage of men had masturbated to orgasm by age ten (even though the majority had attempted self-stimulation, stopping short of orgasm). Between ages ten and fifteen the

[14]"A married lady who is a leader in social-purity movements and an enthusiast for sexual chastity, discovered, through reading some pamphlet against solitary vice, that she had herself been practicing masturbation for years without knowing it. The profound anguish and hopeless despair of this woman in face of what she believed to be the moral ruin of her whole life cannot well be described." (Ellis, H. [1942], Vol. I, Part One, p. 164.)

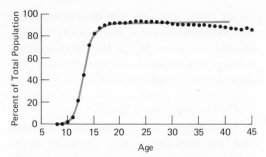

Figure 9.6. Accumulative incidence curve for masturbation by males (data corrected for U.S. population). From A. C. Kinsey *et al., Sexual Behavior in the Human Male* (Philadelphia: Saunders, 1948), p. 502. Courtesy of the Institute for Sex Research.

incidence curve climbed dramatically and then leveled off as it approached age twenty. Practically every man who was ever going to masturbate had already done so by this age. The curve did not go beyond 92 percent; 8 of every 100 males never masturbated to orgasm.

The female pattern was quite different (see Figure 9.7). First, the curve never rose beyond 62 percent: a graphic restatement of what we have already discussed. Second, the curve climbed only gradually to this high point. Up to the age of forty-five years, more and more women were still discovering this outlet by

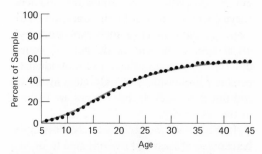

Figure 9.7. Accumulative incidence curve for masturbation to orgasm by females (curve for masturbation short of orgasm omitted). From A. C. Kinsey *et al., Sexual Behavior in the Human Female* (Philadelphia: Saunders, 1953), p. 141. Courtesy of the Institute for Sex Research.

experiencing orgasm through masturbation for the first time.[15]

What was the weekly frequency of masturbation among men? As we noted in connection with total outlet, age and marital status made a great deal of difference. In boys from puberty to fifteen years old, among whom this practice reached a peak, the mean frequency of masturbation was twice a week. If we consider the "active population" only, that is, only those who actually had masturbated sometime or other, then the weekly mean was 2.4 times. These figures decreased steadily with age: In the total unmarried population, the forty-six- to fifty-year-old group averaged fewer than one orgasm every two weeks; in the active population the mean was 1.2. Frequencies for married men were very small. There was no mean higher than once every two or three weeks.

How often did the average male masturbate? In the active unmarried population frequencies ranged from almost twice a week (in the post pubertal group up to fifteen years) to about once every two weeks (in the forty-six- to fifty-year-old group). In "active" married groups the rates were much lower. In no age group did an average married male masturbate more than once a month. Medians were consistently lower than were means, and both averages declined with age.

These frequencies must be understood within the context of the wide range of variation. There were men (apparently healthy) who never masturbated or did so only once or twice in their lives. Others may have averaged twenty or more such orgasms a week over many years.

The average (mean and median) frequencies for the active female sample were quite uniform

---

[15] At age twelve about 12 percent of females and 21 percent of males had experienced orgasm; by age fifteen 20 percent of females and 82 percent of males; and by age twenty, 33 percent of females and 92 percent of males had done so.

at various age levels (up to the mid-fifties) and did not show the steady decline with age that was characteristic of males. The average unmarried woman, if she masturbated at all, did so about once every two or three weeks; the median for her married counterpart was about once a month.

The range of variation in frequency of female masturbation was very wide. In addition to many who never masturbated, some masturbated yearly, monthly, weekly, or daily, and some occasionally reached staggering numbers of orgasms in a single hour. These few individuals inflated the female means to two or three times the corresponding medians.

The prevalence and frequency of masturbation showed a number of interesting associations with other factors beside age and sex. We shall now briefly examine some of them.

Masturbation and Social Class. The better-educated person (especially if female) was more likely to masturbate. Only 89 percent of males with only grade-school educations masturbated sometime in their lives. In the group with no education beyond high school 95 percent masturbated; for those with college education the figure was 96 percent. The corresponding figures for females were 34, 59, and 60 percent.

The frequency of masturbation showed definite correlation with education among males and was highest among college-educated groups. Females did not show this correlation. Although a woman's social background (as measured by education) may have influenced her decision whether or not to masturbate, it did not affect the frequency.

Masturbation was clearly a very important outlet for the better educated: It was used by almost all college-educated males and nearly two-thirds of the females. It constituted not only the chief source (60 percent) of male orgasms before marriage but also almost 10 percent of orgasms following marriage. More than two-thirds of college-educated men masturbated at least sometime after marriage.

These differences in frequency of masturbation can be explained by several factors. First, better-educated people are less fearful of masturbation as a health hazard. In their social circles masturbation may be openly condoned or at least not seriously condemned. At less-educated levels there are strong taboos against masturbation and for that matter against all sexual practices other than coitus. To many in this group masturbation seems not only unhealthy but also unnatural and unseemly. They find it difficult to understand, for instance, why a married man with ready access to a woman would ever want to masturbate.

An additional factor is the difference in class attitudes toward premarital coitus. Although better-educated people have gradually relaxed restrictions against premarital relations, they are probably still less permissive than are their counterparts in lower classes. The greater reliance on masturbation may then arise partly from aversion to its alternatives rather than from direct preference for it.

Adult masturbation is sometimes viewed as a product of "hypocritical" attitudes and sexual inhibitions characteristic of Western (particularly Anglo-Saxon) societies. The less educated among these groups are assumed to be less handicapped by such cultural distortions and closer to living under more "primitive" and therefore more "natural" conditions. The data from other cultures (and from behavioral studies of animals) do not substantiate these allegations.

Masturbation and Marriage. We noted in Chapter 7 that masturbation accounted for far greater shares of total outlet for single people than for those who were married—as would be expected. In fact, we may legitimately ask why married people masturbate at all.

The predominant reason for both sexes is the temporary unavailability of the spouse—through absence, illness, pregnancy, disinclination, and so on. Of all the alternatives to marital coitus (other than abstinence and nocturnal orgasm) masturbation is the least threatening to the marital relationship.

There are other instances in which masturbation may actually be preferable to coitus. A man may then be able to give freer reign to his fantasies, whereby, if he is simply after sexual release, he may circumvent lengthy and tedious courting of a demanding and exacting wife. If he has potency problems, it saves him repeated humiliation. A woman, on the other hand, may find coitus unsatisfying and may attend to her own sexual needs through self-stimulation. As an autoerotic activity masturbation provides a person with full and complete control without the obligations and restraints necessary in dealing with other people.

Masturbation and Religion. As most interpreters of Jewish and Christian moral codes have condemned masturbation, let us see what effect this condemnation has had on actual behavior. Interestingly, men and women seem to have been influenced differently. The very high prevalence of masturbation among males indicates that religious belief has not had a significant effect. A man may feel less or more guilty about masturbating, but sooner or later more than nine out of ten men indulge in the practice. There is a difference, however, in how often they do so. The more religious men (particularly Orthodox Jews and practicing Roman Catholics) in the Kinsey sample did masturbate somewhat less often. The highest frequencies were among religiously inactive Protestants.

Among women masturbation was definitely less widespread among the more devout (41 percent) than among the nondevout (67 percent). The degree of devotion seemed more important than the particular denomination. In contrast to men, once a woman had engaged in this practice, she did not seem influenced by her religious beliefs in how often she used it.

Even though the devout female was less likely to masturbate, this practice accounted for a higher proportion of her total sexual outlet than it did for her nondevout counterpart. Masturbation still apparently provided a "lesser evil," in comparison with alternatives like premarital coitus.

Miscellaneous Factors. Boys who reached puberty at a younger age were more likely to masturbate and to do so more frequently than were boys who reached puberty later. The same did not apply to girls.

Women born after 1920 were more likely (by about 10 percent) to masturbate than those born before 1900. Among males there was a slight increase in the lower educational groups in these two age categories. Otherwise, no substantial changes seem to have occurred in the masturbatory activities of successive generations.

Differences in background seemed to make some difference for women but not for men: Urban women were more likely to masturbate, but there were no differences in how often they did so. The practice also accounted for a smaller percentage of the total outlet of urban women.

It is quite clear from these findings that masturbation is so compelling a method of sexual release for men that most practice it to some extent, regardless of diverse social characteristics. But among women such differences seem to be of considerable moment.

Cross-Cultural Variations

Masturbation is as nearly universal a phenomenon as is coitus but, like all human behavior, subject to cultural variation. European masturbation patterns seem very similar to those of the United States. Is masturbation a predominantly Western practice? The anthropologist Mantegazza (whose writings were prominent in the 1930s) called Europeans a "race of masturbators." He reasoned that Western civilization simultaneously stimulates and represses sexuality and that restrictions on nonmarital coitus compel people to masturbate instead. Let us see what the historical and anthropological records show.

Masturbation has been documented for many ancient cultures, including the Babylonian, Egyptian, Hebrew, Indian, and Greco-Roman. Greeks and Romans believed that Mercury had invented the act to console Pan after he had lost his mistress Echo.[16] Zeus himself was known to indulge occasionally.[17] Aristophanes, Aristotle, Herondas, and Petronius refer to masturbation.[18] Classical attitudes, nevertheless, seem to have been ambivalent: Demosthenes was condemned for the practice, whereas Diogenes was praised for doing it openly in the marketplace.[19]

Condemnations by medieval theologians (penance for as many as forty days) acknowledge that the practice was current. Muslim theologians regarded it as a Christian vice and prayed for mercy upon any of their own who fell into this error.

During the past century the existence of the practice among some illustrious men has been grudgingly acknowledged. Jean Jacques Rousseau, Nikolai Gogol, and Johann von Goethe, for instance, were known to be "victims" of the "vice" by their own admission. Their apologists have pointed out, however, that these men would never have carried it to "excess," their unusual faculties could bear the damage, and

so on, the message being that mere mortals should abstain.

Masturbation is reported by Ford and Beach for about forty primitive cultures but is probably much more widespread.[20] Most groups seemed to disapprove of it for adults. For instance, Trukese men (monogamous fishermen of the Caroline Islands) were said to masturbate in secret while watching women bathe. Men of Tikopia (Pacific island agriculturists) and of Dahomey (West African agriculturists and fishermen) masturbated occasionally, even though both cultures permitted polygamy.

Female masturbation also occurred, but infrequently; it was generally disapproved. Vaginal insertions seemed more common than clitoral stimulation among some primitive people: African Azande women used wooden dildos (and were severely beaten if caught by their husbands); the Chukchee of Siberia used the calf muscles of reindeer; Tikopia women relied on roots and bananas; Crow women used their fingers, and so did the Azanda of Australia.

Among the Lesu (polygamous tribesmen of New Ireland) female masturbation was condoned. Powdermaker reported:

> Masturbation . . . is practiced frequently at Lesu and regarded as normal behavior. A woman will masturbate if she is sexually excited and there is no man to satisfy her. A couple may be having intercourse in the same house, or near enough for her to see them, and she may thus become aroused. She then sits down and bends her right leg so that her heel presses against her genitalia. Even young girls of about six years may do this quite casually as they sit on the ground. The women and men talk about it freely, and there is no shame attached to it. It is a customary position for women to take, and they learn it in childhood. They never use their hands for manipulation.[21]

---

[16] Parke (1906), p. 373.

[17] Frazer, trans. (1898).

[18] Aristophanes finds it unmanly but acceptable for women, children, slaves, and feeble old men.

[19] Ellis, H. (1942), Vol. I, Part One, p. 277.

[20] Ford and Beach (1951).

[21] Powdermaker (1933), quoted in Ford and Beach (1951), p. 158.

Anthropological reports also indicate that, even where masturbation occurs, it does not seem to be very frequent. The fact that adults of both sexes masturbate in primitive cultures is, however, more relevant than is the purported frequency of the practice in any of them. Information from anthropological field notes is nevertheless hardly comparable to the results of thorough and systematic population surveys. Until such rigorous surveys are conducted cross-culturally, we cannot discuss comparative rates with any certainty.

Masturbation among Animals

Self-stimulation is quite prevalent among animals.[22] Among males of many species masturbation to the point of orgasm has been documented. It is less certain for females, whose capacity to reach orgasm is much less developed.

Self-stimulation can be observed among subprimates. A sexually aroused porcupine, for instance, holds one forepaw to its genitals while walking about on the other three paws. It may also rub its sex organs against various objects; one captive male was observed hopping about with a stick between its legs, showing obvious signs of arousal.

Dogs and cats lick their penises before and after coitus; elephants use their trunks; captive dolphins rub their erect penises against the floor of the tank, and one male has been observed stimulating itself by holding its penis in the jet of the water intake. Comparable activities have been noted among rats, rabbits, horses, bulls, and other animals.

A curious practice has been observed among red deer, whose antlers apparently become erotically sensitive during rutting season.

This act is accomplished by lowering the head and gently drawing the tips of the antlers to and fro through the herbage. Erection and extrusion of the penis from the sheath follow in five to seven seconds. There is but little protrusion and retraction of the penis and no oscillating movements of the pelvis. Ejaculation follows about five seconds after the penis is erected, so that the whole act takes ten to fifteen seconds. These antlers, used now so delicately, may within a few minutes be used with all the body's force behind them to clash with the antlers of another stag. These mysterious organs are a paradox; at one moment exquisitely sensitive, they can be apparently without feeling the next.[23]

Self-stimulation is quite common among primates. Captive male apes and monkeys manipulate their penises by hand or foot and also take them into their mouths or rub them against the floor. Masturbation does not occur only in captivity; free spider monkeys manipulate their genitals with their tails, and adult male rhesus monkeys have been observed masturbating to the point of orgasm in the presence of receptive females.

Female mammals of subprimate species apparently masturbate only rarely. During the breeding season some may manipulate their vulvas, rub them against various objects, walk about astride sticks, and so on; the types of activity are quite similar to those of the males. Self-stimulation, furthermore, appears to serve more than merely autoerotic functions, for the genital secretions left on objects or even on the ground by a female in heat attract and excite males.

Masturbation is definitely less frequent among female primates than among males, both in the wild and in captivity. Females can be seen fingering or rubbing their genitals but often only perfunctorily. Even when such activity is clearly autoerotic, it does not lead to definitely observable orgasms. Observers have also noted that, in contrast to subprimate females, who act as do the males of their own species, subhuman female primates use methods closer to those of women than to those of males of their own species. Here is a description of the type of self-stimulation that some female apes indulge in.

Adult female apes sometimes devote considerable energy and ingenuity to the achievement of vulvar stimulation. In one instance a full-grown chimpanzee was playing with a

---

[22]The data presented in this section are from Ford and Beach (1951), pp. 159-161.

[23]Darling (1937), quoted in Ford and Beach (1951), p. 161.

mango. First she placed the fruit upon her external genitals. Then, apparently dissatisfied with the results of this procedure, the animal put the mango on the floor, sat down upon it, turning, twisting, and rubbing awkwardly with her hands and continually varying her position, "as though to improve her technique of producing genital friction." Subsequently, the chimpanzee raised and lowered her body repeatedly, bumping her genitals against the fruit. Later she explored the vagina with a finger and also inserted a pebble into the orifice.[24]

Masturbation and Health

"There is really no end to the list of real or supposed symptoms and results of masturbation," according to Havelock Ellis, who was himself ambivalent about the practice.[25] Insanity; epilepsy; various forms of headaches (in addition to "strange sensations at the top of the head"); numerous eye diseases (including dilated pupils, dark rings around the eyes, "eyes directed upward and sideways"); intermittent deafness; redness of nose and nosebleeds; hallucinations of smell and hearing; "morbid changes in the nose"; hypertrophy and tenderness of the breasts; afflictions of the ovaries, uterus, and vagina (including painful menstruation and "acidity of the vagina"); pains of various kinds, specifically "tenderness of the skin in the lower dorsal region"; asthma; heart murmurs ("masturbator's heart"); and skin ailments ranging from acne to wounds, pale and discolored skin, and "an undesirable odor of the skin in women" are all supposed consequences of masturbation.

There is, of course, no evidence to support any of these or any other claims of physical harm resulting from masturbation. Yet for more than 200 years (from the dawn of the Age of

Enlightenment) and until recently these dire effects have held an unshakable place in the beliefs of the medical elite in the Western world. The historical emergence of these notions is worth reviewing.

From the time of Hippocrates physicians have voiced their concern that overindulgence in sex is detrimental to health (Chapter 12). Only in the last 250 years, however, has masturbation been singled out as a particularly harmful activity. Before the eighteenth century we can find only occasional references to masturbation in medical texts. Early in the eighteenth century a book entitled *Onania, or the Heinous Sin of Self-Pollution* appeared in Europe. The author was probably a clergyman turned quack who peddled a remedy along with the book. Although the work became very popular throughout Europe (and is referred to in Voltaire's *Dictionnaire Philosophique*), it appears to have had no immediate impact upon medical opinion.

Then in 1758 *Onania, or a Treatise upon the Disorders Produced by Masturbation* by the distinguished Swiss physician Tissot appeared. It reiterated and amplified the claims of the former work. Tissot's views, coming from an unimpeachable authority, seem to have found ready acceptance. Despite rebuttals and accusations that he was exploiting his medical reputation to further his private moral points of view, the book became a standard reference. By the end of the eighteenth century the "masturbatory hypothesis" of mental disease and assorted ills was well entrenched. The further progress and eventual discrediting of these notions have been described by Hare.[26]

What about the psychological aspects of masturbation? As current views have been strongly influenced by psychoanalytic concepts, it may be best to examine first the reasoning

[24]Bingham (1926), quoted in Ford and Beach (1951), p. 163.
[25]Ellis, H. (1942), Vol. I, Part One, p. 249.
[26]Hare (1962).

behind some answers to questions about what masturbation means and what its consequences are.

Masturbation has received a great deal of attention in psychoanalytic theory. There are references to it in almost every one of the twenty-three volumes of Freud's collected works. The same is true of the writings of other analysts, and W. Stekel has devoted an entire volume to this topic.[27]

Freud believed that autoeroticism involves much more than Ellis envisaged when he proposed the term. Freud included, for instance, activities like thumb sucking. As for masturbation, he divided it into several phases (Chapter 8): first, the self-stimulation of early infancy, which lasts only a short while; then further such activity before the age of four; then suppression until the onset of puberty and the beginnings of adult sexuality; and finally, either continuation into adulthood or replacement by heterosexual coitus.

Freud found childhood masturbation (the second phase) of critical importance as a potential cause of neurosis. He believed that its effects "leave behind the deepest (unconscious) impressions in the subject's memory, determine the development of his character, if he is to remain healthy, and the symptomatology of his neurosis, if he is to fall ill after puberty."[28]

His reasoning is that early infantile masturbation is no more than innocent self-exploration, that the infant obtains pleasure from it but is too young to be blamed or even to comprehend blame, and that masturbation is therefore conflict-free. During the next phase the child (at about three years old) is going through the critical oedipal stage; he is now capable of

fantasies, and when he resumes masturbation incestuous wishes become linked to it so that he feels guilty and fears punishment.

In addition to these inner changes, the environment also now treats him differently: A child of four is expected to behave properly, and masturbation is considered improper. He is told to stop, threatened, perhaps ultimately punished. Parents may actually imply that harm will come to his genitals if he persists. The child is bewildered: Are the threats directed at the act or at the fantasies (of which most parents are quite oblivious)? What will happen to him? What should he do? From this welter of unconscious conflicts under a facade of childhood innocence his psychological future takes shape.

At puberty infantile conflicts reemerge and must be resettled, this time for adaptation to the world of adults. Masturbation now becomes a testing ground for adult sexual behavior, a way of becoming acquainted with one's equipment, of rehearsing future sexual behavior, and of releasing sexual tensions. In time, there is a gradual switch from the autoerotic to the sociosexual sphere—masturbation is abandoned for the more mature and fulfilling outlet of coitus but is resumed when coitus is unavailable.

Masturbation, viewed within the framework of psychoanalytic theory, is thus a universal and normal activity of childhood and adolescence and a legitimate adult outlet when coitus is not possible. It is considered harmful, however, when it engenders guilt and anxiety—and symptomatic of sexual immaturity when it is preferred to heterosexual intercourse.

It is possible to argue that, on the basis of the phylogenetic and cross-cultural record, masturbation is a biologically and psychologically legitimate sexual outlet. Population researchers may point out that by condemning adult masturbation psychoanalysts impute at least some degree of emotional disturbance to

---

[27] Stekel (1950).

[28] Freud, *Three Essays on the Theory of Sexuality* (1905), in Freud (1957-1964), Vol. VII, p. 189.

a vast segment of the population with no other independent evaluation of their behavior and feelings.

Despite the general condoning of the practice, (at least for adolescents) by the medical profession, doctors often finish by noting that one should not carry the practice "to excess." Excess is not defined, and what the harm will be is not specified. This vagueness reflects the discredited but not discarded notions of former times.

Masturbation is still not quite "respectable," even though it is openly discussed in literary and popular works.[29] The polite tolerance of earlier marriage manuals toward the practice does, however, seem to be giving way to unabashed endorsement by writers of current popular sex manuals.[30]

---

[29] For example, Roth (1967).

[30] *"J"* (1969), pp. 38–52; *"M"* (1971), pp. 60–68.

For most adults, sexual intercourse is generally what sex is all about. Sexual intercourse is not the only sexual outlet, of course, and substantial numbers of people obtain their sexual pleasures through other means. Some do this out of preference and others because coitus is not legitimately available to them.[1]

Lower animals copulate in accordance with their physiological drives, and so does man. Yet millennia of evolutionary development have endowed the sex act with profound psychological and moral significance for man. Intercourse is a complex interaction between two individuals that can be understood only within the overall context of their relationship.

Sexual intercourse is not just orgasm. It is a union between two individuals acting in a social context in accordance with their physiological and psychological needs. This is implied in the terms "coitus" and "intercourse." It is also significant that the most common English vernacular for sexual intercourse also means to cheat, trick, take advantage of, and to treat unfairly. In its various forms it also stands for inferior, unpleasant, difficult, confusing, blundering, wasteful, disorganized, in trouble, "neurotic." The same word which expresses our desire to make love also expresses dismay, annoyance, or anger. Our very language thus betrays our ambivalence and the fact that sexual encounters involve far more than the gratification of our erotic needs.

Foreplay

Foreplay, in one form or another, is a universal prelude to coitus. Even lower animals engage in some courting before intercourse. In the West foreplay usually consists of more or less the same activities engaged in during petting, except that here they lead to sexual intercourse.

Marriage manuals are replete with instructions on techniques of sexual arousal, apparently on the assumption that people do not know what to do beyond the most rudimentary kiss and caress. Even if this assumption were correct (which it is not), to give erotic advice without belaboring the obvious or sounding silly is very difficult. Actually, most of us do seem to manage our sexual activities without benefit of

---

[1] "Coitus" or "coition" (Latin for "going together") is the specific term for heterosexual intercourse. "Sexual relations" and "sexual intercourse" are less specific since homosexual pairs may also be said to be having sexual relations and there can be nonvaginal forms of heterosexual intercourse. However, common usage has made these terms (as well as "making love" and numerous colloquial expressions) synonymous.

CHAPTER

10

SEXUAL INTERCOURSE

formal instruction. Given fundamentally healthy and accepting attitudes, a couple innocent of sexual experience will learn fast enough.[2]

Instruction in erotic techniques may nevertheless be useful for those of us who are anxious about sex and unsure of ourselves. Even when nothing new is said, the written text inspires confidence actually to do what we already know about. Those who wish to go beyond ordinary levels of sexual competence may also want to learn from the experiences of others who are more imaginative and resourceful.

Because of the wide range of preferences and differences in levels of responsiveness, we shall deal here primarily with general principles of effective sexual arousal and shall restrict our description of specific techniques to only a few examples.

Psychological Context

Excluding sadomasochistic relations, in which sex serves aggressive purposes, most people require certain minimums of affection and trust before they can engage in satisfactory sexual encounters. Many profess and some actually believe that unless they are "in love" they cannot engage in sex without cheapening the act. This issue has, of course, profound moral as well as psychological significance.

Discussions of sexual arousal and coitus must be understood within this larger emotional context. For a person who is deeply in love, the mere presence or the slightest touch of his beloved can be unbearably stimulating; in other cases intense love may be entirely devoid of erotic content. Still others may achieve high levels of sexual gratification without benefit of such intense emotions. But even then there is usually some reaction to the partner as a person beyond physical sexual interest.

Nothing could be more appropriate than expressions of affection during foreplay, and few measures are more effective in arousing a partner. Such sentiments, however, sometimes become prepayment for sexual favors rather than manifestations of genuine feeling.

Even though expressions of affection are more meaningful when they are spontaneous, some people cannot help trying to extract such assurances at every turn; others are in turn guilty of mouthing passionate endearments for pragmatic ends. There are of course many ways of expressing affection and all (not just the verbal forms) should be recognized.

The prelude to coitus may be as pleasurable as coitus itself. A certain mix of seriousness (but not heavy drama) and lightheartedness (but not comedy) is often the most effective mood. There is, of course, no absolute standard, and different occasions require different attitudes. Some couples enjoy chasing each other around, wrestling on the floor, tickling each other, and jump into each other's arms amid screams and giggles. Others prefer a more subdued mood, with voices gentle and hushed and movements restrained. Although a certain element of romance may be cherished at these moments, it is also notable that some couples can proceed right to coitus after only a few perfunctory caresses.

The effective methods of approaching one's partner are just as variable. The popular vision of the strong, virile male who firmly but gently takes charge offers one example. A man may be equally successful, however, with a more

---

[2]There is an extensive literature of sexual instruction in the form of "marriage manuals." Some of these are translations of ancient erotic works but mostly they have been written in the West during the past hundred years or so, usually by physicians or other professionals. Since these books number in the thousands and some have sold millions of copies, they obviously have been responsive to a wide public need even though they tend to be inaccurate in various ways. For current professional views concerning their usefulness, see "Do Marriage Manuals Do More Harm than Good?" (1970).

diffident approach, moving slowly but with finesse. There is also no one way in which a woman ought to behave. Sex calls for honesty and mutual concern, not stereotypes.

There are various ways of approaching sex, but it is perhaps best simply to "be oneself," though emphasizing one's assets. Yet it is difficult to drop all pretense without a feeling of mutual trust. To "be oneself" and to accept the other person as he is, however, are only the beginning. As incompatibilities and differences are unavoidable, both partners must also be willing and able to accommodate each other's idiosyncratic needs—but only up to a point. Some relationships may be incompatible and are best abandoned. People may be so hopelessly dominated by neurotic conflicts that they need to mature or change before they can engage in sexual intercourse responsibly and satisfactorily.

It is natural to look for simple physical means to ecstasy, and we are annoyed when instead we are offered psychological generalities. Nevertheless, if one aspires to become an accomplished lover, the search for buttons and levers will have to be abandoned. There is no denying the importance of knowing where the nerve centers are, but the current that feeds those circuits is emotion.

Sex does not operate within a psychological vacuum, and the range of possible emotional reactions varies tremendously, depending upon circumstances and the relations of the individuals. As we cannot possibly deal here with even a fraction of these variations, we shall assume in this chapter that we are dealing with physically healthy and affectionate couples with legitimate reasons for engaging in sexual intercourse.

The following arousal techniques are not limited to foreplay, of course, and can continue while coitus is in progress. The male usually takes the more active role in these activities primarily because they stimulate him. There is

no reason, however, why women cannot be just as active if this behavior leads to mutual enjoyment.

Techniques of Arousal

A clear understanding of which parts of the body respond to which types of stimulation is a prerequisite for becoming a competent lover. The information on "erogenous zones" and the body's responses to sexual stimulation offered earlier (Chapter 3) is relevant here. Of the innumerable activities that may be included in foreplay, we shall single out a few that are generally found to be quite effective and are acceptable to most people.

Kissing. Erotic kissing is a ubiquitous component of sex play in many, but not all, cultures.[3] It is both an expression of sexual desire and an effective erotic stimulant. Although it takes several forms, it generally involves the tongue and the inside of the mouth. "A humid kiss," says an ancient Arabic proverb, "is better than a hurried coitus." Erotic kissing, like coitus, builds up gradually and requires sensitivity and timing.

Initially kissing involves mostly lip contact. A light, stroking motion (*effleurage*) may be used in alternation with tentative tongue caresses and gentle nibbling of the more accessible lower lip. Gradually, as the tongue becomes bolder, it can range freely in the mouth of the partner, who may suck on it (*maraichinage*). The use of the tongue in erotic kissing is sometimes referred to as "French kissing," but as Figure 10.1 illustrates, this is a far more

---

[3]There are important differences even within the various social classes in a given culture. In the Kinsey sample, for instance, 77 percent of the college-educated males but only 40 percent of those with only grade-school educations reported practicing the erotic, or deep, kiss. Simple lip kissing is much more frequent and was reported by almost all (99.4 percent) of the married male Kinsey respondents.

Figure 10.1. Mochica pottery. Courtesy of William Dellenback and the Institute for Sex Research.

universal form of foreplay and unlikely to have originated in a single culture.

This type of voluptuous kissing not only serves as a prelude to coitus but may also continue right through it. Occasionally an ardent couple may start with a deep kiss and not break oral contact until coitus is over.

Kissing, of course, need not be restricted to the sexual partner's lips. Any part of the body may be similarly stimulated although the neck, ear lobes, breasts, inside of the thighs, fingertips, palms of the hands, and so on, as well as the genitals, have a higher erotic potential, as discussed earlier (Chapter 3).

Kissing is practiced in many other cultures, but in some societies it is unknown, at least in

a form familiar to us.[4] Tinquians (monogamous Philippine agriculturists and headhunters) and Balinese used to bring their faces together and smell each other ("rubbing noses"). The Thonga of Mozambique (primitive agriculturists), on the other hand, seemed to be revolted by the Western kiss: "Look at them—they eat each other's saliva and dirt."[5]

Behavior resembling human kissing can also be observed in primates. Immature chimpanzees, for instance, occasionally press their lips together as a prelude to further sexual exploration. Bingham has also reported that during coitus a male chimpanzee would occasionally suck vigorously on the female's lower lip.[6] Oral contact during sexual activity also occurs in other animals, for example, mice (males lick the females' mouths), sea lions (they rub mouths), and elephants (males insert the tips of their trunks into their partners' mouths).

Oral-Genital Stimulation. An exceedingly effective but somewhat controversial erotic stimulant is the "genital kiss."[7] It involves oral stimulation of the genitals and is a fairly widespread though unevenly distributed practice. In the Kinsey samples almost half the college-educated males but fewer than 5 percent of those with grade-school educations reported having stimulated their wives in this manner.

---

[4] For a discussion of cross-cultural aspects of kissing see Opler (1969).

[5] Ford and Beach (1951), p. 49.

[6] Bingham (1926), in Ford and Beach (1951), p. 49.

[7] The Dutch gynecologist Van de Velde boldly (for his time in 1926) favored this practice. It was he who coined the term "genital kiss," in preference to the technical terms "cunnilingus" (to lick the vulva) and "fellatio" ("to suck") for the oral stimulation of female and male genitals respectively (Van de Velde [1965], pp. 154–156). Some sex manuals provide explicit instructions on oral-genital stimulation. See, for example, "J" (1969), pp. 119–123, and "M" (1971), pp. 110–116.

Women reciprocated much less frequently. Almost 60 percent had never attempted it, and the rest had done so only infrequently. Female reluctance may have resulted from shyness, ignorance of what to do, or fears of indecency or perversion. The possibility that a man might ejaculate in the process may have been a further deterrent, though some women have no hesitation in deliberately bringing a man to orgasm in this fashion.

Again, there is no standard procedure for oral-genital contacts. Usually a man gently caresses the clitoris, the minor lips, and the area of the introitus with his tongue, occasionally sucking and nibbling at them. The saliva produced in this process serves as an additional lubricant. In the male the glans is the primary focus of excitement; gentle stroking of the frenulum with the tongue and lips mouthing and sucking the glans while firmly holding the penis, and grasping and pulling gently at the scrotal sac with the other hand are some of the means of stimulation. These activities must be conducted with tact and tenderness, since few people appreciate a tooth-and-nail assault.

A couple may engage in mutual oral-genital contact ("sixty-nine") as a prelude to coitus or for its own sake (see Figure 10.2). It is not unusual for a woman to achieve multiple orgasms from genital stimulation before intercourse begins. The man thus need not fear leaving his partner unsatisfied during coitus and can time his own orgasm as he wishes.

Oral-genital stimulation is repulsive to some people. If the genitals are clean, objections are difficult to support on hygienic grounds. A person is not obliged to perform or submit to such activity, of course, if it does not appeal to him, but to carry judgments beyond personal preference and to make legal or moral issues out of them is another matter.

Oral-genital contact is also reported in other

Figure 10.2.   Fantasy, attributed to P. Breughel.

societies. Among the Aranda, Ponapeans, and Trukese, for instance, both men and women have been reported to stimulate their partners in this way. In other groups only one or the other sex is permitted to do so.

Oral stimulation of female genitals is quite common among primates, and females reportedly respond with obvious gratitude. Stimulation of the male organ, however, is less well documented. Quadrupeds rely on their mouths quite frequently during sexual activity. Their activities include smelling, licking, mouthing, and so on.

Tactile Stimulation. Tactile stimulation is another important method of sexual arousal. Fondling and caressing are most common, but scratching and gentle slapping can also be effective. The areas to be stimulated are again the "erogenous zones," though, as we indicated earlier, each person has his own unique eroto-genic map.

Kissing and caressing operate on the same physiological principle: The object is to stimulate the sensory receptors on the surface of the skin. In fondling, deeper tissues are also stimulated and the erotic response is somewhat different. Actually these approaches are interchangeable. For example, the lips can be stimulated through gentle caressing by the fingertips and the lips and tongue can be used in turn to caress some other part of the body.

Tactile stimulation can be greatly enhanced if surfaces are moist. The mouth has a natural advantage over the hands in this regard but saliva can also be used quite effectively to moisten the area to be caressed. Even more effective is the use of lotions. Any hand lotion that has a pleasant scent for both partners will do. Apart from their physical effects, lotions provide additional advantages. Whereas ordinary caresses may be cursory and fleeting, when lotions are used, foreplay is prolonged, becomes more deliberate, and helps the participants to stimulate each other unabashedly rather than furtively. Even its "messiness" may have an arousing quality, possibly because of its association with the genital fluids. Further on (Chapter 12) we shall discuss the use of lotions in the treatment of sexual inadequacy.

The effectiveness of fondling female breasts is well known in many cultures.[8] Breast stimulation can be enhanced of course by using both the mouth and hands. The nipples, though the most responsive parts, need not be the exclusive focus of attention. Most women also enjoy more general fondling, mouthing, and caressing of their breasts, particularly if they are proud of

them. The size of the breast has no relation to its sensitivity, and a small-breasted woman must not be assumed to be less sensitive in this area.

Tactile stimulation of the genitals is, of course, particularly exciting for most people. In the Kinsey sample, 95 percent of males and 91 percent of females reported manually stimulating the genitals of their sexual partners. Males tended to be more active in this regard. The techniques of genital stimulation during foreplay are similar to those employed in autoerotic activities (see Chapter 9).

Occasionally a person will stimulate himself during foreplay or even coitus. If he feels free enough, he can thus demonstrate to his partner how best to stimulate him. The more a couple is able to communicate, the less is the need for extraneous instruction.

Stroking the anal orifice and inserting fingers into the rectum are appreciated by some and rejected by others on aesthetic and other grounds. To suspect underlying homosexual motives in all such anal insertions is questionable.

Since each person knows best what is most exciting to him, there is much that can be learned from autoerotic activities that would be useful in foreplay. These can then be modified and supplemented with additional techniques of stimulation that become possible by the presence of a partner. Tactile stimulation of the inner thighs, buttocks, and genitals, for instance, can be most effectively combined with oral stimulation of these parts.

When natural vaginal lubrication is inadequate, it is often recommended that the couple use a coital lubricant (for example, "K-Y jelly"). In these cases the jelly need not be applied just prior to intromission. Preferably it should be used much earlier during coital foreplay when it not only lubricates the introitus but greatly enhances tactile stimulation of the clitoris and the adjoining structures. There is no reason, of course, why women with adequate natural

---

[8] In the Kinsey sample 98 percent of respondents reported manual stimulation and 93 percent oral stimulation of female breasts by the males. Stimulation of the male nipples is rare in heterosexual contacts.

vaginal lubrication cannot also use these jellies for their erotic enhancement.

Despite differences in individual responsiveness, some general principles are worth bearing in mind. Most people find it best to start slowly and with the less sensitive areas. Some do crave rough handling, but many others do not. As no one objects to tenderness, it would seem preferable to start gently and to become more forcible as appropriate rather than to startle and offend at the beginning.

Sensitive surfaces respond best to gentle stimulation, whereas larger muscle masses require firmer handling. Once an area has been singled out for stimulation, it should be attended to long enough to elicit arousal. Frantic shifting from one part of the body to another can be as ineffective as monotonous and endless perseverance. If stimulation is to be effective, it must be steady and persistent. Its tempo and intensity may be modulated, but sexual tension must not be permitted to dissipate. The task of erotic arousal requires patience and is not always free of tedium. Yet effective lovers manage to sustain a sense of novelty and a feeling of excitement as if each time were the first time.

Other Means. Several additional considerations are important. First is the matter of timing. The correct technique applied to the right place at the wrong time will fail to arouse. The same stimulus may be experienced as unpleasant or painful at one stage yet catapult a person to peak excitement at another. Correct timing in turn requires the ability to gauge excitement.

The necessity for effective communication is obvious to most people, but it is often difficult to achieve. Almost everyone will complain when in pain, but most of us are much more reluctant to ask for enhancement of pleasure for fear of seeming forward, lascivious, or perverted. Wishes are sometimes more easily communicated simply by guiding the partner's hand or otherwise indirectly.

Expression of emotion during lovemaking should be no cause for shame. It is a time to let oneself go. Furthermore, a woman who wishes to enhance her partner's excitement and pleasure can most effectively do so by letting him know how she feels. The awareness of a woman's arousal fills a man with pride and provides proof of his competence as a lover. The sighs and moans, squeaks and squeals, grunts and groans of sex are also songs of love.

The erotic potential of pain is well known. Even ordinary versions of foreplay and coitus involve enough physical activity to result in some pain. Within limits and with certain partners mild pain from bites and scratches can be quite stimulating. It will be recalled from Chapter 3 that the threshold of pain is higher during sexual excitement, and this type of stimulation is usually attempted during advanced stages of lovemaking.

Although either sex may lead in lovemaking, usually the male is more aggressive. Psychoanalysts ascribe a certain degree of passivity and "normal masochism" to females.[9] Whether these tendencies (if in fact present in women) are biologically or culturally determined, is debatable. Women can be just as aggressive as men during lovemaking and may compensate for their weaker muscles by using their longer fingernails. It is sometimes difficult to draw the line separating the judicious use of pain as a normal stimulant from its pathological applications in sadomasochistic activities (Chapter 11).

There are wide cultural variations in the sexual use of pain. In some primitive groups sex is a violent affair in which either the male or the female may be the active party. Animal studies clearly demonstrate the deep phylo-

---

[9]Deutsch (1944–1945), Vol. II, p. 277.

genetic roots of the erotic functions of pain. The mating behavior of most animals has a definite aggressive component. The males are the ones who invariably bite, paw, and sometimes injure their partners. The females do not reciprocate.

There are many additional techniques of stimulation. Indian manuals have lengthy discourses on bites, nail marks, slaps, and blows that may prove baffling to most of us. Tickling is another activity to which people react differently.[10] A basic acceptance of oneself and one's partner as individuals, unabashed pride in the body and its sexual functions, the conviction that sex is moral and honorable, and some knowledge of the basic (rather than the exotic) sexual functions are what generally count most in sex.

How long does foreplay usually last? Preferences seem to vary widely among individuals and cultures. The Lepcha and Kwoma, for instance, proceed to coitus without much ado. Trobrianders may spend hours in foreplay. Western "marriage manuals" devote much attention to the necessity of foreplay in preparing the woman for intercourse. Some even specify various time periods as irreducible minimums.[11]

It seems best to leave the length of foreplay to each couple to decide. Aside from preferences, different circumstances require different amounts of preparation. Physiologically, full erection and adequate vaginal lubrication indi-

cate readiness. Psychologically, a couple is ready when both members feel a mutual urge for sexual union.

Intercourse

Making love has been compared to a game of chess: The moves are many, but the ending is the same. Coitus proper starts with the introduction of the penis into the vagina. It can be achieved from a variety of postures, and intercourse involves various types of movements. Even though there is more to making love than coital mechanics, understanding the physical basis of the act is helpful. The relationship between male and female sexual organs during face-to-face intercourse is illustrated in Figure 10.3; the theme was also treated by Leonardo da Vinci five centuries ago (see Figure 10.4).

Until recently, a great deal of attention was focused on the relative positions of the sexual organs during coitus, with special reference to whether or not the clitoris came into "advantageous contact" with the penis. Current research has shown that, because of the movement of the clitoral hood, it is immaterial whether the clitoris is stimulated directly by the penis (which is difficult at best) or indirectly (by friction with its own overhanging skin; see Chapter 3). It should also be recalled that, contrary to popular belief, there is no evidence that the sizes of the sex organs of male or female have any bearing on the quality of the sex act (Chapter 2).

Although discussions of the mechanics of coitus suggest that their main contribution is to enhance the physical aspects of intercourse, the benefits are in fact mostly psychological. Some of us approach sex with uncertainty and a tendency to hurry. In experimenting with various approaches, we become more deliberate, controlled, and purposeful. This effort implies care and concern for the partner, so that intercourse literally fits the meaning of the term: an

---

[10]For a discussion of the sexual significance of tickling see Kepecs (1969).

[11]Among married couples in the Kinsey sample the lengths of time involved in foreplay were three minutes or less in 11 percent, four to ten minutes in 36 percent, eleven to twenty minutes in 31 percent, beyond twenty minutes in 22 percent, and some couples spent several hours each day in erotic play (Kinsey *et al.* [1953], p. 364).

It is also of interest that in cases where coitus was preceded by twenty minutes or more of foreplay only 7.7 percent of the wives did not experience orgasm. Where penile intromission lasted sixteen minutes and longer, only 5.1 percent of the wives failed to reach orgasm (Gebhard [1968]).

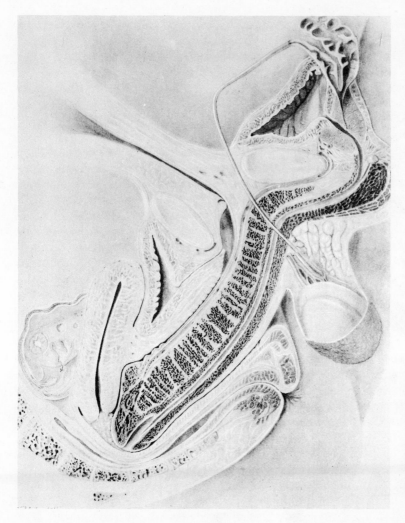

Figure 10.3. Male and female genitals in face-to-face coitus. From Robert L. Dickinson, *Atlas of Human Sex Anatomy,* 2nd ed. (Baltimore: Williams & Wilkins, 1949), figure 142. Copyright © 1949 by The Williams & Wilkins Co., and reprinted by permission.

interaction between two people. Involving the female partner more actively increases her enjoyment, as she becomes a willing participant rather than a submissive object. When she takes some of the initiative, he in turn is reassured that he is giving as much pleasure as he is feeling. Knowledge of and experimentation with sexual techniques can thus greatly enrich a sexual relationship.

A second advantage is obtained from the variety of possible postures. Married couples especially sooner or later begin to find sex a bit monotonous. "Marriage," Honoré de Balzac wrote, "must continually vanquish a monster that devours everything: the monster of habit."[12] The imaginative use of different positions can be an antidote to habit, though sustaining real variety year after year is difficult to do.

Various coital positions do, of course, also yield different physical sensations, and, though

---

[12] Quoted in Van de Velde (1965), p. 45.

Figure 10.4. Leonardo da Vinci, figures in coition.

most of us are able to improvise, some of us need the inspiration and information that come from knowing about the experiences of others. Finally, it is important to know how conducive to impregnation a given position is likely to be. Such knowledge is helpful to a couple that is trying to conceive a child, but no posture is reliable as a contraceptive measure.

It is important to recognize that simply trying different coital positions offers no sexual panacea. But it is difficult to imagine any actual harm that might result from it. After all, most people have enough sense not to proceed in the face of pain or discomfort, no matter how elegant or exotic their embrace.

There is nothing mysterious or magical about coital positions. Experimentation shows one approach to be more exciting at one time and others under other circumstances. There is no "position to end all positions," and the search for mechanical perfection is endless and pointless.

A certain agility is indispensable to both partners if they wish to explore the limits of coital gratification, but sex should not become a series of gymnastic feats. There is a story of an Oriental courtesan who had attained such perfect control that she could engage in coitus while holding a cup of tea on one uplifted foot. Although the difficulty of such tasks is apparent, their purpose is less clear.

Another potential drawback is that reading about coital techniques can result in a "cook-book" approach to lovemaking, which robs the act of the spontaneity that ought to be its hallmark.

Many marriage manuals, both ancient and contemporary, give such detailed instructions that the reader becomes overwhelmed by the apparent complexity of the act and cannot help but wonder how millions of people ever manage to accomplish it all by themselves. Illustrations of coital postures are no less bewildering, particularly some of those from the Far East (see Figure 10.5). The complexity of Indian sexual practices prompted the sixteenth-century Arab sage, Sheikh Nefzawi, to comment: "This position, as you can perceive, is very fatiguing and very difficult to attain. I even believe that the only realization of it consists in words and designs."[13] Looking at such illustrations one almost gets the impression that the participants are locked in position with only the penis

moving in and out like a piston, whereas coitus, of course, involves continuous movement.

To speak of coital positions is thus misleading, for we are actually dealing with general approaches, rather than specific postures. During face-to-face intercourse, for instance, a woman lying on her back will stretch her legs out, then pull them up halfway or bring her knees close to her chest for a while, then stretch them out again, and so on. Even when more marked shifts in posture occur, one position flows into another, and sexual activity never loses its fluid quality.

Approaches

Despite the innumerable erotic postures described in love manuals, the basic approaches to coitus are relatively few. The couple may stand, sit, or lie down; the two may face each other, or the women can turn her back to the man; one person can be on top, or both can lie side by side.

Figure 10.6 illustrates some of the more common coital approaches and obviates the need for detailed descriptions.[14] (Also see illustrations in Chapter 13.) Instead we shall examine the relative advantages of these various alternatives.

Face-to-Face. The primary advantage of face-to-face approaches is the opportunity for direct interaction. The partners can gaze into each other's eyes, fully communicating their feelings through speech and facial expressions. They can also kiss and nibble at each other while joined together. This approach allows for numerous alternatives.

In the traditional and most commonly used approach in the Western world, the woman lies

[13]Nefzawi (1964 ed.), p. 132.

[14]Sex manuals are replete with such descriptions. See, for instance, Van de Velde (1965), Chapter 11; Nefzawi (1964 ed.), Chapter 6; and Harkel (1969).

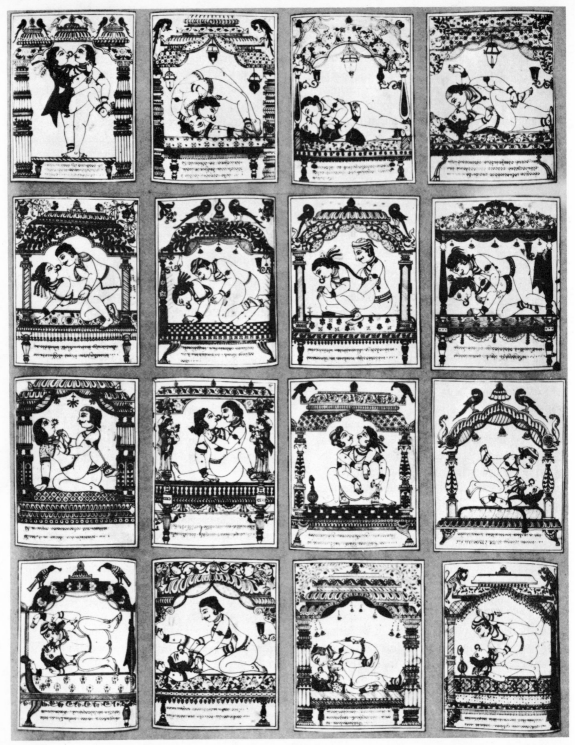

Figure 10.5. Pages from a nineteenth-century Orissan posture-book. Reprinted by permission of G. P. Putnam's Sons and Weidenfeld & Nicholson Ltd. from *Erotic Art of the East*, ed. Philip Rawson, p. 43. Copyright © 1969 by Philip Rawson.

on her back with the man on top of her. But, Figure 10.6 (A, B, C, D, E) shows that considerable variety can be achieved within this basic arrangement, depending upon the position of the woman's legs.

Sequence A offers a convenient starting point for coitus. As the woman pulls her legs up and opens her thighs, the vaginal introitus becomes accessible. Either partner then spreads the lips and guides the penis in. The couple is now fully engaged. Coitus may go on in this manner for a while, or the woman may extend (C) or flex (D) her legs. Extending them provides support for the penis by tightening the vaginal orifice around it. There is thus maximum friction and little likelihood that the penis will slip out as coitus continues. This position is, therefore, useful when erection is relatively weak. Its disadvantage is that penetration is not deep.

When the woman flexes her legs (D) the effect is the opposite, and deep penetration is possible. Placing a pillow under her lower back makes this alternative more comfortable. Once the couple is established in this position, the woman's legs may be placed in a number of ways: She may simply hold them up as illustrated (D) or place them on the man's shoulders. He may hold them under his arms. Or she may entwine her legs around his back and lock her feet together, which gives her excellent leverage for moving her pelvis to meet his thrusts or simply for sustaining muscular tension.

The specific advantage of having the man above is simply that it is most acceptable to many people. The man can be the more active participant: He makes love to the woman. Women who appreciate being pinned down by strong male bodies and submitting to active lovemaking also find this position satisfying.

Coitus in this position (particularly as in A or B) is the most likely to lead to pregnancy. The optimal pooling of the ejaculate in this approach has been described earlier (see Chapter 5). In order to maximize the chance of conception, the woman must maintain this posture for a while after coitus, and the man should not withdraw abruptly.

There are also several drawbacks to these positions, however. If they are used exclusively, sexual interest may eventually diminish. The man's weight can also be a problem: He can support himself (B), but a really heavy man will still be a considerable burden on the woman. Furthermore, in this position the man's hands will not be free to stimulate his partner.

More serious is the restriction that such positions impose upon the woman's movements. Although she can move her legs, her pelvis remains largely immobilized or can be moved only with considerable effort.

Just as many variations are possible if the woman lies on top of the man (Figure 10.6, G, H, I). Her weight is usually less of a problem, and she has the opportunity to express herself fully by regulating the speed and vigor of her movements and the depth of penetration. Many women find it easier to achieve orgasm in this manner. Furthermore, a man is less likely to be immobilized by her weight and is therefore less handicapped than she would be underneath.

The primary disadvantages of this set of alternatives are psychological. Some men feel threatened by being placed in the "passive" or "feminine" position, and many women may be too inhibited to become active partners in coitus. These attitudes are changing, however. Whereas only about one third of those born before 1900 in the Kinsey sample had engaged in this variant, more than half of those born later than 1900 reported having done so.

A host of other alternatives is available to the partners when they lie on their sides (Figure 10.6, K, M, N). Penetration is somewhat more difficult in these positions and requires that the woman lift her upper leg. Partners may effect union in one of the other positions and then roll onto their sides.

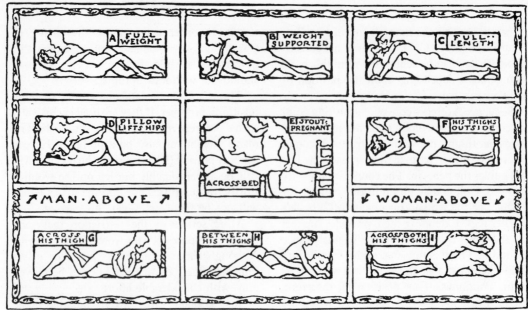

COITAL·POSTURES·OR·PATTERNS·IMPORTANT·FOR·ADJUSTMENT·AND·INSTRUCTION
AS·SEEN·FROM·THE·SIDE

AS·SEEN·FROM·ABOVE

Figure 10.6. Coital positions. From Robert L. Dickinson, *Anatomy of Human Sex Anatomy,* 2nd. ed. (Baltimore; Williams & Wilkins, 1949), figures 159c and 159d. Copyright © 1949 by The Williams & Wilkins Co., and reprinted by permission.

The primary advantage of this approach is the comfort it provides by eliminating weight on either partner. The participants lie side by side, with their legs intertwined in one of several ways. Penetration is, however, shallow and movements are restricted. Coitus tends to be prolonged and leisurely. Ovid commended this approach above others: "Of love's thousand ways, a simple way and with least labor, this is: to lie on the right side, and half supine."[15]

The prone face-to-face approaches provide a rich variety of alternatives, allowing either partner to take the active role. Depending upon excitement, fatigue, body build, and agility, each partner has the opportunity to give and obtain pleasure. An important advantage of all prone postures is that the postorgasmic lassitude can be accommodated effortlessly.

Sitting and kneeling positions involve deliberate attempts at variety, for couples cannot simply "roll" into these positions but must set them up.

In seated intercourse (see Figure 10.6, L) the man sits in a chair or on the edge of the bed. The woman stands in front of him and lowers herself onto his erect penis. By keeping her feet on the ground she can control her pelvic movements up and down. Or she may achieve deeper penetration by straddling him and perhaps locking her feet behind the chair. His pelvic movements are restricted, but his hands are entirely free.

In the kneeling position (Figure 10.6, E) the man controls the pelvic thrusts. Being on solid ground gives him excellent leverage, which he cannot achieve lying down unless he pushes against the frame of the bed. Pushing the toes down into the bed is not very effective. The kneeling position is often recommended for a woman's first coitus. The superior control of the man, the angle of penetration, and the

---

[15] Ovid, quoted in Van de Velde (1965), p. 227.

exposed position of the woman in combination are said to make the rupture of the hymen least painful for her and easiest for him.

There is another, famous approach in this category: The woman straddles the man lying on his back and lowers herself onto the erect penis. She can then lean forward or backward. His legs may be extended or flexed enough to provide support for her back. As her feet rest firmly on the bed, her control of movement is excellent. The ancient Romans were reportedly fond of this position and women boasted of how they "rode" their partners (some writers still call this position the "attitude of equitation"). Many experts consider it, of all possible approaches, to have the maximum voluptuous potential.

Penetration, when the couple is standing face to face, is difficult. If, however, the woman can lift one leg high enough, it is possible. She may then wrap her legs around his waist while he supports her buttocks. Ancient manuals call this position "climbing the tree."

A very satisfactory variant of the kneeling position (Figure 10.6, E) involves an arrangement in which the man stands. His partner must be higher up, as on top of a table. As he is squarely on his feet, with both hands free, he has maximum control of his movements and is able to engage in protracted coitus. Ejaculating while standing constitutes no problem for most men, but the postcoital phase is not very comfortable.

Rear Entry. The dominant form of coitus among animals is from the rear—and for that very reason it is shunned by many people (in the Kinsey sample, only about 15 percent reported having tried it). In addition to the variety that they provide, the rear-entry positions make it easy for the man to fondle the woman's breasts and stimulate her genitals manually. This ability is of major importance when clitoral stimulation is necessary for the woman to achieve orgasm. In all other positions, though manipulation of the clitoris is possible, it tends to be difficult and interferes with full contact between the partners.

These positions have no serious disadvantages. It is true that they somewhat isolate the partners, who cannot conveniently see each other. On the other hand, close and comfortable body contact is easy to achieve—no other position will allow a woman to curl up as snugly in a man's lap.

It was generally maintained until recently that the rear-entry approach bypassed the clitoris and left it unstimulated by the penis. Direct observations have now shown that the movements of the clitoral hood during coitus stimulate the clitoris, no matter what the direction of entry (see Chapter 3).

Rear entry is possible, of course, while lying down, sitting, or standing up. When a woman is lying on her face, coitus is possible, but penetration is not deep. Coitus in this manner may be impossible for obese people. If the two lie on their sides (usually on the left), however, intromission is not difficult. This method is very restful and is suitable for coitus during pregnancy or ill health, when exertion is better avoided. In the sitting versions the man is astride the woman's buttocks. Or the chair position already described (see Figure 10.6, L) may be modified so that she has her back turned to him.

The rear approach allows many other variations in the woman's position. She can go down on all fours or even put her head down ("knee-chest position"). Penetration is easy, and the man's hands are free to roam over her buttocks, inside her thighs, on her genitals, over her breasts, and so on.

The standing rear approach is possible, provided that the woman bends over forward to facilitate intromission. A historically well-known variant is the "wheelbarrow," in which a standing man enters from behind while the

woman is in the knee-chest position: He then lifts her legs up and proceeds with coitus.

Cross-Cultural Variations. The standard face-to-face posture with the man on top may indeed be called the "missionary position," but it also constitutes the most common approach for natives of several dozen primitive cultures. Other positions are widely used too, though one or two variants tend to be dominant in a given culture. Rear approaches are never standard practice. The position in which the woman squats over the man is widely recognized as providing her with maximal stimulation.

There is also considerable variation in who takes the more active role. Some primitive peoples are quite similar to those of the West in this respect. The Chiricahua Apaches, for instance, even shared the Victorian notion that a woman, besides being passive, should display no emotion during coitus. On the other hand, the Hopi, Trukese, and Trobrianders considered an inactive female apathetic and a poor sexual partner.

Movements

In contrast to that of sexual approaches, the importance of coital movements has been generally neglected. Pelvic thrusts during coitus are a mammalian characteristic. Typically they start with penetration, build up momentum, and culminate in orgasm. Man is heir to this behavior, but he can also improve upon it. Both male and female can control the depth of penetration, as well as the speed and vigor of coital thrusts, in order to prolong and intensify the pleasure of both partners.

The way in which penetration is performed sets the tone for the act. This initial step calls for gentle firmness and confident deliberateness. Even when the vagina is properly lubricated, the introitus may still be tense. The glans must first be placed firmly against it, but the area is highly sensitive, and a little patience may be required before the orifice relaxes. A skilled lover may not penetrate even then but may keep moving his glans in the introitus until the woman shows through her own pelvic thrusts the unmistakable signs of wanting deeper penetration.

Coital movements, like positions, have an almost infinite variety, often shading into one another. Generally the initial thrusts are slow, deliberate, and progressively deeper. Thrusts and counterthrusts may then follow various patterns. The man can thrust and withdraw; then the woman does the same. Or they may thrust and withdraw simultaneously. These movements may be rhythmic or not, fast or slow, with shallow or deep penetration, and so on. It is possible, of course, for a movement to be executed by only one person while the other remains relatively passive. Some recommend a nine-stroke rhythm: nine shallow thrusts, then one full lunge, or nine full lunges followed by a shallow thrust.

In all these movements, variation and steady work must be artfully combined with an element of surprise. Frantically rushing through pattern after pattern is as bad as monotonous concentration on one, unless the partners prefer it that way, in which case their choice should supersede the combined advice of all experts.

As coitus progresses, the penis may be thrust completely into the vagina and be rotated inside (like a pestle in a mortar).

The motions described are merely illustrations. These and other movements must be coordinated with the various approaches. Some movements are quite versatile; others can be used only with particular approaches. Perhaps the most important dictum in this connection is that control of coital movements should be as much a prerogative of the female as of the male. During sexual intercourse the genitals must cease to be the exclusive possessions of

the male or female and must become instead shared organs.

Prolonged sexual intercourse is generally viewed as desirable. Many techniques have evolved to extend it, primarily by helping the man to delay ejaculation.[16] Because of their greater capacity for multiple orgasms, females have no need to hold back and may go on having orgasms as long as men can sustain their erections. If a man is capable of multiple orgasms, ejaculation comes later in each successive union.

Ejaculation may be delayed through mental distraction (thinking of something else or looking the other way) or through deliberate checks on the build-up of muscular tension (slowing coital movements, pausing entirely, consciously relaxing). It is also helpful to minimize friction, particularly on the glans. In short, when excitement seems to be mounting out of control, one follows the opposite of what we have described as effective methods of erotic stimulation. How long to sustain coitus is a matter of individual judgment. Sexual intercourse is not a contest of endurance. The only criterion is optimal mutual gratification.

Finally, another much-lauded accomplish-

---

[16] The ultimate in control of ejaculation is required for the performance of *karezza,* or *coitus reservatus,* which has enjoyed sporadic popularity in various parts of the world, including the nineteenth-century Oneida colony in upstate New York. In *karezza* intercourse proceeds as usual, but actual ejaculation is delayed indefinitely. Those who have mastered this technique claim that they can reach a dozen or more sexual climaxes without ejaculation. It has also been suggested that such males actually experience retrograde ejaculation (see Chapter 3) during the act. Besides enhancing sexual pleasure, *karezza* is sometimes believed to be a source of "spiritual enrichment." In physiological terms, if sexual tension is not adequately dissipated, the accompanying vasocongestion persists for a long time. If this occurs repeatedly, it may lead to pelvic pathology. Incidentally, coitus reservatus is not to be confused with coitus interruptus, where the male simply withdraws prior to ejaculation (see Chapter 6 and Lehfeld [1968]).

ment is mutual orgasm. There is much to be said, of course, for the joint experience of orgasm, as long as it does not become the overriding criterion of a successful sexual encounter. Such preoccupations mar sexual enjoyment. Actually there is also some advantage to entering the climax separately. If the woman experiences orgasm several times, the last may be made to coincide with the male's ejaculation.

Are some orgasms "better" than others? Even in physiological terms, orgasm is not a uniform experience, particularly among females (see Chapter 3). The subjective perception of orgasm also varies between individuals and in the same person at different times. Although we have no objective criteria to assess the psychological intensity of orgasm, experience would indicate that some orgasms are perceived as more pleasurable and gratifying than others. It is safe to assume that a host of psychophysiological factors determine this. The identity of the partner and the circumstances under which coitus is taking place all contribute to the mood of the individual, which greatly colors his perceptions. But in addition, physical factors evidently play a role. These may include the time interval since the preceding orgasm, level of fatigue, length and nature of foreplay, and so on. While it is reasonable to assume that these factors are significant, we do not know as yet with sufficient certainty how and why they are important. On this matter every person is his own expert.

Uncertainties in this regard do not generally inhibit marriage manuals from dispensing advice. Some of this advice has plausible physiological explanations, the rest is more mythical, which is not to say that it cannot influence behavior. In the first category are recommendations to heighten the sexual climax through stimulation that supplements the sensations of orgasm. A woman can, for instance, gently squeeze the man's testicles or press against the root of the penis during his orgasm. Likewise, the man may continue to stimulate the clitoral area during the woman's climax. Often the supplemental stimulant induces mild to moderate pain: a slap on the buttocks, squeezing the thighs, as well as pinching, scratching, or even biting may be stimulating to some at this time. There are more enterprising alternatives as well. One marriage manual recommends placing a cold towel or an ice pack on the genital area at the moment of orgasm.[17] Apart from their unavoidable physical impact, whether or not such adjuncts to lovemaking are experienced as pleasurable will depend, of course, on the participants' conception of what lovemaking is all about.

Circumstances

There is a general human preference for privacy during coitus. Why is not clear. It is true that man is vulnerable to attack at such a time, but animals generally do not seem to mind copulating in front of one another. When two partners are bothered by a third animal, they will, of course, try to elude it.

In various cultures coitus occurs in or out of doors, depending upon which affords more privacy. For the sake of novelty and additional excitement, some venturesome couples in our society occasionally make love on the beach or in other natural settings. Sometimes simply using a room other than the bedroom fulfills the same function.

Bedrooms are usually furnished with some thought to romantic atmosphere. Most often provisions are made for soft lighting; less often mirrors are positioned strategically so that the partners can observe themselves. Only rarely is a couple bold enough, however, to place a mirror on the ceiling or in some other place where its exclusively sexual function would be

---

[17]Eichenlaub (1961), pp. 107–108.

obvious. Besides, not everyone finds this prospect stimulating. There is, of course, no end to the refinements that can be added—sound systems, erotic art, and so on.

Animals also respond better in certain settings. In fact, many fishes and birds can mate only under certain environmental conditions. Some male mammals may restrict their contacts with females to their own territories. There is a general tendency to seek sex where it has been enjoyed before. In novel situations animals are also apprehensive and easily distracted from sexual aims.

The preferred times for coitus vary in different cultures. Practical, as well as psychological, considerations play a role, of course. Most couples in our culture make love at night because it is convenient within the routine of everyday life. But it is unwise to always relegate coitus to the very last waking moments of the day, for a certain amount of stamina and alertness are essential for real pleasure. It is also advisable occasionally to change the time to the morning or the middle of the day, simply for variety.

In the animal world copulation occurs during the active period of the day. Subhuman primates, for instance, are diurnal animals, and both sex and eating occur in broad daylight. Man's shift to a nocturnal sexual pattern is probably the result of cultural influences.

Nudity during coitus is also subject to cultural and individual preference. Men generally obtain far more excitement from looking at female bodies than women do from looking at men. Women may also, however, prefer to make love naked because it enhances intimacy.

Some couples make love in front of mirrors, usually at the men's instigation. Although some may see implications of voyeurism in this behavior, it seems harmless and even desirable if it enhances coital performance.

Should intercourse be planned or spontaneous? Some people claim that coitus requires preparation as does any other activity. Apart from practical considerations, they believe that anticipation heightens excitement. Others cannot even bring themselves to take contraceptive measures because they imply forethought.

Relatively few of us have the energy, the need, or the means to stage a major production each time that we engage in sex. On the other hand, far too many people reduce making love to the level of routine, as regular and uninspiring as brushing their teeth and going to the bathroom.

Some of the most exciting sexual encounters may well occur on the spur of the moment and in the least likely of places. Nevertheless, the realities usually require some advance planning if the act is to have more than ordinary significance. As in most everything else in life, virtuosity in sex requires that natural gifts be supplemented by preparation and practice.

The Aftermath

Coitus does not end with orgasm. The final phase is one in which the physiological effects of excitement recede and the individual feels sexually satiated. The physical manifestations during this stage of detumescence and its behavioral components have been described earlier (see Chapter 3).

Marriage manuals devote considerable attention to this phase. Men are warned not to dismount abruptly and turn their backs, or to go to sleep; rather they are told to disengage themselves gradually with endearments and tender caresses. Such advice is predicated upon the assumption that women are slower to become aroused, more difficult to satisfy, and require longer to return to a quiet state; it is then the men's responsibility to see to it that the activities of foreplay, coitus, and afterplay are prolonged appropriately.

It would be altogether simpler if these gender-specific sex roles could be put aside once and for all. Men and women can be full-fledged and equal partners in coitus. They are active or passive, depending upon mutual preference and nothing else; who is on top and who is at the bottom, who caresses whom, and so on ought to be dissociated from notions of masculinity and femininity, and under no circumstances should lovemaking become an arena for competition. Once the fundamental equality of the sexes is acknowledged, it becomes relatively simple to agree on a mutually acceptable postlude to coitus.

These remarks presuppose that both partners have reached orgasm. But sometimes one partner, more often the woman, lags behind. Until she is able to catch up, no matter what happens during afterplay the outcome will be relatively unsatisfactory. Because the male is less frequently able to have multiple orgasms, it is generally preferable that the woman's climax comes first, or simultaneously with his. When occasionally the man's climax precedes the woman's, and he feels unable or disinclined to have a second erection, there is no reason why the woman should not be brought to climax by noncoital stimulation.

The aftermath of coitus may signify the end of an episode of sexual activity or it may simply be an interlude between two acts of intercourse where afterplay imperceptibly merges into foreplay again. Even nonconsecutive acts of coitus are to some extent linked together through memory. In a letter to her husband Abelard after years of enforced separation, Heloise writes:

> Truly, those joys of love, which we experienced together, were so dear to my soul that I can never lose delight in them, nor can they vanish from the mirror of my remembrance. Wheresoe'er I turn, they arise before me and old desires awake.[18]

---

[18]Quoted by Van de Velde (1965), p. 251.

Intercourse and Marriage

Of all the social correlates of sexual intercourse, marriage is undoubtedly the most important. Coitus is the predominant sexual outlet for married persons. Sex is universally approved within marriage; in most Western societies marriage is the only context where it is permissible. Although there certainly is much more to marriage than sex, the adequacy of conjugal sex has tremendous bearing upon the quality and permanence of the marital relationship.

The family is the basic unit in most social organizations. Its form and nature may vary across cultures, but it serves the same fundamental needs. Major functions are to ensure readily available sexual intercourse in a setting of mutual affection and trust and to provide for the care of offspring that may result from such union.

The institution of marriage is timeless, complex, and taxing. There have been efforts, both voluntary and forced, to alter or even to eradicate it. They have failed in the past, but experiments continue.[19]

There has been much speculation about the origins of the human family, and there have been many attempts to trace its evolution. Particularly interesting are recent studies of subhuman primate groups in their natural habitats. In all this research the role of sex in the formation of family bonds has been duly noted, but its exact nature is a matter for debate. One thing is clear: Animals engage in sex because it is enjoyable or reduces tension. They do not do so in order to procreate; they can

---

[19]Sparta, Nazi Germany, the Soviet Union, and Communist China tried unsuccessfully to abolish marriage on a national scale. Various American communal groups, like the Oneida colony of a century ago, have done so on a smaller scale (see Bishop [1969] and Chapter 18).

hardly be expected to associate coitus with pregnancy causally.

Important as the institution of marriage may be, however, it is not the object of our immediate interest here. Nor are we primarily concerned at this point with the critical moral and legal issues involved in sex outside marriage, which we shall deal with in Chapters 16 and 17. Instead, we shall examine here the available information on contemporary sexual behavior. As marital coitus is of such vital concern, we shall begin with it and examine its characteristics in greater detail; then we shall turn to coitus outside marriage.

Marital Intercourse

As we would expect, practically all married people have sex with their spouses. Some do so rather infrequently, however, and a few never have coitus in years of marriage—often because of physical inability (perhaps of psychological origin) or, for instance, because one or both partners are homosexuals who have married for social reasons.

Important as marital coitus is for most people, it frequently does not seem to fulfill all their sexual needs. We have already examined (see Chapter 7) to what extent marital coitus was supplemented by other sexual outlets in various age groups in the Kinsey samples. Coitus accounted for about 90 percent of the total sexual outlets of married males, but only about 85 percent of total outlets involved coitus with their wives. The remaining 15 percent of total sexual outlets involved extramarital coitus, homosexual contacts, masturbation, nocturnal emissions, and animal contacts. Obviously, each individual male did not divide his sexual activities in just this way. Some had only marital coitus, others only one additional outlet, and so on.

The relative insufficiency of marital coitus became more apparent when all males, regardless of marital status, were considered as a group. Although about two-thirds of the adult male population is married at any given time, marital coitus accounted for fewer than half the orgasms (46 percent) experienced by all males.

Nor did marital coitus account for the total sexual outlets for women. Up to the mid-thirties, the proportion of female orgasms resulting from conjugal sex was similar to that of the married male group (about 85 percent). Other outlets then seemed to become more prominent, so that by the late forties only slightly more than 70 percent of total sexual outlets resulted from marital coitus. Males did not show a comparable change with age.

For the vast majority of married people whose primary outlet is conjugal sex, how often to engage in it is a pertinent question. Although most couples settle this issue in a mutually satisfactory manner, for some it remains a matter of conflict. The average (median) frequency of coitus for younger married people in the Kinsey samples was almost three times a week. By the age of thirty this figure had dropped to about twice a week, by the age of forty to once every four days, by the age of fifty to once a week, and by the age of sixty to once every twelve days (couples who abstained from marital coitus were excluded from the sample). These averages conceal the wide differences among people's sexual activities. Some couples make love sporadically, others every night, and a few several times a day.

Marital intercourse does not occur with clockwork regularity, nor is it entirely erratic. After allowance for periods of illness, pregnancy, menstruation, and so on, most couples settle into some form of sexual routine after a few years of marriage.

Marital intercourse offers special joys as well as special problems. Ideally a husband and wife form a compatible pair, and their sexual life meshes harmoniously with their overall relationship. In reality marriages fall short of this ideal for large numbers of people, as divorce rates and conflict-ridden households attest.

It is impossible to arrive at a consensus on the relative importance of the sexual and other aspects of marriage. People admit to having married for predominently romantic or sexual motives, but soon enough their interactions come to revolve around the more prosaic business of everyday living. The arrival of children often spells the end of any reserves of energy and interest that the couple may have.

Marital sex varies in different relationships. Sometimes a passionate sexual bond continues between husband and wife into very old age. More often marital sex takes on the attributes of uninspired home cooking: It is wholesome and available and, as one is paying for it, one may as well eat it. Occasionally marital sex becomes a nuisance at best and a torment at worst.

We are all acquainted with the endless caricatures of marital boredom: the man with the fat and ugly wife who yearns for the joys of bachelorhood and the woman with the dull-witted and wilted husband who dreams of romance. If these fates await us, why marry? One cynical reason is that the available alternatives are hardly more cheerful: the lonely bachelor nursing stale drinks at a bar, the white-haired casanova still making a fool of himself, the aging seductress being passed around from man to man, and so on.

Even when we take a less gloomy and more realistic approach, there is no escaping the fact that sex within marriage is no guaranteed source of unbounded joy. Nor, for that matter, is sex outside marriage necessarily an endless lark. What intensifies sexual problems within marriage is that the couple is bound together by profound social ties and expectations. When a man fails sexually with a casual acquaintance, he need not see her again; the husband must face his wife at the breakfast table. If a single woman finds coitus unsatisfactory, she can change partners or forget about it. A wife cannot exercise these options without serious risk to her marriage and in some cultures to her survival.

For our purposes here, it is not unreasonable to assume that most of us are likely to find marriage or a comparable permanent relationship sufficiently appealing, even on non-sexual grounds, to enter it. How then can we best manage the sexual aspects of such a relationship?

First, some consideration should be given to this matter before entering into such an intimate association. The wisdom of ages condemns the man or woman who marries from sexual infatuation alone. Such an act is comparable to buying a car or a house because one likes its color, but in marriage the risks are greater than in a business transaction. Yet should one disregard the sexual attributes and attitudes of the intended mate? In certain cultures, in which sexual restrictions within marriage are less binding (usually for the men), one can afford to do so when the nonsexual rewards are sufficiently enticing. This alternative is possible but more problematic in the West.

The physical attributes of a potential mate are fairly apparent. Besides, today increasing numbers of individuals have extensive sexual contact, including intercourse, before marriage. One would imagine that such intimacy would serve to screen out the more incompatible matches, but current divorce rates and the persistence of sexual problems in troubled marriages suggest that it does not.

There is then some reason to distrust our superficial judgment in such matters and to attempt to look more deeply into the potential strengths and weaknesses of the proposed union, taking into account both sexual and other factors. One common mistake is to assume that "things will change" after marriage. Usually they do not. Superficial fears and concerns, inexperience, and lack of knowledge can indeed be overcome within a rewarding relationship. Many women start to achieve orgasm only after a year or more of marriage. But deep-seated sexual aversions, marked disparities in sex drive, and fundamental sexual orientations do not change so easily. We may choose to embark on a serious relationship despite such problems, but we ought to at least do so with our eyes open.

It is ironic that we take great pains to ensure that people are properly qualified to perform certain professional or occupational tasks, yet we assume that partnership in marriage and parenthood are tasks for which everyone is congenitally suited. People would be spared much grief if marital sexual counseling preceded marriage, rather than following it.

Sustaining a vigorous and rewarding marital sex life is not so difficult if the basic ingredients of trust and affection are there, along with reasonably favorable economic and social circumstances. Some ways of coping with difficulties will be described in Chapter 12.

Correlates of Marital Intercourse. It has been generally assumed that husbands are more eager for coitus than their wives, although one can find the same type of informal evidence to substantiate the opposite claim. It is not even possible to obtain consistent information from spouses as to how often they do have coitus.

In the Kinsey survey husbands tended to report lower coital frequencies than their wives, which Kinsey interpreted as indirect evidence that men would prefer more frequent intercourse than their wives.[20]

As we have already shown, age has a direct bearing on the frequency of marital coitus: As age advances, rates decline. Obviously, part of the decline results from biological changes

associated with aging, but the reductions in coital rates are greater than that in total sexual outlets, which means that marital coitus is to some extent replaced by other outlets. Some of this decline, then, must also be caused by the "aging" of the marital relationship itself.

There is no correlation between the frequency of marital sex and social class as determined by educational level or parental occupation. The percentage of total sexual outlets involving coitus does, however, vary with class. Among men with elementary-school and high-school educations in Kinsey's sample it steadily increased in importance with age. The married college-educated male, however, instead of dropping other outlets (extramarital affairs, masturbation, and so on) relied on them increasingly, so that by his late forties intercourse with his wife provided only two out of three of his orgasms.

Among women of all educational groups marital coitus progressively yielded to other outlets as they grew older, but the tendency was particularly marked among college-educated women.

Decade of birth had no bearing on coital frequency (though it did have an important relation to whether or not orgasm was achieved, as we shall discuss later), nor did the age at which adolescence had begun. Religious affiliation or devotion did not affect the frequency with which women engaged in marital coitus. Men who were less devout, however, were almost one-third more active in marital coitus. For both sexes conjugal sex was more predominant and other outlets much less used.

Nonmarital Intercourse

The primary importance of coitus outside of marriage lies in its social and moral implications. In strictly physiological terms it is immaterial of course, whether or not the sexual partners are married to each other. But in individual cases sexual performance can be very

[20]For a discussion of conflicting estimates of coital frequency, see Levinger (1970).

much influenced by social and moral considerations.

A detailed discussion of the moral issues involved in sex outside marriage will not be attempted here (Chapters 1 and 17 treat them at some length). Instead, we shall briefly outline a few of the more salient psychological and social considerations and discuss the figures reported by Kinsey and his associates on the prevalence and correlates of nonmarital intercourse.

Sex outside marriage can be discussed as a whole for certain purposes. On the other hand, there are important distinctions between premarital, extramarital, and postmarital sex. For example, in the first and last instances, where the person has never married or is separated, divorced, or widowed, there is no third party to consider. Extramarital relations are usually complicated by concern about the spouse.

Despite important historical and cultural differences, sex outside marriage seems to have always coexisted with sex within marriage and sex as such is, of course, older than marriage. The more pertinent questions refer to variations in the prevalence of these practices and in our attitudes toward them.

Premarital Intercourse. Premarital coitus has posed one of the thornier social problems in the West, particularly regarding women. Since the individuals involved are usually young, parents and society have assumed protective attitudes to prevent mistakes by young people that would wreak harm to personality, career, marital prospects, and so on. However, social attitudes may be rapidly changing and the increased availability of contraceptives is significant in this regard. The effective separation of sexual from reproductive functions is bound to have repercussions in public attitudes. In our discussion of psychosexual development (see Chapter 8) we indicated some of the ways in

which various societies regulate sexual behavior before marriage. On some college campuses at least, the prevalent attitudes toward premarital sex appear to be much more open and flexible than those in the past. For many, premarital coitus no longer carries its former stigma although promiscuity seems to be neither common nor generally approved. Some students seem concerned if they do not feel ready for intercourse while in college even though they engage in considerable sexual activity short of it.[21]

Several decades ago, the Kinsey survey revealed what was for many Americans a staggering fact—that half of all the women in the sample had had sexual intercourse before marriage. Most often (46 percent of respondents) premarital intercourse involved only engaged people who subsequently married. Among males the rates of premarital coitus were even higher but less surprising. In the group with only elementary-school educations, practically every male (98 percent) had had coitus before marriage; in the more educated groups, the percentages were lower (85 percent for high-school graduates and 68 percent for those with college educations).

Premarital coitus usually occurred irregularly and rather infrequently. Males had intercourse, on the average, once every two weeks, females once a month or so. Premarital intercourse accounted for a third of the male outlets in the early twenties but a somewhat smaller proportion of the female outlets. The proportion remained the same for males in their mid-forties but rose to more than 40 percent for women in that age group.

The prevalence of premarital intercourse was markedly related to educational level and age at marriage (the older the person, the more likely he was to have already had coitus) for

---

[21] Student Committee on Human Sexuality (1970), p. 11.

males but much less so for females. There was little relation to parental occupational class for either sex.

Of women born before 1900 only 14 percent had had premarital sex; among those born later than 1900 this figure had almost quadrupled. Men did not show this generational difference. Premarital sex was more common among both sexes in urban areas. It was also distinctly less common among the more devout.

Intercourse between unmarried people most often occurred in the woman's home. Each act generally lasted longer than marital intercourse did, though the couple was less apt than were married people to experiment with coital positions.

Extramarital Intercourse. Extramarital intercourse, like premarital intercourse, has been traditionally condemned in the West yet it has never been suppressed successfully. Currently, extramarital relations appear to be quite prevalent in the West. In extramarital coitus the participants are usually older than in premarital coitus and are therefore less subject to social controls. On the other hand, an additional complication is posed by the uninvolved spouse.

Why would a person with access to a spouse wish to engage in coitus with someone else? This question has tormented moralists as well as the spouses of adulterous men and women. The answers are many: Some are all too obvious, yet none is entirely satisfactory. Judgments of extramarital intercourse are often qualified by circumstances: Enforced lengthy absences, chronic debilitating illness, unhappy unions that persist for a variety of nonsexual reasons, and the like are viewed by some as mitigating factors. Yet at other times there are no such externally visible explanations and one assumes that one or both spouses are motivated by the search for variety and excitement. All too often extramarital affairs fulfill poorly

realized neurotic needs or are thinly veiled attempts to humiliate or otherwise hurt the marital partner.

In the Kinsey sample, about half the men and a quarter of the women admitted that by age forty they had had at least one extramarital affair each. Like premarital coitus, this outlet was generally irregular, occurring only once every one to three months; it accounted for fewer than 10 percent of total outlets.

Extramarital coitus was somewhat more prevalent among less-educated males, particularly before age twenty-five. It was higher among better-educated women after the age of twenty-five. (These figures do not, of course, mean that these two groups were having affairs with each other.) There was no relation to parental occupational class.

Women showed a definite generational difference. By the age of twenty-five, only 4 percent of those born before 1900 had had coitus with men other than their husbands. This proportion increased in successive generations to 12 percent for those born between 1920 and 1929. As would be expected, the more devout were less likely to be unfaithful to their spouses. The length of involvement in extramarital affairs and the number of partners involved varied, of course. About 41 percent of women with this experience reported one partner, but about an equal percentage had had affairs with two to five men.

Many different criteria are used to assess extramarital intercourse. Some consider the element of honesty to be the paramount factor. Others maintain that what the spouse does not know cannot hurt. It has been generally believed that extramarital relations reflect weaknesses in the marital relations and are detrimental to the institution of marriage. Currently there are counterclaims that some extramarital relations can actually enrich and strengthen a marriage. As a result, some writers now differentiate between healthy and disturbed reasons for having extramarital relations.[22] Rational analyses of the social aspects of extramarital behaviors do not necessarily satisfy, of course, the moral questions in these issues.

Postmarital Intercourse. Sexual relations involving the separated, divorced, or widowed are in general less socially controversial than premarital or extramarital coitus. These individuals tend to be emancipated from parental control and society tends to extend them some special consideration. And, of course, there is no uninvolved spouse to be considered. These social attitudes permit the widowed or divorced more freedom but also place them in special situations. The women in this group in particular resent being viewed as easy sexual prey. In the Kinsey sample the statistical characteristics of sexual behavior in this group generally fell somewhere between the patterns of married and single persons.

Cross-Cultural Variations

The available information on other Western or industrialized societies, though scanty, indicates that patterns of coitus are not much different from those that we have described. Despite the common fantasy that individuals in primitive groups conduct their sex lives as they please, the fact is that in every known society there are restrictions on sexual activity, including the universal practice of marital coitus.

Preliterate societies are generally more permissive in allowing extramarital coitus and concurrent conjugal ties between one man and several women (polygyny) or, less commonly, between one woman and several men (polyandry). Marital ties are also much less formal

or binding. Liberal attitudes toward sexual behavior may also be reflected in the free public representation of sexual themes (see Figure 10.7). On the other hand, these groups have numerous restrictions on sexual expression, even between husband and wife, that are unheard of in Western communities.

For instance, in some societies, when one partner is ill, intercourse is forbidden to the relatives as well. In an epidemic a chief of the Bena (polygynous Tanzanian agriculturalists) might even extend the prohibition to everyone in the community. Periods of abstinence may be required before, during, or after ordinary seasonal activities like hunting, fishing, and farming. Sometimes the prohibition is very specific: Women in Ila (polygynous Zambians, with multiple forms of sustenance) were expected not to engage in coitus before brewing beer or sowing crops; men, on the other hand, had to abstain when smelting iron. Sexual restrictions are sometimes imposed in time of war. In many societies men are required to abstain before battle and in a few communities after they return as well. The wives are expected to remain chaste. A number of other restrictions seem to be universal. In almost all societies one is expected to wait for some time before remarrying after the death of a spouse. This waiting period may be short or many years long, clearly defined and enforced or vague and supported only by public opinion.

The reasoning behind some of these prohibitions is not always clear. The lassitude following coitus is not conducive to immediate aggressive behavior or to back-breaking labor, but these aftereffects of orgasm are short-lived. In times of stress and conflict it is necessary to command all one's strength, whereas sexual intercourse seems to divert attention. Sex is sometimes used as an antidote to anxiety or depression. There thus seems to be a general feeling that recourse to the comforts of sex distracts attention from the main social issues.

---

[22]See Ellis, A. (1969). Neubeck, ed. (1969) includes other essays on extramarital relations. For a range of professional opinions about the significance of extramarital relations, see "The Significance of Extramarital Sex Relations" (1969).

Another popular notion is that sex and aggression are antithetical ("make love not war").

The frequency of coitus varies among societies and undoubtedly within each group also. We have already reviewed these data in Chapter 7.

Animal Intercourse

Animals and men are not quite comparable in this regard, of course, for animal sexuality is largely controlled by physiological conditions independent of social constraints, at least in the human sense. It is interesting, however, to examine such behavior for these very reasons. As animal sexuality is not perennial, the following frequencies are those for the periods when both sexes are responsive.

A male animal usually has several females and sometimes an entire harem at his disposal. We might conclude that males are more highly sexed. The performance of Alaskan seals during the breeding season is particularly impressive. For as long as six weeks a single male will forgo food to copulate with scores of females that come to him to be impregnated. Among domestic animals one bull is sufficient to inseminate a large number of cows.

However, most females have higher capacity for copulation. If allowed, a cow will continue to copulate as long as she is in heat. The same is true of cats, dogs, and various primates. Males will copulate several times in succession and then lose interest; females remain receptive as long as they are in heat. Among free-ranging rhesus monkeys a single female during an estrous phase of about nine days, will daily take on male after male, each of whom retires after three or four ejaculations. She will thus copulate fifty or sixty times during this period—but without orgasm as far as can be ascertained.

The information contained in this chapter is an introduction to the topic of sexual intercourse. In Chapter 12 we shall turn to problems of sexual malfunctioning, primarily difficulties

Figure 10.7. Intercourse: grass figures from Mambilla, Northern Nigeria. Such grass figures are made by adolescent boys near springs where girls come to get water. The grass in the figures is rooted in the ground, but stones, sod, bunches of grass, and so on are used to construct breasts and genitals. Boys compete to see who can make the best figures. This activity takes place during November and December when the grass is high and the figures are subsequently destroyed during the dry season. Photograph (taken in 1949) and information provided by Dr. Gilbert D. Schneider, Ohio University.

in sexual intercourse. Subsequent chapters deal with the subject of sexual intercourse in considerable detail from various cultural and social perspectives.

The sexual life of man has many facets. Even though heterosexual intercourse is the preferred mode of sexual expression for most adults, many people also engage in other forms of sexual behavior in addition to nearly universal activities like erotic fantasy at one time or another; some do so exclusively.

Such departures from standard coital practices have generally been known as *sexual deviations*. Those who object to implications of pathology prefer the term *sexual variations*. This conflict over terminology reflects current uncertainties in the evaluation of such behavior. There is no serious disagreement, of course, when the activity is flagrantly bizarre or demonstrably harmful. The conflict does not center on necrophilia or sex murder but rather on such behavior as homosexual contacts in private between consenting adults or coitus between a man and a woman who is underage only in a technical sense.

Aberrant sexual behavior has preoccupied man for a long time. There are references to such practices in the oldest historical records. More recently an extensive literature has developed, particularly around the theme of homosexuality. Unfortunately, most such works abound in stereotypes and speculations.

Our approach in this chapter will be pre-dominantly descriptive, and, in view of the many types of behavior possible, it will have to be cursory. We have already dealt with some of these topics in earlier chapters and shall return to them in subsequent ones.

There is a common tendency to conduct discussions of sexual deviations in the manner of a tour through the zoo. The following considerations must therefore be emphasized.

First, although it is convenient to call individuals "homosexuals," "voyeurs," and so on, it is much more useful to speak of homosexual or voyeuristic *behavior* and of people who have had various degrees of such experiences. The sex life of man consists not of "pure" types of behavior but of combinations of various activities at various times. Furthermore, even when some individuals are oriented predominantly in one of these aberrant directions, to label them accordingly is to exaggerate their differences from other people to the point of caricature.

Second, many types of aberrant behavior exist in all shades and gradations and are exceedingly common (even though we may not be conscious of them). Again, we are not mainly interested in the bizarre: Although few of us are necrophiliacs or child molesters, there is a range of voyeuristic-exhibitionistic and sado-masochistic activity, for instance, that is part

VARIATIONS AND DEVIATIONS IN SEXUAL BEHAVIOR

of common heterosexual experience and that we do not—and have no reason to—label "deviant" or "pathological."

Judgments on sexual behavior are just as appropriate as are judgments on other forms of human activity. Not all sexual behavior is equally adaptive, healthy, socially desirable, moral, and so on. Such judgments, however, ought to be made with great care. Experience shows how arbitrary they can be and how easy it is to inflict unnecessary hardship upon people whose main offense may consist in being different.

As the title of this chapter suggests, we consider certain activities as mere variations on and others as pathological deviations from the norm of sexual behavior. We shall make no attempt to follow such distinctions here, however. How such judgments are made has been discussed in Chapters 1 and 7 and is further elaborated in Chapters 16 and 17. As most of the professional literature calls such behavior "deviations," we shall also use this term more frequently. But our objective at this point is primarily to describe rather than to condone or to condemn.

CLASSIFICATION OF SEXUAL DEVIATIONS

The first attempt at a comprehensive review of sexual aberrations was undertaken by the Viennese psychiatrist Richard von Krafft-Ebing, who published his classic *Psychopathia Sexualis* in 1886. Freud's own formulations, to be discussed here, appeared in 1905 in his *Three Essays on the Theory of Sexuality* (see Chapter 8).

Freud based his classification of sexual aberrations on the assumption that among adults any form of sexual behavior that takes precedence over heterosexual intercourse represents a defect in psychosexual development. Freud labeled the person from whom sexual attraction emanates the "sexual object" and what one wishes to do with the object the "sexual aim." In a healthy, or mature, sexual relationship an adult of the opposite sex would thus be the sexual object and the wish for coitus the sexual aim.[1]

It then follows that deviations from this pattern can take one of two forms: deviations in the choice of sexual object and deviations in the choice of sexual aim. In the first instance, the alternative object could be an adult of the same sex (as in homosexuality), a child (as in pedophilia), a close relative (as in incest), an animal (as in zoophilia), an inanimate object (as in fetishism), or even a dead body (as in necrophilia). In the second instance, instead of seeking (and when permissible engaging in) coitus, the individual would prefer to watch others having coitus (voyeurism), to expose his own genitals (exhibitionism), to inflict pain (sadism), or to suffer pain (masochism). When deviation involves choice both of object and of sexual aim, it is usually designated by the choice of object. In classifying a sadomasochistic homosexual relationship, homosexuality is considered the more important characteristic.

This classification is not primarily concerned with the social significance of these various aberrations and would label as deviations certain widely accepted practices like oral-genital contacts and even kissing as ends in themselves when legitimate access to coitus is available. Freud's primary interest was not in these deviations as such but in their theoretical signifi-

---

[1] The use of the term "object" in this context is not intended to imply that people are or should be used as inanimate objects. Applied to persons, "objects" means individuals who fulfill essential functions in the gratification of others. For further discussion of this concept see Engel (1962), p. 17.

cance for his conceptions of infantile sexuality and psychosexual development. Our use of Freud's classification system is primarily pragmatic; the system is convenient and widely used, and adoption of it does not necessarily imply acceptance of Freud's related theories.

DEVIATIONS IN OBJECT CHOICE

Homosexuality

Of all the possible deviations homosexuality is the single most important. It is the most common and in some ways the most problematic. As there is also more available information on homosexual activities than on any other deviation, we shall discuss it in greater detail. Homosexuality is generally viewed either as a life style, as an illness, or as a criminal offense.[2]

As a Way of Life

Homosexuals, like heterosexuals, have not one but many life styles. Some are conventionally married men and women who occasionally indulge in furtive homosexual affairs; others live openly as homosexual couples. If the individual is a teacher or an employee of the U.S. State Department he may live in constant fear of losing his job, but as a prominent literary figure he may make his fame and fortune by expressing his homosexuality.

Homosexuals are widely distributed throughout the country and are found in all socioeconomic strata. After all, among males only, we are dealing with an estimated 2 million people (2 percent of the male population) who indulge in exclusively homosexual behavior and an even larger group for whom homosexual acts constitute one of several sexual outlets.

In our brief review here we shall touch only upon the more salient aspects of life in the homosexual community, or the "gay crowd," as a certain group of homosexuals prefers to be known. This community represents a subculture in our society, one in which the life style encompasses many activities beyond sexual ones. Because of certain important differences, we shall discuss the life styles of male and female homosexuals separately.

Among Males. The behavioral characteristics of male homosexuals are highly influenced by their vulnerability to harassment, censure, and persecution by society. As only in certain areas of large cities can homosexuals be observed behaving in relative freedom, we cannot speak with confidence of how homosexuals would behave if they were left alone. At present, the typical homosexual is psychologically isolated from society, dependent upon other deviants for sexual expression, and ruled by a concealed but complex system of social relations and reciprocal obligations, even though this pattern may be rapidly changing in some parts of the country.

The first criterion for differentiating among homosexual life styles is thus whether a man is a covert or an overt homosexual. Covert homosexuals are to be found within the full range of occupations in our society. They "pass" for heterosexuals in most of their business and social relationships. They may even be married, parents, and in most other respects indistinguishable from the rest of the population. They may lead "double lives" or restrict

---

[2]The term "homosexual" is derived from the Greek *hom*, "the same," rather than from the Latin root *homō*, "man." It has numerous synonyms, both vernacular and technical. Some, like "homophile," reflect attempts to eliminate pejorative connotations. Others, like "bisexuality" and "inversion," reflect particular etiological points of view. All these terms are correctly applicable to either sex, but common usage tends to reserve them for males and to apply "lesbianism" to sexual activities between females.

their homosexual behavior to periods when they are away from home, as do men who participate in extramarital heterosexual affairs.[3]

Overt homosexuals constitute a smaller group. They have given up all pretense and openly rely upon the homosexual community for gratification of their sexual needs. These men work in professions in which they are either tolerated or in which there are no penalties (and perhaps even some advantages) for being homosexual.[4] They tend to be defiant of the heterosexual world and willing to face it only on their own terms. An overtly homosexual hairdresser, for instance, has been quoted as follows:

> Rosenstein can go to hell as far as I care. She works you to the bone if she can get away with it. She told me I run around the place like a regular pansy. So I told her I am a pansy and if she doesn't like it she can get somebody else to do her dirty work for her. I knew she wouldn't fire me. All the ladies ask for me and I don't have to pretend to nobody.[5]

Overt and covert homosexuals tend to shun each other. The former consider the latter hypocrites, and the latter shun the former to protect themselves. If a person does not blatantly display his homosexual way of life, can we identify him through physique, dress, mannerisms, and so on? The answer is generally "no." Probably the most common misun-

derstanding of male homosexuals is reflected in stereotypes that portray them as "effeminate," "swishy," "faggots," or "fairies." There are individuals who fit these stereotypes, to be sure, and within the gay crowd they are known as "queens." But these men represent only a very small proportion of the homosexual population and are by no means appreciated by the rest. Some gay bars will actually refuse admission to "queens in drag," that is, dressed in flagrantly effeminate fashion. Currently, the term "queen" is said to be losing its more negative connotations and to be becoming synonymous with "gay."

At the other extreme, some homosexuals make a point of looking and acting extremely "masculine." Some are body-building enthusiasts with formidably muscular torsos. Others may be career military officers, with all the trappings of power and authority. (There were reportedly high proportions of homosexuals in the Nazi *Wehrmacht* and among cowboys in the old American West.)

Most ordinary homosexuals look and act as do ordinary people. Not that homosexuals cannot effectively identify one another. People who must communicate covertly develop systems of cues involving dress, mannerisms, and so on. Male homosexuals tend to be more innovative in and conscious of dress, and the heterosexual population often unwittingly adopts their styles. The homosexual significance of the style then becomes completely lost, of course. Similarly, just as most homosexuals are neither effeminate nor unusually masculine, not all men who have limp wrists or speak in high-pitched, lisping voices or are physical-culture enthusiasts are necessarily homosexual. Guessing games based on such superficial traits are quite futile and misleading. Masculinity and femininity are culturally defined attributes (and not clear ones at that) that have no demonstrable correlation with sexual orientation.

Male homosexuals generally have short-term

---

[3] When a public figure or a group of respectable citizens is exposed as homosexual, there is inevitably a major public scandal with far-ranging repercussions. For two journalistic accounts see Stearn (1961), *The Sixth Man*, and Gerassi (1967), *The Boys of Boise*.

[4] Certain occupations seem to have larger proportions of homosexuals. Oft-cited examples are the fashion industry and the legitimate theater. There are, however, no "homosexual" or "heterosexual" occupations, and people of both orientations may be found in practically all lines of work. For a discussion of the occupational choices of homosexuals, see Leznoff and Westley in Ruitenbeek, ed. (1963), pp. 162-174.

[5] Ruitenbeek, ed. (1963), p. 166.

relationships, though some ties may be very intense.[6] Whatever the explanation, this fact has an important bearing on the life style of the male homosexual. As his affairs tend to be short, he needs frequently to find new partners. To find them, many homosexuals thus go "cruising" in search of "tricks" or "pickups." Every major city has its known homosexual hangouts. Some are public places like parks, bus depots, and men's rooms. Others are special "gay bars" or "clubs." The police are usually aware of these hangouts but ignore them unless there is political pressure for a crackdown or when a homosexual strays beyond the areas of tacit toleration. As the occasional and uninformed homosexual is more likely to make such mistakes, it is often he rather than the confirmed and experienced practitioner who is arrested.

Quite frequently the threat to the homosexual from his fellow homosexuals is at least as serious as the threat from the police. Blackmail, extortion, and beatings have been quite common, and the victim cannot usually bring himself to seek protection from family, friends, or the police. Homosexual prostitutes who prey on older men, who must rely increasingly on paid services, are notorious in this respect. Many of these young men justify their behavior, as do many female prostitutes, as simply "giving people what they deserve." A male prostitute may not even consider himself homosexual, for he presumably participates only for money.

Important as life around certain bars is for most homosexuals, such behavior is not unique to them. Female prostitutes and heterosexuals of both sexes looking for "one-night stands" operate in much the same way. The actual approaches used are also quite similar: The prospective partner is spotted, subtle and less subtle cues are exchanged, and the couple may have a drink or two; the couple becomes progressively intimate and leaves together or arranges to meet somewhere.

For those ignorant of homosexual ways, it is difficult to understand such relationships. It is easier if we forget for a moment that such an encounter is between members of the same sex and simply try to reconstruct what would transpire in a comparable situation between a man and a woman. Homosexuals, like heterosexuals, may be shy and inhibited or forward and aggressive. Witty homosexuals tell witty jokes, and uncouth homosexuals tell vulgar jokes; some are subtle in their approaches, others clumsy; and so on.

Even more mystifying to many people is what homosexuals actually do when they are together. The answer is that they do what is physically possible, including everything that men and women do except participate in vaginal intercourse. Kissing and petting are the usual preliminaries, followed by mutual genital stimulation. The two primary activities leading to orgasm are oral-genital contact (singly or mutually) and, less frequently, anal intercourse. With practice and the use of lubricants the anus can readily admit an erect penis and even considerably larger objects that also figure in homosexual encounters at times.[7] What char-

---

[6]Homosexual jealousy is notorious. It is said to be more common among male than among female homosexuals. Some homosexuals ascribe it to their being in a closed and persecuted community and anticipate that it will be less prevalent as attitudes toward homosexuals change.

---

[7]Anal intercourse is called "sodomy" in American legal parlance (it is called "buggery" in England). The term also includes certain other acts in some jurisdictions (see Chapter 16). The word "sodomy" is derived from the Old Testament town of Sodom. As related in Genesis 19, the Sodomites were so depraved that on one occasion they surrounded the house of Lot, insisting that he release to them two male houseguests: "'Bring them out' they shouted, 'so that we can have intercourse with them.'" Lot, who had offered shelter to the two strangers, felt bound by his obligation as host to protect them even at the price of offering to the crowd his two virgin daughters instead. The Sodomites' homosexual advances should have

acterizes an act as homosexual is not the act itself but the fact that the partners are of the same sex.

There is no "homosexual act" that cannot be performed by a heterosexual couple. By the same token, homosexuals claim that anal intercourse is just as "real" and satisfying as is vaginal coitus. Whatever its rewards, anal intercourse also carries some of the same penalties as does vaginal intercourse. Venereal disease, for instance, is readily transmitted in this way, and promiscuous homosexuals have some of the highest rates of such disease in the country.

There is considerable preoccupation with assigning "active" and "passive" roles to members of a homosexual pair. Parallels are drawn, for instance, between vaginal and anal intercourse, in which the one who inserts the penis is considered the active, dominant, or "masculine" partner and the other the passive, receptive, or "feminine" one. Such distinctions are generally not useful and in oral-genital contacts they are quite meaningless.

In practice, only a small minority of male homosexuals show definite preferences for one role over the other. One study[8] of a group of male homosexuals showed that 46 percent practiced all forms of sexual activity and varied their roles (between inserting and receiving insertion) depending upon wish for variety, the preferences of the partners, and so on. Of this group half the members expressed some preference for one role or the other, but half insisted that they had no preference at all. The remaining 54 percent of the group showed some inclination for certain activities (like fellatio)

over others, but of the total sample only 20 percent could be said to show distinct preferences for given activites, as well as for particular roles. Quite frequently homosexual partners switch roles during a sex act or engage in mutual oral-genital contacts, further blurring possible distinctions between active and passive roles.

Despite these findings, important conclusions continue to be drawn from such spurious distinctions. Some psychiatrists, for instance, attempt to link them to character traits and histories of psychosexual development. Judges tend to be harsher with the "active" partners. Homosexuals themselves are no exception: Some men in fact claim that they are not homosexual at all because they exercise exclusively "masculine roles" in their encounters with other men.

Life around gay bars is by no means the only, or even the standard, homosexual life style. Some homosexual men abhor the very thought of such circles. Their affairs may be conducted in the privacy of elegant settings, with all the gentility and accouterments of the most idealized heterosexual romance. Others may meet in public toilets, where one stranger brings another to orgasm in the most expeditious manner possible, just as some heterosexual men may engage in coitus with prostitutes in dark alleys.

Of the many other "types" of homosexuality we shall mention only two: "latent homosexuality" and "deprivation homosexuality." The "latent" homosexual is a man with strong but poorly repressed homosexual tendencies. Most of the time he is unaware of such feelings and only occasionally do homosexual fantasies and impulses cross his consciousness. Occasionally he may succumb to them, perhaps under the influence of alcohol, and subsequently he may feel extremely guilty. Sometimes these tendencies are quite apparent to all but the latent homosexual himself. Some latent homosexuals, in unconscious efforts to rid themselves of such

---

been left unmade, for the two strangers turned out to be angels of the Lord, who subsequently utterly destroyed the town, sparing only Lot and his family. Homosexual advances continue to be risky undertakings, as most men who are not so inclined tend to feel highly insulted when approached.

[8] Hooker (1965), pp. 24–52.

impulses, become virulent critics of homosexuality (a "reaction formation"). On rare occasions such impulses threaten to "break through," and the man may have episodes of intense anxiety and personality disorganization ("homosexual panic"). The homosexual who is conscious of his impulses may feel guilty but does not suffer such intense apprehension.

The term, if not the concept, of latent homosexuality has been a source of considerable confusion. Whereas clinicians have some general understanding of what it means, it can cause unnecessary concern to a person who experiences fleeting homosexual thoughts, which are quite common. Such thoughts are not diagnostic of latent homosexuality. To wonder what something might be like does not mean to aspire to it (see Chapter 9).

"Deprivation homosexuality" ordinarily involves heterosexual men who turn to homosexual contacts when deprived of women, most often in the armed forces or in jail. It can be argued theoretically that deprivation alone is not enough to reverse a man's sexual orientation and that these men may in fact have been latent homosexuals all along. Be that as it may, some men do engage in homosexual acts in jail, for example, but not on the outside.[9]

Homosexuality in prison is a complex and grim topic that cannot usefully be discussed separately from prison society as a whole, including its internal organization and codes of conduct. For some men homosexual contacts become the only way to counteract desperate loneliness behind bars. For others it is a means of establishing their positions in the prison pecking order: Some dominant inmates have "girls" in their service as a sign of status, just as in some cultures mistresses are obligatory for men who have "arrived." Finally, in a group

seething with aggression, homosexual acts often become imbued with a ferocity to which many a man with no homosexual leanings becomes the helpless victim.[10]

Much of the popular literature on homosexuality deals with its relatively flagrant aspects and the revelations of its more vocal representatives. Material from clinical sources is vast but involves only homosexuals in treatment, who may or may not be representative of the homosexual population at large.[11]

To counteract what they consider distorted images of homosexuals, various private groups have been organized. The best-known, until recently, was the Mattachine Society (named after medieval court jesters, who were fearlessly outspoken), a national organization with chapters in many major cities and a predominantly but not exclusively homosexual membership. The purpose of such groups is to promote fair and equal treatment for homosexuals and to protest the oppression and abuse to which they have been subjected, as have other minorities. The Mattachine Society holds meetings, arranges lectures, and issues several publications (for example, *Homosexual Citizen* and *Mattachine Newsletter*).

More recently important changes appear to be taking place in the homosexual world as part of the "gay liberation movement." Organizations like the Gay Liberation Front and the Gay Activist Alliance are much more open and forcible in their efforts to acquaint the public with their cause.[12]

The beginnings of gay liberation as a

---

[9]To avoid these activities, prison authorities in some countries (for example, Mexico) and in one state in this country (Mississippi) permit conjugal visits to married prisoners in special cottages on the prison grounds.

[10]For a revealing report see Davis in Gagnon and Simon, eds. (1970), pp. 107–124.

[11]In addition to various specific references on homosexuality, some of which we shall mention later on, see West (1968); Ruitenbeek, ed. (1963); Karlen (1971).

[12]This new attitude is partly reflected in the proliferation of such homosexual publications as *Gay, Come Out, The Advocate, Gay Power, Gay Flames, Gay Sunshine, San Francisco Free Press, Vector,* and so on.

movement go back to June 1969, to a riot by homosexuals at a gay bar in Greenwich Village that was reportedly precipitated by police harassment. Immediately following that riot the first Gay Liberation Front was organized in New York City. There are currently an estimated fifty or so such groups but no national Gay Liberation Front as yet. Despite the common name, these organizations vary widely, from moderately conservative to very radical in orientation.[13]

Despite these differences, there is generally far greater readiness among homosexuals in these groups to come out into the open. On a number of college campuses, for example, there are semiformal homosexual organizations that make no effort or pretense at concealing their identity. At least among younger homosexuals there is now a tendency to shun gay bars and other traditional hangouts in favor of dances and other social and political functions. There are also gay communes, "consciousness-raising groups," and various alliances with other "liberation movements" in pursuit of common goals.

These often dramatic changes in attitudes both inside and outside the homosexual community are, of course, not uniform throughout the country. In some cities police officers participate in encounter sessions with homosexuals in an effort to further mutual understanding.[14] In others homosexuals continue to live in constant fear of the police. In view of these disparities, it is impossible to describe general patterns of homosexual life. Much of what is said in this chapter, for example, may be applicable to some parts of the country but out of date in others, or true of some subgroups but not at all of others.[15]

---

[13] Kameny (1971).

[14] "Cops Meet the Gays." *San Francisco Chronicle,* May 10, 1971, p. 1.

[15] Information about current changes in the homosexual world has been provided by Stephen A. Robins.

Among Females. The majority of lesbians, like their male counterparts, are indistinguishable from the general population in physique, dress, and mannerisms. Despite the points of contrast to be discussed, much of what we have said about male homosexuals also applies to females. Some of the differences between the life styles of female and male homosexuals simply reflect role expectations for men and women in general, as in vocational opportunities, for example. Other distinctions are less specific: Lesbians form more lasting ties, operate in less differentiated subcultures, and are generally far less often detected and harassed.

There are a few gay bars and clubs in large cities that cater to lesbians, but even there differences in atmosphere and activities can be detected. The lesbian rarely goes to a gay bar looking for a pickup. She usually goes with a friend to socialize, exchange gossip, have a few drinks, and dance. (Dancing and petting are often restricted to private backrooms, where only customers known to the management are admitted.)

There is a much greater tendency among lesbians to pair off and to live as couples in relatively stable relationships. Such relationships are often called "marriages" and may be sealed by exchanges of wedding rings. Roles are somewhat more clearly defined in lesbian relationships, and one partner usually takes the more "masculine" role, as "head of the family," with protective responsibilities. This form of relationship is most clearly visible between the "butch" and "femme" (or "fem"). The butch (or "bull dike") is in a sense the counterpart of the male queen. She wears masculine pants and shirts, cuts her hair very short, and may even be employed in some predominantly male occupation like truck driving. Although she is quite aggressive and masculine in appearance and manner, such a woman can still pass in the straight world as simply a "masculine woman." It is less common in our society to suspect or to identify lesbianism, whereas there is widespread suspicion of effeminate males. The "femme" or feminine member of the couple is typically feminine in dress, mannerisms, and general appearance. She is the more passive member of the couple and, if she works, is more likely to have a job as a secretary, a waitress, or some other traditionally female occupation.

When it comes to sexual activities, the distinctions between butch and femme tend to blur, though some lesbian couples do preserve particular roles in lovemaking. A few may even imitate heterosexual intercourse, with one partner wearing a dildo (see Chapter 9). These activities, however, despite common belief, are very rare. In fact, they are more often performed by prostitutes (who may or may not be lesbians) for the benefit of male customers. Incidentally, though it is not uncommon for prostitutes and call girls to be lesbians, they sell their services mainly to men rather than to women. It is usually more difficult to find deprivation homosexuality among females, for men are rarely lacking to satisfy their heterosexual needs. Female liaisons in jails are common but often exist as quiet relationships without the violence characteristic of males in prison.

A more common type of lesbian relationship involves two girls who live together in a close and mutually dependent relationship but not as butch and femme. Usually both are employed and may be schoolteachers, salesgirls, nurses, businesswomen, and the like. Although the initial meeting may have occurred in a lesbian bar or club, more often the two have met at work, school, or through mutual friends. Two women may live together for ten years or more and never arouse the suspicions of their neighbors or families, much less of casual acquaintances, which is not true for men in a similar situation. Consequently the lesbian is subject to relatively little harassment or social pressure, except for the occasional well-meaning friend or relative who insists on arranging hetero-

sexual dates for her. The lesbian couple tends to lead a self-contained social life, going to the movies, the beach, the theater, or shopping together and occasionally entertaining gay (male or female) or straight couples. Needless to remark, women friends may also live together and do all these things without being lesbians.

Lesbian sexual activities consist primarily of kissing, caressing, fondling and oral stimulation of the breasts, mutual masturbation, and oral-genital contacts. *Tribadism* is an exclusively lesbian but not particularly common practice in which the genitals are mutually stimulated as one woman lies on top of the other and simulates coitus.

Lesbians with heterosexual experience claim that orgasms achieved through homosexual activities are incomparably more satisfying. The Kinsey study did in fact reveal a higher incidence of orgasm among lesbians than among heterosexual women. One explanation is that lesbians have a natural advantage over male partners, who often have foggy notions of female anatomy and sexual functioning.

The literature on lesbianism, though less extensive than that dealing with male homosexuality, is, nevertheless, still quite large.[16] Lesbian organizations are more recent in origin and remain less prominent than their male counterparts. The best known has been The Daughters of Bilitis (founded in 1956), which draws its name from a book of prose poems by Pierre Louys, which appeared in 1894 and purported to be a translation from the Greek of Sappho's love poems to a courtesan named Bilitis. The general aims and functions of this society are comparable to those of male homo-

---

[16]For a review of the theme of lesbianism in literature see Chapter 14 and Foster (1958). Almost all books on male homosexuality also deal with lesbians. Most of this writing is done by men. Some notable exceptions include the relevant chapters in Deutsch (1944-1945) and de Beauvoir (1952). Two well-known novels on this theme are *Claudine à l'école* by Colette (1948-1950) and *The Well of Loneliness* by Radclyffe Hall (1928).

sexual organizations. These women, however, claim double social disadvantages, being both female and homosexual. *The Ladder: A Lesbian Review* is the society's official publication. Changes similar to those affecting male homosexuals are also currently affecting lesbian groups. Liberation movements among women, however, tend to be primarily concerned with the protection of women's rights in general, rather than of lesbians' rights in particular. Even though most members of women's liberation groups may be strictly heterosexual, there are those who maintain that women will never be free as long as they continue to rely on males for their emotional and sexual needs. These issues are discussed further in Chapter 18.

The Frequency of Homosexuality. There had been surveys of male homosexuality before the Kinsey study, but it was the latter that brought to light how widespread the use of this sexual outlet was. In fact, the findings about homosexuality and premarital sex caused the most furor when Kinsey's work was published. His data are still rejected by some people, even though his challengers have no quantitative information of their own. One criticism is that, because of Kinsey's tolerant view of homo-

sexuality, a disproportionate number volunteered as subjects for his study, thus swelling the figures. At any rate, it should be recalled that even under the best circumstances Kinsey's findings cannot be taken as representative of the country as a whole, nor are they current. But they are still the most extensive data available and therefore will be outlined here.

The Kinsey volumes on the male and the female contain exhaustive tables and graphs on the various facets of homosexual contacts. We can present only two of them. Excluding homosexual activity before puberty (which about 60 percent of males had experienced), Kinsey found that by age forty-five about 37 percent of males had had at least one homosexual encounter leading to orgasm. For females this figure was 13 percent. Such activity was much more common among single people of both sexes (at age forty-five about 50 percent of single males and 26 percent of females) than among married people (by age forty-five about 10 percent of married males and 3 percent of females).

The extent to which these people participated in homosexual activities varied greatly. Kinsey never said nor implied that every second male was a practicing homosexual. Actually he avoided calling anyone "homosexual," preferring to describe variable frequencies of homosexual contact, with or without other sexual outlets.

The only reasonable way that Kinsey thought this data could be conceptualized was by placing everyone on a heterosexual-homosexual behavior rating scale (see Figure 11.1). People in categories 0 and 6 were exclusively heterosexual (0) or homosexual (6) in both their physical contacts and erotic interests. Those in categories 1 and 5 had predominant heterosexual (1) or homosexual (5) orientations, with only incidental interest in the other sex. Categories 2 and 4 included those in whom a clear preference for one sex coexisted with a lesser but still active interest in the other. Finally, people with approximately equal heterosexual and homosexual interests constituted category 3. In computing these ratios Kinsey departed from his own definition of sexual outlets (activities leading to orgasm) and considered as relevant all erotic responses, physical

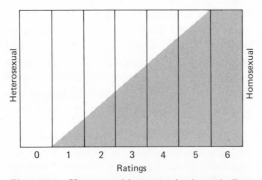

Figure 11.1.   Heterosexual-homosexual rating scale. From A. C. Kinsey *et al., Sexual Behavior in the Human Female* (Philadelphia: Saunders, 1953), p. 470. Courtesy of the Institute for Sex Research.

as well as psychic, whether they had culminated in orgasm or not.

This rating scale indicates not the amount of sexual activity but only the ratio between two sexual orientations. A person with 100 heterosexual and 10 homosexual experiences would be placed closer to the heterosexual end of the scale than would someone with 10 heterosexual and 5 homosexual contacts during a comparable period of time. The man with ten homosexual contacts would thus be "less homosexual" than would the man with only five homosexual contacts.

Individuals were found to be unevenly distributed within these seven categories. The whole notion of such categories is itself artificial: The categories in fact overlap very much, so that we are actually dealing with a continuum, rather than with discrete entities. The figures in Table 11.1 must be understood in that sense. The ranges of percentages resulted from different ratios in various subgroups. With the exception of the exclusive categories (0 and 6), the percentages in Table 11.1 are not for discrete groups but for ranges of behavior. Categories 1-6 thus include those who have exhibited some homosexual behavior, as well as more extensive contacts all the way to the exclusively homosexual.

These figures are rather startling both because of the absolute numbers involved and because of the implications of placing everyone on a continuum and thus "contaminating" large segments of the population that would like to think of themselves as exclusively heterosexual (a claim that only 50 percent of males in the Kinsey sample could make). These considerations moved Kinsey to write:

> Males do not represent two discrete populations, heterosexual and homosexual. The world is not to be divided into sheep and goats. Not all things are black nor all things white. It is a fundamental of taxonomy that nature rarely deals with discrete categories. Only the human mind invents categories and tries to force facts into separated pigeon-holes. The living world is a continuum in each and every one of its aspects. The sooner

Table 11.1. Heterosexual-Homosexual Ratings (ages 20–35)*

Category		In Females	In Males
		(in percentages)	
0	Entirely heterosexual experience		
	Single	61–72	53–78
	Married	89–90	90–92
	Previously married	75–80	
1-6	At least some homosexual experience	11–20	18–42
2-6	More than incidental homosexual experience	6–14	13–38
3-6	As much or more homosexual experience than heterosexual experience	4–11	9–32
4-6	Mostly homosexual experience	3–8	7–26
5-6	Almost exclusively homosexual experience	2–6	5–22
6	Exclusively homosexual experience	1–3	3–16

*From data in Kinsey et al. (1953), p. 488.

we learn this concerning human sexual behavior the sooner we shall reach a sound understanding of the realities of sex.[17]

The findings from other studies in the United States and other countries (like Sweden and Germany) come close to the Kinsey figures for exclusive homosexuals: 2–4 percent of the adult male population. Further substantiating evidence comes from the American armed forces, which reject or discharge about 1 percent of their inductees for this reason. Although some people may pose as homosexuals in order to avoid military service, incomparably larger numbers of homosexuals remain in the armed forces and do not appear in this figure. Figures for females are generally much smaller (0.5 to

[17] Kinsey et al. (1948), p. 639.

1 percent of the female population). In most breakdowns the proportion of female homosexuals is only about a third as great as that of the male group.

Exclusively homosexual men and women regard themselves and are regarded by others as true homosexuals. For the rest of the population the question of who is and who is not homosexual is impossible to answer (and, according to Kinsey, unnecessary to pose). The law condemns a man for a single homosexual offense. Some men with high rates of homosexual activity disclaim the label for one reason or another. A working compromise among some clinicians and social scientists is to define homosexuals as people whose primary source of sexual gratification is through this outlet and to discount those with sporadic and transient homosexual involvements.

Bisexuals and Transsexuals. The two terms "bisexual" and "transsexual" are often mistakenly applied to homosexuals. "Bisexual" applies to people who engage in both homosexual and heterosexual activities. They would be classified in the middle range of Kinsey's homosexual-heterosexual scale. These people claim, however, that they are not "basically" one way or the other and do not simply alternate sexual objects occasionally. Rather, they claim a permanent need for relations with both sexes, to enjoy the best of two worlds as it were. Other people may view them as standard homosexuals who are simply rationalizing their activities. Because of their dual orientations, they are sometimes called "AC-DC" (for "alternating" and "direct" current) and may exhibit conflicts over their ambivalent sexuality.

Transsexuals, on the other hand, are different from homosexuals in important ways, even though they are often lumped together on the basis of behavioral similarities. The transsexual is a person (usually a male) who wishes to be, or sincerely believes that he is, a member of the opposite sex. Some males say that they have always felt themselves to be "women in male bodies" and trace such feelings to their childhoods. Although the transsexual often engages in homosexual (as well as heterosexual) relations, these activities are not homosexual in their view. After all, if a man feels himself to be woman, who else is he/she going to have sex with?

In contrast to the hostility and derision toward women that many male homosexuals express, the transsexual male claims to like women and would prefer to be a full-fledged woman himself. To this end he does everything possible, with occasionally astounding results. The ultimate aim for many of these biological males is a "sex change" operation, in which the penis and the testes are removed and an artificial "vagina" is created through reconstruction of pelvic tissues. The individual thus altered can have "vaginal" coitus. Contrary to occasional newspaper reports, however, pregnancy is absolutely impossible. A full transplant of ovaries and uterus has never been attempted, though it is not beyond the realm of possibility.

Most "sex change" operations involve changing males to females, and some make international news. Christine Jorgensen, a former American serviceman, offers the best known example. These operations are now performed in a few medical centers in this country. Applicants are carefully screened to eliminate those with serious mental derangements and those who might have second thoughts after the surgery. If the applicant has not already had hormone treatments, he must undergo them first. The resulting changes are marked but reversible, so that the patient's reactions can be further evaluated before the irrevocable step of surgery is taken. Even then some transsexuals, much to their own chagrin, may be disillusioned with the results of surgery, and severe psychological repercussions are not uncommon.

The very concept of a sex-change operation

raises numerous moral and medicolegal problems. For instance, the surgeon may be prosecuted under "bodily mayhem" laws, though such charges are unlikely to be pressed. Or a judge may refuse to grant changes in legal status (because the person remains genetically male), thus condemning newly made "women" to live under men's names.

Cross-Cultural Comparisons. Homosexual behavior has existed at all times in all parts of the world. But what such behavior has meant in any given culture is more difficult to assess. The Old Testament is explicit in its condemnations. The prevalence of homosexuality (particularly among males) in classical antiquity has been much belabored, often as justification for later behavior. The tutorial relationships between older and younger Greek men did have a sexual component. Some Greek cities had regiments of lovers fighting side by side. Homosexual behavior was also, however, subject to censure and penalties in classical Greece, depending upon the ranks and relationships of the men involved. Greek democracy was not free from the all-too-universal proclivity for letting some people but not others indulge in aberrant behavior.

The same generalization applies to homosexual behavior among primitive peoples: It is apparently universal but varies widely in prevalence, acceptance, and significance. Of seventy-six societies surveyed by Ford and Beach[18] about a third disapproved of homosexual behavior, and such activity was reported as absent, rare, or covert. Penalties ranged from derision to death.

The balance (64 percent) approved some forms of homosexuality. For instance, among the Konang (the most numerous and powerful tribe on the Alaskan coast) some male children were reared from infancy to occupy female roles in all activities. After maturing such a male was actually married to an important man in the community and regarded as a "shaman" (endowed with magical powers).

Other institutionalized forms of male homosexuality have been observed among various groups (including the warrior Mohave Indians of the Southwest[19]). In these communities some men went through special ceremonies and were received into a special class called "berdaches," "alyhas," or "shamans." Not only did they dress and function as women, but some also went so far as to pretend to menstruate or to become pregnant. They "married" men who might also have female wives and occupied respectable positions in the group.

There is relatively scant reference in either the historical or the anthropological record to female homosexuality. One exception is, of course, the work of Sappho, who lived on the Greek island of Lesbos (from which comes the term "lesbianism) in B.C. the sixth century. Her poems extolled the virtues of the love of women for each other. Sappho was also a proponent of women's rights and had a school for young women, in which poetry, dancing, music, and art were taught.

Most primitive societies do not have terms in their languages for such women. A few, however, accept female homosexual activities as normal, particularly mutual masturbation and the use of artificial penises. Among the Dahomean tribe of Africa, frigidity in a married woman was attributed to lesbian activities, and a similar belief was held in Haiti.

Some forms of deprivation homosexuality may well have existed in the harems of Oriental potentates and wealthy men, whose many wives and concubines were segregated in the custody

---

[18] Ford and Beach (1951), pp. 129–133.

[19] Devereux (1937), pp. 498–527.

of eunuchs. Among these basically heterosexual women the use of artificial penises was possibly more common than among those with basically homosexual orientations.

Cross-cultural data, fragmentary as they may be, generally contradict simple explanations of homosexual behavior as arising only when heterosexual outlets are unavailable or blocked by inhibitions and restrictions. The historical emergence and functional explanations of homosexual behavior remain generally obscure.

Cross-Species Comparisons. Sexual contacts between members of the same sex is widespread among mammals. Again the exact significance of such behavior varies. Animals, in common with men, engage in sexual activities for reasons both sexual and nonsexual (as part of establishing dominance categories, for example).[20] Some animals do not go beyond sniffing or licking the genitals of other animals of the same sex or playfully trying to mount them. Other behavior is flagrantly sexual. For instance, there have been observations of anal intercourse between male macaque monkeys both in captivity and in the wild. Sometimes the "passive" male is observed masturbating while the more "dominant" male is copulating with him.

Deprivation homosexuality has been demonstrated in various species. For instance, when a group of rats is segregated so that there is no access to animals of the opposite sex, homosexual activities, including oral-genital contacts and mounting behavior, will occur after a certain period of time. Depending upon the length of deprivation, the animals may or may not resume heterosexual activity when the sexes are mixed again. The longer the period of segregation, the less is the likelihood that heterosexual activity will be resumed when the

opportunity becomes available. But, as among humans, deprivation is not a necessary condition for homosexual activity.

Haphazard interpretations of animal behavior can be as misleading as can references to cross-cultural data out of context. Although much remains to be learned from both types of comparisons, two general conclusions are quite clear: First, homosexual behavior is never the dominant sexual outlet in any human society or animal species. Second, references to certain kinds of behavior as "natural" and to others as "unnatural" are difficult to substantiate on the evidence of what actually occurs in nature.

As an Illness

Many psychiatrists and other professionals consider homosexuals in general to be emotionally disturbed or ill. This judgment is based on both theoretical grounds and clinical experience. Homosexuals are viewed as having suffered stunted psychosexual development or as having been conditioned to respond to inappropriate sexual objects. They are considered unhappy, immature, and neurotic, unable to achieve satisfying sex lives and missing the rewards of mature heterosexual relationships, parenthood, and family life. Some even consider them pernicious characters who not only endure but also cause suffering.

It is reasonable to assume that homosexuals who seek psychiatric help are neurotic and unhappy people: Why else would they seek such help? But, of course, the same reasoning applies to heterosexuals who seek psychiatric treatment. What is less clear is whether or not homosexuals who express no need for clinical assistance are as badly off, that is, whether their claims of contentment (provided that they are not harassed) are justified, or simply pretense.[21] At any rate, homosexuality in the West, as in

---

[20] For a review of homosexual behavior among animals see Ford and Beach (1951), pp. 134–143. For a critique of earlier evaluations of animal homosexual behavior see Kinsey *et al.* (1953), pp. 448–451.

[21] For a challenge to definitions of homosexuality as a clinical entity, see Hooker in Ruitenbeek, ed. (1963), pp. 141–161, and Kameny (1971).

most of the rest of the world, creates formidable problems of adjustment for the individual, especially in authoritarian countries.

If one accepts the notion that homosexuality is an illness (apart from the problem of social reactions to it), then one can legitimately ask what causes it. As for other forms of deviant behavior, there are many theories of causation but none that can be generally accepted. At present we simply do not know with any certainty what factors are the critical determinants in homosexual (or heterosexual) behavior. The theories to be discussed here have been chosen primarily to reflect current thinking on this problem.

Biological Causes. Physical examinations, chromosome studies, and endocrine studies have so far failed to identify any particular biological difference between homosexuals and heterosexuals. There is thus no evidence to date that biological factors determine object choice. The author of one large-scale study of identical twins has claimed a genetic basis for homosexuality.[22] He has shown that all the identical twins studied were concordant for homosexuality (that is, if one twin was homosexual, so was the other). Among fraternal twins the degree of concordance for homosexuality was not statistically significant. This study has been criticized on the grounds that similarities in environment were not taken into consideration, and other investigators have failed to replicate its findings.

This lack of evidence does not, however, mean that none will be forthcoming. Many researchers remain convinced (as Freud was) that there is a genetic or constitutional predisposition toward homosexuality and that the life experiences of the individual serve either to reinforce or to extinguish it.

One theory involves the concept of *infantile*

bisexuality, in which elements of both masculinity and femininity are assumed to be present at birth and the balance between them to be determined by genetic and hormone factors. In Chapters 4 and 5 we discussed the different proportions in which male and female sex hormones are present in both sexes. There is a steadily growing body of evidence indicating that behavior and anatomy are both influenced by the relative amounts of sex hormones present.

Psychological Causes. Recent psychological studies have focused on the family relations of young boys who become homosexuals.

A study by Bieber and his colleagues compared 106 male homosexuals with 100 male heterosexuals.[23] Although the fact that all the subjects were undergoing psychoanalytic treatment renders generalization from these data questionable, the findings are consistent with general observations about the families of many (but not all) homosexuals. Essentially the pattern found was that of a dominant mother and a passive father. The mother has further been described as overprotective and unusually intimate with her son. (Gebhard and his colleagues, among others, have shown that homosexuals are usually only children, youngest children, or youngest sons.)[24] The father, when present, has been described as detached, unaffectionate, and hostile toward his son. It has been hypothesized that such parents tend to inhibit the expression of masculine behavior in their sons. The domineering mother is said to prohibit the expression of heterosexual impulses except when directed toward herself, as she is jealous of any interest that her son shows in any other female. The boy whose father is aloof

---

[22]Kallman (1952).

[23]Bieber *et al.* (1962). The psychoanalytic literature on homosexuality is quite extensive. A classic reference work is Fenichel (1945). More recent reviews can be found in Bieber *et al.* (1962) and Marmor, ed. (1965).

[24]Gebhard *et al.* (1965).

or openly hostile lacks a masculine figure with whom he can identify and whose behavior he can use as a model. In later life the boy retains a fear of heterosexual relationships and a frustrated need for the masculine (paternal) love that he failed to receive as a child.

Psychoanalytic attempts to unravel the dynamics of homosexuality start with the assumption that all children are "polymorphously perverse" and that for various reasons some do not outgrow and repress these infantile perverse tendencies (see Chapter 8). The reasons may include, for instance, unresolved oedipal ties (to avoid conflict, the child may have become sexually attached to the parent of the same sex and may carry this pattern into his adult life) or castration anxiety (in which males consort with males because the sight of female genitals evokes earlier fears that they too may lose their penises; and in which females may prefer relations with each other to avoid being reminded that they lack penises). These conflicts, though simply stated here, are quite complex and submerged in the unconscious.

Critics of the theory that homosexuals harbor unconscious fears of women claim that it makes just as much sense to say that heterosexuals are plagued by unconscious fears of men. Furthermore, the pattern of intense involvement with the mother and a poor relationship with the father is also not always present in a homosexual's background.

Explanations based on learning theories use the same concepts of conditioning and so on that we discussed in Chapter 8: that pleasant and painful experiences shape sexual orientations, which then remain subject to continuing modification. Although superficially quite plausible, these explanations are also by no means clearly supported by objective studies.

That childhood experiences are important is beyond doubt, but what specifically is relevant is more difficult to pinpoint. The notion that boys who are forced into homosexual activities by older men ("homosexual child molesters") necessarily become homosexuals when they grow up, is difficult to evaluate. Some follow-up studies seem to show that it is unfounded. However, in the Gebhard sample a quarter of the homosexual adults in prison had had, as children, sexual contacts with adult males.[25] "Tomboyishness" and preference for sports or "being one of the boys" in young girls are not correlated with women's choice of women as sexual partners in adulthood. (But adolescent girls who become involved in frequent or prolonged "crushes" on other girls or older women may be exhibiting early homosexual tendencies.)

Treatment. For those who view homosexuality as a pathological condition, improvement or "cure" means changing the individual's orientation to a heterosexual one. Relatively few such "cures" have been reported. There are several reasons why.

First, many homosexuals do not consider themselves abnormal or sick and thus do not seek treatment. When they come to psychiatrists for problems of anxiety or depression, they may pay lip service to the need to resolve their "sexual problems" without any real intention of changing their orientations. What they want is relief of their symptoms. Whether or not homosexuals are more prone to such symptoms and, if so, whether or not such distress is inherent in homosexuality or results from the pressures that they experience as members of an "outlawed" minority are open to question. Certainly some homosexuals develop problems of anxiety, depression, and so on for the same reasons that heterosexuals do.

A small percentage of homosexuals is apprehended and forced to undergo treatment by

---

[25]Gebhard *et al.* (1965), p. 356. For additional information on the effects of early homosexual experiences see Westwood (1960), pp. 24–39, and Doshay (1969).

court order, either in state institutions or as a condition of probation. As we might suspect, such individuals are little motivated to change and will usually "play along" in therapy in order to satisfy the law. Occasionally homosexuality is associated with more serious disorders like paranoid schizophrenia. Treatment is then oriented mainly toward the larger disorder.

There are, finally, some individuals who seek psychiatric treatment of their own volition, genuinely eager to change their sexual orientations. The results of treatment in such situations is determined by several variables, for example, how long the patients have been homosexual and whether or not they have had heterosexual experiences. Some psychiatrists believe that changing the sexual orientation of homosexuals is either unnecessary or unrealistic and consequently gear their treatment to helping individuals become "better adjusted" homosexuals so that they will no longer be dissatisfied with their orientations. "Cures" in this sense are more likely than those involving personality reorientation, but there are also reports of homosexuals who have been "cured" in the latter sense. Therefore it is also misleading to claim that there is "no cure" for homosexuality.

Even though some psychiatrists are openly hostile to homosexuals, the more general attitude is one of tolerance. This attitude is expressed in a famous letter from Freud to a mother who had requested treatment for her son.

April 9, 1935

Dear Mrs. X

I gather from your letter that your son is a homosexual. I am most impressed by the fact that you do not mention this term yourself in your information about him. May I question you, why do you avoid it? Homosexuality is assuredly no advantage, but it is nothing to be ashamed of, no vice, no degradation, it cannot be classified as an illness; we consider it to be a variation of the sexual function produced by a certain arrest of sexual development. Many highly respectable individuals of ancient and modern times have been homosexuals, several of the greatest men among them (Plato, Michelangelo, Leonardo da Vinci, etc.). It is a great injustice to persecute homosexuality as a crime, and cruelty too. If you do not believe me, read the books of Havelock Ellis.

By asking me if I can help, you mean, I suppose, if I can abolish homosexuality and make normal heterosexuality take its place. The answer is, in a general way, we cannot promise to achieve it. In a certain number of cases we succeed in developing the blighted germs of heterosexual tendencies which are present in every homosexual, in the majority of cases it is no more possible. It is a question of the quality and the age of the individual. The result of the treatment cannot be predicted.

What analysis can do for your son runs in a different line. If he is unhappy, neurotic, torn by conflicts, inhibited in his social life, analysis may bring him harmony, peace of mind, full efficiency, whether he remains a homosexual or gets changed. If you make up your mind he should have analysis with me (I don't expect you will!!) he has to come over to Vienna. I have no intention of leaving here. However, don't neglect to give me your answer.

Sincerely yours with kind wishes,

Freud

P.S. I did not find it difficult to read your handwriting. Hope you will not find my writing and my English a harder task.[26]

---

[26]Freud (1951), p. 787. Freud's compassion is quite apparent in this letter—but so is his apparent uncertainty whether or not homosexuality as such is an illness. He first remarks that homosexuality "cannot be classified as an illness" but then contrasts it with "normal heterosexuality" and shows that he is less than sanguine about the prospects of developing "the blighted germs of heterosexual tendencies." We must not forget, however, that this document is a letter to a concerned mother, rather than a scientific paper.

As a Criminal Offense

The relation between sexual behavior and the law is the subject of an entire chapter in this book (see Chapter 16). We shall therefore deal only briefly here with the personality features of homosexuals who are arrested. These sex offenders (like the neurotic who is under psychiatric care) may or may not be representative of the general homosexual population.

The dealings of the law with homosexuals tend to be quite arbitrary. Arrests may occur during sudden raids on gay bars. Homosexuals who cruise in "off limits" areas or those who make public spectacles of themselves are generally picked up not by potential lovers but by the police. The latter also sometimes trap homosexuals by pretending to be potential contacts. Finally, a youngster arrested for some other offense may reveal, during interrogation, his homosexual links with older men. Who is arrested and who escapes also depends upon police officers' conceptions of who are the "active" members of given pairs. Convicted homosexuals are, ironically enough, usually sent to jails where homosexuality is much more rampant than it is outside. Women are rarely arrested on such charges.

On the basis of their extensive study of male sex offenders, Gebhard and his associates have offered this summary of data on homosexual offenders against adults (as distinguished from homosexual offenders whose contacts are with children or other minors, to be discussed later).

> Despite the fact that the homosexual offender vs. adults was not infrequently an only child or the youngest child in the family, he got along very badly with his father and not well with his mother. Nevertheless, there are evidences that he was unusually partial to his mother.
>
> His social life during childhood was quantitatively good: he had numerous friends of both sexes. He also engaged in a good deal of prepubertal sex play which even at this early date was preponderantly homosexual. An even more

impressive omen is the fact that over a quarter of these offenders had, as children, sexual contact with adult males.

> Two other childhood phenomena probably played an important role in their lives. First, their childhoods were often marred by illness, and, second, they reached puberty earlier than any other group. This latter fact may be of extreme importance, for it means that these boys were faced with strong sexual urges at an age when society makes no provision for any expression of sexuality.
>
> The homosexual offenders vs. adults seem to have had the strongest sex drive of any groups if frequency of activity is taken as a measure. This is particularly evident in adult life in the amount of masturbation, which suggests an urgency that could not brook the delays inherent in obtaining any sociosexual activity.
>
> The adult heterosexual lives of these men were comparatively stunted. Petting began at a late date, there was little of it, and the techniques were rather restrained. Only two thirds had had premarital coitus, a percentage surpassed by other groups at far younger ages. The relative lack of heterosexual activity stemmed in large part from disinterest, which is also reflected in the small proportion who ever married.
>
> These offenders were strongly homosexual: nine out of ten had had more than incidental homosexual contacts and three quarters had had extensive experience, which not infrequently was quite promiscuous.
>
> The homosexual offenders vs. adults, as a group, do not appear particularly criminal or dangerous. They do not damage society, they merely do not fit into it.[27]

Pedophilia

The pedophile (from the Greek, "lover of children") is someone who uses children for his sexual gratification.[28] Pedophilia is a serious

---

[27]Gebhard *et al.* (1965), pp. 356–357.

[28]The definition of a pedophile depends upon the definition of a child. The laws of many states define "child molesting" and related offenses like "statutory rape" to

legal offense; almost all pedophiles who are arrested are male. They may be interested in either prepubescent males or prepubescent females but usually not in both.

The heterosexual pedophile is usually pictured as a stranger who lurks about the school playground, abducts an unsuspecting little girl, takes her by force to some secret place, and ravishes her. The facts rarely fit this stereotype. Studies have shown that in about 85 percent of such incidents the pedophile is either a relative, a family friend, a neighbor, or an acquaintance. He makes advances to the child either in her home, where he is visiting or living (as an uncle, stepfather, grandfather, or boarder) or in his own home, where she is used to visiting or is enticed by promises of candy or other treats. (Seventy-nine percent of such contacts occur in homes, 13 percent in public places, and 8 percent in cars.) Physical damage to the child occurs in only 2 percent of instances, though threats of force or some degree of physical restraint is present in about one-third of instances in which arrests and convictions follow.

The entire pedophiliac episode is often quite brief, and, though there may be a series of such episodes before the child reports them to her parents, it is unusual for a prolonged or intimate relationship to develop. (In this sense, the story of Vladimir Nabokov's *Lolita* is atypical.)

Actual sexual contact most often consists of the man's taking the child on his lap and fond-

ling her external genitals. Intercourse is rarely attempted because, among other factors, these men are often impotent. (Coitus is attempted in about 6 percent of instances, but intromission is achieved in only about 2 percent.)

Individuals involved with little girls (heterosexual offenders against children) tend to be older than is any other group of sex offenders, with the exception of those involved in incest. The average age at conviction is thirty-five, and 25 percent of these offenders are over forty-five. About 5 percent are actually senile individuals whose judgment is impaired through mental deterioration; 15–20 percent of offenders are mentally retarded, and their behavior can be considered as attempts to socialize with girls at similar mental levels. Treatment of such men is obviously difficult, for it is rather unlikely that a man with a child's mentality can establish a satisfactory relationship with an adult woman. Through the use of aversive conditioning techniques, however, he can sometimes be trained to stay away from children.

The majority of heterosexual offenders with children are, however, neither senile nor mentally defective; 70–80 percent have been married at some time in their lives. They tend to be conservative and moralistic, and some require alcohol before they can commit their offenses. They usually do not have criminal records, with the exception of possible previous convictions for molesting children.

The homosexual pedophile obtains sexual gratification through the use of young boys as sexual objects. Although this activity is viewed by some people as a variation of adult homosexuality, it is uncommon and scorned by the vast majority of homosexuals. Most homosexuals confine their sexual activities to other adults.

Homosexual pedophiles also do not usually molest strangers, and the boys with whom they become involved are most often relatives or the sons of acquaintances. In addition, contacts are sometimes made through youth organizations.

---

include victims up to the ages of sixteen, eighteen, or even twenty-one. Sexual involvement with even a postpubescent fifteen-year-old girl, however, is usually a different sort of activity from what we describe here as pedophilia. In the former the "victim" may actually have been the seducer, and the "offender" may have misjudged the age of his sexual partner, because of her physical appearance or because she lied about her age. Gebhard *et al.* (1965) define a child as younger than twelve years old, a minor as between thirteen and fifteen years old, and an adult as more than sixteen years old. These age limits correspond well with stages in biological maturation. All statistical references in the rest of this chapter are from this work unless otherwise specified (see Chapter 1 for further information about this research).

The popular notion that better police surveillance will prevent such crimes is thus difficult to justify.

Sexual activities with a young boy may include fondling and masturbation of the boy, mutual masturbation, fellatio, and *pederasty* (anal intercourse with a child).

Homosexual offenders against children generally show deficiencies in socialization and interpersonal relationships. They often say that they prefer the company of boys because they feel uneasy around adults. Their average age when they commit their offenses is 30.6 years, and only 16 percent are married at this time. Their sexual experiences have usually been predominantly but not exclusively homosexual.

Child prostitution (male and female) has existed in various parts of the world, but it is now rare in most countries. The child molester, especially when he uses force, arouses strong aversion and anger in the community. Even in jail he is so poorly tolerated that he must be isolated from other inmates. Sexual contacts between adults and children in other countries have been discussed in Chapter 8.

Incest

Incest is very rare but of great social significance. It is one sexual offense that is universally condemned, but it does occasionally occur, and historical and literary records include some well-known examples.[29]

The term "incest" (from the Latin for "impure," or "soiled") is commonly used for sexual relations between parents and offspring. In this sense it is much more common between fathers and daughters than between mothers and sons. Actually incest includes all sexual relations between a person and his close relatives (for example, siblings, grandparents, uncles, and aunts). The taboo is extended to cousins in some but not in all groups. (The Roman Catholic and Greek Orthodox churches prohibit marriage between first cousins, but such marriages are permitted by many Protestant churches, as well as by Judaism and Islam.)

The incest taboo is generally assumed to have evolved very early in mankind's life in an attempt to safeguard the integrity of the family unit, for sexual competition within it would be highly disruptive (as it is when incest does occur). Furthermore, mating outside the family has been important in the formation of larger social units held together by kinship ties. The proposition that the incest taboo arose from recognition of the genetic dangers of inbreeding (through concentration of disease-carrying recessive genes) is much less plausible.[30]

Whatever its precise origins, prohibitions against incest are now universal. Ford and Beach came to the conclusion that:

> Among all peoples both partners in a mateship are forbidden to form sexual liaison with their own offspring. This prohibition characterizes every human culture. This generalization excludes instances in which mothers or fathers are permitted to masturbate or in some other sexual manner to stimulate their very young children. A second exception is represented by the very rare cases in which a society expects a few individuals of special social rank to cohabit with their immediate descendants. The Azande of Africa, for example, insist that the highest chiefs enter into sexual partnerships with their own

---

[29]The story of Lot and his daughters is told in Genesis 19 and that of Oedipus in the tragedy *Oedipus Rex* by Sophocles. The circumstances in both stories are extraordinary. Lot and his daughters are the only survivors of the cataclysmic destruction of Sodom and Gomorrah, and the apparent motivation of Lot's daughters in intoxicating and seducing their father is to ensure the continuity of their family line. Oedipus (see Chapter 8) is not even aware that the queen whom he has married is his own mother.

---

[30]For an analysis of the functional significance of the incest taboo, see Murdock (1949). For a sociological review, see Weinberg (1963).

daughters. In no society, however, are such matings permitted to the general populations.[31]

Similar exceptions for intermarriage between siblings were also made among the Incas and the ancient Egyptian pharoahs (Cleopatra was the offspring of and herself a partner in such matings). Incidentally, 72 percent of the societies surveyed by Ford and Beach were found to have more extensive incest prohibitions than is common in the West: Sometimes they were broad enough to exclude half the population as potential sex mates for a given individual.

The role of incestuous wishes in the psychoanalytic scheme of psychosexual development is well known and has been discussed in Chapter 8.

The only data on offenders of incest laws available from the Gebhard study is on father-daughter relationships. The ages of the daughters at the time of the offenses were correlated with some characteristics of the fathers. Fathers who became sexually involved with prepubertal daughters tended to be passive, ineffectual men who drank excessively. The sexual contacts involved either fondling the external genitals or oral-genital contacts.

Offenders against maturer daughters tended to be religious, moralistic, and often active in fundamentalist sects. (They were rated as the most religious of all the groups of sex offenders studied by Gebhard and his colleagues.) They were poorly educated and had a median age of forty-six at the time of the offense. Activity culminated in coitus in 91 percent of instances, and in only 8 percent did the daughters clearly resist the advances of their fathers, whereas 58 percent clearly participated voluntarily (either encouragingly or passively).

Charges of incest are usually pressed by wives, but sometimes the daughters go directly to the police. Often an incestuous relationship has been continuing for some time and then is suddenly discovered by the wife or is reported by the daughter because she is angry at her father for some unrelated reason.

Animal Contacts

Sexual contacts with animals (*zoophilia,* or *bestiality*) were by far the least prevalent of the six components of total sexual outlet studied by Kinsey. Even though 8 percent of adult males and 3 percent of females reported such contacts with animals, their activities accounted for a fraction of 1 percent of total sexual outlets. In some groups, however, such behavior was relatively common: Among boys raised on farms as many as 17 percent had had at least one orgasm through animal contact after puberty.

Mankind has a long history of intimate associations with animals in many aspects of life, including the sexual ones (see Figure 11.2). This theme has been an important source of fantasy and an inspiration for many works of art. Classical mythology abounds with tales of sexual contacts between the gods disguised as beasts and apparently unsuspecting goddesses and mortals. Zeus, for instance, approached

Figure 11.2. Petroglyph in a cave in northern Italy. From E. Anati, *Camonica Valley* (New York: Alfred A. Knopf, 1961), p. 128. Reprinted by permission.

---

[31]Ford and Beach (1951), p. 112.

Figure 11.3.   Leda and the Swan (after Michelangelo). Courtesy of The National Gallery, London.

Europa as a bull, Leda as a swan (see Figure 11.3), and Persephone as a serpent. From such unions issued the many half-man, half-beast denizens of the mythological woods: satyrs (half-goats), centaurs (half-horses), and minotaurs (half-bulls), to name only the most familiar.

Historical references are also plentiful. Herodotus mentions the goats of the Egyptian temple at Mendes, which were specially trained for copulating with human beings. More often, we find references to animals as sexual objects framed as prohibitions. The Hittite code, the Old Testament, and the Talmud specifically prohibit such contacts for males, and the Talmud extends the prohibition to females. The prescribed penalties tended to be severe (death for both human and animal participants; see Leviticus 20). Such sanctions remained in effect in Europe throughout the Middle Ages and, indeed, until fairly recently. In 1468 one Jean Beisse was convicted of copulating with a cow and a goat: Jean, the cow, and the goat were all burned at the stake. In 1601 sixteen-year-old Claudine de Culam was convicted of copulating with a dog: Both were hanged and their bodies burned. In 1944 an American soldier was convicted at a general court-martial of sodomy with a cow and sentenced to a dishonorable discharge and three years at hard labor: This time the cow was spared.

The animals and the specific activities involved in these sexual encounters vary widely. Copulation with dogs is well documented, but other purported combinations strain our credulity: Some Indian illustrations, for instance, may have been intended symbolically rather than literally. Common sense suggests that the animals most often used would be those usually found on farms and in homes and that the most common activity would be some form of masturbation or intercourse.

In the Kinsey sample general body contact with animals was more often reported by women, whereas men were more likely to have masturbated the animals. Oral-genital contacts, involving the animals' mouths and the human genitals, were reported by both sexes, but coitus with animals was more common among men and very rare among women.

We hear and read about "sex dogs" that are specially trained and sold for purposes of zoophilia, but such tales are difficult to document. There have, however, been (and are quite likely to continue to be) establishments that feature exhibitions of coitus between prostitutes and dogs (or even donkeys). These activities fascinate men more than they do women.

Group Sex

Many people are attracted by the idea of having sex with more than one other person at a time. Illustrations of such activities are plentiful in the erotic art of classical Greece, (see Figure 13.5) and in that of the Far East. The theme has also been much exploited in erotic literature.

Although sex orgies are not new, they have in all likelihood been indulged in only by occasional men of wealth or by small and special groups. Recently it has been claimed that "group sex" is quite common among more typical segments of the general population. Although it no doubt occurs among "swingers,"

there is no way of quantifying the actual prevalence of such practices. At the level of fantasy many people are no doubt intrigued by the notion, and "underground" films exploit the theme frequently.

The participation of several couples in simultaneous coitus does not meet the definition of a deviation, for neither choice of object nor means is necessarily aberrant. The practice does raise questions of exhibitionism and voyeurism, however, for sex is ordinarily conducted in private.[32]

When one person takes more than one partner at a time, then the definition of deviation seems applicable. When three people are involved (one male and two females or the opposite), the practice is known as *troilism*. As simultaneous coitus is impossible in the first instance and highly impractical in the second, usually some combination of coitus with oral-genital stimulation is adopted. All other versions of "group sex" are variations on this theme.[33] Group sex may be exclusively heterosexual, homosexual, or mixed. It may also include homosexual behavior that would otherwise be unacceptable: two males who would otherwise not touch each other may do so in the process of sex play with the same woman. Or two men having coitus with the same woman successively may be striving to achieve physical contact between their own genitals, as it were, by placing their penises in the same vagina in rapid succession. Overt homosexual contact is rare in males, but common in females.

---

[32] Among animals the sight of copulation is sometimes quite arousing to nonparticipants. When "public" sexual activity breaks out in an animal group, it may lead to violent conflict. It has been suggested that prohibition of public sex among human beings arose from fears that it would excite bystanders and result in uncontrollable sexual activity and disruption of the group.

[33] A serious effort to study the practice of group sex was recently reported by an anthropologist (see Bartell, 1971).

Fetishism and Transvestism

In fetishism the sexual object is an inanimate article.[34] Most often it is a piece of clothing or footwear. Parts of the body may also take on fetishistic significance, however. The boundary between normally erotogenic objects or parts of the body and fetishes is frequently quite nebulous. Practically all heterosexual males, for instance, are aroused by the sight of female underwear. Each man is also partial to particular portions of the female anatomy besides the genitals. There is an intermediary group in whom such partiality becomes quite pronounced. For example, a man may become so preoccupied with the shape of a woman's legs or her provocative stockings and garters that he loses sight of the woman as a whole. It is only when a man becomes clearly focused on these paraphernalia or body parts to the exclusion of everything else, however, that we can speak with confidence of fetishism.

This deviation, at least in the sense in which the term is generally used, is an almost exclusively male one. The attachment of women to jewelry or furs, for instance, is excluded because women obtain no conscious sexual gratification from these objects.

In principle, any article or body part can become endowed with fetishistic meaning, but some objects are more commonly chosen than are others. The attraction may arise from the shape, texture, color, or smell of the article or from a combination of these features. Most fetishes fall into two categories: "feminine" objects that are soft, furry, lacy, pastel-colored (like pink panties with frilly edges) and "masculine" objects that are smooth, harsh, or black (like chains and leather garments). The latter category is more often associated with sado-masochistic fantasies and practices.

What do fetishists do with these objects? Most incorporate them into masturbation sequences. Some may actually ejaculate into or over their fetishes. A fetish can also become associated with some other deviant practice, as we have noted. For example, a masochist may require that he be whipped by a woman wearing spike-heeled shoes, black garters, and so on.

Some fetishes may be so disguised or so far removed from actual sexual objects that the source of their erotic significance is hardly apparent, even to the fetishist himself. Outward circumstances can be quite misleading, however. For instance, a man may masturbate with female underwear because he has no access to a woman and the feminine garment helps him in his fantasies. In this sense, the underwear is more a masturbation aid than a fetish.[35] The key criterion, as for most deviations, is whether the choice of object is "voluntary" or resorted to only in the absence of feminine company.

Fetishism is explained according to two processes: learning by association and symbolism. In the former a person "eroticizes" certain nonsexual objects because of their frequent associations with actual sexual parts and functions or because of chance associations under emotionally charged conditions. For example, when a boy has his first glimpse of the female genitals in conjunction with other sights, sounds, and activities, some of the latter may

---

[34] The word "fetish" means an artificial, or fake, object. Anthropologists apply it to objects that are believed by primitive peoples to have magical power. In a more general sense it includes any article that is valued beyond its intrinsic worth because of superstitious or other meanings ascribed to it.

[35] There is a sizable industry that caters to the market for such masturbation aids, the most sophisticated of which is a life-size and presumably lifelike doll of inflatable rubber or plastic. The simpler models are sold openly as "party gags." More sophisticated ones are advertised as "hard-to-get items"; they come equipped with "pubic fur," "vagina," and "clitoris," and so on. See Thompson (1967), p. 142. The use of dolls, conventional or otherwise, in fetishism is sometimes called *puppetophilia.*

become indelibly impressed on his mind, even to the extent of overshadowing the primary stimulus. We also learn, of course, to value certain parts of the body over others simply by growing up in given cultures.

Psychoanalytic theorists find this sort of explanation inadequate. "The foot fetishist," Fenichel wrote in reference to one of Freud's cases, "who became fixated on the incident of seeing his governess expose her foot had some unconscious reason why the sight of a foot, ordinarily innocent enough, aroused his sexual excitation." [36] The unconscious reason in this case was the boy's castration anxiety: He realized that the governess had no penis, which revived his earlier fears that he might lose his own (in retaliation for his incestuous wishes). Then he saw the woman's naked foot; the shape of the foot and its nakedness combined to suggest a penis. The foot then became equated in his mind with the penis; the governess thus had a "penis," and the boy's fears were allayed, but in the process the female foot became "eroticized" in his mind. Such a process occurs in the unconscious. The boy, as an adult, has no notion why female feet (or, by association, stockings, garters, shoes or similar sights, shapes, smells, and so on) excite him. The fetish usually, as in our example, symbolizes the penis but may also represent the vagina or even objects like feces and urine associated with "pregenital" activities.

Human responses to body smells and products vary widely. Most people learn to find such odors and sights offensive and sexually repellent (except that vaginal secretions during excitement are frequently stimulating to men). Occasionally, however, the opposite occurs, and a person becomes highly aroused by filth ("mysophilia"), feces ("coprophilia"), and urine ("urophilia"). The sound of a woman urinating

is intriguing to many males, but the deviant may be exclusively preoccupied with such elimination functions. It is said that in some exclusive Continental brothels, a man could, for a fee, watch women defecate into transparent toilet bowls.

Transvestism, though a separate deviation, is closely linked to fetishism, for the transvestite (also usually a man) achieves sexual gratification through wearing the clothing of the opposite sex. Again appearances can be quite misleading, however. Some "transvestites" are actually transsexuals: As far as they are concerned, they are wearing the clothes of their own sex. Others are homosexuals using female clothing to attract other homosexuals. Then there are socially accepted instances in which men dress as women, as in amateur burlesque skits or Japanese Kabuki plays.

Only a small proportion of transvestites in the Kinsey data were overt homosexuals or even consciously inclined toward homosexuality. These apparently heterosexual men claimed simply to enjoy wearing women's clothing, and it was not unusual for their mothers to have dressed them as girls in childhood.

Others

A number of additional deviations in object choice deserve brief mention. Necrophilia is the sexual use of corpses. It is exceedingly rare and usually involves psychotic men. Literary and artistic references to love and death are sometimes interpreted as suggestions of necrophiliac fantasies, as in Edgar Allan Poe's:

> I could not love except where death
> was mingling his with beauty's breath.

Practices like kleptomania and pyromania are much more common. The first involves compulsive stealing without much interest in the nature and intrinsic value of the objects stolen. The pyromaniac suffers from irresistible im-

---

[36] Fenichel (1945), p. 341.

pulses to set fires. In both instances the deviant may actually experience sexual arousal. If not, the erotic nature of the activity is nevertheless inferred.

Other special designations are not useful. "Gerontophilia," for instance, refers to sex with a considerably older person. There may or may not be much to be said for such activities, but hardly anything is gained by making "perversions" out of them.

DEVIATIONS IN SEXUAL AIM

The deviations in object choice discussed in the preceding section involve relatively distinct entities: Males, females, animals, and inanimate articles are distinct and mutually exclusive classes of objects. Aberrations in aim are far more difficult to characterize, for differences between the "normal" and the "deviant" are more quantitative than qualitative.

The activities to be considered are described as they occur in the context of adult heterosexual relationships. When they coexist with deviations in object choice, they are classified according to the latter. Deviations in sexual aims are rare in their "pure" forms and are most common among men.

Voyeurism

Leofric, Lord of Coventry in the eleventh century, agreed to remit an oppressive tax if his wife, the Lady Godiva, would ride through the town naked on a white horse. The lady, a benefactress of monasteries and a friend of the poor, consented. Out of respect and gratitude everyone in town stayed behind closed doors and shuttered windows during her ride— everyone, that is, except Tom the tailor, who peeped and went blind. At least, that is the way the legend goes.

Only the very naïve would be surprised to hear that men are usually erotically aroused at the sight of uncovered female bodies. When such exposure is accompanied by movements, it can be even more exciting. Women, as a rule, are not so fascinated or aroused by the sight of male nudity. Male interests are widely indulged through "girl watching," attending burlesque shows, and so on. Such behavior is often loosely called "voyeuristic" but does not constitute a deviation.

Strictly speaking, voyeurism is viewed as a deviation when it is preferred to coitus or indulged in at serious risk. It is socially unacceptable when the person is observed without her knowledge and would be offended if she became aware of it.

The typical voyeur is not interested in ogling his own wife or girl friend. In 95 percent of incidents he observes strangers. What draws him to peep through their windows is in large measure the danger and excitement entailed. The practice is culturally widespread (see Figures 11.4 and 13.20).

Voyeurs tend to be young men (the average age at first conviction is 23.8 years). Two-thirds of them are unmarried, one-fourth are married, and the rest are either divorced, widowed, or separated. Very few show evidence of serious mental disorders, and alcohol or drugs are usually not involved in their deviant behavior (only 16 percent of Gebhard's sample was drunk at the time of offense, and none was under the influence of drugs). The voyeur usually takes great care not to be seen by the object of his attentions, and most voyeurs are reported to the police by passersby or neighbors, rather than by the women themselves. Voyeurs are also known to have fallen off window ledges or been shot as burglars.

In intelligence, occupational choice, and family background "peepers" tend to be a heterogeneous group. They are, however, more likely to be the youngest children in their families. The single most common characteristic of this group of sex offenders is a history of grossly deficient (both in quantity and in quality) heterosexual relationships. Most voyeurs do not have serious criminal records, but many have histories of minor offenses (misdemeanors). As a rule they do not molest their victims physically.

Psychoanalysts predictably link such behavior to the primal scene: parental coitus observed by the offspring. Their deviance is then explained as an effort to go back to the physically traumatic scene in order to gain mastery over it. Fenichel refers to a case in which the voyeur would wait while a couple engaged in coitus in an adjacent room. The voyeur would then begin to cry, and the woman would leave her partner and rush to him. Only then could he engage in coitus.[37] Many voyeurs are just as content watching solitary females undress. They frequently masturbate while watching or immediately thereafter.

Figure 11.4. Japanese bathing scene (eighteenth century?). Artist unknown.

Exhibitionism

The word "exhibitionist" is a good example of the arbitrariness and confusion with which certain terms, and the concepts that they embody, have come to be used. The drunken man who fleetingly exposes his genitals to a passing woman while urinating in a dark alley is an exhibitionist (for practical purposes, only if she takes offense). A woman who spends hours on end undressing herself to musical accompaniment or cavorts naked on a stage in front of a paying audience is "exhibitionistic" in her behavior but not an "exhibitionist" (see Figure 11.5). The male behavior carries a stiff prison sentence; the woman is permitted to make her living this way. However badly females may fare in other areas of sexual behavior, when voyeurism and exhibitionism are concerned the law is on their side. A woman undresses in front

of an open window, and a man looks up at her: He is a voyeur. The roles are reversed: Now he is an exhibitionist.

The mating behavior of animals, as well as of men, includes a great deal of "exhibitionistic" activity. Society permits and expects a certain amount of enticement by women, from coquettish exposure of an ankle to unceremonious baring of her buttocks; and, depending upon the time and the place, either may be appropriate.

Exhibitionism is a deviation when an adult male obtains sexual gratification from exposing his genitals to women or children who are involuntary observers, usually complete strangers. In a typical sequence the exhibitionist drives or walks in front of a passing woman with his genitals exposed. He usually, but not always, has an erection. Usually, as soon as she has seen him, he flees. Sometimes he wears a coat and exposes himself periodically while riding on a subway or bus. Or he may stand in a park and pretend that he is urinating.

[37]Fenichel (1945), p. 348.

Figure 11.5. Thomas Rowlandson, *Untitled.*

The exhibitionist, in common with the voyeur, does not usually attack or molest his "victim." His gratification comes from observing her reaction, which is predictably surprise, fear, disgust, and so on. Women who keep their calm foil his attempt. (For the same reason, a nudist camp, where he would hardly be noticed, does not attract this type of deviant.) Some men ejaculate at the scene of exposure; others merely enjoy psychic release. Others become highly aroused and masturbate right afterward.

The average age of the exhibitionist ("the flag-waver" in prison slang) at conviction is thirty years. About 30 percent of arrested exhibitionists are married; another 30 percent are separated, divorced, or widowed; and 40 percent have never been married. The exhibitionist often describes a compulsive quality in his own behavior, triggered by feelings of excitement, fear, restlessness, and sexual arousal. Once in this state, he feels "driven" to find relief. Despite previous arrests and convictions, he tends to repeat his behavior. One-third of the offenders in this category in the Gebhard study had had four to six previous convictions, and 10 percent had been convicted seven or more times.[38]

The exhibitionist seems to need to display and reaffirm his masculinity, and sometimes an element of sexual solicitation (rarely realized) is present as well. Exhibitionists do not usually show signs of severe mental disorder, and alcohol and drugs are involved only in rare instances. Psychoanalytic explanations are based on reactions to castration fears.

Although usually not classified with exhibitionism, the practice of making obscene telephone calls is similar to it in some ways. The caller is usually a sexually inadequate person, who can have sexual interchanges with women through this apparently safe (though progressively less so as detection mechanisms are improved) method. His pleasure is also derived from eliciting embarrassment and intense emotion. Telephone companies recommend that the recipient of an obscene call remain calm and either hang up immediately or alert the operator by means of a second telephone to trace the call to its source and have the caller arrested.

In a similar category are men who try to shock women by using obscenities or telling off-color jokes. There is, of course, no absolute criterion for determining what is obscene. The important factor is not the word used or the content of the story but its intended impact on others.

Sadomasochism

Even though our individual and collective security depends upon understanding and defending against aggression, we know relatively

little about it. To what extent is it an inborn drive? If it is learned, how is it learned? There is a vast literature on the topic, but few conclusions have been generally accepted. This uncertainty applies also to the interrelation of sex and aggression.

The sex act entails a certain degree of force. In the animal world sexual encounters include varying amounts of force. Nips and bites are often inflicted (usually by the male) during copulation; among skunks and minks such biting may be savage. Most sexually active people make judicious use of force in lovemaking but rarely to the point of causing pain. Scratching and "love bites" do occur between ardent lovers, but they are inflicted in the heat of passion and are not calculated to make the partner suffer. As noted earlier, the threshold of pain perception is raised during sexual excitement, so that one is less aware of pain.

Aggressive fantasies are also quite common. They may take the form of dreams, daydreams, or fleeting thoughts (see Chapter 9). Most often they revolve around the theme of rape. A man may harbor such thoughts about a variety of women, and the imagined responses may range from playful resistance to humiliating submission. Women, too, have such fantasies, often mixed with fear but not without elements of enjoyment.

Certain spectator sports have been compared to the cruel gladiatorial combats of Roman times. The responses of most people who enjoy such spectacles are not overtly sexual: Only a rare individual has an erection while watching a particularly bloody boxing match. It is, nevertheless, worthwhile to speculate on whether or not such public wallowing in violence serves deep-seated needs that may be sexually tinged.

Although the term is often used loosely, "sadism" as applied to sexual deviation is restricted to instances in which the individual needs to inflict pain in order to achieve sexual

---

[38]Gebhard *et al.* (1965), p. 394.

satisfaction. Masochism, also frequently used loosely, is applied to instances in which the individual must be subjected to pain in order to achieve such satisfaction.[39] These two aber-

rations will be discussed jointly, for they are mirror images of the same phenomenon. Although occasionally innocent people are harmed by sadists or inadvertently satisfy the masochistic needs of others, in general sadists and masochists use each other as partners.

As sexual deviations, sadism and masochism tend to be discrete. That is to say, a sadist does not wish alternately to whip someone and then to be whipped himself (see Figure 11.6). At an unconscious level, however, the conflicts that result in one or the other of these impulses may be quite similar. In psychodynamic terms it is therefore common to think of sadomasochism

[39]These terms are derived from the names of two historical figures who wrote on these respective themes. The first was the eighteenth-century French nobleman Donatien-Alphonse-François, Marquis de Sade; the second was the Austrian Leopold von Sacher-Masoch (1836–1905), also a nobleman of rather involved ancestry. The works, as well as the biographies, of both men are widely known. For a summary of both lives, see Ellis, H. (1942), Vol. I, Part Two, pp. 116–119. This volume also has an extensive review of the historical and anthropological literature in the section entitled "Love and Pain" (pp. 66–188).

Figure 11.6. Mauron, *The Cully Flaug'd* (eighteenth-century illustration for *Fanny Hill*).

as a form of behavior in which sex and pain become pathologically attached.

It is neither possible nor necessary to catalogue the infinite variety of obvious, as well as startling, devices that have been imagined and sometimes (though very rarely) actually used in sadomasochistic sexual encounters.[40] The depredations of Nero and Caligula, as well as those of lesser deviants and tyrants, are well (perhaps too well) known. We shall therefore briefly describe only those sadomasochistic practices that are still fairly commonly encountered.

Both in this country and abroad a person can pay to have himself whipped. This type of service is usually provided by specialized prostitutes and is more likely to be found in large cities. It is far more difficult to find someone who will submit to such treatment for money, for there are certainly easier ways to earn a living.

The overwhelming majority of sadomasochistically oriented people restrict their activities to reading special magazines that feature either cartoons or photographs of women dressed in leather and spike-heeled shoes trying to look menacing as they gag, bind, chain, whip, and variously "torture" their victims. Red paint is substituted for blood in the color photographs. The readership of these magazines is largely harmless.

Sadists who are more apt to act out their impulses are another matter. At their mildest sadistic men merely soil women ("saliromania") or cut their hair off. At their worst they may rape, mutilate, and kill.

The masochist poses no serious threat to society and is rarely arrested. Even though women are believed to be naturally somewhat masochistic, the sexual deviants in this category are also usually male.

Psychiatric and forensic writings are replete with case histories of sadomasochism, but literature conveys better the atmosphere of such activities, as illustrated in the following parody from *Myra Breckenridge*. The narrator is Letitia Van Allen:

> It began upstairs when he tore my clothes off in the closet. Then he raped me standing up with a metal clothes hanger twisted around my neck, choking me. I could hardly breathe. It was exquisite! Then one thing led to another. Those small attentions a girl like me cherishes . . . a lighted cigarette stubbed out on my derriere, a complete beating with his great thick heavy leather belt, a series of ravenous bites up and down the inner thighs, drawing blood. All the usual fun things, except that this time he went beyond anything he had tried before. This time he dragged me to the head of the stairs and raped me from behind, all the while beating me with his boot. Then, just as I was about to reach the big O, shrieking with pleasure, he hurled me down the stairs, so that my orgasm and the final crash with the banister occurred simultaneously. I fainted with joy! Without a doubt, it was the completion of my life.[41]

Rape

Rape is an ancient phenomenon. Some men use force only to achieve their sexual aims (usually coitus). They are not interested in hurting the women. Other rapists use more force than necessary and it is sometimes difficult to tell whether the primary purpose of the attack is sexual or aggressive. Even though there is usually a sadistic element in rape, rapists may be differentiated in general terms from sadists if sadism is defined more strictly as a

---

[40] Another whole sphere of behavior is generally known under the title "psychic," or "moral," sadism and masochism. It involves the inflicting and suffering of psychological pain, with concomitant sexual pleasure dimly perceived.

---

[41] Vidal (1968), p. 270.

deviation rather than as a character trait. For example, most sadists rely on masochists or prostitutes, whereas rapists assault unwilling victims. Also the rapist usually has overt sexual aims (most often coitus or oral-genital contact), whereas the sadist may be content with the pleasure obtained from inflicting pain with or without genital involvement. Rapists are generally younger men (the average age is 24.5 years at the time of first offense), and their victims are young women (the average age is 24 years, but 3 percent are 50 years old or older). Alcohol figures prominently in more than half these attacks.

Even though accounts of sexual assaults in the press tend to be sensationalized, rapists do constitute a significant threat to women, par-

ticularly in large cities. Very rarely do we read about a group of women forcing a man to have coitus with them at knife point. A more serious threat to men is the young woman who goes along with the sex act half-heartedly and then decides that she has been raped.

The sex murderer is a dangerous and terrifying person (Figure 11.7). He usually tortures and sexually assaults his victim before killing her. Such men, who are very seriously deranged (often psychotic) may also mutilate the corpses or have further sexual contact with them. Every decade brings a few of these "lust murderers," who keep entire cities in chilling terror until apprehended.[42]

What is it that drives people to violent sexual activities with unwilling partners? Unfortunately most answers are only conjectural. The personality and family profiles drawn by Gebhard and his associates are revealing but do not permit conclusions about causation. For instance, heterosexual aggressors against children tend to be intellectually dull and the victims of broken and unhappy homes. They have few and poor relationships with adult females and rely heavily on prostitutes for sexual partners. They tend to use alcohol excessively. Offenders against minors (twelve to fifteen years old) have equally unfortunate home backgrounds, and many have criminal records. They are usually amoral, aggressive young men who seek whatever immediate gratification they can find, regardless of the ultimate consequences. The aggressor against adults is similar in his unconcern about the welfare and rights of others. Most such men have generally sociopathic orientations. They violate women in the same way that they help themselves to other people's property and use whatever force is necessary to do so. Some are flagrantly dis-

Figure 11.7. Franz Masareel, *Sex Murder*. Book illustration, *Ginzberg L'Enfer*, p. 185.

[42]For two relatively recent cases, see Freeman (1955), *Catch Me Before I Kill More*, and Frank (1966), *The Boston Strangler*.

turbed, but a few are ordinary people who occasionally act impulsively or misjudge situations.

To understand sexual violence, we must therefore understand the overall problem of sociopathy and criminality. The mixture of sex and aggression is but one facet of this problem. People who need to inflict or suffer pain in order to obtain sexual gratification may be wrestling with various unconscious conflicts. For instance, some people who feel that sex is bad and dirty must first suffer in order to enjoy it (or must inflict pain as punishment). The conflict that psychoanalysts believe is central to all perversions, castration anxiety, is thus also relevant to sadism: The cutter of women's hair may be symbolically castrating others in defense against his own fears. Freud's study "A Child Is Being Beaten"[43] is a classic in the psychoanalytic literature on sadomasochism.

---

[43] Freud (1957-1964), Vol. XVII, pp. 175-204.

As everyone experiences physical ill health and mental turmoil at one time or another, it is realistic to view a certain amount of illness as a natural part of life. In addition to the ordinary wear and tear on our bodies and minds, we are all subject to certain common ailments, as well as to some less common and more serious disorders. Some knowledge of these matters is helpful in allaying worry and discomfort, as well as in alerting us to the presence of danger signals.

A vast number of disorders may affect the sex organs and sexual functioning. Furthermore, the sex organs may suffer secondary effects from general systemic diseases. Several medical specialties are involved in the treatment of these various disorders. Gynecology deals with disorders of the female sexual or reproductive system. Most male disorders are treated by urologists. When syphilis was more prevalent and more difficult to treat, syphilology was a separate medical specialty. Because syphilis has many skin manifestations, these syphilologists often were also dermatologists, or skin specialists. Finally, because most sexual malfunctions (like impotence and frigidity) have no demonstrable physical basis and are believed to result from psychological conflicts, psychiatrists often treat them.

We shall deal primarily with four types of sexual disorder in this chapter: first, some very common, mild, but nevertheless irritating conditions; second, venereal diseases; third, certain serious conditions the early recognition of which may save lives; and, finally, primary disturbances of sexual functioning.

Minor Disorders

A very common minor disorder of the female reproductive organs is leukorrhea, characterized by a whitish vaginal discharge, which almost every woman experiences at some time in her life. Leukorrhea is not a discrete disease entity but rather a condition that has multiple causes. Infectious organisms commonly cause it; a protozoan called *Trichomonas vaginalis* accounts for about one-third of these conditions. A man may harbor this organism in the urethra or prostate gland without symptoms, and it is therefore customary to treat sexual partners simultaneously with a drug called metronidazole (*Flagyl*) to prevent reinfection.

A yeast-like organism called *Candida albicans* is another frequent cause of vaginal irritation and discharge. Candida infections are particularly common among diabetic women and during pregnancy. Although not usually serious, they can be rather annoying, especially when they involve itching skin on the thighs.

CHAPTER

12

SEXUAL DISORDERS

They are sometimes difficult to cure but usually respond to treatment with mystatin (*Mycostatin*) suppositories.

Leukorrhea may also be related to alterations in hormone balance (during pregnancy or menopause) or to irritation from foreign bodies (like a contraceptive device). Irritating chemicals in commercial douche preparations may also cause vaginal discharges. For that matter, frequent douching of any sort is likely to increase the production of vaginal mucus. Most gynecologists do not recommend regular douching for healthy women. For those women who wish to douche occasionally (as after menstruation) a mildly acid solution (for example, two tablespoons of vinegar in a quart of water) is usually recommended. Alkaline (soda) douches should be avoided because they interfere with the normal chemical balance of the vagina.

There is no male counterpart to leukorrhea. Urethral discharges in males almost always result from venereal disease. Frequent urination and difficulty initiating urination may be psychologically caused, but if they persist a physician should be consulted.

Venereal Diseases

The term "venereal" comes from the Latin *venereus*, "pertaining to Venus," the goddess of love. Venereal diseases are propagated through sexual intercourse. We shall discuss the two diseases that account for the vast majority of cases: *gonorrhea* and *syphilis*. It is tragic that, though ready cures for both these diseases are available in the form of penicillin and other antibiotics, incidence has been rising in recent years, particularly among young people who do not avail themselves of proper treatment.[1]

Gonorrhea

Gonorrhea is an infection caused by the bacterium *Neisseria gonorrhoeae* and can affect a variety of mucous-membrane tissues. This microorganism does not survive without the living conditions (temperature, moisture, and so on) provided by the human body and is transmitted from human being to human being during contact with infected mucous membranes in sexual intercourse. There has never been a documented case of gonorrhea contracted from a public toilet seat (or from shaking hands with an infected individual).

Ancient Chinese and Egyptian manuscripts refer to a contagious urethral discharge that was probably gonorrhea. The ancient Jews and Greeks thought that the discharge represented an involuntary loss of semen. The Greek physician Galen (A.D. 130–201) is credited with having coined the term "gonorrhea" from the Greek words for "seed" and "to flow." For centuries gonorrhea and syphilis were believed to be the same disease, but by the nineteenth century a series of experiments had demonstrated that they were two separate diseases. In the most dramatic of these experiments a physician inoculated himself with gonorrheal pus and failed to develop the symptoms of syphilis. In 1879 A. L. S. Neisser identified the bacterium that causes this disease and now bears his name.

In males the primary symptom of gonorrhea (known also as the "clap" or "strain") is a purulent, yellowish urethral discharge. The usual site of infection is the urethra, and the condition is called *gonorrheal urethritis*. The discharge from the tip of the penis appears

---

[1] In California, for instance, there were 14,697 *reported* cases of gonorrhea in 1955 and 35,700 reported cases in 1964. There were 6,802 reported cases of syphilis in 1955, 12,191 in 1964. The incidence has continued to rise since then, and no one knows how many additional cases go unreported (*Control of Communicable Diseases in California*, California State Department of Public Health, 1966).

within three to ten days after contraction of the disease, and is usually accompanied by burning during urination and a sensation of itching within the urethra. The inflammation may subside within two or three weeks without treatment or it may persist in chronic form. The infection may spread up the genitourinary tract to involve the prostate gland, seminal vesicles, bladder, and kidneys. In 1 percent of cases the disease spreads to the joints of the knees, ankles, wrists, or elbows, causing gonorrheal arthritis, a very painful condition.

More than 90 percent of cases clear up immediately with prompt treatment (usually penicillin by injection). The discharge often disappears within twelve hours after treatment, though a thin flow persists for a few days in 10–15 percent of patients.

Gonorrhea can usually be prevented by one of two methods: use of a condom and thorough washing of the sex organs and genital area with bactericidal soap or solution after sexual exposure or a single dose of penicillin or other appropriate antibiotic within a few hours after exposure.

In females the symptoms of gonorrhea may be mild or absent in the early stages. The primary site of infection is usually the cervix, which becomes inflamed (*cervicitis*). The only early symptom may be a yellowish vaginal discharge. Not all such discharges are gonorrheal, however. Microscopic examination and bacterial culture of the discharge are required for definitive diagnosis. Treatment with penicillin is usually effective if the disease is recognized and treated promptly.

If left untreated, however, the infection may spread upward through the uterus to involve the fallopian tubes and other pelvic organs. Often this spread occurs during menstruation, when the uterine cavity is more susceptible to gonorrheal invasion. Acute symptoms—severe pelvic pain, abdominal distension and tenderness, vomiting, and fever—may then appear during or just after menstruation. Again treatment with antibiotics usually brings about a complete cure, but if the disease is not treated or is inadequately treated, a chronic inflammation of the uterine tubes (*chronic salpingitis*) ensues. This condition is accompanied by formation of scar tissue and obstruction of the tubes and constitutes a common cause of infertility in females, particularly those who frequently contract gonorrhea, for example, prostitutes.

Until recently a common cause of blindness in children was *ophthalmia neonatorum*, a gonorrheal infection of the eyes acquired during passage through infected birth canals. Instilling penicillin ointment or silver nitrate drops into the eyes of all newborn babies is now compulsory and has helped to eradicate this disease.

Syphilis

It is commonly believed, though the belief has not been thoroughly substantiated, that syphilis was brought to Europe by Columbus and his crew after their first voyage to the West Indies. It is true that, within a few years after Columbus' return in 1493 from his first voyage to the New World, epidemics of syphilis spread across Europe with devastating effects. History suggests that the Spaniards introduced the disease to the Italians while fighting beside the troops of Alfonso II of Naples. Then in 1495 an army of mercenaries fighting for Charles VIII of France conquered Naples and engaged in a bit of celebrating before returning to France, Germany, Switzerland, Austria, and England, taking the disease along. By 1496 syphilis was rampant in Paris, leading to the passage of strict laws banishing from the city anyone suffering from it. In 1497 all syphilitics in Edinburgh were banished to an island near Leith. In 1498 Vasco de Gama and his Portugese crew carried the disease to India, and from there it spread to China; the first epidemic in that country was reported in 1505. Outbreaks of syphilis in Japan later followed the visits of European vessels.

The New World origin of syphilis is confirmed by the discovery of definite syphilitic lesions in the bones of Indians from the pre-Columbian period in the Americas. There are no comparable findings in the bones of ancient Egyptians, nor are there any clear descriptions of the disease in the medical literature of the Old World before Columbus. Physicians in the early sixteenth century did not have a name for the disease, but the Spaniards called it the "disease of Española" (present-day Haiti). The Italians called it "the Spanish disease," and the French called it "the Neapolitan disease." As it spread to many countries, it acquired the name *morbus Gallicus,* the "French sickness," a name that persisted for about a century. The term "syphilis" was introduced in 1530 by the Italian physician Girolamo Fracastoro, who wrote a poem in Latin about a shepherd boy named Syphilus who caught the disease as a

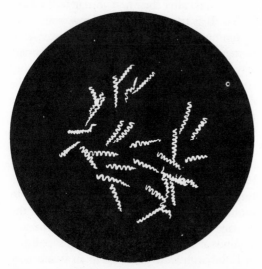

Figure 12.1. Typical organisms of *Treponema pallidum* from tissue fluid in a dark field. The length of each is about ten microns. From Jawetz et al., *Review of medical microbiology,* 9th ed. (Los Altos, Calif.: Lange Medical Publications, 1970), p. 220. Reprinted by permission.

punishment from the gods (for having insulted Apollo). As this name was ethnically neutral, it gradually became accepted as the proper term for the dread disease.

Various historical figures have been afflicted by syphilis, as indicated by records of their physical appearances and symptoms. Columbus himself died in 1506 with symptoms typical of advanced syphilis, involving the heart, extremities, and brain. It is generally accepted that the first four children of Catherine of Aragon, first wife of Henry VIII of England, all died of congenital syphilis, leaving only one survivor, the future "Bloody Mary." (Mary died at age forty-two, of complications of congenital syphilis, it appears). Henry's disappointment over not having a male heir undoubtedly played a role in his insistence upon legalizing his second and subsequent marriages, which led to the break between England and Rome.

It was not until 1905 that the microorganism that causes syphilis was identified. German investigator Fritz Richard Schaudinn identified and named *Spirochaeta pallidum,* describing it as a "slender, very pale, corkscrew-like object" (see Figure 12.1). (The name *Treponema pallidum* is now the technically correct one, though "spirochete" is more commonly used.)

In its late stages syphilis can involve virtually any organ or tissue of the body, producing myriad symptoms similar to those of other diseases, which led the famous physician Sir William Osler to call it the "Great Imitator." The early stage, however, is marked by a primary skin lesion at the site of contact and known as a *chancre.* The chancre (pronounced "*shank*-er") is a hard, round ulcer with raised edges and is usually painless. In the male it commonly appears somewhere on the penis, on the scrotum, or in the pubic area (see Figure 12.2). In the female it usually appears on the external genitals (see Figure 12.3), but it may appear in the vagina or on the cervix and thus escape detection. It may also appear on the

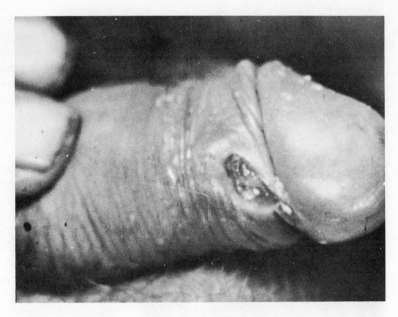

Figure 12.2. A chancre of the penis. Note the raised, hard appearance of the ulcer. From A. I. Dodson and J. E. Hill, *Synopsis of genitourinary disease,* 7th ed. (St. Louis, Mo.: The C. V. Mosby Co., 1962), p. 201. Reprinted by permission.

mouth or elsewhere on the skin. As syphilitic infections in men may begin at other sites than the penis, condoms do not necessarily provide protection against them. And, as it is usually not apparent that someone is a carrier of syphilis, the only sure way to avoid the disease is to know before sexual contact whether or not the anticipated partner has had a negative blood test for syphilis—an unlikely question to ask as a prelude to making love. The point is, however, that casual sexual contacts are more likely to expose one to syphilis (or other venereal disease), for, statistically, the greater the number of sexual partners, the greater the probability of encountering someone who is a carrier. For example, prostitutes have higher venereal disease rates than the general population.

The chancre appears two to four weeks after contraction of the disease and, if not treated, usually disappears in several weeks, leading to the illusion that the individual has recovered from whatever he thought he had. Actually this chancre is usually only the first stage in the development of a chronic illness that may

ultimately be fatal. Treatment with penicillin when the chancre occurs cures most cases, and relapses after proper treatment are rare.

When syphilis is untreated, the "secondary stage" becomes manifest within weeks after the healing of the chancre. There is usually a generalized skin rash, which is transient and may or may not be accompanied by such vague symptoms as headache, fever, indigestion, sore throat, and muscle or joint pain. Many people do not associate these symptoms with the primary chancre.

After the secondary stage, all symptoms disappear, and the so-called "latent period" begins. During this period, which may last for years, the spirochetes burrow into various tissues, particularly blood vessels, the central nervous system (brain and spinal cord), and bones.

About 50 percent of untreated cases reach the final, or "tertiary," stage of syphilis, in which heart failure, ruptured major blood vessels, loss of muscular control and sense of balance, blindness, deafness, and severe mental disturbances can occur. Ultimately the disease

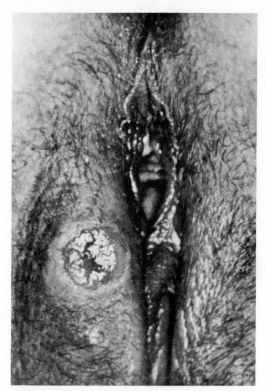

Figure 12.3. A large chancre on the labia majora. Primary syphilis in the female is not usually this obvious. From R. S. Weiss and H. L. Joseph, *Syphilis* (Baltimore: Williams & Wilkins, 1951), p. 73. Copyright © 1951 by The Williams & Wilkins Co., and reprinted by permission.

Children with congenital syphilis are prone to impaired vision and hearing, as well as to certain deformities of the bones and teeth. Treatment with penicillin can alleviate many of the manifestations of congenital syphilis if it is initiated early in infancy.

Cystitis

Cystitis is an infection or inflammation of the bladder. It is not a venereal disease, but its occurrence in women is sometimes associated with sexual activity. (It is so common among newlywed women, for instance, that the term "honeymoon cystitis" has been used to describe it.)

The bacteria that invade the bladder through the urethra are not usually caught from the sexual partner but are normally present on the genital skin of the infected person. Women are more prone to cystitis because of their significantly shorter urethras, compared to those of males. The primary symptom of cystitis is frequent and painful ("burning") urination. It may subside spontaneously in a few days, but it is advisable to receive proper antibiotic treatment because untreated infections may spread from the bladder to the kidneys, causing a much more serious condition—*pyelonephritis.*

Cancer of the Sex Organs

The most common cancers in both sexes involve organs of the reproductive system.

Of the Breast

Cancer of the breast[2] is the most common form of cancer in women. It is extremely rare in women under age twenty-five but increases

can be fatal, but treatment with penicillin even at late stages may be beneficial, depending upon the extent to which vital organs have already been damaged.

Syphilis can be transmitted to the fetus through the placenta; hence the mandatory blood tests to identify untreated cases of the disease before marriage and before the birth of a child. Treatment with penicillin during the first half of pregnancy can prevent congenital syphilis in the child. Nine out of ten pregnant women who have untreated syphilis either miscarry or bear stillborn children or living children with congenital syphilis.

---

[2]Although not technically sex organs, the breasts are part of the reproductive system and are highly sensitive to sex hormones, as noted in Chapter 4.

steadily in each decade thereafter. Ultimately, at least 5 percent of all women develop cancer of the breast. The cause of this disease is unknown, but it is clear that breast cancers respond to sex hormones. The spread of this cancer is thus accelerated by increased estrogen secretion during pregnancy. We noted in Chapter 6 the apprehension of some investigators that the long-term ingestion of hormones in birth-control pills may stimulate the growth of breast cancer, but a definitive answer to this question will not be available until sufficient women have taken the pills for twenty years, permitting follow-up studies about 1980.

Removal of the ovaries is often beneficial in treatment of breast cancer, as is treatment with the male sex hormone testosterone. Of course, the primary treatment is surgical removal of the breast (*mastectomy*).

Cancer of the breast can be fatal, but with early diagnosis and treatment the prognosis is much more favorable. About 45 percent of patients with cancer of the breast are still alive five years after the initial diagnosis, and about 30 percent survive ten years or more. Early diagnosis and treatment are often missed because cancer of the breast begins with a painless lump in the breast, which may go unnoticed for a long time, until spread of the disease produces other symptoms. Hence the need for breast examinations at regular intervals and surgical biopsy of any questionable lump.

Of the Cervix

Cancer of the cervix is the second most common type in women. About 2 percent of all women ultimately develop it. It is very rare before age twenty, but the incidence rises over the next several decades. The average age of women with cancer of the cervix is forty-five. This disease is more common in women who have been sexually active and have borne children. The disease is very rare among Jewish women, which has given rise to the theory that

smegma, which tends to collect under the foreskins of uncircumcised males (Jewish males are usually circumcised) may play a part in the development of cancer of the cervix.

Cancer of the cervix may present no symptoms for five or ten years, and during this period treatment is extremely successful. The well-publicized Pap smear test (which women should undergo annually) is the best means now available for identifying cancer of the cervix in the early stages (when it is most susceptible to treatment). From the patient's point of view, the Pap smear is an extremely simple test to perform. The physician simply takes a specimen of cervical mucus with a cotton-tipped swab and makes a "smear" of this material on a glass slide. The procedure is quick, simple, and painless. The smear is then stained and examined under a laboratory microscope for the presence of cancerous cells.

As cancer begins to invade surrounding tissues, irregular vaginal bleeding or a chronic bloody vaginal discharge develops. Treatment is less successful when the cancer has reached this stage. If treatment (surgery, radiation, or both) is instituted before the cancer spreads beyond the cervix, the five-year survival rate is about 80 percent, but it drops precipitately as the disease reaches other organs in the pelvis. The overall five-year survival rate for cancer of the cervix (including all stages of the disease) is about 35 percent. The comparable figure for ten years is about 26 percent.

Of the Prostate

Cancer of the prostate is the most common form of cancer in men. Nevertheless, it rarely causes death. (A study of causes of deaths of British men over fifty years old showed that cancer of the prostate was the cause in only 1.38 percent of the sample.) There are two reasons for this low mortality rate. First, cancer of the prostate is rare before age fifty and uncommon before age sixty, 70–80 percent of cases occur between the ages of sixty and eighty, and about 25 percent of men in the ninth decade of life have cancer of the prostate. By that time they are likely to die of other causes, like heart disease, rather than of cancer. Second, most cancers of the prostate are relatively small and grow very slowly. Only a minority spread rapidly to other organs.

Cancer of the prostate, like cancer of the breast, is responsive to sex hormones. Androgens stimulate its growth, and surgical castration (removal of the testicles) is thus part of the treatment for this disease. Furthermore, estrogens slow the growth of prostatic cancer and are often given as part of the treatment, again highlighting the physiological antagonism between estrogen and androgen (compare the use of testosterone in treatment of cancer of the breast). Whereas administration of androgen to women causes "masculinization" (beard growth, deepening of the voice, enlargement of the clitoris) and increases the sex drive, administration of estrogen to men may cause "feminization" (enlargement of the breasts), impotence, and loss of libido.

The initial symptoms of prostatic cancer are similar to those in benign enlargement of the prostate (see Chapter 4). They include frequent urination, particularly at night; difficulties initiating urination; and difficulties emptying the bladder. These symptoms largely result from partial obstruction of the urethra by the malignant growth. Early in the course of the disease libido may increase, and frequent erections (related to increased androgen secretion?) may occur. Later on, however, there is usually a loss of sexual functioning. A tentative diagnosis of cancer of the prostate can usually be made on the basis of a rectal examination (palpation of the prostate through the rectum), the history of symptoms, and certain laboratory tests. A prostate examination should certainly be part of an annual physical checkup for any

man over fifty, for, as with other cancers, the prognosis is much more optimistic when it is diagnosed and treated early.

Of the Penis

Cancer of the penis is rare in the United States, accounting for about 2 percent of all cancer in males. It is interesting, however, because of its apparent relation to circumcision. Cancer of the penis almost never occurs among Jews, who undergo ritual circumcision within the first two weeks of life, as do most Christians in this country. This disease is also rare, though somewhat less so, among Muslim men, who usually undergo circumcision before puberty. On the other hand, in areas of the world where circumcision is not common, cancer of the penis is much more prevalent. It accounts for about 18 percent of all malignancies in Far Eastern countries, for instance. The usual explanation, though it has not been confirmed, is that circumcision prevents accumulation of potentially carcinogenic secretions, or possibly a virus, around the tip of the penis (the usual site of this type of tumor).

Sexual Malfunctioning

Competence in sexual intercourse is not an all-or-none phenomenon, and there is no absolute scale on which to evaluate it. No one is expected to be able to copulate at will with anyone, anywhere, anytime. Normal functioning entails considerable fluctuation in sexual desire, and it is expected that performance will occasionally falter. Beyond a certain ill-defined boundary, however, the extent or frequency of failure—whether at the level of desire, performance, or gratification—must be considered malfunction.

Probably no other human disturbance entails more silent suffering. Even when a person marshals enough courage to seek help, it is difficult to know where to turn. As no one dies of sexual distress (though impotence does drive some people to suicide) and fertility may not be disturbed, the main and apparently tolerable loss seems to be erotic gratification. Actually the toll in unhappy marriages and unfulfilled lives is incalculable.

Types of Sexual Malfunctioning

Difficulties in sexual intercourse are not discrete disease entities, even though the specific labels attached to some of them may give that impression. Rather, they belong on a continuum in which physical, psychological, and social influences interact. Problems of men and women should also be viewed jointly, for many difficulties in sexual intercourse are caused by interpersonal difficulties.

The manifestations of sexual apathy and lack of gratification in coitus are similar in the two sexes, but the difficulties in actual performance differ because of the peculiarities of the sexual apparatus of each sex. Among men the primary problems are impotence and inability to delay ejaculation. If an erection is achieved and sustained there is very rarely any difficulty in achieving orgasm, and pain is almost never an issue. For women the main difficulties are failure to attain orgasms and painful intercourse.

Apathy. It is expected of healthy men and women that they will wish to engage in sexual intercourse with someone, sometime, someplace, even though they may elect not to carry out this wish or may be prevented from doing so. Beyond this stipulation, judgments of the intensity of sexual desire are arbitrary (see Chapter 7).

A most important factor in sustaining sexual desire is the satisfaction gained from coitus itself. If, for whatever reason, a person finds the experience distasteful, painful, or merely tedious, the incentive to join in it is, of course, much weakened.

In its mildest form, sexual apathy is simple indifference. A person forgoes sexual intercourse for extended periods because he or she does not feel like having it, despite propitious circumstances and willing partners. Sometimes the person is so preoccupied with other events and activities that sex is understandably set aside for awhile. But it is also possible that these other activities are at least unconsciously aimed at avoiding sex. In treating marital difficulties it is necessary to determine when a person is making unreasonable demands upon a harassed marital partner and when a sexually apathetic partner is deliberately becoming exhausted before bedtime.

More often, sexual apathy is part of a general listlessness, perhaps resulting from concrete external causes or from a general depression reflecting internal conflicts. Sexual apathy is not restricted to mere listlessness, however. A person may feel consciously uneasy about coitus and may actively seek to avoid it. Perhaps the experience has been uncomfortable and dissatisfying, or feelings of guilt and shame may have overbalanced the pleasure and joy in the act. Some people actually dread coitus, out of disgust or fear.

The Effects of Sex on Health. The beliefs that one has about the effects of sex on health often exert an important influence on one's sexual functioning. Therefore, we shall briefly digress at this point to examine a number of longstanding popular notions. While many of these notions have been formally discarded, the same basic concerns influence current thinking.

Man seems always to have attributed peculiar significance to semen, and Hippocrates, among other authorities, commented on its "precious" character. Pythagoras called it "the flower of the blood." It has also been considered an emanation of the brain and even a product of the soul, rather than of the body (Epicurus). As late as the turn of the twentieth century medical textbooks, though disavowing these notions, seriously declared that loss of an ounce of semen equaled a loss of forty ounces of blood.[3]

From such premises it would be easy to conclude that masturbation is a wasteful and debilitating practice and that "excessive" intercourse leads to ill health. Criteria for "excessiveness" and "ill effects" have, of course, varied. The following excerpt is from a medieval document by Moses ben Maimon (Maimonides; 1135–1204), but we need not search long to find similar notions even in current medical circles:

> Effusion of semen represents the strength of the body and its life, and the light of the eyes. Whenever it (semen) is emitted to excess, the body becomes consumed, its strength terminates, and its life perishes. . . . He who immerses himself in sexual intercourse will be assailed by (premature) aging. His strength will wane, his eyes will weaken, and a bad odor will emit from his mouth and his armpits. . . . His teeth will fall out and many maladies other than these will afflict him. The wise physicians have stated that one in a thousand dies from other illnesses and the (remaining 999 in the thousand) from excessive sexual intercourse. Therefore, a man must be cautious in this matter if he wishes to live wholesomely. He should not cohabit unless his body is healthy and very strong and he experiences many involuntary erections. . . . Such a person requires coitus and it is therapeutic for him to have sexual intercourse.[4]

There is no evidence that in a person of average health sexual activity leads to either debility, premature aging, or ill health. Furthermore, for all practical purposes, "excessive"

sexual experience is impossible: Sooner or later the person will be sated, his body will respond less readily, and his activity will come to an end. Debauchery may involve a great deal of sex, but it also involves excessive drinking, eating, fatigue, and insomnia: No one questions that these factors undermine health.

Interestingly, the very opposite view—that regular sexual outlets are essential to good health—has also been popular. There may be much to be said for regular sexual outlets, but their indispensability to physical health remains to be demonstrated.

The problem is entirely different for older or sick people. Orgasm places considerable strain on the cardiovascular system: People who would react adversely to any kind of exertion would also suffer from the physiological strain of the sexual activity. Occasionally, increased blood pressure may cause a stroke. Death as a result of heart attack or rupture of a cerebral vessel during coitus also occurs, but rarely. With caution and common sense, people in less than perfect health can enjoy sex without adverse effects. Even heart-transplant patients have resumed sexual activity only months following surgery.

Coital Inadequacy in Males. Disturbances in male performance are generally called "impotence" ("lacking of power"). In addition to the simple inability to have an erection, the term covers partial or weak erections, inability to sustain an erection long enough to penetrate, and orgasm before or right after entry (premature ejaculation) as well as the very rare condition in which an erect penis fails to ejaculate (ejaculatory impotence). The last two conditions can also be appropriately considered as disturbances of ejaculation. Men who are potent in autoerotic or other noncoital activities but unable to consummate coitus are also considered impotent. It is customary to separate primary from secondary impotence, though

---

[3]Parke (1906), p. 379.

[4]Maimon, in Rosner (1965), p. 372.

such distinctions are not always consistent. The most common one is between men who have never been able to have an erection that would permit coitus (primary impotence) and those who are impotent only in some situations.[5]

Again there is no absolute scale against which to evaluate male performance. Obviously a man must keep his erection long enough to penetrate and reach a climax. Beyond such minimal criteria, judgments can be only relative. A penis that is powerless in one instance may perform adequately in a better-lubricated vagina, a relaxed introitus, a more accessible position, and so on.

The length of intercourse preceding orgasm is also not always related to the gratification obtained by either partner. Generally, of course, the longer that a man can delay ejaculation, the greater is the opportunity for the woman to achieve orgasm. But, again, some women may be gratified by practically any potent man, whereas others would not respond no matter how long the man could continue. Judgments of male potency must, therefore, be based on performance with a hypothetical woman of average receptivity and ordinary responsiveness. The more practical question in marital conflicts is not whether or not a man is sufficiently potent in the abstract but whether or not he is potent enough to satisfy his wife.

In view of these ambiguities, accurate assessment of the prevalence of impotence is impossible. Most figures quoted in surveys include only individuals with long-standing and nearly complete impotence.

Erectile impotence affects about 1 of every 100 males under thirty-five years of age, but the inadequacy is chronic and totally incapacitating in only some of them. At seventy years of age about one in four males is impotent. The

progressive decline of potency with age is fairly general, though some men retain their potency into old age. Failure to ejaculate is very rare and affects no more than 1 in 700 men of all ages.

Impotence resulting from aging or from actual physiological disturbances tends to be generalized. Impotence resulting from psychological causes may also be general, or it may be specific to certain situations and interactions. Some men are impotent only during coitus with their wives, with women other than their wives, or with women with certain types of physical appearance or personality. Sometimes it is the inhibitions that are specific, but, conversely, sometimes erection is possible only if equally special conditions are fulfilled. These conditions may be relatively simple (total darkness) or may revolve around such intricate rituals as the woman's wearing black stockings fastened to a special type of garter and so on.

Erectile potency and sexual desire usually go together. The problem is worse, of course, when desire persists despite physical failure. In the rare condition known as "priapism" (see Chapter 3), the opposite is true—erections do not reflect sexual desire and may actually be painful.

It is difficult for most men to imagine a more humiliating and despairing problem than impotence before old age. The damage is far more than mere loss of sexual pleasure. Male notions of masculinity and even personal worth are so closely linked to potency that any malfunctioning is almost certain to shatter self-esteem.

Premature ejaculation may or may not be associated with failures of erection. Armed with the finding that three out of four men reach orgasm within two minutes of intromission and that most male animals do so even sooner, the Kinsey group made light of premature ejaculation as a form of sexual malfunctioning.

Although it may be impossible to set exact time limits to define normal functioning, there

---

[5]For clinical purposes a man may be considered secondarily impotent if his attempts at coitus fail in one out of four instances. Masters and Johnson (1970), p. 157.

is no mistaking the fact that a significant number of men (and their partners) complain of inability to delay ejaculation until some measure of deliberate mutual enjoyment has been obtained. It is small comfort to them to realize that subhuman primates ejaculate even sooner. Especially when their own orgasms may even precede penetration, the whole point of sexual intercourse may seem lost. The impotent man has been derided in the literature of many lands:

> When such a man has a bout with a woman, he does not do his business with vigor and in a manner to give her enjoyment. . . . He gets upon her before she has begun to long for pleasure, and then he introduces with infinite trouble a member soft and nerveless. Scarcely has he commenced when he is already done for; he makes one or two movements, and then sinks upon the woman's breast to spend his sperm; and that is the most he can do. This done he withdraws his affair, and makes all haste to get down again from her. . . . Qualities like these are no recommendation with women.[6]

Coital Inadequacy in Females. Disturbances in female sexual performance are generally called "frigidity," though the difficulty may include sensitivity to pain, as well as sexual coldness or unresponsiveness. Problems of frigidity, like those of impotence, can be either general or restricted to specific situations, partners, and so on. Women, however, feel less pressure to achieve orgasm at coitus as frequently as men do, partly because coitus can take place when a female is unresponsive but not when the male is and also because women continue to be sexually subservient in Western society. This situation is changing, however (see Chapter 18).

In its mildest form, frigidity is simply failure to attain orgasm, even though coitus itself is pleasurable. Unless they are made to feel inadequate, many such women do not even feel that they have sexual difficulties.[7]

More typically, a woman goes through the motions of sexual intercourse but "feels nothing." To placate and satisfy her partner, she may actually be quite active sexually, and she may attain considerable gratification from his expressions of affection, from body contact, and from other aspects of lovemaking, even though erotic pleasure as such is absent.

In some women frigidity leads to frantic and promiscuous sexual experimentation, partly as a conscious search for satisfaction but also as a manifestation of complex unconscious mechanisms, which we shall discuss later. Frigidity may involve more than passive neutrality. Sexual intercourse is often marred by vague apprehension, outright fear, or even revulsion and disgust. Paradoxically some of these unpleasant affects may coexist with considerable sexual excitement.

Pelvic pain is a common complaint among women, and sometimes it causes problems in coitus. It may be experienced at penetration, during intercourse, or afterward. Pain and fear of pain may be indistinguishable, particularly in the first instance. When pain occurs only during intercourse, it is less likely to be confused with fear of pain. Pain after coitus usually takes the form of a dull ache associated with irritability. When pain is felt or anticipated, a certain amount of muscular tension is inevitable. As the pelvic muscles surrounding the introitus become spastic, penetration becomes difficult and sometimes (as in vaginismus) impossible.

There is one definition of frigidity that is open to question: the orthodox Freudian one in which only "vaginal orgasm" is considered

---

[6]Nefzawi (1964 ed.), p. 110.

[7]In "extremely happy marriages" 4.4 percent of the wives have not experienced orgasm in marital coitus (Gebhard, 1968).

evidence of mature sexual functioning. As we noted earlier (Chapter 3), there is no physiological basis for a distinction between vaginal and clitoral orgasms; increasing numbers of psychoanalysts are now willing to concede this point. For practical purposes, as long as a woman achieves orgasm and is satisfied with intercourse, it seems futile to argue along these lines.

Achievement of coital orgasm seems to have been correlated with various factors (age, age at marriage, length of marriage, frequency and technique of coitus) in the Kinsey sample.[8] Among married women, whose opportunities for coitus were greatest, one out of four failed to reach orgasm during sexual intercourse. Other studies have produced widely divergent figures.[9] The likelihood that a woman would reach orgasm during sexual intercourse seemed unrelated to techniques of foreplay and coitus. Religious background also made no difference, nor did the age at which adolescence had begun.

There was some positive correlation with age and social class. Older (up to middle age) women, more educated women, and women whose parents were in higher occupational classes were all more likely to attain orgasm. Marrying young seemed to be a deterrent: The group that had married by twenty years of age least frequently responded with orgasms. There was also a marked positive correlation with the length of marriage. Only half had experienced coital orgasm within the first month of marriage. But this percentage rose steadily with time: 63 percent in the first year, 71 percent in the fifth year, and 85 percent by the twentieth year of marriage.

The likelihood of orgasm during marital coitus also appeared to be markedly correlated

with premarital experience of orgasm through either masturbation, petting, or coitus. Also the incidence of coital orgasm was shown to have steadily increased in the younger generation.

Failure in Coital Gratification. How do we determine whether or not an act of intercourse with orgasm has been satisfactory? The question is not rhetorical, even though it may be impossible to answer. Any experienced person can testify that not all coital orgasms are the same, and some may complain that, though they are potent or responsive, they are not enjoying sexual intercourse enough.

Enhancing coital gratification is an ancient quest, and we have described some ways in which it can be accomplished. As the only criterion is subjective experience, however, complaints cannot easily be evaluated as symptoms of sexual malfunctioning. Sometimes the problem is one of unrealistic expectations.

In the current preoccupation with sex and its exploitation for commercial purposes, some men and women have come to expect of every orgasm an earth-shaking experience. Ordinary and otherwise perfectly acceptable levels of gratification leave them disappointed. The only cure for this problem is to recognize that the body cannot necessarily deliver everything that the imagination calls for.

Sometimes, however, orgasm is experienced with markedly diminished pleasure. The problem may be fear of experiencing strong affect and resulting loss of emotional control. It is also possible that genuine neurophysiological disturbances may be present, even though we are as yet unable to identify them.

Causes of Sexual Malfunctioning

Sexual functioning is vulnerable to disruption from biological, psychological, and cultural causes. At least in theory the interaction of forces from all three areas can occur. In practice, however, we identify the disorder accord-

[8]Kinsey *et al.* (1953).
[9]Kinsey *et al.* (1953), p. 375, footnote 22.

ing to the dominant cause only. The causes of sexual malfunctioning can thus be subsumed under several categories: organic, psychogenic (intrapsychic or interpersonal), and cultural.

Organic Causes. Sexual inadequacy is known to arise from demonstrable physical causes. In these instances psychological factors may contribute or be present as secondary reactions to the malfunction itself, but they are not the primary causes. Organic causes may be natural or pathological. A prime example of the former is the aging process. Its effects on sexual functioning are discussed in Chapter 3. Organic causes other than aging account for only a minority of instances of sexual malfunctioning.

Among pathological causes are certain diseases of the nervous system and endocrine disturbances. Many lesions are easy to correct; others may be the initial manifestations of more serious illnesses requiring urgent medical attention.

Intrapsychic Causes. The vast majority of sexual malfunctions in both sexes result from psychological problems, internal conflicts primarily related to past experiences. When these conflicts dominate a person's sex life to the extent that inadequate performance is the rule, then the causes can be considered primarily intrapsychic. On the other hand, when the sexual problem seems to be part of a larger conflict between two specific people, it is more convenient to label it "interpersonal." This distinction, though arbitrary, has practical merit in treatment. Intrapsychic causes must be dealt with as such. As veterans of successive divorces discover, when marital partners change the conflicts may remain the same. Interpersonal conflicts also ultimately result from intrapsychic problems, but the latter may be more circumscribed and require no special attention. Treatment may then be focused on the relationship between two individuals rather than upon the individuals themselves.

The psychological causes of sexual malfunctioning are innumerable and not specific to types of disturbances: The same conflict may cause sexual apathy in one man, impotence in another, and premature ejaculation in a third. The same lack of specificity is characteristic of women.

It is generally agreed that anxiety and depression are detrimental to sexual functioning. But how such emotional disturbances are generated and what constitutes sufficient psychological cause are matters of controversy. It would be impossible to review here all the possible intrapsychic causes of sexual malfunctioning even according to only one school of thought. The following discussion therefore offers only a series of illustrations that may convey some idea of the range of significant intrapsychic problems.

First of all, it is important to distinguish between anxiety and depression in response to external reality and in response to no apparent such cause. The damaging effects of fear—of discovery, of pregnancy, of venereal disease, or of injury during rape—are obvious. Other fears may be more subtle. A woman visiting her family or in-laws may be uneasy or apprehensive about engaging in sex with her husband if there is any chance that they will be overheard. Loss of sexual interest in response to personal or community tragedies, financial and other worries, sickness in the family, and so on is also quite understandable.

Most sexual problems arising from reality factors tend to disappear as the primary problems are resolved or as the person adapts to them. Sometimes, however, sexual inadequacy outlasts the original cause and becomes entangled with other internal conflicts.

In most established patterns of malfunctioning, specific external causes are difficult to identify (and, of course, there are many instances in which such circumstances cause no sexual disturbance). We ascribe these disorders to the influence of forgotten events from the past operating as repressed conflicts or as faulty learning.

Learning theorists have proposed a variety of models to explain the genesis of sexual malfunctions. Central to many is the mechanism of conditioning, in which the affect associated with an experience determines one's future reaction to a similar situation. Sometimes the antecedents of the experience are easy to trace. A sexually adequate man suffers a mild heart attack during coitus; thereafter the very thought of sex makes him anxious. Another man develops a prostate infection, and sexual intercourse becomes painful; gradually his potency declines, even though his infection is cured and he experiences no further pain.[10]

More often, malfunctioning results from a complex series of learning experiences. The transmission of certain sexual attitudes and values to children—like teaching that sex is dirty or dangerous—is one example. The adult may have forgotten specific or implied parental admonitions and punishments, but their damaging effects on his sexual performance persist.

Psychoanalysts offer extensive explanations of the intricate intrapsychic conflicts behind sexual malfunctioning. In contrast to the view that the key lies in faulty learning, psychoanalytic interpretations emphasize unconscious conflicts that influence behavior. For instance, conflicts arising from unresolved oedipal wishes may be major causes of difficulties in both sexes. Castration anxiety is a common explanation for failures of potency among males. The person who retains repressed and unresolved incestuous wishes from the oedipal period (Chapter 8) may unconsciously reexperience these forbidden and threatening desires when he attempts to engage in coitus. He feels tremendous guilt and primitive childhood fear of punishment in the form of genital mutilation. Under these circumstances he cannot perform—by losing his potency he obviates the necessity for engaging in the incestuous (symbolic but very real for him) act and its dire consequences.

When a man's impotence applies to coitus with his wife but not with a prostitute, he may unconsciously be equating the former with his mother and therefore failing. Men who distinguish between "respectable" women (to be loved and respected) and "degraded" women (to be enjoyed sexually) are said to have "madonna-prostitute complexes."

The female counterpart to this conflict, according to psychoanalytic theory, involves the father. As all men or certain types of men (defined by marital status, body build, or any of innumerable other characteristics) may be unconsciously identified with the father, the result may be to avoid coitus with any man, or at least to feel no pleasure in it. When no emotional involvement occurs, the woman is less likely to feel guilty about her incestuous conflict.

Another important area of intrapsychic conflict involves sexual identity. A man who identifies with women and a woman who resents her femininity may fail to function adequately because intercourse requires them to act in accordance with "biological" roles, which clash with their self-images. Strong fixed attitudes against certain coital positions and various other idiosyncratic inhibitions are related to this problem.

Finally, there is the threat of loss of control. As orgasm implies a certain abandonment of self-control, some men and women fear that other dangerous impulses will also be released. At times this fear is experienced consciously

---

[10] Wolpe and Lazarus (1966), p. 102.

as a fear that the vagina will be torn or that the penis will be "strangled" by the vagina (*penis captivus*).[11] Usually the apprehension is vague, not even consciously felt; the man simply fails to have an erection, and the woman fails to reach orgasm.

Some sexual difficulties result from fundamentally nonsexual conflicts. Some people experience primitive fears, for instance, of being engulfed, of losing their boundaries as individuals. Sexual penetration and the feeling of dissolution during orgasm may evoke such fears and can therefore be exceedingly threatening.

Interpersonal Conflict. It takes two to make love. Apart from moral considerations, an irreducible minimum of affection and intimacy is required if any mutual gratification is to emanate from intercourse. Some people insist that anything short of deep love cheapens the act; others find this view utopian or naïve.

Interpersonal conflicts are extensions of intrapsychic problems, but sometimes the pathology takes the form of a particular type of relationship. There is no end to the kinds of interpersonal conflicts that interfere with sex. Some people even claim that the quality of sexual intercourse is the best indicator of the nature of the overall relationship.

Intense disappointment, muted hostility, or overt anger will obviously poison sexual interaction. Subtle insults are just as detrimental. Women, for instance, are quite sensitive about being "used." If a man seems to be interested predominantly in a woman's body and neglects her thoughts and feelings, she will feel that she is being degraded to the level of an inanimate object.

Many women inevitably associate coitus with

---

[11] Among dogs certain anatomical features make it possible that a male be unable to withdraw its fully erect penis from the vagina. Such "locking" cannot occur in humans under any circumstances.

being exploited, subjugated, and so on. That some colloquial terms for coitus are also used in the latter sense clearly demonstrates this point (see Chapter 10). It is natural for a woman who feels this way to rebel by failing to respond.

Women have often risked pregnancy in exchange for gratification of deeply ingrained needs for love and security. Consequently any male behavior before or during intercourse that even remotely implies unconcern and insensitivity may make a woman reluctant to respond, even though she deprives herself of pleasure as well.

The attitudes most detrimental to the male's enjoyment are those that threaten his masculinity. Lack of feminine response, nagging criticism, and open or covert derision rarely fail to have an impact on male enjoyment. A man who feels overburdened by a dependent wife may also react negatively if her sexual requirements appear to be endless too. Women have sometimes used sexual apathy vindictively and to obtain what they want. These weapons, though effective, are double-edged swords.

The human mind is subject to such twists and turns that individual sexual responses may seem paradoxical and unpredictable. Some people respond sexually only when they are humiliated or hurt, and what would be inimical to an ordinary relationship becomes for them a prerequisite for potency and responsiveness. Often these people have such harsh consciences that enjoyment is only possible for them after punishment and pain.

Cultural Causes. Even though the blessings and burdens of a culture are unevenly distributed among its people, no one is entirely exempt from cultural influences. But, though it would be foolish to deny the impact of prevalent sexual mores upon individual functioning, particularly upon the development of sexual attitudes in childhood, sweeping indictments of the mores of particular cultures are difficult to substantiate and reflect the absence of a true cross-cultural perspective.

In this country, for instance, a great deal has been made of the damaging effects of Victorian attitudes, especially upon female sexuality. And the demands and anxieties of the modern world, the hectic pace of living, and the increasing assertiveness of woman are blamed for sapping men's virility.

Although the detrimental effects of such forces upon sexual functioning may seem obvious enough to some people, it is nevertheless preferable to have more evidence before stating the causal relations categorically. What is most misleading is the common implication that at other times or in other places conditions have been better. Eastern cultures in particular are held up to us these days as models of sexual good sense. It is perhaps helpful to realize that the average Indian has never heard of the *Kama Sutra* and that knowledge of Persian love manuals is restricted primarily to scholars of Islamic literature (many of whom happen to be Westerners). Nor have the Eastern peoples simply lost the precepts embodied in these works, for only an aristocratic minority ever did have the opportunity to enjoy them.

Not that various doctrines have not warped Western sexual attitudes in the past and do not continue to do so at present. Our public attitudes toward sex are indeed often ignorant, bigoted, and hypocritical. Some people think that we have recently become tasteless and shameless as well.[12]

Guilt certainly interferes with sexual functioning, but is guilt always and necessarily bad? Goethe at least did not think so: Once, when he attempted to make love to a willing maid at an inn, his potency failed him, and he wrote and told his wife about it, apparently grateful

that he had been prevented from being unfaithful.

Nevertheless, those who mistake their sexual weaknesses for strength of moral fiber ought to be aware that neurotic conflicts may lurk behind their scruples. Religions may be sexually restrictive, but none frowns upon sexual enjoyment under the proper circumstances.

In our progressively secular society it is claimed that shame is replacing guilt as the primary social inhibitor.[13] Some people argue that in Western society the premium on competence and success, combined with an over-emphasis on sex, creates a formidable hurdle to enjoyment. Orgasm becomes a challenge, rather than the natural climax of coitus. Inability to achieve it, or failure to reach a certain intensity, and having to rely on clitoral stimulation or some other technique become not only signals of sexual incompetence but also reflections of personal inadequacy.

Treatment of Sexual Malfunctioning

Sexual malfunctioning may be mild and transient or may present formidable challenges to treatment. The remedies for sexual inadequacies that can be treated range from fairly simple educational programs and self-help to highly specialized, intensive, lengthy therapy. Although, for purposes of clarity, we shall describe various methods of treatment as separate entities, in practice these approaches are both deliberately and inadvertently combined.

Sex Education. Even though instruction should ideally precede and prevent the formation of erroneous sexual notions and warped attitudes, most of us do remain educable to the end of our lives. In the treatment of sexual malfunctioning, the educational approach has

---

[12] Tyrmand (1970).

[13] Ellis and Abarbanel, eds. (1967), p. 451.

two main goals: imparting information and changing attitudes.

In addition to basic data on anatomy, sexual functioning, coital techniques, methods of enhancing pleasure, and other topics presented in this book, there are other kinds of information that may be useful in overcoming milder forms of sexual inadequacy. For example, when a man is often impotent or a woman responds with difficulty, intercourse should be attempted only under the most favorable conditions: when both partners are well rested, relaxed, secure in a comfortable setting, and with plenty of time. If there are interpersonal problems, a time when strain and antagonism are at a minimum must be chosen.

Although the couple should start with the expectation that intercourse will be mutually satisfactory, it is unwise to approach it with grim determination. The primary objective must be mutual enjoyment, with or without sexual intercourse. A given sexual encounter may thus go no farther than kisses and caresses, or orgasm may be achieved without intercourse. Sexual gratification through intercourse can then come when both partners are ready, neither forced nor anxiously anticipated.

When a man's problem is impotence, he should not even attempt penetration unless a reasonably strong erection is present. A semierect penis may become flaccid when it bends and twists against the resistance of the vaginal opening, and this loss of erection further destroys self-confidence. A woman who is apprehensive or unresponsive should not be penetrated until she is well lubricated (naturally or with an artificial lubricant) and has been aroused at least to some degree. If she can reach orgasm without intercourse, it is best that she do so first or that she admit the penis only when she has reached the peak of excitement.

Advice of this sort sooner or later borders on the objectionable. Some women may prefer to go without orgasms rather than touch their own genitals or have their partners stimulate them manually or orally. Those who are determined to overcome the problem must face the fact that for them orgasm requires specific efforts, some of which may seem rather indelicate. Couples with sexual problems must also forget about mutual climaxes and other such expectations until their basic functioning has been straightened out.

A somewhat controversial but effective sexual stimulant is fantasizing during coitus. Thinking about someone else or some other form of sexual activity may be quite arousing, and it may be the only way that a woman can reach orgasm. The objections are, of course, obvious. But this aberration seems sufficiently innocuous to be permissible, given the fundamental aim of reaching orgasm. Also the hope behind all these suggestions is that once proper sexual functioning has been established, they will be less and less necessary.

Levels of sexual excitement can be controlled to a large extent by the person's thinking. When he is distracted, sexual excitement fades; when he dwells on the exciting and pleasurable aspects of his activity, sexual tension mounts. It is imperative, however, that individuals not become preoccupied and anxious about what is happening.

Marital Counseling. The kind of information that we have outlined is readily available from books, magazines, public lectures, and so on, but it is difficult to assess the effectiveness of such material. For people with serious sexual problems, more direct and personal instruction is often necessary.

When sexual difficulties arise in a casual relationship, the most common remedy is simply to forget about the other person and to look for a new partner. It is almost always married couples who come for joint assistance, because of what is at stake in their relationships. Hence the term "marital counseling."

The marital counselor is most often a clinical psychologist or a psychiatric social worker. General practitioners and clergymen also do a great deal of marital counseling, though they may call it something else. Psychiatrists and gynecologists often offer marital advice to their patients, as divorce lawyers do to their clients. In addition, particularly in certain family-oriented cultures, older, respected members of the community may be called upon for guidance. Although issues more general than sexual incompatibility may be involved, the sexual aspects of the relationships also come under scrutiny.

Systematic marital counseling involves much more than information and advice. The whole relationship between the couple becomes the focus of attention. The pre- and post-marital sexual histories of the individuals are examined. The genesis of the sexual incompatibility is carefully uncovered and its corollaries are separated out. As the partners come to understand the basis of their sexual difficulties, they may gradually gain control of the negative factors and make the necessary adjustments. When sexual difficulties are secondary to other conflicts, they may receive only cursory attention, but otherwise they are a primary focus. It is important that the counselor make this distinction clear as early as possible so that everyone involved is working toward the same goal.

Perhaps the single most important key to the solution of interpersonal sexual difficulties is to prevent the bedroom from becoming a battleground. The couple must learn that, though the tendency to carry other conflicts into the sexual realm is very tempting, it must be resisted. When a person feels angry and hurt, he naturally does not want to engage in sex, and these feelings cannot be helped. But often one or the other partner deliberately and consciously retaliates by depriving the mate sexually or by simply going through the motions apathetically. This tactic is classic. Indeed in cultures in which wives are totally dependent upon their husbands, it may be their only effective weapon. But otherwise there is less justification for its use.

In addition to the various types of marital therapy, several couples may be treated together in group therapy, in encounter groups, in marathons, and so on. To a great extent the value of such methods depends upon the skills of the particular group leader and the motivations of the participants.

Psychotherapy. Broadly defined, "psychotherapy" includes all methods of psychological treatment that do not involve drugs or other physical means. There are, of course, many types of psychotherapy, involving differing theoretical assumptions and clinical techniques.

Behavior therapy is based on learning theory. Sexual inadequacy is considered an illness in itself, rather than a symptom of some underlying disorder; the goal is to eliminate it. Behavior-therapy techniques are many, and are aimed at reduction and control of anxiety, breaking down inhibitions, undoing faulty learning, and replacing it with more effective approaches to sex through assertive training, systematic desensitization to previously learned fears or phobias, and related approaches.[14]

In supportive psychotherapy the aim is to provide the patient with an opportunity to express himself, to share his feelings, and to ventilate his resentments within a secure and positive relationship with the therapist. Although the patient may reveal a great deal about himself, no effort is made to link this information with forgotten childhood experiences. Rather, the therapist concentrates on the current and the conscious. As he comes to represent a respected and loved figure to the patient, the

---

[14] Illustrations of the use of these methods can be found in Wolpe and Lazarus (1966).

therapist is often able to alleviate guilt, shame, and suffering merely by accepting the patient as he is. In this context a great deal of relearning can also occur.

In insight-oriented psychotherapy, the most intense form of which is psychoanalysis, the goals of treatment are much more ambitious. The sexual complaint is considered merely a symptom. Its elimination, though important, may be considered secondary to achieving basic understanding and reorganization of the personality structure.

Psychoanalysis involves intricate, detailed, and lengthy exploration and analysis of the patient's past, psychological defenses, repressed conflicts, dreams, and relationship with the analyst (transference)—in order to help him gain insight into the unconscious roots of his conflicts and sexual symptoms.[15]

Physical Therapies and Mechanical Aids. All the methods of treatment described so far are slow, complex, often expensive, and not always effective. It would be so much easier if sexual disorders could be dealt with by simple methods, but no such methods are yet generally available.

The treatment of physical defects and other organic causes is primarily a medical matter. Some of these problems (like pain from infections) are simple to treat, whereas others are incurable. In dealing with sexual disorders, sex hormones, except in rare instances, are useless. Aphrodisiacs and "nerve tonics" are generally worthless and may even be harmful.

Tranquilizers may be helpful in allaying overt anxiety, but they do nothing for the calm, frigid woman or for the placid, impotent man. Alcohol, in moderate amounts, may help to

relieve anxiety and to loosen inhibitions, but beyond a certain limit even the most virile man will have trouble having an erection under its influence.

Miscellaneous other physical and mechanical methods have been used with varying degrees of success. Men prone to premature ejaculation, for instance, can use condoms to reduce the sensitivity of the glans and thus to retard excitement and orgasm. A more effective, but also more inconvenient, alternative is the application of a local-anesthetic ointment to the glans about half an hour or so before intercourse. It has recently been reported that squeezing the glans between thumb and two fingers will avert orgasm and permit the man to go on with coitus. This technique will be discussed later.

Finally, there are extreme measures, to provide men with mechanical supports so that they can achieve penetration: splints that can be attached to the penis to carry the flaccid organ into the vagina. They permit a couple to carry on a semblance of intercourse, and an impotent but fertile man can thus impregnate his wife. Sometimes, after using splints, a man gains enough confidence and potency to dispense with them (they are therefore sometimes called "coitus-training apparatus").

A man who has lost his penis through trauma or surgery may have recourse to a penile prosthesis, actually a dildo, which he attaches. Before cringing at the thought of such devices, it is well to contemplate the despair of men in such predicaments.

Frigid women may be aroused with mechanical vibrators. Again the hope is that once they become conditioned to experiencing orgasm, they will be able to enjoy intercourse.

Some years ago, the gynecologist A. H. Kegel devised a set of pelvic exercises to help patients control the leakage of urine that sometimes follows childbirth ("stress incontinence"). His patients spontaneously reported that their sexual functioning had also improved. These Kegel

---

[15] There is a vast literature on psychoanalytic technique and the methods of treatment derived from it. Succinct presentation of this material can be found in Colby (1951) and DeWald (1964).

exercises are said to be quite effective in strengthening the muscles around the vaginal orifice (the *pubococcygeus*) and thus facilitating orgasm. The simplest way for a woman to learn them is first to identify the main muscle involved by voluntarily interrupting the flow of urine a few times. The exercises consist simply of flexing this same muscle ten times in a row six times a day at the beginning and working up to longer periods. The objective, as in all other forms of exercise, is to strengthen the muscles through repeated use.

A timeless remedy that combines many aspects of these various therapies is to put the sexually inadequate person in the hands of an experienced lover. Moral considerations aside, some men and women are driven to this alternative, first to find out whether or not the failures are really their own and then perhaps to learn from the experience. The proverbial whore with the heart of gold, the knowing woman who seduces the tremulous young man, and the older man who initiates the virgin are well known literary and folk figures. Some sex specialists actually hire women who assist in the treatment of impotent men in this way.

The Reproductive Biology Research Foundation Program. The therapeutic approaches described so far have been used by many clinicians in generally unsystematic fashion, and the results have been either poor or poorly evaluated. Recently the same team that pioneered the research in the physiology of orgasm has reported on a more systematic program for the treatment of sexual malfunctioning.[16]

Their approach combines well-tried methods with certain novelties. It has the outstanding merits of brevity (two weeks) and generally good rates of success. The results have ranged from the spectacular (100 percent cure for vaginismus) to the somewhat disappointing (40 percent failure for primary impotence which is most difficult to treat). This program is based on the conviction that there is no such thing as an uninvolved sexual partner. Treatment therefore always and necessarily involves a pair and never a single individual. Furthermore, a therapeutic team composed of a man and a woman conducts the treatment. The procedure requires that the problem couple move from home to live near the treatment center for the duration of the treatment, under as pleasant and relaxed circumstances as possible.

The first step is to take a detailed history from each partner. Then the partners are instructed (never commanded) to explore a little at a time their latent erotic capabilities: to disrobe in the privacy of their bedroom, to caress and explore each other's bodies in a gentle and pleasurable manner. Gradually over the two-week period interactions become more intimate, and eventually they culminate in intercourse. These physical activities in private alternate with detailed discussion with the therapists. Successes and failures are analyzed with candor, in a nonthreatening, nonjudgmental manner. Ultimate success comes when it does: There is no fixed schedule, no pressure to perform.

The key tasks are to convince the couple that sex is a natural function that requires no heroic effort but only a relaxed, accepting attitude. No one is at fault, and there is no uninvolved partner. Each must learn to give, as well as to receive, to involve himself in sex rather than to remain an observer. Orgasm will come in time; there is no need to seek it anxiously. These and similar attitudes are conveyed, along with an objective, factual approach to the sex organs and their functions.

Within this psychological framework the problem couple is instructed in specific physical techniques. As already indicated, the first task

---

[16] Masters and Johnson (1970). For a summary of this work, see Belliveau and Richter (1970).

is to learn to stimulate the partner effectively, as well as to be able to respond to such stimulation. The use of lotions has been found very useful in this respect. Interestingly enough, those who were repelled by the use of such lotions (ordinary products like hand lotions) were more likely not to respond to treatment.

After the couple has become adept at such general body stimulation, it gradually engages in active genital play. When the presenting problem is premature ejaculation, it is recommended that the woman sit comfortably on the bed and that the man lie on his back facing her, his body extended between her legs.[17] This position provides her with easy and full access to his genitals. After appropriate stimulation, when the man achieves full erection and is about to ejaculate, the woman holds the glans between her thumb and two fingers and squeezes it firmly for several seconds.[18] The woman then resumes genital stimulation, and the procedure is repeated. Gradually the man is able to maintain increasingly longer periods of erection. Next the woman straddles him and gently lowers herself onto his erect penis.[19] After intromission she remains motionless in order to minimize stimulation. If the man nevertheless feels the urge to ejaculate she withdraws and averts orgasm by the squeeze technique; then she reinserts the penis. By this method the

man is able to maintain his erection intravaginally without premature ejaculation.

The treatment for impotence follows the same general pattern. The first task is to bring the man to erection. He is encouraged to communicate to the woman specifically what he finds arousing. When he has achieved erection the couple is discouraged from attempting coitus at first; instead they continue to engage in relaxed and pleasurable foreplay. Only after sufficient confidence has been attained is intromission attempted in the same position described for treating premature ejaculation.

When the presenting symptom is orgasmic dysfunction in the woman, the couple goes through the same preliminaries, but then the male becomes more active in stimulating his partner. A suitable position is with the man comfortably seated on the bed and the woman between his legs with her back turned to him, thus providing him with ready access to both her breasts and her genitals.[20] During coitus, however, the partners resume exactly the same approach as for male inadequacy. In both instances the woman takes the initiative and the more "active" role in coitus.

These researchers were able to locate numerous physical causes (infections, poorly healed lesions, and so on) for painful coitus (dyspareunia). Hence their recommendation of a most careful gynecological evaluation of such problems at the outset. Vaginismus responds very well to gradual dilation of the introitus.

[17] Belliveau and Richter (1970), p. 116, figure 4.
[18] Masters and Johnson (1970), p. 104, figure 4.
[19] See Belliveau and Richter (1970), p. 119, figure 5.

[20] See Belliveau and Richter (1970), p. 177, figure 7.

PART
3
CULTURE

Erotic images have pervaded art from its earliest beginnings. The connection between sex and image has been so constant and so close that it has led militant enemies of sex, at various times in history, to reject all art as being necessarily tainted by carnality. And while it is now customary to laugh at this view, it may still be useful to examine whether it does not contain a grain of truth. There is reason to suppose that all art involves some erotic motivation, though this need not express itself openly. The unacknowledged erotic motive may, rather, contribute a special energy and pleasure to the work and be felt by the viewer as vitality. It is possible for erotic tensions to operate subliminally in such harmless contexts as, for example, portraits or landscapes. They may affect the form of these works, their qualities of color and shape, without becoming manifest in their content. Some Freudian psychologists have claimed that art is sublimated sex, that it feeds on energies which would "normally" be released directly into sexual activity, and that its function is to divert these energies into other, socially acceptable channels.

Whether this is in fact more specially true of art than it is of other kinds of work need not concern us. But if it is true of art at all, then a further observation is called for, namely that the evidence of history suggests that the sexual energies spent in making art appear to be male. It is clear, at any rate, that in the past several thousand years, and under the most varied cultural conditions, men have always and everywhere been the artists and that when art has explicitly expressed sexual attitudes, it has always expressed characteristic male attitudes. So universal have been the dominance of the male artist and the masculine interest in art that we are tempted to conclude that art is an expression of male sexuality.[1]

The parallel between biological and artistic creation has had an important bearing on the character of primitive art. The origins of erotic art, as of all art, lay in magic belief and ritual. In early cultures, the role of the artist was that of a life-giver. The most important quality of his work was not its beauty or its resemblance to reality, but its magical potency, its possession of independent life and influence on the surrounding world. The view of art as a form of magical generation continued in the beliefs and practices of later, higher cultures. The story of the creation of Adam from a lump of clay,

---

[1][The above remarks about male supremacy in art must be evaluated in the context of the circumstances under which women have had to live and work. See Woolf (1929). HAK.]

THE EROTIC IN ART
by Lorenz Eitner

Figure 13.1. "Venus" Lespugne (Haute-Garonne, France), Early Stone Age, bone carving.

women with strongly accentuated breasts and hips (see Figure 13.1). Some of these sculptures seem to represent pregnant women; they thus resemble cave paintings showing pregnant animals from the same period. It is probable that these images were made to promote the fertility of the tribe and the herd. They were not meant to be merely likenesses of reality; rather they were intended to *be* reality, brought into effective being out of dead matter in magical fulfillment of a wish. Their sexual character was twofold: They were intended as instruments of fecundity and were themselves products of a process resembling human reproduction.

The great abundance of sexual references in prehistoric and primitive art does not reflect a mood of carefree hedonism in early civili-

as recorded in Genesis, exemplifies such a survival, and so do the Egyptian carved funerary effigies, which were intended to serve as substitute bodies for the homeless souls of the dead—the Egyptians' descriptive term for sculptor was "he who keeps alive." According to Greek myth, Daedalus, the inventor of sculpture, made figures which were so powerfully alive that they had to be chained to their bases, and Pygmalion carved the statue of a girl who, with Athena's help, came to life under his chisel and in time became his bride. A trace of the ancient beliefs seems to linger in modern clichés which liken the production of art to conception, pregnancy, and birth.

Origins in Magic and Ritual

Among the oldest known representations of the human body, dating from the Early Stone Age, are sculpted figurines and reliefs of

Figure 13.2. Phallic monument, the Dedication of Karystos (from the Sacred Road on the Island of Delos), fourth-third century B.C.

zations, but a concern with urgent human needs and most particularly with the preservation of life itself. Sexual art at this stage was magical art, having very little to do with individual experience or pleasure. Sexual imagery served to explain the mysterious origins of human life, the motion of the sun and the moon, the cycle of the seasons, and man's existence after death. The advent of an agricultural economy and village life provided the base and the need for communal ritual: festivals requiring the use of magic images and instruments. The basic connection between agriculture, with its reliance on fecundity, and the early growth of culture helps to account for the prevalence of sexual content in early art, as well as in early myth, drama, and dance. From prehistoric times cult objects have often been given the form of sexual organs. The veneration of the phallus found

expression in the suggestive shapes of wooden posts or stone shafts, in Egyptian obelisks, Greek *omphaloi,* Hindu *lingams,* and other such monuments from many different civilizations (see Figure 13.2). Phallic idols were enshrined in sanctuaries or carried in ritual processions. Sexual symbols adorned weapons, tools, and pottery, and were worn as fetishes or amulets (see Figure 2.6). Representations of sexual acts were less common but no less widely distributed. They have been found in Neolithic cave drawings, in the aboriginal art of Australia and Africa, and in the ceramic sculpture of Peru.

The beginnings of Greek and Roman civilization offer impressive examples of the influence of early agrarian fertility cults on the subsequent development of art and literature. The fields and flocks of rural Greece were guarded by phallic pillars or statues. Priapus,

Figure 13.3. Satyr pursuing a nymph, painting on an Attic red-figure amphora by Oltos, early fifth century B.C. Louvre, Paris.

god of animal and vegetable fertility, was venerated in the form of herms with erect phalluses. Dionysus, god of cultivation, of wine, and of passion, was celebrated in processions of phallus bearers. Faunus, the Latin god of cattle, and Fauna, his female counterpart, were believed to lurk in the fields and forests and were embodied in images expressive of benign, animal sensuality. Pan, Silenus, and the lustful satyrs, often shown in a state of sexual excitement, invaded the arts and the theater from the beginning. The rampaging of these nature spirits, their pursuit of women, their drunkenness and wild fornication furnished subjects for the drama, for painting, and for sculpture. Greek painted vases of the Archaic period (seventh–sixth centuries B.C.) abound with lusty scenes of copulation in settings of bacchic revelry or satyr play (see Figure 13.3). These scenes sometimes adorned objects of daily use, suggesting a high-spirited lasciviousness astonishing to modern minds, but their connection with old, ultimately sacred traditions made them respectable—even holy—in their time.

Works of cult-inspired sexual art from widely separate regions and periods show enormous varieties of types and styles, but they have in common that each tends, within its own cultural setting, toward the formal abstraction and stereotype repetition that characterize primitive or archaic art everywhere. They do not express the individuality of particular artists, but embody the rules laid down for art and sex by the different civilizations which produced them. In this, they simply reflect the general restrictions which bound all early art. Slowly unfolding conventions, rather than the individual will of artists, governed subject matter and style. Painters and sculptors were not free to choose. Similarly, all early cultures restricted the expression of sexuality. Men and women were not free to act according to their individual impulses. Thus the treatment of sex in art remained, throughout most of history,

under a double restraint. Sexuality could be openly expressed only when it was legitimized by an important social concern, such as religious ritual. And even then it could be expressed only in forms sanctioned by the various artistic traditions. When sexual activity was represented in art, as, for example, in Greek priapic scenes or in Hindu temple sculptures, the context was always religious and the manner of representation severely stylized and conventional. It is questionable whether works of this kind should be called "erotic." They belong, rather, to religious art, for their sexual character, however blatant, is secondary to their sacred or ritual function.

The same is true of the ceramic sculptures of the Mochica culture of Peru (*c.* 400–1000 A.D.), often described as works of "erotic realism" but actually ritual objects in a highly formalized archaic style (see Figures 2.5 and 10.1). Some of these clay vessels take the shapes of figures with grotesquely enlarged sexual organs; others serve as bases for figures of men and women or animals engaged in sexual intercourse. The variety of positions, including anal coitus and fellatio, is impressive, but it is clearly not the result of the sculptors' personal caprice or observation. The vases fall, rather, into well-defined groups, each marked by the constant repetition of certain stock motifs. Realism is limited to a narrow range of types and gestures. These sculptures were made as grave offerings; their function was probably similar to that of the erotic funeral art of other archaic cultures, such as that of the Etruscans.

Secular Erotic Art

To the modern observer, detached from these ancient traditions or totally ignorant of them, the distinction between religious convention and secular invention often remains obscure. Sexual scenes or symbols from early cultures may speak to his artistic and erotic

Figure 13.4. Temple reliefs, sixteenth century A.D., Srirangam Temple, Trichinopoly, India.

sensibility, to his private self, so persuasively that he overlooks their conventional, functional, and public character. But the members of the culture which these works were made to serve did not consider them as aesthetic objects made for appreciation, nor did they think of them as erotic, in the modern, banal sense of the term. There is a sharp difference, at any rate, between the tribal craftsman who carves a phallic image to replace an older, worn-out cult object, necessarily imitating it as closely as he can, and the contemporary experimental sculptor in Paris or Los Angeles, who constructs a large penis in fiberglass with a forthcoming exhibition in mind. Regardless of how these two works may strike the detached viewer (who may well prefer the primitive carving) they cannot be fairly measured on the same scale of meaning and quality. The tribal

craftsman would find the work of the cosmopolitan artist puzzling and perhaps offensive, unless, by chance or design, it happened to conform to the conventions of his tribe. He would, at any rate, judge both works by what he considered their effectiveness, as a cobbler would judge a pair of well-made shoes. His own work would certainly pass the test of utility. Whether or not it also has aesthetic qualities in the eyes of the alien observer is a matter of chance.

An important difference between religious art with sexual content and secular erotic art is that only the latter can qualify as obscene. Hindu temple sculptures (Figure 13.4) or primitive fertility idols offer forthright sexual displays, but they are obscene only when deliberately taken out of their context. In its own culture, the sexual idol fulfills a sacred function; transported to another setting—a gathering of suburban matrons, for example—it may become obscene, but the obscenity will reside not so much in the object as in the false presentation of it.

Obscenity results from the violation of prohibitions. In tradition-dominated cultures, such violations are unlikely to occur, for ordinary men are not strong enough to challenge the rules, and the men in power usually have little interest in changing them. The earliest historical instance of a conscious sharp break in religious and artistic tradition is associated with the heresy of the Egyptian pharaoh Ikhnaten (Amenophis IV) who ruled in 1379–1362 B.C. Ikhnaten overthrew the powerful priest caste and consolidated the innumerable cults of Egypt in a unified worship of the sun god Aten. He moved the capital of his empire to a newly founded city, Akhetaten (Tell el 'Amarna), and here sponsored an art which ran directly counter to the formality and conservatism of Egyptian custom. For nearly 2,000 years, Egyptian art had clung to archaic formality, observing severe restraint in dealing

Figure 13.5. Love play, painting on an Attic red-figure Stamnos, fifth century B.C. Louvre, Paris.

with erotic themes and refraining from the representation of female nudity. The art of Ikhnaten's court, by contrast, was vividly unconventional in the observation of nature and direct in the display of intimate human situations, even those involving the royal family. While the painters and sculptors of Akhetaten avoided the outright representation of sexual acts, they treated the female nude with a sensuous warmth that struck conservative Egyptians as obscene, especially when the artists committed the sacrilege of showing the queen Nefertiti and her princesses in scandalous nakedness. The brief period of emancipation ended with the life of Ikhnaten and was followed almost immediately by a relapse into strict conventionality.

The episode of Ikhnaten's heresy was an exception. It reflected the extremely static quality of Egyptian culture, with its archaic traditions that could be disturbed only by an all-powerful individual. Normally, the opportunity to experiment with artistic and sexual conventions which is a prerequisite for erotic art (and obscenity) arose in those more permissive and dynamic civilizations which allowed men to be critical of sexual taboos and to think of breaking them. The degree of individual awareness and independence which this requires can exist only in societies at a very advanced stage of development. As long as art stands for the generally shared convictions of a society, as it does in its primitive and archaic phases, its morality remains unquestioned. Only when it becomes the particular concern of an elite or of private individuals does it begin to raise moral problems. The makers or patrons of erotic art in such highly developed and secular societies as those of Hellenistic Greece, Imperial Rome, or postmedieval Europe took liberties with sexual conventions knowing that they were treading on dangerous ground. They knew that they were likely to come into conflict with strong currents of belief and feeling. They saw the lines, drawn by law or public opinion, which define the limits of tolerance. To exceed these limits was to risk censure, and this risk constituted a powerful temptation. It lent to erotic art the attraction of the forbidden, the power to arouse, to shock, or to offend. Obscenity has an edge of impudence or defiance; it is stimulated by restraints.

The most common types of obscenity in art are pictures of the sexual organs (see Figures 13.31, 13.32, and 13.33), of intercourse (see Figures 13.14 and 13.15), and of "perverse" behavior (see Figure 13.21). What makes them obscene is that they openly portray aspects of sex that are regarded as shameful or as strictly private. Prohibitions against offensive art are, in fact, only extensions of prohibitions against offensive sexual behavior. They are quite clearly not rooted in basic human nature but are taken from codes of morality that differ from culture to culture and from period to period. There is scarcely a part of the human body of which the exposure or representation has not, at some time or in some place, been considered indecent. Some cultures take pains to conceal the genitals and the breasts, others leave these bare but cover the posterior, still others are concerned with covering the navel, the feet, or the face.

When artists, freed from religious restraints, become able to challenge and violate these prohibitions, vast new opportunities open before them. They can now address themselves directly to the frustrated sexual curiosities and appetites of their fellow men. In the West this point was first reached by the Greeks at the beginning of the Classical period. The treatment of erotic themes in Greek art, from the late sixth century B.C. on, shows a gradual shift in meaning and spirit. The sacred awe which had once surrounded the symbols and myths of sex gradually gave way to comedy. Satyrs became figures of fun, their pursuits and copulations a source of ribald entertainment. The Olympian gods themselves took on a more human form, and their love exploits began to resemble the experiences of mortals. As its religious significance lessened, Greek erotic art began to reflect secular attitudes and personal feeling. The change is evident in the new conceptions of traditional myths, but it is even more apparent in scenes taken from the pleasures of common life which were often used by the vase painters and the makers of incised mirrors and other objects of luxury. They concern the lovemaking of young men and courtesans, orgies of gymnastic complexity (see Figure 13.5), and occasionally pederasty. Perhaps not quite all of these representations were entirely without spiritual significance. Paintings of sexual intercourse on the walls of Etruscan tombs suggest that images of decidedly profane appearance could still hold meanings which would make them appropriate to a serious, and perhaps sacred, purpose. But the majority of these scenes in later Greek art seem to lack such special meanings. They appear to be no more than objects of lustful contemplation, detached from any religious or cultural concern. What qualities these erotic images have are aesthetic, reflecting the spirit and skill of individual artists or craftsmen and the tastes of their patrons. They run the gamut from routine work of crude execution—perhaps the earliest examples of commercial pornography—to work of the most aristocratic beauty. Many of them were undoubtedly meant to be obscene in representing sexual behavior which, unhallowed by religious associations, was commonly regarded as indecent.

Full nudity, both male and female, had been

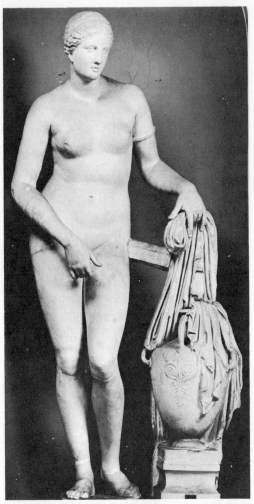

Figure 13.6. Aphrodite, Roman copy after the Aphrodite of Cnidos by Praxiteles, the original dating from *c.* 349 B.C. Copy in the Vatican, Rome.

attention to parts of the body which now took on the charm of the forbidden. The statues of the gods, particularly those of Aphrodite and the other divinities of love, were treated with a sensuous refinement clearly meant to make them attractive to the individual beholder. The powerful erotic appeal of the cult statue of Aphrodite which Praxiteles (*c.* 370–*c.* 330 B.C.) carved for a sanctuary at Knidos was attested by the ancient writers and in countless imitations by later Greek and Roman sculptors (see Figure 13.6). "They say," wrote Pliny the Elder, "that a certain man was once overcome by love for the statue and, having hidden himself in the shrine at night, embraced it, and left a stain on it as indication of his lust."

The Classical Tradition

In Greek art of the Hellenistic period (fourth–first centuries B.C.), work of erotic subject matter and erotically charged style constituted a major specialty, carried on by many artists, some of them of the highest accomplishment (see Figure 13.7). Much of their production continued, often in a slightly sweetened or trivialized form, the inventions of such earlier innovators as Praxiteles. On a lower level, numerous manufacturers of erotic trifles and petty decorative work supplied the cities of the Mediterranean and sent their wares beyond the frontiers of the Greek world. The importance of the Hellenistic period in the development of erotic art lay less in the originality of the work it produced than in the formation of a vast secular repertory which influenced all later erotic art in Europe, notably in Rome, and left its traces in the art of North Africa, the Middle East, and India.

The Greeks created the prototypes of erotic art in the West in works of such compelling power that the very notion of physical beauty and attraction forever after bore Hellenic features. The Roman contributions to this tradi-

taken for granted in earlier Greek art. When the subject matter justified it, as it did in the representation of certain gods, the entire body could be shown, without self-consciousness or shame. This innocence began to disappear from art during the fourth century B.C. Nakedness became an attraction which was deliberately exploited. Gestures of modesty came to be used, ostensibly to conceal, but actually to draw

tion were technical and social, rather than strictly artistic. Workshops throughout the Roman empire multiplied the images which Greek art in its late decline had already reduced to the level of easily copied banality. The Roman art industry, commercial in essence, produced work which varied in quality, depending on the social class and purse of the customer for which it was made. When it addressed itself to the elite, it affected Greek refinements and often achieved high technical finish; when geared to popular demand, it often fell into slapdash perfunctoriness. The mythological tradition continued in work of large scale, in mural painting, relief, and sculpture. Vestiges of the original religious function of erotic art survived in scattered instances, such as the sarcophagi reliefs which symbolized death in the guise of the love of Artemis for the sleeping Endymion or in the representation of a Dionysian initiation rite, including the unveiling of the sacred phallus, in the Villa of the Mysteries at Pompeii. The strain of profane eroticism, on the other hand, is profusely represented by simple scenes of copulation on the walls of Pompeiian houses of prostitution, on oil lamps, vases, and cut gems. These straightforward exhibitions of the various coital combinations, instructional in their effect on the viewer, rather than aphrodisiac, express a distinctly Roman sense of fact: Latin prose, in contrast to the Greek poetry of sex.

The erotic licentiousness of ancient art did not go unopposed. Currents of resistance to it were always present among the more tradition-bound populations of the Empire. The recoil from pagan eroticism was strong in the East, among Semitic sectarians, in Greece, among the adherents of the Stoic and Cynic philosophies, and even in Rome itself, where patriarchal traditions of austerity and modesty were in constant conflict with cosmopolitan freedom. The rise of Christianity coincided with the spread of ascetic practices throughout

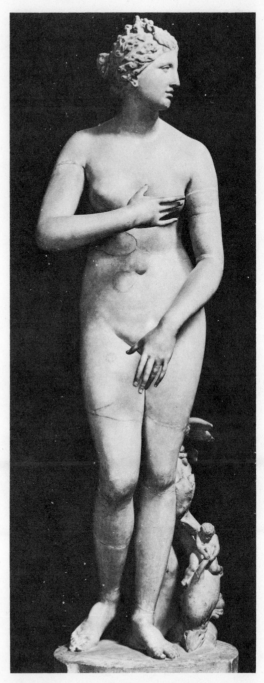

Figure 13.7. Aphrodite, so-called "Medici Venus," Hellenistic, *c.* third century B.C. Uffizi, Florence.

Figure 13.8. Eve, *c.* 1240, portal sculpture from the Cathedral of Trau, Dalmatia, by Magister Radovan.

gentile and Jewish communities of the Empire. From the second century A.D. onward, the popularity of licentious art declined. When, in the fourth century A.D., Christianity became the official religion of the state, its communities devoted themselves to the suppression of every kind of idolatry and unchastity. The makers of erotic art fell under a double ban, so formidable that it put an effective stop to their work.

Driven underground, the gods of antiquity haunted the Middle Ages in the form of demons and spirits. Nothing illustrates the moral and psychological revolution which Christianity achieved more clearly than does this transformation of the erotic myths of Aphrodite, Dionysus, and Pan into nightmare fantasies of guilt and fear.

Sexual subject matter in medieval art remained, literally, marginal; it found its way obscurely into the sculpted decorations of churches or crept into the borders of illuminated pages. The odium of paganism weighed as heavily against the representation of nudity or of erotic scenes as did the fear of obscenity. When nude bodies had to be shown, as in scenes of the Fall of Adam and Eve or of the Last Judgment, they were stiffly schematized to remove from them any taint of sexuality (see Figure 13.8). No fresh observation altered these stunted stereotypes as they passed from generation to generation, the mere ghosts of the Classical models from which they had once been adapted. Only toward the close of the Middle Ages did artists begin to treat the nude more frankly, allowing themselves a closer look at the antique and at reality and daring to express a shy delight in the beauty of the human body. Sexual subjects, on rare occasions, entered medieval art without Christian sanction. Small reliefs of women exposing their genitals are sometimes found inconspicuously placed on the facades of churches, relics of pre-Christian protective magic. Among the carvings on choir stalls and in the marginal decorations of devotional books small, obscene figures sometimes lurk, personifying evil or sin, but serving perhaps also as an entertainment for the worshiper's wandering mind.

It is idle to speculate on what might have been the course of medieval art, if the Christian attitude toward sex had been accepting, rather than hostile. The example of Hindu temple sculpture of the period corresponding to that of the European cathedrals proves that it is possible for a highly evolved religion to promote a sensuous, or even an openly sexual, art (see Figure 13.4). The temples in the Deccan region of India, especially those at Khajuraho (tenth century A.D.), Bhubaneswar (eleventh century A.D.), and Konorak (thirteenth century A.D.), are profusely covered with figures carved in high relief, shown in a bewildering variety of poses: dancing, playing instruments, and

making love. The pliant, voluptuously proportioned bodies of the women, consorts of gods and heroes, hint at their descent from distant Hellenistic origins. The scenes of sexual activity are quite explicit. Lined up in long rows, nearly always erect, the couples seem to move in a slow dance as they embrace, their bodies joined in every conceivable sexual combination. Although their features conform to a type, they are far removed from the schematism of genuinely "early" art. The best of these sculptures have an expressive freedom and variety, arising from subtleties of formal handling, which show them to be the work of conscious artists, schooled in a sophisticated milieu. Although their purpose was certainly religious—their sexual character has been interpreted as a reflection of Tantric Hinduism which prescribed sexual activity as a form of worship—they

Figure 13.9.   *The Birth of Venus, c.* 1480, by Sandro Botticelli (*c.* 1444–1510). Uffizi, Florence.

Figure 13.10. Venus, c. 1530, by Titian (1477?–1576). Uffizi, Florence.

cannot simply be classed with primitive fertility idols. They stand alone in the history of world art as a forthright assertion of sexuality on a grand and public scale, reconciling instinctual drive with religious purpose, intimate experience with monumental form.

Revival of Erotic Art in the Renaissance

In the West, ecclesiastic sponsorship excluded erotic art. It was only when secular patronage reappeared in the course of the fifteenth century that artists recovered the freedom to deal with subjects forbidden by the Church. The cultural and social revolution known as the Renaissance transformed the ideological function and social base of art. The process of secularization which European art underwent in the fifteenth and sixteenth centuries invites comparison with the secularization of Greek art 2,000 years before. The difference was that Greek art had evolved organically from primitive and archaic sources, developing ideas and forms out of its own continuity, while European art of the Renaissance, emancipated from its own recent tradition, could claim an ancient heritage—the achievement of Greece and Rome, triumphantly rehabilitated and ready to be regained. But this possession was not to be shared by all classes of society. Christian art had been an instrument of spiritual salvation, controlled by the Church but addressed to all mankind. The secular art of the new age was an intellectual luxury, the entertainment and privilege of an educated elite. This fact helped to liberate the makers of art from doctrinal restraints and inspired them with fresh daring and independence of mind. But it also cut them off from the common people and forced them to cater to a small and capricious class.

As subjects taken from ancient history, myth, and poetry began to compete with religious subject matter, the interest of secular patrons was directed particularly to those aspects of ancient culture that Christianity had banned or buried. Protected by the general rehabilitation of antiquity, specifically erotic themes reappeared in early Renaissance art. Humanist scholarship now legitimized the nudity of Venus, as Christian theology had formerly, with some reluctance, sanctioned the nudity of Eve. From tombs and rubble-filled vaults, treasure hunters brought to light statues and paintings of splendid, sensuous beauty. The artists chose them as their models, and in their own works tried to restore these divinities to their appropriate settings. The loves of the gods; their feasts and triumphs; the old fables of pursuit, disguise, seduction, and abandonment thus reentered the repertory of art. From this effort of recovery and revival came the prototypical images of modern erotic art: Botticelli's *Venus*, seaborne in perfect nakedness (see Figure 13.9); Giorgione's *Venus*, asleep in a wide landscape; Michelangelo's *Leda* embracing the swan; Correggio's *Io* held by the cloud-shape of Jupiter, and many more. Endlessly recopied or

Figure 13.11. Feast of the Gods, second half of the sixteenth century, by a Flemish Mannerist (attributed to F. Floris). Reims Museum.

adapted and broadcast through the medium of prints, these faces, bodies, and attitudes furnished the basic stock of erotic types in subsequent Western art.

The sensuality which warmed the mytho-logical compositions of Raphael and Titian was tempered by decorum and emotional reticence (see Figure 13.10). In the works of the following generation the erotic flavor sometimes sharpened to an uncomfortable intensity. The

Figure 13.12. Amorous Feast, engraving by the Master of 1465. Louvre, Paris.

subjects that these so-called Mannerists chose were often obscure and of labyrinthine complexity (see Figure 13.11). Olympian and Biblical trappings served as an appeal to sexual curiosity; intricate allegories or pedantic fables offered occasions for erotic teases turning on clever half-concealment of sexual organs in tangles of interwoven limbs. Although it had originated in Italy, Mannerism had a long after-life in the French School of Fountainebleau and in the Netherlands. It has a special interest for the history of erotic art as an instance of the influence of sexual fantasy on the formation of a style. The tumescent fullness or flaccid languor of Mannerist figures, the curious deformations of breasts, hips, and buttocks which Mannerism grafted onto the classical ideal, the weird dimplings, buddings, and undulations with which it enlivened bodies all express a pervasive obsession with sex. At its best, the erotic drive in Mannerism produced work of great expressive force; at its worst it led to stale affectation and unintentional humor.

Besides this classical strain in the erotic art of the Renaissance, there existed another, more popular one of bawdy imagery, drawn from the

Figure 13.13. The Mixed Bath, engraving by Virgil Solis (1514–1562).

Figure 13.14. *Pair of Lovers,* late copy after an engraving by Marcantonio Raimondi, based on designs by Giulio Romano.

reality of common life (see Figures 13.12 and 13.13). Particularly in the countries of the North, inexpensive prints of the brawlings and couplings of peasants, mercenaries, and prostitutes in taverns, markets, or public baths enjoyed wide circulation. In contrast to the elegant lasciviousness of courtly eroticism, these Rabelaisian subjects were meant to appeal to middle-class taste. They were conceived in an earthy vernacular, without aesthetic pretensions. Their robust obscenity reflects the mood of folk humor in scenes of greed, sottishness, and vanity. There is not a trace in them of the exalted pantomime of passion and seduction. The sexual situation is never described in the form of a sensuous or aesthetic experience. The emphasis, instead, is wholly on grotesque be-

havior, sharply, often sardonically observed, on loutish pursuit, pratfall, and lifted skirt. From the sixteenth century onward, this realistic strain of "low" erotic genre, reminiscent of antique satyr burlesque, continued as an important alternative to the grander traditions of erotic art.

License and Puritanism

The relative freedom from restrictions that made these works possible also encouraged the production of trivial erotica, often based on antique precedent, which exploited the widespread taste for pictorial obscenity. The example of Roman pornography inspired many modern imitations, of which Giulio Romano's

(1499–1546) famous pictures of the positions of sexual intercourse (painted before 1524) were an early and influential instance (see Figure 13.14). The beginning of modern commercial pornography can be traced to this time. It was strongly assisted by the technological developments that permitted graphic reproduction in the form of woodcuts, engravings, and etchings (see Figure 13.15).

The protest against licentious, soul-corrupting images began immediately upon the revival of secular pagan art in the early Renaissance. The successive movements of reform which came to be directed against the worldliness and moral decay in Renaissance society all included demands for the control of artistic excesses, of nudity or indecency, particularly when they marred religious subjects, and for curbs on the production of erotic art. The more radical campaigns for moral regeneration, such as Fra Savonarola's severe regime of penance in Florence during the last years of the fifteenth century, went to the logical extreme of including all art that was not strictly devotional in the general ban on vicious luxuries. Throughout Europe, the recoil from the Renaissance effort of intellectual emancipation and secularism expressed itself in recurring moods of repentance and in retreat into austere piety. The outlook that has come to be called "puritan," with its fear of sex and suspicion of art, took form in this Lenten phase of the Renaissance. It has ever since been a main influence on the struggle against obscenity in art (which could conceivably be fought on very different grounds) and has shaped the strategies of restraint, censorship, and suppression which continue to be in use today.

The Reformation was, on the whole, hostile to the figurative arts, though by no means everywhere and not always on moral grounds. At the court of Saxony Lucas Cranach (1472–1553) painted voluptuous nudes for his Protestant patrons, as well as portraits of his friend Martin Luther. In other parts of northern and central Europe, especially those over which Calvinism had gained control, the Reformation's opposition to "idolatry" seriously restricted the role allowed to the arts or forbade them altogether. In the countries that had remained Catholic the movement of reform led to the formulation of detailed rules to safeguard the decency of art. In 1524 Marcantonio Raimondi was imprisoned for having engraved Giulio Romano's pictures of the positions of intercourse. In 1559 Pope Paul IV ordered some of the nude figures in Michelangelo's *Last Judgment* in the Sistine Chapel to be covered; seven years later, further figures in this fresco were clothed by order of Pope Pius V. The

Figure 13.15. Satyr and Nymph, c. 1590, engraving by Agostino Carracchi (1557–1602).

Council of Trent (1545–1563) formulated rules of artistic decency. Thereafter the Inquisition, aided by numerous and ubiquitous eccelesiastical authorities, was particularly charged with the enforcement of these rules. In 1573 the painter Paolo Veronese had to defend himself before an Inquisitional tribunal against the charge of having introduced offensive details into his *Christ in the House of Levi.* Faced by these severe controls and by the mounting pressure of popular disapproval, few men cared to own and few artists to produce work of an openly sexual character.

Compared to the preceding century, the seventeenth century was not an age of license in the arts. When artists occasionally ventured beyond the bounds of the permissible, their action usually reflected the desire of a self-assured and powerful patron, rather than their personal daring. At the Spanish court, Diego Velasquez (1599–1660) painted a single nude Venus, posed chastely in back view. The Fleming Peter Paul Rubens (1577–1640) permitted himself much greater freedom (see Figure 13.16). His powerfully sensuous nudes proclaim a very virile interest in sex and were certainly meant to give erotic pleasure, but they stop far short of the insistent lewdness and affectation of much Mannerist painting. Rembrandt (1606–1669) drew and etched several small erotic subjects, couples in the act of love, treating them with such gentle truthfulness and gravity as to appease the Grand Inquisitor himself (see Figure 13.17). This seriousness and intensity also appear in those of his Biblical scenes that have erotic overtones and that might, in other hands, have yielded nothing more than a superficial attractiveness. Rubens and Anthony van Dyck were perhaps attentive to conventions and to censorship, though it is difficult to believe that these seriously hampered the irrepressible Rubens; Rembrandt evidently followed only his intuition. Because of the vigor, truth, and depth of the conception of sex

Figure 13.16. Andromeda, c. 1638, by P. P. Rubens. Staatliche Museen, Berlin.

and because of their avoidance of the conventional, Rembrandt and Rubens ought to be ranked among the few great masters of erotic art in the West. The fact that in the pictorial anthologies of "erotica" they tend to be overshadowed by lesser artists, whose work leaves little to the imagination, only illustrates the triviality of the notion that eroticism in art consists of exposure and display, rather than of expression.

The Eighteenth Century

The early decades of the eighteenth century witnessed a thorough liberalization of the manners and tastes of the cosmopolitan elite which set the tone of art. A new style of life took shape at the court of France among nobles and cultivated bourgeois by whom the long-awaited death of Louis XIV was greeted as a liberation, and from there it spread to other capitals and courts. The new generation looked with contempt on the stoic and martial virtues of the preceding age, which they judged to have been barbaric, rather than grand, and cultivated instead the subtler graces of a polished social existence. The old authorities lost their terror and the prohibitions and penalties which had hemmed in the more intimate and irregular indulgences, especially the sexual ones, faded rapidly. At no other period of Western history has erotic art been more warmly cherished and promoted more officially than in the years from about 1720 to about 1780. The effect of this tolerance was not only to increase the number of erotic works, but also to raise their general level of quality by making it possible for artists of high ability to devote themselves to such subjects without embarrassment or fear.

The period produced only one painter, Watteau, who can be compared with Titian, Correggio, or Rubens as an artist of the erotic, but it sustained hundreds of talented specialists in amatory subjects. Never before had so much ingenuity and invention been lavished on rosy, dimpled nudities and on the endless pantomime of seduction and copulation. Never since that time has pornography in the West attained such genuine grace and charm. What saved Rococo art from vulgarity, though not always from monotony or insipidity, was the tact of the aristocratic society for which it was made. It is important to bear in mind how completely class-determined was the morality which this

Figure 13.17.   The Fourposter Bed, 1646, etching by Rembrandt.

Figure 13.18.   Nude Girl, c. 1740, by F. Boucher. Staatliche Gemäldesammlung, Munich.

art reflected. While the elite had achieved an almost unlimited freedom in sexual matters, harsh punishment still threatened sexual offenders of the inferior social orders—the penalty for convicted homosexuals of the lower classes was death by quartering.

Antoine Watteau (1684–1721) invented a form of pictorial love poetry, the *fête galante*, in which modern men and women in elegant fantasy dress are shown celebrating in Arcadian groves guarded by the statues of pagan gods. With great subtlety, his paintings combine elements from the two main traditions of erotic imagery, antique myth and modern genre. Pater, Lancret, and a host of lesser artists

imitated and often coarsened Watteau's inventions, which were given additional wide currency by reproductive prints. Francois Boucher (1703–1770) carried on the grander manner of the Venetian and Flemish masters (see Figure 13.18). He exploited the fables of the gods and nymphs with amiable cynicism, extracting from them all the sexual stimulation they would yield. The insincerity of his paintings adds something to their attractiveness; travesty is as much a characteristic of his style as is the unanatomical gracefulness of his nudes which often recall, in their elongations and undulations, the sensual monstrosities of Mannerist art. Jean Honoré Fragonard (1732–1806) also made playful use of antique motifs, as in his famous etchings of satyrs, but most of his many erotic subjects had contemporary, rural, and popular settings (see Figure 13.19). They are notable for their wit; their interest often hinges on some explosive incident, on a prank, surprise, or struggle. Compared to Fragonard's nervous vivacity, Boucher's displays of flesh seem placid. Sex contributed to the work of Fragonard an excitement which heightened the tone and animated the form; it was his inspiration, rather than merely his material.

On a much lower level the journeymen of erotic art—painters, decorative sculptors, and countless engravers—fabricated their petty depravities (see Figure 13.20). They were at their most insipid in fantasies of putti and turtle doves and at their best in observations of contemporary high or low life. Rarely, one of them ventured from the agreeably trivial into the dangerous area of perversion and cruelty, reminding us that the age of Fragonard was also that of the Marquis de Sade (see Figure 13.21). The function of much of this production was evidently aphrodisiac; many erotic pictures seem calculated, in the choice of situation and of view, to appeal to voyeur curiosity. We know from his *Memoirs* that Casanova used lewd pictures as aids in his schemes of seduction.

Toward the close of the eighteenth century,

Figure 13.19. The Surprise, c. 1770, by H. Fragonard, Gallimard collection, Paris.

Figure 13.20. Erotic scene, *c.* 1780, by an anonymous French artist.

the surfeit of licentious pictures began to bore and irritate the public. Having reviewed the annual *Salons* for many years, Diderot was finally moved to write:

> I am no Capucin, but I confess that I should gladly sacrifice the pleasure of seeing any more attractive nudities, if I could hasten the moment when painting and sculpture, having become more decent, will compete with the other arts to inspire virtue and purify manners. I think I have seen enough tits and behinds. These seductive things interfere with the soul's emotions by troubling the senses.

Lewdness went out of fashion, suspected of contributing to the corruption of society. A few artists still carried on important erotic work at the very end of the eighteenth century, among them the bizarre Henry Fuseli (1741-1825), who cast his sometimes perverse sexual fantasies in a style which verged on Mannerism

(see Figure 13.22), and Thomas Rowlandson (1756-1827), who continued with inexhaustible verve the Rabelaisian tradition of erotic genre. But the day of libertinism had passed. The pose of virtue, in its heroic or sentimental forms, became the favorite affectation in the arts on the eve of the French Revolution.

Periods of highly developed civilization tolerate, in their most permissive moods, an erotic art which expresses the artist's personal view. The eighteenth century offered artists unusual freedom, liberal patronage, and a ready market for work of erotic subject matter. The result was a vast production of *sujets libres,* ranging in frankness from the mildly suggestive

Figure 13.21. Flagellation scene, *c. 1770,* etching from Caylus, *Thérèse Philosophe.*

to the vehemently pornographic and in quality from hackwork to work of genius. But it is noteworthy that nearly all the pornography is of very inferior quality, while the erotic work of Watteau, Boucher, and Fragonard very rarely goes to the point of hard obscenity. This is not only of the eighteenth century. Very little of the pornography produced in the West during the past three or four hundred years has high artistic quality. In the anthologies of erotic art the great artists of these centuries are sparsely represented, mostly by work of remarkable mildness, while worthless pornography abounds.

What was it that kept strong-minded artists, working in fairly tolerant societies, from going more often beyond the "bounds of decency?" It can hardly have been prudery or fear of censorship. More likely they were inhibited by a difficulty inherent in art itself. Unsublimated sexuality, like absolutely literal visual representation, appears to deny a fundamental necessity of art, namely that of aesthetic transformation. The artist's purpose, even his erotic purpose, is most completely fulfilled not by the simple presentation of a subject but by the manner of its formal expression. The more serious the artist, the more likely he is to become absorbed in questions of form and to shift his attention from the simply factual to the more complex aesthetic interest of his subject, impelled not by moral or social considerations, but by the demands of art. It is in this transformation of raw fact into expressive form that the artist's individuality asserts itself in the deliberate choice of arrangements, in omissions, emphases, and many other stylistic decisions. The partial frustration of libidinal satisfaction carries a great compensation. While straightforward pornography may satisfy the voyeur's immediate demand for "realism," its ultimate effect tends to be monotony and boredom. Erotic art, by contrast, holds more intense and lasting pleasures.

That stylization need not lead to blandness is shown by Japanese *shunga* paintings and woodcuts, dating from the late seventeenth to the early nineteenth century, which present scenes of coitus with the most flamboyant bravado (see Figure 13.23). Derived from the illustrations of Chinese bridal books and novels, the Japanese art of *shunga* developed into a very

Figure 13.22. Love Play, c. 1775, drawing by Henri Fuseli. Museo Horne, Florence.

Figure 13.23.   Two Lovers, c. 1790, colored woodcut by Utamaro.

distinctive national specialty. It reached its finest point in the polychrome woodcuts—usually composed in series of twelve plates—of such masters as Harunabu (*c.* 1725-1770), Utamaro (1753-1806), Hokusai (1760-1849), and Eisen (1791-1848). These prints are one of the very rare instances in art history (Greek erotic vase painting being another) in which explicit sexual subjects have been raised to the highest level of art. The *shunga* artists' emphasis on the mechanics of copulation is uncompromising. They show men in upgathered robes who expose enormous sexual organs and use them, like swords, to penetrate women who submit to their attack, enshrouded in elaborately pleated and patterned kimonos. These formal arrangements are endlessly varied and display a richness of invention, a subtlety, and a daring which overwhelm the viewer. It was, no doubt,

a great boon to the Japanese artists that convention did not require them to show their couples in the meagerness of nudity, but allowed them to spread about their figures magnificent contrivances of colored stuffs. This highly artificial stylistic device, above all, gave to their pictures that intense beauty which the Chinese counterparts of *shunga*, composed of piteous, shrunken nudities, totally lack.

Decline of Erotic Art in the Nineteenth Century

The various movements which dominated European art in the nineteenth century, from neoclassicism and romanticism to the various forms of naturalism and realism, were not favorable to the development of a vigorous erotic art. While serious artists had difficulty in dealing with sexual themes, the commercial mass-production of pornography, stimulated by advances in printing technology and by an expansion of the market, rapidly took on the proportions of an industry. About the middle of the century photography began to compete with cheap prints and illustrations and gradually supplanted them on the market of erotic trash. The sheer volume of production was immense. Most of it was of low quality, the hasty routine of tenth-rate hacks, proletarians of commercialized sex, whose job was merely to feed the hungry presses. Paradoxically, the demand for obscenity rose in proportion to the spread of the

Figure 13.24. Pair of Lovers, c. 1816, drawing by Th. Gericault. Private collection, Paris.

morbid prudery that had by 1820 begun to replace the fairly tolerant attitudes that had persisted through the early years of the century. The systematic repression of sexual impulses gradually so sensitized civilized men to erotic suggestion that the sight of an ankle and, it is said, even of a chair leg could arouse "impure" thoughts in them. The guilt and hypocrisy with which prudery burdened people of every class, and by no means in Victorian England only, poisoned the atmosphere of intellectual life and spread its contagion throughout the arts. It drove eroticism into the sweatshops of pornography and flooded the world with sickly and repulsive pictures which disturbed the minds of anxious adolescents. It also filled public art exhibitions with tantalizing nudes posing as Greek goddesses or Christian martyrs, a form of academic pornography, the last, weak echo of the classical tradition of erotic art.

Equally repelled by *salon* and sewer, many artists of the early nineteenth century were ill at ease with sexual subjects. Some of them, William Turner (1775-1851) and Théodore Géricault (1791-1824), for example, dwelt in their private work on explicitly sexual fantasies, but never allowed them to enter their exhibitable work (see Figure 13.24). Eugène Delacroix (1798-1863) found release for his sensuality in scenes of carnage and suffering. His most daring erotic invention, the *Death of Sardanapalus* (1827) is an orgy of lustful destruction. Jean-Antoine Ingres (1780-1867), too, drew energy from the thwarting of his erotic impulses. The sense of tension in his work is strongest when he deals with the female body, for which he felt a keen attraction (see Figure 13.25). He often showed it in complete nudity, but at the same time removed it from the sphere of earthly satisfaction by means of a glacial over-stylization.

Next to the work of these artists of high rank whose eroticism, overshadowed by tragic conflict, remained within the bounds of "decency"

Figure 13.25. The Turkish Bath, c. 1859–1863, by J. A. Ingres. Louvre, Paris.

as the time understood them, the work of such lesser men as Tassaert, Deveria, and Gavarni, who sometimes overstepped these bounds, today seems harmlessly "spicy," quaint, and dated. About 1840, a strong taste for the rococo brought about a revival of elegant frivolities in the manner of Boucher and Fragonard. One of the participants in this revival was Francois Millet (1814–1875), later to become the pious chronicler of peasant life, whose early erotic works reveal an unsuspected vein of bucolic jollity.

Among the few significant artists of the period to win a reputation for obscenity was Gustave Courbet (1819–1877). As a painter of the erotic, he was handicapped by a self-imposed program of realism that ruled out the free-ranging fantasy from which erotic art normally springs. The challenge of realism tempted him to try literal erotic painting: His most uncompromising essay in this vein is the close-up portrait of a woman's abdomen. Since realism excluded imaginative transformations or stylistic artifice, it had to concentrate on the

material reality of body and on the actuality of event. Applied to erotic art, its logic would have required the quasi-documentary portrayal of actual sex acts. Courbet never went to this extreme, but he came close to it in two paintings, the so-called *Sleep* (Figure 13.26) and its sequel, *Awakening,* both of which, oddly, represent pairs of nude women in situations suggestive of lesbian intercourse. Despite their convincing materiality, Courbet's paintings seem far less erotic than, for example, the artificial nudes of Boucher or even those of the Mannerist painters.

Courbet's attempt to apply still-life realism to erotic subjects found few imitators. Edouard Manet (1832–1883) took his nudes from the tradition of Raphael and Titian, and—in mockery of the *salon* painters—put these hallowed stereotypes into strictly modern settings and situations (see Figure 13.27). His *Olympia* (1863) translated a familiar image—that of the recumbent Venus—from the harmlessness of its accustomed, art-historical associations into hard, scandalous reality. The process is exactly the reverse of the idealization commonly used by artists of the time to decontaminate dangerous subjects: By taking his nude from its artistic context, Manet recharged it with erotic interest.

Realism, one of the dominant currents in the development of nineteenth century art, was commonly blamed by contemporaries for what they saw as a drift into sensuality and vulgarity. Actually, as far as the visual arts were concerned, its effect was almost the opposite. Optical realism put serious difficulties into the path of erotic art, for scenes of sex in painting and sculpture can seldom be simply representational and are almost never based on direct observation. They tend, rather, to be projections of fantasy and daydream. In virtually all the main traditions of art, the typical image of the sex act, even when superficially "realistic," contains a large element of distortion and schematization. In order to stimulate the viewer's interest and to make clear the mechanism of sexual union, artists have always found it necessary to resort to suggestive artifice and fiction. Represented literally, copulation offers little more than the appearance of shapelessly heaped bodies and tangled limbs. Realist artists sought to avoid this difficulty by concentrating on the more easily communicated public aspects of sex. Constantin Guys (c. 1805–1892), trained as a pictorial journalist, brought a reporter's curiosity to the scenes of prostitution and vulgar entertainment which he often drew (see Figure 13.28). His interest in these subjects was sociological, rather than sexual. He recorded the atmospheres of brothels, restaurants, and gambling houses, characterizing their inhabitants with a keen eye for the meaning of costume and gesture. After him, Edgar Degas (1834–

1917) and Henri de Toulouse-Lautrec (1864–1901) painted or drew intimate portraits of brothel life or of individual prostitutes, sometimes with clinical sobriety or ironic humor, rarely with any sense of pleasure (see Figure 13.29). These pictures are, in a sense, the last descendants in the lineage of mundane erotic genre which began with the love feasts of the Greek vases and continued in the jolly peasant obscenities of modern printmakers from Beham to Rowlandson. But to relate Degas and Lautrec to this tradition is to recognize the change in the spirit of erotic art during the nineteenth century. The macabre sexual allegories of Felicien Rops (1833–1898) are works of fantasy, rather than of observation, but they address themselves to the social realities of crime, prostitution, and disease (see Figure 13.30).

Figure 13.26.   Sleep, 1867, by G. Courbet. Petit Palais, Paris (Photo Bulloz).

Figure 13.27. Luncheon on the Grass, 1863, by E. Manet. Louvre, Paris.

Their strident obscenities are rhetorical, and their message is a form of Calvinism couched in pornographic terms.

The last 100 years have not been a golden age of erotic art. The reasons lie not in prudery or censorship but in the condition of art itself. The gradual decline of figure painting, the devaluation of subject matter, the artists' preoccupation with formal problems, and the resulting trend toward abstraction have all contributed to making erotic themes irrelevant to the main, progressive currents of modern art. Impressionism which represented the outlook of the most cultivated and liberal segment of the middle class in the decades of 1870–1890 was not suited to erotic subjects; in terms of Impressionist perceptions and stylistic devices, they were hardly paintable. Only Auguste Renoir (1841–1919) seriously made the attempt, but most of his compositions of nudes date from before or after his rather brief involvement with true Impressionism. The most innovative artists of the period therefore contributed much less

to the battle against Victorian morality than their literary friends.

Erotic Art and the Modern Movements

Curiously enough, the more conservative and tradition-oriented artists of the time, the Pre-Raphaelites and Symbolists, for example, were less handicapped in this respect than their radical colleagues. It was they who promoted the neoromantic reaction against materialistic realism and insisted on the primacy of the imagination, on mystery, emotion, and expressive style. They thus created the conditions that brought about the brief flowering of erotic art during the last years of the nineteenth century. Among its typical exponents were the aesthetes and exquisite stylists, such as Aubrey Beardsley (1872–1898) who drew elegant depravities in a perversely pure pen-and-ink manner (see Figure 11.5), and the Austrian painter Gustav Klimt (1862–1918) whose embracing lovers, magnified to mural format and surrounded by cascades of luminous colors, have the solemnity of Byzantine icons (see Figure 13.31). Equally characteristic of this period were the sentimentalists of sex, the yearners after Eternal Truth and strugglers against Ugliness, who had a fondness for grandiloquent allegory. Auguste Rodin (1840–1917) occasionally reflected their spirit in his sculptures of straining nudes through whose pantomime he sought to express vast notions, such as the eternally masculine and feminine or the tragic conflict of the sexes, but in his life drawings he could be extremely straightforward (see Figure 13.32).

The problematical aspects of sex were an obsessive preoccupation with literary men and social thinkers of the time; the troubled concern with sexual matters stimulated the development of psychology and opened new sources of subject matter for art. The work of the Norwegian painter Edvard Munch (1863–1944) epitomized the neurasthenic anxiety that overshadowed the treatment of sexual themes in serious art around 1900. The note of calamity and doom which he and other artists of his generation introduced into themes of love constituted a distinctive, modern contribution to erotic art. It continued in some of the work of the Expressionists and reached an extreme in the paintings of Egon Schiele (1890–1918) in which sexual excitement sometimes rises to an intensity so close to pain that it gives them the appearance of martyrdoms, rather than scenes of love. Jules Pascin (1885–1930), a quieter temperament, brought to erotic subjects a macabre humor and a delight in the grotesque that are apt to chill the viewer's senses (see Figure 13.33). A strain of inverted puritanism runs through a great deal of the licentious art of the post-Victorian age.

The rise of abstractionism in the twentieth century was bound to have an adverse effect on erotic art, for it is difficult to refer to sex in totally nonfigurative terms. Some artists tried to find a way around this difficulty by resorting to suggestive shapes and colors, following tradition or their own intuition, which would convey sexual suggestions to the viewer's mind or stir his subconscious. These suggestive, abstract forms have always been used in art, particularly in primitive art, and their unrid-

Figure 13.28. Prostitutes and Soldiers, c. 1855, drawing by C. Guys. Petit Palais, Paris.

dling has long been a sport for anthropologists and iconographers. What has defeated most modern attempts to use such forms for the expression of private meanings is their tendency to remain vague and ambiguous when not defined by conventions, as they are in primitive art. There is no imaginable shape which cannot in some way be interpreted as a male or female symbol, or as a symbol of both male and female sex. A simple vertical line can be seen as an erect penis or as the opening of the vagina. The qualities of roundness or angularity, or hollowness or solidity, tallness or horizontality can all be read as sexually significant. Circle, oval, triangle, and square can take on the most various meanings. Red has sometimes been used

as a male, sometimes as a female color, white and blue, according to some traditions, have a definite sexual significance as well. The possibilities are endless, but their power to arouse genuine erotic responses seems very limited. In this respect figurative art appears to have a clear advantage over abstraction. Suggestive, biomorphic forms have, nevertheless, become a commonplace in twentieth century art, from the movement of Dada in the 1920s to that of Funk in the 1960s, from the paintings of Miro (see Figure 13.34) to those of Arshile Gorki, and from the sculptural "concretions" of Arp to those of Bellmer. The Surrealists made extensive use of such forms, often combining them with shreds of literal representation torn

Figure 13.29. Two Women, c. 1879, monotype by E. Degas. Courtesy Museum of Fine Art, Boston.

Figure 13.30. Sailors' Bar,
1875, drawing by F. Rops.
Private collection, Paris.

from classical or romantic contexts.

Eroticism, inseparable from traditional associations, from myth, and from figure, has in
the main been a conservative influence on
twentieth-century art. Those artists who have
been most strongly motivated by it have usually
been led to man-centered, representational

work, and often to quasi-classical style. The
sculptures of Gaston Lachaise (1886–1935)
illustrate the effect of total absorption in the
sexual attraction of the human body on an
artist's work (see Figure 13.35). Lachaise's
powerful female nudes range in type and expression from the serenity of Aphrodite to the

Figure 13.31.   Reclining Woman, c. 1910, drawing by G. Klimt. Mr. and Mrs. Nathan Oliveira collection, Stanford.

Figure 13.32.   Nude, c. 1910, drawing by A. Rodin. Witt collection, London.

or portrait, to which certain stylistic and thematic usages were appropriate. Their adoption of traditional forms has perhaps expressed a desire to be free, on occasion, from the obligation of strenuous nonconformity and self-expression and a wish to deal with the explosive subject of sex in a spirit of artistic detachment.

Modern art is for elite tastes; it has no mass

Figure 13.33.   Girl Reading, c. 1915, watercolor by J. Pascin. Stanford Museum, Stanford.

ferocity of primitive fetishes. In Picasso's work, the recurring returns of erotic subjects seem like intervals of relaxation between periods of strenuous experiment. The classical style in which he has conceived many of these compositions and his frequent choice of motifs from ancient mythology, Minotaurs, satyrs, and nymphs, prove how close a link exists in his mind between the erotic and this particular tradition. Much the same can be said of Matisse, who clung throughout his life to certain stock motifs from the classical repertory—that of the recumbent Venus, for example—as if these were inseparable from the very idea of erotic art. Both artists treated the erotic as a special genre, as a subject matter type, not unlike landscape following. Serious work with sexual content produced by modern artists is generally too obscure, too encumbered with formal problems, and too mild to satisfy the amateurs of pornography. There is no large-scale production of graphic sexual entertainment for the middle- and low-brow audience, as there is in literature, mainly because there would not be enough profit in such a production. Pornography is essentially a business; it requires a solid economic base, and this sculpture, painting, and the graphic arts no longer provide. They have ceased to be an effective vehicle for commercial pornography. Film and photography have taken over this function. They offer more to the single-minded voyeur and do not fatigue him with aesthetic irrelevancies. Besides, they are

Figure 13.35.   Elevation, c. 1925, bronze sculpture by Gaston Lachaise. Stanford Museum, Stanford.

less expensive to make and much easier to sell. Venturesome dealers or publishers sometimes try to put the work of serious artists on the pornographic market, but the results are usually disappointing both to the entrepreneurs and to their unwary clients. Greek vase paintings and the erotic prints of Picasso are less profitable because they are less popular than are simple "dirty" pictures. What little obscenity now and then comes from the world of art is peripheral;

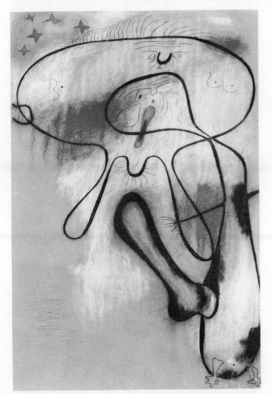

Figure 13.34.   The Lovers, 1934, by Joan Miro. Courtesy Philadelphia Museum of Art, Philadelphia.

it plays a larger role in gallery publicity and promotional literature than in the work of artists. The relatively small amount of frankly commercial pornographic "art" which continues to be made, despite the shrinking demand, has little importance; the mass production of a few efficient photographic studios has had more impact on the popular mentality of our time than all the hand-made pornography in the world.

The recognized harmlessness of erotic art has kept censors from paying much attention to it. In 1912 the Austrian painter Egon Schiele was tried and imprisoned for obscenity. His case was something of a historical landmark, for in the decades since, very few artists, working in cosmopolitan centers and under conditions of reasonable political freedom, have suffered serious persecution on moral grounds. Censor-ship, once so formidable, has had little effect on the progressive art of the twentieth century. In provincial localities, zealots have sometimes forced their notions of decency on artists and public. The totalitarian states—Fascist Italy, Nazi Germany, Spain, Russia, and China—did control, or still do control, the purity of their art, for reasons which are political, rather than strictly artistic or moral. Fascist and Commu-nist dictatorships alike have insisted that art be uncomplicated, inoffensive, and ideologically correct. Obscenity, in their view, is merely one symptom of a basic decadence. In curing the root evil, which is individual freedom, these regimes have removed their nations from participation in the mainstream of twentieth-century art and have granted their peoples and their artists the comforts of insularity—untroubled by erotic fantasies.

Erotic literature is literature about *eros* (ἔρως), both the god of love and love itself. To distinguish erotic love from monotheistic love of god, love for one's neighbor, or the kind of love typified in Gertrude Stein's remark "Toasted Suzy loves ice cream," we may define it as *sexual* love, the reflection upon and performance of acts involving the genitals of human beings in conjunction with those of other human beings, animals, or objects. The greatest erotic literature, not surprisingly, treats woman's love for man and man's love for woman.

Most of the masterpieces of world literature that treat such love leave the physical aspects beyond embraces undescribed. Censorship apart, it may be that most writers who have set out to glorify love have feared the comic potential in what Shakespeare called "the beast with two backs" and have preferred to keep the loins of their idealized lovers draped. Ovid's *Heroides* (*c.* 10 B.C.), a series of imaginary letters between great lovers, typically treats Hero and Leander and Dido and Aeneas in ideal terms, though there is more carnality between Paris and Helen:

> . . . you seemed fit spoil for the great hero to steal away, when, after the manner of your race, you engaged in the sports of the shining palaestra, a nude maid mingled with nude men. . . . If you must needs have been rendered up, I should first at least have taken some pledge from you; my love for you would not have been wholly for naught. Either your virgin flower I should have plucked, or taken what could be stolen without hurt to your virgin state. . . .[1]

Alexander Pope's *Eloisa to Abelard* (1717) applied Ovid's form to the famous twelfth-century lovers, straining the language to describe heights of amorous passion ("In seas of flame my plunging soul is drowned") but refrains from referring to carnal acts. Vergil's *Aeneid* is quite parallel: His Dido is all passion, and the scene in which she gains Aeneas's body is stirring, though quite unspecific: "To the same cave came Dido and the Trojan chief. Primal Earth and nuptial Juno gave the sign; fires flashed in Heaven, the witness to their bridal, and on the mountain-top screamed the Nymphs."[2]

Equally reticent are Dante's Paolo and

---

[1] Ovid, *Heroides* (Loeb Library trans.; 1914), p. 209. Compare "taken what could be stolen" (*quod poterat . . . rapi*) with de Sade's Justine among the robber band. Text translations, where not otherwise noted, are my own.

[2] The last clause is a beautiful touch: "summoque ulularunt vertice Nymphae." Vergil, *Aeneid*, in *Works* (Loeb Library trans.; 1916), IV, pp. 165–168.

CHAPTER

14

THE EROTIC IN LITERATURE
by Strother B. Purdy

Francesca, whose fall was accompanied by the reading of erotic literature:

That book, and he who wrote it, was a pander. That day we read no further.

(*Inferno* V, 137–138)[3]

But Shakespeare rarely leaves us in doubt that lovemaking involves more than kissing and holding hands. Cleopatra, for example, is both feminine ideal ("Age cannot wither her, nor custom stale/ Her infinite variety") and sexual partner, who "made great Caesar lay his sword to bed:/ He plough'd her, and she cropped." Her speech has a noble frankness unknown to Francesca and Eloisa: "Is he on his horse?/O happy horse, to bear the weight of Antony!/ Do bravely, horse!"

More typical, and very beautiful, are the metaphors of "The Song of Songs":

I am the rose of Sharon, and the lily of the valleys. . . . My beloved is mine, and I am his: he feedeth among the lilies. . . . Thy lips, O my spouse, drop as the honeycomb: honey and milk are under thy tongue; and the smell of thy garments is like the smell of Lebanon . . . the joints of thy thighs are like jewels, the work of the hands of a cunning workman. Thy navel is like a round goblet, which wanteth not liquor: thy belly is like an heap of wheat set about with lilies. Thy two breasts are like two young roes that are twins. . . .[4]

There is a parallel in the sensual Sanskrit romances, in which the most exquisite allusions and similes at once convey an intense erotic feeling and disguise the fact that the embraces remain unspecified. Bāṇa's *Kādambarī* (A.D. mid-seventh century) is written with inimitable voluptuousness. When the heroine, Kādambarī, timidly offers betel nut to the hero, Chandrāpīda, the language is so powerful that

the erotic stimulation might have been too much for the reader had the events described been of more intimate character:

The hand Chandrāpīda stretched out, by nature pink, as if red lead had fallen upon it from the flapping of his triumphal elephant, was darkened by the scars of the bowstring . . . its fingers by the forthflashing rays of his nails seemed to run up hastily, to grow long and laugh, and the hand seemed to raise five other fingers in the five senses that, in desire to touch her, had just made their entry full of love. Then contending feelings took possession of Kādambarī as if they had gathered together in curiosity to see the grace at that moment so easy of access. Her hand, as she did not look whither it was going, was stretched vainly forth, and the rays of its nails seemed to hasten forward to seek Chandrāpīda's hand; and with the murmur of the line of bracelets stirred by her trembling, it seemed to say, as drops of moisture arose on it, "Let this slave offered by Love be accepted," as if she were offering herself, and "Henceforth it is in thy hand," as if she were making it into a living being, and so she gave the betel.[5]

The erotic quality of great Western love poetry, of lyric forms like sonnet, song, and epithalamium (often addressed to specific women), approximates that of classical Sanskrit writings. Gaius Valerius Catullus (born 84 B.C.) set a standard with his poems recording an unhappy infatuation with Clodia, wife of Q. Metullus Celer, that was seldom matched later. One of the notable exceptions is the "To His Coy Mistress" by Andrew Marvell (1621–1678), which successfully emulated Catullus' Poem 5 ("Let us live, my Lesbia, and love") and even surpassed it. But, in accordance with a pattern that became increasingly established and the source of much degradation in Western erotic taste, Catullus concentrated

---

[3] Dante, *The Inferno* (Ciardi trans.; 1954).
[4] King James version, 2:1, 16; 4:11; 7:1–3.

[5] Bāṇa, *Kādambarī* (1956 ed.), p. 148.

almost all his direct description of carnality in separate satirical poems.

Not many serious literary treatments of heterosexual love in the West have escaped the extremes of sublimation and degradation. One of the best attempts to describe the realities of a man and a woman in love is D. H. Lawrence's *Lady Chatterly's Lover* (1928). This novel emphasizes what is most positive in sexual intercourse, the pleasure and the sense of union with another person, the hopeful creation of new life. But at the same time it contains passages like the following:

> . . . she lay with her hands inert on his striving body, and do what she might, her spirit seemed to look on from the top of her head, and the butting of his haunches seemed ridiculous to her, and the sort of anxiety of his penis to come to its little evacuating crisis seemed farcical. Yes, this was love, this ridiculous bouncing of the buttocks, and the wilting of the poor insignificant, moist little penis. This was the divine love! After all, the moderns were right when they felt contempt for the performance. . . . Cold and derisive her queer female mind stood apart. . . .[6]

This attitude, according to Lawrence, was typical of the "modern woman," who had become a monster of will. The male struggle against the feminine will and the modern industrialism that gave it birth are perhaps the central themes of Lawrence's work, and in *Lady Chatterly's Lover*—the only one of his books with explicit scenes of sexual intercourse—the penis is celebrated as the corrective instrument. Lawrence's eroticism was tied to a message, and that message, though meant to bring sexual happiness, has so much of the anti-intellectual, anti-industrial, and anti-feminine in it as to be unpalatable today.

Less self-conscious, less detailed, but every bit as frank in their celebration of heterosexual love are many of the stories in *The Thousand and One Nights* (*Alf Laylah wa Laylah*), compiled in Arabic from Arabian, Persian, Egyptian, and other sources in the ninth to the fifteenth centuries. Sex is presented in a cultural framework that is strange and in some ways repellent to the modern Western reader but quite without conflicts over looking at oneself from outside. The dominant descriptive pattern is what might be called "metaphorical flourish":

> Thereupon she pressed him to her bosom and he pressed her to his bosom and the twain embraced with closest embrace, and she took him and, lying down on her back, let down her petticoat trousers, and in an instant that which his father had left him rose up in rebellion against him and he said, "Go it, O Shaykh Zachary of shaggery, O father of veins!"; and putting both hands to her flanks, he set the sugar-stick to the mouth of the cleft and thrust on till he came to the wicket called "Pecten." His passage was by the Gate of Victories and therefrom he entered the Monday market, and those of Tuesday and Wednesday and Thursday, and, finding the carpet after the measure of the daisfloor, he plied the box within its cover till he came to the end of it.[7]

Carnality is strong but perceived through a dense medium of rhetoric:

> . . . he kissed her and embraced her and threw himself upon her as the lion upon the lamb. Then he sheathed his steel rod in her scabbard and ceased not to play the porter at her door and the preacher in her pulpit and the priest at her prayer-niche, while she with him ceased not from inclination and prostration and rising up and sitting down, accompanying her ejaculations of praise and of "Glory to Allah!" with passionate movements and wrigglings and claspings of his member and other amorous gestures. . . .[8]

---

[6]Lawrence, *Lady Chatterly's Lover* (1957 ed.), p. 205.

[7]Burton, trans., *The Thousand and One Nights*, "The Tale of Ala al-Din and Abu al-Shamat," (Luristan ed.; n.d.), IV, pp. 51-52. All further excerpts are from this edition.

[8]*The Thousand and One Nights*, "The Tale of Ali Shar and Zumurrud," IV, p. 227.

Physical details are sparingly employed, for this literature is one of stock situations and formalized language. The physiology and psychology are those of types, not of individuals, and are not dwelt upon except in extreme instances—a man who falls senseless from love, a penis too large to carry, baboons and demons as lovers—which belong to the realm of magic and the supernatural.

Another, shorter masterpiece of world literature, the sixteenth-century Chinese *Chin P'ing Mei* (*The Golden Lotus: The Tale of Hsi-mên and His Six Wives*), sets equally delightful, and more realistic, descriptions of love against a social panorama that is very nearly the match of that in *The Thousand and One Nights*. Whereas in the Arabic work exaggeration and reliance on the supernatural reduce the descriptive scope, in the Chinese work the criminality of Hsi-mên and his women, especially Golden Lotus, narrows the focus to a series of thefts, bribes, and murders. Nevertheless, the psychological characterization is so adept that Hsi-mên is among the more attractive characters of world fiction; when he dies we feel, along with his wives, that the world has become empty. Scenes like those in which he enjoys his new pleasure garden and the one in which he takes dinner on a snowy day with all six of his wives to celebrate his return to the bed of his first wife, Moon Lady, are so perfect that they leave the reader with a longing for such a superior way of life! The erotic passages partake of this cultural elevation; even though the hero is a demon of lust and the action is centered amid a group of women pent up in a harem, the focus on character is never overshadowed by interest in the genitals or by obsessive emphasis on sexual acts. Music, dance, poetry, and delicately ambiguous conversation surround the love bouts, along with the most delicately imaginative indelicacies, like the hair-woven supporter presented to Hsi-mên by one admiring wife and the device employed by

another to save him the effort of rising from bed to urinate.

Scenes of sexual intercourse are sometimes treated with simple directness:

> Without giving her time to object, he carried her to old woman Wang's bed, took off his clothes and, after unloosing her girdle, lay down with her. Their happiness reached its culmination.[9]

At other times the approach is humorously metaphorical:

> They laughed and played together till the flush of desire mounted to their brows and the passion in their hearts made them tremble. Then they performed the mystery of clouds and rain, and did whatever the wine inspired.[10]

And at still other times description is generously detailed:

> He kissed the girl and threw his arms about her. Then pulling the bolster aside he placed her on the bed, threw her legs over his shoulders and set to work, for his instrument was ready. It was not long before the girl's love juices began to flow so freely that his trousers were wet. He withdrew his penis, took some powder from the box, applied it to the end, and returned to the assault. The powder confined the liquid and things became better. The girl held his penis in her anus and spoke to him caressingly while he, inflamed by the wine he had drunk, put his legs together and violently pushed onward. He thrust in nearly three hundred times, to the point that her hair was shaken down about her shoulders and her tongue was so feeble she was unable to speak. Hsi-mên was scarcely breathing, but suddenly his semen flowed and he experienced the supreme pleasure. . . .[11]

---

[9] Egerton, trans., *The Golden Lotus* (1939 ed.), I, p. 67. All further excerpts are from this edition.

[10] *The Golden Lotus,* I, p. 233.

[11] *The Golden Lotus,* IV, pp. 42–43. The term *suci amatorii* ("love juices") shows the sad fact that the true psychology of sex was no better observed here than in the majority of erotic works.

Views of Women

As Erotic Toys

It is well at this point to consider the main views of women presented in heterosexual erotic fiction. Central to such fiction is the idea that women are somehow the repositories of love, creatures who exist in order that love may exist. Byron directly echoed Ovid's "Hero and Leander" when he wrote, 1,800 years later:

Man's love is of man's life a thing apart,
'Tis woman's whole existence. . . .[12]

As Richard Burton noted, in his "Terminal Essay" in *The Thousand and One Nights*, "Women, the world over, are what men make them."[13] What men have first, or predominantly, made of women is objects of lust, erotic toys. This attitude is so common in literature, erotic or otherwise, eastern or western, that it can be taken as the norm. Stories of great lovers often elevate the woman's role, giving her a real personality and presence, but her greatest act is generally some exaggeration of submission: the suicides of Dido and Juliet, the twenty-year wait of Penelope, the incorruptible chastity of Damyantī and Sītā. On the other hand, the "greatest lovers" (Casanova, Don Juan) are always men, for "great" in this sense means multiple sexual conquests, something allowed a man but not a woman; women of such conquests are treated as "celebrated courtesans" like Thaïs or sinister figures like Messalina. The women with whom Don Juan wins his reputation are, of course, utter ciphers, as well identified by number as by name ("In Italy six hundred and forty, in Germany two hundred and thirty-one"). They have no character or living presence because they cannot be allowed to hinder the narrative, which is of the Don's progress from one conquest to another.

The woman as erotic toy is presumably the essence of the role of the prostitute. The prostitute is the "slave of love" par excellence. She must do her purchaser's bidding without question, submit to whatever domination he chooses to impose, and so forth; she is a living erotic dream, combining utter amenability with convenient departure at daylight. The sadistic Husson of Kessel's novel *Belle de Jour* (1928) expresses this fantasy, describing a whorehouse as a place "a man can inflict any desire he has . . . [where men are] stripping and taking their slaves, just as they like, without any control."[14] Houses of prostitution do not always live up to such dream expectations: The girls are fully prepared to see that the slave master pays, and on a rapidly ascending scale, for "any desire" and "just as he likes." In general, he must have a very active imagination to see himself in any role but that of customer. Any man can visit a whorehouse any day and discover this truth for himself; perhaps it is for this reason that what may be called the "literature of prostitution" (*Hetärenliteratur*) is often considerably more matter-of-fact than are other kinds of erotic literature. It involves the only kind of love in which business plays a central role and carries that dollar-and-cents practicality along with it (for a recent example, see Robert Gover's *One Hundred Dollar Misunderstanding*). Dreams like that of Husson come true only in the literature of sadism, as fantasy perversions of heterosexuality.

Nevertheless, a good deal of distortion can occur within the matter-of-fact representation of a whore's life: Two main varieties are found in two eighteenth-century English *Hetärenromane* with parallel plots, *Moll Flanders* and

---

[12]Byron, *Don Juan* (1819–1824), I, 194, in *The Poetical Works of Lord Byron* (1912), p. 647.

[13] *The Thousand and One Nights*, X, p. 192.

[14]Kessel, *Belle de Jour* (1967 ed.), pp. 46–47.

Fanny Hill. Defoe's *Moll Flanders* (1722), one of the first, and often called one of the greatest, English novels, offers a good example of the prostitute to whom money is paramount. The heroine is a clever, resourceful woman who has been "twelve years a whore, five times a wife (whereof once to her own brother), twelve years a thief, eight years a transported felon in Virginia, at last grew rich, liv'd honest, and dy'd a penitent." That is a fair description of the bewildering variety of incident in the book and a fair indication of its capacity to cater to a combined interest in crime, sex, and moral convention. Defoe's tremendously successful mixture of erotic, economic, and moral factors, perfectly summed up in "whore . . . grew rich . . . dy'd a penitent," the formula of having one's cake and getting to eat it too, has unfortunately set a pattern for thousands of novels since, and a major, if not the major, part of the treatment of sex in Anglo-American culture.

In that *Moll Flanders* has had a success not unconnected with its erotic content, it is surprising to see, on close inspection, how the erotic element is actually reduced in it. Of making love to the Elder Brother, Moll says, "We had, after this, frequent opportunity to repeat our crime. . . ."[15] The "crime" is sexual intercourse between her and the man who has proposed marriage to her. Moll ends by taking £500 from the Elder Brother to marry the Younger Brother, and after this auspicious beginning to her adventures we hear far more about money than about love. That Moll should be money-minded, a shopkeeper in a world of shopkeepers, and capable of viewing sex as criminal—parallel to thievery in that it involves breaking the law for money—probably more truly reflects the psychology of whoredom than do many novels of this kind. The effect, however, is totally unerotic, one in which the excitement of money displaces that of sex.

Erotically Hyperion to Defoe's satyr is John Cleland's *Memoirs of a Woman of Pleasure* (1749), popularly known as *Fanny Hill,* which offers an example of the whore to whom "love is paramount." It was also written in London, not many years after *Moll Flanders,* and also purports to be the true story of a whore written by herself. It offers parallel descriptions of the downward path, fears of jail, accumulation of money, and final happy marriage, with attendant warnings about the folly of vice and the wisdom of virtue. Cleland's tale, however, is thoroughly erotic, romantic, unrealistic, and aristocratic rather than bourgeois in outlook, a blithe, unmaterialistic celebration of sex and true love relatively untouched by hypocrisy. Whereas Defoe's work led into, and in fact served as a basis for, the English novel, Cleland's work led nowhere, for it has been almost throughout its history a banned book, difficult to obtain and forbidden to literary criticism.

Foremost in *Fanny Hill* is simply the act of sexual intercourse, sufficiently detailed to be fairly considered the book's raison d'être. Cleland's language is playfully Latinate, but when the critical moment arrives he never leaves his reader in doubt about what is happening:

> . . . Her thighs were still spread, and the mark lay fair for him, who now kneeling between them, display'd to us a side view of that fierce erect machine of his, which threaten'd no less than splitting the tender victim, who lay smiling at the uplifted stroke, nor seem'd to decline it. He looked upon his weapon himself with some pleasure, and guiding it with his hand to the inviting slit, drew aside the lips, and lodg'd it (after some thrusts, which Polly seem'd even to assist) about half way; but there it stuck, I suppose from its growing thickness: he draws it again, and just wetting it with spittle, re-enters,

---

[15] Defoe, *Moll Flanders* (Modern Library ed.; 1926), p. 22.

and with ease sheath'd it now up to the hilt, at which Polly gave a deep sigh. . . .[16]

Such passages, with which the book is plentifully supplied, are almost without exception humorous and joyful. Innocence is the book's main characteristic—an innocence that allows prostitution, true, but prostitution such that it is hard to take it seriously. It is also difficult to accept Fanny herself, whom many details give away as the wish-creature of her author, a projection of male fantasies of sexual delight. The presence in Fanny's speech of learned reference, as well as stock misogyny ("Violent passions seldom last long, and those of women least of any," p. 116) and her elaboration on the beauty of another woman's breasts (p. 194) betray Cleland. Both Fanny's sexual physiology and her psychology are inaccurate: She derives intense erotic stimulation from the sight of a penis and rates each one according to its size; she describes female orgasm according to the "spending" theory; she dwells on the sexual prowess of men.

In comparing *Fanny Hill* to *Moll Flanders* we find an irony that is repeated again and again in the history of Western literature: The "realistic" book distorts reality by leaving out sex or, rather, leaving it in only as a darkly hinted "criminal" motivation; the erotic book is steeped in a fantasy centered upon male satisfaction and tends imperceptibly—and even against the wishes of competent authors like Cleland and Lawrence—to dominate the action to the point of distortion. *Moll Flanders* tells us nothing about a whore's life but the deceit and the money; *Fanny Hill* tells us only man's dreams of what a whore's dreams of sex might be. But at least the sex is there in *Fanny Hill*, unsuppressed by the modesty of an author who posits a modest whore.

---

[16] Cleland, *Memoirs of a Woman of Pleasure* (1963 ed.), p. 73. All further excerpts are from this edition.

There are many European "dialogues of courtesans," beginning with Lucian's *Etairikoi Dialogoi* (*c.* A.D. 150): for example, *Elegantiae latini sermonis seu Aloisia Sigaea* by Nicholas Chorier (1622-1692) and *I Ragionamenti* by Pietro Aretino (1492-1556). It is difficult now to understand their traditional rating as *erotica classica*. In *Ragionamenti* Nanna tells Antonia a group of hilarious stories—one of nuns serving dildos at their dinner table, another of a woman who has herself sent to jail for life so that she can enjoy the enormous phallus of a fellow prisoner—and then settles down to a serious discussion of the trade of whoring: how to get rid of a bully, how to give a Frenchman those endearing little extra attentions that he demands, and so forth. Crudity and intellectual banality seem equally matched in these deathless works.

Stranger by far, though, is the fantasized whore who became a prominent feature of the romantic and postromantic literature of Europe: the Virtuous Sinner, the Whore Worth Saving, a peculiar mixture of Christian doctrine (any soul can be led to grace), love ethic (love conquers all and sanctifies all acts), and sadism (the whore is "saved" and then used by the rescuer at his will). Another marked characteristic of works on this theme is the ease with which the lover who seeks to save becomes a masochistic figure, collaborating in his own degradation, although he originally set out to end the degradation of his loved one. The most famous and most influential such work is Alexandre Dumas Fils' *La Dame aux Camélias* (1848), the forerunner of *Irma la Douce, The Nights of Cabiria, Sweet Charity, Never on Sunday,* and *The World of Suzie Wong.* It is the sad story of the love of Armand Duval, a young bourgeois with little money, for one of the great Parisian courtesans of his day, Marguerite Gautier, who lives and spends lavishly and thus requires a series of rich customer-lovers, rather than penniless young men.

Nevertheless, the two fall in love, and Marguerite takes up life in a cottage, in order to be with Armand. But they are tragically separated, and "consumption" (tuberculosis), which has racked her from the beginning of the action, dispatches her. Marguerite is noble throughout, suffering moods of melancholy over her approaching death and the shame of her status as a kept woman.

But the erotic effect of the novel is questionable; the emphasis on suffering, whether Armand's tears (no lover in fiction sheds more tears than does Armand) or Marguerite's bloody coughs, is too great. There are fleeting moments of eroticism and some odd touches like Marguerite's bouquets of camellias: white twenty-five days of the month and red the other five! The emphasis throughout is upon life as suffering, a vale of tears. The tacit assumption is that its natural consummation lies in beholding the death of a beautiful woman. In that sense the woman is once again toy or cipher, but less for the satisfaction of the man's lust than for that of his self-esteem, his need for power. Armand's existence, for all his dedication to Marguerite, is entirely selfish; he is like a child watching himself cry in the mirror. What ultimately gives him away is the speed and violence with which he accepts Marguerite's letter of dismissal (actually dictated by his own father); without even trying to obtain an explanation, he directs against her a series of insults and humiliations of the most sadistic refinement. When she comes in tears to beg his forgiveness, he lies with her and then pays her as a common whore. He never sees her again alive.

The effect of such a "classic love story" upon the modern reader is not quite that of the intended celebration of love, particularly if the reader has had the benefit—perhaps the shattering experience—of reading Fyodor Dostoyevsky's *Notes from Underground* (1864), a ruthless and devastating investigation of such sentimentality and its underlying sadism that makes us wonder that any one had the temerity to present the save-the-whore theme in literature again.

As Demons

La Dame aux Camélias celebrates a kind of heterosexual love, then, but in it the concept of woman as erotic toy undergoes a subtle change suggesting a variation in the usual relations between man and woman. Marguerite is passive—dying, tormented by creditors, and dependent upon the love of Armand—yet she exerts a powerful force on the lives of many men. She is both victim and victimizer, a siren whose call bends the will of men to her own. Armand takes, in his passion, a suppliant position, giving vent to such effusions as "I would give ten years of my life to weep for one hour at her feet" [17] and at one point even signing over his income to her. She tells him that he must carry out her every wish without question if he wants her love, and, as he rapturously agrees, he accepts a camellia for his buttonhole—in effect donning her livery. It is not a large step from this attitude to the view of woman as a powerful figure, the temptress who lures to destruction, *femme fatale*, Lilith, lamia, the demon succubus, *La belle dame sans merci*, and, finally, Sacher-Masoch's Wanda, cruel mistress of the whip.

The whore of demonic power, who toys with men, rather than being their toy, stands forth clearly in two other famous French novels at opposite ends of the Romantic movement: the abbé Prévost's *Manon Lescaut* (1731) and Émile Zola's *Nana* (1880). Chronologically *Manon* is quite close to *Moll Flanders*, from which it borrows some plot details, but it depicts a full-blown romantic passion quite foreign to Defoe's prosaic whore and her mercantile world. Money means nothing to Manon, pleasure everything. As even in an aristocratic

---

[17] Dumas, *La Dame aux Camélias* (1956 ed.), p. 49.

atmosphere, however, it takes money to buy pleasure, Manon will do anything for money, particularly if the thing itself—making love to men—is itself pleasurable. She has little other motivation, and wildly improbable escapades succeed one another as the chevalier des Grieux, fully aware of her faithlessness and his own fatuity, follows her to his ruin and her death. Prévost, whose purpose is moral, he tells us, rather than erotic, describes des Grieux as "a blind young man who refuses to be happy, in order to precipitate himself voluntarily into the worst misfortunes."[18] But the novel is neither as pessimistic nor as masochistic as such descriptions lead us to expect. Life is not a travail for Manon and des Grieux, as it is for consumptive Marguerite and tearful Armand; it is a lottery with about equal chances for misery and happiness. The figure of des Grieux looms as large in the literature of love as does that of Goethe's Werther, the sorrowing suicide; he is the victim par excellence of the demonic woman, tempted from the life and standards of a gentleman into cheating, theft, murder, and the existence of a fugitive—all for love and the world badly lost.

But after *Nana* the mold is broken: She is the demon whore with such a vengeance that she resembles an elemental destructive force, rather than a woman; the sentimentality of *La Dame aux Camélias* is corrected so thoroughly that it is difficult to decide whether or not *Nana*, for all its heavily erotic setting, is not finally antierotic to the point of shrill misogyny. Here is Nana, onstage as the "Blonde Venus," presenting herself to the open-mouthed men of Paris:

> She was in effect naked. She was naked with a quiet audacity, confident of the all-powerfulness of her flesh. A light gauze covered her, her round

shoulders, her Amazonian breasts, the rosy tips of which stood out raised and firm as lances, her broad hips moving voluptuously. . . . She was Venus rising from the waves . . . when she raised her arms, the golden hairs of her armpits were visible. There was no applause. No one laughed now; the grave faces of the men were bent forward, their nostrils contracted, their mouths uncomfortably parched. A gentle current, laden with a secret menace, seemed to flow. . . . Nana continued to smile, but with the sharp smile of a destroyer [literally, "eater"] of men.[19]

Her destruction of a half-dozen of these men, on a suitably grand scale, follows, resembling Diana's massacre of the children of Niobe more than the wiles of a mortal woman. Nana's scorn for her lovers increases in direct proportion to the amounts that they spend on her, until she reaches the apex of living in a palatial mansion furnished by a great nobleman while haughtily spurning him in order to amuse herself with a lesbian prostitute. Her house "seemed to be built over an abyss, into which men with all their property, their persons, even their names, disappeared without leaving the smallest dust speck of a trace."[20] With destructive glee she smashes all the expensive presents that men have brought to her on her birthday, and as a final triumph she forces her noble lover, Count Muffat, to undress and crawl around on all fours, spitting, barking, and scratching on command and soiling the gold-embroidered court uniform that he has worn to her house from attendance upon the Empress.

In one of Zola's most striking metaphors Nana is a giant *mouth*, eating up the countryside, swallowing farms, villas, fields, mills, streams and forests; she "eats" men, but it is apropos to recall that Fanny Hill calls vaginas "our nether mouths." Nana has no role apart from that of her vagina. If her fearsomeness

---

[18]". . . un jeune aveugle qui refuse d'être heureux, pour se précipiter volontairement dans les dernières infortunes." Prévost, *Manon Lescaut* (1965 ed.), p. 4.

[19]Adapted from Zola, *Nana* (Vizetelly trans.; 1948 ed.), pp. 26–27.

[20]Zola, *Nana* (1938 ed.), p. 31.

is a misogynistic conception, the excitement of her domination is surely masochistic. Baudelaire's *Les Fleurs du Mal* recognized this feeling as a wish for death:

You trample men to death, and mock their clamour
Amongst your gauds pale Horror gleams and
    glances,
And murder, not the least of them in glamour,
On your proud belly amorously dances.

The dazzled insect seeks your candle-rays,
Crackles, and burns, and seems to bless his doom.
The groom bent over his bride as in a daze,
Seems like a dying man, to stroke his tomb.[21]

As Wily Adulteresses

The woman with *furor uteri*, who is rarely if ever sexually satisfied, becomes the wily adulteress in marriage, and it is her exploits, rather than those of her erring husband, that are the major preoccupation of what might be called the "literature of adultery." *The One Thousand and One Nights* are set within a framework of adultery: When Shah Zaman sets out to visit his brother, King Shahryar, he has reason to return unexpectedly to his palace and there finds his wife asleep in the arms of "a black cook of loathsome aspect and foul with kitchen grease and grime." He cuts them into four pieces with one blow of his sword and sets out again. At his brother's palace he happens to spy Shahryar's queen, in the absence of her lord, call in "a big slobbering blackamoor," who, "winding his legs around hers, as a button loop clasps a button . . . threw her and enjoyed her." He sadly concludes that no man in the world is safe from the malice of women and tells his brother, who promptly cleans out his harem in a general bloodbath and concludes in his turn that "there never was nor is there one chaste woman upon the face of the earth."[22]

Shahryar then evolves his uniquely bloodthirsty scheme for avoiding further cuckoldry: He marries a new woman every night, and in the morning she is executed. After three years the maiden Shahrazad becomes his wife in order to save the women of the kingdom: She begins her 1,001 nights of story telling, breaking off in mid-story each night, thus piquing the king's curiosity and earning a delay in her execution. We should hardly have expected that Shahrazad would tell the king stories of the faithlessness of women, but then how could she have held his interest? Her stories of sexual exploits do in fact rely heavily upon the very behavior that originally put the king into his murderous frame of mind. Examples are "The Woman's Trick against Her Husband" (keeping the fish that he gave her to cook alive in a jar while she goes off with her lover, so that when he accuses her she shows him the fresh fish and denies that she was ever gone), "The Woman Who Made her Husband Sift Dust,"[23] "The Confectioner, His Wife, and the Parrot,"[24] and many others in the section called "The Craft and Malice of Women."

Another Arabic classic, *The Perfumed Garden of the Shaykh Nefzawi* (*Al Roud al atir wa nuzhat al khatir,* c. 1400) includes few stories that do not concern the marital deceits of women. Even the section "Concerning Women who Deserved to be Praised" is taken up mainly with the story of the Negro Dorerame and the lengths to which women of high estate will go to enjoy his outsized charms; it ends with the reflection that "a man who falls in love with a woman imperils himself, and exposes himself to the greatest troubles."[25] The section "On the Deceits and Treacheries of

---

[21] Baudelaire, *Les Fleurs du Mal* (1952 ed.), p. 28.

[22] *The Thousand and One Nights,* I, pp. 4, 6–7, 14.

[23] *The Thousand and One Nights,* VI, p. 143.

[24] *The Thousand and One Nights,* VI, p. 132.

[25] Nefzawi, *The Perfumed Garden* (1963 ed.), p. 116. All further excerpts are from this edition.

Women" manages to stretch credibility somewhat farther. We hear of a man brought to his own wife by a careless panderer and of how she manages nevertheless to put him in the wrong ("Story of a Deceived Husband Being Convicted Himself of Infidelity"), of a woman who marries one man for the day and another for the night ("Story of the Woman with Two Husbands"), and of similar marvels.

The parallels in theme and plot between *The Perfumed Garden* and *The One Thousand and One Nights* are not surprising, but it is remarkable to see how closely European literature of the fourteenth to sixteenth centuries, in which the dominant erotic form is the simple, coarse prose tale, resembles them. Boccaccio's *The Decameron* (*c.* 1350) is the best collection of these tales, ranging over magic, travel in distant lands, feats of arms and chivalric valor, and amorous exploits; among the last it returns again and again to the quicksilver nature of the married woman. One wife who confesses to a priest lies about the advances of a certain man so that the priest will rebuke the man and inadvertently notify him of her interest (day 3, story 3); another wife cannot see why she should not dispose as she sees fit of what is left after her husband is satisfied (day 6, story 7); still another sets her husband to watch at the door while she brings her lover in by the roof (day 7, story 5); a fourth lets her lover lie with her while her husband watches from a tree, convinced that he is seeing an illusion (day 7, story 9); and so on. Most of these situations seem more grotesque than erotic; the author's misogyny and affectation of pity for married men crudely exaggerated.

Yet Boccaccio was essentially a skillful writer; except for Geoffrey Chaucer, those who imitated his erotic style were not. Chaucer's *Canterbury Tales* (*c.* 1375) treats adultery in parable form. "The Merchant's Tale," about an old man who marries a young woman and is cuckolded, uses Boccaccio's device of having the husband see his wife and her lover lying together while persuaded that he is not. "The Miller's Tale" gives us the immortal Alisoun, supple and slender as a weasel, who fools both lover and watchful husband; "The Shipman's Tale" tells of a wife who finds her husband insufficiently "fresshe abedde" and turns to whoring:

This faire wyf acorded with daun John
That for thise hundred frankes he sholde al nyght
Have hir in his armes bolt upright. . . .
(lines 313–315)

Rather less competent are *Les Cent Nouvelles Nouvelles* (*The Hundred Tales,* *c.* 1450, possibly written or compiled by Antoine de la Sale), in which one wife covers her husband's one good eye so that her lover can escape the bedroom (tale 16), one locks her husband in a chest all night while she lies with her lover (tale 27), one has two lovers and her husband in the house at once (tale 34), one has her lover throw slops on her from a window so that she will have an excuse to enter his house (tale 37), one makes her husband think that he dreamed giving her a fish which she had already given to her lover (tale 38), one lets her lover do everything but kiss her, as she has promised fidelity to her husband with her mouth (tale 48), and many others play similar tricks.

This view of married women is common in Oriental literature too. *Jou-p'u-t'uan* (*Flesh Prayer Mat*) by Li Yü, a minor Chinese erotic classic published in 1634, takes it more or less for granted that wives whose husbands are away, are of lower social class, or are sexually lacking, will welcome the advances of men like the Before Midnight Scholar, the lustful hero. The Sanskrit *Vetalapañcavimsati* (*Twenty-Five Tales of a Vampire,* a part of Somadeva's *Kathāsaritsāgara,* A.D. 1081) includes the "Tale of the Parrot" (the third story), to illustrate how "females are of intolerable audacity, immoral and wicked"[26]; the adulterous wife has her nose bitten off by a *vetala* (demon) that enters the corpse of her lover and then manages to have her husband sentenced to death for mutilating her.

Even twentieth-century Western literature includes this theme, though in altered form. It may be that we are now moving toward a view of love as superior to the bonds of marriage (exactly the view of the early European Romantic movement), so that a woman will be *expected* to hold a prosaic husband, no longer "fressh abedde," whether Leopold Bloom, Lord Chatterly, Henry Miles, or Philip Quarles, in lower esteem than the man who brings her middle-aged fulfillment and other such delights.

The Joys of Iconoclasm

Besides adultery there are other forms of heterosexual love that, because they are forbidden, hold a certain charge of sexual interest. Incest is one of them in many cultures; pedophilia is another, less common but equally beyond the pale in the modern West; erotic sacrilege once provided a powerful thrill to jaded senses. The variations of sodomy, fellatio, and cunnilingus have long had similar special appeal. As far as erotic literature goes and leaving to one side considerations of social causation, portrayal of such special activities is necessary, for depictions in art of experiences that everyone has had cannot be counted on to sustain interest.

Incest between brother and sister is the forbidden union that has attracted the greatest literary talents and intellectual ingenuity. The English poet Percy Bysshe Shelley (1792–1822) placed it in a framework of Platonic philosophy and in an intellectual form whose real basis is its attraction not only for those who want to

have sexual intercourse with forbidden objects but also for those who dream of transcending the separation of the sexes. The perfect partner in the recreation of the original and superior human being mentioned in Plato's *Symposium* is thus the woman with whom one was born (the closest approximation to the birth of Eve from Adam's rib): one's sister and ideally one's twin sister. The physical resemblance between brother and sister is a basis for changes in sex roles and in union the siblings can form a third, new existence. Shelley, in contrast to Byron, had no ideally amorous sister; he attempted to treat Emilia Viviani as one. In *Epipsychidion* ("little co-soul," 1821), he exclaims "Would we two had been twins of the same mother!" (line 45) and addresses the lady as "Spouse! Sister! Angel!" He projects for her and the protagonist a life together that is at the same time chaste, pastoral, and thoroughly, not to say self-righteously, erotic:

Our breath shall intermix, our bosoms bound,
And our veins beat together; and our lips
With other eloquence than words, eclipse
The soul that burns between them, and the wells
Which boil under our being's inmost cells,
The fountains of our deepest life, shall be
Confused in Passion's golden purity. . . .
(lines 565–570)

The climax is notable for its beautiful combination of physical and intellectual elements:

We shall become the same, we shall be one
Spirit within two frames. . . .
One hope within two wills, one will beneath
Two overshadowing minds, one life, one death,
One Heaven, one Hell, one immortality,
And one annihilation. . . .
(lines 573–574, 584–587)

The poem ends with something very close to description of the act, as well as the emotion, of love: "I pant, I sink, I tremble, I expire!" (line 591).

In contrast, William Faulkner's *The Sound*

---

[26] Somadeva, *Vetalapañcavimsati* (1956 ed.), p. 31.

and the Fury (1929) and Thomas Mann's *Blood of the Walsungs* (1905) may be cited as outstanding evocations of brother-sister love from the opposite (negative) point of view.

Incest between mother and son has also been given exceptional literary treatment, but again eroticism is usually displaced by horror: One lies with one's mother not because of the lust that her person inspires but because one is driven by malign fate, the will of the gods, a desire for utter damnation, or the like. Oedipus thus was driven to unwitting marriage with his mother so that his sin of hubris might be punished. He blinds himself, and she commits suicide when they discover what they have done. Shakespeare's Hamlet comes to an equally tragic end attempting to avenge the murder of his father, for he is tormented by visions of his mother's sexuality. Her "incestuous sheets" he never enters; he constructs a picture of imaginary incest (the queen has married her husband's brother), of life "in the rank sweat of an enseamed bed, stew'd in corruption, honeying and making love over the nasty sty," with which to torment himself. Faulkner's Quentin Compson does the same.

Father-daughter incest is also generally the subject of tragedy rather than of erotic sport, though with less impressive literary results. Among the most notable examples are Shelley's *The Cenci* (1820), F. Scott Fitzgerald's *Tender Is The Night* (1934), and Ralph Ellison's *Invisible Man* (1947). Terry Southern and Mason Hoffenburg's *Candy* (1964) is a more recent attempt to turn a father's lust for his daughter to comic ends.

Akin to the lust of parent for child is the lust of an adult for a child, *paedophilia erotica*. In its heterosexual form it usually involves a male adult's pursuit of a female child. Its literary embodiment is common in idealized form, in which the love is considered impossible by the lover, who therefore remains suspended with his beloved in a childhood world. Lewis Carroll's books, in their setting of harmless picnic excursions and child photography, offer one of the most affecting and fascinating examples. When the man decides to force the child into adult sexuality, moral convention is so directly opposed that an erotic description with more than pathological appeal is almost impossible. It is difficult to be certain of the intention of such a passage as this one from *Mémoires d'une Procureuse Anglaise* (*c.* 1890, possibly by Edward Sellon), but it seems dubious in the extreme:

> . . . that unusual taste Sir Charles had for young girls, a taste that increased over the years to the extent that, in the end, he would no longer endure those of 12 or 13 years of age, but demanded infants of 6 or 7. . . .[27]

Although many inferior erotic works like Frank Harris' *My Life and Loves* bear traces of heterosexual pedophilia, there is only one masterly work that centers on it: Vladimir Nabokov's *Lolita* (1955). In the convention of the modern novel, Nabokov's emphasis is on the psychology behind the action: Humbert Humbert as a child loved and lost a girl, who has since remained engraved in his mind, crippling his adult life and sexual tastes. When he accidentally meets the twelve-year-old Lolita, it is as if his past has been restored to him. In his "adult disguise" he compares her feature for feature with his "dead bride" and finds her perfect:

> It was the same child—the same frail, honey-hued shoulders, the same silky supple bare back, the same chestnut head of hair. A polka-dotted black kerchief tied around her chest hid from my aging ape eyes, but not from the gaze of young memory, the juvenile breasts I had fondled one immortal day. And, as if I were the fairy-tale nurse of some little princess (lost, kidnapped, discovered in gypsy rags through which her nakedness smiled at the king and his

---

[27] Sellon (?), *Mémoires d'une Procureuse Anglaise* (n.d.), p. 7.

hounds), I recognized the tiny dark-brown mole on her side. With awe and delight (the king crying for joy, the trumpets blaring, the nurse drunk) I saw again her lovely indrawn abdomen where my southbound mouth had briefly paused; and those puerile hips on which I had kissed the crenulated imprint left by the band of her shorts—that last mad immortal day behind the "Roches Roses." The twenty-five years I had lived since then tapered to a palpitating point, and vanished.[28]

The fantasy here is very beautiful, a recapture of the lost past parallel to that of Proust's À la Recherche du Temps Perdu, in the hands of a writer very nearly as skilled. But Humbert and Lo's transcontinental honeymoon turns ghastly and ends in a murder that is—a tribute to the bewildering range of tone in this book—perhaps the most comic in all literature. Humbert's last feelings about Lolita are sentimentally guilt-ridden and colored by loathing for his own flesh:

> I loved you. I was a pentapod monster, but I loved you. I was despicable and brutal, and turpid, and everything, mais je t'aimais, je t'aimais! And there were times when I knew how you felt, and it was hell to know it, my little one.[29]

Lolita is nearly unique among erotic works; it explores the psychology of the male with malevolent acuity, deliberately focusing upon a repulsive form of sexual activity in order apparently to expose human frailty the more savagely and to underline the pain of life—yet with such verve and charm that we are willing victims and greedily join in. There is no more convincing argument of the superior sexual charms of immature girls than that offered by Humbert!

Sacrilege, the profanation of sacred things,

has naturally many other motives and forms besides the sexual. Its capacity to excite has declined with the decline of religious belief, but it has figured strongly in the history of erotic literature, especially in the West, where the dominant religious doctrines have strongly associated sexual pleasure and sin. It is, in fact, the dominant character of countless medieval and Renaissance works, the "merry tales" devoted to the activities of monks and nuns. The Decameron includes such stories as that in which "Fra Alberto giveth a lady to believe that the angel Gabriel is enamoured of her and in his shape lieth with her sundry times."[30] Piacevoli Notti by Giovanni Francesco Straparola (published in 1550-1554) includes the story of the priest who hides from the woodcarver whom he has cuckolded by posing as a crucifix. Les Cent Nouvelles Nouvelles regales us with nuns critical of penis size (tale 15) and monks who take tithes in the form of sexual intercourse (tale 32), "cure" their "fingers" by vaginal insertion (tale 95), and are put to flight or beaten by outraged husbands (tales 52, 61, 76).

The cleric as sexual psychopath, rather than simply as lustful sinner, became something of a fixture in eighteenth-century Gothic literature. The protagonist of M. G. Lewis' The Monk (1796) is both rapist and murderer, and the book served as a model for scores of other horror writers. Kidnapping, torture, rape, and murder are carried out on a grand scale by the brothers of the Benedictine abbey in de Sade's Justine (1791) and are echoed in Restif de la Bretonne's Anti-Justine (1798), which poses the uniquely disgusting figure of the monk Foutamort ("Fuck-to-death").

Most works of antireligious (anti-Christian) eroticism seem to deny the validity, and even the possibility, of chastity, demonstrating that

---

[28]Nabokov, Lolita (1959), pp. 38–39.

[29]Nabokov, Lolita (1959), p. 259.

[30]Boccaccio, The Decameron (Modern Library ed.; n.d.), day 4, story 2, p. 317.

those who profess chastity are necessarily hypocrites. Yet they have generally left the chaste God and his virgin mother untouched; neither the seductively intellectual de Sade nor the wholly unpretentious, anonymous author of *The Autobiography of a Flea*, who merely describes a whole gallery of priapic priests, has gone any farther. The better-written and better-known chronicles of misbehavior within the cloister, like Alessandro Manzoni's "La Monaca di Monza" (in *I Promessi Sposi*, 1825) and Denis Diderot's *La Religieuse* (1780), go no farther than to demonstrate that enforced chastity is a tragedy for those without the special psychological equipment for accepting it. Lawrence, on the other hand, took as his subject in "The Man Who Died" (1931) the sex life of Christ himself, setting out to prove the harmfulness of chastity at the very source, so to speak. After rising from the dead, Lawrence's Christ meets a priestess of Isis and learns the importance of physical passion. His intellectual awakening is followed by a physical one, the climax of the story:

> He untied the string on the linen tunic, and slipped the garment down, till he saw the white glow of her white-gold breasts. And he touched them, and he felt his life go molten. "Father!" he said, "why did you hide this from me?" And he touched her with the poignancy of wonder, and the marvellous piercing transcendency of desire. "Lo!" he said, "this is beyond prayer." It was the deep, interfolded warmth, warmth living and penetrable, the woman, the heart of the rose! My mansion is the intricate warm rose, my joy is this blossom![31]

Several heterosexual practices also appeal to the taste for the forbidden. Cunnilingus, analingus ("rimming"), fellatio, and anal intercourse are, with bestiality, collectively defined by law as sodomy in many parts of the English-speaking world. The inhabitants of the city of Sodom, of course, were utterly destroyed for their sinful sexual habits. Martial makes frequent mocking reference to the "cunnilingue"; he reports having asked such a man at the baths, for instance, to be sure not to wash his head, for that would dirty the water far more than would the immersion of the rest of his body. De Sade includes the act only to heighten his satanism, one suspects; even Frank Harris, that apostle of sexual enlightenment, reports using it only when advancing age brings his potency down from its former heights.

Heterosexual fellatio also occurs seldom in literature and is almost never the central erotic effect—with one notable exception, Martial's beautiful little poem about the ship-wrecked husband whose wife has taken a vow to participate in fellatio with him if he returns safe:

When Diodorus, for the Tarpeian crown
Was traveling to Rome, Egypt left behind,
Philaenis vowed, for the safe return of her husband,
That she, innocent girl, would lick
That which even the chaste Sabine women love.
His ship shattered by grim tempests
Plunged beneath the waves, overwhelmed by the
    deep,
To claim the vow, Diodorus swam to shore.
O tardy and sluggish husband!
If *my* woman had made that vow on shore
I would have returned before setting out![32]

Reference to fellatio has become common in modern erotic literature, but the tendency to consider it a degrading act, suitable, along with cunnilingus, for taunts is as common to The Fugs and *Screw* as it was to their medieval predecessors. Analingus and anal intercourse are now common in erotic films, but remain rare in literature.

---

[31] Lawrence, *The Tales of D. H. Lawrence* (1948 ed.), p. 1135.

[32] Martial, *The Epigrams of Martial* (Loeb Library trans.; 1920), II, p. 101.

Erotic Humor

Homosexuals are often mocked, and once in a very great while masochism, sadism, or fetishism is given humorous treatment, but the literature of erotic humor is almost entirely heterosexual. Indeed, heterosexual relations are probably the richest source of comedy in literature.

The simplest kind of sexual humor involves neither plot nor character but only physiology. Much of it depends upon surprise, the adventitious intrusion of erotic reference, the sudden turning of a nonerotic remark, situation, or object into a sexual reference. The riddle is one of the oldest and most obvious examples: "What's the lightest thing in the world?" (expectation of some element known to geology or physics); "A penis—even a thought can lift it" (sudden turn to sexual reference). The Old English *Exeter Book* (*c.* A.D. 1000) contains, along with religious poetry, riddles like this one:

> I have heard of something growing in a corner, swelling and standing up, raising its covering. At that boneless thing a proud-hearted bride grasped with her hands; a prince's daughter covered that swelling thing with her robe.[33]

The solution is "lump of dough" for the uninitiated and "penis" for those in the know.

The erotic intrusion need not be confined to riddles; comic songs and rhymes often begin on a nonsexual tack, then suddenly veer into direct sexuality, as in this seventeenth-century French example:

> How Liza sings—like an angel!
> But that's too little praise,
> Say rather, to do her justice,
> Liza sings as well as she fucks![34]

This approach transforms every object and reference into a potentially sexual object or reference. The greater the apparent incongruity, the greater the comic effect. The prize for an individual instance must go to François Rabelais (1494–1553), whose Panurge suggests to Pantagruel (*Pantagruel,* Chapter XV), as they discuss building a great wall around Paris, that it be built of female genitals, for they receive any attack and are never daunted.

This example from Nathanael West's *Miss Lonelyhearts* (1933) is worthy of Rabelais:

> . . . when he reached the park, he slumped down on a bench opposite the Mexican War obelisk.
>
> The stone shaft cast a long, rigid shadow on the walk in front of him. He sat staring at it without knowing why until he noticed that it was lengthening in rapid jerks, not as shadows usually lengthen. He grew frightened and looked up quickly at the monument. It seemed red and swollen in the dying sun, as though it were about to spout a load of granite seed.
>
> He hurried away. . . .[35]

In more subtle writers effects are achieved more expressionistically: The sexual obsession projects itself almost imperceptibly upon the landscape. Nabokov's *Lolita* is one great network of such correspondences, in which automobiles, tennis and chess games, motel signs, insects, and even patterns of light and shade cue the reader to the body and movements of the desired young girl.

In the West the most familiar comic-erotic character types are derived from Greek and Roman comedy. Central among them is certainly the phallic *miles gloriosus* ("boasting soldier"), of whom Rabelais's Panurge is a fine example, as he anticipates the arrival of 150,000 whores, fair as goddesses, and promises that "this afternoon . . . there [shall] escape not one unbumped by me, breasted and jummed after

---

[33] In Loth, *The Erotic in Literature* (1962), p. 59.

[34] Fleuret and Perceau, eds., *Le Cabinet Satyrique* (1924 ed.), I, p. 113.

[35] West, *Miss Lonelyhearts* (1933), p. 33.

the ordinary fashion of man and woman in the Venetian conflict." [36] One of the doughty heroes of *The Perfumed Garden* takes upon himself the task of deflowering eighty young virgins without ejaculating, and another easily sustains an erection for thirty days and thirty nights. The Police Chief of Jean Genêt's *Le Balcon* (1956) plans to erect a statue to himself in the form of a giant penis—his plans, like those of most such braggart heroes, come comically to naught.

The cuckold is the most prominent figure of fun in medieval and Renaissance literature. He is funny in direct proportion to the drubbing that he receives, to his humiliation. There is little or no inquiry into his or his wife's motives in *The Decameron* or *Cent Nouvelles Nouvelles:* It is sufficient that he be a husband to be a cuckold. When a wife hides her lover in a jar and then tells her husband that he came to buy it and is inspecting it, he believes her (*The Decameron,* day 7, story 2); when a husband is locked all night in a clothes chest so that his wife may entertain her lover, he thinks only of his discomfort and is not suspicious (*Cent Nouvelles Nouvelles,* 27). Verisimilitude is the last consideration in such tales.

A necessary companion to the cuckold is the wily adulteress treated comically. The usual male point of view in erotic literature does not recognize that all men are inclined to break vows and betray trusts, but in most erotic comedy this much and more is universally assumed about women. Panurge is proclaimed a cuckold by everyone whom he meets or consults, even before he has selected his bride (*Pantagruel,* Book III) for under the fickle moon *cosi fan tutte* (so do they all); as Byron patronizingly remarked, love is women's only business, and therefore a woman can hardly be expected to go a lifetime on only one encounter,

affair, or partner. The story of the Devil's, or Hans Carvel's, ring is representative of both thought and style on this point; the extent to which its profundity has been appreciated is obvious from its inclusion in Ariosto's Fifth Satire, Rabelais' *Gargantua and Pantagruel,* La Fontaine's *Nouvelles en vers,* Prior's "Hans Carvel," and elsewhere. It is a story that apparently just could not be told too often. A husband dreams that the devil comes to him and offers him a magic ring, saying that as long as he wears it it will be impossible for his wife to cuckold him without his knowledge. He puts the ring on and wakes to find his finger deep within the vagina of his sleeping *Frau.*

The comic female in greater works, like those of Shakespeare, is genuinely in love—Kate the Shrew, the Beatrice who teases Benedick—but the majority of the novellas, as well as Rabelais's work, are tinged with a childish misogyny. They reflect the view of males who are disconcerted by the fact that there are two sexes—and thus women to intrude upon and spoil the fun of fighting, questing, loafing, whittling, and just hanging around with the fellows.

The headstrong young lover must also be mentioned, for he is the source of a wide range of literary figures: Mephistopheles as handsome charmer (as in Goethe's *Faust* and Lovelace of Richardson's *Clarissa*), Don Juan, Arab prince, Latin lover. Romeo, Pyramus, the *Innamorato,* Leander have less charm but feel truer passion. As comic material the young lover is generally ardent but naïve, an exponent of the kind of idealism that is a natural target for the comic view of life. A superior specimen is Chaucer's Absolon, the parish clerk of "The Miller's Tale": neat, clean, and fashionably dressed, with beautiful hair, and able to dance "in twenty manere" and to stay up all night serenading the women of the town. He is a regular tomcat but doomed to discomfiture, as we sense when Chaucer tells us "he was somdeel

---

[36] Rabelais, *Pantagruel,* in *Works* (n.d.), p. 379.

squaymous of fartyng, and of speche daungerous." He is, in other words, just too pretty and too pleased with himself not to be pushed in the mud. When he comes at night to the window of the beautiful wife of the carpenter and calls for a kiss:

> . . . at the wyndow out she putte hir hole,
> And Absolon, hym fil no bet ne wers,
> But with his mouth he kiste hir naked ers
> Ful savoury, er he were war of this.
> Abak he stirte, and thoughte it was amys,
> For wel he wiste a woman hath no berd.
> He felte a thyng al rough and long yherd,
> And seyde, Fy! allas! what have I to do?"
> "Tehee!" quod she, and clapte the wyndow to.
> (lines 3732–40)

Absolon takes a remarkable revenge with a shaft of heated iron, but he is finished as a lover.

Erotic Autobiography

Closely related to erotic humor is the autobiography given over largely to details of the writer's sex life. The writer is generally male, the tone boastful, and the outcome often unintentionally humorous. The *Mémoires* of Jacques Casanova (1725–1798) are the most famous of the Western erotic autobiographies and have served as a model for many subsequent efforts. The main characteristics of the type are all there: a general air of mendacity, despite professions of utter frankness; a dubious assertion of the literary value of what is being written; a moral and emotional callousness that permits the use of women as a kind of superior masturbation device, to be set aside and taken up again at will; and a dominating vanity that both justifies the whole ("I write to tell the life story of an important man / great lover of my times") and supplies the unintentional humor, akin to that of the *miles gloriosus*.

Casanova's affair with Mlle. XCV (Miss Wynne) is an example. He woos her ardently but to no avail. She loves another, by whom she is pregnant, and is being forced by her family into marriage with a man whom she loathes; she is entirely too preoccupied to respond to the overtures of our hero—that is, until terror of possible discovery of her pregnancy forces her to seek aid from whatever quarter. Casanova sees his advantage and presses it, inventing on the spur of the moment an alchemical abortive agent—guaranteed *if* it is administered to the womb on the tip of the male organ. In a few weeks the patient, near suicide, agrees to the treatment, which Casanova decrees must be carried on repeatedly over several days. Her earlier haughtiness has been replaced by gratitude; she has come to believe in what she formerly spurned, for it offers her only hope. Casanova admits that he found his lies difficult to sustain—the situation is like that of playing an elaborate practical joke on a person who is dangerously ill—and the sadism of his behavior is not softened by the explanation that he offers: "Though I loved her . . . I could not be sorry in the slightest that I had fooled her. . . . It was a slight sop to my self-esteem" [!][37] The story does not end there, however. When the treatment shows itself to have been ineffective, he arranges for Miss Wynne to be secretly received at a convent. This thoughtful action leaves the members of her family distraught, for they have no idea what has happened to her, even whether she is dead or alive, but they do know that M. Casanova had been coming to the house every day to see her. The scenes that follow between him and the frantic mother, in which he disclaims all knowledge of the girl's whereabouts and even offers to join in the search for her, not only lack erotic interest but also are

---

[37] "Je ne me faisais pas le moindre reproche de l'avoir trompé . . . c'était une petite vengeance d'amour-propre." Casanova, *Mémoires* (1958–1960 ed.), IV, pp. 84–85.

morally appalling. His arrest and narrow escape from a murder charge are a fitting climax to the series of deceits, at each new stage of which Casanova plays the part of "a man of honor." That he appears in some passages even to have fooled himself adds only the most dubious kind of literary interest.

Frank Harris' *My Life and Loves* (1922–1925) must be mentioned because it is the most famous Casanova-like narrative in English and because it is erotic narrative with repeated and detailed descriptions of heterosexual intercourse. But Harris, with his incessant boasting, his parade of fabrications in which he makes and breaks men and nations, and his autodidactic show of spurious learning, makes Casanova seem, by contrast, the spirit of truth and generosity. Needless to say, Harris, in company with all the other erotic autobiographers, has a feeble conception of what love is, and his erotic drama often fails of its intended effect. (Oscar Wilde said of him: "Frank Harris has no feelings. It is the secret of his success.") To sum up his feelings for Sophy, the American mulatto whom he preferred above all other women and fearlessly took about in defiance of Jim Crow laws, he writes, "Sophy was the pearl of all the girls I met in this first stage of my development."[38] And as for the erotic lore! Schoolboys would laugh at paragraphs like this one, which makes a sideshow barker's spiel sound as learned as Masters and Johnson:

> There in Athens I learned new sex-secrets which may perchance interest even the Philistines, though they can be learned in Paris as well, and will be set forth simply in the second volume of these "confessions," which will tell the whole "art of love" as understood in Europe, and perhaps contain my second voyage around the world and the further instruction in the great art

which I received from the adepts of the East— unimaginable refinements, for they have studied the body as deeply as the soul.[39]

The unimaginable refinements fail, alas, to make their appearance in the second volume or anywhere else in Harris' work: The secret of his sex life is perhaps that he equates lovemaking with making money (conquest and investment) and money itself with sperm (emphasizing the virtue of thrift).[40] As young Frank forges ahead to wealth and fame in the United States, he comes upon alarming evidence of the harmful effects of wet dreams (squandered capital) and heroically aids his friend and mentor Professor Smith of Kansas to overcome them by tying up his "unruly member" nightly with whipcord. Harris finds dramatic corroboration of his theory in the story that Honoré de Balzac (unfortunately deceased before he could receive the benefits of Harris' treatment) had once told Theophile Gautier that he could not conceive (sic) a great story for at least a fortnight after having a wet dream.[41] When Harris is in Heidelberg, amazing the German scholarly world, he naturally recognizes a relation between mental acuity and semen reserves:

> At first I thought there must be some virtue in the climate; but one wet-dream made me realize that the power was in the pent-up semen. . . . I realized that I had already seriously diminished my capital of vigor, so to speak. . . . I resolved to restrain myself vigorously and get back to my former vigor. . . .[42]

He resolves to be more careful about investments too; no longer will just any girl be

---

[38] Harris, *My Life and Loves* (1963 ed.), p. 205. All further excerpts are from this edition.

[39] Harris, *My Life and Loves,* p. 213.

[40] See Marcus, *The Other Victorians* (1966), who calls Harris "distasteful and untrustworthy" and notes this capitalism of sexuality (pp. 94 and 244).

[41] Harris, *My Life and Loves,* p. 241.

[42] Harris, *My Life and Loves,* pp. 267–268.

able to drain him of his precious vital fluid. Around the corner lies *Dr. Strangelove;* it is not surprising that a man with such ideas has little to offer us in those other passages in which he describes his experiences in the arms of women. Over his loveless marriage, undertaken for money and social position, he draws a veil, unconsciously illustrating the "paradox" of the Don Juan type, who knows all the secrets of the Orient to make any woman delirious with joy but can never make a woman happy.

A great deal of *My Secret Life,* the anonymous erotic autobiography by "a Victorian gentleman," perhaps Henry Spencer Ashbee (1834–1900), the famous bibliographer of erotic literature,[43] seems to parallel Harris' work. Again we find a monotonous succession of conquests unskillfully described; an inability to treat women in any way but as objects, with the accompanying greater interest in *labia majora* than in *labia oris* (lips of the mouth); a tacit assumption that his endless flow of words is of unusual literary value; and an utter lack of awareness of what he is doing or why he is doing it. But *My Secret Life* has greater literary value than does *My Life and Loves:* The lies and boasts about business affairs, politics, great men, and so on are almost all absent, as is sham sexual theory. Perhaps the explanation is that "Walter," the protagonist, had an assured social position and nothing to prove, whereas Harris was a scrambling "self-made" man.[44]

Social position, however, lends an unhappy quality to Walter's narrative, for he preys upon servants, female dependents, and others who fear punishment, unemployment, or simply starvation. Harris, at least, wins his women by his charm. Walter's utter lack of self-examination and social responsibility enables him to describe for us his forcible penetration, amounting to rape, of a ten-year-old girl without comment—after all, the girl's "protector" was in the room and had been paid handsomely.

My Secret Life has little literary interest, and its value as data of sexual performance is much diminished by the impossibility of knowing how much is fact and how much fantasy. It is the story of a pathetically obsessed man burdened with a pathological condition that leaves him time for nothing in his life, as far as we can see, but the unending pursuit of sexual contact. Don Juan was, by contrast, a scholar, social leader, and patron of the arts. A not always well-concealed hostility to women may be Walter's motivating spring; there is a revealing scene in which he suddenly decides to resume sexual relations with his hated wife, whom he generally avoids as if she were the plague (note the parallel to Harris' unhappy marriage). "I have frigged myself in the streets before entering my house, sooner than fuck her," he explains.[45]

> Then a dread came over me. I had fucked a common street nymph, and in the sperm of a common sailor, both might have the pox,—what more probable? . . . . Fear of the pox kept me

---

[43]This is the identification most fully advanced by Legman, in *The Horn Book* (1964) and in his introduction to *My Secret Life* (1966). Legman bases his argument partly on the belief that Ashbee could hardly have been ignorant of *My Secret Life* yet failed to list it in his bibliographies—perhaps too clever by half.

[44]The question of whether *My Secret Life* is genuine autobiography or fiction is discussed at length by Legman in his introduction to it and by Marcus in *The Other Victorians* (1966). Both conclude that it is genuine. They believe that Walter may possibly have had the 1,200 women he claims, along with all those inheritances, and that his narrative has all the ineptitude of a true story.

But it is extremely hazardous to decide on the basis of ineptitude (are there no badly told fictions?), as well as naïve to think it is impossible for Walter to have been indulging in fantasy simply because he wrote anonymously. History is full of "secret diaries" most carefully composed for later, even posthumous, publication, and it may be doubted that many men have ever written 100 pages, not to mention 2,359, with no expectation that they would be read.

[45]*My Secret Life* (1966 ed.), p. 364.

awake some time. Then the scene I had passed through excited me so violently, that my prick stood like steel . . . an irrepressible desire for cunt . . . made me forget my fear, my dislike of my wife, our quarrel, everything else,—and jumping out of bed I went into her room.

"I shan't let you,—what do you wake me for, and come to me in such a hurry after you have not been near me for a couple of months,—I shan't . . ."

But I jumped into bed, and forcing her onto her back, drove my prick up her. It must have been stiff, and I violent, for she cried out that I hurt her. . . . But I felt I could murder her with my prick. . . . While I fucked her I hated her. . . .[46]

As Walter's only form of self-examination is to look or feel to find whether or not he has an erection, he is naturally content with his own explanation for renewing relations with his wife. He is quite unaware of the motivation that makes this scene revolting: He thinks that he has contracted a disease and unconsciously decides to give it as a perfect present to his wife. The overlay of unconscious sadism in the book is a little too thick for the reader's enjoyment.

Henry Miller, perhaps the best-known contemporary eroticist, seems to have cast the greater part of his considerable output of erotic fiction in the form of autobiography. His friend Lawrence Durrell has lavish praise for what he calls Miller's "seven volume autobiography," presumably including *Tropic of Cancer* (1934), *Black Spring* (1936), *Tropic of Capricorn* (1938), *The Rosy Crucifixion* (*Sexus*, 1949; *Plexus*, 1953; *Nexus*, 1960), and *Big Sur* (1956). Miller is the most imaginative and literate of the autobiographers; rather than simply telling his life story, he uses it as a framework for erotic fantasy. *Tropic of Cancer*, the most widely read of his books, is a portrait of the artist as a young dog cocking a leg at the world, for

Miller's eroticism is Rabelaisian in the poorer sense: all-consuming and basically infantile, amusing but centered on feces, nails, hair, bad smells, farts, belches, "dirty words," and all the other aspects that fascinate the adolescent who has discovered sexuality but not yet put it into perspective.[47] As does Walter, Miller feels a need to break all taboos, to write and say "fuck . . . cunt . . . fuck" as often as possible in order to demonstrate his freedom and originality. Miller is especially burdened by the latter for, whereas Walter is totally unconscious of the monotony in his repetitious descriptions, Miller is an artist, determined to dazzle us with his imaginative force:

> You can stuff toads, bats, lizards up your rectum. You can shit arpeggios if you like, or string a zither across your navel. I am fucking you, Tania, so that you'll stay fucked. And if you are afraid of being fucked publicly I will fuck you privately. I will tear a few hairs from your cunt and paste them on Boris' chin. I will bite into your clitoris and spit out two franc pieces. . . .[48]

This writing is literate, Rabelaisian, but the disorder only apparent in Rabelais is genuine here: A zither strung across an anus makes Rabelaisian sense as a windharp; strung across a navel it makes no sense. Biting into a clitoris is painful by suggestion and the coins are impossible to connect to the act in any sensible way. Walter's insertion of money into a whore's vagina has both point (the vagina is the source of her wealth) and wit (a modern Zeus, he pours gold into Semele's "lap"). Miller forcibly joins

---

[46] *My Secret Life* (1966 ed.), pp. 675–676.

[47] The effect of this attitude is such that Reiss in *Erotica! Erotica!* (1968), p. 455, calls Miller "antisex": "Millers Werke sind nicht erotisch, erregend, aufregend, sondern deprimierend. Das Leben erfüllt Miller mit Ekel—und wie er es darstellt, erfüllt es auch uns mit Ekel. Und mit Verzweiflung." ("Miller's works are not erotic or exciting or agitating, but dispiriting. Life fills Miller with aversion, and the way he represents it, it fills us with aversion too. And with despair.")

[48] Miller, *Tropic of Cancer* (1961 ed.), p. 9.

images from Hieronymus Bosch, James Joyce, and Walt Whitman to echoes of Rabelais with mixed surrealistic and naturalistic intent. Reality is disordered for aesthetic effect but at the same time truth is claimed.

The temptation to celebrate the self and phallic fantasy is seldom resisted in erotic autobiographies, which are more often works of fiction than of fact. Most of the value of works like those by Harris and Casanova, whose claim to our attention is their supposed revelation of truth, is thus nullified. Miller, on the other hand, claims imaginative and fictional value, but the important detachment of author from character that we find between Marcel Proust and his Marcel and between Donleavy and his Ginger Man is absent.[49] The erotic *picaro* is most successful when frankly fictional and treated comically, as in the *Jou-p'u-t'uan;* otherwise he is unintentionally comic and his lies a source of annoyance to the discerning reader.

Homosexuality

Homosexuality in literature has had to be presented, more often than not, in disguise—a code language or some other form of indirect representation. One of the greatest modern novelists, Marcel Proust (1871-1922) thus depicts the central, homosexual love affair of *À La Recherche du Temps Perdu* (*Remembrance of Things Past*, 1923-1927) as one between Marcel and Albertine, rather than Albert. He openly describes only the contemptible Baron de Charlus and, in a surprising revelation near the end, the manly aristocrat Robert de St.

Loup, as homosexuals. The view of the homosexual in the society in which Proust lived is expressed by Marcel, his *persona:*

> [They are a] race upon which a curse weighs and which must live amid falsehood and perjury, because it knows the world to regard as a punishable and a scandalous, as an inadmissable thing, its desire . . . which must deny its God. . . .[50]

Proust's contemporary André Gide (1869-1951) also wrote his best novels with characters disguised as heterosexuals, but he made an open statement and justification of homosexuality in *Corydon* (1924), a treatise on homosexual love. Oscar Wilde (1865-1900) kept his homosexuality out of most of his writing, confessing to "the love that dare not speak its name" only in court and perhaps in the little known "Teleny."[51] We search the poetry of Arthur Rimbaud and Paul Verlaine in vain for an acknowledged description of their stormy love affair. Aubrey Beardsley (1872-1898), better remembered for his erotic drawings, did produce a pallid, childish fairy tale, *Under the Hill*, based on the Tannhäuser legend; in it masturbation, effeminacy, and homosexual sodomy are given pride of place. And Walt Whitman, in *Leaves of Grass* (1855-1892), boldly sang of his love for men (especially firemen), as well as for women, but in chaste terms. Gautier, in *Mademoiselle de Maupin* (1835) flirts with describing homosexuality; the hero dramatically announces, "I love a man!" but the situation is undermined by the fact that the man, as in Shakespeare's comedies, is a female transvestite. Shakespeare himself, writing in a relatively tolerant age, very successfully

---

[49] I interpret *for* Miller here; on the point of autobiography versus fiction in Miller's work, see Wilson, *The Shores of Light* (1952), pp. 708-709; Booth, *The Rhetoric of Fiction* (1961), p. 367.

[50] Proust, *Cities of the Plain* (1932 ed.), p. 13.

[51] This story, published in Girodias, ed., *The Olympia Reader* (1965), pp. 459-469, is too badly written to be believably attributed to Wilde. But see Hyde (1966), pp. 152-156.

veiled what may be the expression of homosexual love in his sonnets, and *Hamlet* can as well be called "the play of a homosexual" as can *Who's Afraid of Virginia Woolf*? Either claim is ridiculous without biographical evidence. Even Restoration comedy left the subject pretty much alone; Sir John Vanbrugh's *Relapse* (1696) touches on it lightly in one scene, and the Earl of Rochester's *Sodom* (1684) is about the only other example.

In medieval Europe homosexual works were even rarer, perhaps because of the more barbarous punishments then inflicted for homosexual acts—certainly not because of a scarcity of homosexual passion. The tolerance of Greece and the Roman Empire is well known. In Greek literature there is ample representation of the kind of love that Zeus bore for Ganymede and Achilles for Patroclus, who could say, as David said to Jonathan, "thy love to me was wonderful, passing the love of women" (II Samuel 1:26). Plato's *Symposium* (*c.* 384 B.C.) offers a variety of attractive justifications for homosexuality, the most celebrated of which is that of Aristophanes, who asserts that there were originally three sexes—men, women, and men-women, whom the gods split in two, and the halves go about seeking each other: men seeking men, women seeking women, and men and women seeking each other. Homosexuality, both male and female, is thus as much in the order of nature as is heterosexuality. *The Greek Anthology* (a collection of poetry from *c.* 200 B.C. to A.D. 500) offers some of the high points in the literary portrayal of the beauty of men and boys, especially in Strato's *Musa Puerilis* (Book XII), under which heading have been collected homosexual epigrams by many hands. Perhaps nowhere else, except in some Persian lyrics, are young boys so celebrated as love objects. The legendary ideals are Patroclus, Amor (Aphrodite's son), and, most often, Ganymede:

I see not lovely Dionysus. Has he been taken up to heaven, Father Zeus, to be the second cup-bearer of the immortals? Tell me, eagle, when thy wings beat rapidly over him, how didst thou carry the pretty boy? has he marks from thy claws?[52]

Love in the night brought me under my mantle the sweet dream of a softly-laughing boy of eighteen, still wearing the chlamys; and I, pressing his tender flesh to my breast, culled empty hopes. Still does the desire of the memory heat me, and in my eyes still abideth sleep that caught for me in the chase that winged phantom. O soul, ill-starred in love, cease at last even in dreams to be warmed all in vain by beauty's images.[53]

Eastern literature offers nothing quite like the licentious homosexual freedom of Petronius Arbiter's *Satyricon* or Martial's acid gibes at homosexual life, but it does have a long tradition of references to homosexual love. The *Kama Sutra* (*c.* A.D. 400), the earliest surviving Sanskrit love manual, includes instructions for the homosexual courtesan (excised from most English translations). The *Gulistan* of Sa'di (*c.* A.D. 1240), often called its Persian counterpart, contains songs of lament, in the style of the *Musa Puerilis,* over the arrival of chin hair upon catamites' cheeks and also testifies to harsh social attitudes toward homosexual doings: When the Qazi of Hamdan (Chapter V, story 20) is caught in bed with a boy, he is sentenced to death.

The One Thousand and One Nights includes several homosexual tales, including that of Kamar al-Zaman, in which we are treated to witty arguments against heterosexuality in the form of little couplets and quatrains. This one is certainly the clincher:

---

[52] Strato in Meleager, *et al., The Greek Anthology* (Loeb Library trans.; 1918), IV, no. 67, p. 313.

[53] Meleager in *The Greek Anthology* (Loeb Library trans.; 1918), IV, no. 125, p. 345.

The penis smooth and round was made with anus
   best to match it;
Had it been made for cunnus' sake it had been
   formed like hatchet![54]

The subject is again debated in "The Man's
Dispute with the Learned Woman Concerning
the Relative Excellence of Male and Female,"
in which Abu Nowas tells us that "The least
of him [the superior male partner] is being free/
From monthly courses and pregnancy."[55] Another story of Abu Nowas, however ("Abu
Nowas with the Three Boys") tells how Harun
al-Rashid catches him in compromising circumstances and condemns him to death.[56] He
saves himself by his wit, as does the Qazi in
Sa'di's *Gulistan.*

Two seventeenth-century European works
are famous as daring paeans to homosexuality,
and particularly to anal intercourse: the Earl of
Rochester's *Sodom* (1684) and Ferrante Pallavicino's *L'Alcibiade Fanciullo a Scola* (*Young
Alcibiades at School,* 1652).[57] Rochester's play
tells of a king (probably James I of England)
who gives over his kingdom to homosexuality:

   I do proclaim, that Buggery may be us'd
   Thrô all the Land, so Cunt be not abus'd.

Developing a line of thought parallel to that
of the *Musa Puerilis,* he explains,

   Faces may change, but Cunt is but cunt still,
   And he that fucks is slave to woman's will.

Courtiers and soldiers obey his words with
alacrity, and the women are left with nothing
but "dildoes and dogs"; we are treated to
several scenes of the latter as the play pursues
its course. It has no literary merit, and its only

raison d'être is apparently a childish pleasure
in violating as many social taboos as possible.

L'Alcibiade Fanciullo a Scola is far superior,
written with a wit considerably less crude and
following a logical progression from the beginning, when a tutor takes his charge in hand,
to the end, when the tutor triumphs in the boy's
seduction and deprives him of his "anal virginity." The action proper consists of a series
of arguments and counter-arguments, as the
tutor describes in lofty terms the social, historical, and biological factors favoring sodomy
and the student replies as eloquently with the
opposite point of view. One striking passage
expresses an unusual aspect of the homosexual
fear of woman, her menses, the *vagina dentata,*
and so forth: The tutor depicts the female
orifice as a place so large as to cause "a
labyrinthine horror" of entering and becoming
lost. When men and women make love, he adds,
their stomachs are uncomfortably and un-
naturally pressed together; the curve of a man's
lower abdomen is perfectly suited, on the other
hand, to the matching shape of a boy's rear.

Of the many other attempts to recreate the
spirit of *The Greek Anthology* most are beneath
critical notice. One is spuriously attributed to
Byron, a defense of sodomy entitled *Don Leon,*
with *Leon to Annabella: An Epistle from Lord
Byron to Lady Byron.* Byron could hardly have
written such bad poetry, amusing as parts of
it may be, with its mixture of homosexual
expression and neoclassical poetic diction. Here
is the narrator on the subject of his Greek boy:

Another Daedalus I taught him how
With spreading arms the liquid waste to plough
Then brought him gently to the sunny beach,
And wiped the briny moisture from his breech.[58]

Greater poetry and truth are to be found in
those parts of some predominantly heterosexual

---

[54] *The Thousand and One Nights,* III, p. 303.

[55] *The Thousand and One Nights,* V, p. 156.

[56] *The Thousand and One Nights,* V, p. 64.

[57] Pallavicino's authorship has been questioned by Burton
(*The Thousand and One Nights,* X, 214*n.*), and Aretino
has been suggested as the author.

---

[58] *Don Leon/Leon to Annabella: An Epistle from Lord Byron
to Lady Byron* (n.d.), p. 27.

works that treat homosexuality: *My Secret Life, Ulysses,* and *Women in Love.* The American William S. Burroughs has provided some startlingly imaginative homosexual scenes, of which the following paragraph is a representative sample:

> Lines of brain wave and electric discharge from erogenous zones appeared on screen shifted back and forth across each other in permutating grills welding two brains and bodies together with vibrating feedback—The screen shifted into a movie—Bradley was lying naked with the attendant on the cot—The divide line of his body burned with silver flash fire shifting in and out of the other body—rectal and pubic hairs slipping through composite flesh—penis and rectums merged on screen and bed as Bradley ejaculated. . . .[59]

Nabokov, another contemporary of large ability, wrote of the homosexual world in *Pale Fire* (1962), and Allen Ginsberg's poetry (*Reality Sandwiches,* 1963; *T. V. Baby Poems,* 1967; *War Poems,* 1968) has recreated much of the spirit of Whitman, with more explicit homosexual references.

But, as modern Western literature is dominated by Joyce, Proust, Kafka, Faulkner, and Mann, so the artistic representation of the homosexual is dominated by Proust—and by Mann. Both writers see him as a tragic figure, and no work better illustrates this view than does Mann's *Der Tod in Venedig* (*Death in Venice,* 1912), which tells of a great but aging German writer who falls in love with a beautiful young Polish boy vacationing, as he himself is, in Venice. On the day that the boy leaves the city the writer dies. The story is one of the most brilliant, profound, and disturbing in literature—disturbing because it invokes the shades of Socrates and Phaedrus and associates them with disease and dishonesty, the cosmetic beauty of Venice that hides a rotten and crumbling interior, unnatural practices, and death. The old man cannot leave the city and the boy, even though he knows that the city is in the grip of the plague. He cannot speak the boy's language, nor does he dare to approach him. He only watches, and when he recognizes that he can watch no more his abasement and his life end together:

> . . . Tadzio . . . was barefoot and wore his striped linen suit with the red breast-knot . . . he paused again, with his face turned seaward; and next began to move slowly leftwards along the narrow strip of sand the sea left bare. . . . Once more he paused to look: with a sudden recollection, or by an impulse, he turned from the waist up, in an exquisite movement, one hand resting on his hip, and looked over his shoulder at the shore. The watcher sat just as he had sat that time in the lobby of the hotel when first the twilit grey eyes had met his own. He rested his head against the chair-back and followed the movements of the figure out there, then lifted it, as it were in answer to Tadzio's gaze. It sank on his breast, the eyes looked out beneath their lids, while his whole face took on the relaxed and brooding expression of deep slumber. It seemed to him the pale and lovely Summoner out there smiled at him and beckoned; as though with the hand he lifted from his hip, he pointed outward as he hovered on before into an immensity of richest expectation.
>
> Some minutes passed before anyone hastened to the aid of the elderly man sitting there collapsed in his chair.[60]

Female homosexuality has made even more shadowy appearances in literature. In the West, Sappho of Lesbos (born *c.* 612 B.C.) is the eponymous heroine of the race of women who love women, as celebrated as are the goddess Diana and her band of scornful virgins or Hippolyta and her Amazons. Unfortunately

---

[59] Burroughs, *The Ticket That Exploded* (1968 ed.), p. 73.

[60] Mann, *Death in Venice* (1955 ed.), p. 83.

very few of her poems have survived, and those mostly in fragments, which scholars have filled out with educated guesses, as in "To Gongyla":

[Come hither tonight] I pray, my rosebud Gongyla, and with your Lydian lyre; surely a desire of my heart ever hovers about your lovely self; for the sight of your very robe thrills me, and I rejoice that it is so. Once on a day, I too found fault with the Cyprus-born—[whose favour I pray these words may lose me not, but rather bring me back again the maiden whom of all womankind I desire the most to see.][61]

It was perhaps this poem that inspired Ezra Pound to write his "Papyrus," an imitation of a Sapphic fragment that reminds us what Sappho's work really is for us: a few beautiful fragments, like the hand of a statue found in the sea:

> Spring. . . .
> Too long. . . .
> Gongula. . . .[62]

Few women writers have followed Sappho. Virginia Woolf gives a fleeting portrait of the lesbian Miss Kilman in *Mrs. Dalloway* (1925), a woman's version of *Ulysses;* Radclyffe Hall's *The Well of Loneliness* had a *succès de scandale* in the late 1920s; and France has given us Célia Bertin and Françoise Mallet. But male writers have generally dominated this literature and filled the gaps in feminine descriptions of lesbianism. An example of the resulting distortion is Lawrence's *The Fox,* which confidently assigns his philosophy of male and animal power to a lesbian relationship, so that we see a woman playing the male role in order to assert her personality and her right to an independent life. But she is not meant to be independent; when the fox appears (and later a man), she is caught. Her happiness too is swept away; all nature,

even falling trees and errant poultry, conspire to drive her into submission to the male.

For a sample of the lurid male view of lesbian practices, the acts that Lucian refused to enlarge upon in his *Dialogues of Courtesans,* we can cite the anonymous *The Way of a Man with a Maid.* It is a sadistic fantasy, sometimes advertised as "one of the most famous underground novels of Victorian England" but probably written after World War I. Its narrator lures women into his power and then forces them into lesbian acts—for example, cunnilingus and mutual orgasm by pelvic friction—and, almost without exception, once introduced to these practices the women become fervent devotees, even while remaining totally subservient to the heterosexual demands of the narrator, to whom the heroine writes as follows:

"Come, darling!" I whispered. In a moment she was on the bed by me with parted legs; I got between them and on her, and in each other's arms we lay spending, she sometimes on me, I oftener on her, till we fell asleep still clasped against each other! Oh, Jack, you don't know what a good turn you did us yesterday afternoon!

Today Fanny is another person, so sweet and gentle and loving! An indescribable thrill comes over me when I think that I have this delicious girl at my command whenever I feel I'd like to be—naughty! You must come and see us soon, and have some tea, and my maid and me!

> Your loving sweetheart
> Alice[63]

The style of this work is a delicious parody comparable to Joyce's mock *Sweets of Sin* ("Frillies—for him, for Raoul!"), but it is difficult to be precise about the psychology of sexual parody. Lesbianism itself remains ill defined in erotic literature. As different as *The Way of a Man with a Maid* is from *The Fox,* both treat women as mere projections of male

---

[61] Sappho in *Lyra Graeca* (Loeb Library trans.; 1922), I, p. 217.

[62] Pound, *Personae* (1926), p. 112.

[63] *The Way of a Man with a Maid* (1968 ed.), pp. 149–150. See also Legman, *The Horn Book* (1964), p. 489.

sexuality; in one male power can break up lesbian love, and in the other male power can initiate it.

Sadomasochism

Sadism and masochism are both descriptive and affective terms, which makes them difficult to separate from each other in the literature of erotic punishment. Kafka's *In der Strafkolonie* (*In the Penal Colony*, 1919) offers the most horrifying association of sadism with religion and political power in literature, but at its climax the chief torturer suddenly strips himself naked and lies down in the machine in rapt expectation of twelve hours of torture and then death. Defining sadism according to type of literary work is also difficult. Is the murder mystery a sadistic form?[64] Certainly the fictional private detective is free to be openly erotic and sadistic, using the power of his discoveries to extort money, favors, or sexual satisfaction from his victims, whom he teases with hopes of bargains and escape before he turns them over to the police. In the novels of Mickey Spillane this is done; the detective even takes over the role of executioner as well: The detective-hero of *I, the Jury* (1947) allows the beautiful but guilty girl to strip herself seductively before him, then shoots her in the abdomen. As she lies on the floor in death agony, groaning "How could you?" he replies "Easy."[65]

The contemporary relative of the detective is the international spy, once considered a dishonorable sneak but now painted as an admirable combination of physical strength, rampant heterosexuality, and cunning. Ian Fleming's James Bond is the archetype, using his physical strength to administer crippling beatings and his virile charm to seduce endless women. He too is an executioner, with a special license to kill. His excesses, like those of the detective, are, of course, always provoked—to set our minds at rest about what would otherwise be highly pathological behavior. Bond is unthinking; when the pain that he inflicts and endures is explained by philosophical antimorality, a reasoned justification of murder and torture, we have the heroes of de Sade's novels. The literature of seduction, with its hero type the "gay betrayer," is a stop along the way.

Paramount among novels of seduction is Choderlos de Laclos' *Les Liaisons Dangereuses* (*Dangerous Acquaintances*, 1782), based on Richardson's *Clarissa Harlowe* (1748). The hero, the vicomte de Valmont, and his confidant, the marquise de Merteuil, sweep aside the Richardsonian veil to expose the motivation of criminal sexuality. They take three main victims: a young and innocent girl of good family, her true love, and a mature and virtuous married woman. Only the last is allowed the comparatively noble escape of death; she never has to face her husband after having fallen victim to the supersubtle devices of Valmont. And when Valmont takes her she is unconscious; in this respect and in meting out final punishment *ex machina* (Valmont, like Richardson's Lovelace, is killed in a duel), Laclos evades the full implications of the improbable that he so clearly shows as possible—human viciousness in complete control of the lives of the innocent.

There is no escape from the implications in the works of Donatien-Alphonse-François de Sade (1740-1814), which are unique in the annals of erotic literature for their elaborately rational description and justification of the most disgusting crimes. "Whatever is, is right," cry de Sade's heroes, "therefore it cannot be wrong—nay, it is imperative—that I enact my

---

[64] Legman, *Love and Death* (1963), *passim,* carries the argument that the detective story, the murder mystery, and related fictional forms are sadistic a little further than most critics do, but in a manner that is intelligent and provocative.

[65] Spillane, *I, the Jury* (1948), p. 144.

innermost desires." These desires are fulfilled with a magical efficacy that attests the extent to which fantasy rules de Sade's palaces, dungeons, and bedrooms. In *La philosophie dans le boudoir* (*Philosophy in the Bedroom*, 1795) the fifteen-year-old virgin Eugénie is no sooner introduced to debauchery and its philosophical justification than she takes them up with gusto, offering herself freely as partner in a round of anal, vaginal, and oral intercourse with flagellation, cunnilingus, and fellatio; she climaxes her afternoon by assisting at the rape of her own mother by a syphilitic valet. She then sews up her mother with a large needle and heavy thread, in order to ensure the operation of the infection. The effect would be greater, however, if the characters presented had a little more resemblance to genuine human beings, even insane ones.

The same extreme fantasies dominate *Justine, ou les malheurs de la vertu* (1791), de Sade's most famous work. That it shows a world in which evil triumphs and innocent virtue receives one hopeless defeat after another is not the main trouble with *Justine,* for, after all, the same theme was delineated in the classic novel on which *Justine* was probably modeled, Voltaire's *Candide* (1759). But cruelty so dominates the sexual scenes as to totally overshadow *any* imaginable sexual pleasure. As de Sade wrote from a desire to shock more than from any other motive, we read him to test our own shockability, rather than to derive vicarious sexual pleasure—unless, of course, we delight in the idea of being masturbated while watching a woman bled to unconsciousness (as does the comte de Gernande), of lowering a naked woman on a rope into a pit full of rotting corpses and masturbating over her (as does Roland), or of timing an orgasm to coincide with the decapitation of a beautiful woman (as does Monseigneur):

> He calls me to him, begins with two or three kisses whereby our mouths are obliged to unite; he seeks my tongue, finds and sucks it and his, running deep into my throat, seems to be pumping the very breath from my lungs. He has me bend my head upon his chest, he lifts my hair and closely observes the nape of my neck.
>
> "Oh, 'tis delicious!" he cries, squeezing it vigorously; "I've never seen one so nicely attached; 'twill be divine to make it jump free." [66]

The marquis de Sade is not the only writer who has described the erotic thrill in torture and death. Only Octave Mirbeau (1850–1917), however, in his *Le Jardin des Supplices* (*Torture Garden*, 1899), matched and even surpassed the master in horror, presenting a fevered dream of torture as art and death as orgasm that ranks high among the most frightful books ever written. Mirbeau's central figure, the English Miss Clara, has all the characteristics of a de Sade hero: She mocks and lives above law, convention, and morality, and she sees the agony of others as life's only pleasure ("le sang . . . est le vin de l'amour").[67] Her late-nineteenth-century world does not give her the freedom of de Sade's ancien regime, however, and she must live in China to gratify her tastes. She is a *voyeuse*, rather than a participant. She merely watches the Chinese executioners torture and kill their victims, falling into trance-like states of orgasmic climax that nearly kill her each time that she experiences them. At the same time she exerts a baneful spell on the susceptible males who come within her reach: The narrator becomes her slave, crying out "take me where you please . . . to suffer . . . to die . . . it makes no difference!"[68] His fate is adumbrated by the old Chinese master torturer, who boasts of making one sex into another with his knives.[69] Drained of even his

---

[66] Sade, *Justine* (1965 ed.), pp. 706–707.

[67] Mirbeau, *Le Jardin des Supplices* (1935 ed.), p. 153. All further excerpts are from this edition.

[68] Mirbeau, *Le Jardin des Supplices,* p. 95.

[69] Mirbeau, *Le Jardin des Supplices,* p. 169.

will to live, the narrator decides, as he watches Chinese prostitutes throw themselves onto the bronze *phalloi* of a monstrous idol (it goes without saying that Mirbeau's China is purely imaginary), that *la luxure* can bring about "la plus sombre terreur humaine et donner l'idée véritable de l'enfer."[70] Sadism is alone among erotic forms in having that ability.

Death takes a milder form in works of mainly masochistic character, for it has less horror than seductive appeal as the ultimate punishment, the one that cannot be outdone. Burroughs' fascination with what might be called "the hanging game" is an example; it recurs again and again in his essentially comic erotic novels, *Naked Lunch* (1959), *The Soft Machine* (1961), and *The Ticket That Exploded* (1962):

> Johnny is led in, hands tied, between Mary and Mark. Johnny sees the gallows and sags with a great "Ohhhhhhhhhhh!" his chin pulling down towards his cock, his legs bending at the knees. Sperm spurts, arching almost vertically in front of his face. . . .[71]

Essentially parallel is Kafka's *Das Urteil* (*The Judgment*, 1916), in which the son masochistically accepts his father's condemnation to death, leaping off a bridge as the traffic streams across it, a streaming that Kafka identified in a letter as "eine starke Ejakulation."[72] Even de Sade's master torturer, Roland of *Justine*, felt an overmastering desire to experience this final thrill, the orgasm that accompanies one's own death.

But it would be a mistake to assume that all sadomasochistic works demonstrate fascination with death. There is a large subgenre of works about whipping, ranging from the kind that leads to disfigurement to mild application of the birch as a prelude to normal intercourse—from *The Story of O* to *Venus Schoolmistress*. But it has more often been the schoolmaster who has applied the rod since ancient times, frequently in homosexual passion for the boys that he punishes. As the anonymous author of *Don Leon* cries, somewhat hypocritically (for his is a poem of homosexual passion):

Flog, lechers, flog, the measured strokes adjust: 'Tis well your cassocks hide your rising lust.[73]

A prominent fantasy in flagellant literature is the masochistic one of a man being beaten by a woman. A piece entitled "Hints on Flogging" (one of *The Whippingham Papers*)[74] states that "one of the great charms of birching lies in the sentiment that the floggee is the powerless victim of the furious rage of a beautiful woman." It is also the theme of the archetypal work in the literature of masochism, Leopold von Sacher-Masoch's *Venus in Pelz* (*Venus in Furs*, 1888). The narrator, Severin, so insistently subjugates himself to the woman he loves, the beautiful and imperious Wanda, that he arouses in her a demon of sadistic lust, and she plies the whip upon him with a will. She becomes *la belle dame sans merci*, but finally tires of the role and, in a conclusion both unconvincing and instructive, abandons poor Severin for a more normal lover.

Eros Deprived

Minor forms of sexuality, those that deprive the god Eros of his due, also generally take a minor role in literature. There are some exceptions: In *My Secret Life* masturbation combined with voyeurism is revealed as a genial specialty, whereas Faulkner uses it for shock value in *Sanctuary*, and in Joyce's *Finnegans Wake*, the world's grandest and most impenetrable erotic

---

[70] Mirbeau, *Le Jardin des Supplices*, pp. 234–235.

[71] Burroughs, *Naked Lunch* (1959), p. 96.

[72] Related in Brod, *Franz Kafka* (1946), p. 159.

[73] *Don Leon*, lines 920–921.

[74] *The Whippingham Papers* (1888), p. 4. This work is a collection of flagellant pieces, each with separate pagination, attributed in part or whole to Algernon Swinburne.

novel, it is *probably* the haunting, shameful secret of Humphrey Earwicker. Mark Twain took masturbation as the subject for his comic "Address to the Stomach Club," as did Philip Roth for *Portnoy's Complaint.* The most attractive masturbator in English fiction is Leopold Bloom of *Ulysses;* the most malign (though sympathetic) is Humbert Humbert of *Lolita.*

The fetishist scenes in erotic literature are also essentially masturbatory. "How beautiful are thy feet with shoes, O prince's daughter," exclaims the poet of "The Song of Songs," but he gives no indication of preferring the shoes to the lady, as does the old man in Mirbeau's *Journal d'une femme de chambre* (*Diary of a Chambermaid,* 1900), who takes Célestine's shoes to bed with him as aids in masturbation and dies with one so firmly fixed in his mouth that the angry owner must use a razor to free it (a typical Mirbeauesque detail!). Also related to masturbation is the use of female shoes, boots, and corsets as symbols of restraint in sadomasochistic works; the laces or straps are progressively tightened as erotic frenzy mounts.

From there it is but a short step to transvestism, most common among males and sometimes a prelude to heterosexual intercourse. Byron's Don Juan assumes the garments of a houri in order to gain entrance to the harem, as well as to save his life; Louvet de Couvray's Faublas (*Les Aventures du chevalier de Faublas,* 1787) is so convincing in women's clothes that he manages to gain entry to ladies' bedchambers and to enjoy their favors while their husbands sleep nearby. Casanova also employs this ruse, as do the hero of the tale of the Scottish Washerwoman (tale 45) in *Les Cent Nouvelles Nouvelles* and Meriton Latroon of Richard Head's *The English Rogue,* described in *The Life of Meriton Latroon* (1665). Heterosexual though they may be, most such incidents imply that womanhood is an inferior position. When the full masochistic potential is exploited, transvestism becomes an expression of the death wish, as when Bacchus in Euripides' *Bacchae* (*c.* 407 B.C.) encourages King Pentheus to don female garments and to go out to the bacchantes, who then tear him limb from limb. When Herakles assumes the robe of Queen Omphale, he only illustrates how low a great hero can fall. This fantasy is given free rein in the anonymous *Miss High Heels* (1931) but in few other works of any literary interest. Dennis-Evelyn, the boy-girl of the title, is made the legal ward of a cruel female relative, who is made still more ferocious by the knowledge that he, rather than she, is to inherit the family riches. She punishes him by forcing him to wear female clothes and even sends him to a girls' school (some straining of verisimilitude is necessary here!). If he is "good" he will be allowed to resume male dress and status upon reaching his majority, but he is, of course, "bad" and must be punished; gloves, corsets, and especially shoes are lovingly extolled the while as implements of restraint. Protesting but at the same time consenting, Dennis-Evelyn is finally condemned to lifelong femininity; his relative assumes his property and, symbolically, his penis as well. Transvestism of this type has as its real end change of sex; its masochistic basis is revealed in Joyce's *Ulysses,* when Bloom imagines exchanging sexes with a brothel madam:

Bello

. . . What you longed for has come to pass. Henceforth you are unmanned and mine in earnest, a thing under the yoke. Now for your punishment frock. You will shed your male garments, you understand, Ruby Cohen? and don the shot silk luxuriously rustling over head and shoulders and quickly too.

Bloom

(Shrinks) Silk, mistress said! O crinkly! scrapy! Must I tiptouch it with my nails?

Bello

(Points to his whores.) As they are now, so will you be, wigged, singed, perfumesprayed, rice-powdered, with smoothshaven armpits. . . . You will be laced with cruel force into vicelike corsets of soft dove coutille, with whalebone busk . . . your figure . . . will be restrained in nettight frocks, pretty two ounce petticoats . . . the frilly flimsiness of lace round your bare knees will remind you. . . .[75]

"Real" sex change, the depiction of a man becoming a woman or the reverse, also has played a small but recurrent role in erotic fiction. Its results usually reflect the unhappy desperation that brings it about: We may say that Gore Vidal's *Myra Breckinridge* (1968) derives fleeting satisfaction from raping a man with an artificial phallus, but from then on "her" story is a ghastly parody of erotic pleasure of any kind. Catullus' *Attis* castrates himself in a religious-erotic frenzy, but on the morrow "she" must face a mutilated future. Virginia Woolf's *Orlando* (1928) changes sex as he-she lives through 350 years of English history, and Ovid's Iphis is changed into a man just in time to claim a bride on their wedding day (*Metamorphoses,* book IX), but these books are erotically lifeless fantasies.

The final insult to Eros is the literature of antisex, works that make erotic reference only to express disgust and loathing. Aldous Huxley's *After Many a Summer Dies the Swan* (1939) is peopled with images of copulating baboons and equates human vanity and desire for immortality with evolutionary degradation. On the last page the fifth Earl of Gonister, 201 years old and transformed into an ape, has intercourse with his housekeeper in the foul underground pit where he is kept. The Yahoos of *Gulliver's Travels* reveal in their naked and filthy antics Swift's horror of sex; he married the woman who loved him but could not bring himself to consummate their marriage. Robert Burton's *Anatomy of Melancholy* (1621), a great compendium of learning and opinion on a thousand subjects, takes a gloomy view of woman and her charms and offers a sure "Cure of Love-Melancholy" in passages like the following:

. . . separate her from her clothes: suppose thou saw her in a base beggar's weed, or else dressed in some old hirsute attires out of fashion, besmeared with soot, colly, perfumed with opoponax, sagapenum, asafoetida, or some such filthy gums, dirty, about some undecent action or other . . . if you reflect what issues from her mouth and nostrils and other orifices of her body you will say that you have never seen worse filth. Follow my counsel, see her undressed. . . . As a posy she smells sweet, is most fresh and fair one day, but dried up, withered, and stinks another.[76]

Burton knew his Juvenal well, as did Swift; Juvenal's sixth satire (*c.* A.D. 110) offers a diatribe on the infidelity, jealousy, dishonesty, ignobility, anger, spite, and general worthlessness of women of such severity that it can serve as a very powerful antidote to love:

For a husband to order his wife on board ship is cruelty: the bilgewater then sickens her, the heavens go round and round. But if she is running away with a lover, she feels no qualms; then she vomited over her husband; now she messes with the sailors, she roams about the deck, and delights in hauling at hard ropes. . . .[77]

As disgusting as this passage may seem, it is merely frivolous in comparison to the spirit of Hamlet ("Man delights not me: no, nor woman neither") that fills so much twentieth-century literature. The most influential poetry of

---

[75] Joyce, *Ulysses* (1934 ed.), pp. 523–524.

[76] Burton, R., *The Anatomy of Melancholy* (1949 ed.), III, pp. 207–208.

[77] Juvenal, *Satires* (1961 ed.), p. 91.

T. S. Eliot, *The Love Song of J. Alfred Prufrock* and *The Waste Land,* depicts upper-class love as lifeless and lower-class love as disgusting, whereas Samuel Beckett, a recent winner of the Nobel Prize for Literature, places love, along with life itself, in a featureless landscape of despair. As for sexual intercourse, it reaches its tragicomic nadir in *Malone Dies* (1951):

> There sprang up gradually between them a kind of intimacy which, at a given moment, led them to lie together and copulate as best they could. . . . The spectacle was then offered of Macmann trying to bundle his sex into his partner's like a pillow into a pillow-slip, folding it in two and stuffing it in with his fingers. But far from losing heart they warmed to their work. And though both were completely impotent they finally succeeded, summoning to their aid all the resources of the skin, the mucus, and the imagination, in striking from their dry and feeble clips a kind of sombre gratification.[78]

Only the past holds hope for such characters, for they were once young; the same is true for those of Eliot, Proust, and Nabokov. But it has been left for two writers more dramatically affected by the horrors of modern politics to imagine sex with all its pleasures, even those accompanied by guilt and shame, completely eliminated. Arthur Koestler's *Age of Longing* (1951) depicts the application of Pavlovian principles to the orgasm, with appropriately revolting effects; George Orwell's *1984* (1948) projects a state-run campaign to gain control of the forces of sexual frustration (exactly what Huxley showed seventeenth-century religion doing in *The Devils of Loudon,* 1952) so that sexual pleasure can be transformed into politically controllable hatred and the act of intercourse drained of meaning, physically on a par with an enema.

That is a discordant note on which to end;

---

[78] Beckett, *Malone Dies* (1962 ed.), p. 108.

civilization may very well not survive its present capabilities, but should we therefore deny ourselves cakes and ale? Children must be born in the meantime, whether or not we succeed in controlling the excesses inherent in the procedure. If the world's erotic literature has one message to give, it is that to be human is to be sexual—no better and no worse. And there are things worse.

Bibliography

The literature of analysis and criticism of erotic fiction is plentiful, but without the established and reliable standards, historical accuracy, and methodological clarity of literary criticism in general. This literary criticism has confined itself to uncensored works for the most part and to the nonerotic aspects of those works. Erotic bibliography has also suffered from the public disesteem that has forced clandestine printings, threatened the reader, dealer, or collector with police action, and deprived the author and scholar of the rewards for accuracy and imagination available in the other areas of literature. Thus the leading works in the erotic field are often curious in method, distorted in emphasis, and undependable both in matter of fact and in matter of judgment. Paramount among erotic bibliographers in English, and a typical case in point, is H. S. Ashbee, who privately printed and published, under the *nom de plume* of Pisanus Fraxi, three large volumes of quaint and curious erotic lore, *Index Librorum Prohibitu* (sic)/ *being*/ *Notes bio-biblio-Iconographical and critical,*/ *On*/ *Curious and uncommon books* (London, 1877), *Centuria Librorum Absconditorum* (same subtitle, London, 1879), and *Catena Librorum Tacendorum* (same subtitle, London, 1885). These are disorganized, unindexed, idiosyncratically analytic, and uniquely valuable for their mass of information on nineteenth-century and earlier works of an erotic nature in European languages. G. Legman's *The Horn Book: Studies in Erotic Folklore and Bibliography* (New York, 1964) is a modern exemplar, as idiosyncratic and as erudite as Ashbee; like Ashbee, Legman does not profess to cover erotic literature but to deal with those elements of the subject that he knows about and that interest him. His carefully researched studies of many erotic classics make his *Horn Book, faute de mieux,* the most valuable available study in English. Legman's ancillary studies are also worth mentioning, such as *Love and Death: A Study in Censorship* (New York, 1963), which presents an extreme argument for the dire effect of repressed sex upon popular literature and culture, especially in the area of sadism, but is intelligent and provocative.

Other books of wide scope generally fall short of the *Horn Book,* but they do have individual excellencies: David Loth's *The Erotic in Literature* (New York, 1962) is a breezily written survey with much attention to censorship in England and America. H. M. Hyde's *A History of Pornography* (New York, 1966) again treats the law and censorship more than it does the literature, but is a good general history. Eberhard and Phyllis Kronhausen's *Pornography and the Law: The Psychology of Erotic Realism and Pornography* (New York, 1959), while unsuccessful in applying a standard of "hard core" pornography vs. "erotic realism," gives an intelligent survey. A. Mordell's *The Erotic Motive in Literature* (London, 1919) applies a Freudian approach to literature through psychology, tracing motifs such as that of Oedipus through mainly English works. Morse Peckham's *Art and Pornography* (New York, 1969), one of the "Studies in Sex and Society" series of the Institute for Sex Research at Bloomington, Indiana, gives a lengthy and detailed application of the author's personal theory of culture and value to a number of erotic works, convincingly explodes several *idées reçues,* and demonstrates the cultural value

of erotic literature. Wayland Young's *Eros Denied: Sex in Western Society* (New York, 1964) gives a survey of erotic literature somewhat weakened by the common censorship-orientation; it is self-consciously free in language but consciously structured with an ambitious classification of erotic literature by kinds. Paul Tabori's *The Humor and Technology of Sex* (New York, 1969) is journalistic, unscholarly, and unindexed, but gives a long chapter covering erotic literature. However, it should be mentioned before going further that probably the best overall survey of the field is Paul Englisch, *Geschichte der erotischen Literatur* (Stuttgart, 1927), which concentrates on German literature and neglects the East, but gives a scholarly and responsible presentation of such a vast quantity of material that it has no equal. It is complemented but not rivalled by several other German studies, Carl von Bolen's *Erotik des Orients* (Teufen a/R, 1955) and *Geschichte der Erotik* (Wien, 1951), neither of which is devoted to literature and both of which are rather uncritical of cultural generalities, and Curt Riess' *Erotica! Erotica!/Das Buch der verbotenen Bücher* (Hamburg, 1968), which is not as bad as its title makes it sound and includes a number of contemporary writers that Englisch could not have included.

Books like those of Legman and Englisch, and all those mentioned so far in general, stand in high relief against the dim and well-populated background of works on erotic fiction of the lowest standard, efforts less of scholarship than of pandering to gullibility and salaciousness. An example is Ralph Ginzburg's *An Unhurried View of Erotica* (New York, 1958), in which a minimum of material of any kind is assembled with no concern for literary quality, confident layman's sociology of sex, and unquestioning repetition of the hoariest fables about erotic works and their authors. Almost as silly is R. G. Reisner's *Show Me the Good Parts: The Reader's Guide to Sex in Literature*

(New York, 1964), which gives some thought to subject headings and shows some common sense, particularly in its section on "Unwarrented Reputations," but otherwise devotes itself to works like *The Carpetbaggers* and *Return to Peyton Place.* And cited too often to ignore is that nineteenth-century curiosity of misinformation, F. K. Forberg's *Manual of Classical Erotology* (*De Figura Veneris*, originally written in 1844 and republished in 1966 by Grove Press), which offers culled and mistranslated erotic bits from classical authors accompanied by fantastic physiological commentary (that the breath of a cunnilingue is unbearable, for example). Forberg, whom we presume to have been a chaste bachelor, cites Martial as his authority for this particular observation, yet he is unaware that Martial was joking.

Finally, there are many works of smaller scope that are most often reliable and unobsessed by the censorship-mentality: S. K. De, *Ancient Indian Erotics and Erotic Literature* (Calcutta, 1959) is a survey by a noted Sanskrit scholar, somewhat vitiated by his old-school tendency to rate Sanskrit works lower than European ones and to chastely avoid direct mention of physicality. David Foxon, *Libertine Literature in England 1660–1745* (London, 1964) is a mainly bibliographical study of several eighteenth-century classics. Stephen Marcus, *The Other Victorians: A Study of Sexuality and Pornography in Mid-Nineteenth-Century England* (New York, 1966, no. 1 of the ISR "Studies in Sex and Society") gets into difficulties over what is "pornography" versus what is "literature," but is a landmark work of scholarship where none had been before. More responsible, though less imaginative than Legman, its central feature is a lengthy and valuable discussion of *My Secret Life.* H. Hibbet's *The Floating World of Japanese Fiction* (London, 1959) and C. T. Hsia's *The Classic Chinese Novel* (New York, 1968) treat several of the erotic Chinese and Japanese masterpieces with professional skill and informed judgment. Another work of primarily literary scholarship, which helps to fill in another part of the history of erotic literature, is Mario Praz' *The Romantic Agony* (Oxford, 1933), by now the classic study of satanism, sadism, and derived decadent themes in European literature of the nineteenth century. A last example of the more general approach may suitably be Denis de Rougemont's *Love in the Western World* (New York, 1956), which imaginatively, perhaps over-ambitiously, treats the Tristan and Isolde legend and its European literary progeny, tracing the connections between romance and adultery, courtly love and the idealization of women.

"Il n'est pas de film sans amour."

Ado Kyrou

"'Alles ist möglich.' Das ist die Weltanschauung des 'Kinos.'"

Georg Lukács

If it is correct that sexual behavior is mainly learned rather than instinctive, then the greatest teacher of sex to modern man has been the motion picture. By 1963, 200 million people were seeing American films every week, and the film industries of India and Japan were exceeding those of the United States in output.[1] From their inception, films have been primarily erotic vehicles: Films of romance outnumber all other kinds, and films without love interest are rare; young lovers are usually the central figures and greatest "stars." According to a charming story, the first projector for private use was bought by the Shah of Persia in 1900 so that he might show himself blue films, and thus the die was cast.[2]

It may be noted that current terms for the erotic classification of films are crude and imprecise. "Blue," or "stag," films are generally confined to direct depiction of sexual acts, are short, and are not shown in theaters. The use of "blue" for "obscene" (thus distinct from "true blue," "bluestocking," "bluenose," and "blue law") has an obscure history and is perhaps connected to blue gowns worn by imprisoned prostitutes in England at one time, to the concept of taboo (as "make the air blue"), or to that of excess ("blue blazes, blue streak"). Only since a recent U.S. Supreme Court decision (Stanley *v.* Georgia, 1969) has the simple possession of blue films been relatively safe from prosecution.

"Commercial," or "feature," films are shown in theaters, are usually ninety minutes long plus or minus twenty minutes, and are subject to industry codes of erotic censorship, often altered by court decisions, like U.S. *v. I Am Curious (Yellow)*, 1968, and social pressure groups, like The League of Decency.

"Underground" films, like blue films, are generally the work of directors without studio or industry support whose themes and values are often subversive of those of studio and industry. Their erotic content is in some instances as great as that of blue films, but their range of subjects is wider and their directors (Andy Warhol, Stan Brakhage, Kenneth Anger,

[1] Houston (1963), p. 72.
[2] Kyrou (1957), p. 235.

THE EROTIC IN FILM
by Strother B. Purdy

Ed Emshwiller, and others) neither are, nor desire to be, anonymous.

Even though the short history of the cinema means that there are a relatively small number of films of interest—in contrast, for example, to the number of erotic literary works—there are nevertheless so many that we cannot possibly give the *history* of erotic film in this chapter. We shall instead discuss a selection of what may be considered classic expressions of the erotic on film, attempting to cover the main psychological and dramatic types. We shall include few films of specialized erotic interest (*The Leather Boys, The Killing of Sister George, Staircase, The Sergeant,* and so on).

There is also little need to trace progressively greater exposure of human anatomy and closer approach to representation of sexual intercourse in films since 1960. The job has already been done by Arthur Knight and Hollis Alpert in a series of articles in *Playboy*.[3] Furthermore, when we consider that complete nudity[4] and direct representation of nearly every imaginable sex act have existed on film from the beginning, to trace the process by which scenes previously confined to blue films now appear in feature films would require a discussion of censorship. That *I Am Curious* (*Yellow*) presents abbreviated scenes of sexual intercourse cannot be said by itself to advance, to change, or in any way to alter the film as an artistic medium, for both abbreviated and unabbreviated scenes of sexual intercourse have existed in films for years. What can be said is that Vilgot Sjöman made a greater effort to place the erotic scenes within a framework of intellectual curiosity and political opinion. If that effort had been successful his film would

be worthy of attention here; as it is, a shallowly conceived vehicle for scenes of imitated sexual intercourse, his film is not worth attention. The Lumière brothers made a film of a train entering a station; in 1895 it was a wonderful accomplishment, but one did not have to go to the movies to see a train enter a station. Once the novelty of seeing it on the screen wore off one might ask, "So?" Now we can endure only trains that are loaded with characters on their way somewhere, like *From Russia with Love.*

The dependence of film upon literature is so great that we may ask whether or not anything at all can be said here that has not already been said in our chapter on erotic literature. Most films are based on novels or short stories (*Gone with the Wind, The Blue Angel, Blow Up, An American Tragedy, Sunrise, Point Blank, Belle de Jour, Catch-22, Women in Love,* and so on), and those that are not always have written scripts, or "books," which in some cases (*Love Story, Patton, 2001*) even become books *after* the films. The classic love stories, like *Camille, Nana, Carmen,* and *Anna Karenina,* have been filmed time and time again. Why should they be discussed as films when they have already been discussed as literature? The most important reason is that film is the only "total" art form, the only one that includes sound, pictures (sometimes in color), and story, that combines the speech and action of the legitimate theater with the stability of a finished work, while enjoying the complete freedom from time and space that characterizes literature. It can use literature in printed or dramatized form; it can use painting, sculpture, and music.

Less important, but significant, is that film, when it uses literary sources, invades the role of the reader. Literary works are abstractions, unrealized until read, as are symphonies until they are performed. Conscious or unconscious interpretation is made by a person who reads a book and remembers selected parts of it

---

[3] Knight and Alpert (1965–1969).

[4] The roots of the motion picture itself may be considered to lie in the sequential projection of still photographs of the naked human body in movement done by Eadweard Muybridge in 1880.

afterward. What the author thought is never fully known; what each reader thinks is different from what the author thought and what every other reader thinks. From his own reading the film director[5] forms a new work of art in his total medium. Therefore it is the director's vision that we share and explore in a film, rather than that of the author; the director is thus the crucial innovative artist in film. A director who "faithfully" films a literary work surrenders his artistic originality and most of his power; if the work is a great one, like *War and Peace,* it resists translation anyway. Who can know or do what Tolstoy would have done with film? A director's own conception of *War and Peace* would no longer resemble the novel and would be unsatisfactory in another way. Great books thus generally engender poor films; the literary sources of great films (like *Intolerance, Potemkin,* and *La Strada*) are usually poor things in their own right; thus no great film is approachable, except for purposes of contrast, through its literary source. For that reason we cannot feel that we have satisfactorily discussed any topic taken up by the film, whether it be history, political science, sociology, or sex, if we have kept to its "original" source.

Love and the Stars

In the majority of the world's greatest films, in the sense of "most seen, known, and praised," heterosexual love stories provide either central focus or narrative framework. *The Birth of a Nation, Intolerance, Metropolis, Camille, Gone with the Wind, Citizen Kane, The Blue Angel, Rashomon, Ugetsu, La Strada, Wild Strawberries,* and *The Maltese Falcon* are only a few examples. The exceptions are notable indeed:

Potemkin, 2001, The Passion of Joan of Arc, The Wizard of Oz, All Quiet on the Western Front. We are simply restating the statistical fact that almost everyone is interested in sex and that the number of people more interested in some other one thing is never large or concentrated.

Furthermore, the star system, which amounts to a powerful social concern with the fantasy-lives of a group of film actors,[6] is an almost exclusively romantic-erotic phenomenon. Comedy, as we have noted in Chapter 14, is destructive of fantasy-projection and unconcerned with individuals in roles; only comedians become "great stars" without being erotic—Chaplin, Fernandel, and perhaps one or two more.

With very few exceptions (like Bela Lugosi and Shirley Temple) "stardom" is enjoyed by sexually attractive men and women who enact love on the screen: Greta Garbo, Rudolph Valentino, Marlene Dietrich, Charles Boyer, Douglas Fairbanks, Errol Flynn, Mary Pickford, Lillian Gish, Ronald Colman, Clark Gable, Mae West, Jean Harlow, Frank Sinatra, Marilyn Monroe, Monica Vitti, Marcello Mastroianni, Robert Redford, Sophia Loren, Jeanne Moreau. We might even ask what other role there is for a woman star. She is chosen for stardom because she is beautiful; her beauty has no other dramatic purpose than as an object of love. The male role of greatest prominence is always that of the lover, the one who "gets the girl." The other male roles open—brutal murderer (James Cagney, Edward G. Robinson) or cowboy (William S. Hart, William Boyd), for example—never bring the same fame. And even they are more often than not tinged with erotic interest. Cagney's sadistic treatment of women was an important part of his charm; the monster-ghoul roles of Bela Lugosi and Lon

[5] This is to treat the director as the organizer and unifier of the work of many subordinates, as well as an artist in his own right. Many directors do not, of course, live up to the demands of the role.

[6] How great this identification actually is is pointed out by Morin (1960), p. 166 and *passim.*

Chaney always included, or hinted at, rape or sexual mutilation; the Marx Brothers' antics would be less memorable if Groucho and Harpo's indefatigable attacks on women had been omitted; the cowboy and the Western badman are either killed, or redeemed by the love of good women; even the most appealing of all woman haters, W. C. Fields ("Women are like elephants to me: nice to look at, but I wouldn't want to own one"), found it necessary to pay elaborate court to Mae West.

Love is not the only effective subject matter of the film—*The Last Laugh* and *2001* have proved that—but it is impossible to doubt that filmmaking and lovemaking have been inextricably bound up throughout the history of the medium.

Films and Reality

We imagine film makers to be basically concerned with the problem of "capturing" reality. But film, more than the other arts, can not only catch up with but can also go beyond "reality," which is, after all, only what each of us perceives it to be (what chemical analysis and telescopes reveal are vastly different parallel aspects of reality). The blue film can show us *more* of the literal elements of sexual intercourse than men and women normally see: extended closeups of genitals in contact, as seen from below, above, and between. This process of seeing reaches its logical and final point when the camera of Masters and Johnson records the view from inside a transparent penis as it enters a vagina.[7]

Film is therefore not simply a convention within reality, in the sense that it represents by artificial means what is real. It is something more complicated than that: a convention within a convention (within reality), for it represents by artificial means that which we generally agree represents reality—our ideas and beliefs. It is not necessary to take a Berkeleyan view of the world as the thought of God to appreciate this: It is inherent in the mechanics of vision and photography. Eye and brain, with or without the help of a lens, do not record; they interpret and assign conceptual meaning.

Second, the "capturing of reality" is often most successful when achieved indirectly. Another basic aesthetic principle is that the best way to capture the world of a chess grand master is not necessarily to accompany a real master with a camera (though this approach has been tried by various *cinéma verité* schools, of which the disastrous *Chronique d'un été* [1961] may be taken as a typical product); the best way to show what a riot is about is not necessarily to film a real riot. Experienced reality is annoyingly formless and random; the human brain tends to find satisfaction in imposing order and in order once imposed—in art. True "true" art is therefore not art at all: a real Campbell's soup can, the film of a real sex act. The difference between these two examples is superficial: We can see Campbell's soup cans every day, and we therefore have a low tolerance for one presented as a work of art (and a greater tolerance for one copied in plaster). We see few sex acts daily, so we have an essentially inartistic interest in seeing filmed sex acts.

Aesthetic truth suffers in the interests of censorship here, though; the act of love is as

---

[7] The camera most often sees more than the naked eye, and photographic images therefore seem "more than real." This is especially noticeable in stills, however, which are outside the time dimension, whereas motion pictures are temporal experiences. The lens "sees" impartially, registering every difference in light reflection; the eye sees "intellectually," being directed by the brain to select certain kinds of information and to reject the rest. Hearing is parallel. A mechanical impartial sound track of a forest encounter may produce speech drowned out by crackling leaves and twittering birds; it must be carefully tuned to approach human hearing, which usually filters in favor of speech. Some contemporary directors, like Andy Warhol, deliberately use uncontrolled film sound, though whether for aesthetic reasons or from laziness is not clear.

natural and fit a subject for film as for any other representational art. Jules Dassin's *Phaedra* (1962), which cuts to fireplace flames, rather than showing Melina Mercouri and Anthony Perkins making love, is a better film than is *Cream Cheese*, which has long scenes of love-making. *Phaedra* retells the classical story of Phaedra and her stepson Hippolytus, for whom she conceives an unfortunate passion in the absence of Theseus, her husband and his father. In Euripides' *Hippolytus* (428 B.C.) she hangs herself when he chastely rejects her advances, and Theseus, upon his return, asks Neptune to send a monster from the sea to frighten the boy's chariot horses and thus to kill him. In Racine's *Phèdre* (1677) Phaedra's maid falsely accuses Hippolytus of initiating the seduction; Theseus has Neptune kill him in the same way, and Phaedra then commits suicide. Dassin translates events from both plays to modern Greece, making Theseus (Raf Vallone) a ship-owner reminiscent of contemporary shipping tycoons and the chariot and horses of Hippolytus (Anthony Perkins) an ultrafast sports car. This Hippolytus and his stepmother (Melina Mercouri) do commit the incest-adultery from which the ancients shrank and decide on joint suicide when they are discovered. *Cream Cheese* (anonymous, *c.* 1960) is an undistinguished, typical blue film, devoted to sex acts between a man and two women on a bed, with additional thematic material clumsily added in the form of a symbol (a package of cream cheese), a cat, an electric dildo, and the rudiments of a plot (at the beginning, one girl is vacuuming the carpet while the other sports with the gentleman).

The superiority of *Phaedra* does not result from avoidance of what some film critics call the "inartistic and ridiculous" expedient of showing the act itself.[8] *Phaedra* is the better

film because its lovemaking is part of a larger construct (the plot of incest tragedy) and because the shot of flames suggests abandonment to passion, the fall from responsibility and honor into love and death. It shows more of the human condition than does *Cream Cheese* and instructs while it delights. But *Cream Cheese* is superior in one respect: The act of love, the central act of life, is revealed, rather than concealed. The camera can suggest more than it can show, but what it *can* show and what it *may* show should not be confused.

In film things *are* what they seem on the level of photographic representation; the images are always simply shadows on a screen, so that mental images and photographic images are equivalent. The latter are not seen more or less clearly despite or because of the former; rather the two are related by visual transformations.

Relevant is the career of the great romantic director Josef von Sternberg (Viennese, 1894-1969) including *The Last Command* (1928, with Emil Jannings), *The Blue Angel* (1930, with Jannings and Marlene Dietrich), *Morocco* (1930, with Dietrich and Gary Cooper), *Dishonored* (1931, with Dietrich and Victor McLaglen), *Shanghai Express* (1932, with Dietrich and Clive Brook), and *The Devil Is a Woman* (1935, with Dietrich and Lionel Atwill). No other director has so mastered the eroticism of lighting and gesture; perhaps no other director had such an instrument as the Dietrich of 1930-1935. *The Blue Angel* (*Der Blaue Engel*, made in Germany), the first and best of the Dietrich films, tells the story of Professor Rath, a middle-aged bachelor who finds his *gymnasium* students ogling pictures of Lola Lola, chanteuse at a local cabaret, "The Blue Angel." He sallies forth to rebuke the hussy, blundering into the backstage world thronged by her admirers and customers (including his own students), and ends more dan-

---

[8] "A film director cannot show his audience a couple making love—not because it would be immoral but because it would be inartistic and ridiculous—but he can symbolize it in many ways" (Stephenson and Debrix, 1965, p. 205).

gerously ensnared than they. When he comes to class late, having spent the night with Lola, the boys greet him with shouts and taunts and ribald drawings on the blackboard. Heedless of the scandal, he proposes to Lola, who accepts him in astonishment. Having lost his academic position, he accompanies her on the road tour of her sleazy company; when his savings are spent, her interest in him declines, and he sinks by degrees to the debasement of peddling her pictures to customers and, finally, to playing the clown onstage in the town where he had taught. Breaking off this performance, he makes a mad attack on Lola and the handsome Mazeppa, who are fondling each other in the wings. Easily repulsed, he rushes out into the snowy night, makes his way to the *gymnasium*, and collapses there at his old desk, utterly broken, staring out into the dark and empty room. If Lola Lola appears as an angel to the professor, we must see her so; when she is revealed as a devil, we must see her so. She is *visually* transformed, regardless of the possibility that we sense her devilish nature from the beginning.

If one believes that the devil is a woman, then in film one will attempt to express the idea visually both in her image and in her actions. One must present what Edmund Spenser could only describe in *The Faerie Queene*. We see her through the eyes of a bewitched (or bedeviled) Lionel Atwill, the

Figure 15.1. Von Sternberg's *The Blue Angel* (1930): the unchallenged master portrayal of a man's sexual degradation. Courtesy of Janus Films and the Museum of Modern Art Stills Archives.

director's alter ego, or those of Cesar Romero or Glenn Ford. We may seem to be claiming that all film is expressionistic, and perhaps almost all the classic films of love are. When acting seeks to imitate reality, the filming must be expressionistic; on the other hand, when acting is stylized or allegorical, as in silent films, the visual recording of expression and gesture can be no more than neutral recording.

Woman's dual nature is also strongly apparent in the work of Fritz Lang (German, 1890-   ) which includes some of the greatest films ever to deal with love, though on a legendary, or abstract, scale: *Der Müde Tod* (1921), *Die Nibelungen* (1924), and *Metropolis* (1926). Others of his famous films are *M* (1931), *Ministry of Fear* (1945), and *The Big Heat* (1953).

Metropolis, a vision of the future and the *2001* of its day, depicts the empire-city of an industrialist-ruler; the masters live in gilded excess in skyscrapers and penthouse gardens while the workers and the machines they tend are kept underground. By accident Freder, the industrialist's son, catches a glimpse of the workers' underworld and, in horrified sympathy, joins it, offering assistance to Maria, a lay saint who rallies the afflicted and is recognized as a leader by the workers. But his father orders the evil genius and master technician, Rotwang, to make a robot in the likeness of Maria, to test her in a naked dance before a large party of men (they run wild), and to program her to stir the workers to a revolt that will justify his putting them down once and for all. This ruse works beyond the master's expectations: He is threatened with total ruin as the rebels wreck the main dynamo, cutting off all electric power and flooding the underground city where they live. The robot next appears amid a crowd of merrymakers in the upper city, urging them to come out and "watch the world going to the devil" (at her unveiling by Rotwang, Death had left his place before a gallery of statues of the Seven Deadly Sins in the cathedral and had entered the city, swinging his scythe). The

workers, thinking that their children have been drowned in the flood (though actually they have been saved by the true Maria), turn on their leader, stream into the upper city, and capture her. They carry her to the cathedral and burn her at the stake, falling back in horror as, amid the smoke and flames, she turns back into a thing of steel. Meanwhile Rotwang has found the true Maria at the cathedral and chases her, fearing that the mob will kill him if it sees her next to his replica. He carries her to the cathedral roof, pursued in turn by Freder. They grapple desperately, and Freder throws him to his death, thus saving, and winning, the girl. Freder then acts as mediator between "brain and hand," his father and the leader of the workers, forcing them to pledge with a handclasp a new order of social justice.

The real woman and the devil are separate here, the situation allegorical; there is no need to include more than the simplest representation in the film. But Lang adds expression and gesture as well: He has Brigitte Helm assume a slightly crooked stance and a twisted leer instead of a smile. The effect is less than subtle but horribly effective, and the scene in which she is transformed again into the metal monster whence she came has all the horror of watching a young girl turn into an ancient crone, as in Frank Capra's *Lost Horizon* (1937), or of imagining a girl turning into a hideous witch in folklore. This mythic quality leaves directors like von Sternberg in *The Devil Is a Woman,* Robert Rossen in *Lilith,* or Roger Vadim in *Et Dieu créa la femme,* far behind, caught within the limitations of "realism."

This is a reversal of the equation of Carl Dreyer's powerful but conventional *Passion of Joan of Arc* (1928),[9] in which woman becomes

---

[9] The Dane Carl Dreyer (1899-1968) made *The Passion of Joan of Arc* in 1928 as a silent film, telling with simplicity and few subtitles the story of the trial and execution of the saint. It focuses on the faces and symbolic patterns that embody the girl's thoughts as she nears death, and

saint in the fire at the stake; and it is more complex, with the added term of the machine. Lang's innocent girl crouches in the shelter of the city's cathedral as her false form is burned, revealing the horror beneath the flesh. Lang was probably not consciously presenting either an erotic philosophy like that of D. H. Lawrence (burning away the false exterior with the fires of lust) or like that in Marshall McLuhan's *Mechanical Bride* (the machine providing a successfully deceptive ersatz eroticism). His obvious and superficial theme is socio-political, but the erotic power of the images sweeps it aside: Scenes in *Metropolis*, like the burning at the stake and the party at which the false temptress is unveiled and dances before a delirious crowd of tuxedoed *aristoi*, take on an independent life of their own. This is powerful evidence that the director who tries to use erotic images in the service of an intellectual message is likely to find his message overturned and scattered by them, and himself a Phaeton trying to control the horses of the sun.

Film illusion, including eroticism, outweighs film realism: The film that takes advantage of the camera's ability to serve as the mind's eye, rather than as simply the eye alone, has true power. Von Sternberg's Dietrich films hover on the edge of this power, but finally fall short of it, as do those of Cecil B. De Mille, Orson Welles, Jules Dassin, and Alfred Hitchcock, for all their "magical" effects. They remain tied to the literary tradition. D. W. Griffith[10] relied heavily on literature but could push the film to an approximation of its natural power, as Lang, Ingmar Bergman, Federico Fellini, and Jean-Luc Godard (in exceptional instances) have been able to do.

Ingmar Bergman (Swedish, 1918–   ), like Griffith, effortlessly overcomes his tendency toward heavy literary-theatrical direction, capable of spoiling any film, by means of skillfully constructed erotic images. They are not all pleasant, but few moviegoers have forgotten the rape in *The Virgin Spring*, the woman in the water with the soldiers in *Naked Night*, the masturbation scene in *The Silence*, or the castle meeting in *The Hour of the Wolf*. The last is a particularly good example of erotic illusion as film metaphor. The protagonist, painter Johan Borg, has come to a lonely island with his wife to work and to rid himself of obsessive memories—of his previous marriage, of his relationship with the child of that marriage, of a disastrous love affair with a woman, Veronica Vogler, who exercised demonic power over him. He finds the island inhabited with the very people he came to avoid—or, as we begin to suspect as events take a bizarre turn, he fantasizes them as inhabitants. He sees himself killing his son; he sees an old woman threaten to take off her hat and her face with it; he sees the baron walking on the walls; and, finally, he sees his innermost desire, the naked body of Veronica stretched out in expectation of his arrival. His world has narrowed to the illusion of her body's presence, and, as he reaches forward to grasp her she smilingly ridicules him—this is not an assignation, but a trap—and disappears. He is destroyed. The barrier between illusion inside the mind and outside it has been broken down, and there is nowhere for him to locate himself. In spiritual terms we may say that he is damned; in psychological terms he is hopelessly disoriented; he disappears too, we see him no more. His innocent wife is apparently left alone on the island, speaking into the camera. The film may have a literary parallel

---

the thoughts of men who could wreak such horror. The film continues to be considered one of the ten best ever made.

[10] The American David Wark Griffith (1875–1948) was the greatest film pioneer; he either introduced or first used effectively the full-length film, the closeup, cross cutting between action and reaction or between parallel narratives, the moving camera, the flashback, the long shot. In short, he can be said to have done more than anyone to make film an independent art.

Figure 15.2.   Bergman's *The Virgin Spring* (1959): the full horror of rape. Courtesy of Janus Films and the Museum of Modern Art Stills Archives.

in the vision of the body of Helen of Troy from Goethe's *Faust,* but because its terms are primarily visual the woman's body becomes the *primary* symbol and the primary reality in illusion.

Luis Buñuel's *Belle de Jour* (1968) is another outstanding example of erotic illusion in the modern film.[11] Like Joseph Strick's *The Bal-*

cony, Resnais' *L'année dernière á Marienbad,* and Fellini's *Giulietta degli Spiriti,* it places erotic acts and relationships in a deliberately puzzling area between dream and waking, coming closer thereby to a grasp of their real nature. Here the illusionist within the illusion is a frigid young wife (played by Catherine Deneuve) with masochistic longings. In Joseph Kessel's undistinguished novel *Belle de Jour* (1928), which served as the starting point for

[11]Luis Buñuel (Spanish, 1900–   ) has had the longest productive career of all film directors, from the pioneer surrealist film, *Un Chien Andalou* (1928), to the hit of the 1970 Cannes film festival, *Tristana.* His savage attacks on the established church and state, particularly *Viridiana*

(1961), *El Angel Exterminador* (1962), and *Simon of the Desert* (1965), use sexual imagery with shocking effect.

Figure 15.3. Bergman's *The Hour of the Wolf* (1968): Borg (Max von Sydow) unveils the illusory body of Veronica Vogler. Courtesy of Janus Films and the Museum of Modern Art Stills Archives.

the film, she simply builds herself a secret life as a whore, taking her place among the inmates of a brothel during the day and going home before her husband returns from work. She is inevitably found out, her husband is crippled in a scuffle with her underworld lover, and she is forced to live the rest of her life in shame and despair as his nurse. In Buñuel's hands the illusion and the eroticism take over, becoming as in life more powerful than the daylight rationality that is supposed to rule them. Like *The Hour of the Wolf, Belle de Jour* has no ending, only a cessation of the series of trans-

formations which has progressed through erotic fantasy to a point at which Belle's husband is crippled but seems to arise cured; the coach that bore her to dream torture delights rolls by, visible to her *and* to her husband, but it no longer contains her double. Can she have been stripped and flogged by her husband, who then turned her over to his coachmen with orders for them to take their pleasure? No, that was a dream. Can she then have been a whore and been ruthlessly forced by a succession of brutal men? Her husband's having been shot and blinded by her gangster lover is proof that she

Figure 15.4. Dolores del Rio in a mid-1920s publicity still: The "mask of beauty," an essentially immovable and type-characterizing device, was most suitable to the silent film but lasted well beyond it. Courtesy of the Museum of Modern Art Stills Archives.

was, for it was at the whorehouse that the gangster met, wooed, beat, and won her. But the husband rises from his wheelchair, takes off his dark glasses, and smilingly advances to embrace her! Was the life of prostitution only a fantasy then as well? Buñuel leaves us simply with the images, as her imagination might have supplied them, refusing to order them. All the male figures in the film are dramatically subordinate to the woman, yet what she thinks, what reasons she may offer are finally irrelevant to the male erotic fantasy (that of Kessel, that of Buñuel, that of the male audience) that makes use of *her*. As one woman remarks to another in Jarrell's *Pictures from an Institution,* "We are cakes that must think, *How nice to eat me!*"

Woman's central presence as a *body* in film, as a sexual and physical object, is thus coupled with her sexual role as the center of male illusion, the symbolic presence that is never fully captured by Aristotelian logic or physical reality. The part of the body that is visually capable of expressing both facets is the face, and, though women's breasts and legs began to take on an almost fetishistic character in the 1940s, and the late 1960s saw something of a return to total female nudity in movies, it can be said that, from the invention of the closeup to the present day, the faces of beautiful women have dominated films—and thus have come to play a role in art and life that they had not previously had. Makeup, not to underline character, but as a "mask of beauty,"[12] became the badge of Western woman, reaching its latest evolution just before 1960 and the shift to the less artificial in American design and manner.

[12]The phrase is borrowed from Morin (1960), p. 21.

This line of faces, from Theda Bara and Dolores del Rio to Marlene Dietrich, from Dietrich to Ava Gardner, and from Gardner to Monica Vitti and Catherine Deneuve, has been dominant. Studied in closeup, these faces are static but powerful, heavily made up, detached from their bodies, often expressionless. Another line, of bodies, stretches from the priestesses of Isis in *Intolerance* to Rita Hayworth to Marilyn Monroe and Brigitte Bardot and Ursula Andress and Anouk Aimée and Natalie Wood; it also involves mouths and eyes sharing with breasts, legs, and hips an opening and closing rhythm. This tradition has become more prominent in the last decade.

Conventions of Love

That the face has had such a long rule reflects the particular power of convention in film (partly because of the Hollywood studio system), so great that it can be called "the tyranny of form." S. D. Lawder has also called it the "tyranny of Griffith's genius."[13] Films began with the unquestioning use of literary conventions: scenes built around speeches between characters; plotting of events to demonstrate theme and character; exteriorization of thought; dependence on "action." Though most of the innovative possibilities within the medium had been worked out by 1920, and at least tentatively employed in subsequent years, directors and producers generally preferred to follow familiar, proved, commercially successful, and basically literary devices. Only recently has this tyranny of form showed signs of cracking, but that too has been partly in response to literary influences like those of the *nouveau roman*.

Speech has been one of these imposed conventions. Once sound had been commercially established, the treatment of love began to

center on the use of conversation: The lovers *told* their love. The silent blue film escaped this theatrical tendency. The films of Mae West (*I'm No Angel, She Done Him Wrong,* and others) included delightful erotic badinage ("Is that a gun in your pocket, honey, or are you just glad to see me?") and the filmed versions of fine drama (like *Blithe Spirit* and *The Taming of the Shrew*) benefited from the original dialogue, but the general run of romantic films emphasized saying and telling. Boyer's "Come with me to the Casbah" and Dietrich's "I think I am falling in love with you," both delivered with pregnant mournfulness, thrilled hearts all over the world and stimulated latent "bovaryism" in filmgoers. But they fell far short of the medium's erotic potential.

Among modern directors, Michelangelo Antonioni (Italian, 1912–   ) has most clearly broken with this convention: His lovers, Monica Vitti and her partners in films like *L'Eclisse, L'Avventura,* and *Il Deserto Rosso,* communicate more through silence than through speech. Such communication is possible only in film, thanks to the closeup, and in life, which is filled with long silences. When speech becomes secondary, the visual elements increase in importance, along with the sense of physical presence. The question whether or not Antonioni's films have gone too far in this direction and lost the control necessary for art does not lessen the value of his reintroduction of silent gesture.

Again, because of films' tendency to follow where literature leads, the romantic plot, in which the events of a love affair are causally and chronologically linked, has been prominent in the history of erotic motion pictures. Love has its story, a pattern to be comprehended logically. Life, of course, is not made up of "stories," which, in the artificially structured and rigorously polished forms that producers have preferred, imprison actors in frameworks of the lowest common literary denominator: O. Henry effects like neat and surprising end-

---

[13] Lawder (1968), p. 33.

Figure 15.5.   L'Avventura (1959): an inferior male in the company of Monica Vitti, Antonioni's superstar for his series of love-nothingness films; expressionless beauty in a moral-erotic vacuum. Courtesy of Janus Films and the Museum of Modern Art Stills Archives.

ings; key roles assigned to dogs and children, with thematic and philosophical summaries delivered by the children; pairs of lovers illustrating copybook virtues and vices, in ghastly travesty of *Anna Karenina;* and so forth. See, for example, Warner Brothers' *Sweet November,* starring Sandy Dennis and Anthony Newley:

Each month of the year, Sara Deever, a Brooklyn Heights girl who leases apartments and sublets them at a profit, shares her bohemian flat with a different man with a different conformist hang-up. In this way, she feels, she will have helped someone to attain greater fulfillment while

she, in turn, will be assured of always being remembered. ("People must be remembered, otherwise they were never here at all.") One day in October, she meets a staid British-born box manufacturer named Charlie and invites him to be her "November." Intrigued by both the offer and the girl, Charlie accepts. As the days pass, Charlie finds himself not only losing his inhibitions but also falling in love with the unconventional Sara. But when he asks to be allowed to stay beyond November, Sara firmly tells him that he must leave, as all his predecessors have done, on the last day of the month. Then Charlie learns from a neighbor and friend, Alonzo, that Sara is dying from a fatal illness for which there is no remedy. Overcoming his grief, Charlie begs

Sara to seize whatever happiness she can by letting him remain. But, although she knows that for the first time she is truly in love, Sara tells Charlie that he must go. On the last night of the month, Sara packs Charlie's bags and waits for "December" to arrive. When he does, Charlie kisses Sara goodbye and reminds her that she will never be forgotten—"I've got you with me all the rest of my life."[14]

In such a triumph of plotting the only thing there is *not*, of course, is life.

At the very beginning of this plot dominance, D. W. Griffith broke away with the fugal plot of *Intolerance* (an experiment he did not repeat). *Intolerance* (1916) sets a sordid story of love in the slums against the ennobling background of historical and heroic events on three levels: the fall of Babylon; the life of Christ; the Massacre of St. Bartholomew's Day. Toward the end of the period of the dominant plot Delannoy and Cocteau, working out of the surrealist tradition established by Buñuel, did something to extend plot into mythic parallel, and thereby to supersede it. Delannoy's *L'Eternel Retour* (1943) retells the story of Tristan and Isolde, and Cocteau's *Orphée* (1949) sets the myth of Orpheus, in modern France.

Kurosawa's 1950 Japanese masterpiece *Rashomon* showed the way to something more complex: the story of a rape visually embodied in four conflicting versions that finally cannot be interpreted because no key with which to evaluate them is provided. Resnais and Robbe-Grillet's *L'année dernière à Marienbad* (1961) also presents a love affair, including a possible rape, but it deprives the viewer of every conventional point of reference in logical reality and chronology, so that he must rely solely on his intuition to tell him whether any given scene represents what actually happened before or

after any other scene. The result is the perfect abstraction of love, for the presentation of this affair is not only free from plot (it is impossible to know what happened last year at Marienbad, whether or not anything happened at all, or whether the "now" is actually that last year) but also free from speech (there is little conversation between the lovers); it emphasizes illusions that support love in life: The action takes place in the mirrored corridors and labyrinthine gardens of a supposed nineteenth-century *hôtel de grande luxe*.[15]

Nothing seems more natural, or even more correct, than that the film should present love as visual and aural experience, to be seen and heard. But this notion is also bound up with artificial limitations of form, derived from the nineteenth-century theater that the first films copied. If the lady does not show her love with her smile, she must speak it; by 1935, she both smiled and spoke, in order to leave no doubt in our minds. We do indeed, in our daily lives, wish both to hear and to see those we love, but we also do a great deal of thinking, and our lovers think too. They think about our thinking, as well as about their own, and we think about theirs. Cannot the film somehow represent such thought? Can it not do what the novel does easily and the theater rather stiltedly, by means of the soliloquy? The motion picture was not very old before Griffith used the device of panning to an actor's face as he stands lost in thought, then cutting to the subject of the thought. He used it quite literally: If the girl is thinking of her lover, we see the lover doing something, just as we see him in any other sequence in the film. By the time of F. W.

---

[14] *Film Facts* (1968), p. 29.

[15] Our discussion of love in this film parallels Robbe-Grillet's theory of the *nouveau roman*. It is interesting that this theory is so suited to the writing of films that Robbe-Grillet has found himself writing not *romans* (novels) but *ciné-romans* (film-novels), which can in effect serve as shooting scripts.

Murnau's *Last Laugh* (1924)[16] thoughts and dreams had taken on fantasy shapes as in our living dreams; in films like *Beauty and the Beast* (1947) and *Hamlet* (1948) psychoanalytic theory, the modern attempt to interpret dreams and unconscious symbols, became established. Hitchcock's long series of films, including *Spellbound* and *Psycho,* use this symbolism so thoroughly that, as in *I Confess,* the sex act itself is kept hidden, even repressed (as is the body in *Rope*), subordinated to the tortured imaginings of the murderer or of his victim.

This approach is eminently Freudian and eminently suited to the mystery-thriller form, which involves murder and very commonly the problem of hiding, and subsequently discovering, the corpse. As the unconscious resists the Freudian analyst's efforts to bring its contents to light, the "body" of sexual repression resists discovery with all the cunning that the sick man can bring to bear. Hitchcock has thus been able to work inside a censored film industry that rigorously curbs erotic material but lets violence take almost any form,[17] for his work "censors" in the same way, returning again and again to the theme of the hidden corpse (in the manner of Clouzot's *Diabolique*) that keeps cropping up (as in *The Trouble with Harry*). We are not intruding here upon psychological territory with guesses about connections between murder and love (as they are so strongly indicated in *Psycho*) but are merely noting perhaps the most popular form of sexual sublimation in film, in which a hidden end (possession of the woman's body) and a proclaimed end (finding the corpse and the perpetrator) are parallel. The action of the film is to hunt for clues that lead to both goals at once.

A particularly clear example is offered by John Huston's *The Maltese Falcon* (1941), in which the murderer and the desirable girl turn out to be the same person. If the murder mystery and the courtship plot cannot converge, they must at least parallel each other, as in *Rear Window,* where the thrill of murder revealed is vicarious and guilt-free. In both cases an imaginative need—perhaps one created by the film and its literary antecedents, perhaps not— is satisfied and imaginative pleasure is given.

The murder mystery has proved one of the most successful film forms; it has also been a prime locus for the association of sexual pleasure with crime and punishment. No convincing proof that this connection results from censorship has ever been put forward, though it seems logical to argue that restricting portrayals of normal sexuality forces the resort to abnormality because there is no way to make sex go away. The argument is that, when a director cannot show men and women in bed together, sexual caresses more charged than the kiss, or more of a woman's body than can be seen in public, then he is forced to seek alternate means to release the charge of sexual energy held in frustrated stasis by the mere image of the girl, to show her strangled, shot, stabbed, or brutalized. In some film forms, a woman may be strapped to an operating table for some horrible surgical procedure, embraced by a python or a gorilla or a nameless blob, crucified, thrown to the lions in the arena, or tortured and mercilessly flogged.

The trouble with this argument is that it is simplistic and Utopian, suggesting a solution

---

[16] F. W. Murnau (1889–1931), along with G. W. Pabst and E. A. Dupont, is one of the few directors who could be compared with Fritz Lang in the great 1920s period of German Expressionistic film; like Lang, Murnau also made films that have remained landmarks of the medium, particularly *Der Letzte Mann* (*The Last Laugh,* 1924) and *Sunrise* (1927). Nearly as great, in the opinion of many critics, are his *Tartuffe* (1925) and *Faust* (1926).

[17] Macdonald (1969) points out that Hitchcock's practice matches the tastes of American censors perfectly: "In *Psycho* they see nothing wrong in showing with intimate, suggestive detail a helpless woman being stabbed to death, but had Mr. Hitchcock ventured to show one of Janet Leigh's nipples, that would have been a serious offense against morality and decency" (p. 51).

parallel to "if we can stop poverty we can stop crime." Crime and criminal (or painful) sex obviously have attractions apart from their apparent utility in gaining release from monetary or sexual insolvency. Rich juveniles steal, and the James Bond films, along with their numerous imitators, provide as much or more sadism than did earlier and far more rigorously censored films—in combination with all the new, "healthy" freedom of sexual representation: We see Bond atop women in bed and women willingly divesting themselves of their garments in the throes of passion. We also see women punched in the jaw and murdered through the blocking of the skin pores with gold paint (*Goldfinger*), drugged into helplessness (*From Russia with Love*), machine-gunned from the air (*You Only Live Twice*), shot in the back while dancing, strapped to a bed for a torture session (*Thunderball*), and so on.

On the other hand, a classic mystery thriller like Lang's *Ministry of Fear* (1945) manages its erotic appeal (Ray Milland's romance with the beautiful blonde refugee played by Marjorie Reynolds) and its suspense entirely without *psychopathia sexualis*. Overt sex is restricted to amorous glances and one long kiss, but it has its effect—or had its effect, for it does seem excessively prudish by contemporary standards. Clearly, in artistic representation rewards and expectations are closely allied. In an atmosphere of contact absence, one long kiss is Paradise; in an atmosphere of contact freedom, one long kiss is an affront to one's sense of sophistication (when do they take off their clothes?). Art for those who create it is, like life, mainly a matter of game-playing: The very fact that the rewards in the game stay forever the same (in the context of our discussion sexual intercourse is the archetypal prize) forces constant changes in the rules as a means of avoiding boredom. The differences between the intellectualized chess game of murder and sex in *Ministry of Fear*, and *From Russia with Love*, which starts with

a chess game but soon abandons it for physical contact, are necessary in a sense. If the treatment of sex in *From Russia with Love* had been permitted in films in 1945, by 1963 it would have become tedious, and change would have been necessary. We laugh at the Victorians for their sexual attitudes, forgetting that they were playing the same game and had tired of the earlier set of Restoration rules, which we now proclaim as the "new freedom."

Homosexual Themes

Women are not always on the receiving end of violence in bloodthirsty films; they are only the most dramatically effective victims, and their mistreatment almost always brings immediate sexual responses from men. When the violence is predominantly between man and man, as in Westerns, war films, and murder mysteries, the sexual component is less easily defined. There is nothing especially sexual in a policeman's shooting a suspect or a gangster's mutilating another gangster, no matter what specific sexual feelings the perpetrators may have at the time. There is something specifically homosexual, however, in the persecution of *Billy Budd* by the mate Claggart; this persecution, which ends in the deaths of both men, is in effect a courtship. Open treatment of homosexuality has been avoided through most of the history of film (*Mädchen in Uniform* is apparently one of the few exceptions before the 1960s, when films like *The Fox, Staircase, The Killing of Sister George*, and *The Sergeant* appeared), but there are many examples of disguised or sublimated homosexuality. The humiliation and flagellation so common in films about sailing ships, Roman galleys, mutinies at sea, and the persecutions of drill sergeants, prison warders, and shop foremen belong in a gray area—with a slight push by the director or writer the sexual element dominates.

A rather interesting example is Charles

Vidor's *Gilda* (1946), Rita Hayworth's most celebrated vehicle and therefore associated in the popular mind with the upper reaches of ideal heterosexuality. Yet the film is considered by some critics, mainly on the Continent, to have a homosexual theme. Once we examine this interpretation, it seems quite appropriate to the relationship between a nightclub owner (Mundson, played by George Macready) and an adventurer (Johnny, played by Glenn Ford) in which the former required utter fidelity and constant attendance from the latter, presumably the better to run the club, and in which there are to be "no women mixed up." As Mundson later tells Gilda, "We make our own love, Johnny and I." Johnny bitterly rebukes Mundson for his sudden marriage to Gilda, an American girl with whose shady past Johnny is familiar. He determines to protect Mundson from this noxious female influence and orders her to leave the city, once he feels he has accumulated sufficient evidence of her infidelity. Mundson's own flight, necessitated by a murder in which he is involved, forestalls this action; when he apparently dies in a plane crash, leaving Gilda his heir, Johnny marries her. The much-abused girl is hardly prepared for what happens on her wedding night: Johnny takes her to an apartment where he has installed a large portrait of Mundson and leaves her there alone. "You were unfaithful to him when he was alive," he says with bitter scorn, "now that he is dead you will be faithful to him." Johnny imprisons her with elaborate and sadistic thoroughness, frustrating all her efforts to escape and get a divorce, and the marriage remains unconsummated—until a surprise ending shows both that they have been in love all along. They leave together for the United States and eternal happiness. But until these last moments *Gilda* is a woman hater's film: Gilda is continually insulted ("There are more women than anything else in the world, except insects") and slapped in the face by Johnny.

In Hitchcock's hands the murder mystery has produced other such tentative hints at homosexual passion: both *Rope* (1948), which recreates the Leopold-Loeb murder, and *Strangers on a Train* (1951) put male characters with mutual homosexual attractions at the center of the action but refrain from showing them in sexual attitudes.

Things were far different in the 1960s, when underground films began to achieve wide university and even commercial circulation. Warhol's *Vinyl, Nude Restaurant,* and *I a Man* tend more to lengthy discussion than to sexual activity, but homosexuality is their main theme. Anger's *Scorpio Rising* employs rapid intercutting of (faked) shots of sodomy and fellatio with long, and heavily meaningful (to the initiated), views of motorcyclists lovingly pulling on their trousers and boots, heavy belts, and black-leather jackets. There are other examples, just as representative of unconscious humor. It remained for the master Fellini, with his *Satyricon* (1970), to present male homosexual love in images of intense beauty. His Encolpius' pursuit of the beautiful boy Giton and the slow development of his rivalry with Ascyltos, a muscular rowdy, into a deeply felt masculine companionship are the more affecting for the nightmare horror of the events in which they are set; they bring to the film a long delayed flowering of homosexual erotica.

The Blue Film

It must not be forgotten that during all these years the lowly and little-discussed blue-film industry has been treating sex of all kinds directly and sometimes successfully. Aside from the general lack of acting and directing talent, the main limitation of the form is its inherent incapacity to relate to life without, and around, the sexual component. Representation of any other fact of life or human character but sexual intercourse is omitted. As if to symbolize this failure, the average blue film shows a bed, a windowless room, and two or three people without clothing. The sense of sequestration provided by the setting may suggest furtiveness, for guilt and the expectation of punishment have long been shared by actors and audiences of these films, especially when the former are masked and the latter worried about possible police raids. There have been changes in these films as well since the 1950s. Color has brought a greater liveliness to many blue films; the actors today are younger, the girls prettier, and the sexual activities accompanied by expressions of pleasure, a pleasure mixed, perhaps, with a desire to shock, *épater les bourgeois,* that mixes ill with the attitude of sexual freedom the films seek to present. It is probably too early to expect an intellectual liberation within the form to accompany the physical one; suffice it to say that the departure of the tattooed sailors and veteran whores of the earlier period is not to be lamented.

The main market for blue films has traditionally been heterosexual, and very few of them feature male homosexuality, but there are interesting homosexual tints to the overall picture. The standard films of heterosexual intercourse, like *Do Me Again, Really Finished,* and *100 Per Cent Lust,* focus for long sequences on the male organ in all its glory, which, in any other context, say a "boys' magazine," would be condemned by most males as deviant entertainment.

These three American films are typically plotless, giving the impression of having been cut in one-reel lengths from an endless loop of filmed intercourse. Technical innovation and a more complex theme distinguish *Magic* (anonymous American, *c.* 1955), in which two (clothed) women are gossiping on a couch, presumably about sex, for when one of them snaps her fingers at the coffee table a dildo appears on it, then a real penis. The girl who is left out of the ensuing action snaps *her* fingers

at an empty space in the room and a naked man appears. Also noteworthy is *Bare Interlude* (French, *c.* 1935), which features the preparation of what looks like a sacramental meal by the heroine; and the probably unique *Buried Treasure* (Hollywood, *c.* 1930), an animated film dramatizing a number of episodes of barnyard humor. *Hotel Mamie Stover* starts with a long and expertly directed masturbatory strip tease by a girl reading the title book on a bed, before she is joined by a lesbian partner. *Tunnel of Love* shows two lesbians, of well-differentiated characters, in a bout of love play that is outstanding for its convincing display of passion. Despite its lack of all but the simplest structure, it is one of the cleverest combinations of *cinéma vérité* and directed acting in blue films.

It is not unusual for a blue film to build to a climax of sorts, in which two men enter one woman at once or stimulate her at once—not strictly heterosexual behavior. But many blue films, like *Hotel Mamie Stover, Tunnel of Love,* and *La Femme au Portrait,* have lesbian themes, and they are often several cuts above their competitors in quality. The view of homosexuals as "more sensitive" and less crude than their heterosexual counterparts is featured in *La Femme au Portrait* (French, 1940s). The oafish male, who takes a swig of whiskey, pounds himself on the chest, and makes a big mark on the wall each time that he achieves orgasm, is played against the sweeter, gentler, and more aesthetic relationship between the girl and the woman in a picture that she has wheedled the man into buying at a street market. In the finale the two women escape together into the picture, leaving the uncomprehending male sitting crowned with horns.

The film version of Lawrence's *The Fox* is hardly different from *La Femme au Portrait* in theme but far closer to life in event, and this characteristic emphasizes the paradoxical nature of the blue film. For the blue film deals with the source of our mystery: It presents us with bodies, genitals, and acts of love, including orgasms. It is thus beyond periods, styles, and changes in taste. We may laugh at the lady of *The Casting Couch* (c. 1919)[18] in her "teddies," but when she takes them off we do not laugh. But the blue film ultimately cannot present love or the erotic in any but the least rewarding way. It has its appeal, for, as the Kronhausens have testified, the average person retains an interest in erotic art no matter how crude and repetitious and "obscene" he may find it.[19]

We cannot safely predict that commercial films, for all their increasing nudity, will ever entirely take over the sphere of blue films. It is simply a cultural fact that blue films are made under conditions least rewarding to creativity and that their subject matter to a large extent forbids creativity. Sexual intercourse is, in mathematical terms, a "well-defined system." Cleopatra's infinite variety lies not in her genitals but in her mind. The degree to which curiosity is heightened and boredom defeated (the ultimate goals of art) is in inverse proportion to the relentless closeness of the camera to the penis entering and being withdrawn from a vagina. The erotic power of an individual motion picture is therefore never predictable from "the amount of sex" in it.[20] The equation is rather an infinitely subtle combination of light and shade, allusive gesture and speech. It is no accident that the blue film has remained a silent form through the last forty years of

sound, surely not only because of economics but also because the complexity and suggestive sexuality of speech are basically foreign to it.

The form of films shifts in response to shifts in the cultural assumptions of audiences, and the delicate aesthetic balances achieved at given moments are not repeated. For this reason, movies like *Foolish Wives* and *The Devil Is a Woman* are never replaced by movies like *Some Like It Hot* and *Gilda;* all remain in a continuum.

Rape and Death

As a final comment on the nature of the blue film, we can note that sadomasochistic elements are almost never successful in blue films, whereas they are staples in normal commercial films. Blue films offer sexual "reality," without the acting, aesthetic distance, and creative imagination of normal films. The blue film is thus inextricably bound by its own limitations. If action is faked, as in "pulling" blows with a whip, technical and imaginative poverty betray the film into laughability (as in *An English Tragedy* [mid-1930s], which totally fails to recreate its literary source, *The Way of a Man with a Maid*). If the director sticks to "reality," the result is superficially exciting but finally disappointing, for the erotic appeal of sadomasochism is not that of watching real torture; it is that of imagining oneself inflicting or experiencing torture. The male actors in such "realistic" films almost never have erections.

Sadomasochism is always faked in commercial films and is therefore always, to a greater or lesser degree, imaginative. It can be highly successful, as in *Rosemary's Baby* (directed by Roman Polanski, 1968), but it can also fail, as in most of Vincent Price's adaptations of E. A. Poe and the lesser features shown on the drive-in circuit. The scene of the diabolic conception in *Rosemary's Baby* has few rivals in blue films. The Institute for Sex Research

---

[18] *The Casting Couch* is of interest for its early date, its use of subtitles, and its rigorously straightforward enactment of one of the most famous erotic themes of Hollywood life, the kind of *droit du seigneur* that agent, director, or producer supposedly wields over the aspiring actress.

[19] Kronhausen and Kronhausen (1964), p. 327.

[20] This type of assessment is the basic error of much film criticism, like that of Knight and Alpert, which tacitly assumes that the erotic power of films increases over time and that cataloguing instances of breast and thigh exposure, approaches to sexual intercourse, and so on demonstrates this increase.

has a fragmentary German film of a black mass (*c.* 1930), featuring a cast of, comparatively speaking, "thousands" (about twenty-five), torches, cloaks, masks, a high priest, and a wide range of victims. It involves a certain amount of Satanism, but it is close to unique.

But erotic flagellation, torture, mutilation and sacrilege are esoteric and peripheral to rape, the simplest, most common, and most dependable sadomasochistic activity in films. Frequently rape is suggested by stalking, the same kind of inexorable hunt on which the mystery-detective film is based. In that the thrill is in the hunt and subsequent capture, it is erotically immaterial whether the girl is merely raped, or raped and killed. Murder is generally combined with rape for greater dramatic effect and because the difficulties of handling a simple rape are infinitely greater. In cases of attempted rape, of course, the problem does not arise; fright is the only emotion that actor or audience need deal with. Griffith set the tone in *The Birth of a Nation* (itself representing the birth of an art form), in which two attempts of rape are both foiled melodramatically, the first when the white virgin jumps off a cliff to escape the black rapist and the second when a white man rescues her. The rape threat has thus been parallel to the death threat from the beginning: Pearl White tied to the railroad tracks or to a board headed for a circular saw recurs as Phoebe Zeitgeist on the Bullet Line track. She is the woman helplessly awaiting violation. She will either be saved or die, for rape is traditionally equated with death (indeed, it is "worse than death," which is why Griffith's white virgin backs off the cliff). In rape films the victims, and especially young girls, are like birds with broken wings—better put out of their misery (offscreen). We can discharge pity and terror in their absence; if they remain and talk, what can they do and say?

The rape-death device is erotically satisfying to a common type of sadism; it is therefore present even in films of great distinction, like Kurosawa's *Rashomon.* The latter conforms to the main corollary: If the raped woman does not die, she must at least be morally or psychologically destroyed. In *Rashomon* all the men's (the bandit's, the husband's, the woodcutter's) stories of the forest encounter agree on one specific point: that the woman showed a steep moral decline after having been raped. In Buñuel's *Viridiana* (1961), nearly as great a film as *Rashomon,* we are free to conclude that Viridiana's rigorous religious faith, her stern virtue, and her naive desire to do good have all been undermined, if not destroyed, by her experience of rape by the very beneficiaries of her charity. And even in Vittorio de Sica's *La Ciocara* (*Two Women,* 1960), steeped in hardboiled Italian neorealism, the raped daughter becomes an immediate convert to whoredom, psychotic as well. It is a cliché of sadist literature that, once given a taste of force, the average woman is immediately converted to debauchery. William Faulkner's novel *Sanctuary* (filmed as *The Story of Temple Drake* in 1933) turns upon this point; if the idea really does nag at the edges of our consciousness, it is no wonder that most rape films dispose of the victims as rapidly as possible.

Bergman's *Virgin Spring* (*Jungfrukällen,* 1959) uses the traditional combination of rape and murder in a film of such beauty that it can serve as exemplar of the type. The long and detailed rape scene is violent and horrible, but erotically powerful too. That power is more disturbing than the violence, for to feel it is to feel complicity in crime. That the rape is followed by murder functions here as a kind of release, for the act of murder draws off, simplifies, and concentrates the human guilt that we are forced to share. The dark girl, Ingeri, a foil for the bright, blonde innocence of the Virgin, has been raped and has survived. She *may* survive, for she is associated with paganism and the forces of evil. The fate of the dark girl,

Figure 15.6.   Kurosawa's *Rashomon* (1950): an uninterpretable rape. Courtesy of Janus Films and the Museum of Modern Art Stills Archives.

the prostitute, is irrelevant to the erotic illusions cherished in Western society. But those illusions are harder, in the end, on the pure-white virgin. She must die, poor lamb, so that her innocence may be preserved and so that our sadistic impulses may be satisfied.

Erotica Minora

A minor but not uncommon erotic theme in films is transvestism. Chaplin transformed himself into a remarkably convincing woman by means of costume changes in two early short films, *The Masquerader* (1914) and *A Woman* (1915). The plots are hazy at best, but the

miming is excellent and the uses to which it is put clearly erotic. As a woman Charlie *vamps,* is openly seductive. When great directors like Buñuel, in *Viridiana,* or Bergman, in *Now about These Women,* use transvestism, it is with equally frank recognition of its erotic potential. The common disguises of the erotic excitement in treating a man as a woman or a woman as a man are two: first, pretense to comic, sinister, or other motives for the disguise, and, second, exaggeration into camp, overplaying the vamping and feminine mannerisms in order to render the whole situation farcical, rather than erotic.

In the first category are Hitchcock's *Murder*

Figure 15.7. Chaplin in *A Woman* (1915). Courtesy of the Museum of Modern Art Stills Archives.

(1930), in which the murderer is a transvestite trapeze artist, and *Psycho*, in which the murdering son is dressed as his mother, as well as Robert Hamer's *Kind Hearts and Coronets*, a *tour de force* of role-switching. Comic roles are generally motivated strictly by demands of the plot; Cary Grant in *I Was a Male War Bride* (1949) and Jack Lemmon and Tony Curtis in *Some Like It Hot* (1959) have no alternative but to don female garb.

The latter film is actually an example of camp drag: Once they have been "required" to change clothes because they are hunted wit-

nesses of the St. Valentine's Day massacre, Curtis and Lemmon develop wildly seductive mannerisms, Lemmon in particular parodying the head tossing, hip swinging, and eyelash batting of a drag queen (see the documentary *The Queen*, 1968). Nevertheless, the characters are made up to be *unconvincing* as women, as in *Charlie's Aunt* (filmed in 1941 with Jack Benny), in which socks and garters show below the skirts, so that there is tension between the erotic and the absurd. This tension is necessary, for in *Some Like It Hot* the main character remains in drag almost from beginning to end, and Wilder must be credited as one of the few directors ever to have brought off nearly two hours of such exposure. Most transvestite scenes are simply vignettes, or, as in *Myra Breckinridge* (1970), a woman is cast in the role of the man in drag, thus short-circuiting the whole effect. Wilder was also honest, or "daring," enough to suggest at the very end of his film that Lemmon's passionate lover, the millionaire roué played by Joe E. Brown, has known all along that he has been courting a member of his own sex and is not going to let "her" escape on that account. As Brown whisks Lemmon off to his yacht for the getaway, along with the now happily heterosexual couple of Curtis and Marilyn Monroe, he refuses to listen to any number of confessional hints from Lemmon about the impossibility of their marrying. Baffled and a little desperate, Lemmon finally blurts out, "I'm a man!" Brown, with an expression at once bemused and a little sinister, replies, "Nobody's perfect."

Wilder's sex comedies are very much of their time, restricted to innuendo and misunderstood situations (looking like lust but turning out to be something less wholesome—greed, pride, or deception for deception's sake); this approach, in the hands of less talented directors, marked the final development in the 1950s of those old standbys of American erotic art, the dirty joke and the virgin tease. The aging teen-ager Doris Day, who spends nights in bachelors' apartments (and pajamas) but never does anything that a lady would not do, is the living symbol of this period of American film culture. The Playboy bunny is her counterpart, offering a superabundance of unavailable sex and the manners of a courtesan with the vows of a Vestal. The man in drag is an even better symbol: You had better not touch, or you'll find something that you didn't expect. On the other hand, if you knew all along, you have the laugh on "straight citizens" and are in on something both clever and sterile.

The long sequence in *A Funny Thing Happened on the Way to the Forum* (1966) in which Zero Mostel chases a man (Jack Gilford), whom he has himself dressed in drag, through a softly lit glade while a love song swells on the sound track, as well as the final scene, in which two of the three brides being claimed by eager husbands are men in drag, suggests a different kind of transvestism, tasteless and ultimately anti-erotic. No one is trying to fool anyone for a sexual purpose, yet the whole thing has a leering quality, even a little of which can spoil the fun inherent in the comedy of Terence and Plautus and the marvelous, imaginative camera work of Nicholas Roeg.

In films the erotic is always accompanied by the antierotic or at least always gives rise to it. It might be argued that a surfeit of the erotic in films of the 1950s and 1960s has caused a revulsion from sex in the work of some directors. Perhaps a medium as erotic as film contains within itself the seeds of its own denial; the erotic images a sensitive and capable director can wield with overpowering effect drive him by their very excess to a corrective bitterness and withdrawal. Erich von Stroheim made *Blind Husbands* (1918), then *Foolish Wives* (1921), both according to his "universal formula of sophisticated sex, seduction, and intrigue in a Continental setting."[21] Then in 1923 he made *Greed,* an adaptation of Norris'

---

[21] Finler (1968), p. 12. Erich von Stroheim (born in Vienna 1885; died 1957) brought an exacting craftsmanship to Hollywood films, but ultimately Hollywood refused to pay for it, and he was relieved of his directorial duties. His films were never released in their extravagant full-length versions; even so, *Blind Husbands* (1918), *Foolish Wives* (1921), *Merry-Go-Round* (1922), *The Merry Widow* (1925), and *The Wedding March* (1926) remain among the classic films of seduction and intrigue, whereas *Greed* (1923) is considered one of the most remarkable film adaptations of a novel. Stroheim also had a long acting career, working under both Griffith in *The Birth of a Nation* (1915) and Jean Renoir in *La Grande Illusion* (1937); he perfected the character of the cruelly dashing military officer, often a competent seducer, into an archetype.

McTeague, which, as far as we can tell without having seen it, greatly emphasizes the relation between sex and money and between both and death. Male rivalry over a woman ends with the woman murdered and one rival alone and on foot in the middle of Death Valley, handcuffed to the corpse of the other.

Aspects of Ewald André Dupont's *Variety* and von Sternberg's *The Blue Angel*, both of which spell out the degradation in store for a man who lets himself be enthralled by a woman, can be considered antierotic. This antieroticism is, of course, comparable to the anticrime sentiments in films filled with photogenic machine-gunnings and beautiful gangster limousines, proclaiming the while that crime does not pay. But the man who takes Lola Lola or Berta-Marie seriously is going to find himself anaesthetized to feminine charm.

Variety (German, 1925) reveals, within the framework of a prison interview, how the trapeze artist "Boss" Huller (Emil Jannings) came to realize that he was being cuckolded by the young and pretty Berta-Marie (Lya de Putti) whom he worshiped, even going so far as to darn her stockings for her. Her seducer was the handsome and dashing Artinelli, who had brought the two of them into big-time circus work. Huller was stunned and broken to see a mocking sketch of himself as a cuckold on a café table, but he steeled himself to take revenge. In a dizzying trapeze sequence, set in the Berlin Wintergarten, he thought to drop Artinelli into the crowd far below but could not do it. The end came soon after, however, when he knifed Artinelli in a hotel room and gave himself up to the police.

When Antonioni made a series of films in the 1960s that threatened the conventions of film love and romance, his concepts were not totally new or totally untried by his contemporaries. For instance, Fellini's *La Dolce Vita*, the film that came to be considered the key to affluent postwar society, expresses a loathing for the sexual amusements of socially prominent but useless people; the more sensitive individuals (like Steiner) are driven to suicide or (like Marcello) to self-destruction of a more subtle kind. Nevertheless, the film holds out the touchingly innocent figure of Paola, the girl on the beach. In Fellini's work love is often distorted but never denied. The more coldly intellectual Antonioni, on the other hand, sees "eroticism as a disease of our age." [22] That his *L'Avventura, La Notte,* and *L'Eclisse* treat only the rich, idle, and spoiled does not prevent their powerful depiction of emptiness from having a corrosive effect upon the romantic nature of film in general.

L'Ecclisse (1961) begins and ends with the heroine's recognition of her own loneliness and the mutual failure of communication in a love affair, a recognition that is underlined throughout the film by long silences and distant shots of the empty spaces between buildings, like the empty spaces, physical and otherwise, between people. *Il Deserto Rosso* (*The Red Desert*, 1964) adds color, and scenes of lovemaking, to approximately the same situation, an alliance between a man and a woman in which neither finds, or is even able to seek, anything definable. The lovemaking is mindless, lacking even the exaggerated posturings of the early silent era; all the antierotic boredom, false starts, and *voies sans issue* of life itself are here, but they are more devastating when enlarged by the medium. When illusion is so thoroughly undermined, the erotic is not simply subdued; it is destroyed. Withdrawal to a higher plane, a life without feeling, is the only solution to the dramatic situations in these films. They remain a curious monument to joylessness, too well made to ignore but too blankly pessimistic to take seriously.

---

[22] "Eroticism: The Disease of Our Age," *Films and Filming*, January 1961, p. 7.

Marriage and Romance

Marriage has generally resisted erotic treatment in films, as it has in literature. It more
often yields comedy or serves as background
to adultery, for these two treatments render it
at least a little exciting. But even comic excitement is tinged with scorn, and adultery reflects
upon the erotic insufficiency of marriage. The
comic marital pair is generally ludicrously ill
matched (as are the psychiatrist and his wife
in *What's New, Pussycat?*) or in some other way
prevented from entertaining thoughts of love
(Fellini, in his comic masterpiece *Lo Sciecco
Bianco*,[23] treats a bride and groom with great
tenderness but keeps them separated throughout
the action). Comic and serious aspects of married love and adultery have been successfully
mingled in only a very few films, among them
Marcel Pagnol's minor classic *La Femme du
Boulanger* (*The Baker's Wife*, 1938). The priest
brings back the errant wife of the baker, the
villagers save him from suicide, and through
their joint efforts bread is baked once more;
the erotic here, as elsewhere, lies only in the
illicit, in the scenes between the wife and her
young paramour.

This observation can be generalized: The
main excitement of love as shown in art lies
in courtship, the sexual approaches that previously unacquainted people make to each other.
Marriage does not usually include courtship,
and it cannot therefore provide the excitement
that films need. Adultery, on the other hand,
combines courtship with danger and is therefore
an exceptionally good subject. With a few other
themes, like jealousy and separation, it can
introduce courtship into marriage, usually in the
guise of the husband's efforts to regain the
affections of his wife. Bergman's *A Lesson in
Love* is a well-made example of such a film;
Murnau's *Sunrise* (1927)[24] is the most beautiful
yet made.

When sexual intercourse itself is the subject
of a film, the equation is vastly altered; it no
longer makes a difference what the legal status
of the lovers is. There is at least one blue film
with a setting of married life, but it is quickly
breached and forgotten as the film moves into
illusionless recording of intercourse. The most
powerful combination of illusion, expectation,
curiosity about the unknown, and promise of
delight is still to be found in courtship. Because
films have catered to the most popular illusions—that there is love at first *sight*, that
accidents may bring lovers together or rend
them apart but that their relationship has been
uniquely predestined—the dominant film form
has been, and still is today, the romance. From
Broken Blossoms to *A Man and a Woman*, from
Song of Love to *Elvira Madigan*, romance has

[23] *Lo Sciecco Bianco* (*The White Sheik*) is about a couple who come to Rome for their honeymoon, planning to meet relatives who live there and to seek an audience with the Pope. The wife's head has been quite turned by reading of the dashing and amorous White Sheik, a Valentino figure in the photo-comics, and she sneaks out of the hotel while her husband is napping and goes to the magazine's office. She foolishly follows the actors on their day's shooting, accepting a lift in their truck, and is unable to return to the city until the middle of the night. She has met the Sheik, even acted with him, and has found him to have feet of clay (as well as a termagent wife). Meanwhile the distraught husband searches wildly in all directions, fending off his wondering relatives by pretending that his bride is resting in their hotel room. After many poignant and hilarious incidents, including a suicide attempt by the wife, who feels utterly shamed and compromised, the two are reunited in time to make the papal audience.

[24] A married farmer (George O'Brien) becomes infatuated with a city woman who is vacationing in his village. She tempts him to murder his wife (Janet Gaynor); he starts to do so but relents at the last minute. His wife flees in hysterics; he catches her up in the city and manages, in several touchingly beautiful scenes, to win back her confidence. Returning home in their boat, they are swept overboard; he reaches shore, but she is lost. He goes mad with grief; then she is found and carried in, alive, by an old fisherman. She glances feebly and lovingly at her husband, the sun rises, and a cart passes, carrying the city woman whence she came.

carried the day. Love viewed romantically, rather than from the point of view of sexual realism, is what films have been about: the bodies of women presented in a framework as structured as that of medieval courtly love. The film has given our era, after all, its religion of love!

At the height of the celebrations in Babylon in Griffith's *Intolerance*, the Princess Beloved is shown seated on a throne at the end of the palanquin bearing King Belshazzar. She places a rose in a tiny chariot drawn by two doves

and sends it across the short space to his side. He lifts up the rose and holds it out to her, as she smiles and looks down. This formal, highly artificial gesture encapsulates the Babylon that Griffith wished to present: the home of justice and law, magnanimity, and the spirit of love. He has been so successful in this idealization in "the greatest film of all time,"[25] that, when, amid the death and destruction of

---

[25] Franklin (1959), p. 20.

Figure 15.8.   Griffith's *Intolerance* (1916). Despite its defects, this film is one of the best ever. The rose has just been delivered by the dove-drawn chariot, and the king holds it up, illuminating the ages with a gesture of love's promise. The actors are Serena Owen as the Princess Beloved and Alfred Paget as Belshazzar, the king. Courtesy of the Museum of Modern Art Stills Archives.

Figure 15.9.   Stairway to Heaven (1946): sentimentality enhanced by technicolor effects. The dead aviator stands before God (in the judge's wig and white robes) and the Council of Heaven; his intermediary is the living girl who loves him and for whose sake he will be returned to life. Courtesy of Rank Film Sales, Inc., and the Museum of Modern Art Stills Archives.

the city, he inserts a shot of the doves, with their little chariot still attached, cowering amid the ruins of the throne room, the effect is unbearably pathetic.

Another such rose appears in *Stairway to Heaven* (1946), with *The Red Shoes* (1948) and *The Tales of Hoffman* (1951) part of a remarkable efflorescence of the romantic film in Britain immediately after World War II. In *Stairway to Heaven* God and Love are brought into powerful alliance: After a long argument in the Grand Council of Heaven, it is decided

that a dying British aviator played by David Niven is to be granted a new lease on life because an American girl has fallen in love with him. Her love is demonstrated by one of her tears, brought to Heaven on the rose into which it fell. Challenged to prove his own love for the girl, Niven cries, "Give me fifty years and I'll show you!" The message is clear: On earth as in heaven love conquers all. For is God not love?

In this view there is little difference between romance and religion; the apocalyptic visions that end Griffith's epic films and that end the Beatles' *The Yellow Submarine* suggest that "All You Need Is Love." Thousands of other films, some of them very fine, operate from the same fundamental premise. Fellini's *La Strada* is a notable example, one of the great modern films. Its settings and characters are supplied by the neorealist movement in post-World War II Italian films, but its philosophy is anything but realistic. It is instead an allegory of divine love, in which animal man (Zampano, played by Anthony Quinn) is offered the pearl without price, the pure love of an innocent (Gelsomina, played by Giulietta Massina), and throws it away. It is the greatest crime:

Zampano's boastfulness, infidelity, thievery, even murder could all have been atoned for had he been capable of love. At the end—alone, a burden to himself and others—in the dark night of his soul, he becomes capable.

At the opposite end of the scale of illusion, in the land of enchanted palaces and magical effects where no pretense to realism is made, is Cocteau's inimitable *La Belle et la Bête* (*Beauty and the Beast*), which celebrates the same kind of love. In it, as in the lavish but crude *Pandora and the Flying Dutchman* (starring James Mason and Ava Gardner, 1951), the heroine holds the key that can release the lonely, loveless man from the curse that binds him—as

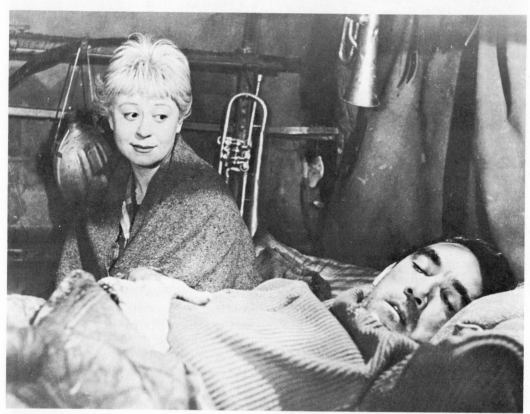

Figure 15.10.   Fellini's *La Strada* (1954): Gelsomina (Guilietta Massina) and Zampano (Anthony Quinn). Courtesy of Audio Brandon Films and the Museum of Modern Art Stills Archives.

Figure 15.11.   Cocteau's *Beauty and the Beast* (1947): magical folklore cast in magical images. The film is in sharp contrast to the deliberate ugliness of *La Strada,* but it makes the same point—that unselfish giving of oneself in love is the clue to life and its greatest prize. Courtesy of Janus Films and the Museum of Modern Art Stills Archives.

it bound Zampano. The impotence of evil against pure love is here highlighted through the universal appeal of folklore. Beauty holds the key to our desires; we desire her body and something more as well, something only vaguely definable as happiness. Films are naturally adapted to capitalize on that vagueness.

Erotic and Other Images: *Persona*

In the preceding discussion we have shown the film dominated by its erotic elements, as a naturally erotic art form. This natural eroti-

cism distinguishes it from literature, which can present anything that can be thought—as long as it can be put into language. In our view, unless erotic elements are rigorously excluded from a film, they will spread through it as if they were an infection, taking on a life of their own and superimposing themselves upon any other ideas that the director may have intended. A great enough artist can subdue any such elements to his plan, but film directors have managed to subdue sex only in rare instances. Such instances are worth study because of the light that they can shed on the relations between

Figure 15.12. The metaphysics of the erotic: Bibi Andersson and Liv Ullmann, the lovers of *Persona* (1967). Courtesy of Janus Films and the Museum of Modern Art Stills Archives.

art and eroticism. This chapter can suitably conclude with a look at one such film, which in its mastery of sexual elements, reflects a view of the film medium itself: Bergman's *Persona* (1967).

At first glance, *Persona* appears to be a film about courtship between two women, a famous actress (Elizabeth Vogler) who has suffered a nervous breakdown and a naive young nurse (Alma) assigned to care for her. The actress's withdrawal into psychosis is partly caused by recognition of her own loathing for her husband and child; the nurse is vaguely unhappy, having had a series of unsatisfying relationships with men, culminating in her present engagement to

a man whom she does not love. The lesbian atmosphere is heightened by other elements: The doctor who treats the actress and directs the nurse is also a woman, efficient and slightly masculine; the only man who appears is Vogler, Elizabeth's husband, a blind phantom who attempts unsuccessfully to penetrate the closed circle that the two women, nurse and patient, have created in their retreat to the lady doctor's island.

When Alma discovers, from reading an unsealed letter, that Elizabeth is only playing with her, rather than responding seriously to her adoration, she turns cruel, sacrificing her professional responsibility to her desire for

THE EROTIC IN FILM 419

revenge. The extent of that revenge—the deliberate sealing off of the sick woman in her psychosis—betrays the depth of the passion that has given rise to it. But this action lies on the uppermost surface, the obviously erotic level—if anything in this subtle film can be called obvious. The women exchange a few shy caresses, but the most erotic moment in the film is that in which Alma *tells* Elizabeth of sunbathing naked with another girl and of how they called two young boys on the beach over to make love to them.

Beneath the surface of the film lurks the question of the identity behind the mask (*persona*) that each individual assumes in life. The actress has made her career by assuming one mask after another with great success, until her sudden collapse and withdrawal from all roles, which is embodied in her refusal even to speak. She has therefore left a hole in the surface, an opening toward which the nurse, with her adolescent longing for something more romantic and exciting than life as she knows it, is slowly drawn. At one point she says to the actress, "When I saw you in your film, I wanted to be like you." Now we see her moving into Elizabeth's identity almost unconsciously. In effect, from wanting to have what she loves (but does not recognize herself as loving), she moves to becoming what she wants. What she loves is what she wants to be, and her love is ultimately narcissistic. At the beginning she fears Elizabeth's strength (the literary source of the film is August Strindberg's *Den Starkere*); at the end she is the stronger, the one to be feared. She has taken the identity that she wanted, has traded masks with Elizabeth. When the husband appears in the dream, he addresses Alma as if she were Elizabeth, while Elizabeth watches mutely; when we see, in flashback, the scene in bed with Vogler during which Elizabeth begins to lose her grip on the world, it is not she but Alma who is in bed with him. At this point Alma is ready to tell Elizabeth the story of what she (Elizabeth) thought and felt while she was

bearing and then abandoning her child. The strain in this process is intense; we penetrate beyond concern with sex to concern with identity, past a woman's relation to a man to her relation to another woman, then to her relation to herself. In life we play sexual roles, but we like to think that we do not play roles to ourselves, that our identities are secure. That is the second mask, or the second conventional illusion to be punctured by this film. The first was the mask we hold up to others, the second is the mask we hold up to ourselves, or show ourselves in the mirror.

As the women merge their identities, speaking each other's thoughts[26] and gazing into the camera with their heads side by side, we move beyond concern for both sex and identity to the final question, to their final positions at the edge of the abyss. Into this abyss Elizabeth has looked suddenly during a performance, and she has decided to perform no more. All human identities finally merge in that of existence—do they exist or don't they? Which is, put simply: Who is alive and who is dead? Very few works of art reach this level of intensity, particularly when encumbered with erotic distractions. Yet Theo in Gautier's erotic novel *Mademoiselle de Maupin* sums up: "Very often the meaning of life is that it is not death. That is all." Recognition of this truth permits us to penetrate the last mask in *Persona*, represented by the image of the burning Vietnamese monk whom Elizabeth sees on the hospital television set. One pushes through this mask at a terrible risk, for to penetrate the boundary between life and death is to enter death, and to risk, in metaphysical terms, a living death. Alma goes first, and draws Elizabeth after her: She climaxes her journey of the soul by repeating to Elizabeth, who has suffered a relapse and is now back in

---

[26]This stage is reached when Elizabeth comes to Alma seated at the table and apparently says, while Alma thinks she (Alma) is saying to herself, "You must go to bed or you'll fall asleep at the table."

the hospital, the word "nothing," and forcing her to repeat it. That is the end for them, but it is not the end of the film, which has been considering itself, as it were, while it has been considering these two women. It starts and finishes by showing the electrodes of the projector drawing together to make the fierce arc light and drawing apart as darkness takes over. It reviews, in short sequences, its own progression, as film, from those early shorts in which death appeared as a comic skeleton jerkily chasing a man in pajamas around a bedroom; it appears to physically tear and break during the confrontation between Elizabeth and Alma over broken glass left on the path; it is therefore separate throughout, as film, as a strip of celluloid, from what it is showing, in a Brechtian *Verfremdungseffekt*, as if to say "Here is what I can do, but notice that I am doing it; you are not in it, but outside." It forces us out of the film dream, the unwinking acceptance as reality of what is only art.

The final mask is worn by the director of the film, the master of illusion. To dispel the illusion of reality by forcing us to see his film as a film, then to dispel the erotic illusion by forcing us to look past it to the life behind it, then to dispel the illusion of life by forcing us to look at the death beyond it, is unusual, uncomfortable, possibly a metaphysical error. Most directors conceal the mystery so as to keep it effective; Bergman's unveiling of it is brutal and shocking, but all the more revelatory for that, and a necessary step in the modern process of learning, and seeing, and knowing sex in the movies.

Bibliography

While numerous insights concerning sex and film have been published over the years by psychologists, anthropologists, novelists and film critics in other contexts, the specialized study of film eroticism has been pursued only sporadically and without outstanding result. But we note here several titles from the small specialized literature for the considerable interest they hold in part and in sum, and because most of them develop parts of the subject well beyond the confines of this chapter. Probably the best book is Ado Kyrou, *Amour, Érotisme, et Cinéma* (Paris: Le Terrain Vague, 1957), rambling, poorly indexed, with numerous misprints, opinionated and superficial in places, but full of insight in others. Edgar Morin, *The Stars* (trans. from French by Richard Howard; New York: Grove Press, 1960) is equally imaginative and provocative, though tied to the star cult and its effects outside of film. G. Lo Duca, *Die Erotik im Film* (Basel, 1965), offers an intelligent classification of material and numerous illustrations from film stills. Raymond Durgnat, *Eros in the Cinema* (London: Calder and Boyars, 1966), is a lively survey of a large number of films, several of which are studied in detail. Durgnat's rather carefree sociological generalizations are outweighed by his sensitivity to film technique. Of limited value, but containing useful information, are Alexander Walker's *Sex in the Movies* (Baltimore: Penguin Books, 1969), a survey of stars and censorship; Jean Boullet, *La Belle et la Bête* (Paris, 1958), a survey of monsters used to act out erotic fantasies on women in films; and Gerd Osten and Artur Lundkvist, *Erotiken i Filmen* (Stockholm, 1950), a short but wide-ranging study. Jim Henri, *The World's Most Sensual Films* (Chicago, 1965), is fatuous and journalistic, but offers a glimpse in English of the apparently unbridled sadism in the Japanese film. The Knight and Alpert series in *Playboy* magazine, "The History of Sex in Cinema" (April 1965–January 1969) is invaluable documentation.

Introduction

It is a fair assumption that most readers of this book are guilty of having broken one or more of the many laws governing sexual behavior in our society. Consider the following data from the Kinsey study of male sexual behavior: At some time 85 percent of men had engaged in premarital intercourse, 59 percent had participated in oral-genital contacts, 70 percent had had intercourse with prostitutes, 30–45 percent had been involved in one or more extramarital affairs, 37 percent had participated in homosexual activities, an additional 10–15 percent had been exclusively homosexual for prolonged periods (three years or more), and 17 percent of those raised on farms had had intercourse with animals.[1] All this behavior is prohibited by criminal laws; considered collectively, the number of sexual offenders among the male population appears to have exceeded 95 percent of all males. Kinsey declared:

> Only a relatively small proportion of the males who are sent to penal institutions for sex offenses have been involved in behavior which is materially different from the behavior of most of the males in the population. But it is the total of 95 percent of the male population for which the judge, or board of public safety, or church, or civic group demands apprehension, arrest, and conviction, when they call for a clean-up of the sex offenders in a community. It is, in fine, a proposal that 5 percent of the population should support the other 95 percent in penal institutions. The only possible defense of the proposal is the fact that the judge, the civic leader, and most of the others who make such suggestions, come from that segment of the population which is most restrained on nearly all types of sexual behavior, and they simply do not understand how the rest of the population actually lives.[2]

The following transcript from a recent court hearing in California illustrates this point rather vividly. The defendant, a minor, was accused of having committed incest with his sister.

IN THE SUPERIOR COURT OF THE STATE OF CALIFORNIA, IN AND FOR THE COUNTY OF SANTA CLARA, JUVENILE DIVISION, HONORABLE XXXXX, JUDGE, COURTROOM NO. 1.

In the Matter of XXXXX, a minor, No. XXXX

STATEMENTS OF THE COURT

San Jose, California   Sept. 2, 1969

---

[1]Kinsey *et al.* (1948), pp. 391–392.

[2]Kinsey *et al.* (1948), p. 392.

SEX AND THE LAW

APPEARANCES:

For the Minor: XXXXX, ESQ., Deputy Public Defender

For the Probation Department: XXXXX, ESQ., Court Probation Officer

Official Court Reporter: XXXXX, C.S.R.

Sept. 2, 1969   10:24 a.m.

The Court: There is some indication that you more or less didn't think that it was against the law or was improper. Haven't you had any moral training? Have you and your family gone to church?

The Minor: Yes, sir.

The Court: Don't you know that things like this are terribly wrong? *This is one of the worst crimes that a person can commit. I just get so disgusted that I just figure what is the use? You are just an animal.* You are lower than an animal. Even animals don't do that. You are pretty low.

I don't know why your parents haven't been able to teach you anything or train you. [You] people, after 13 years of age, it's perfectly all right to go out and act like an animal [*sic*]. It's not even right to do that to a stranger, let alone a member of your own family. I don't have much hope for you. You will probably end up in State's Prison before you are 25, and that's where you belong, anyhow. There is nothing much you can do.

I think you haven't got any moral principles. You won't acquire anything. Your parents won't teach you what is right or wrong and won't watch out.

Apparently, your sister is pregnant; is that right?

The Minor's Father, XXXXX: Yes.

The Court: It's a fine situation. How old is she?

The Minor's Mother, Mrs. XXXXX: Fifteen.

The Court: Well, probably she will have a half a dozen children and three or four marriages before she is 18.

The county will have to take care of you. You are no particular good to anybody. We ought to send you out of the country. . . . *You belong in prison for the rest of your life for doing things of this kind. You ought to commit suicide. That's*

what I think of people of this kind. You are lower than animals and haven't the right to live in organized society—just miserable, lousy, rotten people.

There is nothing we can do with you. You expect the county to take care of you. *Maybe Hitler was right. The animals in our society probably ought to be destroyed because they have no right to live among human beings.* If you refuse to act like a human being, then, you don't belong among the society of human beings.

Defense Attorney: Your Honor, I don't think I can sit here and listen to that sort of thing.

The Court: You are going to have to listen to it because I consider this a very vulgar, rotten human being.

Defense Attorney: The Court is indicting the whole [ethnic] group.

The Court: When they are 10 or 12 years of age, going out and having intercourse with anybody without any moral training—they don't even understand the Ten Commandments. That's all. Apparently, they don't want to.

So, if you want to act like that, the county has a system of taking care of them. They don't care about that. They have no personal self-respect.

Defense Attorney: The Court ought to look at this youngster and deal with this youngster's case.

The Court: All right. That's what I am going to do. The family should be able to control this boy and the young girl.

Defense Attorney: What appalls me is that the Court is saying that Hitler was right in genocide.

The Court: What are we going to do with the mad dogs of our society? Either we have to kill them or send them to an institution or place them out of the hands of good people because that's the theory—one of the theories of punishment is if they get to the position that they want to act like mad dogs, then, we have to separate them from our society.

Well, I will go along with the recommendation. You will learn in time or else you will have to pay for the penalty with the law because the law grinds slowly but exceedingly well. If you are going to be a law violator—you have to make up your mind whether you are going to observe the law or not. If you can't observe the law, then, you have to be put away.

STATE OF CALIFORNIA, COUNTY OF SANTA CLARA ss.[3]

This judge's verbalizations are admittedly atypical, and he was duly censored. His attitude, nonetheless, may be widely shared.

Many people are unaware of the existence of laws that define everyday sexual experiences as crimes. One of the purposes of this chapter is simply to point out the existence of these statutes, for potentially they affect almost everyone in the population. Perhaps this effort seems hardly worthwhile, for these laws are largely "dead"; they are so rarely enforced as to be inconsequential. But, as we shall demonstrate later, their very existence "on the books" allows for their occasional capricious application, which ill serves the interests of society, the individual, and the law.

Let us consider briefly how and why these laws came to be written in the first place. It is useful first to examine the general rationale behind the writing of criminal laws. Packer has listed several ideal criteria for justifying the use of criminal sanctions against certain behavior:

(1) The conduct is prominent in most people's view of socially threatening behavior, and is not condoned by any significant segment of society.

(2) Subjecting it to the criminal sanction is not inconsistent with the goals of punishment.

(3) Suppressing it will not inhibit socially desirable conduct.

(4) It may be dealt with through even-handed and nondiscriminatory enforcement.

(5) Controlling it through the criminal process will not expose that process to severe qualitative or quantitative strains.

(6) There are no reasonable alternatives to the criminal sanction for dealing with it.[4]

Another professor of law has put the issue of sexual ("morals") offenses somewhat differently:

What truly distinguishes the offenses commonly thought of as "against morals" is not their relation to morality but the absence of ordinary justification for punishment by a non-theocratic state. The ordinary justification for secular penal controls is preservation of public order. The king's peace must not be disturbed, or, to put the matter in the language of our time, public security must be preserved. Individuals must be able to go about their lawful pursuits without fear of attack, plunder, or other harms. This is an interest that only organized law enforcement can effectively safeguard. If individuals had to protect themselves by restricting their movements to avoid dangerous persons or neighborhoods, or by restricting their investments for fear of violent dispossession, or by employing personal bodyguards and armed private police, the economy would suffer, the body politic would be rent by conflict of private armies, and men would still walk in fear. No such results impend from the commission of "morals offenses."[5]

We cannot begin to understand the precepts embodied in the sex laws of our society without understanding something of the Judeo-Christian tradition of sexual ethics described in Chapter 17. It will become apparent as we quote from specific statutes in a typical American penal code that the laws pertaining to sexual behavior are, for the most part, not directed toward "the preservation of public order" as are most criminal laws. Rather, they embody a particular ethical point of view of sexual behavior: that the sole purpose of sexual activity is reproduction. When we recognize that a majority of legislators held this point of view

---

[3] The italics are added.

[4] Packer (1968), p. 296.

[5] Schwartz (1963).

when these laws were written, it is not difficult to understand how such activities as masturbation and homosexuality came to be designated as criminal offenses. Other notions arising from the particular ethical and religious backgrounds of the founders of Anglo-American society are also embodied in law, including the opinion that sex in general is evil and the belief that having more than one spouse at a time is wrong.

Some lawyers and legislators have questioned the constitutionality of laws directed toward enforcement of the views of a particular religion, in light of the provisions in the U.S. Constitution for separation of church and state. But until recently very few were willing to voice such questions openly because of the risk to their reputations and careers. When a legislator seeks to overturn a law that makes intercourse between an unmarried couple a crime, it is far too easy for a political opponent to say that he must also favor free love, sin, and thus "corruption" in general. Few men are willing to subject themselves to such charges, particularly if they must run for elective office periodically.

But, aside from the question of the constitutionality of laws governing sexual behavior, several other objections can be raised. Packer has stated them:

(1) Rarity of enforcement creates a problem of arbitrary police and prosecutorial discretion.

(2) The extreme difficulty of detecting such conduct leads to undesirable police practices.

(3) The existence of the proscription tends to create a deviant subculture.

(4) Widespread knowledge that the law is violated with impunity by thousands every day creates disrespect for law generally.

(5) No secular harm can be shown to result from such conduct.

(6) The theoretical availability of criminal sanctions creates a situation in which extortion and, on occasion, police corruption may take place.

(7) There is substantial evidence that the moral sense of the community no longer exerts strong pressure for the use of criminal sanctions.

(8) No utilitarian goal of criminal punishment is substantially advanced by proscribing private adult consensual sexual conduct.

The only countervailing argument is that relaxation of the criminal proscription will be taken to express social approval of the conduct at issue. There is little enough, as we have seen, to that general proposition. It becomes peculiarly vacuous when addressed to this issue, where the social taboo is so much stronger than the legal prohibition. It does not pay a statute much of a compliment, a justice of the Supreme Court once remarked, to say that it is not unconstitutional. It may also be said that it does not express much approval of a behavior pattern to say that it is not criminal.[6]

Because of these widely recognized objections to our present sex laws, The American Law Institute, when preparing its *Model Penal Code*, recommended the abolition of all laws governing sexual activities performed in private between consenting adults. The reasoning behind this recommendation is apparent in this comment:

The Code does not attempt to use the power of the state to enforce purely moral or religious standards. We deem it inappropriate for the government to attempt to control behavior that has no substantial significance except as to the morality of the actor. Such matters are best left to religious, educational and other social influences. Apart from the question of constitutionality which might be raised against legislation avowedly commanding adherence to a particular religious or moral tenet, it must be recognized, as a practical matter, that in a heterogeneous community such as ours, different individuals and groups have widely divergent views of the seriousness of various moral derelictions.[7]

---

[6]Packer (1968), p. 304.

[7]The American Law Institute (1955), Article 207.1, comment.

A distinction can be made among three general categories of sexual behavior, all of which are subject to criminal sanctions in most of the fifty states at the present time. The first includes the sexual behavior of consenting adults in private. Many if not the vast majority of authorities on criminal law believe that such activities should be legalized.[8] The second category includes offenses involving force or violence (for instance, rape), offenses against children ("child molesting"), and offenses that present a public nuisance (for instance, exhibitionism). Legal opinion is almost unanimous that such offenses should remain under criminal sanctions. No one, obviously, favors the legalizing of forcible rape (though some revision of the laws pertaining to statutory rape may be in order in some states). The third category of offenses is the most controversial at the present time; it includes those offenses that involve commercial exploitation of sex (prostitution and the sale of pornography).

In this chapter we shall discuss some of the specific offenses included in each of these three categories and compare existing American statutes[9] with those of the *Model Penal Code* and with some from other countries. We shall attempt to describe how existing laws are usually enforced and shall present arguments for and against their retention in our society.

Laws Pertaining to Consenting Adults

Fornication

On June 13, 1969, a jury in Paterson, New Jersey, found a man and a woman guilty on three counts of fornication; that is, the defendants were convicted of a crime of sexual intercourse between consenting unmarried adults. According to Municipal Judge Ervan F. Jushner, "I saw a crime being committed when an unmarried woman walked into my courtroom pregnant." There were three counts of fornication in the indictment, for the woman had already borne three illegitimate children. The couple was convicted under Section 2:133-1 of the *New Jersey Statutes,* which reads, "Any person who shall commit fornication shall be guilty of a misdemeanor, and be punished by a fine not exceeding $50, or imprisonment not exceeding six months, or both." The defense attorneys argued that this couple was being prosecuted not for fornication but because they were poor and sought welfare for the support of the children. It certainly seems likely that the prosecution in this case, as in so many others involving sex offenses, was not directed toward eliminating the behavior specified in the charges. The intention was most likely to punish this couple for having had illegitimate children whom it could not support adequately.

The use of illegitimate pregnancy as evidence of fornication is not limited to New Jersey. Pennsylvania's statutes specifically state, for instance, "If any unmarried woman has a child born of her body, the same is sufficient to convict her of fornication."[10]

In those states where fornication is prohibited by law, the offense is usually a misdemeanor, punishable by a fine, which may be as small as $10 (Rhode Island) or as large as $500

---

[8] In 1962 Illinois became the first state to revise its criminal code along the lines suggested in the Model Penal Code. Specifically, oral-genital contacts and anal intercourse between consenting adults (of the same or opposite sex) in private and sexual acts with animals are no longer criminal offenses. Connecticut has made similar changes, effective in October 1971. New York and Kansas have made some revisions in their sex laws, and a few other states are considering similar action.

[9] For convenience, we shall refer primarily to the California Penal Code, for in most respects it is typical of the codes in other states as they apply to sexual offenses. When there are wide disparities among states we shall note them, and we shall quote from codes of states other than California in specific instances.

---

[10] *Pennsylvania Statutes,* Title 18, Section 4506.

(Texas). In Arizona, however, the statute defines fornication as a felony punishable by imprisonment for not more than three years. The offense is, however, defined as "living in a state of open and notorious cohabitation," one of several variations among state statutes defining fornication.[11] In some states, for instance, a single act of intercourse between two unmarried adults is an offense. In other states there must be evidence of repetition or of cohabitation. In such a state a couple living in a stable relationship may be penalized, but the promiscuous individual has not violated the law.

An interesting aspect of some fornication laws is the differences in application to males and females. A married woman who has intercourse with a single man is more likely to be charged with adultery if she is prosecuted. On the other hand, a married man who has intercourse with a single woman is likely to be charged with fornication, a lesser crime in most states and no crime at all in some states. The rationale behind this distinction dates back to Roman law. It reflects concern for property rights; the illicit sexual activities of a married woman were viewed as more serious because they raised the possibility of the introduction of a fraudulent heir into the family. A man might then end up unwittingly supporting a child that was not his own.

The difference between fornication and statutory rape is based on the age of the girl. When the girl is under a certain age (varying from fourteen to twenty-one, depending upon the state), the crime is defined as statutory rape rather than as fornication; only the male is then considered guilty of the offense, even if the girl has been a willing partner.

Our society is unique in many aspects of its sex laws, particularly those defining sexual intercourse between unmarried consenting adults as *criminal* behavior. Other societies may condemn it as immoral, some may set certain limits on it, and others may encourage it; yet most of our states define it as a crime. As we have noted earlier, however, the majority of men and women in our society do engage in sexual intercourse before marriage.

The American Law Institute has not included a fornication statute in the *Model Penal Code*. Nor has it recommended a seduction statute, which is common in existing criminal codes. The California seduction statute reads as follows:

> 268. *Seduction.*—Every person who, under promise of marriage, seduces and has sexual intercourse with an unmarried female of previous chaste character, is punishable by imprisonment in the State prison for not more than five years, or by a fine of not more than five thousand dollars, or by both such fine and imprisonment.

It should be noted that the male can usually escape prosecution for seduction by marrying the girl. If she is under age, however, he may still be prosecuted for statutory rape, even though a legal marriage may have occurred since the offense.

Marital Sexual Activities and Divorce

Most people assume that whatever varieties of sexual activities in which a married couple engages in the privacy of its own home are legal. This assumption is incorrect. Almost all sexual activity that may occur between husband and wife, with the exception of kissing, caressing, and vaginal intercourse, is defined as criminal in virtually every state of the union. Oral-genital contacts (cunnilingus and fellatio) and anal intercourse (sodomy), in particular, are so defined. In most states they are felonies and carry severe penalties. The California statutes read as follows:

> 288a. *Oral Sex Perversion.*—Any person participating in an act of copulating the mouth

---

[11] Arizona Code, Section 43-402.

of one person with the sexual organ of another is punishable by imprisonment in the state prison for not exceeding 15 years, or, by imprisonment in the county jail not to exceed one year.

286. *Sodomy—Punishment.*—Every person who is guilty of the infamous crime against nature, committed with mankind or with any animal, is punishable by imprisonment in the state prison not less than one year.

In some states oral-genital contacts, anal intercourse, and intercourse with animals are all included under single sodomy laws and are labeled "crimes against nature." The rationale for these laws should be clear from the discussion of "crimes against nature" in Chapter 17, which we can anticipate here: The natural purpose of sex is reproduction, and therefore any sex act that does not include the potential for conception is a sin (crime) against the laws of nature. A few states even include mutual masturbation under sodomy, for the same reason. We have already presented data from the Kinsey studies and other studies to show that many married couples do practice forms of sexual expression other than vaginal intercourse either as part of foreplay or for occasional variety.

It is unlikely that the average married man suspects that his marital sexual activity will ever be held against him. Even if he knows that a certain behavior is illegal, as long as he and his wife perform it in private, who can substantiate any charge? It turns out, however, that a wife may be all too willing to offer such evidence, in order to win a divorce on grounds of cruelty. Or she may simply be angry at her husband and looking for vengeance. In 1965 a woman in Indiana had a major quarrel with her husband of ten years. In the heat of her anger she filed a complaint of sodomy against him. She did not accuse him of having used force. Before the case came to trial the woman changed her mind and sought to withdraw the charge. She was not allowed to do so because sodomy is an offense against the state, and the state proceeded to prosecute. The husband, stunned by the whole affair, was convicted and sentenced to a term of from two to fourteen years in the state prison. After serving three years of his sentence, he was released when the U.S. Seventh Circuit Court of Appeals overturned the conviction on a technicality in the proceedings. The law itself was not challenged. So far the only landmark decision involving the constitutionality of laws governing the activities of married couples has been the 1965 decision by the U.S. Supreme Court in the case of Griswold *v.* Connecticut. The court ruled that a law prohibiting the use of birth-control devices by married couples was unconstitutional on the grounds that the right to marital privacy excludes such prohibitions. The *Model Penal Code* recommends the legalizing of all private consensual marital relations.

The law also deals with the frequency of intercourse between a married couple.[12] For example, if no intercourse at all has occurred, the law provides for annulment of the marriage on these grounds. A man's impotence or a woman's refusal to engage in sexual intercourse with her husband has long been held sufficient grounds for annulment, though the historical reasoning is somewhat different in the two instances. The impotent male's inability to have intercourse has been held to nullify the reproductive purpose of marriage. To some extent the same notion applies to the unwilling female, but there is also an additional reason. Wives have been traditionally viewed (see Chapter 17) as a

---

[12]At one time, when the law of the Roman Catholic Church was enforced by civil law in Europe, the timing of intercourse and the position to be used (face-to-face, with the woman on her back) were prescribed. All intercourse was forbidden during Lent, for three days before taking communion, and during various religious holidays. In early North America, the Puritans forbade intercourse on Sundays. The birth of a child on a Sunday was considered evidence that the parents had had intercourse on a Sunday. Such a child was viewed as "conceived in sin" and not eligible for baptism.

"remedy for the concupiscence" of the husband. This concept is reflected in the specific exclusion of rapes of wives from rape laws. Even though the husband may have used force and the wife may have been an unwilling partner on a given occasion, legally rape has not been committed (although the husband can be charged with assault and battery in some instances).

Perhaps one indication of the changing view of women's rights is the increasing number of divorces granted to women in the last several decades on the grounds that their husbands' demands for frequent intercourse are unreasonable and constitute cruelty.[13] Judges, however, seem to follow highly personal standards (reflecting their generally advanced age?) in rendering opinions on the "normal" frequency of intercourse for a married couple. For instance, Kinsey has described an opinion upheld by the Supreme Court of Minnesota, in which it was ruled that intercourse on the average of three to four times a week represented an "uncontrollable craving for sexual intercourse" on the part of the husband![14]

As our laws reflect particular religious points of view on the purpose of sex and marriage, it is not surprising that the right *not* to have children has been limited, at least indirectly, by statute. We have already mentioned the decision in Griswold *v.* Connecticut, which finally, in 1965, legalized contraceptives in the one state that still prohibited their use. Abortion, however, remains highly controversial and we will discuss the present state of abortion laws in Chapter 18.

We should also mention the laws governing divorce in our country. Everyone is undoubtedly aware of the high and steadily increasing divorce rate, about 25 percent nationwide and as high as 50 percent or more in some regions. Some jurists blame the high divorce rate on the fact that "our marriage laws and administrative procedures make it far too easy for the immature, the mentally and physically unfit, and the legally disqualified to become married."[15] Some states recognize common-law marriages, which do not require licenses or ceremonies. Under common law a boy over fourteen years old and girl over twelve years old have only to agree that they take each other as husband and wife. Some states require that they live together a certain length of time and require parental consent for marriage if the male is under twenty-one or the female under eighteen. If the partners falsify their ages and manage to obtain a license and marry, however, there is usually nothing that the parents can do to annul the marriage.

Obtaining a divorce is usually far more difficult. Forty-nine of the fifty states require proof of a "marital offense," resulting in the usually unrealistic finding that one party (most often the woman) is not at fault and that one party is "guilty" of the offense, which provides both grounds for the divorce and a basis for awarding property to the "innocent" party.[16] The most common offenses acceptable as grounds for divorce are adultery, insanity, conviction of a felony, conviction of a sex crime, imprisonment, alcoholism, drug addiction, desertion, nonsupport, impotence, general

---

[13] See Kinsey *et al.* (1953), p. 369, for a listing of some examples.

[14] Dittrick *v.* Brown County, 1943: 9 N.W. (2d) 510; quoted in Kinsey *et al.* (1953), p. 370.

[15] Ploscowe (1951), p. 8. See also Slovenko (1965), pp. 16 ff. Slovenko has noted, "It is easier to obtain a marriage license than a driver's license."

[16] The one exception is California, where the law (effective January 1, 1970) provides for dissolution of a marriage on the basis of irreconcilable differences. There are no "guilty" and "innocent" parties, and the property must be divided evenly. This law provides for divorce by consent of both partners, a concept that goes back to Roman law but was abolished when marriage came under the jurisdiction of the Roman Catholic Church.

cruelty, physical cruelty, and mental cruelty. Residence requirements vary from six weeks (Nevada) to five years (Massachusetts, though only three years are required if the person suing was a state resident when he married). Many states have restrictions on remarriage, particularly for the "guilty" party. South Dakota, for instance, prohibits the remarriage of an adulterer during the lifetime of the ex-spouse. Such restrictions can be evaded, however, by remarrying in another state and then returning home, for the courts recognize a marriage as valid as long as it is valid in the state where it was performed.

Adultery

Our laws on sexual offenses reflect several sources, but the Judeo-Christian tradition is most prominent. In particular, the early American settlers brought with them the traditions of the English courts, which had a long history of attempting to regulate sexual behavior. From the thirteenth century until the time of Oliver Cromwell and the Puritan Revolution (1640), sexual offenses were handled by the English ecclesiastical courts. Although they condemned all imaginable forms of "illicit" sexual behavior and punished offenders with fines or jail sentences, the ecclesiastical courts were notably ineffective in modifying the sexual activities of the general population. (They did not always receive support from royalty either, for at times the kings and their courtiers were the most notorious offenders.) The English Puritans abolished the ecclesiastical courts and made sexual offenses like adultery and incest capital crimes punishable by death in the common-law courts (adultery had not previously been a common-law offense).[17] The Puritans of the Massachusetts Bay Colony also made

adultery a crime punishable by death, but as the limited colonial population might have been nearly decimated by enforcement of this law, it was rarely invoked; in 1694 the death penalty was replaced by public whipping and the enforced wearing of the letter "A," immortalized by Nathaniel Hawthorne in *The Scarlet Letter*. Connecticut went a little farther and prescribed that an adulterer should have the letter "A" branded on his forehead with a hot iron. Pennsylvania took a middle course, providing for branding only after the third conviction (prison sentences of one year or more were prescribed for the first and second offenses).

The penalties have diminished over time, but adultery is still a criminal offense in most states.[18] It is a misdemeanor punishable only by fines in some states,[19] but elsewhere it is a felony punishable by lengthy prison terms varying from one to five years. The penalties for adultery tend to be more serious than those for fornication, presumably because of the threat to the family that extramarital affairs pose. Adultery is also the only offense that is considered sufficient grounds for divorce in every state in the union where an offense is required (that is, excluding California).[20]

We have already noted that under Roman law (and also under English common law) adultery was defined only as intercourse with a married woman. A married man who had intercourse with a single woman was not guilty

---

[17] The ecclesiastical courts were restored by Charles II of England in 1660, but their power and influence were gradually curtailed.

[18] Exceptions are Arkansas, Louisiana, Nevada, New Mexico, and Tennessee, which do not have specific statutes and penalties for adultery.

[19] The maximum fine in Maryland is $10.

[20] In New York, where adultery was the only legally acceptable grounds for divorce until recently, it was common practice to arrange fraudulent evidence of adultery in order to obtain a divorce. A witness would be hired to give false testimony about an affair with the husband, or a situation staged with "another woman" would be witnessed by someone hired to do so. (Professional "other women" were available for fees of $10 and up.)

of adultery. American courts have, however, tended to hold the view adopted by the English ecclesiastical courts: that either a married man or a married woman having intercourse with someone other than his or her spouse is guilty of adultery. At least this definition is applied in divorce cases. But paradoxically, perhaps, this law is almost never applied to prostitution. A married man having intercourse with a prostitute is rarely prosecuted for adultery.

The *Model Penal Code* does not include adultery as a criminal offense, though certain extramarital contacts involving minors (under sixteen years old) or seduction ("a promise of marriage which the actor does not mean to perform"[21]) are still included as offenses.

Homosexuality

Homosexuality per se is legal in all the states. It is only specific homosexual *acts* that are defined as crimes. It is no crime to be sexually attracted and oriented toward members of the same sex. In fact, the laws defining various common homosexual acts (oral-genital contacts, anal intercourse, mutual masturbation) as crimes do not specify the sexes of the participants. These acts, as we have already noted, are crimes under the laws of most states, whether performed by a man and a woman, two men, or two women.

The penalties for these offenses can be quite severe, but in practice relatively few homosexuals are arrested and convicted under these laws because most homosexual acts are performed in private and are thus protected by the search-and-seizure provisions of the U.S. Constitution. When an arrest is made for a specific homosexual act, the latter usually has occurred in a public place (rest room, park, automobile, theater), and in about 90 percent of instances the act is oral-genital

contact. Although this offense is often defined as a felony, judges in some states (for instance, California) have the discretionary power to reduce the charge to a misdemeanor (and in California they usually do). (Judges do not, however, have this prerogative when the offense is anal intercourse.) In general, and for a first offense in particular, the individual convicted of a homosexual act is fined, given a suspended jail sentence, and placed on probation. As Hoffman has noted (in reference to California), "The judges realize that putting a homosexual into prison is like trying to cure obesity by incarceration in a candy shop."[22]

But only a minority of homosexual arrests are made for specific sexual acts; the majority are for solicitation or loitering in public places. The pertinent California statutes read:

> 647. *Disorderly Conduct Defined—Misdemeanor.*—Every person who commits any of the following acts shall be guilty of disorderly conduct, a misdemeanor:
>
> (a) Who solicits anyone to engage in or who engages in lewd or dissolute conduct in any public place or in any place open to the public or exposed to public view.
>
> (b) Who loiters in or about any toilet open to the public for the purpose of engaging in or soliciting any lewd or lascivious or any unlawful act.
>
> 650 ½. *Injuries to Persons, Property, Public Peace, Health or Decency; False Personation for Lewd Purpose.*—A person who willfully and wrongfully commits any act which seriously injures the person or property of another, or which seriously disturbs or endangers the public peace or health, or which openly outrages public decency, . . . for which no other punishment is expressly prescribed by this code, is guilty of a misdemeanor.

One survey conducted in the Los Angeles area indicated that 90–95 percent of all homo-

---

[21] The American Law Institute (1962), Section 213.3(1)d.

[22] Hoffman (1968), p. 91.

sexual arrests were for violations of section 647(a) of the California Penal Code.[23] The most controversial aspect of the majority of these arrests is the use of policemen as "decoys." Usually a young police officer dressed in casual clothes loiters in a public rest room or similar location for the express purpose of enticing homosexuals to solicit "a lewd or lascivious" act. The arrest is usually made by a second police officer stationed nearby. The decoy then serves as witness against the defendant. The controversy revolves around the accusation that police decoys are involved in *entrapment;* that they induce people to commit illegal acts that they would not otherwise commit. Certainly most homosexuals would not knowingly solicit police officers, but that point is irrelevant under the law. If an individual has a predisposition to commit a particular offense, it is not illegal for a police officer to *entice* that person to commit the offense.

In addition to the issue of enticement versus entrapment, there is the question whether or not police decoys serve a useful function and represent a worthwhile investment of police manpower. As most homosexual soliciting that does occur in public places is quite subtle, achieved through certain signals, gestures, or brief remarks that have significance only to other homosexuals (or to policemen trained in the jargon of the gay world), it seems unlikely that such behavior constitutes a significant enough offense to the public decency to justify such measures. Hoffman, in fact, has argued "that putting out as decoys police officers who are young, attractive, and seductively dressed, and who engage in enticing conversations with homosexuals is itself an outrage to public decency.[24] We can argue, of course, that the use of police decoys serves to deter public homo-

sexual soliciting, but the argument is unconvincing because the express purpose of using decoys is to promote such behavior in order to achieve arrest, rather than to prevent it.

We have so far been discussing only homosexual activities between males, for, as we noted in Chapter 11, female homosexuals are not usually subject to the same sanctions as are males. With only a few exceptions (Georgia, Kentucky, South Carolina, and Wisconsin), the laws do not distinguish between male and female homosexuals, but in actual practice females are almost never arrested or prosecuted for homosexual activities. The Kinsey study reviewed all the sodomy convictions in the United States from 1696 to 1952 and failed to find a single one involving lesbians. In a review of all the arrests in New York City over a period of ten years, the Kinsey researchers found "tens of thousands" of arrests and convictions of male homosexuals but only three arrests of females for homosexual offenses; all three cases had been dismissed.[25] Many factors contribute to this difference in treatment; some of them have been touched upon in Chapters 11 and 17. Lesbians tend to engage in less public sexual behavior, lesbian activities are not considered as "sinful" as are male homosexual activities, and the law in general tends to be more protective of female sexual activities (with the exception of prostitution).

For poorly substantiated reasons, male homosexuals are regarded as more threatening to society than are lesbians. Police officers seem to think that homosexuals are more likely to commit crimes of violence and crimes against children than are other individuals. Although massive studies like that conducted by Gebhard and his associates at the Institute for Sex Research[26] have not confirmed this belief, it is still

[23]Hoffman (1968), p. 84.
[24]Hoffman (1968), p. 87.
[25]Kinsey *et al.* (1953), p. 485.
[26]Gebhard *et al.* (1965).

commonly held. One result is the practice of requiring the registration of convicted homosexual offenders. Various states have in their criminal laws provisions similar to the following:

> 290. *Person Convicted of Certain Lewd Crimes Must Register with Sheriff—Facts to State.*—Any person who, since the first day of July, 1944, has been or is hereafter convicted in the State of California of the offense of assault with intent to commit rape or the infamous crime against nature, under Section 220, or of any offense defined in Sections 266, 267, 268, 285, 286, 288, 288a, subdivision 1 of Section 647a, subdivision 3 or 4 of Section 261, subdivision (13) (a) or (d) of Section 647, or subdivision 1 or 2 of Section (14) 314 of this code, or of any offense involving lewd and lascivious conduct . . . shall within 30 days after the effective date of this section or within 30 days of his coming into any county or city, or city and county in which he resides or is temporarily domiciled for such length of time register with the chief of police of the city in which he resides or the sheriff of the county if he resides in an unincorporated area.

This requirement renders the convicted homosexual susceptible to being "picked up for questioning" whenever a "sex crime" is committed in the area in which he is living. Identified homosexuals are also subject to "purges" like that in the U.S. State Department and other government agencies in the 1950s. Homosexuals are generally prohibited from holding jobs that require security clearance or involve the handling of "sensitive information." This requirement is based not simply on the idea that "perverts" are unreliable but also on the belief that homosexuals are more vulnerable to extortion and blackmail. Legalizing homosexual acts between consenting adults would not necessarily change this situation. Homosexuals would probably still be vulnerable to blackmail because of the probable effects of public disclosure of their activities: Whether criminal or not, homosexuality is still widely condemned in our society.

Nevertheless, there is a growing trend toward legalizing homosexual behavior. *The Wolfenden Report*, based on a ten-year study by Great Britain's Committee on Homosexual Offenses and Prostitution, was issued in 1957 and provided powerful impetus to this trend. The document has been so widely discussed and has had so much influence that it seems appropriate to quote directly some of its crucial arguments and recommendations.

> 53. In considering whether homosexual acts between consenting adults in private should cease to be criminal offenses we have examined the more serious arguments in favor of retaining them as such. We now set out these arguments and our reasons for disagreement with them. In favor of retaining the present law, it has been contended that homosexual behavior between adult males, in private no less than in public, is contrary to the public good on the grounds that—
>
> (i) it menaces the health of society;
> (ii) it has damaging effects on family life;
> (iii) a man who indulges in these practices with another man may turn his attention to boys.
>
> 54. As regards the first of these arguments, it is held that conduct of this kind is a cause of the demoralization and decay of civilizations, and that therefore, unless we wish to see our nation degenerate and decay, such conduct must be stopped, by every possible means. We have found no evidence to support this view, and we cannot feel it right to frame the laws which should govern this country in the present age by reference to hypothetical explanations of the history of other peoples in ages distant in time and different in circumstances from our own. In so far as the basis of this argument can be precisely formulated, it is often no more than the expression of revulsion against what is regarded as unnatural, sinful or disgusting. Many people feel this revulsion, for one or more of these reasons. But moral conviction or instinctive feeling,

however strong, is not a valid basis for overriding the individual's privacy and for bringing within the ambit of the criminal law private sexual behavior of this kind. It is held also that if such men are employed in certain professions or certain branches of the public service their private habits may render them liable to threats of blackmail or to other pressures which may make them "bad security risks." If this is true, it is true also of some other categories of person: for example, drunkards, gamblers and those who become involved in compromising situations of a heterosexual kind; and while it may be a valid ground for excluding from certain forms of employment men who indulge in homosexual behavior, it does not, in our view, constitute a sufficient reason for making their private sexual behavior an offense in itself.

55. The second contention, that homosexual behavior between males has a damaging effect on family life, may well be true. Indeed, we have had evidence that it often is; cases in which homosexual behavior on the part of the husband has broken up a marriage are by no means rare, and there are also cases in which a man in whom the homosexual component is relatively weak nevertheless derives such satisfaction from homosexual outlets that he does not enter upon a marriage which might have been successfully and happily consummated. We deplore this damage to what we regard as the basic unit of society; . . . We have had no reasons shown to us which would lead us to believe that homosexual behavior between males inflicts any greater damage on family life than adultery, fornication or lesbian behavior. These practices are all reprehensible from the point of view of harm to the family, but it is difficult to see why on this ground male homosexual behavior alone among them should be a criminal offense.

56. We have given anxious consideration to the third argument, that an adult male who has sought as his partner another adult male may turn from such a relationship and seek as his partner a boy or succession of boys. We should certainly not wish to countenance any proposal which might tend to increase offenses against minors.

57. We are authoritatively informed that a man who has homosexual relations with an adult partner seldom turns to boys, and vice versa, though it is apparent from the police reports we have seen and from other evidence submitted to us that such cases do happen.

58. In addition, an argument of a more general character in favor of retaining the present law has been put to us by some of our witnesses. It is that to change the law in such a way that homosexual acts between consenting adults in private ceased to be criminal offenses must suggest to the average citizen a degree of toleration by the Legislature of homosexual behavior, and that such a change would "open the floodgates" and result in unbridled license. It is true that a change of this sort would amount to a limited degree of such toleration, but we do not share the fears of our witnesses that the change would have the effect they expect. This expectation seems to us to exaggerate the effect of the law on human behavior. It may well be true that the present law deters from homosexual acts some who would otherwise commit them, and to that extent an increase in homosexual behavior can be expected. But it is no less true that if the amount of homosexual behavior has, in fact, increased in recent years, then the law has failed to act as an effective deterrent. It seems to us that the law itself probably makes little difference to the amount of homosexual behavior which actually occurs; whatever the law may be there will always be strong social forces opposed to homosexual behavior. It is highly improbable that the man to whom homosexual behavior is repugnant would find it any less repugnant because the law permitted it in certain circumstances; so that even if, as has been suggested to us, homosexuals tend to proselytize, there is no valid reason for supposing that any considerable number of conversions would follow the change in the law.

60. We recognize that a proposal to change a law which has operated for many years so as to make legally permissible acts which were formerly unlawful, is open to criticisms which might not be made in relation to a proposal to omit, from a code of laws being formulated *de novo*, any provision making these acts illegal. To

reverse a long-standing tradition is a serious matter and not to be suggested lightly. But the task entrusted to us, as we conceive it, is to state what we regard as just and equitable law. We therefore do not think it appropriate that consideration of this question should be unduly influenced by a regard for the present law, much of which derives from traditions whose origins are obscure.

61. Further, we feel bound to say this. We have outlined the arguments against a change in the law, and we recognize their weight. We believe, however, that they have been met by the counter-arguments we have already advanced. There remains one additional counter-argument which we believe to be decisive, namely, the importance which society and the law ought to give to individual freedom of choice and action in matters of private morality. Unless a deliberate attempt is to be made by society, acting through the agency of the law, to equate the sphere of crime with that of sin, there must remain a realm of private morality and immorality which is, in brief and crude terms, not the law's business. To say this is not to condone or encourage private immorality. On the contrary, to emphasize the personal and private nature of moral or immoral conduct is to emphasize the personal and private responsibility of the individual for his own actions, and that is a responsibility which a mature agent can properly be expected to carry for himself without the threat of punishment from the law.

62. We accordingly recommend that homosexual behavior between consenting adults in private should no longer be a criminal offense.[27]

The laws of many Western countries (for example, France, Belgium, West Germany, the Scandinavian countries, and Great Britain) are based on the principles recommended in *The Wolfenden Report*. In the United States, we noted earlier, Illinois (in 1961, effective in 1962) and Connecticut (in 1969, effective in

---

[27] *The Wolfenden Report* (1963), pp. 43–48.

1971) have adopted similar laws. The Soviet Union, along with the rest of the United States, remains one of the few countries that still have strict proscriptions against homosexual acts. We have already described (Chapter 11) the attitudes of various primitive societies toward homosexuality.

The Law and Sexual Psychopaths

It is generally agreed that sex offenses that involve force or children or that constitute some sort of public nuisance should continue to be prohibited by law. The authors of *The Wolfenden Report* and the American Law Institute, for instance, support this view. There is disagreement among legislators, psychiatrists, and other professionals, however, on how offenders should be dealt with under the law. People who commit offenses of the sort to be described in this section are generally designated legally as *sexual psychopaths*. It should be made clear that the term "sexual psychopath" does not correspond to any particular disease constellation generally recognized by psychiatrists. Rather, it is a legal term that poses some of the same problems as does the legal term "insanity," which also does not correspond to any particular form of mental illness. The elements that seem to constitute sexual psychopathy under the law include compulsiveness, repetition, and a certain bizarre, or disconcerting, quality in sexual behavior. Under most relevant statutes, then, a man who commits a single rape is much less likely to be considered a sexual psychopath than is a man who has exhibited his genitals in public on several occasions.

Thirty of the fifty states and the District of Columbia now have laws applicable to sexual psychopaths. The first state to pass such a law was Michigan, in 1935, but this law was subsequently declared unconstitutional. The first laws of this kind to be upheld by higher courts were those of Illinois (1938) and Minnesota (1939).

There are two very significant aspects to these laws. First is the *indeterminate sentence,* under which the sexual psychopath can be imprisoned or hospitalized for the rest of his life (or for any lesser period). The indeterminate sentence is apparently acceptable on the grounds that society must be protected from habitual sex criminals. The procedures for imposing such a sentence, however, pose problems related to the constitutional rights of the offender.[28] The law assumes that the prison or hospital superintendent and the courts will release the sexual offender when there is no longer reasonable cause to believe that he constitutes a menace to society, but this assumption is not always justified. The duration of the sex offender's incarceration is subject, among other variables, to the personal attitudes of the prison warden, hospital superintendent, or judge. The official desire to put a sex offender away indefinitely is based at least partly on other mistaken assumptions, one of which is that sex offenders have a high rate of recidivism. This is not the case. The only group of individuals convicted of major crimes that has recidivism rates lower than those of sex offenders are those convicted of homicides. Among the 7 percent of sex offenders who do repeat their offenses the majority are nonviolent offenders: voyeurs, exhibitionists, and homosexuals.[29] Furthermore, every study of sex offenders has shown that, contrary to another popular notion, they rarely show patterns of progression to more serious or more violent sex crimes. Exhibitionists do not eventually become rapists, nor do child molesters eventually become "sex killers." When a rapist has a record of previous criminal offenses, it often consists of nonsexual crimes like assault and burglary. Those rare individuals who commit the sort of highly publicized sex murder and mutilation that may lead to general crackdowns on all "sex perverts" are usually extremely disturbed or psychotic.

The second significant aspect of the laws on sexual psychopaths is their recognition of sex offenders as mentally ill, in some sense, and in need of treatment or rehabilitation, rather than punishment. Particularly when the earlier sexual psychopath laws were enacted, this recognition was quite revolutionary. Provisions for treatment are usually tied to the indeterminate sentence, so that the sex offender is sentenced to confinement and treatment until he is no longer considered a menace to society.

Although many states have laws on sexual psychopaths, these laws are seldom applied. One reason is the ways in which many of them are written. The potential for double jeopardy is frequently so great that courts are reluctant to enforce such laws, especially when the statutes provide that an individual need only be accused of or charged with a sex offense to be institutionalized as a sexual psychopath.[30] Under these laws, the individual may, after his release from a state hospital where he has been committed for treatment, be tried and sentenced to prison for the same offense for which he was committed to the hospital. Under postconviction laws the individual must be tried and convicted of a sexual offense *before* sexual-psychopath proceedings may be instituted; the latter then come under civil, rather than criminal, law. If the convicted sex offender is deemed a sexual psychopath, as the result of examination by

---

[28] Bowman and Engle (in Slovenko, 1965, pp. 757–778) discuss such legal problems as denial of due process and equal protection, especially the rights to counsel, jury trial, and appeal, as well as the rights to notice of a hearing, personal attendance at the hearing, subpoenaing of witnesses, and cross-examination.

[29] Report of the New Jersey Commission on the Habitual Sex Offender, quoted in Slovenko (1965), p. 140.

---

[30] Ten of the thirty states with laws pertaining to sexual psychopaths do not require conviction of a sex offense before commitment as a sexual psychopath. The individual, if arrested, may be committed without a trial.

expert witnesses (usually two psychiatrists), he may then be committed to a state institution for treatment. Even under most of these post-conviction laws, however, the individual can still be sentenced to prison for the original offense after his period of involuntary hospitalization.

California has made the greatest use of the legal concept of sexual psychopathy and has established a special institution (Atascadero State Hospital, Atascadero, California) for the treatment of offenders. Most other states do not offer special facilities for sex offenders and do not have professional personnel specifically trained to treat such individuals.

We shall briefly describe here some legal aspects of specific sexual offenses that fall under the general rubric of sexual psychopathy. Details on the kinds of individuals and behavior patterns involved in these offenses have already been described in Chapter 11.

Public Nuisance Offenses

Those acts subsumed under the general category of public nuisances include exhibitionism, voyeurism, and transvestism. They do not involve physical contact with victims, and indeed the victims of voyeurism may be totally unaware of the crimes and of the people committing them. These acts are viewed as criminal on the grounds that they offend public decency, disturb the peace, and tend to subvert and corrupt the morals of the people. The greatest controversy over this general category of offenses involves exhibitionism. Here is a typical statute:

> 314. *Indecent Exposure.*—Every person who willfully and lewdly, either
>
> 1. Exposes his person, or the private parts thereof, in any public place, or in any place where there are present other persons to be offended or annoyed thereby; or
>
> 2. Procures, counsels, or assists any person

so to expose himself or take part in any model artist exhibition, or to make any other exhibition of himself to public view, or the view of any number of persons, such as is offensive to decency, or is adapted to excite to vicious or lewd thoughts or acts, is guilty of a misdemeanor.

Upon the second and each subsequent conviction under subdivision 1 of this section, or upon a first conviction under subdivision 1 of this section after a previous conviction under Section 288 of this code, every person so convicted is guilty of a felony, and is punishable by imprisonment in state prison for not less than one year.

Various problems in the wording of such laws are apparent. One is that a person can be convicted of indecent exposure for an offense that occurs in comparative privacy, as long as someone present claims to have been offended. There have also been instances in which no one present was offended, yet the person or persons involved were convicted of "indecent exposure." These cases have usually involved people bathing in the nude at nudist camps or sunbathing in their own backyards.[31]

There has also been some controversy in the courts over what portions of the anatomy constitute "private parts." Most courts draw an absolute line at the limits of pubic hair (which has led some "bottomless" dancers in California to shave their pubic hair in an effort to circumvent this definition). Traditionally a woman's breasts, with the exception of the nipples, have not been considered "private parts" under the law; hence the use of "pasties" by strip teasers. Recent court decisions in several states, however, have declared that the breasts, including the nipples, do not constitute "private parts," thus affirming the legality of "topless" dancers in certain jurisdictions.

The *Model Penal Code* does not differ sig-

---

[31] Ploscowe (1951), p. 160.

nificantly from present laws, except that the word "genitals" is substituted for "private parts."[32]

Crimes against Children

Sexual offenses involving minors are subject to severe sanctions in every state, though prosecution is often difficult because the only witnesses are children, who are not always able to provide the reliable, consistent evidence necessary for conviction. Although the following California statute is typical in providing for long prison sentences for child molesters, in practice the disposition in California courts is usually made under the provisions of the laws related to sexual psychopaths:

> 288. *Exciting Lust of Child Under Age of Fourteen.*—Any person who shall willfully and lewdly commit any lewd or lascivious act including any of the acts constituting other crimes provided for in part one of this code upon or with the body, or with any part or member thereof, of a child under the age of fourteen years, with the intent of arousing, appealing to, or gratifying the lust of passions or sexual desires of such person or of such child, shall be guilty of a felony and shall be imprisoned in the State prison for a term of from one year to life.

The definition of a child or minor in these statutes varies somewhat from state to state. The American Law Institute proposes that minority be defined as being less than sixteen years, provided that the offender is at least four years older than the other person.[33]

Although child molesters are almost always males, the children involved may be either male or female, depending upon the orientation of the pedophiliac. The behavior involved most often consists of fondling the genitals, but may also include mutual masturbation, oral-genital

contacts, intercourse, or pederasty (see Chapter 11).

A special type of sexual offense against a minor is incest. The law usually treats incest in special statutes prohibiting marriage or sexual activity between immediate family members and relatives of varying degrees of consanguinity. The offense is a felony and punishable by as much as fifty years in prison in some states. Of all *reported* sex offenses incest is probably the least common, accounting for 3–6 percent of the total reported sex offenses in various jurisdictions. The actual incidence is probably significantly higher, however, at least among certain segments of the population. In one study of delinquent adolescent girls, the incidence of sexual relations with fathers or stepfathers was found to be 15 percent.[34] For obvious reasons, people are more reluctant to report family members than strangers to the police, particularly when they are—as they usually are—the main or sole family breadwinners. (The most common type of incest is between father and daughter, the next most common is between brother and sister, and the least common is between mother and son.)

Rape and Related Offenses

Sexual intercourse with a woman other than a spouse under conditions of force or threat of violence is considered the most serious of all sexual offenses under the criminal law. In sixteen states the penalty for rape may be death or life imprisonment, and in twenty-seven other states prison terms of from twenty years to life may be imposed. Although capital punishment has not been ordered often in recent years, from 1930 to 1948 316 men were executed in the United States for rape. In addition to long prison terms, the laws of many states provide for

---

[32] The American Law Institute (1962), Section 213.5.

[33] The American Law Institute (1962), Section 213.3(1)a.

[34] Halleck in Slovenko (1965), p. 683.

"asexualization" (castration) or involuntary sterilization of rapists.

The California statute is less vaguely worded than are those of many states, yet it does illustrate some of the problems in defining rape:

261. *Rape—Acts Constituting.*—Rape is an act of sexual intercourse, accomplished with a female not the wife of the perpetrator, under either of the following circumstances:

1. Where the female is under the age of eighteen years;

2. Where she is incapable, through lunacy or other unsoundness of mind, whether temporary or permanent, of giving legal consent;

3. Where she resists, but her resistance is overcome by force or violence;

4. Where she is prevented from resisting by threats of great and immediate bodily harm, accompanied by apparent power of execution, or by any intoxicating narcotic, or anesthetic, substance, administered by or with the privity of the accused;

5. Where she is at the time unconscious of the nature of the act, and this is known to the accused;

6. Where she submits under the belief that the person committing the act is her husband, and this belief is induced by any artifice, pretense, or concealment practiced by the accused, with intent to induce such belief.

262. *Minor Under 14 Presumed Incapable of.*—No conviction for rape can be had against one who was under the age of fourteen years at the time of the act alleged, unless his physical ability to accomplish penetration is proved as an independent fact, and beyond a reasonable doubt.

263. *Essential Elements—Penetration.*—The essential guilt of rape consists in the outrage to the person and feelings of the female. Any sexual penetration, however slight, is sufficient to complete the crime.

264. *Punishment.*—Rape is punishable by imprisonment in the State prison not less than three years, except where the offense is under subdivision 1 of section 261 of the Penal Code, in which case the punishment shall be either by imprisonment in the county jail for not more than one year or in the State prison for not more than 50 years, and in such case the jury shall recommend by their verdict whether the punishment shall be by imprisonment in the county jail or in the State prison; provided, that when the defendant pleads guilty of an offense under subdivision 1 of section 261 of the Penal Code the punishment shall be in the discretion of the trial court, either by imprisonment in the county jail for not more than one year or in the State prison for not more than 50 years.

One difficulty involves the question of consent by the female. Whereas a woman who has been rendered unconscious by a drug or a blow on the head or who is mentally retarded or seriously ill mentally may be clearly incapable of having given responsible consent, the issue is not usually that clear. A man may have intercourse with a woman whom he has met at a party at which both have been drinking heavily. That the man was drunk at the time is no defense, yet the woman can claim that, because she was drunk (even though voluntarily), she was incapable of giving responsible consent, though she offered no resistance. The man will usually be convicted of "forcible rape."

The question of how much resistance the female must put up varies under the laws of the different states. Some courts require evidence of considerable physical resistance, but others do not, on the grounds that a woman may have been paralyzed by fear or may have realized that resistance was useless and might even have brought greater injury.

The most controversial aspect of rape laws is the age of the female. Under California law, for instance, intercourse with *any* female under eighteen years of age, even with her consent, constitutes rape, by definition: so-called "statutory rape." The majority of rape convictions are for statutory rape, rather than for violent sexual intercourse with adult women. The justification for ignoring consent in rape cases involving girls under a certain age is given in this court opinion quoted by Ploscowe:

> The intention of the law is to protect unmarried girls from carnal copulation, such intercourse being fraught with peril to the morals of the community and to the well-being of the individual. With the age of consent fixed at eighteen years, it may not confidently be stated that all girls under that age do not comprehend what they are doing when they consent to intercourse. The law, however, deals with all, and not with individuals. In law, the act of intercourse, or the attempt to have intercourse, is without their consent, and against their will. The state says that they do not consent, or that their apparent consent shall be disregarded. It offers resistance for them. It deals with the case as *rape*; not as a mere statutory offense. A rape with consent is an anomaly. . . .[35]

The age of consent varies from state to state, but sixteen and eighteen are most common. In Tennessee the age of consent in this connection is twenty-one, yet a girl can obtain a marriage license when she is sixteen. If a married girl under twenty-one has an affair with another man, he may be prosecuted for rape, rather than for adultery. (There are such cases on record.) The law often fails to recognize that a girl of seventeen or even younger may be quite experienced and aggressive sexually. She may even lie about her age and say that she is eighteen, especially if she also looks much older than she is. None of these factors can be used as a defense against a charge of statutory rape in most states. In a few states, however, that a girl is promiscuous or a prostitute may be used as a defense against such a charge.[36]

The American Law Institute recommends that the age for statutory rape be less than ten years.[37] A male who had intercourse with a girl under sixteen would be guilty of the lesser offense of "corruption of minors," provided that he were at least four years older than the girl.[38] These recommendations would eliminate the present possibility that a boy involved in an adolescent love affair can be convicted of a felony and sentenced to a long prison term. It is not unusual in such a situation for the girl to be more mature and to have encouraged the boy until she became pregnant or her parents discovered the relationship. The characterization of such a boy's behavior as felonious rape seems quite unrealistic.

Commercial Exploitation of Sex

Prostitution

The only sexual offense for which women are prosecuted to any significant extent is prostitution. In itself this phenomenon is interesting, for prostitution, as we shall define it for purposes of this discussion,[39] is a profession of women who perform sexual acts for men who pay for them—and for the most part men write and administer the law in our society. Prostitution can exist only because of the demand for such services by men, and its extent is obviously correlated with the size of the male population without other readily available sexual outlets, as is attested by the large numbers of prostitutes near military bases.

The history of prostitution has been the subject of many volumes,[40] and we shall not attempt to cover it here. Suffice it to say that prostitution has always existed, despite repeated attempts to eliminate it. In various ancient

[35] Case of People *v.* Gibson, 1922, 232 N.Y. 458, 134 N.E. 531; in Ploscowe (1951), pp. 179–180.

[36] In some states, such as California, a similar defense may be used against a charge of seduction.

[37] The American Law Institute (1962), Section 213.1(d).

[38] The American Law Institute (1962), Section 213.3(1)a.

[39] Other less common forms of prostitution include provision by men of paid sexual services for women and homosexual prostitution (see Chapter 11).

[40] See, for instance, Henriques (1962–1963).

cultures prostitution was associated with religious rites, so-called "sacred" or "temple" prostitution. Commercialized prostitution, as we know it today, goes back at least to ancient Greece. Solon is credited with having been the first public official to establish, in 550 B.C., licensed public houses of commercial prostitution. The taxes from these brothels were used to build a temple to Aphrodite.

The term prostitute comes from the Latin *prostituere,* meaning "to expose" and implying the offering of one's body for sale *passim et sine dilectu* (indiscriminately and without pleasure), in the words of Roman law.

The arguments for and against legalized prostitution have changed very little over the centuries. The following passage, written almost 100 years ago, might just as easily have been written last year. It illustrates romantic, moralistic, and realistic points of view:

> While giving all credit to the more honest or unthinking propounders of this legislation [to legalize prostitution], it will scarcely be questioned that there are some who advocate it on grounds which are miserably selfish, dastardly, and cruel. These persons almost openly profess that man must have his irregular passions gratified at any cost, and that if need be, every generation must supply its holocaust of women to gratify them. A process of natural selection, determined by poverty, and further controlled by police and surgical regulations, will regulate the quantity and manner of the supply. It may even be (in the opinion of these persons) not indecorous to spare a passing sigh for the poor unfriended victim demanded for man's lust, and ever and anon sacrificed as a substitute for the good and the rich. This state of mind cannot be represented more adequately than by citing the language of Mr. Lecky, the historian of "European Morals" (vol. ii. p. 299): "Herself (the prostitute) the supreme type of vice, she is ultimately the most efficient guardian of virtue. But for her, the unchallenged purity of countless homes would be polluted, and not a few, who, in the pride of their untempted chastity, think

> of her with an indignant shudder, would have known the agony of remorse and of despair. On that one degraded and ignoble form are concentrated the passions that might have filled the world with shame. She remains, while creeds and civilisations rise and fall, the eternal priestess of humanity, blasted for the sins of the people."

It is scarcely possible to comment with ordinary self-restraint on such a mischievous abuse of rhetoric as this whole passage displays. It exhibits in its most intense form the living genius of the whole class of legislation which is now being reviewed. The picture it presents is that of an endless vista of dissolute husbands in the midst of happy, wealthy, and virtuous homes; husbands, wives, and children all contentedly subsisting by virtue of a daily immolation of outcast and downtrodden women. The picture is as false as the conception of humanity is unworthy. Bad men do not fill the world less with shame because they are cruel and cowardly enough to sacrifice to themselves the poor and the weak in the place of the rich and the strong. Virtue and chastity are robbed of their meaning when they can be only purchased and secured at the price of another's degradation.

The following extracts from an address on surgery, delivered before the American Medical Association at Detroit, in the United States, by Professor Gross, of Philadelphia, in 1874, under the title, "Syphilis in its relation to the National Health," exhibit similar views in their latest form, as they are found to prevail among some sections of the medical world, and also indicate the policy by which it is sought surreptitiously to adjust society in conformity with such views:—"Sexual intercourse is an imperious necessity, implanted in our nature, for the gratification of which man will brave any danger, however great, to health and even life. Whether descended from the ape, or whether created in the image of his Maker, he is still an animal, who, but for the humanising influences of civilisation and Christianity, would be more savage and degraded than the wildest beast of the forest. If this postulate be admitted, it requires no argument to prove that *prostitution is an essential necessity of society.*

"One very great difficulty in regard to the practical operation of a licensing law would be the forming of a bill of an entirely unexceptional character. Great judgment and care would be necessary in the selection of a proper title; if this be offensive, or too conspicuous, it would at once call forth opposition. My opinion is that the entire subject should be brought in, as it has been in England, under the head of the 'Contagious Diseases Acts,' a phrase not likely to meet with serious objection, as it would serve as a *cloak* to much that might otherwise be distasteful to the public. The word 'licensing' should not be used at all in this connexion, as its purport is liable to be misunderstood, many persons supposing that the 'licensing law' is designed to encourage and extend prostitution.

"In reflecting upon this subject, I am sometimes inclined to believe that prostitution is the normal condition of the human race; or if we reject this proposition, so offensive to good taste, it must be admitted, beyond the possibility of doubt or cavil, that the practice is so interwoven with our social system as to form an essential part of it.[41]

Despite various dissenting voices, the prevailing opinion in our society is still that prostitution is a social and moral evil and should be subject to criminal sanctions.

Prostitution is usually not viewed as evidence of psychopathology by either psychiatrists or the courts. The Diagnostic Manual of the American Psychiatric Association lists prostitution under a category called "Social maladjustments without manifest psychiatric disorder."[42] Unlike most types of male sex offenders, prostitutes are not included under the provisions of sexual psychopath laws. Sufficient data does not exist to allow one to make any generalizations about psychological disorders among prostitutes. There does seem to be a higher incidence of lesbianism and of mental deficiency among prostitutes as compared to the general population of women. Most prostitutes come from broken homes and have less than optimal family relationships. The sex life of the prostitute also seems to be less than optimal. Most prostitutes do not experience sexual satisfaction or orgasm in their relations with clients, although they will often simulate a passionate response in order to please the customer. According to one study, most prostitutes experience orgasm only through solitary masturbation or lesbian activities with another prostitute.[43]

The laws dealing with prostitution are many and encompass various types of behavior and many individuals connected with organized prostitution beside the "solo practitioner." The most common form of prosecution by far, however, is for the offense of soliciting. Soliciting is often quite broadly defined to include a wide range of activities, as in this Colorado statute:

> Any prostitute or lewd woman who shall, by word, gesture or action, endeavor to ply her vocation upon the streets, or from the door or window of any house, or in any public place, or make a bold display of herself, shall be guilty of a misdemeanor, and shall be fined not more than $100, or imprisoned in the county jail for not less than ten days nor more than three months, or both.[44]

Most arrests are made when prostitutes solicit customers or plainclothes police officers on streets or in public places like bars or hotels. The experienced prostitute is very careful in the wording of her offer, in order to avoid arrest. She will mention no sexual activity at all but will speak vaguely of "wanting to have a good time" or "some fun." She will also be

---

[41]Amos (1877), pp. 17-20.

[42]American Psychiatric Association (1968), pp. 51-52.

[43]Caprio and Brenner (1961), p. 251.

[44]*Colorado Statutes Annotated* (1935), Chapter 48, Section 214.

wary of speaking directly of fees for services to be rendered. Instead she may mention that she needs a certain amount of money for some new clothes or to support her sick mother. These ploys are not always successful, however, and courts have sustained convictions when there was sufficient reason to believe, on the basis of circumstances and general behavior, that the women had been soliciting, regardless of whether or not they specifically "offered their bodies for hire." Usually a convicted prostitute is fined and then released to resume her occupation. This system obviously does not deter the prostitute much. Instead it functions as a sort of excise tax, the cost of which is passed on to the customer.

It has often been suggested that the customer should be arrested along with the prostitute as an accomplice to an illegal act. Customers are rarely arrested, however, and in most states using the services of a prostitute is not a specific crime, though it may fall under the provisions of more general statutes covering fornication or adultery, for example. There is strong resistance to penalizing customers, and the rationalization for continuing the present system is interesting:

> It has been put to us with some force that the present law is unjust in that it selects a special class of women, designates them "common prostitutes" and provides penalties solely for them, leaving their customers unpunished. It is argued that if there were no customers there would be no prostitutes, and to seek to punish the prostitute while the man is uncondemned is the negation of justice. We should agree that from the moral point of view there may be little or nothing to choose between the prostitute and her customer. But, as we have explained above (and as most of our witnesses would agree), it is not the duty of the law to concern itself with immorality as such. If it were the law's intention to punish prostitution *per se,* on the ground that it is immoral conduct, then it would be right that it should provide for the punishment of the

man as well as the woman. But that is not the function of the law. It should confine itself to those activities which offend against public order and decency or expose the ordinary citizen to what is offensive or injurious; and the simple fact is that prostitutes do parade themselves more habitually and openly than their prospective customers, and do by their continual presence affront the sense of decency of the ordinary citizen. In doing so they create a nuisance which, in our view, the law is entitled to recognize and deal with.[45]

Beside the prostitute and her customer others are usually involved in the enterprise of prostitution. They are often those who profit most from the business and are usually viewed as the major exploiters of prostitutes. They include procurers, pimps, operators and "facilitators" of houses of prostitution, and those who "traffic in women." The activities of all these individuals are generally prohibited by either state or Federal law.

The procurer, or panderer, coerces women into houses of prostitution or otherwise entices them into becoming prostitutes. The coercion need not be physical but must involve some element of intimidation or fraud, to distinguish it from pimping, which involves soliciting customers for a prostitute or receiving her earnings. The relationship between the prostitute and the pimp is superficially voluntary, but the prostitute who attempts to sever the relationship is apt to be threatened or intimidated to such an extent that she quickly changes her mind.

Those who operate houses of prostitution or in any way contribute to the running of such enterprises are subject to prosecution in most jurisdictions. This category may include madams or business managers, landlords, taxicab drivers on commission to transport customers, and any other employees of such oper-

---

[45] *The Wolfenden Report* (1963), pp. 143-144.

ations. Enforcement of these laws has led to an apparent decline in the number of brothels in the country in recent years, but many continue to operate under the guise of Turkish bath houses, massage parlors, and other legitimate businesses. (In addition, there has been an apparent increase in the number of call girls operating out of apartments "by appointment only," available at higher prices than those charged by "streetwalkers" who "turn tricks" in motel rooms, cars, or less private places.)

Bringing women into the country or transporting them across state lines for the purpose of prostitution are now Federal offenses under certain provisions of the Immigration and Nationality Act and the Mann Act (also known as the Federal White Slave Act). The Mann Act (U.S. Annotated Code, 1925, Title 18, Section 398) defines as a felony any act of transporting or aiding in transportation (for example, furnishing travel tickets or means of transportation) of a female for prostitution "or for any other immoral purpose."[46] The latter clause provides for prosecution when no prostitution is involved. Men have been convicted under the Mann Act for crossing state lines with their girlfriends and then having intercourse. Lovers who live near state borders are obviously particularly susceptible to such offenses. A dissenting judge in one such case commented:

> Today another unfortunate chapter is added to the troubled history of the white-slave-traffic act. It is a chapter written in terms that misapply the statutory language and that disregard the intention of the legislative framers. It results in imprisonment of individuals whose actions have none of the earmarks of white slavery, whatever else may be said of their conduct.[47]

[46] The offense is punishable by a $5,000 fine, five years in prison, or both.
[47] Cleveland v. U.S., 1946, 329 U.S. 14, 67 Sup. Ct. 13.

There are those who argue that criminal sanctions against prostitution have obviously not eliminated it any more than Prohibition eliminated the consumption of alcohol, that the law has simply forced it underground and into the hands of gangsters and the criminal underworld. It can also be argued that, if prostitution were legal, there could be regular medical supervision and licensing of prostitutes, leading to lower venereal-disease rates. There is no question that there is a high incidence of venereal disease among prostitutes. The difficulty with any system of periodic medical examinations is that a woman can be free of infection on examination and can then contract syphilis or gonorrhea from her very next customer and pass it on to all subsequent customers until the time of the next examination. Prostitutes certainly constitute the major reservoir for the microorganisms that cause venereal disease. Contact with a prostitute is the usual source of venereal infection among military personnel in particular.

Among the male civilian population contacts with prostitutes account for a relatively small percentage of total sexual outlet. Kinsey found that only 3.5–4 percent of the total sexual outlet of his male sample involved sexual relations with prostitutes. About 69 percent of the white male sample in the Kinsey study had had contact at some time or other with prostitutes but often only isolated experiences. About 15–20 percent had had relations with prostitutes more than a few times a year during a period of up to five years at some time in their lives.

But even though prostitution represented only a small *percentage* of the total sexual activity of the population, the *absolute number* of contacts with prostitutes was enormous. Kinsey estimated a total of 1,659,000 such contacts per year per million population in the United States. Put in terms of a community of 500,000 people, this figure comes to about 16,000 acts of prostitution a *week*. The magnitude of the problem that these figures present for law-enforcement officials is staggering. Full-scale enforcement of the laws governing prostitution is obviously doomed to failure, yet it seems unlikely that any major change will be made in the direction of more enforceable laws. The American Law Institute recommends, in general, maintenance of the status quo.[48] The *Model Penal Code* supports the concept that prostitution, whether carried on in private or in public, is criminal.[49] It also appears to re-affirm the concept of prostitution as a "status crime," that is, one in which the individual does not have to commit an act of prostitution to be guilty of an offense but has only to be identified as a prostitute to be considered guilty.

Pornography

Whereas relatively little public sentiment on regulating prostitution is apparent today, the public concern about pornography[50] and pornography laws, both pro and con, is considerable. Pornography laws have a relatively short history, dating back only to the nineteenth century. The concern of the law with obscenity seems to be correlated with the development of mass communications, widespread literacy and availability of books, and the invention of the camera. In the United States the single most significant law designed to prevent the dissemination of pornographic materials is Section 1461, Title 18, of the U.S. Code,

adopted in 1873. This law has been named for its primary advocate, Anthony Comstock, then Secretary of the New York Society for the Suppression of Vice.[51] Under the Comstock Act it is a felony knowingly to deposit in the U.S. mail any obscene, lewd, or lascivious book, pamphlet, picture, writing, paper, or other publication of an "indecent character."[52] Enforcement of this act comes under the Inspection Service of the U.S. Post Office Department.

There is particular concern about material sent through the mail because it is believed that the mail provides the "smut peddlers" with easy access to children. Concern about this issue among legislators can be sensed from the following excerpt from *The Congressional Record:*

> There is a black plague sweeping the Nation more devastating than the one that ravaged Europe in the Middle Ages. Its principal victims are children and adolescents, although like its ancient predecessor, it destroys adults as well. Clergymen, educators, sociologists, city, State, and Federal law-enforcement agencies are hard pressed to curb it—and often disagree as to method.
>
> The children's plague is pornography. Its name, however, is legion: obscenity, sexual depravity, sadism—the entire spectrum of carnality usually in printed or photographic form, or both. It is sold by the ton primarily to ele-

---

[48] The American Law Institute (1962), Sections 251.2, 251.3.

[49] The *Model Penal Code* does specifically except private mistresses supported by their lovers.

[50] Pornography is also known as "obscenity," "smut," "filth" and in Judge John M. Woolsey's words "dirt for dirt's sake." Judge Woolsey ruled that James Joyce's *Ulysses* could be admitted through U.S. Customs because it seemed to offer more than "dirt for dirt's sake." "In spite of its unusual frankness, I do not detect anywhere the leer of the sensualist. I hold, therefore, that it is not pornographic." United States *v.* One Book Called *Ulysses,* 5 Fed. Supp. 182 (S.D.N.Y. 1933).

[51] Comstock was an active crusader. His annual report in 1881 showed that in the first eight years of the existence of the Society for the Suppression of Vice he had confiscated 203,238 obscene pictures and photographs; destroyed 27,584 pounds of books; seized 27 framed obscene pictures from the walls of saloons; confiscated 1,376,939 obscene circulars, catalogues, songs, and poems plus 7,400 microscopic pictures designed for use in pocket charms and knives; and obtained mailing lists used in the distribution of pornography with a total of 976,125 names and addresses (Kilpatrick, 1960, p. 243).

[52] The question of whether or not first-class mail, particularly personal letters, is exempt from this act has been the subject of several Supreme Court opinions. Although the Court has ruled that first-class mail is private, it has also ruled that the mailing of an obscene letter is a violation of the law.

mentary and high school boys and girls. Approximately 1 million children are being solicited by mail order pornographers each year, according to the U.S. Post Office Department, which last year received 70,000 separate complaints from parents. The commercial filth by mail is estimated to be a half-billion-dollar-a-year racket and growing more lucrative by the day, thanks to hobbling court decisions, light prison sentences and fines, and public apathy.

Side by side with the mail-order smut peddlers are the incredibly prolific publishers of obscene paperback books and magazines considered to gross at least a billion dollars annually.

Those concerned declare that no act of subversion planned by the Communist conspiracy could be more effective in shredding the Nation's moral fabric than the lethal effects of pornography. While it is not impossible that some of the material now sold is Kremlin inspired, ironically the Reds need not work too hard at this. They are well aided by thousands of amoral, dollar-crazed Americans, many of them militant in defense of their constitutional rights to pander to man's baser passions and their consequent fallout: perversion and depravity. . . .

J. Edgar Hoover, Chief of the Federal Bureau of Investigation, attributed the Nation's rising sex crimes directly to commercial pornography:

"We know that in an overwhelmingly large number of cases, sex crime is associated with pornography. We know that sex criminals read it, are clearly influenced by it. I believe pornography is a major cause of sex violence." . . .

The Kefauver committee reports uncounted instances of obscene circulars sent to children as young as 10 or 12. The mail order sin merchants hunger for better and newer mailing lists, particulary those of school children and teenagers who, once "hooked" in the manner of dope addicts, form a faithful and steady market for future purchases. . . .

Its effect in a classroom is electric. One nun in a midwestern suburb said: "We can always tell when this stuff is making the rounds. You can sense it in the room. When this happens we question each pupil individually until we uncover the rotten truth." . . .

The advertising copy of most mail order rot plainly is intended to produce one return first of all: names. Names and addresses. "The racket will take the willing sucker for just as much as the sucker can be taken," writes Kilpatrick. "Preying upon adolescents, curious girls, sex-hungry old men, the pornography factories will fill any order that promises a ready profit." The filth merchants aim the bulk of their garbage at the so-called normal male animal. However, should he tire of photos and movies he can readily obtain novelties, playing cards, peephole viewers, jigsaw puzzles, erotic recordings, suggestive statuettes, and lewd chinaware. . . .[53]

In all the rhetoric on pornography it is not always clear exactly what sort of material people are including under the term. In the history of American literature we can note that Hawthorne's *The Scarlet Letter,* Mark Twain's *Huckleberry Finn,* and Henry Miller's *Tropic of Cancer* were all condemned as obscene at the time of their publication. Furthermore, some people distinguish between erotic works of art, literature, and the cinema that have at least potential cultural merit (see Chapters 13, 14, and 15) and those produced purely for commercial exploitation and "utterly without redeeming social value" (sometimes called "hard-core pornography"). These and other issues led the U.S. Supreme Court to provide a new definition of obscenity in the landmark case of Roth *v.* United States.[54] The Roth case also addressed itself to the question of whether or not the Comstock Act violates the First Amendment provision that "Congress shall make no law . . . abridging the freedom of speech, or of the press." On the constitutional question, the Court clearly stated that "ob-

---

[53] From a report introduced by Senator Kenneth Keating of New York, *Proceedings and Debates of the 87th Congress, First Session,* Vol. 107, No. 150 (August 29, 1961).

[54] 354 U.S. 476 (1957).

scenity is not within the area of constitutionally protected speech or press."

In defining obscenity the Court laid down four essential elements: First, the material must be viewed in terms of its potential appeal to *the average person* (a modification of earlier definitions as obscene of material that would affect only certain "susceptible" individuals); second, *contemporary community standards* are to be applied (the court acknowledged that standards vary from generation to generation); third, *the dominant theme* of the material and the content must be *taken as a whole*, rather than out of context (it had previously been customary simply to present isolated "vulgar" quotes or pictures from a book, for example, without reference to the overall theme; under such a rule the Bible itself could be found obscene because of its descriptions of women's breasts, as in *The Song of Solomon*, and of episodes of adultery, like that of King David; pictures of nudes in a magazine extolling the virtues of nudism for health purposes have become legal under this new definition; fourth, the *appeal* must be *to prurient interest* (this requirement is applicable to content, as well as to the *intentions* of authors, publisher, and so on; a typical obscenity statute (that of California) written since the Roth case defines "prurient interest" as "a shameful or morbid interest in nudity, sex, or excretion, which goes beyond customary limits of candor in description or representation of such matters and is matter which is utterly without redeeming social importance."[55] Publishing, distributing, selling, and various related offenses are also considered crimes if the material involved is judged to be obscene by these standards.

The justifications for obscenity laws are generally three. Legislators and judges declare that pornography is damaging to children, causes increases in the numbers of sex crimes, and has deleterious effects on the morals of the population by causing sexual arousal in otherwise normal people. We shall comment briefly on each of these three issues.

There are no significant scientific data that either prove or disprove the notion of possible damage to children from pictures or books portraying or describing sexual activities. Although few argue seriously in favor of distributing "hard-core pornography" to children, the question of the benefits and dangers of early exposure to material dealing with sexual functioning, anatomy, reproduction, and so on in sex-education classes at the elementary-school level is one that must, for the present at least, be settled by common sense. There are no reliable empirical data on this subject.

There is a substantial body of knowledge on the relation of pornography to sex crimes, particularly as reported in the Gebhard study,[56] which has confirmed the reports of police officers and other law-enforcement officials that sex offenders often have pornography in their possession or admit to having seen pornographic materials. The cause-and-effect relation that so many have assumed, however, has not been established. In the Gebhard study the use of pornography by sex offenders was compared to the experiences of a normal control group and to those of a group of prisoners who were not sex offenders. There were *no differences* among the three groups in use of, possession of, or exposure to pornography. Within each group variations in use and exposure to pornography were related primarily to age, socioeconomic class, and educational level. A further important finding was that sex offenders were not prone to greater sexual arousal from view-

---

[55] The *Model Penal Code*, Section 251.4(1), uses similar wording but omits the phrase "without redeeming social importance."

[56] Gebhard *et al.* (1965), Chapter 31.

Table 16.1 Sexual Response in Normal Subjects to Various Forms of Erotica

		Definite or Frequent	Sometimes	Never	Number of Subjects in Study
Viewing portrayals of nudes	Male	18%	36%	46%	4191
	Female	3%	9%	88%	5698
Viewing commercial films	Male	6%	30%	64%	3231
	Female	9%	39%	52%	5411
Viewing burlesques and erotic floor shows	Male	28%	34%	38%	3377
	Female	4%	10%	86%	2550
Observing portrayals of sex acts	Male	42%	35%	23%	3868
	Female	14%	18%	68%	2242
Reading literary materials (e.g., romantic novels)	Male	21%	38%	41%	3952
	Female	16%	44%	40%	5699
Reading erotic materials (e.g., specifically sexual stories)	Male	16%	31%	53%	4202
	Female	2%	12%	86%	5523

Source: Compiled from data in Kinsey *et al.* (1953), Chapter 16.

ing pornography than were other groups of males.

This point leads us to the third and final issue: How susceptible are normal individuals to sexual arousal from various forms of erotica, and is such arousal an evil that should be prohibited by law?[57] There is no doubt that viewing or reading erotic materials is sexually arousing for a significant percentage of the population, particularly males. The Kinsey data on this subject are typical of the findings of other investigators (see Table 16.1). Should this fact be a source of concern for those responsible for criminal law? It has been the source

of such concern because of the assumption that sexual stimulation may lead normal individuals to commit illegal sex acts. But there is no particular reason to believe that sexual stimulation of a normal individual will lead to anything other than fantasies and normal sexual activity. If we accept the notion that there is nothing inherently wrong or criminal in the expression of human sexuality, then this argument is without substance.

Children are continually exposed to the graphic details of fighting, violence, and killing on television and in other media. It is paradoxical that our laws seem to be more preoccupied with prohibiting the stimulation of sexual activity than with prohibiting the stimulation of aggressive or violent behavior.

---

[57] For a review of more than 250 articles on this subject, see Cairns, Paul, and Wishner (1962), pp. 1008-1041.

Introduction

So far we have confined ourselves mainly to a factual and analytical presentation of such topics as the biological structure and function of the sexual organs, the expression of human sexuality in a wide variety of sexual behavior, and the sexual themes and feelings expressed in art, literature, and films. We turn now to moral questions, questions about what we *should* do. Morality involves value judgments and questions of right and wrong. It is one thing to discuss how a contraceptive method works but quite a different thing to discuss whether or not one should use it or whether or not its use should be limited to those who are married, whose lives would be endangered by pregnancy or childbirth, or who already have "too many" children.

The general impression is that a significant change in attitudes toward sex and morality has been occurring in recent years. The impression is probably correct, though it is difficult to document. We noted in Chapter 1 a poll of 1,600 Americans conducted by Louis Harris in 1969, which shed some light on this question.[1]

---

[1] "Changing Morality: The Two Americas, A Time–Louis Harris Poll" (1969).

The sample included a cross section of educational, income, occupational, and religious groups. One finding was that traditional sexual "sins" were considered far less reprehensible than were other kinds of behavior. Such surveys are indicative of people's attitudes toward sex and morality but not necessarily of their behavior. We could base a set of moral principles on such data if we were willing to subscribe to the notion that what is right is defined by what most people believe is right, just as some social scientists define "normal" sexual behavior by the behavior patterns of the majority of people. But even in a democratic society majority opinion is not always right in the moral or ethical sense. There are standards, to which we all refer at some time or other, that go beyond the consensus and reflect belief in certain principles or moral guidelines, whether the specific issue is sexual behavior, business practices, or war.

In Western societies, the tradition most influential in shaping sexual morality has been the Judeo-Christian tradition. Whether or not we agree with this tradition, we simply cannot deny its tremendous influence, even in the present-day United States. Most of our current laws governing sexual behavior reflect this tradition, and many people who flatly reject the Judeo-Christian ethic on intellectual grounds

SEX AND MORALITY

find themselves still subject to it at an emotional level. It is not at all unusual, for instance, to talk to unmarried young people of both sexes who are engaging in premarital intercourse and see nothing wrong in their behavior yet find themselves *feeling* guilty about it.

In recent years there has been heightened interest in the philosophies and religions of the East. Similarly, some Western thinking and practices have been introduced in Asian countries, largely through movies and contact with our armed forces. There has also, however, been strong resistance, in both East and West, to new or different standards of behavior, particularly those in the emotionally charged areas of sexuality. Passionate kisses and nudity on the screen have caused Western movies to be censored in India, and women have been arrested for wearing miniskirts in Taiwan. Western dances have been condemned as "vulgar" by the Nationalist Chinese government. Conversely, mixed nude bathing, an old custom in Japan, has hardly caught on in the United States yet, nor has the practice of legalized prostitution that exists in some countries in the Orient.

In this chapter we shall examine the historical development of the Judeo-Christian ethic in connection with sexual and related behavior. We shall then discuss a series of specific sexual issues and shall try to show how we approach these issues in moral or ethical terms. It is not our aim to espouse one set of values over another but rather to describe the kind of reasoning that culminates in a widely held moral principle.

The History of Western Sexual Morality

The Jewish Tradition

Attitudes toward Marriage and Family. A high regard for marriage and children is a prominent theme in early Hebraic teachings. In particular, the notion of procreation as a pri-

mary obligation of man is fundamental to the Old Testament and the Talmud, and this notion has been preserved to the present day by the Roman Catholic Church. Probably no other single doctrine has had as many ramifications for sexual behavior as has the doctrine that the purpose of sex and marriage is reproduction. In the very first chapter of the first book of the Old Testament it is written:

> So God created man in his own image, in the image of God he created him; male and female he created them. And God blessed them, and God said to them, "Be fruitful and multiply, and fill the earth and subdue it; and have dominion over the fish of the sea and over the birds of the air and over every living thing that moves upon the earth.[2]

The belief among the ancient Jews that they in particular should multiply, in order to propagate God's chosen people, is repeatedly mentioned in the Old Testament. For example, God tells Abraham, "I will indeed bless you, and I will multiply your descendants as the stars of the heavens and as the sand which is on the seashore."[3] Similar promises were made to Abraham's son Isaac and to Isaac's son Jacob.

The Talmud stresses the religious obligation to marry and to raise a family. The unmarried person was at best pitied, and for a man to remain single indefinitely was considered unnatural and immoral. A Jewish woman was expected to bear children, and, indeed, if she failed to do so after ten years of marriage she could be divorced on those grounds alone. Furthermore, a man had an obligation to see that the family name was carried on:

> If brothers dwell together and one of them dies, the wife of the dead shall not be married outside the family to a stranger; her husband's brother shall go in to her, and take her as his wife, and

---

[2]Genesis 1:27–28.

[3]Genesis 22:17.

perform the duty of a husband's brother to her. And the first son whom she bears shall succeed to the name of his brother who is dead, that his name not be blotted out of Israel.[4]

Marriage was to be entered into early but not lightly. Eighteen was the recommended age for males, shortly after age twelve (at which age minority status ended) for girls. Jews had a particularly high regard for the institution of marriage (and still do, if judged by the low divorce rate among Jews compared to those among adherents of other faiths, especially Protestants). They were encouraged to be cautious and to give a great deal of thought to the selection of marriage partners. In contrast to the prearranged marriages, often with partners never seen in some Oriental cultures, rabbinic law stated, "A man is forbidden to take a woman to wife without having first seen her, lest he afterwards perceive in her something objectionable and she becomes repulsive to him."[5] Furthermore, marriages were believed to be divinely arranged and sanctioned. According to an old story recorded in the Midrash:

> A Roman lady asked a Rabbi, "In how many days did the Holy One, blessed be He, create the universe?" "In six days," he answered. "What has He been doing since then up to the present?" "He has been arranging marriages." "Is that his occupation? I, too, could do it. I possess many male and female slaves, and in a very short while I can pair them together." He said to her, "If it is a simple thing in your eyes, it is as difficult to the Holy One, blessed be He, as dividing the Red Sea!"[6]

The Jews were apparently very supportive of newlyweds and favored a sort of extended honeymoon. "When a man is newly married, he shall not go out with the army or be charged with any business; he shall be free at home one year, to be happy with his wife whom he has taken."[7]

Attitudes toward Women. Although Jewish women were accorded great respect in their roles as wives and mothers, males had the upper hand in property rights and divorce. A woman could be divorced by her husband without her consent on the grounds that he found something "unseemly" or "indecent" about her,[8] but a woman could not divorce her husband without his consent. There was a division of opinion on the interpretation of this law, and by A.D. the first century there were two fully developed schools of thought. The School of Shammai took the view that the law applied only in instances of adultery by the woman, but the School of Hillel took a much broader view, which encompassed such grounds as poor cooking and less beauty than that of another woman. Gradually, however, Jewish women were accorded equal rights under Jewish law regarding divorce and property ownership.

Boys were clearly preferred to girls as offspring, however. Some of the reasons for this preference given in the Talmud sound familiar to present-day parents:

> In a quotation from Ben Sira, which the Talmud preserved: "It is written, A daughter is a vain treasure to her father. From anxiety about her he does not sleep at night; during her early years lest she be seduced, in her adolescence lest she go astray, in her marriageable years lest she does not find a husband, when she is married lest she be childless, and when she is old lest she practice witchcraft." The same thought is contained in the explanation of the words of the Priestly Benediction: "The Lord bless thee and

---

[4] Deuteronomy 25:5–6.

[5] Kiddushin, 41a (Babylonian *Talmud*); in Cohen (1949), p. 164.

[6] Bereshith Rabba, LXVIII, 4; in Cohen (1949), p. 164.

[7] Deuteronomy 24:5.

[8] Deuteronomy 24:1; Mishna Gittin, Chap. 9, no. 8, in Cohen (1949), p. 167.

keep thee'—bless thee with sons, and keep thee from daughters because they need careful guarding."[9]

Nevertheless, feelings of tenderness and responsibility toward all children prevailed, as did a belief that all children were truly gifts from God:

> It happened that while the Rabbi [Meir] was lecturing in the House of Study on the afternoon of the Sabbath, his two sons died at home. Their mother laid them upon a bed and covered them with a sheet. At the termination of the Sabbath, the Rabbi returned to his house and asked where the children were. His wife said to him, "I want to ask you a question. Some time ago a person came here and entrusted a valuable article to my care, and now he wants it back. Shall I restore it to him or not?" He answered, "Surely a pledge must be returned to its owner!" She then said, "Without asking for your consent I gave it back to him." She thereupon took him by the hand, led him into the upper room, and removed the sheet from off the bodies. When he saw them he wept bitterly; and she said to her husband, "Did you not tell me that what has been entrusted to one's keeping must be restored on demand?" "The Lord gave, and the Lord hath taken away; blessed be the name of the Lord."[10]

Rules Governing Sexual Morality. Sexual behavior was strictly regulated by Jewish laws, and the penalties for infractions could be quite severe. Adultery, incest, homosexuality, and bestiality were forbidden, and punishments ranged from social ostracism to death.[11] Contraception was totally forbidden to men and generally to women as well, though some exceptions were made for the latter: "A minor lest

pregnancy prove fatal, a pregnant woman lest abortion result, and a nursing mother lest she becomes pregnant and prematurely wean the child so that it dies."[12]

There seemed to be a very positive feeling among Jews about sexual intercourse, within the confines of marriage, at least, which contrasts rather sharply with the attitude prevalent in the early Christian Church, an attitude that has persisted to some extent until very recent times: that sex per se is intrinsically evil and tinged with guilt.

The Christian Tradition

Origins. As Jesus and his twelve disciples were all Jewish, it might seem reasonable to assume that Jewish sexual traditions were largely shared by them. As Jesus radically departed from some of the major religious tenets and practices of his contemporaries, however, we cannot carry this assumption very far. We shall restrict ourselves to inferences from the biblical record.

Jesus was chaste and celibate, yet he did not shun the company of women from any walk of life, even in a culture in which heterosexual contacts were more or less restricted to members of one's own family. Because of the special circumstances of his life, we cannot assume that he necessarily intended his celibate existence to serve as a model, nor did he ever indicate that he meant it so.

What did Jesus say about sex specifically? We have only a fragmentary record of his teachings, and there is relatively little on this subject. His most restrictive statements are those in the Sermon on the Mount:

> You have heard that it was said, "You shall not commit adultery." But I say to you that every

---

[9] Sanhedrin, 100b (Babylonian *Talmud*); in Cohen (1949), pp. 171–172.
[10] Cohen (1949), p. 171.
[11] Leviticus, Chaps. 18–20.
[12] Cohen (1949), pp. 170–171.

one who looks at a woman lustfully has already committed adultery with her in his heart. If your right eye causes you to sin, pluck it out and throw it away: it is better that you lose one of your members than that your whole body be thrown into hell. And if your right hand causes you to sin, cut it off and throw it away: it is better that you lose one of your members than that your whole body go into hell.[13]

What did Jesus actually mean by these remarks? It is highly unlikely that he was suggesting that one literally blind oneself rather than cast adulterous glances. Such a prescription simply does not fit the overall context and meaning of his sayings. It is relevant that earlier in the same sermon Jesus equally condemned the nursing of anger.[14] As surely no human being can avoid feeling angry at one time or another, it seems that Jesus was using these examples not as actual standards of behavior but rather as illustrations of how wretched and helpless man is apart from God. A minor yet significant point is that Jesus was speaking in a language and idiom that happen to be rich in metaphor.

As far as we know, Jesus made no statements extolling the virtues of sex. In view of the fragmentary record, however, such negative evidence is inconclusive. He did, however, deal with a woman caught in adultery (the Mosaic penalty for which was death by stoning) as follows:

Jesus went unto the mount of Olives. And early in the morning he came again into the temple, and all the people came unto him; and he sat down, and taught them. And the scribes and Pharisees brought unto him a woman taken in adultery; and when they had set her in the midst, They said unto him, Master, this woman was taken in adultery, in the very act. Now Moses in the law commanded us, that such should be stoned: but what sayest thou? This they said,

tempting him, that they might have to accuse him. But Jesus stooped down, and with his fingers wrote on the ground, as though he heard them not. So when they continued asking him, he lifted up himself, and said unto them, He that is without sin among you, let him first cast a stone at her. And again he stooped down, and wrote on the ground. And they which heard it, being convicted by their own conscience, went out one by one, beginning at the eldest, even unto the last: and Jesus was left alone, and the woman standing in the midst. When Jesus had lifted up himself, and saw none but the woman, he said unto her, Woman, where are those thine accusers? hath no man condemned thee? She said, No man, Lord. And Jesus said unto her, Neither do I condemn thee: go, and sin no more.[15]

Jesus was also criticized by his pious detractors for consorting with sinners, including prostitutes. It is also interesting that none of the three great temptations of Jesus was related to sex.[16]

From this fragmentary record theologians, as well as other believers and nonbelievers, have reached all feasible conclusions, casting Jesus in roles ranging from stern ascetic to proponent of free love.

Christianity was based on the teachings of Jesus but did not limit itself to them. Even in the early Church a variety of interpretations and points of view on all matters began to be incorporated into Christian doctrine.

Greek and Roman Influences. Very early in the history of the Church (A.D. the first century), and particularly under the influence of St. Peter and St. Paul, gentiles (non-Jews, especially Greeks and Romans) were incorporated into the Church,[17] and they brought with them the

---

[13] Matthew 5:27–30.

[14] Matthew 5:21–22.

[15] John 8:1–11 (King James Version).

[16] Matthew 4:1–11.

[17] St. Peter, considered by Roman Catholics to be the first head of the Christian Church, had a vision, subsequent to which he preached that God had spoken to him on integration of the Church: "Truly I perceive that God

thinking of Greek and Roman culture about sexuality and morality. On one basic premise the Greeks, Romans, and Jews were agreed, however: that the purpose of marriage was to produce legitimate offspring (the Greeks and Romans on behalf of the state, the Jews on behalf of God).

Both the Greeks and the Romans held women to be inferior and subservient to men. In the early days of the Roman Empire women were treated with perhaps more respect than Greek women had been, but they remained subservient and dependent upon their fathers until they married, after which time they were legally subject to their husbands. By A.D. the second century a gradual lessening of the husband's authority over his wife had occurred, but, rather than improving the quality of married life, it seems simply to have reflected the general corruption of social life during the period just before the ultimate downfall of the Empire. Divorce rates and hedonism greatly increased, and concomitantly family life degenerated. In both Greek and Roman cultures, the double standard was traditional. Men participated in extramarital sexual liaisons (both heterosexual and homosexual, especially among the Greeks), and prostitution was condoned.

In contrast to the prevailing hedonism of the gentile world (at least in the large cities of Greece and Rome; the outlying provinces tended to be more conservative) at the time of Christ there were schools of thought that condemned the common sexual practices of the time and extolled the virtues of asceticism. Particularly in Greece, the Cynics and the Stoics alike tended to renounce the world—including material possessions and marital and sexual relationships—in favor of purity (poverty and chastity, according to some). This ascetic tradition, rather than the hedonistic one, was quite influential in the thinking of the early Christians, as we shall see.

The Teachings of St. Paul. St. Paul stands as the first important Christian teacher on issues of sexual behavior. As discussed earlier, Jesus himself had had relatively little to say on such issues, although we have the distinct impression that he was quite understanding toward those who had been condemned or ostracized for offenses like adultery and prostitution. St. Paul, on the other hand, appears to have considered marriage and sexuality inferior to chastity and celibacy. Defenders of St. Paul point out that he wrote in the belief that the world would end within his lifetime. If the Kingdom of God was at hand, why worry about marriage and family when one should be preparing for the end? Nevertheless, for whatever reasons, St. Paul clearly elevated the single, celibate state to a status of greater purity than that of the married or sexually active state. This elevation was the beginning of a tradition that became very influential in Christian thought over the centuries. St. Paul saw marriage as a relationship to be entered into in order to avoid the sin of fornication and thus appropriate only for those too morally weak to resist venereal temptations. In one of his best-known statements on this subject he said: "To the unmarried and the widows I say that it is well for them to remain single as I do. But if they cannot exercise self-control, they should marry. For it is better to marry than to be aflame with passion."[18]

Regardless of St. Paul's motives, the important point is that he provided a basis for future elaboration of the notion that sex is to be avoided, that abstaining from sexual activity *of any kind* leads to a higher moral state, and that marriage is a concession to the body that should

---

shows no partiality, but in every nation anyone who fears him and does what is right is acceptable to him" (Acts of the Apostles 10:34–35).

[18]I Corinthians 7:8–9. The King James Version reads, "It is better to marry than to burn."

be made only by those deficient in will power. St. Paul suggested that celibacy is not only more pleasing to God but also less anxiety-provoking:

> I want you to be free from anxieties. The unmarried man is anxious about the affairs of the Lord, how to please the Lord; but the married man is anxious about worldly affairs, how to please his wife, and his interests are divided. And the unmarried woman or girl is anxious about the affairs of the Lord, how to be holy in body and spirit; but the married woman is anxious about worldly affairs, how to please her husband. I say this for your own benefit, not to lay any restraint upon you, but to promote good order and to secure your undivided devotion to the Lord.
>
> If any one thinks that he is not behaving properly toward his betrothed, if his passions are strong, and it has to be, let him do as he wishes: let them marry—it is no sin. But whoever is firmly established in his heart, being under no necessity but having his desire under control, and has determined this in his heart, to keep her as his betrothed, he will do well. So that he who marries his betrothed does well; and he who refrains from marriage will do better.[19]

St. Paul advised those who did marry: "Wives be subject to your husbands, as to the Lord. For the husband is the head of the wife as Christ is the head of the Church. . . . Husbands, love your wives, as Christ loved the Church."[20]

The Patristic Period of the Church: St. Augustine. Theologians call the several centuries following the time of St. Paul and extending through the fall of the Roman Empire "the patristic age" because in that period formulation of the doctrines of the new religion was dominated by a small group of men who are known as the "Fathers of the Church."

Included in this group were St. Ambrose, St. Jerome, and St. Gregory (the Great), but the member who most influenced Christian doctrine on human sexuality was St. Augustine.

St. Augustine's personal struggle with his own sexual nature is recorded in his *Confessions.* In brief he had "sowed his wild oats" during the first thirty years of his life; then he had been converted to Christianity and had, in effect, renounced all sexual activity. We find a similar pattern in the lives of St. Jerome and the theologian Tertullian, but the contrast between "before" and "after" is not nearly as striking as in the life of St. Augustine. He was born in A.D. 354 of a Christian mother and a non-Christian father. While still a minor he fathered a child and began a thirteen-year sexual liaison with the mother of his son Adeodatus ("by God given"). During this time Augustine was involved in turn with Manichaeanism (which took a dim view of marriage and even of sexual intercourse), then with Skepticism, and, just before his conversion to Christianity, with Neo-Platonism. Having reached the conclusion that he could not successfully control his own sexual desires, St. Augustine decided to enter a legitimate marriage, and his mistress of many years was exiled to Africa in order to avoid complications. Even while betrothed and awaiting his marriage, however, he found himself taking another mistress to satisfy what seemed to him base but uncontrollable instincts. His conflict during this period is reflected in the oft-repeated prayer of his younger years: "Give me chastity—but not yet."

The turning point in St. Augustine's life came in his thirty-second year, when he read the writings of St. Paul, which convinced him that the highest calling in life was celibacy and total abstinence from sexual activity. He broke his engagement, renounced his mistresses, and was baptized into the Christian Church, much to the delight of his mother, with whom he had been living.

[19] I Corinthians 7:32–38.

[20] Ephesians 5:22–25.

Following his conversion, St. Augustine quickly became an influential member and ultimately a bishop of the Roman Catholic Church. Later in his life, beginning three years after Rome had been sacked by the Vandals in A.D. 410, St. Augustine spent thirteen years writing his monumental *The City of God.* Whereas his autobiographical *Confessions,* in the words of Lord Byron, "make the reader envy his transgressions," St. Augustine associates guilt rather than pleasure with sexuality in *The City of God.* He acknowledges that coitus is essential to the propagation of mankind, but argues that the act itself is tainted with guilt because of the sin of Adam and Eve. Sexual intercourse was thus transformed from something pure and innocent to something shameful—"lust"—by the original sin of Adam and Eve, which was passed on from generation to generation.

18. Of the shame which attends all sexual intercourse

Lust requires for its consummation darkness and secrecy; and this not only when unlawful intercourse is desired, but even such fornication as the earthly city has legalized. Where there is no fear of punishment, these permitted pleasures still shrink from the public eye. Even where provision is made for this lust, secrecy also is provided; and while lust found it easy to remove the prohibitions of law, shamelessness found it impossible to lay aside the veil of retirement. For even shamelss men call this shameful; and though they love the pleasure, dare not display it. What! does even conjugal intercourse, sanctioned as it is by law for the propagation of children, legitimate and honourable though it be, does it not seek retirement from every eye? Before the bridegroom fondles his bride, does he not exclude the attendants, and even the paranymphs, and such friends as the closest ties have admitted to the bridal chamber? The greatest master of Roman eloquence says, that all right actions wish to be set in the light, i.e. desire to be known. This right action, however, has such a desire to be known, that yet it blushes to be seen. Who does not know what passes between husband and wife that children may be born? Is it not for this purpose that wives are married with such ceremony? And yet, when this well-understood act is gone about for the procreation of children, not even the children themselves, who may already have been born to them, are suffered to be witnesses. This right action seeks the light, in so far as it seeks to be known, but yet dreads being seen. Any why so, if not because that which is by nature fitting and decent is so done as to be accompanied with a shame-begetting penalty of sin? . . .

21. That man's transgression did not annul the blessing of fecundity pronounced upon man before he sinned, but infected it with the disease of lust

Far be it, then, from us to suppose that our first parents in Paradise felt that lust which causes them afterwards to blush and hide their nakedness, or that by its means they should have fulfilled the benediction of God, "Increase and multiply and replenish the earth"; for it was after sin that lust began. It was after sin that our nature, having lost the power it had over the whole body, but not having lost all shame, perceived, noticed, blushed at, and covered it. But that blessing upon marriage, which encouraged them to increase and multiply and replenish the earth, though it continued even after they had sinned, was yet given before they sinned, in order that the procreation of children might be recognized as part of the glory of marriage, and not of the punishment of sin. But now, men being ignorant of the blessedness of Paradise, suppose that children could not have been begotten there in any other way than they know them to be begotten now, i.e., by lust, at which even honourable marriage blushes.[21]

As lust (the Latin *concupiscentia*) is inextricably involved in all sexual acts because of original sin, it then follows that chastity is

---

[21] Augustine (1934 ed.), parts 18 and 21.

a higher moral state than is marriage—and certainly a prerequisite for priests and nuns. This view is being seriously questioned today by certain members of the Roman Catholic Church, as it was by Martin Luther in the Reformation. Whereas St. Paul had viewed the married state as inferior to celibacy on the grounds that it was distracting for those who truly wanted to dedicate themselves to God, St. Augustine went a step farther and labeled intercourse, even within marriage, as sinful. Although he recognized that the act of copulation is essential for procreation—the subject of a divine commandment—he believed that the behavior and emotions that accompany intercourse make it shameful. Such behavior and emotions he took to be signs of man's degradation since the Fall. Although one could minimize the sinfulness of coitus by performing it only as part of fulfilling one's *duty* to have children (a notion that even today is not foreign to many people), one could not totally ignore the fact that a child conceived under these circumstances is the product of an act of concupiscence. Hence the need for infant baptism in order to wash away the guilt of lust.

The Middle Ages: St. Thomas Aquinas. The early centuries of the medieval period were the Dark Ages as far as significant new thoughts about sexual ethics are concerned. But, as the Church ultimately assumed jurisdiction over marriage and divorce, previously a function of civil authorities, there ensued a lengthy controversy over the conditions, if any, under which divorce and remarriage could be allowed. Church authorities in Rome held that a lawful, consummated marriage could not be dissolved under any circumstances. Elsewhere, particularly in England, divorce was allowed to Roman Catholics for adultery, and remarriage was allowed when a husband had died or was presumed dead in battle.

By the twelfth century, however, the Roman Catholic Church had clarified and consolidated the official view that it still takes today: that marriages are final. There were a few loopholes, however. A Christian spouse could obtain a divorce from a non-Christian on the grounds that the latter would not convert: the so-called "Pauline privilege," based on St. Paul's statement, "If the unbelieving partner desires to separate, let it be so, in such cases the brother or sister is not bound."[22] Also, in practice, marriages outside the Church did not have quite the same binding force as did marriages performed within the Church. Another loophole involved "consummation" of the marriage, that is, sexual intercourse. Although a marriage was formed by mutual consent as expressed in the marriage vows, it did not become indissoluble until the couple had had intercourse. Consequently, if both parties wanted "out" of a Roman Catholic marriage they could (and still can) seek an annulment on grounds that it had never been "consummated."

By far the most influential writer in the Church during the Middle Ages was the thirteenth-century scholar and theologian St. Thomas Aquinas. An unusually systematic thinker and author, Aquinas spelled out the position of the Roman Catholic Church on questions of sex and morality in such minute detail that essentially nothing new has had to be added since. There is virtually no form of sexual behavior to which Aquinas did not address himself. In his massive work *Summa Theologica,* he has included dissertations on touching, kissing, fondling, seduction, intercourse, adultery, fornication, marriage, virginity, homosexuality, incest, rape, bestiality, prostitution, and related topics. His discussion of "nocturnal pollution" (wet dreams) demonstrates the thoroughness and wide range of

---

[22] I Corinthians 7:15.

argument that he brought to bear on a particular topic:

Whether Nocturnal Pollution Is a Mortal Sin?

We proceed thus to the Fifth Article:—

Objection I. It would seem that nocturnal pollution is a sin. For the same things are the matter of merit and demerit. Now a man may merit while he sleeps, as was the case with Solomon, who while asleep obtained the gift of wisdom from the Lord (3 Kings iii, 2 Par. i). Therefore a man may demerit while asleep; and thus nocturnal pollution would seem to be a sin.

Obj. 2. Further, whoever has the use of reason can sin. Now a man has the use of reason while asleep, since in our sleep we frequently discuss matters, choose this rather than that, consenting to one thing, or dissenting to another. Therefore one may sin while asleep, so that nocturnal pollution is not prevented by sleep from being a sin, seeing that it is a sin according to its genus.

Obj. 3. Further, it is useless to reprove and instruct one who cannot act according to or against reason. Now man, while asleep, is instructed and reproved by God, according to Job xxxiii, 15, 16, "By a dream in a vision by night, when deep sleep is wont to lay hold of men. . . . Then He openeth the ears of men, and teaching instructeth them in what they are to learn." Therefore a man, while asleep, can act according to or against his reason, and this is to do good or sinful actions, and thus it seems that nocturnal pollution is a sin.

"On the contrary," Augustine says (*Gen. ad lit.* xii. 15): "When the same image that comes into the mind of a speaker presents itself to the mind of the sleeper, so that the latter is unable to distinguish the imaginary from the real union of bodies, the flesh is at once moved, with the result that usually follows such notions; and yet there is as little sin in this as there is in speaking and therefore thinking about such things while one is awake."

I answer that, nocturnal pollution may be considered in two ways. First, in itself; and thus it has not the character of a sin. For every sin depends on the judgment of reason, since even the first movement of the sensuality has nothing sinful in it, except in so far as it can be suppressed by reason; wherefore in the absence of reason's judgment, there is no sin in it. Now during sleep reason has not a free judgment. For there is no one who while sleeping does not regard some of the images formed by his imagination as though they were real, as stated above in the First Part (Q. LXXXIV., A. 8, *ad* 2). Wherefore what a man does while he sleeps and is deprived of reason's judgment, is not imputed to him as a sin, as neither are the actions of a maniac or an imbecile.

Secondly, nocturnal pollution may be considered with reference to its cause. This may be threefold. One is a bodily cause. For when there is excess of seminal humour in the body, or when the humour is disintegrated either through overheating of the body or some other disturbance, the sleeper dreams things that are connected with the discharge of this excessive or disintegrated humour: the same thing happens when nature is cumbered with other superfluities, so that phantasms relating to the discharge of those superfluities are formed in the imagination. Accordingly if this excess of humour be due to a sinful cause (for instance excessive eating or drinking), nocturnal pollution has the character of sin from its cause: whereas if the excess or disintegration of these superfluities be not due to a sinful cause, nocturnal pollution is not sinful, neither in itself nor in its cause.

A second cause of nocturnal pollution is on the part of the soul and the inner man: for instance when it happens to the sleeper on account of some previous thought. For the thought which preceded while he was awake, is sometimes purely speculative, for instance when one thinks about the sins of the flesh for the purpose of discussion; while sometimes it is accompanied by a certain emotion either of concupiscence or of abhorrence. Now nocturnal pollution is more apt to arise from thinking about carnal sins with concupiscence for such pleasures, because this leaves its trace and inclination in the soul, so that the sleeper is more easily led in his imagination to consent to acts productive of pollution. In this sense the Philosopher says (*Ethic.* i. 13) that "in so far as certain movements in some degree pass" from the waking state to the state of sleep, "the dreams of good men are better than those of any other people": and Augustine says (*Gen. ad lit.* xii. *loc. cit.*) that "even during sleep, the soul may have conspicuous merit on account of its good disposition." Thus it is evident that nocturnal pollution may be sinful on the part of its cause. On the other hand, it may happen that nocturnal pollution ensues after thoughts about carnal acts, though they were speculative, or accompanied by abhorrence, and then it is not sinful, neither in itself nor in its cause.

The third cause is spiritual and external; for instance when by the work of a devil the sleeper's phantasms are disturbed so as to induce the aforesaid result. Sometimes this is associated with a previous sin, namely the neglect to guard against the wiles of the devil. Hence the words of the hymn at even:

> Our enemy repress, that so
> Our bodies no uncleanness know.

On the other hand, this may occur without any fault on man's part, and through the wickedness of the devil alone. Thus we read in the *Collationes Patrum* (*Coll.* xxii. 6) of a man who was ever wont to suffer from nocturnal pollution on festivals, and that the devil brought this about in order to prevent him from receiving Holy Communion. Hence it is manifest that nocturnal pollution is never a sin, but is sometimes the result of a previous sin.

Reply Obj. I. Solomon did not merit to receive wisdom from God while he was asleep. He received it in token of his previous desire. It is for this reason that his petition is stated to have been pleasing to God (3 Kings iii. 10), as Augustine observes (*Gen. ad lit.* xii. *loc. cit.*).

Reply Obj. 2. The use of reason is more or less hindered in sleep, according as the inner sensitive powers are more or less overcome by sleep, on account of the violence of attenuation of the evaporations. Nevertheless it is always hindered somewhat, so as to be unable to elicit a judgment altogether free, as stated in the First Part (*loc. cit.*). Therefore what it does then is not imputed to it as a sin.

Reply Obj. 3. Reason's apprehension is not hindered during sleep to the same extent as its judgment, for this is accomplished by reason turning to sensible objects, which are the first principles of human thought. Hence nothing hinders man's reason during sleep from apprehending anew something arising out of the traces left by his previous thoughts and phantasms presented to him, or again through Divine revelation, or the interference of a good or bad angel.[23]

In addition to his comprehensive treatment of issues involving sex and morality, which helped to consolidate the position of the Roman Catholic Church on these questions, Aquinas is noteworthy for his reliance on the notion of Natural Law, or "rules of nature." Aquinas based his arguments partly on the Bible, but also on the writings of the Fathers of the Church, and the use of "right reason." In addition, he held the view that God had created the natural world and that, with the exception of the human species, which had been corrupted by the Fall (original sin) and subsequent willful misdeeds, the natural order of things is representative of the way that God had originally intended the world to be. Consequently it is possible to observe the sexual behavior of animals, for instance, and to derive conclusions about what is natural and therefore "right" for man. It is particularly striking, as we shall discuss later in this chapter, that a similar argument is currently being put forth by various eminent anthropologists and ethologists; the major difference is that the behavior of animals (particularly of the subhuman primates) is being viewed today as a standard of *normality,* rather than of *morality.*

Aquinas was greatly influenced by Aristotle

---

[23]Aquinas (1911–1925 ed.), Second Part of the Second Part, Question 154, Article 5.

in his thinking about nature and Natural Law. He also referred to Aristotle for data to support his arguments. Some of the data seem questionable, for instance Aristotle's story of a horse that threw itself over a cliff in horror at the realization that it had mated with its own mother by mistake, thus committing incest. Not only is the story itself questionable, but also the use of such data to support an argument that incest is contrary to nature since animals disapprove of it can certainly be debated.

On the other hand, some of Aquinas' arguments from nature are quite compatible with modern professional thinking. Consider, for instance, the argument against coitus by an unmarried couple:

> I answer that, without any doubt we must hold simple fornication to be a mortal sin. . . . In order to make this evident, we must take note that every sin committed directly against human life is a mortal sin. Now simple fornication implies an inordinateness that *tends to injure the life of the offspring to be born of this union.* For we find in all animals where the upbringing of the offspring needs care of both male and female, that these come together not indeterminately, but the male with a certain female, whether one or several; such is the case with all birds: while, on the other hand, among those animals, where the female alone suffices for the offspring's upbringing, the union is indeterminate, as in the case of dogs and like animals. *Now it is evident that the upbringing of a human child requires not only the mother's care for his nourishment, but much more the care of his father as guide and guardian, and under whom he progresses in goods both internal and external.* Hence *human nature* rebels against an indeterminate union of the sexes and *demands that a man should be united to a determinate woman and should abide with her a long time or even for a whole lifetime.* Hence it is that in the human race the male has a natural solicitude for the certainty of offspring, because on him devolves the upbringing of the child: and this certainly would cease if the union of sexes were indeterminate.

> This union with a certain definite woman is called matrimony; which for the above reason is said to belong to the natural law. Since, however, the union of the sexes is directed to the common good of the whole human race, and common goods depend on the law for their determination, as stated above, it follows that this union of man and woman, which is called matrimony, is determined by some law. What this determination is for us will be stated in the Third Part of this work, where we shall treat of the sacrament of matrimony. Wherefore, since fornication is an indeterminate union of the sexes, as something incompatible with matrimony, it is opposed to the good of the child's upbringing, and consequently it is a mortal sin.

> Nor does it matter if a man having knowledge of a woman by fornication, make sufficient provision for the upbringing of the child: because a matter that comes under the determination of the law is judged according to what happens in general, and not according to what may happen in a particular case.[24]

In essence, then, Aquinas argued that offspring should have both mother and father for optimal upbringing and that, as fornication involves the possibility that a child will be born without defined parents to care for it, fornication is morally wrong *because of the potential deleterious effects upon the child* who may be conceived. Many recent studies have shown higher rates of juvenile delinquency, emotional disturbance, and suicide among young people who have grown up in "broken homes," that is, in homes from which one or both parents are absent because of divorce, death, separation, or other reasons. On the other hand, it may seem that, with the availability of extremely reliable contraceptive methods, this argument against fornication would no longer hold. In practice, however, reliable contraceptive methods are either not available to or are not

---

[24] Aquinas (1911-1925 ed.), Second Part of the Second Part, Question 154, Article 2; italics added.

used by many unmarried people who engage in sexual intercourse; hence the large number of illegitimate babies each year.

In the Middle Ages the view that the highest moral state is chastity, that is, total abstinence from sexual behavior in the usual sense, continued. It is somewhat difficult to appreciate today how widespread this view has been for many centuries, not only in the Christian world but also in other developed cultures and in some primitive societies. The glorification of virginity, as in the cult of the Virgin Mary, was long a popular subject for both secular and religious writers.

Havelock Ellis has written an interesting history of the "chastity movement" during the Christian era, from the beginnings of the Church to the twentieth century.[25] He has described the ascetic and romantic aspects of chastity:

Chastity manifested itself in primitive Christianity in two different though not necessarily opposed ways. On the one hand it took a stern and practical form in vigorous men and women who, after being brought up in a society permitting a high degree of sexual indulgence, suddenly found themselves convinced of the sin of such indulgence. The battle with the society they had been born into, and with their own old impulses and habits, became so severe that they often found themselves compelled to retire from the world altogether. Thus it was that the parched solitudes of Egypt were peopled with hermits largely occupied with the problem of subduing their own flesh. Their preoccupation, and indeed the preoccupation of such early Christian literature, with sexual matters, may be said to be vastly greater than was the case with the pagan society they had left. Paganism accepted sexual indulgence and was then able to dismiss it, so that in classic literature we find very little insistence on sexual details except in writers like Martial, Juvenal and Petronius who intro-

duce them mainly for satirical ends. But the Christians could not thus escape from the obsession of sex; it was ever with them. We catch interesting glimpses of their struggles, for the most part barren struggles, in the Epistles of St. Jerome, who had himself been an athlete in these ascetic contests. . . .

This is the aspect of early Christian asceticism most often emphasized. But there is another aspect which may be less familiar, but has been by no means less important. Primitive Christian chastity was on one side a strenuous discipline. On another side it was a romance, and this indeed was its most specifically Christian side, for athletic asceticism has been associated with the most various religious and philosophic beliefs. If, indeed, it had not possessed the charm of a new sensation, of a delicious freedom, of an unknown adventure, it would never have conquered the European world. There are only a few in that world who have in them the stuff of moral athletes; there are many who respond to the attraction of romance.[26]

Ellis has pointed out that the romantic aspects of chastity were not as mysterious as might appear at first glance—underlying this movement was an element of female protest against subjugation in the traditional marriage arrangements of the times. He has noted that chastity was advocated, not simply as a source of rewards after death or "because the virgin who devotes herself to it secures in Christ an ever-young lover," but also because "its chief charm is represented as lying in its own joy and freedom and the security it involves from all the troubles, inconveniences, and bondages of matrimony."[27]

The Reformation. Ellis has perhaps exaggerated somewhat in his statement that "the Reformation movement was in considerable part a

[25] Ellis, H. (1942), Vol. II, Part Three, pp. 143–177.

[26] Ellis, H. (1942), Vol. II, Part Three, pp. 151–153.
[27] Ellis, H. (1942), Vol. II, Part Three, p. 158.

revolt against compulsory celibacy."[28] Nevertheless, both Luther and Calvin, from the earliest stages of their revolt within the Church, attacked the prevailing notions of chastity, celibacy, and marriage. One of Calvin's arguments sounds not at all dissimilar to those being put forward by certain Roman Catholic priests today:

> In the times which succeeded, a too superstitious admiration of celibacy prevailed. Hence, ever and anon, unmeasured encomiums were pronounced on virginity, so that it became the vulgar belief that scarcely any virtue was to be compared to it. And although marriage was not condemned as impurity, yet its dignity was lessened, and its sanctity obscured; so that he who did not refrain from it was deemed not to have a mind strong enough to aspire to perfection. Hence those canons which enacted, first, that those who had attained the priesthood should not contract marriage; and, secondly, that none should be admitted to that order but the unmarried, or those who, with the consent of their wives, renounced the marriage-bed. These enactments, as they seemed to procure reverence for the priesthood, were, I admit, received even in ancient times with great applause. But if my opponents plead antiquity, my first answer is, that both under the apostles, and for several ages after, bishops were at liberty to have wives: that the apostles themselves, and other pastors of primitive authority who succeeded them, had no difficulty in using this liberty, and that the example of the primitive Church ought justly to have more weight than allow us to think that what was then received and used with commendation is either illicit or unbecoming. My second answer is, that the age, which, from an immoderate affection for virginity, began to be less favourable to marriage, did not bind a law of celibacy on the priests, as if the thing were necessary in itself, but gave a preference to the unmarried over the married. My last answer is, that they did not exact this so rigidly as to make

continence necessary and compulsory on those who were unfit for it.[29]

Luther's arguments against celibacy were somewhat different from those of Calvin. Luther seems to have drawn from his own emotional experiences, as had St. Augustine, in formulating his doctrines. His childhood in Germany had been replete with visions of demons and witches and with severe beatings for the most minor offenses. In 1505, caught in a terrible thunderstorm, he vowed to St. Ann that he would become a monk if his life were spared. He entered an Augustinian monastery and reflected upon his sins. But, in contrast to St. Augustine, he came to the conclusion that the desires of the flesh could be neither conquered nor atoned for by good works, penances, and the like. On the specific issue of celibacy, Luther argued, in the style of Aristotle and Aquinas, that celibacy is not a natural state for man and, indeed, that those who are prone to practice it are inclined to be peculiar. Luther viewed marriage not only as normal but also as a secular arrangement that should fall under the jurisdiction of civil authorities rather than of the Church. Luther himself set an example by being married in his home rather than in a church. He felt strongly that marriage is not a specifically Christian sacrament but rather an institution for all men, established at the time of man's creation, long before the founding of the Christian Church. Although this notion ultimately led to more flexible divorce laws in Protestant countries, Luther himself did not condone divorce and remarriage except in instances of adultery or "desertion" (the latter term has come to be interpreted more and more broadly with time).

The Reformers were influential not only in elevating the status of marriage but also to some extent in removing the onus of sin from sexual

---

[28]Ellis, H. (1942), Vol. II, Part Three, p. 164.

[29]Calvin (1960), Book IV, Chapter XII, Section 27.

intercourse. Calvin departed farther from tradition than did Luther. Wheras Luther viewed the sexual appetite as natural, on the order of hunger and thirst, he still shared some of St. Augustine's feeling that sexual behavior has a certain intrinsic shamefulness. Calvin, on the other hand, viewed sex as something holy and honorable, at least within the confines of marriage. He also challenged the long-standing notion that the purpose of marriage is procreation and put forth the idea that marriage should be a social relationship, in which the wife provides companionship for her husband, rather than serving simply as the mother of his children and as a source of relief for his sexual tensions. Nevertheless, both Luther and Calvin held the notion that women should be subject to male authority, within both marriage and the Church. Underlying this teaching was a belief that women are the inferior of the two sexes. We find repeated reflections of this notion in writings, both religious and secular, throughout the history of Western civilization—from Aristotle's description of women as "deficient males" to Freud's theory that little girls suffer from "penis envy."

The Reformation was an extraordinary challenge to established belief and traditions. Yet exceedingly important changes were actually being brought about throughout the Renaissance as well. This transitional period between medieval and modern times began in Italy in the fourteenth century, spread to other parts of Europe, and continued into the seventeenth century. It was characterized by the revival of classical influences and humanistic attitudes, expressed through an unprecedented outpouring of the arts and literature (see Chapters 13 and 14). Medieval asceticism was rejected in favor of full expressions of romantic and physical love and the human body was glorified. It was also a period of considerable confusion in sexual morals and of sharp contrasts even in the behavior of the popes. Alex-

ander VI (1492-1503), for example, was well known for his worldly interests and illegitimate children. Yet fifty years later Pope Paul IV judged Michaelangelo's nude frescoes in the Sistine Chapel indecent and had clothes painted over the figures in *The Last Judgment.*

It would be impossible to trace here further developments of sexual morality during succeeding centuries. However, two movements will be discussed, albeit briefly, because of their direct bearing on present-day beliefs.[30]

Puritanism. The Puritan movement for religious reform began early in the reign of Queen Elizabeth of England in the sixteenth century. Calvinist in theology, the early Puritans felt that the Church of England was too political and too Catholic. During the intermittent periods of persecution throughout the next two centuries large numbers of Puritans emigrated to New England in search of religious freedom.

To the Puritan, man was by nature weak and sinful and therefore in need of constant self-examination, unremitting self-discipline, and hard work. The Puritan sexual ethic, although severe and uncompromising, was primarily concerned with regulating behavior that threatened the stability of the family unit. Apart from their Biblical faith, as newcomers to a harsh land the Puritans were concerned with survival, and protecting the integrity of the family as the basic social unit was felt to be vital to that end. Therefore, the Puritans were unforgiving of adulterers and quite concerned about sex that might lead to the birth of illegitimate children.

In their eagerness to discourage sexual laxity the Puritans imposed rigid codes of dress and

---

[30]The following sections are in part based on material from a work under preparation by Bryan Strong, Department of History, Stanford University, provisionally entitled, "Sex, Character and Reform in America, 1860-1920: A Psychological Inquiry into American History."

behavior. Activities appealing to the senses were frowned upon. Women accused of witchcraft or of partaking in sexual orgies with Satan faced torture and sometimes death. However, despite these excesses, sexual activity within marriage was not strictly regulated. The Puritans were therefore not "antisexual" in principle but rather were opposed to sexual behavior outside of the bonds they believed to have been ordained by God and society.

The Victorian Era. The reign of another English queen, Alexandrina Victoria (1819–1901) is referred to as the Victorian period. During the two centuries separating the reign of Victoria from that of Elizabeth important changes seem to have taken place in sexual attitudes. For instance, whereas the Puritans were content with restricting sex to marriage, Victorians attempted to restrict sexual behavior within marriage as well. Even the stated basis for the restrictions had changed. The Puritans were concerned with piety: Adultery was a sin against God and a violation of community trust. The Victorians were concerned with "character," health, and how best to harness sex and rechannel it to loftier ends.

How did this remarkable change come about? Since Victorian society was considerably more secular than Puritan communities, religion can hardly be responsible for it. There is some evidence that the more indiscriminate antisexuality within Victorian morality was based on the erroneous medical and scientific beliefs of the time.

Victorian sexual ideology revolved around a theory in which semen was viewed as a vital substance and its spillage a grievous and potentially lethal waste. In principle, it mattered little if a man ejaculated into his wife or into some other woman, although procreative necessities required that some concessions be made in this regard.

This semen theory did not originate in the Victorian period. As was discussed earlier (see Chapter 12), such notions were current long before the nineteenth century. But from this starting point Victorian morality evolved into a code of sexual behavior as well as a theory of human sexuality. In this scheme, men were the sexual beings who victimized women and were in turn victimized by them. In the first instance, men imposed their "beastly" sexual urges upon innocent women who were "pure," asexual beings. In the second case sexually provocative women lured men into wasting their seed. A "moral" man abstained from sex outside of marriage and was highly selective and considerate in sexual expression within marriage. "Moral" women endured these sporadic ordeals and did nothing to encourage them. Pleasure was not an appropriate goal for either sex, but especially not for women.

So far as noncoital sex was concerned, the position of Victorian morality should be predictable. Since these acts served no procreative purpose, they were without any redeeming value whatsoever. Masturbation was particularly bad since it involved the young and, being unrestrained by the need for a partner, most readily led to excessive indulgence.

The semen theory of human sexuality has not been entirely abandoned, even today. It is impossible to say, however, to what extent such attitudes rule people's sexual lives. Even during the Victorian period countless thousands undoubtedly paid no heed (see Chapter 14). Some people today see the shadow of "Puritanism" or "Victorianism" behind any attempt to regulate private or public sexual behavior. Others pine away for bygone days when men were gentlemen, women "pure," and so on, with total disregard for the realities of those periods.

Modern concepts of sexual morality, which allow that pleasure is a legitimate sexual goal, probably date back most immediately to the post-World War I era (and may, in fact, have been influenced by it). We shall next examine some of the important changes that have been occurring since then.

The Twentieth Century and Situation Ethics

Theoretical Background

The diversity of moral viewpoints in pluralistic contemporary societies makes it virtually impossible to pursue our discussion in the same linear fashion followed so far. Furthermore, formal approaches to ethical issues seem to have lost their impact for the average person. With some exceptions, even the clergy have become reluctant to make definitive pronouncements on moral issues. The result is that most of us are left to ascertain for ourselves what is right and what is wrong and "play it by ear," as it were.

Therefore, rather than attempt to review contemporary scholarly thinking in sexual ethics, we shall concentrate on examining some of the forces that have helped shape present-day morality and will discuss the works of a few writers who have reached a wide readership, particularly among the young.

At least two major forces have had profound influence on Western ethics in the twentieth century: science and technology, and World War II.

What can serve as foundation for ethics in an age dominated by an ethically neutral discipline, science? The belief that truth is to be found by means of the scientific method is widespread, and belief in the discovery of truth, moral or otherwise, through divine revelation combined with "right reason," in the tradition of Aquinas and other theologians, has apparently waned as man has glorified the scientific method and the products of technology. Only recently have significant numbers of scientists (still only a minority) voiced the notion that

we have expected more from science than it can offer. Technology can produce internal-combustion engines, but it cannot tell us whether or not the benefits of their availability and use outweigh the harm of the air pollution that they produce. Scientists have given us the power to build nuclear weapons but have not provided guidance in using them. In fact, there are moral problems inherent in the decision even to build them. Yet the scientific community has usually remained aloof from, or above, involvement in such value judgments. The scientist frequently attacks a problem because it is there, as the mountain climber scales Mount Everest simply because it is there. The cardiac surgeon may take on the challenge of developing an artificial heart because it is a challenge to his scientific and technical abilities. The question of the cost of such a device for prolonging lives in an overpopulated, underfed world may be secondary to him.

There has been some attempt to use scientific observations (broadly defined) in arriving at moral judgments, that is, in deciding what is right and wrong. In relation to human sexuality we can cite two examples. In 1929 Mead published her anthropological study of adolescence and sex in primitive society, *Coming of Age in Samoa*.[31] She drew certain implications from her study of sexual-behavior patterns in another culture: A nonpunitive attitude toward sexual experimentation (premarital intercourse) among adolescents leads to happier and healthier acceptance of sexuality in the culture as a whole; as happiness and health are legitimate goals for any society, we should adopt such standards in our own culture.

Another example is British ethologist Desmond Morris' *The Human Zoo*.[32] Rather than observing a primitive culture, Morris drew

---

[31] Mead (1929).

[32] Morris (1969).

on observations of subhuman primates—apes, baboons, and monkeys—comparing their behavior in the wild (in the natural state) and in captivity (in the zoo). He pointed out that the sexual behavior of primates in their natural habitat is quite different from that in captivity. Deviance and perversion appear to be functions of living in overcrowded or other unnatural surroundings. The implication is that normal ("right") sexual behavior is what can be observed in the natural surroundings. Large cities ("human zoos"), according to Morris, are unnatural habitats for man and lead to unnatural ("wrong") sexual behavior patterns.

The second major force that has caused twentieth-century man to rethink traditional morality is World War II. Death camps, atomic bombs, and the Nuremburg trials raised anew many moral questions that are still unresolved. At what point do responsibility and loyalty to the law and the state end, and at what point does one choose other, higher standards? Conventional religious principles have been found wanting, as Miller found in interviews with Christians who had participated in the French and Dutch Resistance forces:

> If the Christian men of the Resistance did not know before they committed themselves, they very soon learned that to participate in the anti-Nazi struggle was to be plunged into a moral maelstrom, in which no rules would help. For to resist one must stay alive, and to stay alive one must forge and cheat. Ration books and passports must be forged or stolen. Even within the Christian group, the traitor or the potential traitor must be liquidated without hesitation if not without compunction, since not only might the lives of the group members depend upon it, but the good cause itself. But drive this to its logical limit, and where does it take us? Presumably if a man may be liquidated as a danger to the good cause, the same man may be tortured to make him yield information vital to the good cause. If he resists torture himself, might it not be effective and therefore necessary to torture his

children before his eyes? Forgery, lying and liquidation: they had had a hand in all of them. Then, said I, is *everything* permitted? The reply was quite clear and quite crucial: "Yes: everything is permitted—and everything is forbidden." In other words, if killing and lying are to be used it must be under the most urgent pressure of social necessity, and with a profound sense of guilt that no better way can presently be found. . . . But notice that the dire decisions which are here involved, while they are not held under the neat restraint of any moral formula, are held under the restraint of Christian compassion. And what good in any event would a formula do? It is in every normal case a bad thing to lie, because it corrodes confidence and breaks community. But from the same group of anti-Nazi fighters I heard of a case in which Jewish refugees from Hitler were being transported to Britain in fishing boats from a North Sea port. On one particular evening the human cargo was aboard and the little ship was waiting for the tide, when a Nazi patrol came by on the dock. They knew the captain well but made a perfunctory inquiry about what he was carrying. Should the reply then have been: "Four Jewish adults, and seven children of diverse ages"? Or does the faith commend compassion, which cannot be guaranteed never to be at war with verbal veracity?[33]

We have taken a slight detour here to demonstrate the background that has led to contemporary rethinking of traditional Judeo-Christian morality. To put it briefly, the notion of a moral rule book that one can follow to the letter, rather than simply conforming to its spirit, may lead to immoral behavior, in the view of many modern theologians. The Ten Commandments say, "Thou shalt not kill" and "Thou shalt not bear false witness [lie]," yet there are specific *situations* in which strict obedience to these principles seems likely to lead to evil consequences, as in the Resistance

---

[33] Miller, A. (1955), pp. 99–101.

during World War II. Should these rules be discarded, so that each individual can be free to decide for himself what is right or wrong each time that he is confronted with a moral decision? Opinion is divided on this point. No ethical system, no matter how complete, can possibly cover every situation. Because every individual human being is in a sense unique, he will be confronted sooner or later with a situation that does not fit the rules or in which the rules conflict. For instance, should an unmarried college girl who is pregnant tell the truth to her overprotective father, who has just had a major heart attack, knowing that the news might kill him? According to the Danish Christian existentialist Sören Kierkegaard, certain special situations call for "suspension of the ethical," that is, a break with the usual universal ethical principles, but such variations, he advises, should be made with "Fear and Trembling" (the title of his essay on the subject). The latter advice seems well founded, especially when we look at the consequences of the flexible approach as put forth in a different way by Friedrich Nietzsche. Conventional moral rules can be put aside by the superior individual (Super-man) when it is necessary to advance his own power, said Nietzsche, and Hitler took that seriously.

And so we come to twentieth-century "situation ethics,"[34] the first attempt in a long time to rethink our approach to ethical questions, particularly those relating to human sexuality. We have chosen to focus on situation (or contextual) ethics here, and particularly on the writings of Joseph Fletcher, for several reasons. Situation ethics appears to be a logical outgrowth of the life and experience of man in the twentieth century and consequently has achieved, in a relatively short period of time,

widespread popularity and acceptance (uncritical acceptance, some thinkers say). In addition, Fletcher, the principal popular spokesman for situation ethics, addresses himself particularly to questions of human sexuality. (For instance, four of the eight chapters on "Situations for Ethical Decision" in his book *Moral Responsibility* deal with problems related to sexuality.) The new morality is particularly an American phenomenon, rooted as it is in pragmatism. Fletcher owes as much to William James and John Dewey, the great American pragmatists, as to such eminent twentieth-century theologians as Reinhold Niebuhr and Paul Tillich.

Situation ethics appears deceptively simple—undoubtedly another reason for its popularity. There is only one fundamental principle: that "whatever is the most loving thing in the situation is the right and good thing."[35] Fletcher sees right and wrong in terms of its effects on interpersonal relationships and love as the one and only guiding principle for moral decisions. "Christian situation ethics reduces law from a statutory system of rules to the love canon alone."[36] That is, one's *attitude* or *intentions* in a given situation determine whether or not his behavior in that situation will be right or wrong. Behavior should be motivated by love of a particular kind (the Greeks distinguished several different kinds)—not *eros*, the passionate love, or desire, commonly associated with sexuality; not *philia*, the brotherly sort of love between friends, which is also emotional to some extent; but rather *agape*, the spiritual love which is manifested by an attitude of concern for one's fellow man with no expectation of receiving something in return. The person who is motivated by *agape* can do no wrong and therefore has no need of rules or laws. Fletcher believes that this teaching is the essence of

---

[34] Situation ethics is also called "the new morality"; indeed, the full title of Joseph Fletcher's book on the subject is *Situation Ethics: The New Morality* (1966).

[35] Fletcher (1966), p. 65.
[36] Fletcher (1966), p. 69.

Christianity. Whether or not it is so is a question for theologians to debate. We shall address ourselves to the question of how this approach works in practice.

We shall discuss specific applications later on in this chapter, but at this point we can offer two generalizations. First, in situation or contextual ethics *any means* is justified by the end (love). According to this approach, even killing may conceivably be the most loving thing to do in a given situation—for instance, killing a baby whose crying endangers the lives of an entire party traveling through hostile territory and facing certain death if discovered. Presumably, then, there are also instances when almost any form of sexual behavior is justified. Fletcher has declared:

> Whether any form of sex (hetero, homo, or auto) is good or evil depends on whether love is fully served. The Christian ethic is not interested in reluctant virgins and technical chastity. What sex probably needs more than anything is a good airing, demythologizing it and getting rid of its mystique-laden and occult accretions, which come from romanticism on the one hand and puritanism on the other.[37]

The second general consideration has to do with the inherent difficulties in applying situation ethics:

> A common objection to situation ethics is that it calls for more critical intelligence, more factual information, and more self-starting commitment to righteousness than most people can bring to bear. We all know the army veteran who "wishes the war was back" because he could tell the good guys from the bad guys by the uniforms they wore. There are those who say situationism ignores the reality of human sin or egocentricity, and fails to appreciate the finitude of human reason.[38]

Miller has made a similar point:

> . . . what the Christian ethos or the Christian spirit requires of us is that we allow ourselves to be tutored by the faith and submitted to the facts: and that since our grasp of the faith is always unsure and our mastery of the facts always partial and limited; since we can neither assess our motives with confidence nor calculate consequences with certainty, we are cast in the end always on the forbearance and forgiveness of God.[39]

The demands that situation ethics places on the individual are tremendous and, perhaps, unrealistic when applied to the general population. This point seems particularly valid in connection with sexual behavior, for situation ethics calls for rational, unemotional appraisal of each situation and its short- and long-term ramifications, a prodigious accomplishment for those who are, by definition, involved in extremely emotional situations. That is, we suggest that even two people who are not in bed may have some difficulty in achieving *agape* while discussing whether or not they *should* go to bed together. Fletcher has cited the following instance:

> A young unmarried couple might decide, if they make their decisions Christianly, to have intercourse (e.g., by getting pregnant to force a selfish parent to relent his overbearing resistance to their marriage). But as Christians they would never merely say, "It's all right if we *like* each other!" Loving concern can make it all right, but mere liking cannot.[40]

Sexuality involves powerful emotions—not only love (*eros*) but also feelings of guilt. The former tends to predominate before and during the sexual encounter, it seems. When a question of morality is involved, however, feelings of guilt tend to appear the following day or even

[37]Fletcher (1966), pp. 139–140.
[38]Fletcher (1966), p. 81.
[39]Miller, A. (1955), p. 101.
[40]Fletcher (1966), p. 104.

months or years later. Guilt feelings may be regarded as the "voice of conscience," but actually their origins are extremely complex and may be totally irrational. Again, we shall leave debates over whether or not conscience is a God-given faculty to the theologians, but we cannot deny the reality of guilt feelings. Situation ethics emphasizes the processes that occur before an act. That the individuals believe *at the time* that what they are about to do is right is the important variable. But what of the potentially painful aftermath of guilt feelings, irrational as they may be?

It seems that the current generation of young people is living in a transitional period, in which there is an overlap between two phenomena. One is the belief that guilt feelings associated with sex are a heritage from past generations and are acquired in childhood; the other is the new morality, intellectual acceptance of the premise that sex in the proper context is good and should not be associated with feelings of guilt. Those who find it difficult to shake their feelings of guilt sometimes seek psychotherapy, implying that the feelings of guilt, rather than the behavior that engendered them, are bad and must be dispelled so that these people will be free to act according to their reason.

The Roman Catholic Church has its own method for dealing with guilt—the confessional. It may work as well as psychotherapy in relieving guilt feelings, but the underlying assumptions are quite different. Take, for instance, the devout girl, who, after due consideration, participates in sexual intercourse with a young man whom she deeply loves and plans to marry. She goes to confession, and the priest, if he is true to the tradition of the Church (as he may not be nowadays) acknowledges that the girl has committed a wrongful act (fornication, which is always wrong in the Roman Catholic view, regardless of the situation) but offers absolution in exchange for a specific penance.

One thing that can be said about the Roman

Catholic confessional and any other "legalistic" system of ethics, secular or religious, is that the individual always knows where he stands in terms of right and wrong. There is no need for the element of "fear and trembling" that Kierkegaard describes, and there are those who argue that the average person either does not want or cannot cope with the vagaries of an unstructured approach like situation ethics. The argument is put rather well by the Grand Inquisitor, as he confronts Christ in a scene created by Ivan, one of the characters in *The Brothers Karamazov:*

> Instead of taking men's freedom from them, Thou didst make it greater than ever! Didst Thou forget that man prefers peace, and even death, to freedom of choice in the knowledge of good and evil? Nothing is more seductive for man than his freedom of conscience, but nothing is a greater cause of suffering. And behold, instead of giving a firm foundation for setting the conscience of man at rest for ever, Thou didst choose all that is exceptional, vague and enigmatic; Thou didst choose what was utterly beyond the strength of men, acting as though Thou didst not love them at all—Thou who didst come to give Thy life for them! Instead of taking possession of men's freedom, Thou didst increase it, and burdened the spiritual kingdom of mankind with its sufferings for ever. Thou didst desire man's free love, that he should follow Thee freely, enticed and taken captive by Thee. In place of the rigid ancient law, man must hereafter with free heart decide for himself what is good and what is evil, having only Thy image before him as his guide. But didst Thou not know he would at last reject even Thy image and Thy truth, if he is weighed down with the fearful burden of free choice? They will cry aloud at last that the truth is not in Thee, for they could not have been left in greater confusion and suffering than Thou hast caused, laying upon them so many cares and unanswerable problems.[41]

---

[41]Dostoyevsky (1950 ed.), pp. 302-303.

It is an age-old problem, the responsibility that accompanies freedom of choice. The more rules or laws that there are to follow, the less freedom we enjoy—but the lighter is our burden of responsibility.

Application to Sexual Behavior: Specific Issues

We shall now describe a few of the most common issues of human sexuality on which different approaches to moral questions seem to clash. The disagreements, as we have tried to demonstrate, are bound up in traditions rooted not only in specific religions but also in culture and in certain underlying assumptions that have persisted in the West for several thousand years. Perhaps the best example of the latter is the assumption that women are inferior to men. This attitude is reflected in many of our customs, our etiquette (men open doors for women because they are implicitly the "weaker" sex), our sex laws (written to "protect" women against men, though they deprive women of certain rights as well), differential opportunities in jobs and professions, and attitudes toward sexual gratification (the secondary importance granted to female orgasm, for instance, and even the notion that there is something intrinsically wrong in a woman's expecting the same degree of sexual gratification as her male partner achieves).

We shall emphasize here the contrast between the "new morality" and the traditional theological-legalistic approach best exemplified by the teachings of the Roman Catholic Church (called simply the "traditional position"). These two approaches to sex and morality represent opposite ends of a continuum, and the reader will probably be able to infer and extrapolate from these two poles where and how other viewpoints fit in. We are well aware that many Roman Catholics disagree with the official position of the Church on questions of sex and morality and are striving for change. Never-

theless, even though the Church's official position may change in the near future, the influence of its traditional attitude can be expected to persist for some time to come.

Sexual Intercourse. The new morality clearly approves of intercourse for unmarried people under certain conditions. Fletcher has offered two principles or guidelines for deciding whether or not the conditions are being met.[42] First, another person must not be hurt or exploited by the sex act. (We wonder if there is not a contradiction in Fletcher's example, cited earlier, in which an unmarried couple might deliberately have intercourse and conceive in order to force the parents into consenting to a marriage—is there not an element of manipulation here?) Second, the decision should be based on concern for the welfare and happiness of those involved. Despite the emphasis on eliminating traditional criteria of right and wrong, notions like "happiness" seem to crop up frequently among exponents of the new morality. The idea of judging the morality of an act by the amount and quality of happiness that it produces was developed by John Stuart Mill in the nineteenth century and by others long before. Probably one of the major practical difficulties with the new morality is how easily it is perverted into the notion that "as long as you like each other and feel happy about what you're doing, it's all right." Fletcher carefully points out that "liking" does not equal "loving" in the sense of *agape,* but it seems that many individuals find the distinction either spurious or too difficult to make.

The traditional point of view on premarital or extramarital intercourse has been quite clear and simple: It is wrong. The very term "premarital" implies an act in anticipation of marriage (as the term "extramarital" implies an

---

[42]Fletcher (1967), p. 138.

act outside marriage) that should be reserved for marriage itself. We have noted earlier in this chapter some reasons why moralists and theologians have traditionally argued that sex and marriage must go together. It is no coincidence that the church most opposed to contraception is also firmly opposed to premarital intercourse. The major objection to premarital intercourse is based on the fact that the resulting child may be deprived of legitimate family life and parental devotion. According to an old limerick:

> There was a young lady named Wilde
> Who kept herself quite undefiled
>   By thinking of Jesus
>   And social diseases
> And the fear of having a child.

Aquinas made it quite clear that premarital intercourse per se (fornication, in his terminology) is not a sin, for heterosexual intercourse properly performed is a natural act and thus does not offend God. In Roman Catholic writings the arguments against fornication are not that the act is offensive to God or harmful to the partners involved but that "the postulated offspring explains why fornication is sin."[43]

We can imagine that there are moralists inside and outside the Church who envisage mass orgies of fornication if the moral sanctions against the use of contraceptives by unmarried people are lifted. Many parents of teen-age daughters express the following dilemma: "Should we offer to help our child obtain birth-control pills knowing that there is the possibility that without them she may have intercourse with her boyfriend and become pregnant? Or should we refuse to help her in this way (even if she asks) on the principle that the fear of pregnancy will discourage her from engaging in intercourse?" There is no easy answer to this dilemma. Even when the avowed aim of the parents (or the university health service) is to discourage fornication by not providing contraceptives, the large annual number of illegitimate pregnancies in this country demonstrates that this approach is not effective. On the other hand, it is conceivable that offering birth-control pills to a girl might encourage her to engage in sexual intercourse when she is not ready to do so in terms of her emotional maturity. The availability of reliable contraceptives, among other factors, has certainly led to a rethinking of the traditional views on intercourse outside marriage in our culture, and at the present time even the theologians, not to mention parents and young people, are having some difficulty in trying to decide what is "right."

Contraception. The use of contraceptives has ramifications in many areas—economic, social, political, and ethical. It is well known that the main ethical opposition to their use comes from the Roman Catholic Church. Its official position has been made quite clear: "Catholics regard the use of contraceptives as an objectively defective moral act so that even when they are used with the right motives (spirit), the action remains immoral."[44] The Roman Catholic argument against the use of contraceptives is based on the belief that any *unnatural* act is sinful. Contraceptives interfere with the natural purpose of intercourse, which is procreation. The rhythm method of birth control (see Chapter 6) is permissible because it does not interfere with any "natural" processes (but it is clearly designed to frustrate the natural processes, as defined by this tradition).

The Catholic Church has been criticized by certain groups that are deeply concerned about population control, though in fact it has been moving gradually toward acceptance of contraceptives. But the argument is being kept

---

[43]Noonan (1967), p. 292.

[44]Thomas (1965), p. 114.

within the framework of the concept of Natural Law, rather than being related to the question of overpopulation. Pope Pius XII, in an address to the Seventh International Congress of Hematology (September 12, 1958) said of birth-control pills, "If a woman takes this medicine, not to prevent conception, but only on the advice of a doctor as a necessary remedy because of a disease of the uterus or the organism, she provokes an indirect sterilization, which is permitted according to the general principle of actions with a double effect." That is, medical treatment of a disease is morally correct, and therefore the use of birth-control pills for treatment of conditions like painful or excessive menstrual bleeding or endometriosis (see Chapter 6) is morally correct, even though contraception occurs as a "side effect" of the treatment. (But do not medicines interfere with the laws of nature? The reply is, "No; it is lawful to correct the defects of nature.") In our experience, some Roman Catholic physicians have tended to broaden the definition of "diseases" treatable by the pill to include menstrual irregularity and premenstrual tension, so that almost any woman who wants to use the pill may do so.

Although the Roman Catholic Church is still struggling with the morality of contraception and clinging to its view that downright "sterilization," whether by chemical, surgical, or other means, is immoral, diametrically opposed points of view have become increasingly popular. The situational view has been summed up as follows:

1. *Making babies is a good thing but making love is, too,* and we can *and should* make love even if no baby is intended. There ought to be no unintended or unwanted babies.
2. The best way to make love without making babies is to prevent their conception; the next best way is to prevent fertility itself; and the least desirable way is to end a pregnancy already begun. *But any of these methods is good if the good to be gained is great enough to justify the means.*[45]

We have discussed the viewpoints and suggestions of experts from other fields, such as biology and agriculture, with regard to contraception and overpopulation in Chapter 6. Some of these experts propose investing the state with the authority to enforce the use of contraceptives, yet these same people condemn the Roman Catholic Church's stand against contraception as rigid, authoritarian, and an invasion of individual human rights. Again the question of individual freedom and responsibility, which we discussed earlier in this chapter, arises. There are always those who claim in the name of God or in the name of Science to have the gift of truth and prophecy; they are all too willing to impose the principles of their "truth," by force if necessary, for "man's own good." An alternative approach is to provide people with the knowledge, means, and *freedom* to exercise a variety of options and then to let them choose for themselves. This approach is based on the assumption that, given adequate information about birth-control methods, access to contraceptives at reasonable cost, and freedom from sanctions for or against the use of contraceptives, most people will make the "right" choices. We do not claim to have the gift of prophecy on this point but venture an "educated guess" that, given the freedom that we describe, most people would choose to have from one to three children, a minority would choose to have more, and another minority would choose to have none at all.

Other Issues. Traditional views of the morality of various forms of sexual behavior are currently being reexamined in the light of new knowledge, new ideas, and new circumstances.

---

[45]Fletcher (1967), p. 123.

The view of homosexuality is one. We have discussed the current trend toward legalizing homosexual activities conducted in private between consenting adults (Chapter 16), which reflects, among other things, a changing morality. In the Christian and Jewish traditions homosexuality was considered immoral because it clearly frustrated the procreational purpose of sexual behavior. In an era when procreation that contributes to population pressures is coming to be viewed as immoral, there is a tendency to view nonreproductive sexual behavior more leniently. This view seems implicitly to have removed some of the onus from certain previously condemned practices. The increasingly permissive attitude toward abortions also reflects this notion.

To some extent, moral attitudes have been influenced by studies like the Kinsey reports, which revealed that large percentages of individuals were performing sexual acts in private that were publicly condemned as perversions. The best example of this influence is the changing attitudes toward masturbation, particularly among males. After condemning it for centuries because it involved "wasting" sperm, which, according to Natural Law, is meant for reproductive purposes, moralists made the awkward discovery that virtually every male is guilty of mortal sin!

Lest we leave the impression that the end result of incorporating into sexual ethics the findings and opinions of biological and behavioral scientists would be the elimination of all traditional standards, we shall cite Morris' opinion of adultery:

> . . . difficulties would not arise if we were a different kind of species, if we laid eggs in the sand like a turtle and left them to hatch out by themselves. But for us, with our heavy parental duties, sexual experiments outside the pair-bond have two dangers. They not only provoke powerful sexual jealousies, but they also encourage the accidental formation of new pair-bonds, to the long-lasting detriment of the offspring of the family units involved. Complex sexual combinations and communes may have worked from time to time, but unqualified successes seem to have been isolated rarities, limited to exceptional and unusual personalities. Only the most ruthless intellectual control by all parties concerned will permit sexual experiments of this kind to operate smoothly.[46]

Certain taboos may well remain with us for a long time to come, but the reasons for observing them may change. The moral quality of behavior cannot be dissociated from motives, regardless of the consequences. As T. S. Eliot has said:

> The last temptation is the greatest treason:
> To do the right deed for the wrong reason.[47]

But there is an equal danger inherent in the new morality: that we may too readily justify doing the wrong thing for the right reason.

---

[46] Morris (1969), p. 92.
[47] Eliot (1935), Part I, p. 44.

Amid all the confusion and unanswered questions about human sexuality one fact is clear: that the attitudes of individuals and societies toward sexuality are subject to change. In Greece, where thousands of years ago the nude human figure was glorified in monumental works of art, the government in the 1960s banned the wearing of miniskirts in public. Conversely the floor-length dresses of women in Colonial America have given way to apparel that provides little more (and sometimes less) covering than does a bikini bathing suit. In fact the present propriety of the appearance of members of both sexes on beaches and in other public places clad in no more than the equivalent of brightly colored brief underclothes represents a change in standards of "public decency" in the United States that has occurred within a span of only a few decades.

Styles of dress are easily observable but not necessarily highly correlated with more significant expressions of individual and cultural attitudes toward sexuality, however. Indeed, reliance on such a superficial index as clothing can be quite misleading, particularly in evaluating the sexual proclivities of a given individual, for choice of clothing involves, among other things, what is available, tendencies to conform to (or to rebel against) current fashion, and aesthetic standards unassociated, at least

consciously, with sexuality. Basing the notion that a "sexual revolution" is taking place in the United States on observation of such phenomena as dress styles, nudity in films, coeducational college dormitories, and liberalized abortion laws seems unwarranted at the present time. Although such phenomena are apparent to all, and impressive to some, they may or may not reflect personal attitudes and private behavior.

In the past few decades the first efforts at systematic scientific investigation of personal attitudes and sexual behavior have been conducted by Kinsey and others. In addition to whatever information such studies can provide about certain aspects of human sexuality, the publication and dissemination of the findings undoubtedly have some effect upon the attitudes and behavior of the public. Hearing that almost all boys masturbate, for example, may well lead a boy to feel less guilty about this activity if he had previously believed it to be abnormal.

Research in areas other than sexual behavior may ultimately also have great influence on sexual activity and related concepts. The biochemical research that led to development of the Pill has made it possible to completely separate sexual activity from concern about reproduction. (The Pill is also administered in such a way as to separate contraceptive from

CHAPTER

18

HUMAN SEXUALITY: CURRENT TRENDS

sexual activity.) It is even possible that the Pill has also contributed to a new awareness of the potential for liberation among women. It is interesting that many of the early advertisements for the Pill in medical journals pictured a woman breaking free of chains.

In this chapter we shall comment on specific recent developments, ranging from the biological to the political, that seem to foreshadow changes in our conceptions and expressions of sexuality.

Sex Hormones

Recent studies tend to confirm the notion that sex hormones play an important role in human moods and behavior. Until recently very little was known about the effects of androgens on human behavior. Female sex hormones have been much more fully studied, and fluctuations in female sex steroids have been quite clearly associated with such symptoms as premenstrual tension, irritability, and certain forms of depression. One reason that research on the effects of male sex hormones in humans has been slow has been the unavailability of simple and accurate methods for measuring these substances in such body fluids as blood. If we are to correlate a certain type of behavior with an excess or deficiency of a particular hormone, a method for measuring hormone levels and comparing them with normal values must be available. For various reasons research funds have been more available for work on female sex hormones, particularly the development of the Pill, because of its more apparent practical applications.

There is now, however, increasing emphasis on the study of male sex hormones and their effects in humans, and methods for conducting such research are being developed.[1] Earlier

methods involved bioassay techniques,[2] which are rather inaccurate. Newer techniques rely on such sophisticated discoveries as gas-liquid chromatography, which permits direct measurement of the actual amount of testosterone present in a blood sample; they are significant improvements over earlier, indirect methods of estimating "androgenic activity."

Further research using these more sophisticated techniques will undoubtedly clarify the role of androgens in the sex drives of men and women. We mentioned in Chapter 4 some of the clinical evidence that has led some investigators to believe that adrenal androgens in women are more significant than are the ovarian female sex hormones. Data continue to accumulate in support of this hypothesis, and one endocrinologist has recently remarked: "It has seemed most reasonable to conclude that the major hormones which are responsible for female sexual drive are the androgens of adrenal cortical origin. If this conclusion is valid, it would then appear that for both men and women the principal erotogenic hormone is androgen."[3]

The possible relation of androgens to aggressive, as well as to sexual, behavior is now being actively explored at several research centers. The effects of androgens on aggressive behavior in animals are well known. Castration, especially before maturation, can produce a docile steer rather than a dangerous bull; similar phenomena occur among animals other than cattle. More subtle effects of androgens are also now being demonstrated; administration of or

---

[1]Lunde and Hamburg (1972).

[2]These techniques involve injecting standard amounts of body fluid, for instance, urine, into an animal known to have an organ sensitive to androgens: perhaps the seminal vesicles of a mouse or the comb of a capon. The growth of the "target organ" resulting from the injection is then measured, and an estimate of the amount of androgenic activity present in the specimen is based on these measurements.

[3]Reichlin (1971), p. 151.

exposure to these hormones during certain "critical periods" of fetal development can *permanently* influence behavior even when there is no subsequent exposure to androgens. A group of investigators at the Oregon Regional Primate Research Center has administered daily injections of testosterone to pregnant rhesus monkeys during the presumptive period of sexual differentiation, which is from about day 39 to day 90 of the 108-day gestation period. Virilized (pseudo hermaphroditic) females and their behavior have been closely studied by this method over a period of several years. Observations of eight such animals through infancy and adolescence have shown that they exhibited behavior that was generally aggressive and more typical of the males of the species. Other forms of social behavior, like grooming, that are not specific to one sex or the other were not effected by the testosterone treatment.[4]

The possibility that androgens like testosterone play a role in human aggression, as well as in sexual behavior, is finally being seriously studied for the first time. One discovery that encouraged this research was the discovery that some males have two Y (male) sex chromosomes each (see Chapter 4). These XYY individuals have been found in greater percentages in prisons and maximum-security psychiatric hospitals than in the general population. In at least some instances the additional Y chromosome seems to be associated with abnormal testosterone levels in the blood. Although it is too early to give definitive answers to some of the questions raised by these findings, one current hypothesis is that the presence of the extra Y chromosome causes excessive production of androgens by the fetal testes, which in turn alters the early development of the brain and nervous system. The individual may thus be sensitized to certain environmental or inter-

nal stimuli that might not otherwise provoke aggressive behavior (or at least not to the same degree). Depending upon the individual's life experiences, in combination with his greater physical size and strength (also mediated through androgens), a predisposition to violent outbursts and other aggressive behavior may result from this hormonal abnormality.

The possibility of attempting to control aggressive behavior in human beings by manipulating androgens has been discussed in the scientific literature, and one conclusion is not surprising: "Because both libido and aggressivity in the human male and female depend upon androgens, their control could never be a popular approach to restraining aggressiveness."[5]

Aphrodisiac Drugs

There is very little current scientific research on the development of aphrodisiacs per se. Yet from time to time aphrodisiac properties are noted as the side effects of drugs developed for other purposes. Two chemically related new drugs have recently been reported to induce or enhance sexual drive in animals and humans. They are levodihydroxyphenylalanine (L-dopa) and p-chlorophenylalanine (PCPA). The latter is reported to increase dramatically sexual behavior and motivation in animal studies, but it has not yet been tested in human beings.[6] L-dopa, on the other hand, has been widely administered to human subjects as treatment for Parkinson's disease, a neurological disorder, and a number of investigators have reported apparent sexual rejuvenation in male patients in their sixties and seventies. Although informal reports of this phenomenon have had wide publicity, the evidence is not overwhelming at

---

[4] Goy (1968).

[5] Rothballer (1967).

[6] Gessa *et al.* (1971).

the present time. A true aphrodisiac drug seems as elusive as is the fountain of youth, yet the search for such a substance has always fascinated man and will undoubtedly continue to do so.

Contraceptives

It appears that any new contraceptive methods in the near future will be for the use of females. The main reason is our relative lack of current knowledge of the male reproductive cycle (sperm production, androgens, and so forth). Although there has been considerable discussion about the development and ramifications of a pill for men, it is not yet on the horizon. Carl Djerassi, the chemist whose discoveries led to the development of the Pill for women (Chapter 6) said recently: "Nothing will stimulate future research on a practical male contraceptive agent more than the discovery of viable and significant chemical leads, but, even in that event, 1984 appears to be an exceedingly optimistic target date for the development of a male contraceptive pill ready for use by the public."[7]

A more likely development, though it too is still some time off, is a "once-a-month" pill for women. It may consist of a chemical that will specifically block or incapacitate the corpus luteum, thus preventing implantation and development of a fertilized egg (see Chapter 4). This mechanism is described as "luteolytic" and differs from the mechanism of the present birth-control pill, which primarily blocks ovulation rather than subsequent events. The advantages of a "once-a-month" pill over the present one include convenience and the probability of fewer side effects. But the cost of developing such a pill is significant. Changes in Food and Drug Administration (FDA)

requirements for the filing of a New Drug Application (NDA), a prerequisite for marketing a new drug in the United States, have increased the time and cost involved in the potential manufacture of a new pill. Most experts in this field would probably agree that the additional safeguards built into the present regulations are worthwhile and necessary to prevent the sort of tragedy that occurred when thalidomide was released for marketing in Europe without sufficient pretesting, an event that resulted in the birth of many deformed babies. The present estimates of time and cost involved in the development of a "once-a-month" luteolytic pill are, however, ten years or more and $7–18 million. The latter figure would vary according to the extent of the toxicological studies of animals required by the FDA for the specific drug in question.[8] Pharmaceutical firms are somewhat reluctant to invest this much time and money in developing drugs that may not ultimately be approved for marketing or, if approved, may not be commercially successful.

Prostaglandins

More than forty years ago, R. Kurzrok and C. C. Lieb of New York reported that injections of human semen into the uterus cause vigorous contractions of uterine muscles. By 1935 it had been shown that the factor responsible for this activity is produced by the prostate gland and seminal vesicles; it was named *prostaglandin* by Swedish physiologist U. S. von Euler. Later it was discovered that there are more than a dozen chemically related naturally occurring prostaglandins, and by 1962 Sune Bergström and his colleagues in Sweden had elucidated the chemical structures of two of them. Subsequently S. M. M. Karim and others at Makerere Uni-

---

[7]Djerassi (1970), p. 947.

[8]Djerassi (1970), p. 944.

versity in Uganda reported that labor can be induced in pregnant women through injection of prostaglandins. Some prostaglandins are more effective than are others; the two most effective are called PGE_2 and PGF_{2a}. PGF_{2a} has the additional property of being luteolytic in certain animals; that is, it interferes with progesterone secretion by the corpus luteum through a mechanism that is as yet unknown.[9] But the possible applicability of this finding in laboratory animals to the development of a new contraceptive pill for humans is purely speculative at present.

The property of prostaglandins that has aroused great interest is their *abortifacient* potential: They induce abortions. In January 1970 a group of investigators from the Karolinska Institute in Stockholm published a preliminary report on the use of prostaglandins to induce therapeutic abortion.[10] In the same month Karim published his first report on the same subject.[11] One year later the Swedish group published a more detailed report based on its experiences with sixty-nine women six to twenty weeks pregnant who had been admitted to hospitals for therapeutic abortions.[12] These reports from Sweden and Uganda have received rather wide publicity and have perhaps created the false impression that there will be an "abortion pill" on the market soon. The fact is that prostaglandins cannot be used orally, nor can they be used casually, because of their side effects. They must be administered in a hospital setting under medical supervision and observation. They are administered by intravenous infusion or via a catheter inserted into the uterus either through the abdominal wall or vaginally. The infusion of the drug takes about

seven hours, and in the Swedish study it led to successful abortion in 94 percent of the early pregnancies (less than eight weeks). Success rates with women in later stages of pregnancy were significantly lower (less than 30 percent), even after longer infusions (thirteen hours.) Karim has reported higher rates of therapeutic abortion with prostaglandins in women who are up to twenty-two weeks pregnant. His method involves continuous infusion of the drug for up to forty-eight hours or until abortion is completed. Even with the significantly increased infusion time the method is not completely successful. Side effects are common, plaguing about 50 percent of patients; they include nausea, vomiting, and diarrhea. At the moment the primary advantage of prostaglandins is that they offer the possibility of nonsurgical abortion, which would be most useful in countries or areas where surgical facilities and personnel are limited or nonexistent. It should also be emphasized that the safety of prostaglandins has not yet been established, particularly with regard to possible long-term complications.

A number of important developments related to biological aspects of human sexuality ranging from aphrodisiacs to abortifacients are thus contingent upon further developments in chemistry, particularly the chemistry of hormones. Given limited resources, policy decisions must be made about which, if any, of these new developments are worth the major investments required to perfect them and to make them safe and available to the general population. So far most decisions about the development of contraceptive pills and abortion techniques have been made by men, yet the "products" that emerge from their decisions are intended exclusively for the use of women. No statistics are necessary to support the obvious: Policy decisions on the deployment of research and development funds, both in the Federal government and in private industry, are made almost exclusively by men. We believe that this

[9] Anderson and Speroff (1971), p. 503.
[10] Roth-Brandel *et al.* (1970).
[11] Karim and Filshie (1970).
[12] Bergstrom *et al.* (1971).

state of affairs is changing as the result of several important psychological and cultural developments of the past decade, which we shall comment upon in the remainder of this chapter.

Women's Liberation

The concentration of economic and political power, as well as more subtle forms of domination and control, in the hands of men reaches so far back into history and is so pervasive across cultures that it is impossible to trace its origins with any degree of certainty. It is probable, however, that the phenomenon had its origins in prehistoric times, when the hunting of large animals by males and the nursing of infants by females were essential to the survival of the species. Whether or not the assignment of roles (man as "breadwinner," woman as caretaker of children) had its origins in such biological factors as the physical strength of the male and the breasts of the female, the perpetuation of these roles has most certainly been related to other factors. Although there is increasing evidence that sex chromosomes and sex hormones influence behavioral as well as anatomical sex differences, there is no evidence to indicate that men are any more or less qualified, by biological sex differences alone, to perform the tasks generally reserved for them in today's societies. And in those still relatively rare instances in which women perform the same tasks outside the home as do men, they are often paid less simply because they are women, which highlights an obvious institutionalization of sexual discrimination that cannot be defended by arguments based on biological differences.

Indeed, some current practices run counter to biological facts. For instance, women clearly have longer life expectancies than do men in the United States, yet most industries have compulsory retirement ages for women employees that are three or more years lower than are those for men. Present policies and laws limiting the number of hours that a woman can work each week and providing for compulsory daily rest periods for women employees date back to the nineteenth century, when women (and children) were often grossly exploited in sweatshops, working long hours for pittances. But the notion that women must be protected and controlled by various legal and social restrictions as children are also implies a social need to set women apart and to define their roles as separate and distinct from those of men. Some people ascribe such practices to noble motives, but others consider them indicative of the oppression of women by men who wish to preserve their own privileged positions in a male-dominated society.[13]

The tradition of male dominance over women is apparent in most social institutions, from the family, in which father is "head of the house," to the government, in which, with occasional rare exceptions (for example, Israel, India, and Ceylon in recent years), men occupy the positions of power. Support for this situation comes from many sources. For instance, in Chapter 17 we noted how the Judeo-Christian religious tradition encouraged male supremacy from the outset. Furthermore, male shortcomings have been handily blamed on the destructive influence of women, from the biblical story of Eve in the Garden of Eden to Freud's conception of the castrating woman.

Many of our beliefs about sex differences are self-fulfilling prophecies in the sense that children are influenced to act in accordance with these beliefs. Parents typically serve as models of "sex-appropriate" behavior, and imitation is one of the most common modes of learning for

---

[13] Millett (1970).

children. Parents also use methods of conditioning (positive and negative reinforcement) to teach children how members of their sex are "supposed to" behave. Consider, for example, aggressive and dependent behavior. Aggressive behavior among boys in our society is typically tolerated and often praised (positive reinforcement), whereas the same behavior is discouraged or punished (negative reinforcement) among girls. The opposite is true of dependence. Boys are encouraged to exert independence, whereas dependency is tolerated and encouraged among girls.[14]

Different standards and expectations for sexual activity also exist though they are currently undergoing change. For instance, the Victorian idea that female sexual activity should primarily be in the service of male needs for sexual gratification is giving way to recognition of possibilities for equal sexual pleasure for men and women. It is currently fashionable to associate Freud with the former idea and Masters and Johnson with the latter. As the statements of all these writers are effects, as well as causes, of their times, they are noteworthy but not necessarily blameworthy. Masters and Johnson have reported that women have greater capacities for orgasmic activity than do males, leading some to infer that the female sexual organ (clitoris) is perhaps "superior" to that of the male. As Kate Millett has put it:

> The clitoris . . . is the only human organ which is specific to sexuality and to sexual pleasure: The penis has other functions both in elimination and reproduction. While the male's sexual potential is limited, the female's appears to be biologically nearly inexhaustible, and apart from psychological considerations, may continue until physical exhaustion interposes.[15]

Sex, Love, Marriage, and Children

Contrary to popular belief, girls are not becoming increasingly promiscuous as part of their move toward liberation. A recent study has revealed that the most significant change in the sexual activity of college-age girls in the past twenty years is that more of them masturbate than did previously.[16]

A widespread current notion is that a new sense of sexual freedom among young people has led to frequent sexual activity for its own sake, divorced from traditional associations with love and marriage. Large-scale studies[17] suggest that sexual-behavior patterns, as well as sexual mores, are indeed changing but not necessarily in the direction of increased promiscuity. It is true that the percentage of unmarried college-age adults, particularly girls, who engage in intercourse has been gradually increasing over the past twenty years, but indiscriminate sexual activity among this same group of young people has not increased. Although marriage is no longer commonly considered a prerequisite for sexual intercourse, there is strong emphasis on some sort of mutual commitment and loving relationship before sexual involvement. Most college girls, though more sexually active than their counterparts in the previous generation, do not become sexually involved with men unless they are in love and often contemplating marriage as well. In this respect they resemble their parents, who also implicitly accepted sexual activity among couples who were engaged. The major difference is that American young people are marrying earlier than their parents did in the 1930s and 1940s.

Many more unmarried college couples live together today than in previous years, but such

---

[14] Maccoby, ed. (1966), pp. 74 ff.
[15] Millett (1970), pp. 117–118.

[16] Simon *et al.* (1972).
[17] Simon *et al.* (1972).

relationships tend to be quite conventionally monogamous, a far cry from the "shacking up" and "one-night stands" that many parents seem to fear. Furthermore, prophecies that coeducational dormitories on college campuses would lead to orgies and wild body-swapping parties have thus far proved false. There is surprisingly little sexual activity among residents of coed dorms, probably because of the sibling type of relationships that seem to develop when boys and girls live, study, eat, watch television, and so forth together. Some members of college coed-living groups actually complain about the "incest taboo" that often develops, and more often than not dating partners are found outside the groups.

Another myth is that the easy availability of the Pill has led to routine use by college girls. Usually a girl has become sexually active before she begins to take the Pill, and many girls—for reasons like embarrassment, guilt, and ignorance—do not use any form of contraception, and consequently many still become pregnant before marriage.

Traditional monogamous marriages oriented around nuclear-family units (husbands, wives, and offspring) are still the norm, though alternative forms of marriage and family styles are being discussed and sometimes practiced. Communal-living groups, in which young families pool their resources and share such tasks as food production, cooking, and child care are not uncommon. A more radical notion is that of renewable marriages. (One proponent of this idea is Margaret Mead.) Specific proposals vary in detail, but the essential idea is of marriage as a limited-term contract, with an option to renew upon mutual consent of both parties at the expiration of each specified interval (for instance, three years).

So far there has been little published discussion of the children of such marriages. Failure to renew a short-term marriage contract, though obviating the stigma of divorce

for the adults involved, might have the same net effect upon children as does divorce at present: the loss of a stable familial environment and the breaking up of emotional attachments to parental figures. It is paradoxical that some of those who are most sensitive to the oppression and exploitation of women seem relatively unconcerned about the rights of children. Only recently has the question whether or not children are entitled to such constitutional rights as due process in courts of law (juvenile courts) been raised. But a question of greater moment is whether or not children have the right to parents who will assume the responsibility for their welfare and nurture. Or should the state (or some other agency) provide child-care centers where children can be left while their parents pursue their own interests? Reports from eastern Europe and the Soviet Union, where state-operated child-care centers have been available for twenty years or more suggest higher incidences of emotional disturbances, difficulties in school, and juvenile delinquency among children raised in such facilities. The effects are most pronounced among children who have spent their earliest years (up to five years) essentially separated from their parents. The underlying problem seems to be either the absence of an opportunity for these children to form affectional bonds with parental figures or repeated disruptions of such bonds once formed.[18]

The development and maintenance of emotional bonds with parents would probably be seriously hampered by some of the schemes for child care currently being proposed by various women's groups. A significant variable is the amount of time each day that the child must be separated from one or both parents. In Czechoslovakia until 1967 parents could leave their children in state-operated child-care

---

[18]Bowlby (1951); Ainsworth (1962).

facilities day and night, if they wished, and take them home only on weekends, if at all. Long-term studies started in the early 1950s have suggested that children raised away from home for such long periods of time suffer a higher incidence of emotional disorders as teen-agers than do children reared primarily at home. These findings led to a revision of Czech policies limiting the time that children can spend in child-care centers to six or eight hours a day.

It is sometimes suggested that the Israeli kibbutzim have provided a working model of communal living in which men and women share the work of production and in which feeding and child-care activities are shared in such a way as to promote the happiness and well-being of both parents and children. In the early days of the kibbutzim, however, there was considerable dissatisfaction with the system, particularly among women, and modifications in the organization and the role of women had to be made. Spiro made the following observations in his study of an Israeli kibbutz:

> The social structure of the Kibbutz is responsible for a problem of . . . serious proportions—"the problem of the woman. . . ." With the exception of politics, nothing occupies so much attention in the Kibbutz. . . . It is no exaggeration to say that if Kiryat Yedidim should ever disintegrate, the "problem of the woman" will be one of the main contributing factors.
>
> In a society in which the equality of the sexes is a fundamental premise, and in which the emancipation of women is a major goal, the fact that there is a "problem of the woman" requires analysis. . . . The Youth Movement from which many Kibbutz values are derived was strongly feminist in orientation. The woman in bourgeois society, it is believed, was subjected to the male and tied to her home and family. This "biological tragedy of woman" forced her into menial roles, such as house cleaning, cooking, and other domestic duties, and prevented her from taking her place beside the man in the fields, the workshop, the laboratory, and the lecture hall.

> In the new society all this was to be changed. The woman would be relieved of her domestic burdens by means of the various institutions of collective living, and she could then take her place as man's equal in all the activities of life. The communal dining room would free her from the burden of cooking; the communal nurseries, from the responsibilities of raising children; the small rooms, from the job of cleaning.
>
> In a formal sense, the Kibbutz has been successful in this task. . . . In spite of "emancipation" which they have experienced in the Kibbutz, there is considerable sentiment among the women . . . that they would prefer not to have been "emancipated." Almost every couple who has left the Kibbutz has done so because of the unhappiness of the woman. . . . At a town meeting devoted to the "problem of the woman," one of the most respected women in Kiryat Yedidim—the wife of a leader of the Kibbutz movement—publicly proclaimed that the Kibbutz women had not achieved what they had originally hoped for; as for herself, after thirty years in Kiryat Yedidim she could pronounce her life a disappointment.
>
> One source of the woman's poor morale is that many women are dissatisfied with their economic roles. . . . When the vattikim (original settlers) first settled on the land, there was no sexual division of labor. Women, like men, worked in the fields and drove tractors; men, like women, worked in the kitchen and in the laundry. Men and women, it was assumed, were equal and could perform their jobs equally well. It was soon discovered, however, that men and women were not equal. For obvious biological reasons, women could not undertake many of the physical tasks of which men were capable; tractor driving, harvesting, and other heavy labor proved too difficult for them. Moreover, women were compelled at times to take temporary leave from that physical labor of which they were capable. A pregnant woman, for example, could not work too long, even in the vegetable garden, and a nursing mother had to work near the Infants House in order to be able to feed her child. Hence, as the Kibbutz grew older and the birth rate increased, more and more women were

forced to leave the "productive" branches of the economy and enter its "service" branches. But as they left the "productive" branches, it was necessary that their places be filled, and they were filled by men. The result was that the women found themselves in the same jobs from which they were supposed to have been emancipated—cooking, cleaning, laundering, teaching, caring for children, etc. . . .

What has been substituted for the traditional routine of housekeeping . . . is more housekeeping—and a restricted and narrow kind of housekeeping at that. Instead of cooking and sewing and baking and cleaning and laundering and caring for children, the woman in Kiryat Yedidim cooks or sews or launders or takes care of children for eight hours a day. . . . This new housekeeping is more boring and less rewarding than the traditional type. It is small wonder, then, given this combination of low prestige, difficult working conditions, and monotony, that the chavera (female member of the Kibbutz) has found little happiness in her economic activities.[19]

The organization of the kibbutzim has undergone further modifications, and it appears that some communal-living groups in the United States are experiencing similar problems in trying to establish a different kind of social organization.

One final observation seems relevant: The traditional roles of wife and mother cannot simply be abolished by decree. Despite technological advances, someone must still prepare food, care for children, and so forth. It seems unfortunate that the values and rewards of such activities, particularly child rearing, have been awarded relatively low status and prestige in our society. Furthermore, the value of many of the more public achievements of men has been often overrated, whereas the importance of the father's role in the raising of children has been sorely neglected. Is flying to the moon really a greater achievement than raising a child in an atmosphere of loving concern? Which requires greater skills and patience? Which, in the long run, is most rewarding to the participants?

Abortion and Sterilization

There is a rapidly growing movement in the United States to legalize abortion on demand. Until recently abortions were illegal except in certain states where they could be performed only when necessary to preserve the lives of the women. Colorado and California were the first states to broaden their laws to provide for abortion under other conditions. The California law, adopted in 1967, provides for therapeutic abortions when there is substantial risk that continuation of pregnancy will gravely impair the physical or mental health of the mother or when the pregnancy is the result of rape or incest.[20] Surveys indicate that about 95 percent of the abortions performed in California since 1967 have been performed under the "mental health" provision of this statute. Psychiatrists are put in the often uncomfortable position of certifying that continuation of pregnancy poses a risk to the "mental health" of the woman (who is usually said to be depressed and likely to commit suicide if the abortion is not granted) when in fact there is usually little, if any, evidence to substantiate this claim. In actual practice the real concerns of the physicians are often overpopulation, the dismal prospects of an unwanted child, or belief that women have the right not to bear children, regardless of the circumstances under which they become pregnant.

Many other states, including Arkansas,

---

[19] Spiro (1956), pp. 221–230.

[20] *California Health and Safety Code,* Chapter 11, Section 25951, Division 20.

Delaware, Georgia, Hawaii, Kansas, Maryland, New Mexico, New York, North Carolina, Oregon, and Virginia, have liberalized their abortion laws since 1967. In 1970 Hawaii became the first state to abolish requirements of a demonstrated risk to the mother's physical or mental health, but its law does provide that the woman must be a resident of the state for ninety days before the abortion. Shortly afterward, in July 1970, a New York law that removed all restrictions except the requirement that abortions must be performed within twenty-four weeks of conception, went into effect. New techniques have made it possible to perform abortions in out-patient clinics when women are in the early stage of pregnancy (twelve weeks or less). A suction device is used to remove the contents of the uterus without surgery. The cost of this procedure is considerably less than that of the traditional "D and C" (dilatation and curettage), which involves mechanical scraping of the uterine walls with a "curet" after the cervix has been dilated. Abortion after the twelfth week of pregnancy is now often induced by injection of a salt (saline) solution into the uterus to induce labor. This procedure must be performed in a hospital, for it is somewhat more complex.

Despite the trend toward legalizing abortion, the subject remains controversial. Moral questions involving the termination of life remain unanswered. Is a twenty-four-week-old fetus a human being? Some women have been startled and upset when aborted fetuses have moved, breathed, and cried, briefly, before all signs of life ceased. Should the state pay for abortions for women who cannot afford them? Should abortion procedures require the involvement of psychiatrists and hospital abortion committees, or should they be strictly private matters involving only pregnant women and their personal physicians? These and other issues will continue to be debated.

A related consideration is that of voluntary surgical sterilization for men and women. Voluntary sterilization is not yet legal in all fifty states,[21] and many states do not even have specific statutes on the subject. As recently as 1950 the Attorney General of California declared that sterilization operations were "violative of the state's social interest in the maintenance of the birth rate." In 1969, however California's Third District Court of Appeals ruled, in Jessin v. Shasta County that "California has no public policy prohibiting consensual sterilization operations and . . . that non-therapeutic sterilization operations are legal in this state where competent consent has been given." It was the first occasion on which an appellate court in the United States had ruled specifically on the legality of nontherapeutic surgical sterilization. Increasing concern about overpopulation and increased awareness of the side effects of the birth-control Pill will undoubtedly be accompanied by a significant rise in the number of sterilization operations performed on men and women in this country for contraceptive purposes.

Obscenity, Pornography, and Censorship

On September 30, 1970, the government-appointed Commission on Obscenity and Pornography submitted its report to the President and Congress of the United States. The Commission recommended that Federal, state, and local laws prohibiting the sale, exhibition, and distribution of sexual materials to consenting adults be repealed. The response to both the report and its recommendations was vocal and frequently negative. President Nixon announced that dissemination of pornography:

> if not halted and reversed, could poison the well springs of American Western culture and civili-

---

[21] States like Utah restrict sterilization to instances in which there is "medical necessity."

zation. The pollution of our culture, the pollution of our civilization with smut and filth, is as serious a situation for the American people as the pollution of our once-pure air and water. I have evaluated that report and categorically reject its morally bankrupt conclusions.

Furthermore, despite such opposition, we are witnessing a steady increase in the portrayal of explicit sexual material in books, in films, and on the stage. At the same time we are seeing superficial indications of desexualization, or "neutering," of social identity as indicated by the increasing similarity of clothes and hair styles for men and women. As opportunities for voyeuristic activities increase, it is possible that the need for individual sexual expression will wane. This hypothesis has been put forth by sociologist Charles Winick:

> Paradoxically, our age of so much libidinization of mass media could be the beginning of an epoch of declining sexual behavior. . . . A society with liberal attitudes toward sexual expression is likely to have less sexual behavior than a culture that places sanctions on such expression. We may identify as the Godiva Principle the proposition that people will be attracted to sex in proportion to the extent to which it is prohibited.[22]

A similar view has been echoed by literary scholar, George Steiner:

> Sexual relations are, or should be, one of the citadels of privacy, the night place where we must be allowed to gather the splintered, harried elements of our consciousness to some kind of inviolate order and repose. It is in sexual experience that a human being alone, and two human beings in that attempt at total communication which is also communion, can discover the unique best of their identity. . . . The new pornographers subvert this last, vital privacy; they do our imagining for us. They take away

the words that were of the night and shout them over the rooftops, making them hollow. The images of our love-making, the stammerings we resort to in intimacy, come prepackaged. From the rituals of adolescent petting to the recent university experiment in which faculty wives agreed to practice onanism in front of the researcher's cameras, sexual life, particularly in America, is passing more and more into the public domain. This is a profoundly ugly and demeaning thing whose effects on our identity and resources of feeling we understand as little as we do the impact on our nerves of the perpetual "suberoticism" and sexual suggestion of modern advertisement. . . . Thus the present danger to the freedom of literature and to the inward freedom of our society is not censorship or verbal reticence. The danger lies in the facile contempt which the erotic novelist exhibits for his readers, for his personages, and for the language.[23]

The battle for abolition of censorship in America appears for most practical purposes to have been won, despite continuing skirmishes centering on specific books, plays, or films. Publishers and producers are finding it increasingly difficult to provoke prosecution on obscenity charges, which used to generate a good deal of free publicity.

Human sexuality has become a very public topic in recent years, discussed, practiced, and exploited more openly than at any previous time in this country's history. It is ironic to hear the greater freedom of sexual expression that exists today described as a "sexual revolution," for sex and revolution have never been partners. A prominent historian of revolutions has observed:

> I can think of no well-established organized revolutionary movement or regime which has not developed puritanical tendencies. . . . The libertarian, or more exactly, antinomian, component of revolutionary movements, though

---

[22]Winick (1970), p. 201.

[23]Steiner (1970), pp. 131–132.

sometimes strong and even dominant at the actual moment of liberation, has never been able to resist the puritan. The Robespierres always win out over the Dantons.[24]

---

[24]Hobsbawm (1970), pp. 38–39.

Although some people extol the virtues of sexuality and others condemn its expression, no human being or society has ever been able to ignore it. Our hope is that future attitudes will be based on knowledge, rather than on ignorance.

Abraham, K. 1948. *Selected papers of Karl Abraham*. London: Hogarth Press and Institute of Psychoanalysis.

Advisory Committee on Obstetrics and Gynecology, Food and Drug Administration. 1966. *Report on the oral contraceptives*. Washington, D.C.: Government Printing Office.

———. 1968. *Report on intrauterine contraceptive devices*. Washington, D.C.: Government Printing Office.

———. 1969. *Second report on the oral contraceptives*. Washington, D.C.: Government Printing Office.

Ainsworth, M. 1962. *The effects of maternal deprivation: A review of findings and controversy in the context of research strategy*. World Health Organization Public Health Paper no. 14. Geneva: WHO.

Allen, C. 1969. *A textbook of psychosexual disorders*. 2nd ed. London: Oxford University Press.

Amelar, R. D. 1966. *Infertility in men*. Philadelphia: F. A. Davis Co.

American Law Institute. 1955. *Model penal code: Tentative draft no. 4*. Philadelphia.

———. 1962. *Model penal code: Proposed official draft*. Philadelphia.

American Psychiatric Association. 1968. *Diagnostic and statistical manual of mental disorders*. 2nd ed. Washington, D.C.: APA.

Amos, S. 1877. *Laws for the regulation of vice*. London: Stevens & Sons.

Anati, E. 1961. *Camonica Valley*. New York: Alfred A. Knopf.

Anderson, G. G., & Speroff, L. 1971. Prostaglandins. *Science* 171: 502–504.

Aquinas, St. Thomas. 1911–1925. *The summa theologica*. Trans. by Fathers of the English Dominican Province. New York: Benziger Bros.

Arey, L. B. 1965. *Developmental anatomy*. 7th ed. Philadelphia: W. B. Saunders Co.

Augustine, St. 1934. *The city of God, book XIV*. Trans. by J. Healey, Intro. by E. Baker. London and Toronto: J. M. Dent & Sons, Ltd.; New York: E. P. Dutton & Co.

———. 1955. *Treatises on marriage and other subjects*. Trans. by C. Wilcox *et al*. Ed. by R. J. Deferrari. New York: Fathers of the Church, Inc.

Bailey, S. 1959. *Sexual relation in Christian thought*. New York: Harper & Row.

———. 1963. *Sexual ethics: A Christian view*. New York: Macmillan Co.

Bāṇa (Banabhatta). 1956. *Kādambarī*. Trans. by C. M. Ridding. Bombay: Jaico Publishing House.

Bartell, G. D. 1971. *Group sex*. New York: Peter H. Wyden, Inc.

Baudelaire, C. 1952. *Les fleurs du mal*. Trans. by Roy Campbell. New York: Pantheon Books.

Beach, F. A., ed. 1965. *Sex and behavior*. New York: John Wiley & Sons.

Beckett, S. 1962. *Malone dies*. London: Penguin Books.

Belliveau, F., & Richter, L. 1970. *Understanding human sexual inadequacy*. New York: Bantam Books.

REFERENCES

Benedek, T. 1950. The functions of the sexual apparatus and their disturbances. In *Psychosomatic medicine,* ed. F. Alexander, pp. 216–262. New York: W. W. Norton & Co.

————. 1952. *Psychosexual functions in women.* New York: Ronald Press.

Benson, R. C. 1968. *Handbook of obstetrics and gynecology.* 3rd ed. Los Altos, Calif.: Lange Medical Publications.

Berelson, B. 1969. Beyond family planning. *Science* 163: 533–543.

Bergstrom, S., Bygdeman, M., Samuelsson, B., & Wiqvist, N. 1971. The prostaglandins and human reproduction. *Hospital Practice* 6 (February): 51–57.

Bieber, I., *et al.* 1962. *Homosexuality—A psychoanalytic study.* New York: Basic Books. (Paperback edition entitled *Homosexuality*: New York: Random House, Vintage paperback.)

Bishop, N. 1969. The great Oneida love-in. *American Heritage* 20 (February): 14–17, 86–92.

Boccaccio, G. n.d. *The Decameron.* Trans. by John Payne. New York: The Modern Library.

Bohannan, P. 1969. *Love, sex and being human: A book about the human condition for young people.* Garden City, N.Y.: Doubleday & Co.

Bonaparte, M. 1953. *Female sexuality.* New York: International Universities Press.

Booth, W. 1961. *The rhetoric of fiction.* Chicago: University of Chicago Press.

Borell, U. 1966. Contraceptive methods—their safety, efficacy, and acceptability. *Acta Obstet. et Gynecolog. Scand.* 45, Suppl. 1: 9–45.

Bowlby, J. 1951. *Maternal care and mental health.* World Health Organization Monograph Series no. 2. Geneva: WHO.

————. 1969. *Attachment.* Attachment and loss series, vol. 1. New York: Basic Books.

Brecher, E. M. 1969. *The sex researchers.* Boston: Little, Brown & Co.

Brecher, R., & Brecher, E. 1966. *An analysis of human sexual response.* New York: New American Library.

Brenner, C. 1957. *An elementary textbook of psychoanalysis.* Garden City, N.Y.: Doubleday & Co.

Brod, M. 1946. *Franz Kafka: Eine biographie.* New York: Schocken.

Broderick, C. B., & Bernard, J. 1969. *The individual, sex, and society: A SIECUS handbook for teachers and counselors.* Baltimore: The Johns Hopkins Press.

Brunner, H. E. 1947. *The divine imperative.* Trans. by O. Wyon. Philadelphia: Westminster Press.

Burroughs, W. 1959. *Naked lunch.* New York: Grove Press.

————. 1968. *The ticket that exploded.* New York: Grove Press.

Burton, R. 1932. *The anatomy of melancholy.* London: J. M. Dent & Sons.

Burton, R. F., trans. n.d. *The thousand and one nights.* Luristan ed. n.p.: "Printed by the Burton Club for subscribers only."

Byron (George Gordon, Lord Byron). 1912. *The poetical works of Lord Byron.* London: Oxford University Press.

Cairns, R. B., Paul, J. C., & Wishner, J. 1962. Sex censorship: The assumptions of antiobscenity laws and the empirical evidence. *Minnesota Law Review* 46: 1008–1041.

Calder-Marshall, A. 1959. *The sage of sex.* New York: G. P. Putnam's Sons.

Calderone, M. S., ed. 1970. *Manual of contraceptive practice.* 2nd ed. Baltimore: Williams & Wilkins Co.

Calverton, V. F., & Schmalhausen, S. D. 1929. *Sex in civilization.* New York: Citadel Press.

Calvin, J. 1960. *Institutes of the Christian religion.* Ed. by J. T. McNeill. London: S.C.M. Press.

Caprio, F., & Brenner, D. 1961. *Sexual behavior: Psycho-legal aspects.* New York: Citadel Press.

Casanova de Seingalt, G. G. 1958–1960. *Mémoires.* Paris: Gallimard.

Chall, L. P. 1955. The reception of the Kinsey report in the periodicals of the United States: 1947–1949. In *Sexual behavior in American society,* ed. J. Himelhoch & S. F. Fava, pp. 364–378. New York: W. W. Norton & Co.

Chamove, A., Harlow, H. F., & Mitchell, G. 1967. Sex differences in the infant-directed behavior of preadolescent rhesus monkeys. *Child Development* 38: 329–335.

Changing morality: The two Americas, a *Time*-Louis Harris poll. 1969. *Time* (June 6), pp. 26–27.

Chertok, L. 1967. Psychosomatic methods of preparation for childbirth. *American Journal of Obstetrics and Gynecology* 98: 698-707.

Churchill, W. 1967. *Homosexual behavior among males.* New York: Hawthorn Books.

Cleland, J. 1963. *Memoirs of a woman of pleasure.* New York: G. P. Putnam's Sons.

Cochran, W. G., Mosteller, F., & Tukey, J. W. 1954. *Statistical problems of the Kinsey report of sexual behavior in the human male.* Washington, D.C.: American Statistical Association.

Cohen, A. 1949. *Everyman's Talmud.* New York: E. P. Dutton & Co.

Colby, K. M. 1951. *A primer for psychotherapists.* New York: Ronald Press.

Colette, S. G. 1948-1950. *Claudine à l'école.* Paris: Le Fleuron.

Collis, J. S. 1959. *Havelock Ellis: Artist of life.* New York: William Sloane Associates.

Cory, D. W. 1964. *The lesbian in America.* New York: Citadel Press.

Crawley, L. Q., Malfetti, J. L., Stewart, E. I., & Vas Dias, N. 1964. *Reproduction, sex, and preparation for marriage.* Englewood Cliffs, N.J.: Prentice-Hall.

Curtis, Helena. 1968. *Biology: The Science of Life.* New York: Worth Publishers.

Daly, C. B. 1966. *Morals, law and life.* Chicago, Dublin, London: Scepter Publishers.

Danté Alighieri. 1954. *The inferno.* Trans. by J. Ciardi. New York: American Library.

de Beauvior, S. 1952. *The second sex.* New York: Alfred A. Knopf.

Defoe, D. 1926. *The fortunes and misfortunes of the amorous Moll Flanders.* New York: The Modern Library.

Dement, W. 1965. An essay on dreams. In *New directions in psychology II*, pp. 135-257. New York: Holt, Rinehart & Winston.

de Rougemont, D. 1956. *Love in the western world.* New York: Pantheon Books.

Deutsch, H. 1944-1945. *The psychology of women.* 2 vols. New York: Grune & Stratton.

Devereux, G. 1937. Institutionalized homosexuality of the Mohave Indians. In *Human biology*, 9: 498-527. Detroit: Wayne State University Press.

DeWald, P. A. 1964. *Psychotherapy: A dynamic approach.* New York: Basic Books.

Dewey, J. 1960. *Theory of the moral life.* New York: Holt, Rinehart & Winston.

Diamond, M., ed. 1968. *Perspectives in reproduction and sexual behavior.* Bloomington: Indiana University Press.

Dickinson, R. L. 1949. *Atlas of human sex anatomy.* 2nd ed. Baltimore: Williams & Wilkins Co.

Dienhart, C. M. 1967. *Basic human anatomy and physiology.* Philadelphia: W. B. Saunders Co.

Djerassi, C. 1970. Birth control after 1984. *Science* 169: 941-951.

Do marriage manuals do more harm than good? 1970. *Medical Aspects of Human Sexuality* 4, no. 10 (October): 50-63.

Dodson, A. I., & Hill, J. E. 1962. *Synopsis of genitourinary disease.* 7th ed. St. Louis: C. V. Mosby Co.

Don Leon/Leon to Annabella: An epistle from Lord Byron to Lady Byron (Attributed to Byron). n.d. London: The Fortune Press.

Doshay, L. J. 1969. *The boy sex offender and his later career.* 2nd ed. Mount Prospect, Ill.: Patterson Smith.

Dostoyevsky, F. 1950. *The brothers Karamozov.* Trans. by Constance Garnett. New York: Random House.

Dumas, A. 1956. *La dame aux camélias.* Paris: Calmann-Levy.

Eastman, N. J., & Hellman, L. M. 1966. *Williams obstetrics.* 13th ed. New York: Appleton-Century-Crofts.

Egerton, C., trans. 1939. *The golden lotus (Chin p'ing mei).* London: Routledge & Kegan Paul.

Ehrhardt, A. A., & Money, J. 1967. Progestin-induced hermaphroditism: I.Q. and psychosexual identity in a study of ten girls. *Journal of Sex Research* 3: 83-100.

Ehrlich, P. A. 1968. *The population bomb.* New York: Ballantine Books.

Eichenlaub, J. E. 1961. *The marriage art.* New York: Dell Publishing Co.

Eliot, T. S. 1935. *Murder in the cathedral.* New York: Harcourt, Brace & Jovanovich.

Ellis, A. 1965. *The art and science of love.* New York: Dell Publishing Co.

————. 1969. Healthy and disturbed reasons for having extramarital relations. In *Extramarital relations,* ed. G. Neubeck, pp. 153–161. Englewood Cliffs, N.J.: Prentice-Hall.

Ellis, A., & Abarbanel, A., eds. 1967. *The encyclopedia of sexual behavior.* New York: Hawthorn Books.

Ellis, H. 1939. *My life.* Boston: Houghton Mifflin Co.

————. 1942. *Studies in the psychology of sex.* 2 vols. New York: Random House. (Originally published in 7 volumes, 1896–1928.)

Engel, G. L. 1962. *Psychological development in health and disease.* Philadelphia: W. B. Saunders Co.

Epstein, L. M. 1968. *Sex laws and customs in Judaism.* Rev. ed. New York: Ktav Publishing House.

Erikson, E. H. 1959. Identity and the life cycle. *Psychological issues.* 1, no. 1. New York: International Universities Press.

————. 1963. *Childhood and society.* New York: W. W. Norton & Co.

————. 1968. *Identity: Youth and crisis.* New York: W. W. Norton & Co.

Eroticism: The disease of our age. 1961. *Films and Filming* (January).

Farnsworth, D. L., & Blaine, G. B., Jr., eds. 1970. *Counseling the college student.* Boston: Little, Brown & Co.

Fenichel, O. 1945. *The psychoanalytic theory of neurosis.* New York: W. W. Norton & Co.

Ferenczi, S. 1936. Male and female: Psychoanalytic reflections on the "theory of genitality," and on secondary and tertiary sex differences. *Psychoanalytic Quarterly* 5: 249–260.

————. 1950. *Sex in psychoanalysis.* New York: Basic Books.

Finkle, A. L., *et al.* 1969. How important is simultaneous orgasm? *Medical Aspects of Human Sexuality* 3, no. 7 (July): 86–93.

Finler, J. W. 1968. *Stroheim.* Berkeley, Calif.: University of California Press.

Fisher, C., *et al.* 1965. Cycle of penile erection synchronous with dreaming (REM) sleep. *Archives of General Psychiatry* 12: 29–45.

Fletcher, J. 1966. *Situation ethics: The new morality.* Philadelphia: Westminster Press.

————. 1967. *Moral responsibility: Situation ethics at work.* Philadelphia: Westminster Press.

Fleuret, F., & Perceau, L., eds. 1924. *Le cabinet satyrique.* Paris: J. Fort.

Ford, C. S. 1964. *A comparative study of human reproduction.* Yale University Publications in Anthropology no. 32. (Reprinted: New York: Taplinger Publishing Co., 1964.)

Ford, C. S., & Beach, F. A. 1951. *Patterns of sexual behavior.* New York: Harper & Row.

Foster, J. H. 1958. *Sex variant women in literature.* Chicago: Muller.

Fraiberg, S. H. 1959. *The magic years.* New York: Charles Scribner's Sons.

Frank, Gerald. 1966. *The Boston strangler.* New York: The New American Library. (Also available as a Signet paperback.)

Franklin, J. 1959. *Classics of the silent screen.* New York: Citadel Press.

Frazer, J. G., Trans. 1898. *Pausanias's description of Greece.* New York: Macmillan.

Freeman, L. 1955. *Catch me before I kill more.* New York: Crown Publishers. (Also available as a Pocket Books paperback.)

Freud, S. 1951. Letter to an American mother. *American Journal of Psychiatry* 107: 787.

————. 1957–1964. *The standard edition of the complete psychological works of Sigmund Freud,* ed. James Strachey. London: Hogarth Press and Institute of Psychoanalysis.

Fromm, E. 1956. *The art of loving.* New York: Harper & Row.

Gagnon, J. H., & Simon, W., eds. 1970. *The sexual scene.* Chicago: Aldine.

Gebhard, P. H. 1968. Factors in marital orgasm. *Medical Aspects of Human Sexuality* 2, no. 7 (July): 22–25.

Gebhard, P. H., Gagnon, J. H., Pomeroy, W. B., & Christenson, C. V. 1965. *Sex offenders.* New York: Harper & Row.

Gerassi, J. 1967. *Boys of Boise.* New York: Macmillan Co.

Gessa, B. L., et al. 1971. Aphrodisiac effect of p-chlorophenylalanine. *Science* 171: 706.

Girodias, M., ed. 1965. *The Olympia reader.* New York: Grove Press.

Goldberg, I. 1926. *Havelock Ellis.* New York: Simon & Schuster.

Gorer, G. 1938. *Himalayan village.* London: Michael Joseph Ltd.

Goy, R. W. 1968. Organizing effects of androgen on the behaviour of Rhesus monkeys. In *Endocrinology and human behavior,* ed. R. Michael, pp. 12–31. London: Oxford University Press.

Graves, R. 1959. *The Greek myths.* 2 vols. New York: George Braziller.

Gulevich, G., & Zarcone, V. 1969. Nocturnal erection and dreams. *Medical Aspects of Human Sexuality* 3, no. 4 (April): 105–109.

Guttmacher, A. F. 1962. *Pregnancy and birth: A book for expectant parents.* New York: Viking Press.

Guttmacher, A. F., Best, W., & Jaffe, F. S. 1964. *Planning your family.* New York: Macmillan Co.

Hall, R. 1928. *The well of loneliness.* New York: Covici Friede.

Hamburg, D. A., & Lunde, D. T. 1966. Sex hormones in the development of sex differences in human behavior. In *The development of sex differences,* ed. E. Maccoby, pp. 1–24. Stanford, Calif.: Stanford University Press.

Hare, E. H. 1962. Masturbatory insanity: The history of an idea. *Journal of Mental Science* 452: 2–25.

Harkel, R. L. 1969. *The picture book of sexual love.* New York: Cybertype Corp.

Harlow, H. F., McGaugh, J. L. & Thompson, R. F. 1971. *Psychology.* San Francisco: Albion Publishing Co.

Harris, F. 1963. *My life and loves.* New York: Grove Press.

Hastings. D. W. 1966. *A doctor speaks on sexual expression in marriage.* Boston: Little, Brown & Co.

Henriques, F. 1962–1968. *Prostitution and society: A survey.* Vol. 1: *Primitive, classical, oriental.* Vol. 2: *Prostitution in Europe and the New World.* Vol. 3: *Modern sexuality.* London: MacGibbon & Kee.

Henry, G. W. 1955. *All the sexes.* New York: Holt, Rinehart & Winston.

Hilgard, E. R. 1956. *Theories of learning.* New York: Appleton-Century-Crofts.

Hill, A. B. 1966. *Principles of medical statistics.* London: Oxford University Press.

Hiltner, S. 1953. *Sex ethics and the Kinsey reports.* New York: American Book-Stratford Press.

Hobsbawm, E. J. 1970. Revolution is puritan. In *The new eroticism,* ed. P. Nobile, pp. 36–40. New York: Random House.

Hoffman, M. 1968. *The gay world: Male homosexuality and the social creation of evil.* New York: Basic Books.

Hooker, E. 1965. An empirical study of some relations between sexual patterns and gender identity in male homosexuals. In *Sex research—new developments,* ed. J. Money, pp. 24–25. New York: Holt, Rinehart & Winston.

Houston, P. 1963. *The contemporary cinema.* London: Penguin Books.

How frequently is sex an important factor in divorce? 1970. In *Medical Aspects of Human Sexuality* 4, no. 6 (June): 24–37.

Hyde, H. M. 1966. *A history of pornography.* New York: Dell Books.

International Planned Parenthood Federation medical handbook. 1968. London: IPPF.

Israel, S. L. 1967. *Menstrual disorders and sterility.* New York: Harper & Row.

"J." 1969. *The sensuous woman.* New York: Lyle Stuart.

Jackson, H. 1966. *Antifertility compounds in the male and female.* Springfield, Ill.: Charles C Thomas.

James, A. G. 1966. *Cancer prognosis manual.* 2nd ed. New York: American Cancer Society.

Janis, I. L., Mahl, G. F., Kagan, J., & Holt, R. R. 1969. *Personality: Dynamics, development and assessment.* New York: Harcourt, Brace & Jovanovich.

Jawetz, E., Melnick, J. L., & Adelberg, E. A. 1970. *Review of medical microbiology.* 9th ed. Los Altos, Calif.: Lange Medical Publications.

Jones, E. 1953. *The life and work of Sigmund Freud.* 3 vols. New York: Basic Books.

Jones, H. W., Jr., & Scott, W. 1958. *Hermaphroditism, genital anomalies and related endocrine disorders.* Baltimore: Williams & Wilkins Co.

Joyce, J. 1934. *Ulysses.* New York: Random House.

Jung, C. G. 1960. General aspects of dream analysis. In *Structure and dynamics of the psyche,* vol.

8. Trans. by R. F. C. Hull. New York: Pantheon Books.

Juvenal (Decimus Junius Juvenalis). 1961. *Satires, with an English trans.* by G. G. Ramsay. London: William Heinemann.

Kallmann, F. J. 1952. A comparative twin study on the genetic aspects of male homosexuality. *Journal of Nervous and Mental Disease* 115: 283–298.

Kameny, F. E. 1971. Gay liberation and psychiatry. *Psychiatric Opinion* (February), pp. 18–27.

Karim, S. M. M., & Filshie, G. M. 1970. Therapeutic abortion using prostaglandin $F_{2\alpha}$. *Lancet* 1: 157–159.

Karlen, A. 1971. *Sexuality and homosexuality.* New York: Norton.

Karpman, B. 1954. *The sexual offender and his offenses.* New York: Julian Press.

Kaufman, I. C., & Rosenblum, L. A. 1969. The waning of the mother-infant bond in the species of macaque. In *Determinants of infant behavior,* ed. B. M. Foss, vol. IV, pp. 41–59. London: Methuen & Co.

Kepecs, J. 1969. Sex and tickling. *Medical Aspects of Human Sexuality* 3, no. 8 (August): 58–65.

Kessel, J. 1967. *Belle de jour.* Paris: Trans. by Geoffrey Wagner. New York: Dell Books.

Kilpatrick, J. J. 1960. *The smut peddlers.* Garden City, N.Y.: Doubleday & Co.

Kinsey, A. C., Pomeroy, W. B., & Martin, C. E. 1948. *Sexual behavior in the human male.* Philadelphia: W. B. Saunders Co.

Kinsey, A. C., Pomeroy, W. B., Martin, C. E., & Gebhard, P. H. 1953. *Sexual behavior in the human female.* Philadelphia: W. B. Saunders Co.

Kleitman, N. 1963. *Sleep and wakefulness.* Chicago: University of Chicago Press.

Knight, A., & Alpert, H. 1965–1969. The history of sex in cinema. *Playboy Magazine.* I. The original sin (April 1965); II. Compounding the sin (May 1965); III. The twenties: Hollywood's flaming youth (June 1965); IV. The twenties: Europe's decade of decadence (August 1965); V. Sex stars of the twenties (September 1965); VI. Censorship and the Depression (November 1965); VII. The thirties: Europe's decade of unbuttoned erotica (February 1966); VIII. Sex stars of the thirties (April 1966); IX. The forties: War and peace in Hollywood (August 1966). X. The forties: War and peace in Europe (September 1966); XI. Sex stars of the forties (October 1966); XII. The fifties: Hollywood grows up (November 1966); XIII. The fifties: Sex goes international (December 1966); XIV. Sex stars of the fifties (January 1967); XV. Experimental films (April 1967); XVI. The nudies (June 1967); XVII. The stag film (November 1967); XVIII. The sixties: Hollywood unbuttons (April 1968); XIX. The sixties: Eros unbound in foreign films (July 1968); XX. Sex stars of the sixties (January 1969).

Knight, R. P. 1943. Functional disturbances in the sexual life of women: Frigidity and related disorders. *Bulletin of the Menninger Clinic* 7: 25–35.

Kracauer, S. 1966. *From Caligari to Hitler: A psychological history of the German film.* Princeton, N.J.: Princeton University Press.

Kronhausen, E., & Kronhausen, P. 1964. *Pornography and the law.* New York: Ballantine Books.

Kyrou, A. 1957. *Amour, érotisme, et cinéma.* Paris: Le Terrain Vague.

Landtman, G. 1927. *The Kiwai Papuans of British New Guinea.* London: Macmillan.

Lawder, S. D. 1968. Film: Art of the twentieth century. *Yale Alumni Magazine* (May).

Lawrence, D. H. 1948. *The tales of D. H. Lawrence.* London: William Heinemann.

———. 1957. *Lady Chatterly's lover.* New York: Grove Press.

Legman, G. 1963. *Love and death: A study in censorship.* New York: Hacker Art Books.

———. 1964. *The horn book: Studies in erotic folklore and bibliography.* New York: University Books.

Lehfeldt, H. 1968. Coitus interruptus. *Medical Aspects of Human Sexuality* 2, no. 11 (November): 29–31.

Levinger, G. 1970. Husbands' and wives' estimates of coital frequency. *Medical Aspects of Human Sexuality* 4, no. 9 (September): 42–57.

Lewinsohn, R. 1958. *A history of sexual customs.* New York: Harper & Row.

Li Yü. 1955. *Jou-p'u-t'uan (The prayer mat of flesh).*

Trans. by H. Lowe-Porter. London: Penguin Books.

Lloyd, C. W. 1964. *Human reproduction and sexual behavior.* Philadelphia: Lea & Febinger.

Loth, D. 1962. *The erotic in literature.* New York: Macfadden.

Lunde, D. T., & Hamburg, D. A. 1972. Techniques for assessing the effects of sex hormones on affect, arousal and aggression in humans. *Recent Progress in Hormone Research* 28: in press.

"M." 1971. *The sensuous man.* New York: Lyle Stuart.

Maccoby, E., ed. 1966. *The development of sex differences.* Stanford, Calif.: Stanford University Press.

Macdonald, D. 1969. *On movies.* Englewood Cliffs, N.J.: Prentice-Hall.

Malinowski, B. 1929. *The sexual life of savages in north-western Melanesia.* New York: Harcourt, Brace & Jovanovich.

Malla, K. 1964 ed. *The ananga ranga.* Trans. by R. F. Burton & F. F. Arbuthnot. New York: G. P. Putnam's Sons.

Mann, T. 1955. *Death in Venice.* Trans. by H. Lowe-Porter. London: Penguin Books.

Manvell, R. 1966. *New cinema in Europe.* London: Studio Vista.

Marcus, S. 1966. *The other Victorians.* New York: Basic Books.

Marmor, J. 1954. Some considerations concerning orgasm in the female. *Psychosomatic Medicine* 16, no. 3: 240–245.

Marmor, J., ed. 1965. *Sexual inversion: The multiple roots of homosexuality.* New York: Basic Books.

——, ed. 1968. *Modern psychoanalysis: New directions and perspectives.* New York: Basic Books.

Martial (Marcus Valerius Martialis). 1920. *The epigrams.* Loeb Library trans. London: William Heinemann.

Masters, W. H., & Johnson, V. E. 1966. *Human sexual response.* Boston: Little, Brown & Co.

——. 1970. *Human sexual inadequacy.* Boston: Little, Brown & Co.

May, R. 1969. *Love and will.* New York: W. W. Norton & Co.

Mead, M. 1929. *Coming of age in Samoa.* New York: William Morrow & Co.

——. 1935. *Sex and temperament in three primitive societies.* New York: William Morrow & Co.

——. 1949. *Male and female.* New York: William Morrow & Co.

Meleager, Strato of Sardis, *et al.* 1918. *The Greek anthology.* Trans. by W. R. Paton. London: William Heinemann.

Miller, A. 1955. *The renewal of man.* Garden City, N.Y.: Doubleday & Co.

Miller, H. 1961. *Tropic of cancer.* New York: Grove Press.

Millett, K. 1970. *Sexual politics.* Garden City, N.Y.: Doubleday & Co.

Mirbeau, O. 1935. *Le jardin des supplices.* Paris: Les Editions Nationales.

Money, J. 1968. *Sex errors of the body.* Baltimore: The Johns Hopkins Press.

Money, J., ed. 1965. *Sex research: New developments.* New York: Holt, Rinehart & Winston.

Montagu, A. 1964. *Life before birth.* New York: New American Library.

——. 1969. *Sex, man and society.* New York: Tower Publications.

Morin, E. 1960. *The stars.* Trans. by Richard Howard. New York: Grove Press.

Morris, D. 1969. *The human zoo.* New York: McGraw-Hill.

Murdock, G. P. 1949. *Social structure.* New York: Macmillan Co.

My secret life. 1966. New York: Grove Press.

Nabokov, V. 1959. *Lolita.* Greenwich, Conn.: Fawcett Books.

Nefzawi. 1964 ed. *The perfumed garden.* Trans. by R. F. Burton. New York: G. P. Putnam's Sons. (London: Neville Spearman Ltd., 1963.)

Netter, F. H. 1965. *Endocrine system.* The Ciba Collection of Medical Illustrations, vol. 4. Summit, N.J.: Ciba.

——. 1965. *Reproductive system.* The Ciba Collection of Medical Illustrations, vol. 2. Summit, N.J.: Ciba.

Neubeck, G., ed. 1969. *Extramarital relations.* Englewood Cliffs, N.J.: Prentice-Hall.

Nilsson, A. L. *et al.* 1965. *A child is born.* Boston: Seymour Lawrence, Inc.

Noonan, J. T., Jr. 1967. *Contraception: A history of its treatment by the Catholic theologians and canonists.* New York: New American Library.

Novak, E. R., & Jones, G. S. 1961. *Novak's textbook of gynecology.* Baltimore: Williams & Wilkins Co.

Nunberg, H. 1969. *Principles of psychoanalysis: Their application to the neuroses.* New York: International Universities Press.

Olds, J. 1956. Pleasure centers in the brain. *Scientific American* 193: 105-116.

O'Neil, R. P., & Donovan, M. A. 1968. *Sexuality and moral responsibility.* Washington & Cleveland: Corpus Publications.

Opler, M. K. 1969. Cross-cultural aspects of kissing. *Medical Aspects of Human Sexuality* 3, no. 2 (February): 11-21.

Ovid (Publius Ovidius Naso). 1914. *Heroides and Amores,* with an English trans. by G. Showerman. London: William Heinemann.

Packer, H. L. 1968. *The limits of the criminal sanction.* Stanford, Calif.: Stanford University Press.

Parke, J. R. 1906. *Human sexuality.* Philadelphia: Professional Publishing Company.

Parker, E. 1960. *The seven ages of woman.* Baltimore: The Johns Hopkins Press.

Parran, T. 1937. *Shadow on the land—syphilis.* New York: Reynal & Hitchcock.

Patten, B. M. 1968. *Human embryology.* 3rd ed. New York: McGraw-Hill.

Pavlov, I. P. 1927. *Conditioned reflexes: An investigation of the physiological activity of the cerebral cortex.* London: Oxford University Press.

Peterson, H. 1928. *Havelock Ellis, philosopher of love.* Boston: Houghton Mifflin Co.

Ploscowe, M. 1951. *Sex and the law.* Englewood Cliffs, N.J.: Prentice-Hall.

Pohlman, E. G. 1968. *Psychology of birth planning.* Cambridge: Shenkman Publishing Co.

Pouillet, T. 1897. *L'onanisme chez la femme.* Paris: Vigot Freres. (Originally published in 1876.)

Pound, E. 1926. *Personae.* New York: New Directions.

Prévost, A. F. 1965. *Manon Lescaut.* Paris: Garnier Frères.

Proust, M. 1932. *Cities of the plain.* Trans. by D. K. S. Moncrieff. New York: Random House.

Rabelais, F. n.d. *Works.* Trans. by T. Urquhart & P. Motteux. London: The Abbey Library.

Rawson, P., ed. 1969. *Erotic art of the East.* New York: G. P. Putnam's Sons.

Reich, W. 1961. *The discovery of the orgone.* Vol. 1: *The function of the orgasm.* New York: Orgone Institute Press. (Originally published in 1942.)

Reichlin, S. 1971. Relationships of the pituitary gland to human sexual behavior. *Medical Aspects of Human Sexuality* 5, no. 2 (February): 146-154.

Reik, T. 1970. *Of love and lust.* New York: Farrar, Straus & Giroux. (Originally published in 1941.)

Repairing the conjugal bed. 1970. *Time* 95 (May 25): 49-52.

Riess, C. 1968. *Erotica! Erotica! Das Buch der verbotenen Bücher.* Hamburg: Hoffman & Campe.

Robbins, S. L. 1967. *Textbook of pathology.* 3rd ed. Philadelphia: W. B. Saunders Co.

Rose, R. M. 1969. Androgen excretion in stress. In *The psychology and physiology of stress,* ed. P. G. Bourne, pp. 117-147. New York: Academic Press.

Rosenbaum, S. 1970. Pretended orgasm. *Medical Aspects of Human Sexuality* 4, no. 4 (April): 84-96.

Rosner, F., trans. 1965. *Mishneh Torah,* "Hilchoth De'oth," chap. IV, no. 19. In *Annals of Internal Medicine* 62: 372.

Rossman, I. 1967. *Sex, fertility and birth control.* New York: Stravon Press.

Rothballer, A. B. 1967. Aggression, defense, and neurohumors. In *Brain Function,* Vol. V: *Aggression and defense,* ed. C. D. Clemente & D. B. Lindsley, pp. 135-170. Berkeley, Calif.: University of California Press.

Roth, P. 1967. *Portney's complaint.* New York: Random House.

Roth-Brandel, U., Bygdeman, M., Wiqvist, N., & Bergstrom, S. 1970. Prostaglandins for induction of therapeutic abortion. *Lancet* 1: 190-191.

Rothschild, L., F.R.S. 1958. Human spermatozoon. *British Medical Journal* 1 (February 8): 301.

Rubin, E., ed. 1969. *Sexual freedom in marriage.* New York: New American Library.

Ruitenbeek, H. M., ed. 1963. *The problem of homosexuality in modern society.* New York: E. P. Dutton & Co.

Russell, B. 1968. *Marriage and morals.* New York: Bantam Books. (Originally published in 1929.)

de Sade, D.-A.-F. 1965. *Justine.* In *The Marquis de Sade: Three Complete Novels.* New York: Grove Press.

Salzman, L. 1968. Sexuality in psychoanalytic theory. In *Modern psychoanalysis,* ed. J. Marmor, pp. 123–145. New York: Basic Books.

Sappho of Lesbos. 1922. In *Lyra Graica,* trans. J. M. Edmonds. London: William Heinemann.

Schwartz, L. B. 1963. Morals, offenses and the model penal code. *Columbia Law Review* 63: 669.

Sellon, E. (?). n.d. *Mémoires d'une procureuse anglais.* London: Boardman & Co.

Sherfey, M. J. 1966. The evolution and nature of female sexuality in relation to psychoanalytic theory. *Journal of the American Psychoanalytic Association* 14, no. 1: 28–128.

Shiloh, A., ed. 1970. *Studies in human sexual behavior: The American scene.* Springfield, Ill.: Charles C Thomas.

The significance of extramarital sex relations. 1969. *Medical Aspects of Human Sexuality* 3, no. 10 (October): 33–47.

Simon, W., Carnes, D., & Gagnon, J. 1972. Manuscript in preparation. New York: Harper & Row.

Skinner, B. F. 1938. *The behavior of organisms: An experimental analysis.* New York: Appleton-Century-Crofts.

Slovenko, R. 1965. *Sexual behavior and the law.* Springfield, Ill.: Charles C Thomas.

Smith, D. R. 1969. *General urology.* 6th ed. Los Altos, Calif.: Lange Medical Publications.

Somadeva. 1956. *Vetalapañcavimsati.* Trans. by C. H. Tawney. Bombay: Jaico Publishing House.

Spillane, M. 1948. *I, the jury.* New York: Dutton.

Spiro, M. E. 1956. *Kibbutz: Venture in utopia.* Cambridge: Harvard University Press.

Spock, B. 1970. *Baby and child care.* New York: Pocket Books.

Stearn, J. 1961. *The sixth man.* Garden City, N.Y.: Doubleday & Co.

———. 1964. *The grapevine: A report on the secret world of the lesbian.* Garden City, N.Y.: Doubleday & Co.

Steiner, G. 1970. Night words. In *The new eroticism,* ed. P. Nobile, pp. 120–132. New York: Random House.

Stekel, W. 1930. *Sexual aberrations.* 2 vols. New York: Liveright Publishing Corp.

———. 1950. *Auto-eroticism.* New York: Liveright Publishing Corp.

Stephenson, R., & Debrix, J. R. 1965. *The cinema as art.* Harmondsworth, Middlesex: Penguin Books.

Stern, C. 1960. *Principles of human genetics.* 2nd ed. San Francisco: H. H. Freeman & Co.

Stoller, R. J. 1968. *Sex and gender: On the development of masculinity and feminity.* New York: Science House.

Student Committee on Human Sexuality. 1970. *Sex and the Yale Student.* New Haven, Conn.: Yale University Press.

Sullivan, P. R. 1969. What is the role of fantasy in sex? *Medical Aspects of Human Sexuality* 3, no. 4 (April): 79–89.

Tepperman, J. 1962. *Metabolic and endocrine physiology.* Chicago: Year Book Medical Publishers.

Terman, L. M. 1938. *Psychological factors in marital happiness.* New York: McGraw-Hill.

Thielicke, H. 1964. *The ethics of sex.* Trans. by J. W. Doberstein, New York: Harper & Row.

Thomas, J. L., S.J. 1965. *Catholic viewpoint on marriage and the family.* Garden City, N.Y.: Image Books.

Thomlinson, R. 1967. *Demographic problems.: Controversy over population control.* Belmont, Calif.: Dickenson.

Thompson, G. 1967. *Sex rackets.* Cleveland: Century Books.

Tjio, J. H., & Puck, T. T. 1958. The Somatic Chromosomes of man. *Proceedings of the National Academy of Sciences* 44: 1222–1237.

Tyrmand, L. 1970. Permissiveness and rectitude. *The New Yorker* 46 (February 28): 85–86.

Udry, J. R., & Morris, N. M. 1968. Distribution of coitus in the menstrual cycle. *Nature* 220: 593–596.

Van de Velde, T. H. 1965. *Ideal marriage.* New York: Random House.

Van Lawick-Goodall, J. 1967. Mother offspring relationship in free-ranging chimpanzees. In *Primate ethology,* ed. D. Morris, pp. 287–346. Chicago: Aldine Publishing Co.

Vatsyayana. 1963 ed. *The Kama Sutra.* Trans. by

R. F. Burton and F. F. Arbuthnot. Medallion ed. New York: G. P. Putnam's Sons.

Vergil (Publius Vergilius Maro). 1965. *Works,* with an English trans. by H. R. Fairclough. London: William Heinemann.

Vidal, G. 1968. *Myra Breckinridge.* Boston: Little, Brown & Co.; New York: Bantam Books.

von Krafft-Ebing, R. 1899. *Psychopathia sexualis.* Trans. by C. B. Chaddock. Philadelphia: F. A. Davis Co. (Reprinted: New York: G. P. Putnam's Sons, 1969.)

Waelder, R. 1964. *Basic theory of psychoanalysis.* New York: International Universities Press.

The way of a man with a maid. 1968. New York: Grove Press.

Weinberg, S. K. 1963. *Incest behavior.* New York: Citadel Press.

Weiss, R. S., & Joseph, H. L. 1951. *Syphilis.* Camden, N.J.: Thomas Nelson.

West, D. J. 1968. *Homosexuality.* Chicago: Aldine.

West, N. 1933. *Miss Lonelyhearts.* New York: Avon Publishing.

Westwood, G. 1960. *A minority: A report on the life of the male homosexual in Great Britain.* London: Longmans, Green & Co.

Weyranch, H. M. 1968. *Life after fifty: The prostatic age.* Los Angeles: Ward Ritchie Press.

The Whippingham papers. 1888. London: Privately published.

Whiteman, R. M. 1969. Multiple orgasms. *Medical Aspects of Human Sexuality* 3, no. 8 (August): 52–56.

Whyte, L. L. 1960. *The unconscious before Freud.* New York: Basic Books.

Wilkins, L., Blizzard, R., & Migeon, C. 1965. *The diagnosis and treatment of endocrine disorders in childhood and adolescence.* Springfield, Ill.: Charles C Thomas.

Wilson, E. 1952. *The shores of light.* New York: Farrar, Straus.

Winick, C. 1970. The desexualized society. In *The new eroticism,* ed. P. Nobile, pp. 201–207. New York: Random House.

The Wolfenden report. 1963. New York: Stein & Day.

Wolpe, J., & Lazarus, A. A. 1966. *Behavior therapy techniques.* New York: Pergamon Press.

Wood, H. C., Jr. 1967. *Sex without babies: A comprehensive review of voluntary sterilization as a method of birth control.* Philadelphia: Whitmore.

Woolf, V. 1929. *A room of one's own.* New York: Harcourt.

World Health Organization. 1968. *Hormonal steroids in contraception.* World Health Organization Technical Report no. 386. Geneva: WHO.

———. 1968. *Intrauterine devices: Physiological and clinical aspects.* World Health Organization Technical Report no. 397. Geneva: WHO.

Yalom, I. D. *et al.* 1968. Postpartum blues syndrome. *Archives of General Psychiatry* 18: 16–27.

Young, W. C. ed., 1961. *Sex and internal secretions.* 2 vols. Baltimore: Williams & Wilkins Co.

Zichy, M. 1969. The *erotic drawings of Mihàly Zichy.* New York: Grove Press.

Zola, E. 1948. *Nana.* Trans. by F. J. Vizetelly. New York: Heritage Press. (Originally published: Paris: Fasquelle, 1938.)

Zuckerman, S. 1932. *The social life of monkeys and apes.* London: Routledge & Kegan Paul.

INDEX